WITNESS of GOD'S VOICE

God's Nurturing of a Prophetic Call

WITNESS of GOD'S VOICE

Autobiography

Angelika Mitikas

Monaca, Pa 15061
United States of America

Monaca, Pa 15061
United States of America

Cover Photo/Design by Angelika Mitikas, (John 7:38-39; Psalm 29:3)
Proofreader: Marie Rivers
Published: November 4, 2022

WITNESS *of* GOD'S VOICE
God's Nurturing of a Prophetic Call
Copyright © 2020 by Angelika Mitikas, All Rights Reserved

The Lord's Consolation
Copyright © 1988 by Angelika Mitikas, All Rights Reserved

All Rights Reserved. No part of this publication may be reproduced, distributed, or transmitted in any form or by any means—scanning, printing, electronic, mechanical, magnetic, photographic—including photocopying, recording, or any other information storage and/or retrieval system, or in any other way, without the prior written permission of the author.

All Scripture quotations, unless otherwise noted, are taken from the (NASB®) *NEW AMERICAN STANDARD BIBLE®*, © Copyright 1960, 1971, 1977, 1995, 2020 by The Lockman Foundation. All Rights Reserved. Used by permission. www.Lockman.org

Scripture quotations marked "NIV" are taken from the Holy Bible, New International Version®, NIV®. Copyright © 1973, 1978, 1984, 2011 by Biblica, Inc.™ Used by permission of Zondervan. All rights reserved worldwide. www.zondervan.com
The "NIV" and "New International Version" are trademarks registered in the United States Patent and Trademark Office by Biblica, Inc.™

ISBN: 978-1-7362566-0-2 Paperback Print
      978-1-7362566-1-9 Hardback Print
Library of Congress Control Number: 2021904342

Editions: 10 9 8 7 6 5 4 3 2 1

I dedicate this book in loving memory of
my precious and beloved mom, Mary,
who is now with our Lord Jesus.

My mom's love and encouragement
had always been a true blessing
from our precious Lord God
that I will always treasure.

Table of Contents

Foreword XI
Acknowledgment XIII
Introduction 15
Chapter 1   My Early Years 17
Chapter 2   Spiritual Journey Begins 26
Chapter 3   Early Bronx 31
Chapter 4   The Concrete Jungle 37
Chapter 5   My Best Friend 42
Chapter 6   Entertainment 47
Chapter 7   Demonic Dabbling 51
Chapter 8   Last Traumatic Experience 57
Chapter 9   Culture Shock 63
Chapter 10   My First Car 71
Chapter 11   My Rebellion 78
Chapter 12   Senior Year 82
Chapter 13   Army Beware 86
Chapter 14   Basic Training 91
Chapter 15   Advanced Individual Training 97
Chapter 16   Fort Benning, GA 105
Chapter 17   Beginning of Drug Abuse 112
Chapter 18   Conflicts With CO 116
Chapter 19   Presence of God 120
Chapter 20   My "D" Day 127
Chapter 21   God's Healing 136
Chapter 22   My New Life 140
Chapter 23   Adventurous Joy Ride 145
Chapter 24   Military Police Raid 150
Chapter 25   Field Training 158
Chapter 26   The Lord's Command 164

Chapter 27	Little Dukey	170
Chapter 28	Deeper Walk With God	174
Chapter 29	End Term Servic	181
Chapter 30	Going Home	186
Chapter 31	God's Refining	190
Chapter 32	God's Tenderness	196
Chapter 33	Obedience	201
Chapter 34	Undeniable Message	205
Chapter 35	My Mom	211
Chapter 36	Mom's Homecoming	216
Chapter 37	Darkly	224
Chapter 38	Darkly Pancakes	229
Chapter 39	True to His Word	235
Chapter 40	My Home	242
Chapter 41	Irreverence	247
Chapter 42	God's Spanking	255
Chapter 43	Beginning of Workers' Comp	261
Chapter 44	Surgery	266
Chapter 45	Second Opinion	271
Chapter 46	The Plague	276
Chapter 47	Conspiracy	283
Chapter 48	Independent Medical Exam	291
Chapter 49	Taking Control	297
Chapter 50	End of Nightmare	305
Chapter 51	Another Hard Lesson	314
Chapter 52	Workers' Comp Rep	321
Chapter 53	New Arena	328
Chapter 54	Union Overview	335
Chapter 55	First Major Issue	339
Chapter 56	Making Waves	343
Chapter 57	Cain's First Tirade	347

Chapter 58	Darkly's Blunders	353
Chapter 59	Performance Reviews	361
Chapter 60	First Board Charge	367
Chapter 61	Good-Faith Gesture	372
Chapter 62	Contracting Out	376
Chapter 63	Vindictiveness	382
Chapter 64	Victory	387
Chapter 65	Contracting Out Arbitration	394
Chapter 66	Our Contract	399
Chapter 67	New War	406
Chapter 68	Another Tirade	414
Chapter 69	Going Over Heads	419
Chapter 70	Darkly's Fate	424
Chapter 71	Ferengi's Agenda	428
Chapter 72	Another Term	436
Chapter 73	Warehouse Job	440
Chapter 74	Assertiveness	446
Chapter 75	Flex Job	453
Chapter 76	Counterproposal	461
Chapter 77	Turning in Cain	467
Chapter 78	Vicious Meeting	475
Chapter 79	Flex Job Arbitration	486
Chapter 80	Unpardonable Sin	495
Chapter 81	Standing Alone	502
Chapter 82	Morphed Campaign	507
Chapter 83	Cannot Be Bought	514
Chapter 84	Retaliation	518
Chapter 85	Union Representation	526
Chapter 86	Unethical Crime	532
Chapter 87	Newbie's Canary	538
Chapter 88	My Arbitration	544

Chapter 89	Contract Negotiations	549
Chapter 90	Finishing Well	558
Chapter 91	Critical Safety Concern	567
Chapter 92	Mockery Meeting	575
Chapter 93	Work Goes On	581
Chapter 94	Initial Issues	586
Chapter 95	Tormented Heart	591
Chapter 96	Enough Was Enough	598
Chapter 97	Meltdown	606
Chapter 98	God's Spiritual Healing	611
Chapter 99	Prophetic Warning	616
Chapter 100	Safety Regression	624
Chapter 101	The Trap	630
Chapter 102	Betrayal	636
Chapter 103	Near Misses	642
Chapter 104	My Grievance Meeting	646
Chapter 105	Divine Ambush	652
Chapter 106	God's Timing	657
Chapter 107	Agenda Against Me	661
Chapter 108	Last Battle	666
Chapter 109	Divine Rescue	672
Chapter 110	Another Nightmare	676
Chapter 111	I Was Done	680
Chapter 112	God's Decision	685
Epilogue		691
Author's Appreciation		697

Foreword

After the Lord God created the Earth, He created the human race in His own image and likeness, and created us all to be equal. Afterward, God had no intention to just sit back and watch His precious creation flounder around trying to make it on their own.

The Lord God's intentions had always been to have an intimate relationship with those who love Him, to be intimately involved with every aspect of their lives, and to be involved in the affairs of our world that He created.

God customizes His relationship, nurturing and disciplining for each of His children according to His purpose, and desires to speak to all His children. But we must be attuned to God's Holy Spirit, and able to discern His voice from all other voices that clutter our hearts and minds, and compete for our devotion.

I have endeavored by God's leading to share my relationship with my Lord with brutal honesty. It may seem as though I have shared every intimate dealing from the Lord for all to read, but I am so thankful to the Lord, that is not the case.

I have changed or omitted the names of individuals and organizations to protect the innocent, the guilty—and me. All words in italics are my thoughts. Deity pronouns are capitalized in reverence to God. Scripture references with periods in the parenthesis do not follow precise quoted Scriptures, but are references of Scripture that was shared. The spiritual battles are included by the leading of God's Spirit, and are not unique to my life. More often than we can know, spiritual battles are raged on our behalf, especially at crucial moments of our spiritual walk with God. (Ephesians 6:10-17; Psalm 91:11.)

The Lord knows my heart's prayer for all those who read this book. May you all be blessed in God's special way.

Acknowledgment

I want to express my utmost love and devotion to the One-Triune Lord God of the Universe, who I owe everything to, and who has been my constant source of love, protection and nurturing throughout my life, and will for all eternity.

I give all thanks, praise, honor and glory to my precious Lord God, for all He has done in and through and for my life.

I will always confess—without apology—that I have no greater joy or purpose in life, but to live with tenacious devotion to my personal Lord and Savior, Jesus Christ, who is the very Incarnate God Almighty.

Jesus Christ died for the sins of the world as the Lamb of God. Anyone who accepts the atoning sacrifice of Jesus on the cross, confesses their sins to Him and asks for His forgiveness, and embraces Jesus into their heart to be their Lord and Savior, is reconciled to God—His Holy Father—and becomes His child.

With my sincere love and appreciation, I want to thank all my dear prayer warriors whose love, prayers and encouragement have carried me through the years as I labored on this book. Our Lord Jesus knows every one of you. My prayer is that He will bless you all abundantly in His special way for your love and faithfulness.

I want to thank my dear cousin, Marie Rivers, with my sincere love and appreciation for her diligence as my proofreader. Marie has been a true answer to prayer, and an invaluable resource and blessing from our Lord Jesus.

Marie, may God bless you abundantly in His special way for your love and faithfulness.

Introduction

*U*nbeknown to anyone but God alone, a tiny life is conceived. As the Lord God of the Universe cradles His little daughter in His arms, He gently speaks to her in His commanding voice she will one day know so well:
"Before I formed you in the womb I knew you, and before
you were born I consecrated you; . . ." (Jeremiah 1:5).

I was twenty years old when I found myself in a trailer with three others partying. The familiar sweet aroma of marijuana smoke permeated the air as I relished the exhilarated high. Weird head music blasted away while the TV played without the sound on. After my third inhaled drag of marijuana smoke, something inside me exploded. I wondered: *Was some other drug put in my drink?* I sat there, unable to move, unable to speak, heart pounding out of my chest. And then I floated out of my body and hovered in the air looking down where my body sat.

Meanwhile, the battle in the spiritual realm over my very existence was approaching a fierce climax. God had given His angelic warriors orders to protect me, whereas the demons, under Satan's orders, were desperate to destroy me.

Once back inside my body, a demonic revelation paralyzed me with fear: I would die that night!

Then I remembered the God to whom I had been praying to since I was a little girl as my mind voiced what my heart knew to be true: *God's here; He'll help me!*

No sooner did I finish acknowledging this truth, God manifested His presence with His overwhelming peace that rushed throughout my entire being instantly obliterating the paralyzing fear within me.

My near-death experience while overdosing was the very first time God manifested His presence to me, but was not to be the last. Soon afterward, God propelled me deeper in my walk with Him.

God had begun drawing me close to Himself while I was yet a little girl. As I grew older, my ignorance with demonic dabbling, my rebellious heart and drug abuse fueled Satan's schemes to draw me away from God to destroy me.

The Lord God proved to be unrelenting in pursuing His demand for first place in my heart and life, and His demand of my perfect obedience to Him. God's prophetic call comes with a dear cost in many different ways that only those who have been so called can relate to. However, His reward of intimacy with such a powerful, precious and holy Triune God, by far exceeds any cost—an intimacy I will never, ever be worthy of.

As God's dealings became progressively severer, He would reveal glimpses of His purpose for my life while making sure I understood without any doubt: God's call on my life will never be on my own merits, my accomplishments in my life will never be through my ability alone, my endurance through all the trials and adversities God allows in my life will never be in my strength alone.

My life belongs to God and was never meant to be about me, but about the Lord God within me, demonstrating His grace and power when I am weakest. Only by the grace of God I am what I am! The Lord has made it known to me, that I will always need His help and blessings to succeed well in anything I do. (2 Corinthians 12:9; 1 Corinthians 15:10; John 15:5; Philippians 4:13.)

This true story is a witness of God's willingness to nurture even the most unworthy and inadequate life for His purpose. It demonstrates God's intimacy, grace and power through losses and hardships, through trials and adversities, through betrayals in battles and triumphs in wars, and only for the praise and honor and glory of the Lord Jesus Christ.

Chapter 1
My Early Years

My parents were as Greek as they come. I have fond memories of festive Greek gatherings with friends and family, and Greek foods and baked goods galore. As the Greek music filled the atmosphere inspiring laughter and exuberant line dancing, an appreciation for being part of this ancient ancestry was engraved in my young heart.

All my grandparents were born in Greece. I never met my paternal grandparents who never left Greece, or my maternal grandfather who came to the United States as an adult, but returned to Greece after he divorced my grandmother to live there after his retirement.

But my maternal yiayia, as grandmothers are called in Greek, was a special part of my young life. She was brought to the United States when she was six years old and never returned to Greece.

My dad was born and raised in Greece, and took part in the guerrilla warfare during WWII fighting the Germans in the mountains and caves of Greece. When Dad immigrated to the United States in his twenties, he settled in New York City where he worked as a bridge painter.

My mom was born in Ohio, but was raised in a small town in Pennsylvania. Mom also settled in New York City while in her twenties, along with her mother, sister and brother. Both my parents were in their late twenties when they met in New York City during the mid-1950s, and married just a few months later.

My brother, Michael, was born sixteen months later in a way that doctors proclaimed was a miraculous birth. Mom was seven and a half months pregnant when she twisted her body while catching herself from a fall carrying grocery bags. This incident was later blamed for the cause of Michael being severed from his placenta. When Michael was born prematurely two weeks later, the placenta came out completely rotten except for a small corner the size of a quarter. My parents were told that the chances of a live birth under such circumstances were one in a million.

I was conceived eleven months after Michael was born. Just after my conception, Mom underwent surgery for hemorrhoids, and afterward, had to sit in extremely hot baths two times a day for several weeks as part of the healing process.

However, before this surgery, Mom had expressed concerns to her doctor that she believed she had conceived a baby. But Mom's doctor blamed her anxiety over the surgery as the cause for her menstrual cycle to stop, and did not perform a pregnancy test. Dad was even more adamant that Mom could not be pregnant. Sonograms or over-the-counter pregnancy tests did not exist at that time.

When Mom knew for sure I had been there throughout her surgery and the hot baths, she went into emotional turmoil for the rest of my life in her womb. She began by being fearful of a miscarriage. When she realized I was still holding on, she was convinced that I was deformed without legs or arms. As Mom shared with me later in life, I never kicked her but only turned around. Without sonograms, Mom had no way of knowing that all my little limbs with complete sets of little fingers and little toes were being perfectly formed.

My Heavenly Father was in complete control even before my conception, and the only One who understood the forces that were against my young life. As I held on to dear life, God protected and nurtured tiny me, and ensured my birth into this world.

From the time I was old enough to understand, every year when my birthday came around, Mom loved to tell me the story of the very beginning of my life journey in this world. And each time she shared this story, God powerfully used her to confirm His presence in my life from even before I was born.

Mom would always begin the story with my conception that only she believed. She would then share all about her ordeal of the surgery and hot baths and concerns afterward that I would not be normal. And she would share her long and painful labor ordeal of a natural birth. Mom would always end the story with a huge smile and her absolute delight that I was her daughter, and would lovingly add, "You are a gift from God to me!"

Mom believed there was a God in Heaven, and I can believe that she cried more than a few prayers to God on behalf of her tiny baby while still in her womb.

I am still amazed by how God orchestrated bringing together two people, whose own parents were from two small islands in the same North Aegean Islands of Greece, to meet here in the United States to become my parents. I could have very easily been born in Greece with a very different life journey than what I was to live in this country.

With these strong ties to the Greek heritage, it is no wonder the Greek traditions and customs, some of which were interesting, became a strong part of my way of life during my early years. Greeks also had bizarre superstitions handed down through the centuries, which I only understood after becoming a born-again Christian were not biblical, and in fact were demonic dabbling.

The "evil-eye" curse is one such superstition that Greeks and other ethnic groups still believe in. There are preventive charms that if worn are believed to ward off this evil-eye curse, as well as spitting on someone three times. While I was young, I was often the victim of Greek adults spitting on me to ward off this evil-eye curse. YUCK!

One interesting Greek tradition my parents followed was naming their firstborn boy and girl after the father's parents. This is why Greek families have whole bunches of cousins running around with the same name. This makes it a little confusing for families when addressing their children in the festive Greek gatherings, but this never seemed to be a deterrent from following this Greek tradition. However, Scriptures support that there are times when God has His own purpose for the names children are given. Michael's real given name is translated "God with us."

My parents also followed the Greek tradition of baptizing Michael and me as babies into the Greek Orthodox Church denomination. Older-generation Greeks also had a strong desire that each of their children would be able to speak Greek fluently. This desire caused Mom to begin her school years unable to speak English, as her parents would only allow her and her siblings to speak Greek while in their home. This was more of my maternal grandfather's doing than Yiayia's. Mom was treated harshly in school because of this communication barrier.

Mom cried to her father asking why she couldn't speak English. He answered that she had a different tongue. When Mom shared this story to me, she described how she dragged a chair to the bathroom, stood on it in front of the mirror, and did a thorough examination of her tongue. She wanted to know for herself how her tongue was different.

This ridicule from teachers and kids for Mom's inability to speak English caused her to stutter when she was young. Thankfully, Mom outgrew her stuttering once she became more skilled in English, but she always remained fluent in speaking, reading and writing the Greek language.

Dad was also adamant that both his children learned to speak Greek while Mom wanted to be sure we learned English well to avoid the communication barrier she experienced in her young life.

My Early Years

Michael had no problems learning and speaking Greek very well at a young age, but it was not the same for me. Although I understood everything that was spoken in Greek, for some reason I could never speak Greek. After Dad tried his best to teach me to speak Greek, according to Mom, he finally declared in his own broken English: "I givlup."

And it was no wonder I couldn't speak Greek; I couldn't even speak English correctly. I slaughtered the pronunciation of words in such a way that only my brother and the kids I played with understood when I spoke. This caused a huge communication barrier with my parents and other adults.

Mom would often use Michael as my interpreter when I was trying to tell her something. Michael often called me Babe from when I could remember, an endearment I will always cherish. As my interpreter, he would grab my chin, turn my whole head towards him and say, "Tell me, Babe."

After repeating to Michael what I was trying to say, he would translate this to Mom, who would then turn to me and ask, "Is that what you want?" At this point, I would just nod yes as my answer.

I went to speech therapy in my early school years, and eventually managed to speak so that others could understand me. Although there are times I still tend to "slaughter" the English language, I've learned to laugh these moments away.

I was very shy and sensitive as a young child, a personality that drastically changed as the years went by, and just a stern look from Mom would upset me. But at the same time, I was very strong-willed and independent. I was perfectly fine wandering off on my own while Mom wasn't looking—and did so often. I think my mom might have been one of the first to put her kid on a leash.

Michael was the total opposite. He would just lose sight of Mom and scream his head off until he found her, or she found him. Amazing how two siblings could be so different.

I have only a few vivid memories from my very young childhood that found their way into that never-to-forget part of my brain. As far back as I can remember, I always loved animals, especially dogs. I would often run up to any dog I saw, whether on a leash or running loose, to hug and pet them. This was not a good habit for a little girl, and on one occasion almost ended in a tragedy for me.

Mom's only sister, Aunt Katrina, also had a son and daughter close in age to Michael and me. Bruno was the oldest, then came Michael with Laura not far behind; I was the youngest of our foursome. Whenever Mom and Aunt Katrina would visit Yiayia at the same time, we four cousins would go on our own for some adventures in her South Bronx neighborhood.

During one such adventurous outing, we came upon a junkyard that had some mean dogs tied up that viciously lunged at us, which caused all four of us to run. The three oldest ran away from the dogs while I ran up to the dogs to hug and pet them. I found out the hard way, junkyard dogs were not always nice to little girls running up to them.

I remember being in the hospital emergency room with multiple dog bites on my back. This could have ended in a more tragic way for me. I wasn't more than five years old when this happened. After this incident, Mom was sure I had learned my lesson and would never again run up to every dog that I would see. But I never learned that lesson; my love for dogs was too strong.

Soon after this dog attack incident, Mom got us a puppy. We were living in a rented bungalow house in the borough of Queens, in a predominantly Greek neighborhood. I remember getting up in the middle of one special summer night only to find this adorable little puppy tied to Mom's bedpost. I was so excited that I just had to wake Mom up to tell her this great news: "Ma, there's a real live puppy in our house! A real live puppy!"

She responded in such a loving way: "Yes, he's a live puppy. Now go back to bed and you'll see him in the morning."

I'm not sure how I was able to go back to sleep after seeing this live puppy in my own house, but I did. We named this mutt Duke, and his addition completed our typical American family.

Another vivid memory happened just a few months later. I was just under six years old on this dreadful Halloween night. I had no way of knowing that there were so many people anxiously searching for me, as they believed I was lost and feared for my safety. When I came back home safe, Dad went into a rage, threw me on a chair, and kept beating me and yelling, "Look what you did to your mother!"

I was crying hysterically as Mom tried with all her might to pull Dad off me, sobbing herself and yelling, "Stop! You're going to kill her!"

When Dad finally left me alone, Mom held me close as we both continued sobbing, both terrified over his rage. I don't remember Dad ever hitting me before that night or anytime afterward. But unfortunately, that trauma of his beating and raging anger would be the only vivid memory I would ever have of my dad.

Soon after this happened, Dad left for Greece on what was supposed to be a short trip to visit his mother, who was not expected to live much longer. Dad made this trip overseas on an ocean liner, which was a huge cargo and passenger ship very different from the cruise ships that are known today. It was the following June when Dad finally came back home.

Just a few weeks later, in the first week of August 1965, our lives changed forever. As Mom told the story, Dad tried waking her up only to hear her say while still in her sleep, that she was picking out gravestones and liked a particular one. Dad took this as an omen that upset him before leaving for work that same day.

Dad also believed, as Mom told me later in my life, that when it was his time to die, he would let out one scream and would be gone.

On this August morning, Dad was part of a painting crew working on the Welfare Island Bridge (known today as the Roosevelt Island Bridge) in New York City. During that time, this bridge had an elevator that was not supposed to be operated during the time workers were around and painting this bridge.

OSHA (Occupational Safety and Health Administration, a federal agency) was not established yet during the days when Dad was working on such safety-critical jobs. OSHA was established in December 1970, and now has mandated procedures that require any equipment that would otherwise pose a hazard to workers working on or around them, to have all energy sources identified and shut off, then tagged and locked out with a physical lock to ensure such equipment could not inadvertently be operated, and by doing so, harm someone.

On this particular day, one of Dad's coworkers had put coffee in the elevator, and then pushed the button to send it down to coworkers below to have during their work break. Dad was in the elevator shaft when the elevator came down. He looked up and let out one scream just before the elevator crushed him to death—it was that quick. Dad's brother and other family friends were working with him on that dreadful day, so the eyewitnesses of the events were truthful to our family. I heard the same story told several times over the years while growing up.

I was also told about the superstitions regarding my dad's death: the omen in the morning before leaving for work, his belief on how his death would happen, and the fact that he was not wearing his evil-eye preventive charm on the day he died. None of these factors had any bearing on the cause of what happened to my dad on the day he slipped into eternity.

Now that I am a born-again Christian, I fully understand the Sovereignty of God over life and death, and what is truth versus superstition that has no validity. I also understand that dabbling in superstition is demonic dabbling that is very dangerous.

However, growing up with Greek parents, and being too young to believe anything different, I learned these superstitions that were very real to Mom and Dad.

On that last day of my dad's life, our lives changed forever. My mom would be raising two young children on her own without any financial or other support from a husband. And I would have a huge void in my young heart with an intense longing for some father authority figure to look up to, to trust and to love.

In the fullness of God's timing, yet far into the future, I would come to know, though not always understand, the intense desire of God to be the only One able and willing to fill this Father authority role in my life.

My spiritual journey with God would soon begin while I was yet a little girl, and in a very special way as God continued nurturing my life for His purpose and call.

"A father of the fatherless and a judge for the widows, is God in His holy habitation" (Psalm 68:5).

Chapter 2
Spiritual Journey Begins

Our beliefs or disbeliefs in God have a huge impact on our decisions and life journey in this world. In God's love for His creation, He gave us all a free will to make decisions for ourselves—and we do. However, all of our decisions come with consequences: sometimes good, sometimes bad.

But this one absolute truth will never change: God is Sovereign. Nothing has ever happened, nor will ever happen, without God allowing it to happen, end of story, period. And for those who love God and are called according to His purpose, God will cause all things to work together for good in their lives. (Romans 8:28.)

My mom believed in God and referred to Him on occasions. She never prayed in front of me or taught me how to pray. Yet, God used her simple belief to plant a mustard seed of faith in my heart that He was real. And that mustard seed of faith was all God needed to grow my devotion to Him.

Just after Dad died, Mom moved us to the Bronx borough in the area known as the South Bronx. Mom wanted us closer to where Yiayia lived. This move caused Michael and me to have a much less than sheltered life during our formative years.

We each dealt with Dad's sudden passing in our own ways. Mom was a stay-at-home mom and depended on Dad's financial support. As Mom grieved the loss of Dad, her health began to decline beginning with developing diabetes.

Michael had a hard time with Dad's death, and showed his grief more emotionally and physically. Although Michael was only eight years old, he and Dad were very close with each other.

I was six when my dad died. Mom kept the trunk that Dad used on his trip to Greece in a closet. For a long time afterward, I would lay awake at night and envision that he would come out of this trunk so we could be a family again, and I could have my dad back. Although I vaguely remembered my dad, my young heart loved and missed him.

The following summer after Dad died, Mom sent Michael and me to Hartley Farms, a Christian sleep-away summer camp in New Jersey, for a two-week stay. I remember the camp was beautiful and peaceful in a country atmosphere with many farm animals, and grass and trees all around; a real contrast to my concrete Bronx neighborhood.

Michael stayed with the boys in one area of the camp while I stayed with the girls in another area. Huge wooden cabins housed all the children, each with an open bay of single bunk beds uniformly arranged in rows. At the end of each bunk bed was a small chest used to keep the belongings each child brought along. But poor little me had no belongings for my own!

My suitcase that Mom so lovingly packed for me with all my belongings came up missing upon my arrival at this camp. Those in charge thought of sending me home because I had no clothes to carry me over the two weeks. But instead, at the leading of the Christian counselors, each of the other young children loaned me some of their clothes during my stay, so I was well provided for.

God had a special purpose for orchestrating my presence at this camp that He made sure came to fruition; nothing was going to frustrate His purpose. These same counselors led all of us children in a simple prayer every night before we went to sleep: "Now I lay me down to sleep. I pray the Lord my soul to keep. If I should die before I wake, I pray the Lord my soul to take."

I didn't understand this prayer back then, but it became the prayer that God had used in a powerful way to draw me closer to

Himself. It was the beginning of my prayer life that would morph, as God's Holy Spirit would lead, all the rest of my life. God used total strangers, who loved Jesus and cared enough about young children, to teach us all how to pray.

There were other fun things we did at this camp. We learned how to swim, made crafts, played games, sang around the campfire while roasting marshmallows, and covered our heads at night to keep the bats out of our hair—and this was for real. But the counselors sharing the love of Jesus, the bedtime prayers, and the generosity of other children sharing their clothes with me who had none, these are what I treasure the most from that experience.

When it was time to go home, and everyone's suitcases were brought down from the attic to be repacked, there was my suitcase with all my clothes and belongings just the way Mom had so lovingly packed them, waiting for me to claim them back.

Once I was home, I was faithful in saying my bedtime prayers every single night. At some point as time went on, I thought I was forgetting some of this prayer that I was taught, as it seemed awful short for a bedtime prayer, as if I knew how long bedtime prayers were supposed to be. So, I added on to this prayer.

But in reality, without knowing it at that time, the Holy Spirit took over teaching me to pray. The Holy Spirit, the Third Person in the Holy Trinity Godhead, who glorifies and honors the Lord Jesus Christ, decided when it was time my prayer life morphed.

My prayer still began in the same way, but now I knew to ask God for His blessings and forgiveness for my sins. And I requested the same on behalf of Mom, Michael, everyone in my family, and my pets—just in case they sinned too. I also asked God to please, let my dad and everyone in my family who died rest in peace, including my pets that died. I was trying to cover everyone as much as my young heart knew how. I was just a little girl reaching out to a God I really didn't know yet.

There were times I fell asleep while watching TV without saying my bedtime prayers. I remember often waking up, and after realizing I didn't pray, I would say my bedtime prayers before going back to sleep. I don't ever remember sharing with anyone about my prayer life or my love for God during that time. It was only much later in life that I understood, it was God's Holy Spirit who was the One nurturing and teaching me in my prayer life as a little girl—it was never really my own doing.

Although my parents made sure I was baptized as a baby, and by this time of my young life I was praying faithfully, I was still falling short of the criteria of being a true born-again Christian. My prayer life was a start, if you want to call it that. And God does honor the prayers and attempts of parents to dedicate their babies to Him, and to raise them believing in Him.

However, at some point in everyone's life, each person must make their own decision to accept Jesus as their Lord and Savior, to be born-again, and to be baptized in obedience to Jesus once they are born-again. I never knew any of this during my formative years. God was just "God" to me.

Mom, Michael and I continued believing there was a God, and believing it was enough to be called Greek Orthodox Christians. Although we did not attend church regularly, Mom tried her best to teach us what she knew about God and our Orthodox faith.

As we got older, Mom would instruct us to fast from all dairy products and meat during parts of the Easter season and on holy holidays, per our Orthodox rules. It was never explained why we had to fast from these foods. I remember grumbling to myself and wondering about the meaning of fasting with no understanding. After I became a born-again Christian, I understood the benefits of fasting as God directed, not as a rule dictated by a religious denomination. The exception to a directed fast from others is a call for unity in God's Spirit for a specific purpose and prayer.

We all used some "colorful metaphors" (profanity), which should never be used by "Christians." But when Michael heard me use that G** D*** curse word, he tattled on me to Mom, even though they often used it too. Mom then admonished me never to say that curse again.

Although Michael and Mom continued to use that curse word, when I slipped soon afterward and used it again, though no one else heard me, I immediately and remorsefully apologized to God directly for saying it. This was another experience that found its way into that never-to-forget part of my brain.

It wasn't until years later that I fully understood, that was the first time God Himself dealt with a serious sin in my life, and admonished me twice to get His point across: first through my mom, and then through the conviction of His Holy Spirit.

The names of God, including Jesus Christ and the Holy Spirit, are precious, holy and powerful; they should never be used in vain, whether casually, as a curse, or in any other way. To use any of God's names in vain are very serious offenses to Him that He hates.

God has also made it very clear that those who use His name in vain will not go unpunished. This warning is part of the Ten Commandments: "You shall not take the name of the Lord your God in vain, for the Lord will not leave him unpunished who takes His name in vain" (Exodus 20:7; Deuteronomy 5:11).

God does give us our own free will with consequences to our choices. But I have learned that God has zero tolerance for some sins in my life, and He makes sure that I understand what those sins are. Using God's name in vain is one of those sins. Although I continued using colorful metaphors, I was very careful never to use God's name in vain.

As my life and spiritual journey continued, my Heavenly Father continued His nurturing and disciplining, even as He was drawing me closer to Himself.

Chapter 3
Early Bronx

When God created the human race, He created everyone in His own image and likeness, and created us all to be equal. Any form of racial or ethnic bigotry is wrong. Any violence resulting from this bigotry is even more wrong.

There are many stories that can be told by the victims of such bigotry. Some of what I will be sharing during my South Bronx life is only my story. I have no regret or resentment today for what I was allowed to experience during my formative young years, but only thanks to God's grace.

Although I was the victim of racial bigotry as one of the very few White kids living in the South Bronx during our last few years there, I don't remember ever hating anyone. But I sure hated the hostility of which I was victim.

When my family moved to the South Bronx in 1965, only God knew that our neighborhood would soon be transformed into a dangerous concrete jungle. My experiences support that there is a loving God who is very capable of keeping His beloved children safe in any circumstance that He allows them to be in. And if God so chooses to allow His children to suffer in some way, He has a perfectly good reason for allowing such suffering.

Our apartment building was built in the 1930s. It had sixty-six apartments, six levels, stairs on each side of the building lobby, and one elevator. The building was also infested with mice and cockroaches, including some rare white cockroaches. The building superintendent once told us that we should be glad we had mice. His reasoning was that the apartment buildings up the block from us had rats. And this was meant to console us!

There were other similar apartment buildings on our block that were built around the same era. But only a few were as large as our building. On the surrounding blocks were some single-dwelling row houses.

I have some fond memories of my early days in our Bronx neighborhood. Surrounded by concrete and almost void of anything green, it became our concrete playground. My friends and I played the normal inner-city street games: handball bouncing off the buildings; chalk-drawn hopscotch on the sidewalks; jump rope; hide and seek between the parked cars, buildings and alleyways. We also had concrete parks with swings, slides, monkey bars and seesaws that we frequented and enjoyed.

There were many neat mom-and-pop specialty stores of that era within one to three city blocks up from our apartment building. Mom had an account at the grocery store just up the block. The butcher shop would custom cut meat per customer orders. There was a deli that carried kosher meat and cheese products. Our corner newspaper-candy store was a great place to buy eggcreams, a New York City chocolate drink made with seltzer water but without eggs. The pizzeria sold one slice of pizza for a quarter. A friend and I would often put our change together to buy one slice of pizza, which the owner was happy to cut in half for us.

We frequented and enjoyed the YMCA and movie theater up the block. And the entrance to the subway station was just two blocks from our apartment building.

During different stages of my life journey in the Bronx, I had an array of racially and ethnically diverse group of friends: Jewish, Irish, Black, Hispanic, Latino, and somewhere in between. We all played together with the differences between us never even registering in our young hearts. Yep, life was good in the early "good old days!"

I started first grade in the Bronx with the following few years of school being pretty much uneventful. Michael was in the third grade. Our elementary school was within walking distance of our apartment building. Average kids were in my classes just trying to learn from teachers who wanted to teach, and everyone seemed nice enough to everyone. But something drastically changed from about my fifth grade on.

Everyone has an inherited sinful nature that our environment and what we indulge in can either starve or nurture. In any school system, this sinful nature can manifest itself in types of "bullies," who target other children as their victims. The environment in which these bullies are brought up in becomes a deciding force as to the intensity of their hostility towards their victims.

Without understanding why at the beginning, I became a targeted victim of many of these bullies. As the hostility grew, it seemed learning in school came to an abrupt halt, and survival became the priority.

I was in the fifth grade when one particular experience found its way into that never-to-forget part of my brain. A Black girl tried to lure me away from the school building before picking a fight with me. I was fearful knowing her intention, and tried my best to avoid this fight. In doing so, I lied by telling her I needed to use the restroom, which I knew would get me back into the school building while hoping to distract from her intention.

My hope was crushed when she made the same claim as she followed me back into the school and then into the restroom. I only pretended to use the restroom, and when I came out, to my dismay, there she was just waiting for me.

She taunted me as we left the school, even as I knew she was going to start beating on me as soon as we were out of range of the school building—and sure enough, she did.

From out of nowhere, a circle of kids surrounded us as she started beating on me. I had only one choice at this point—I needed to fight to defend myself.

Neither one of us knew anything about a real punching match. The spectator kids around us had a comical show to watch, as we were two young girls acting like real maniacs. The fight turned into pulling hair, throwing blows any which way while using any limb available, trying to land at least some blows that would end this nonsense fight. In the frenzy, she landed a blow that blackened one of my eyes.

Finally, the fight ended, but I'm not sure how. She went her way, and I went my way. The spectators dispersed on their own; without a maniac-girl fight to watch, it was time to leave.

This happened right at the start of the Easter weekend. A young boy was nearby while I was walking Duke before visiting family for Easter dinner. When he saw me, he proceeded to gawk at me and would not turn his gaze away. He didn't say anything or laugh at me; he just gawked at me. I was so disgusted with his gawking that I spoke to him in a very mean tone: "What? What are you looking at? You got a problem?"

After giving this some thought later, I pictured the comical scene this boy was gawking at. Here I was, a young girl just out walking my dog, all dressed up in my Easter dress, nice shoes, and wearing a bonnet that garnished the comical addition of my shining black eye to this cute outfit. No wonder he gawked at me. I might have done the same thing to some other kid had they been in my condition with a shining black eye, and I'm sure I would have added a few laughs, if not out loud at least to myself.

By this time in my Bronx days, I too was allowing my environment to nurture my inherited sinful nature. My reactions to behaviors from others were going from defensive, to offensive, to aggressive, and at times without even knowing the true intent of the other person. Had Jesus been my Savior at that time, my reaction to this boy gawking at me should have been different.

Mom visited the school principal over this fighting incident that left me with a black eye, and he assured her that this would be addressed and would never happen again. However, as time went on, more incidents happened and the hostility only got worse.

My sixth-grade school year was the only year I had to ride a public bus to another location for schooling. A bowling alley building was converted into this school, leaving us in classrooms without windows. I didn't have any friends in this school, as we were bused in from many different neighborhoods of the Bronx. By this time, I was definitely way out numbered as a White kid in school and cautious of the other kids. I kept to myself while trying to be as inconspicuous as possible, which only proved to be an impossible dream.

There was a Black boy in my class who started making obscene gestures at me indicating he wanted to have sex with me. This went on for some time, even days, without the teacher being able to stop him.

And so, as inconspicuous as I tried to be during these school days, it was all for naught. When I had enough, and my Greek temper over this boy's obscene gestures got the best of me, I took him down.

By then, my brother had taught me just enough of Judo (a form of martial arts) to land him on his back. I sat on top of him as I held his arms in this stronghold, hurting more his pride than anything else. I didn't want to let him loose until he apologized to me for his obscene gestures he made. But before he did, the teacher pulled me off him.

Later, during a parent-teacher conference, this same teacher confessed to Mom that he didn't want to pull me off this boy because he felt the boy deserved what I did to him. But as the teacher, he felt obligated to pull me off for the sake of the other spectator kids who had circled us.

By this time in my life, I was starting to really hate school and hate living in the Bronx. And the worst was yet to happen!

I continued with my prayer life and growing closer to God, even as the hostility grew. However, I didn't have that intimate relationship with God yet that He longed I would have, that He was calling me to have. I believed that Jesus was the Son of God, but I didn't understand why He came and died on a cross. I was ignorant of the entire purpose of Jesus as the sacrificial "Lamb of God" and His resurrection from the dead.

We celebrated Easter with all the special trimmings of chocolate bunnies, colorful Easter eggs, Greek Easter cookies, family dinners, and Easter outfits with cute bonnets that could garnish shining black eyes. But church was not included, and the true meaning of Easter escaped my understanding.

However, regardless of my inherited sinful nature that was nurtured by my environment, regardless of my ignorance to Jesus and His purpose for dying on the cross for my sins, regardless of my ignorance to God's purpose and call on my life, God was always with me.

God kept His eye upon me, instructing and teaching and counseling me in the way in which I should go. (Psalm 32:8.) I just never knew any of this during my young life growing up in the South Bronx.

Chapter 4
The Concrete Jungle

During the time frame of when I lived in the South Bronx, it was believed to be one of the most dangerous areas of the Bronx. With the "good old days" in my Bronx neighborhood gone, it transformed into a concrete jungle.

And there is only one unspoken, unmistakable, unbreakable law for any real jungle life—survival of the fittest, which includes the ability to run, and to run fast. No matter what type of jungle, this is—The Law, period.

Violence became an everyday occurrence. Drug addicts roamed around peddling their drugs. Snipers shot at people from rooftops. Fluorescent light bulbs were thrown from the roofs aiming for people below. There were even designated "kill-whitey" days, when White kids were thrown into glass picture-windows, shot, knifed, beaten, and only because of being White. And you wouldn't dare keep your apartment door unlocked at any time— you never knew who would walk in.

We even had our very own, well-known neighborhood child molester—and I don't say this lightly. He was a short man who had a flat head for some reason, which made him known as Flat Top. Everyone, including the cops, knew about Flat Top. And all of us kids knew he was to be avoided at all costs.

Flat Top was dangerous and indiscriminate with whom he molested, and yet, he was on the loose with full access to any kid he happened to come across. I'm not sure why when he was so well known for such a dangerous disposition.

One day, when I was about twelve years old, I was taking a jaunt through the jungle neighborhood on a hot and lazy summer afternoon. Little drops of sweat rolled down on my brow. The concrete all around emitted heat waves as the sun beat down on it, making it hotter than it was. While minding my own business, I came upon the predator Flat Top prowling about.

Then he spotted me! Flat Top's mean expression gave me the creeps and caused chills to run up and down my spine. Our eyes made contact, and the next thing I knew without provocation, Flat Top started after me full speed ahead.

As the prey with fear the driving force, I instinctively took off running, mind racing, knowing without any doubt—if this predator caught me, he was going to really hurt me before I turned into dead meat!

Flat Top picked up speed coming after me confirming his obvious evil intent. Fueled by his determination to catch me, I ran faster than ever before in my life, desperately trying to reach my apartment building before I ended up in his clutches.

And then this unexplainable and uncontrollable phenomenon happened to me: Without any warning whatsoever, my legs turned into wet noodles. *How can my legs let me down just when I need them the most to get away from this predator to save my life?*

At this point in our predator-chasing-prey episode, my adrenalin kicked in, and even though my legs were wet noodles from being so scared, they managed to carry me to safety. Thank God that He knew what He was doing when He gave us adrenalin to pick up when our bodies let us down.

There was another suspicious man who stalked me. He was tall, husky, had black hair and mustache, and drove a mustard yellow two-door sedan that to this day, I can still remember his license plate number. All this too found its way into that never-to-forget part of my brain.

This man was a creepy presence, to say the least. I saw him when I was at the laundromat. He would just appear and follow me while I walked to the store. For the longest time, it seemed everywhere I went this man would appear from out of nowhere.

I never told Mom about this man stalking me, and I'm not sure why I didn't. Now I know I should have, and I should have given her his license plate number in case I ever came up missing. Maybe by this time, I was just so used to people eyeing me up and stalking me that he was just another predator prowling about this concrete jungle. But every time I would see him just appear from out of nowhere near me, I would give great thought to his presence.

There were other dangerous situations that surrounded my family during our stay in the Bronx. One night, Yiayia phoned to warn Mom to wait before sending either Michael or me out with Duke for the night. Her warning came after hearing on her police radio band that on the roof of the building right across the street from our building was a sniper shooting at people below.

But the warning phone call for our protection came too late! I was already outside walking Duke while this man had his target practice. God never let up on His providential protection for all my family during our time living in the South Bronx.

Another scary and life-threatening experience involved Mom and Michael one day when I wasn't at home. I had just returned from going to the laundromat with our trusty shopping cart, a two-wheel invaluable device most New Yorkers treasured, and then left to go babysitting for friends of our family.

I left this shopping cart full of the clean clothes in the narrow entry hallway of our apartment just a few feet from our thick, steel entry door. A person with a clear mind could easily squeeze past this shopping cart with little effort. The doorknob on this door was broken, so unless the deadbolts were locked, it would drift back open announcing to everyone that the door was unlocked.

Our apartment was on the first floor and in full view of anyone using the stairs nearby. When Michael left our apartment to put trash in the incinerator, he neglected to lock the deadbolts on this door when he returned. His negligence almost cost Mom, Duke and him their lives.

On this day, a doped-up, evil man was stumbling past our apartment when he spotted the slightly drifted open door enticing him to come in. Taking out his huge knife and clutched in hand, he quietly pushed the door open and slowly entered hoping for a kill and to haul away some loot.

But wait! He came upon an unexpected obstacle that kept him from reaching his victims. Too doped up to realize he could just squeeze past the shopping cart full of clothes, he angrily tackled it with all his might, banging it against the walls in a desperate frenzy to reach his victims while still clutching his huge knife.

This was all the diversion needed to alert our trusty guard dog, Duke, who then commenced with a full-blown attack on this evil intruder. Michael, the boy who often "cried wolf" joking around about scary situations, terrified upon seeing the evil intruder, yelled to Mom in Greek so the man could not understand, "There's a man in our apartment with a knife!"

Believing this was another cry-wolf joke, Mom hesitated, but then realized Duke's alarming attacks justified believing Michael was telling the truth this time. As Duke continued his vicious attack, Michael picked up a seltzer bottle ready to hit the evil intruder on his head.

Mom came from the circle-around of the hallway to the other side, and seeing Michael aiming to use the seltzer bottle, yelled in Greek: "NO! NO! Don't hit him with the bottle; you'll kill him! Just push him out! JUST PUSH HIM OUT!"

A full-blown scuffle was going on now with Michael, Mom and Duke desperately trying to protect themselves from this evil intruder and push him out without getting killed, or killing him in the process.

Meanwhile, in the spiritual realm there was another battle raging on. The demon-possessed, doped-up man brought along a slew of other demons with him. The angelic warriors with orders from God Himself to protect my family, were raging a battle of their own against these demons. The angelic warriors and sulfur-breathing demons were clashing swords and throwing up sparks while the demons spewed out angry words at the angelic warriors.

These spirits swished and swooped all around while the battle continued with Michael, Mom and Duke against this evil intruder. Then finally, the angelic warriors gained the upper hand. With a few final blows, a few final clashes with swords, the demons knew they had lost this battle.

As Michael and Mom finally managed to push out the evil intruder, slamming the steel door closed and locking it securely, the demons whimpered as they limply swished away after him, leaving behind some of their sulfur breaths, hoping for another day of battle for a victory. But the victory for this battle belonged to the angelic warriors of the Most High God.

Mom later confessed her thoughts that were going on all during this battle: "All I could think of was: I just got out of the shower, this man is going to kill me, and I'm in my bare feet."

Chapter 5
My Best Friend

I would never want to give anyone the impression that we were always the victims in the Bronx. Michael and I had our fun too, and played with our own "victims" subject to our harmless amusement.

I had many childhood friends. But my very best friend while growing up in this concrete jungle was Michael. I always looked up to my big brother as only a little sister could. We were always so close with a strong bond of love. We did so much more together than I could ever share that left me with so many fond memories.

Mom would entrust Michael with his little sister and let us loose to go by subway to different areas of the Bronx and the higher-class areas of downtown Manhattan, where we played havoc on the streets of New York City. Looking back, we may have been too young for such escapades on our own, as Michael was only about thirteen. But Michael always had a brilliant sense of direction, and rarely did we ever get lost.

We loved playing hide and seek in Central Park, and enjoyed visiting all the museums. Our favorite stomping ground by far was the American Museum of Natural History, where we always had a blast. We would run up the down escalators, run down the up escalators, run around and hide from each other in the animal exhibit caves, and did other things I should not mention.

We also had fun with the "high-class" people of Manhattan, who we thought were always so well dressed as compared to the average clothing we wore. We would walk close behind them so that those who were coming the opposite direction would think we were their kids.

We would ring the doorbells of the more exclusive apartment buildings in Manhattan, and after doing so, run across the street to watch the doormen as they came out from their stations inside to investigate who were the culprits playing games.

One day, I decided to ring one of these doorbells, and then ran across the street without warning Michael that I did. And sure enough, just as I thought would happen, out came this mean-looking and very angry doorman who grabbed Michael, and then yelled and accused him of ringing the doorbell. I stood and watched on the other side of the street where I was safe, and laughed so hard while Michael got in trouble for something I did.

Traveling the subway system to and from these escapades was an adventure in itself. The New York City Transit Subway is a massive and complex system that to this day, really amazes me. With many floor levels above and below ground, with tunnels, stairways, nooks and crannies everywhere, it was easy to get lost just in the subway system itself. However, I felt safe following my big brother through this maze, and I trusted his brilliant sense of direction, perhaps too blindly.

Michael was always protective of me and often walked with his arm around me unashamed to display his brotherly love. But when we fought, I would turn around and wiggle out of his grip to walk on my own—he would get so mad when I would do this.

Only once can I remember getting lost in the subway system because we were fighting. We ended up getting on the wrong train and left the station with no money for two more tokens to get back on for our trip home. Michael then convinced me to beg total strangers for money to get us back home. Michael always knew just how to manipulate me to do something he would not do himself. Even as I made a feeble protest, I knew I had no other choice. My sense of direction stunk back then (it hasn't improved much in my latter years), and I was totally dependent on Michael to get me back home.

And so, I begged total strangers walking the streets of New York City for the sixty cents we needed to get two tokens to get home while Michael hid around a corner.

Thankfully, we managed to get home safely that day with Mom never the wiser to our adventure. We saw no point raising her concerns about her kids' escapades while on their own playing havoc on the streets of New York City.

There were times traveling on the subway system when things got a little tight—so to speak—and a little aggressive, especially during the famous New York City rush hours. If we missed our time for going home before the rush hour, we found ourselves like two little sardines with a bunch of really big sardines all smashed in one train car.

Most of the time, we were in no hurry to get home, unlike some other New Yorkers who felt that time was of the essence in their travels. One particular episode was so traumatic to me that it too found its way into that never-to-forget part of my brain.

As we were getting on a subway train during rush hour, some mean woman decided I wasn't moving fast enough for her liking. Angrily, she started pounding my back with her fists several times while she pushed me and yelled, "Move it, move it, move it," all in her efforts to move me faster so she could get on the train.

This disturbed me greatly, as I was just a kid minding my own business. Her hostile actions against me were totally uncalled for. After all, we were all going to make it on the train eventually. It was bad enough that I was regularly beaten up by my peers. But to have an adult stranger also beat on me—well, her mean actions could have really traumatized me for life! Thankfully, though, I had a stronger emotional disposition.

Once on the train, this woman squeezed further in and held on to a pole in the middle of the car as we stood sardine smashed in the car. Then our eyes locked with a mean glare at each other. A few minutes later, I saw her actions indicated her stop was coming up next.

There are some opportunities in life that seem to happen just ever so fast without a chance to really think things over. When some of these opportunities happen, you just have to be superfast responding. Otherwise, such priceless opportunities may just slip by you in the blink of an eye.

Such was the case when this mean woman started to exit the train by the same door she pushed me through only minutes before, the same door I was sardine smashed standing up against.

Literally, within microseconds of recognizing such a perfect opportunity came the flooding thought in my brain of—vengeance. Within these microseconds of my brain's thought, my body spontaneously responded without any further communication from my brain. My foot found itself in just the perfect place, at just the perfect precise moment needed right in front of this woman as she exited the train.

With this simple action of my foot, this mean woman flew across the subway platform with her crouched body; arms flailed as she desperately clung to her handbag; body twisted and turned every which way; legs wobbled and almost came out from under her, until she finally caught herself just before a dreadful fall.

As she gathered her composure—pride fatally wounded—she glanced back at the train doors she just exited. Our eyes locked one final time. Hers glared with hatred; mine twinkled with laughter as the train doors started to close.

Through the train door window, I gave her my sweetest and biggest smile I could muster up, and then waved to her goodbye as the train slowly moved away from the station. By the glare of her eyes locked on mine, I had great satisfaction knowing that she understood it was her little punching-bag girl who was the cause of her flying-trip across the platform. But there was nothing more that she could do to harm me.

There is an old cliché: "Revenge is a dish best served cold." But sometimes, you need to serve it hot, real hot, or the opportunity will slip by you in the blink of an eye.

Now that I have confessed this vengeful act of mine that I inflicted on a total stranger for her hostility towards me, without a doubt, I will answer to the Lord Jesus if I leave this story without clarifying His final word and position on His children taking their own vengeance.

God's word declares: "Never take your own revenge, beloved, but leave room for the wrath of God, for it is written, 'Vengeance is Mine, I will repay,' says the Lord" (Romans 12:19).

As I truthfully relate this episode while writing this book, I found myself saying a prayer for the mean woman who I believed I had the right to inflict my vengeance upon.

I didn't accept Jesus as my Lord and Savior when I was growing up in the South Bronx: the criteria for being a born-again Christian. I did not know I should be leaving vengeance up to God at that time in my life.

I prayed to "God" every night. I acknowledged Him often. I even loved Him, but only because He first loved me. However, none of my so-called religious practices and beliefs justified me being a true born-again Christian. But even so, God was in the role as my Father even while I was still in my sin.

The day would come when I would acknowledge the atoning sacrifice of Jesus Christ on the cross, and embrace Him into my heart and life to be my personal Lord and Savior.

Chapter 6

Entertainment

In addition to our escapades riding the subway to the high-class areas of New York City, Michael and I managed to have fun within our own neighborhood. Looking back now, some of what we believed was fun at the time was definitely dangerous and wrong to do. We went about our neighborhood just looking for something to get into. There were many run-down and abandoned businesses, and a few empty lots with small trees and bushes that seemed like a forest to us, that we loved to play around.

Our adventures took us to construction sites that we had to climb over embankments and through barricades to get to, obstacles that were meant to keep kids like us out. One time, we were chased away by some man coming after us with a boulder over his head aiming to throw it at us. What was a difficult embankment to cross over getting to this site, on our get-away, it was as though it wasn't there anymore. Adrenalin is a marvelous body reaction in times of extreme fright and served us well as kids, even though my legs still turned into those wet noodles.

Many times, Duke accompanied us on these escapades in our neighborhood, which meant our get-away trips to safety was a little more difficult. It was very hard to convince a male dog that he could not stop to lift his leg and leave his mark at every fire hydrant or light pole he came across when we needed to run for our lives.

We traveled far and wide in our neighborhood adventures. One day, while playing around the riverbank with Michael ahead of me, he turned around in sudden fear and cursed and screamed at me to "run, run, run," as he took off running for his life.

By this time in our adventurous lives, I knew when Michael screamed at me to run with his face distorted with fear, I ran and asked why later. My only hesitation was a few seconds as my brain registered what he was saying. This was long enough for some older teenagers to come out from behind the bridge wall after us. Apparently, Michael interrupted their drug dealings of some sort—he knew it and so did they. We ran and ran for our lives with our wet-noodle legs until they couldn't carry us any longer. We managed to get away to safety, but this episode was another one put into that never-to-forget part of my brain.

Our neighborhood movie theater was another adventure for us as kids. It was a Saturday all-afternoon affair back in those days, as movie theaters allowed people to stay all day watching the same movie over and over again until they got tired of it and left.

The movie theater was divided into the children section separated from the adult section. On special days, we would sneak into the adult section after the lights were turned off, and armed with our water pistols, would squirt innocent people who sat a few rows in front of us. When they turned around to look behind to investigate the origin of the squirts, we turned around too as though we got squirted and needed to know from where.

On a few occasions, the mean old woman "matron," who never smiled and never had any patience for mischievous kids in her theater, would throw us out of the theater. But this never deterred us from returning the following week.

Over time, movies and TV programs became a major source of entertainment, especially when our neighborhood grew more dangerous. Looking back with what I know now, these forms of entertainment were in reality, becoming idols in my life.

Mom even called the TV Guide my "bible." I went through each newly published TV Guide and marked the programs or movies that I wanted to watch on our black and white console TV.

I loved watching animal shows the best with the movie Born Free being my all-time favorite. Together, Michael and I would watch westerns, military movies, science fiction, and demonic and horror movies. Back in those days, there were plenty of biblical movies aired on TV during the holidays that we also loved to watch.

With each movie and TV program I would watch, something would often stir in my heart leaving an imprint. Sometimes it was a strong patriotic emotion, or demonic fear, or just passion over a story that I would dwell on for days.

What I did not know back then but know now, is that the influences of what we indulge in and allow into our minds and hearts have a huge impact on our attitudes and behaviors in life, and may even prove to be dangerous physically and spiritually.

At one time, after watching a movie about Jesus, I remember dwelling on thoughts that had I been living back then, I would have told everyone that they couldn't crucify Jesus because He was the Son of God. My thoughts of wanting to stop the crucifixion of Jesus only proved my ignorance as to the purpose of the cross for our salvation. I remained ignorant of the Gospel during my entire young life living in the Bronx. Satan also knew of my ignorance of the Gospel and played it well against me.

One Christmas season, the Dickens' Christmas Carol movie made me terrified of dying in my sleep. The spirit of the future showing Scrooge his grave was the culprit. I didn't know a lot about God at that time in my life, but I was sure about one thing: God was in charge as to whom He allowed into His Heaven.

For the longest time afterward, I tried so hard not to fall asleep, terrified that if I died in my sleep without the chance of making any sin in my life right before God, I would not get into Heaven. I didn't understand that everyone was born in sin, and that only by accepting Jesus Christ as my personal Lord and Savior, and accepting His atonement through His sacrifice on the cross as the only payment possible for my sins, would I be granted entrance into God's Heaven.

It was during this time that I asked Mom one of the most profound questions I had ever asked her up until that time: "If I did something wrong and I went to jail and paid for the crime, will I still go to Heaven when I die?"

Mom assured me that I would go to Heaven when I died, but never addressed payment for my sins to get there; I don't believe she understood my concerns. Mom also didn't understand at that time the full Gospel of the Lord Jesus Christ.

One other time after watching a movie about Noah, I found a Bible in our apartment and looked up where God said that He would not destroy the world again. This was another ignorance on my part of God's truths. God promised not to destroy the world again with water. However, Scriptures make it clear that God will destroy the world again, but the next time it will be by fire. (2 Peter 3:7 & 3:10.)

I believe that was the only time I read a Bible up until that time in my life. While doing so, I inadvertently came across God's command to His people Israel not to get tattoos. (Leviticus 19:28.) Although the Jewish laws do not bind Christians, I understood years later, that was the first time God spoke to me through Scripture, and in doing so, shared His heart concerning tattoos. This knowledge would be significant in my life in the near future. I am a firm believer now that there are no coincidences with God.

It is clear to me now that Satan used some of these forms of entertainment in his schemes against me. But there were times when God used them to teach me and draw me closer to Himself. Although God patiently allowed these "idols" in my young life, the Lord knew that at some point in my future walk with Him, He would decide when enough was enough, and then demand that these entertainment idols no longer be a part of my life.

Chapter 7
Demonic Dabbling

It was an adventure in itself living in our small three-room apartment between the layout and the long, winding hallway, and the fact that it was downright messy—but it was a fun messy. There were times our only bedroom was littered with clothes thrown on the floor, food plates scattered around, beds not made, garbage scattered that couldn't find its way to a real garbage can—an environment that was paradise to the cockroaches and mice.

The journey through the winding hallway in our apartment had several turns and led to each room. Our living room and kitchen had two doorways each serving as a circle-around back to the main hallway and only entry door. This circle-around was how Mom reached our evil intruder. Lining the hallway were boxes, a chest of drawers opposite our bedroom door, our refrigerator sat in one corner, and a 55-gallon fiber drum—once used as a moving container—sat in another corner. All these objects in our hallway served as places for "things" to be stored on top that were never able to find a place of their own in our small apartment.

At the very end of this long, winding hallway, just a few feet past our bedroom door, was the room I dreaded the most. It was the room I never wanted to enter alone, let alone stay there alone. But it was also the most needed room. It was—The Bathroom!

For some unknown reason, there were times when I was so afraid to go into this bathroom by myself that I would drag poor Duke in—fully against his will—just so something alive would be in there with me. Sometimes I would run for my life after I flushed the toilet because I expected something to come out after me.

Although our apartment was small and cluttered, Mom still loved to entertain by sharing her delicious dinners with friends and family. I can remember spending a lot of time cleaning up our apartment for these dinner guests, except our bedroom. If any guests dared to open this bedroom door—well, they did so at their own risk.

Yiayia would often come for dinner with a man who was a long-time friend of the family. This man was born and raised in Greece, and claimed to be a clairvoyant: a person who receives their fortune telling knowledge through demonic influences.

After dinner, Mom would use a special coffee pot to make a very thick, rich Turkish coffee served in little cups. After drinking their coffee, each person would swish their cups around to get the dregs on all sides of their little cup before turning them upside down. Before long, the dregs dried creating crisscrossing lines like a road map. Then one at a time, this Greek man would read each person's cup of lines and predict their future.

Although I was never directly part of this fortune telling practice, and never understood or was told what was predicted, I accepted it without any misgivings. While engaging in this man's fortune telling services, we were all dangerously dabbling in demonic activities, even in our ignorance.

Michael and I also played with a Ouija Board. I understood only later in life, that this Ouija Board is believed to be the gateway to the demonic spiritual realm. And we indulged in horror and demonic movies. After watching these movies, I would have a great fear to journey through our hallway, as Michael enjoyed scaring me, especially after watching such movies. I never knew when he would get on top of the chest of drawers, or stand in some corner with an object he used to create a scary shadow, or come out of a dark room with a flashlight shining on his face. Mom kept warning Michael that if he didn't stop scaring me, I could end up having a nervous breakdown.

Poor Duke also had a comical phobia while journeying through our hallway. At certain points of his journey, such as the corner where the 55-gallon fiber drum sat, he would carefully walk past with his head turned upward watching, as if at any moment something would come flying off the drum and land on his head. It took only a few things falling on him—like a roll of paper towels—that started this phobia.

Michael also had a phobia that became an obsession that our entry door was always locked, perhaps because of our evil intruder. However, normally people with such an obsession would only be satisfied if they checked themselves to be sure something was locked. This was not the case with Michael.

I remember so well late one night, our conversation went back-and-forth annoyingly with Michael asking me if our apartment entry door was locked, yet would never be satisfied with my assurance that it was. As our conversation continued, Michael became increasingly insistent that I was the one who needed to get out of bed and check to be sure this door was locked.

After I repeatedly refused to check this door, Michael knew his last guilt-ridden, manipulating comment would get me moving: "Okay, Angelika. If the door isn't locked, and someone comes in and murders us, it's gonna be all your fault."

I don't know why I never told him to get out of bed and check the door himself!

In exasperation, I got out of bed to make the long journey through the winding hallway to check our door while being ever vigilant for cockroaches and mice so as not to squash anything live. After finally reaching our entry door, I found it securely locked.

Now why couldn't Michael come all this way, late at night, braving through cockroaches and mice when they are most active, and check this door himself to make sure it was locked? Because he knew his little sister would do it for him!

I started the long journey through the winding hallway back to our bedroom, but fearful now that this was a trick from Michael to scare me on the way back. While looking down still vigilant so as not to squash anything live, I let out a sigh of relief just before I reached our bedroom door.

But wait! I looked up and took a deep breath. There it was, just a few feet past our bedroom door at the end of this long, winding hallway, the most dreadful room in this apartment. It was looming like some evil passageway to hell itself, just calling to me, enticing me to continue straight ahead and right through its doorway. It was—The Bathroom!

Should I go? I need to go. But NO! I can't go at this time of night; you've got to be kidding me! Where's Duke? I need to wait, at least until daylight. That way there is less of a chance that something will come out after me after I flush the toilet.

My fear of this bathroom at times was so real, that now I believe there was an evil presence that caused this fear. Many nights I would literally barricade our entry door as added security, in addition to making sure the three deadbolts and chain were locked and secured.

I would put our shopping cart up against the front of this door, wrapped a dog chain around it to attach it to a chair, added a ladder and whatever else I could find, just to make sure no one was going to come through that steel door. And I was satisfied that no one could get through my barricade. But no one was able to get out either, which I never thought of back then.

But as much as I made sure our steel-entry door was securely locked and barricaded, making sure the physical evil was kept out, I could not have known at that time the importance of securing our spiritual door. I cannot state strongly enough that any form of dabbling in demonic activities is very dangerous.

All the dabbling with demonic activities that were done in our small apartment: engaging with a clairvoyant, playing with a Ouija Board, practicing superstition, indulging in horror and demonic movies—all these practices were dangerous and invited demons into our dwelling space.

I am not implying that our apartment was "possessed" by demons. However, because of the dabbling in demonic activities, even in ignorance yet unbeknown to any of us, we allowed these demons to be "present," and their influences made a difference in our attitudes and behaviors. The angelic warriors received no help from any of us in their duties of keeping us safe. And because of this, the fierce spiritual battles were many.

In this dreadful bathroom, I believe now there was a demon, or two, or more up in the corner somewhere just waiting for an opportunity to attack. I can say this with some true conviction now that I understand more about spiritual warfare. But in my young life growing up in the Bronx, my knowledge of spiritual warfare was non-existent.

I was probably not more than thirteen years old on this particular day when an incident happened that looking back, would confirm what I just stated. I can imagine the fierce spiritual battle that went on right in this bathroom over my life.

The demons were up there in the tub area battling angelic warriors as fiery swords clashed causing sparks to fly everywhere. As the angelic warriors gained the upper hand and were putting the demons into strongholds, the demons uttered curses with their sulfur breaths in their attempts to prove they were invited there; they had the right to be there; they had the right to destroy my life.

After a few final strong blows from the angelic warriors to the demons, a few more clashes with swords, the demons huddled in the corner whimpering in defeat, breathing hard with their sulfur breaths, exhausted, bound and subdued, but remained present.

Finally, although the spiritual battles would still rage over my life in the years to come, the angelic warriors won this battle. After I got out of the shower and grabbed the towel to dry off, safe where I was standing, the angelic warriors let loose the force they had been holding back that was meant to kill me: The plaster ceiling several inches thick over where I had just seconds ago stood in the tub, came crashing down. With this crash, I jumped, screamed and started crying and trembling all at once.

The demons wanted me dead, as they knew if I died without fully accepting Jesus as my Lord and Savior, I would be spending an eternity in hell with them. The demons also knew that once I fully accept Jesus as my Lord, I would have the authority myself in the name of Jesus to resist and renounce their rights to my life.

The angelic warriors had God's charge and authority given to them regarding protecting my life at all costs. My own dabbling in demonic activities was not helping these angelic warriors at all with their duties. But I only gained this knowledge much later in my life, and only after the fiercest spiritual battle was raged over my very existence in this world.

By the grace and love of God, He was going to protect my life until I fully understood, surrendered and accepted Jesus Christ as my personal Lord and Savior.

Chapter 8
Last Traumatic Experience

Kids can be cruel, and often for no reason. Despite my toughness that would not allow me to back off in situations when I needed to stand my ground, there were times I purposely did my best to avoid confrontation as much as possible.

I had devised a secret passageway as a kid that I used to avoid the mean confrontation with the kids who loitered in front of our apartment building whenever possible. My secret passageway consisted of several obstacles that began with climbing out my building-hallway window and into the courtyard where our superintendent kept his German Shepherd dog; the dog didn't concern me as much as the mean kids. Once out of this window, I went over and down walls, over fences, and through alleyways, until I was on the block over from mine. But there were times when it was difficult to avoid unwanted confrontations.

By the time I was in junior high school, I really hated school for many reasons, but mostly because I was constantly bullied for being White. I was often beat on, laughed at, gobbled at (as white meat on a turkey), and experienced some other things I won't mention. By this time, not only did the kids not care if they learned anything, some of the teachers didn't care if they taught us.

The high school that Michael attended was even worse. The very few White families still left in our neighborhood boycotted the high school because of the racial hate crimes against them. Mom also kept Michael home for this boycott, which only accomplished all these kids losing a full year of schooling.

At the same time Mom was boycotting the high school, in my eighth grade, the junior high school I was attending eliminated lunch periods during the school days. This decision was to address the practice of kids dropping drugs in the drinks of unsuspecting kids during lunch, which caused some of these kids to overdose.

Because there were no lunch periods, the school day was split into three shifts of four hours each; the middle shift overlapped the morning and afternoon shifts. I was scheduled for the morning shift from eight to noon.

One cold winter day at noon, I was walking home from school wearing my winter coat that I wore all during that morning to deter it from getting stolen. My stack of schoolbooks was cradled in my arms. Walking with me were two friends from my neighborhood. Always cautious and on the lookout for dangerous situations to be avoided, I spotted them before they spotted us.

Way up on the corner of the block in the direction we were heading was a huge mob of Puerto Rican kids that had gathered, both boys and girls, and covered the expanse of both sidewalks and street. If I had to put a number to this mob, it would have been well over one hundred and fifty kids.

My South-Bronx-streetwise instincts immediately went into alarm mode. I knew any confrontation with this mob would be deadly. My suggestion to my two friends of turning and going the opposite direction before this mob saw us went unheeded. My Black friend made the deciding statement: "They won't hurt us."

I didn't want to abandon my friends, so I continued our walk towards this mob against my better judgment.

And then they spotted us!

This experience was not only put into that never-to-forget part of my brain, it was engraved in my heart forever. At this point, only God would have been able to prevent what happened next, but for some reason, He chose not to.

I noticed that there were spectators from the row houses across the street on their porches observing everything that was happening. But the real battle scenes would be hidden from their eyes. As this mob approached, the angelic warriors with orders from God Himself to protect me, stationed themselves against the warring demons that were also approaching. This battle would be fierce, but not the fiercest that would be fought over my life.

It was only seconds from when this mob spotted us that they swarmed us like vultures coming upon a kill. It didn't take me long to realize—I was as doomed as a snowball in a hot desert.

As some of them swarmed around me, one girl put her arm around me in a feigned friendship gesture and asked in her sweet tone: "You have any money?"

Instantly, my thoughts went to the twelve cents I knew were in my jean pocket, and just as instantly I made my defiant decision: *I'm not giving her my twelve cents! They're gonna beat me up anyway; they're not getting my twelve cents!* (Twelve cents equated to half a slice of pizza to me.)

About this time, the angelic warriors unsheathed their swords and the demons did likewise. Sparks flew up through the air as swords clashed against swords.

Within seconds after my sweet new friend asked if I had any money, she pounced on top of me and started punching my face and head with tremendous force; the rest of this mob followed suit in a frenzy. The blows and kicks came from everyone as they took turns beating on me anywhere they could. As the kids pounced on me, I clung to my schoolbooks (don't know why, I wasn't learning anything from them) while I tried to protect my face and head from their blows. Then they started beating me down into the street gutter!

Lying in a street gutter with spectators watching across the street was embarrassing. As I tried to save what little pride I had left—as if it mattered—I did my best to get myself up and out of the gutter while still clinging to my school books. But before I could stand fully upright, this mob was beating me back down into the gutter with more force than before.

Meanwhile, the angelic warriors and demons continued raging their fierce battle over my life. As the demons drooled saliva, their sulfur breaths spurred hatred and shouted to this mob in their desperate frenzy to end my life: "Kill her! We want her dead!"

At the same time, a Divine command issued forth by way of a gentle whisper meant only for me to hear. Instantly, thoughts came flooding to me in what I must do to survive this nightmare.

Okay. My thoughts raced for survival as fast as my heart pounded: *They want me in the gutter; I'll stay in the gutter.*

While this mob continued beating and kicking me with all their might, and the spectators across the street continued their entertainment watching this savage attack, I mustered up all my South-Bronx-streetwise instincts I could. With all trace of my pride gone, no further resistance or sound coming from me, as the only course of action that would end this nightmare and still stay alive, I obeyed the thoughts of the gentle whisper: "Play dead."

As this mob was beating me down in the gutter for the second time, I clung tighter to my schoolbooks, closed my eyes, curled into a fetal position as I hit the ground, and let my body go limp.

My winter coat absorbed some of the blows and kicks while it also helped to hide my breathing. As the beating and kicking finally slowed down, I overheard a conversation between two of them: "Is she dead?"

There was a pause before the answer came: "I don't know."

After hearing this conversation, I just lay there dead. My eyes were closed shutting out the terror going on outside around me. My heart pounded fast and hard as my thoughts raced:

Yes! Yes! It's working! They really think I'm dead now. Uh-oh! I can feel their eyes boring into me. They're trying to see if I'm breathing, if there is any life left in me. Okay, don't breathe and don't move. But I have to breathe. Then don't breathe so hard. Why am I still clinging to my stupid books? Do dead people cling to things? Well, I can't let them go now. I can't give anything away that I'm still alive. I need to keep playing dead. I need to keep my eyes closed tight. Just don't move and blow it. They have to leave soon. They won't stick around a dead kid that they killed themselves. They have to be leaving soon!

Once I was believed to be dead, most of the beating and kicking stopped except for one or two more kicks. *Good grief, just leave me alone already! Can't you see that I'm dead now?*

I lost all sense of time as I lay there in the gutter dead. I was so scared, and tried so hard to calm my pounding heart and nerves enough to be still and not show any signs of life. It seemed like forever before I got the nerve to get up and get back home. But until I knew without any doubt that no one from this mob was lurking around anywhere, I dared not move. The last thing I needed was for anyone from this mob to see me resurrect from the dead, for then I would be dead for sure.

So, without so much as twitching a muscle on any part of my face or body, I cracked open my eyes ever so slightly. When I saw feet still moving about, I gently closed my eyes again. I waited a little longer before I tried for another lookout.

Cautiously, without twitching any muscles, I slightly cracked open my eyes again. When I didn't see any more feet moving about this time, I cracked open my eyes just a little bit more for a better lookout. As I got the nerve to open my eyes all the way, I surveyed the area as much as my rolling eyes could see without moving my head or body. *Maybe they're still lurking around somewhere?* I was taking no chances at all at this point.

By this time, the demons were defeated, battered, their egos fatally wounded as they limply swished away following after the mob of kids. The angelic warriors once again won this battle, but they kept their ground standing guard over me.

It was only after I decided it was safe to move my head around for a much better survey of the area that I was satisfied the coast was clear from anyone in this mob.

I rose from the dead, got out of the gutter, and brushed myself off; my schoolbooks had never touched the ground!

I looked around to find where my two friends were. My Black friend was nowhere in sight. I was glad to hear later that this mob left her alone. My Hispanic friend did not fare as well. I found her not far from where I was crying uncontrollably and bleeding on the forehead from this mob's beating. I tried to console her, and then decided it was best for us to walk to my apartment that was closer than hers, and get Michael and Duke so all of us could walk her to her apartment to be sure she got home safe.

That night, I was really hurting all over. But there was nothing anyone could do to gain justice for this savage attack. The spectators would surely not say what they saw. They never offered any help at all, not even while I was dead and waiting for the coast to clear before resurrecting. I remember praying that night as I always did. But I don't remember ever hating those kids.

Jesus Himself told us that we could expect storms, trials and tribulations in the world as the children of God. (John 16:33.) But there comes a time when God finally makes His decision that enough is enough, and removes either the trial from the life of His child, or removes His child from the trial.

In any case, the truth needs to be remembered: God will never leave us nor forsake us. (Hebrews 13:5.) Psalm 138:7 declares: "Though I walk in the midst of trouble, You will revive me; You will stretch forth Your hand against the wrath of my enemies, and Your right hand will save me."

Chapter 9

Culture Shock

As God is my witness, I can honestly say that I have no resentment or regrets for what I experienced during my formative years in the South Bronx; the good times far outweighed the bad times. God always protected my family and provided well for our needs. We didn't have everything we wanted, but we had everything we needed. Growing up together in such an environment bonded our love and kept us close.

I will always treasure within my heart the fond memories of the escapades that Michael and I had growing up. I also have fond memories of outings with us foursome cousins accompanied by Mom and my dear Aunt Katrina. Some of these included trips to the Bronx Zoo and amusement parks, among other special places.

Mom always kept in close contact with Dad's family, and other Greek relatives and friends during those formative years. I will always treasure the memories of the festive Greek gatherings with these loved ones.

I also have fond memories of Uncle Zackary, Mom's only brother who I loved dearly. Uncle Zackary was the one who helped start my hobby with birds. He had accepted the Lord Jesus as Savior just before he passed on into eternity.

Mom was always supportive of my love for animals, and allowed me to have many different pets that included a slew of finches housed in a flight cage, along with other birds, guinea pigs and hamsters. But my favorite pet by far was our trusty guard dog, Duke, a Golden Retriever mix. Unfortunately for Duke, he was also the victim of my ambition for training dogs. I tormented him by creating obstacle courses for him to jump over and through because I wanted him to be trained just like Lassie. Duke accepted everything I did to him well for the most part.

I was also enthralled with African animals. I was convinced that I wanted to be a zoologist when I grew up, and go to Africa to study animals just like the TV programs of Daktari, and Mutual of Omaha's Wild Kingdom. Also on my wannabe list were thoughts of being a Seeing Eye Dog trainer, or maybe spending some time in the Army.

I didn't know it at that time, but my Heavenly Father already had my life planned out according to His purpose. God had given me a special Scripture verse years ago just after I accepted Jesus as Savior, and He continues to use it to remind me of His constant nurturing: "I will instruct you and teach you in the way which you should go; I will counsel you with My eye upon you" (Psalm 32:8).

Now before I move out of the Bronx with my story, I would be remiss if I did not share about a very special family that I was privileged to stay with two weeks at a time, each of my last three summers I lived in the Bronx. This was made possible through a not-for-profit agency in New York City. This agency sponsored inner-city kids with an opportunity to be hosted by a private family in their home who lived in a rural area outside the city or state.

This special family had a beautiful home surrounded by woods and other beautiful homes. I played with so many nice kids in the neighborhood and in an atmosphere foreign to me. I was even given a nice bike to ride during my stay.

However, what really left a lasting imprint on my young heart was their willingness to open their home and their hearts to a kid who was a total stranger, showed me a special love, and provided for my needs during my stay. This whole family always meant a lot to me, even all these years later. Although some of the members have since passed on, I am still in contact with the youngest daughter, Penny, who remains a dear friend of mine.

I was fourteen years old when that last traumatic experience happened with that mob of kids. It was shortly afterward that circumstances changed in our lives that allowed Mom to move us to Pennsylvania, something she had wanted to do for a long time. God had pulled my family out of the South Bronx just before the climax of the worst part of the mid-1970s. And I couldn't have been happier leaving all the violence and hatred behind.

All that I was exposed to during my formative years growing up in the South Bronx had made a huge impact on me going into the rest of my young life. My personality went from being a shy and sensitive child, to always being on guard, defensive, and even rebellious at times. I had my own colorful metaphors that had become part of my everyday language, minus using God's name in vain. I was never deprogrammed from my South Bronx days. It didn't take me long after moving to Pennsylvania to realize that I was the victim of a real culture shock.

A married couple, friends of Mom's, drove all my pets and me to Pennsylvania a few weeks before Mom and Michael arrived. During this time, I stayed with Sophia, another friend of Mom's, who was also Greek. Mom had sponsored Sophia for her marriage many years earlier and had a role in the wedding ceremony. During a Greek Orthodox wedding, the bride and groom each wear a crown. As the sponsor, Mom had the honor of crisscrossing three times these two crowns over the heads of Sophia and her groom. (I shared this wedding ceremonial practice for a later purpose.)

While living with Sophia in a rural neighborhood, I was enrolled in the school of her area during my eighth grade of school. I realized soon after attending this new school that I was way behind in my education. While in an English class listening to everyone discussing nouns, pronouns, verbs, and all the other weird names words were given and their usage in writing, I realized that I was totally lost in what they were discussing.

Well, not much I could do about this now. I'll just have to limp along and hope I catch up somehow. But I never did catch up.

Soon after Mom and Michael arrived in Pennsylvania, Mom found a small apartment for rent on the second floor of a private home. This home was in a small and very old town that still had bricks lining most of the sidewalks and streets instead of concrete.

Because there were still six weeks left to this school year, I was enrolled in this small-town school, which made it three different schools I attended in my eighth grade. This was a huge adjustment in itself for someone who hated school.

This small-town school was still paddling kids as a punitive action. Coming from the Bronx, this was a shocker to me. There was also a strictly enforced dress code in school that prohibited wearing blue jeans or even dress pants, which forced me to wear dresses or skirts to school, something I hadn't done in years. *How am I gonna fight in a dress? Where are we now, in the boondocks somewhere?*

I wore outside summer shorts under my dresses and skirts, which took care of any concerns I had when fighting. And I was prepared to fight in this new school. After all, every school had their bullies. I knew of nothing else up until then but "survival of the fittest," which involved fighting when needed.

In addition to getting over the dress code and paddling kids, I had to deal with another type of communication barrier: *What is a yinz? Everyone knows that word doesn't exist; it's supposed to be youse.* Water was warder, which I still say today (some things never change). I found myself the victim of comical entertainment in this new school because I talked funny, which was better than being bullied because of my race.

But who really were the ones talking funny? I went to speech therapy as a youngster, so I couldn't be the one who was talking funny. Everyone I grew up with in the Bronx talked the way I did.

To make matters worse, I had to take my turn giving a speech in front of the class. *Wow! This never happened in the Bronx!*

Here I was, a New Yorker kid just coming to this small town of Pennsylvania to a strange new school. As I stood in front of these kids and teacher I barely knew with their inquisitive eyes staring straight through me, realization dawned on me: *Now I have to talk in front of these strange people?*

I stood ready to give my speech hoping beyond hope that I would be understood and no one would laugh at my Bronx accent when an unexplainable phenomenon happened: I lost my voice! It was gone just that quick without warning. I couldn't find it anywhere. Extreme fright always seems to be the culprit for these unexplainable phenomena in my life. *But why isn't my adrenalin kicking in now?*

Since I couldn't talk to tell all these inquisitive strange people I couldn't talk, all I could do was stand there and laugh. I was so embarrassed and couldn't stop laughing. And so, from then on, I was known as the laughing New Yorker in school. So much for my first great speech and impression at this new school!

Our school principal attended the Greek Orthodox Church that Mom became a member of. But this made no positive bearing on his attitude towards Michael or me. There were times he would be downright mean to us, especially to Michael. He would antagonize Michael for what seemed like no valid reason, and often called him "boy" in a mean tone instead of using his name. This was when Mom got involved and informed this principal that both her kids had names, and "boy" was not one of them.

This principal did his best to discourage me from taking advanced academic courses in ninth-grade. I knew I was behind by what everyone else seemed to know, but I deserved the chance for a better education. After all, I needed a college degree to be a zoologist before I could go to Africa to study wildlife. In my strong and independent will, I ignored this principal's discouragement and went with the academic courses anyway.

I was amazed that the teachers in this boondocks school cared about teaching the kids, and most of the kids tried their best to do well with their grades; another drastic difference from what I knew growing up in the Bronx.

It didn't take long before I found a nice friend, Arlene, who I managed to corrupt to my Bronx ways. There was a curfew for kids in this small town, which only created a rebellious avenue to entertain. Arlene and I would play havoc on this town after curfew, doing and getting into things that we thought were harmless, but also knew were wrong to do. Instead of running away from child molesters and bully kids, I found myself running and hiding from the cops in this small town as they patrolled the area.

The public transit system in this town and surrounding areas was almost none existent. This was another culture shock coming out of New York City. Mom could never drive a car, and even if she did, she couldn't afford a car anyway. However, the area that we had moved to was where Mom had grown up and lived just before moving to New York in her twenties, and she still had some great friends she had kept in contact with who were more than willing to help us out with transportation when needed.

It was over a year after we moved to this small town that we found a real house to rent. It was dilapidated, but had a small fenced-in backyard for Duke. This was a real treat for us after spending years in a small three-room apartment in a building that housed sixty-six families, and after the first small apartment that we rented here. Mom had warned us that people in this area would just drop by unannounced. So she made sure we kept our homes much cleaner than our Bronx apartment. Yep! I was a real victim of culture shock, to be sure!

Mom was doing her very best raising two teenagers on her own. Her thoughts in moving us to this area of Pennsylvania was to get us out of the New York City crime, violence and drug scenes for our own protection. Mom's only requirement for our schooling was that we would each graduate from high school, since she regretted dropping out in the tenth grade herself. Mom left the choice of college for each of us to decide on our own.

I am guessing that it's not at all that unusual for teenagers to go through a rebellious stage in their lives. Having never raised any kids of my own, I am only going by the experiences of others I know who have raised kids. As I was becoming rebellious after moving to Pennsylvania, Michael was even more so.

Because of the Bronx high school boycott, Michael was put back in the tenth grade our first full school year here. Michael had already started smoking cigarettes in New York, and after we moved to Pennsylvania, he started smoking marijuana and drinking alcohol heavily.

To Mom's disappointment, Michael dropped out of high school in his eleventh year. He enlisted in the Marines but was discharged six weeks later for some reason. One thing led to another, and the next thing I knew, Michael ended up in jail for stealing two vehicles.

The crime and drugs that Mom had wanted to protect us from found us in Pennsylvania. We didn't have bail money for Michael, so he stayed in jail until after his court hearing. He was then put on a special probation program, and had he stayed clean for two years, they were going to wipe out his past convictions and leave him with a clean record. Instead of taking advantage of this golden opportunity given to him, Michael skipped out while on probation.

My only big brother who I loved dearly and looked up to, my very best childhood friend and only partner in the board game

Monopoly, my escapades buddy who I experienced so much with playing havoc on the streets of New York City—became a fugitive.

My heart was not broken—it was smashed to smithereens, never to be the same. The emptiness and grief that I felt losing my brother in this way were in many ways harder than losing my dad. I cried out to God with my smashed heart many nights until I couldn't cry anymore, asking Him why, asking Him to bring Michael back, to change everything that happened so we could be a family again. But I never received any answers to my prayers.

Who is this God to whom I have been praying to all these years? Why would God allow such precious people who I loved so much, to be in my life only for a short time, and then abruptly be taken out of my life?

I really did not know God. I loved Him and prayed to Him ever since I was a little girl. But I really did not know this all-powerful, extremely jealous, all-consuming God. (Hebrew 12:29; Deuteronomy 4:24.)

What I did not understand at that time was, although God is Sovereign, in His love has given us all a free will with our own choices that come with consequences. And sometimes these consequences hurt those we love.

God could have intervened and stopped everything that happened, but He was not obligated to do so. God may have allowed Michael to walk out of our lives as a fugitive, but it was through his own free will that he chose to do so.

Mom loved us both dearly and did her very best raising two children on her own. Having Michael do what he did caused Mom to become distraught to the point that she became physically ill during that time. But speaking for both Mom and myself, neither one of us ever stopped loving Michael. And I held tight to my hopes that Michael would someday come home, and we would be a family again.

Chapter 10
My First Car

Although I continued school while grieving the loss of Michael, as in many losses, life goes on for those left behind. After doing fairly well with my first year of advanced academic courses, I chose to do another year of advanced courses going into senior high school. The subjects that I didn't learn in the Bronx school system were behind everyone now, as we were all supposed to know the basics that were taught.

I had some great friends that made everything more enjoyable going to school. And by the time I was in high school, they did away with the dress code. First, it was dress pants that we were allowed to wear, and eventually blue jeans.

Our high school principal did not like the jeans I wore because they were frayed at the bottom. As a matter of fact, in thinking back, he didn't like anything I wore, as he once asked me if I was trying to be the worst dresser in school.

My outfit often consisted of flannel shirts worn open with designed t-shirts underneath, and frayed bell-bottom blue jeans. The hippie era was slowly moving out during that time, and I caught it just before it left completely.

My friends would often try to hide me from Torpedo, as we named our principal among us, whenever he was coming around so he wouldn't see the way I was dressed and yell at me. I never did like dressing up, but at least my clothes were clean. I would love to get Torpedo's perspective now with the ripped-up blue jeans people wear today that are supposed to be the fashion trend.

During my high school years, God had given me a part-time job that I had prayed for working in the Dietary Department at a local hospital. This job paid well and had great hours after school and on weekends. The job consisted of preparing and cleaning up the patient's food trays. It was not unusual to find someone's teeth or some other gross item on these food trays during the cleanup process, which was done without wearing gloves.

I started this job without owning a car for transportation. There were some days when I was able to get a ride to work. But there were many days I had to walk over a bridge and up steep hills to get to work in the next town over, even in the dead of winter. It took what seemed like forever to save up enough money before I took out a loan for the rest to buy a car.

I remember looking at cars when I was older in the Bronx and came across a fastback Mustang, and thought: *I wouldn't mind having a car like that*. With God being my only Father (and dads usually help their kids buy their first cars), wouldn't you know He remembered my thoughts!

The summer before my senior high school year, I saw this 1969 fastback Mustang with a manual transmission listed in the newspaper for $550, which was a lot of money back then.

The very first car I ever drove was a VW Beetle with a manual transmission. This nice lady friend of Mom's was trying to teach me how to drive this thing, but neglected to tell me one very important trick to driving a manual transmission. I never stalled this Beetle, but I could never understand why we went jerking away each time I let the clutch out.

After getting my driver's license, I drove a friend's manual transmission Pontiac GTO a few times, and as far as I knew I did well. So, I never gave it another thought when this Mustang was listed with a manual transmission.

After a full week of going back-and-forth calling this lady about her son's Mustang while she haggled over the price, as she claimed the newspaper was supposed to list it as best offer over

$550, Mom wanted to get involved by calling her; she didn't like this lady giving me the runaround. My response to Mom's request to get involved was honesty: "Ma, you got a big mouth. You'll mess it all up. Please let me handle this."

Mom tended to be very outspoken and was never a hypocrite. If Mom liked you, you knew it. If Mom didn't like you, you knew that too.

When this lady finally agreed to sell me the Mustang for $550, she and Mom had to meet to sign the transfer papers, as her son Ryan and I were underage. When this meeting took place, lo and behold, Kate looked at Mom with joyful excitement and exclaimed, "I know you!"

Mom and Kate had known each other years before with Mom even attending her wedding. And there was Mom with her ever so truthful and outspoken personality: "Kate, you should have heard all the bad names I was calling you over this past week."

This rekindled friendship of these two old friends lasted for the rest of their lives. God had everything planned out so well. Ryan was even nice enough to drive the Mustang and park it in front of our dilapidated rented house.

By the time I bought the Mustang, I had my driver's license for a year. But I had very few opportunities to drive during that time, and had never driven a car without someone being with me.

But now, after praying and waiting for so long, I finally had my very own beautiful, 1969 powder-blue fastback Mustang with a three-speed manual transmission. The black ripped vinyl seats permeated an odor from years of use with visible dust and dirt embedded. The front dashboard had a huge rip right in the middle. The hand-cranked driver's window had a huge gap from a missing weatherstrip, which prevented it from connecting to the back window when rolled up. The body had rust from years of driving on the salted roads in the winters of Pennsylvania.

As I sat in this car all by myself, I was excited and nervous at the same time, but ready for my maiden drive off. I pushed in the clutch (I knew that much) and turned the key to start the engine (it ran). I fiddled around with the radio (AM stations only, no other media plugins) while trying to get just the right station, at just the right volume, making sure it was blasting out of the windows (car had no air conditioning) so everyone could hear my music as I drove away for my very first solo in my new car (it was seven years old). *Yes! This is my car! My very own car that I waited so long for!*

As I got all set for my maiden drive, I started to let the clutch out and move forward, but to my utter surprise, the car jerked and died. *Wow! What happened? Let me try this again.*

I pushed in the clutch, started the engine again, started to let the clutch out, the car moved a few inches this time, but jerked and died again. *This is not good! This is not how I planned my maiden solo drive off in my new car!*

I was not about to give up. I was determined I was going to drive this car one way or another—I had to. It was my car now. The only car that Mom and I had to get our groceries and do our errands, not to mention get me to work. *Okay, let me try this again. Something must be wrong that I don't know about.*

I never remembered any of the other manual transmission cars I drove stalling out. After numerous attempts at my maiden drive with each time resulting in a stalled engine, the engine finally quit starting. So, at seventeen years old with no mechanical experience, no dad or brother around for help dealing with a dead battery in my first car—I was on my own.

After I picked the brains of those who worked at the local gas station, I tackled my dilemma. I disconnected and removed the battery, put it in my trusty New Yorker shopping cart, and wheeled it several blocks to the same gas station to get recharged. I retrieved the battery the next day using the same shopping cart, and connected it back in the Mustang, and I did all this without getting blown up. Okay, maybe a little exaggeration. But batteries can be dangerous. It's a good thing I didn't know this at that time.

At this point, I swallowed my pride and called Ryan to ask if he would please, come and teach me how to drive this Mustang. By then, both our moms were getting reacquainted after so many years of missing out on their friendship. Ryan was nice enough to give me a one-time crash course on how to drive a manual transmission. *Oh! You mean I have to let the clutch out slow when it starts to grab? Why didn't anyone ever tell me this trick before?*

It was now just five days after getting my first car with only three actual driving days under my belt. I was cruising along peacefully, driving up and down all these hills heading to work to the next town over. I was getting just a little bit more confident with the clutch and letting it out even while being stopped on a hill (hill-assist for manual transmissions didn't exist back then). I was still very inexperienced with driving, but at least I was driving.

I was enjoying my favorite tune as the radio blasted away with two more blocks to go before reaching the hospital where I worked. I made a right-hand turn going up a hill, and the next thing I knew, all at once I heard a loud bang, I got a whiplash jerk, and my Mustang came to an abrupt halt. Bewildered and shaken up some, I got out of my Mustang wondering how this parked car jumped in front of mine.

I surveyed the damage to my Mustang: the front bumper was bent, the grill was crumpled apart, the hood looked like a smashed accordion, all this damage was perfectly centered right in the middle. I surveyed the parked car and noticed only small scratches around the left taillights with none broken. I glanced back at my beautiful, so long-awaited car now with the smashed in front end, and then glanced back at the parked car. *How could this happen?*

There's so much damage to my car, and only scratches to this parked car?

Then I heard it! A loud wailing was coming from somewhere. As the wailing got louder piercing my ears, I turned and saw this woman heading straight for me at a fast trot coming from her house crying and screaming, "My car, my car! What did you do to my car?"

More bewildered thoughts went through my mind now. *Who is this wailing woman?* Now that this woman was actually crying over her car and checking out the damage, realization dawned on me. *Oh! Is this your parked car? Well, why did you park it here? Didn't you know it would be in my road?*

Actually, I couldn't speak to this woman. Instead, I glanced over to the smashed in front end of the car that I worked so hard for and waited so long for, and then glanced back at the wailing woman's car with only a few scratches.

This woman was dramatizing the accident and traumatizing me in the process! Couldn't she see I was just an inexperienced teenager with my first car, and now my first accident?

Really, woman! Get a grip on yourself and calm down. Your car is going to be just fine. I glanced back at my Mustang. *Mine, on the other hand, is not looking so good. Look what YOUR car did to mine!*

I so much wanted to say all this to this woman, but knew better. Looking back, I'm not sure how this woman came at me so fast, or how the cops suddenly appeared at the scene from out of nowhere. But then again, maybe time just stopped? Funny how some things appear differently when you're traumatized.

I didn't go to work that night. My Mustang was still drivable, so I just went home after the cops wrote up the accident report. I managed to wait till I got home before I cried my heart out to the same God to whom I had prayed to for this car.

How could God let this happen, after all my hard work and waiting so long and praying so long for this car? For sure, God knew what this car meant to me. I was blaming God instead of myself, knowing that once again, He could have prevented what happened. But He was not obligated to do so, and He chose not to do so.

After getting the Mustang, I had believed that it didn't matter how fast I would drive, all I had to do was keep steering the car and it would follow along. But I found out differently the hard way.

I had also intended on buying a bag of marijuana once I got a car. Michael had been the one to introduce me to smoking marijuana, but I cannot blame him for my psychological dependence on it later in my life. And God knows and judges our thoughts and intentions of our hearts, and knows what the consequences will be. (Hebrews 4:12.)

I can look back to this accident with a clearer understanding now than what I was capable of as a teenager. I didn't understand growing up how God was in my life as my only Father. It wasn't until many years later that I understood this truth.

As my Father, God used this accident as His discipline rod while knowing my thoughts and intentions, to get my attention and steer me away from my intended plans. Unfortunately, I was a very strong-willed child growing up, and at that point in my life, an even stronger-willed teenager.

In the near future, I would learn firsthand, and again the hard way, just how much stronger God's will is compared to mine, and how much stronger His love for me is compared to my feeble love for Him.

Chapter 11
My Rebellion

My first car accident did nothing to discourage my rebellious plans, but only delayed them. A nephew of a family friend did bodywork on cars on the side. This young man offered to repair my Mustang for a much lower cost than what a real body shop would have charged. However, the lower cost also included a longer time frame before the car would be finished, and entailed scouring around the local junkyards for the parts that were needed.

During our journeys through these junkyards, I came across a black snake. Because I handled snakes during my New York pet shop adventures, I decided to pick it up and play with it. Needless to say, wild snakes are not as tame as pet snakes.

Not wanting to hurt the snake, I didn't grab it tight enough or correctly behind his head. My inexperience with handling wild snakes ended with a visit to the hospital emergency room after the snake turned around and bit me as I held it. After this incident, I bought a snakebite kit. I wasn't planning on handling another wild snake anytime soon, but just in case, I was prepared for the next one. I never learn lessons in life easy!

It was several weeks later before I got my Mustang back from the bodywork repairs. The hood didn't match up with the hood locks, and we never found a grill to replace the crumpled one. The missing grill made my Mustang look like the shark in the movie Jaws when it was coming at you from the front. But I was thankful to this young man for fixing my car, and thankful when I finally got it back. I named my Mustang Pegasus, after the flying white horse in Greek mythology.

After I got Pegasus back, I bought a bag of pot (street name for marijuana), which was one ounce in weight. By this time, many of my high school friends were also getting high smoking pot.

My car accident did not slow down my driving. During one outing with a friend driving around getting high, I took on a race challenge. Beth and I were stopped at traffic lights on a four-lane highway. Less than a mile from these traffic lights was another set of traffic lights in front of a new shopping center, with brand new exit and entrance lanes connecting to this four-lane. Beth was holding the joint (street name for pot rolled up like a cigarette) when this kid drove up alongside Pegasus gunning his racing car engine, just daring for a race. In the excitement of the moment, when the lights turned green, I took him on.

As Beth held the lit joint, she cheered me on: "Go, Ange, go, go, go." Both cars flew across this highway with a posted 40 MPH speed limit towards the second traffic lights that were just turning green; the cars that had been stopped there at the red light had not started to move yet.

Fast approaching these traffic lights, cars still at a standstill, I used these exit and entrance lanes at this shopping center as a go-around to avoid smashing these cars as I flew past them.

If the circumstances with these traffic lights were in any other sequence of changing, or if I wasn't able to use those extra lanes as a go-around, this first car race could have been my last.

This same night while Beth and I continued driving around getting high, a fuel line hanging from Pegasus got punctured as I drove over a curb. Not knowing this, I drove until the engine stalled and stopped Pegasus just before reaching the top of a hill. After Pegasus stalled, another car came flying on the same road and almost hit us. This was a night I would never forget!

Getting high on pot was soon becoming a way of life for me. I believed that I was capable of doing just about anything while I was high, including working my job. And there were at least two other teenage coworkers who also came to work while under the influence of pot or other drugs.

Genesis 1:29 was a Scripture I used as my justification for smoking pot, believing that as a plant, it was a gift from God, and as such, He was okay with me getting high on it. However, I was taking this Scripture out of context. Bondage or addiction to anything is wrong, and what I believed was God's gift, was in reality a deception from Satan himself.

I also continued watching way too much TV and movies. After watching the movie Exorcist, I believed I was being attacked and possessed by Satan when my bed started trembling, as it normally did from a train passing through our town. To counter this demonic attack I was sure was happening, I took what I believed was holy water and sprinkled it over my bed in the sign of a cross; I thought this would ward off any evil spirits trying to possess me.

I wasn't a kid anymore, but I was still very ignorant of God's spiritual truths. I was ignorant to the purpose of why Jesus came and died on the cross, and ignorant of the power of His shed blood for the forgiveness of sins and the destruction of Satan. And once again, Satan knew of my ignorance and played it well against me.

Unbeknown to me at that time, the spiritual battles continued to rage over my life. While Satan used the pot and anything else he could get his hands on to try to destroy me, God continued drawing me closer to Himself through His Son, Jesus Christ.

Then one day, I found myself sitting on a curb talking with a teenage boy who shared about Jesus with me in a way I never heard before. I don't remember his name or how we met, and I never saw him again. I didn't quite grasp everything he said, but I was so excited about what I heard that I shared this with Mom afterward. But Mom's response was not what I expected: "It's okay for you to believe, but you can't be too-too much into it."

I responded, "Oh, okay." I pondered what Mom said, and yet, I didn't want to offend the God to whom I had been praying to all these years, every single night ever since I was a little girl.

Mom believed in God and raised me with strong morals she engraved in my heart that if violated, would be sin to God. *Was it my presentation or my excitement that caused Ma's response?*

During this time, my prayer life began morphing again. I started reaching out more to God and asking Him some difficult questions: "What is life all about? Am I here only to live life and never really understand it? Is pot really Your gift, and are You okay with me getting high smoking it? God, please, I really want to know the truth."

I never expected to hear God's voice speak to me back then, nor at any time in my future. I believed God would speak through circumstances, but in no other way did I believe He would speak.

As my prayer life morphed, so did my love for God, even in the midst of my sinful and rebellious heart. It was during one of these heartfelt prayers while on my knees as a teenager, that I first remember actually telling God that I loved Him.

I always acknowledged God in my life from the time I could remember. I loved God before I knew He loved me, but only because He first loved me. But as a teenager, I did not know that God was my Heavenly Father. I had no understanding that I needed to accept Jesus as my personal Lord and Savior, and no clue of anything regarding God's Holy Spirit. Yet, this same God knew everything about my past, present and future, and knew it all at the same time. God understood everything going on within my heart, how I loved Him and was seeking His truths.

God used that young man to plant powerful seeds in my heart that matured in His timing; even as He so patiently nurtured and protected and disciplined me along my life journey; even as He drew me closer to Himself through His Son, Jesus Christ.

Chapter 12
Senior Year

Before my eleventh grade school year had ended, I found out that I would need eight years of college to become a zoologist. This didn't appeal to me, so I decided to forget about college altogether, and took only the courses that were needed for my last year to graduate high school.

However, I did take a mechanical course for women at the community college before I graduated, as I wanted to learn more about how to work on my own car. I caught on well with this course and really enjoyed working on Pegasus.

I was also attempting to secure a full-time position at the hospital I was working at, and had also put my resume in at a dog kennel that bred German Shepherds. Nothing was working out for me by way of full-time employment, and I wasn't sure what I was going to do after I graduated high school.

A recruiter for the U.S. Army showed up at our high school a few months before I was to graduate. A classmate who enlisted talked me into looking at the possibilities. So I took all the Army tests that were being offered for enlisting. I was hoping to do my best in the mechanical parts, as I thought if I did go in, I would enjoy this field as my MOS (military occupational specialty).

When my test results came out very promising, I started to seriously consider this option. I was always fascinated with all the military movies I had watched, and envisioned someday serving my country that I loved in such a way. I was also sure it would be a great experience.

But there was one obstacle: I really wanted my mom to agree to this. I loved her dearly and would not have joined without her blessings. Her health was declining some, but still, she would have been able to take care of herself at that point in her life.

Mom went with me to speak with the recruiter in another town. As I was driving, I was sharing with her all about the benefits, the experience, the chance to serve my country. Yet, even while trying to convince Mom, I was having doubts myself about joining. I didn't tell Mom my doubts, but just kept talking while my mind was racing: *Is this really what I want to do? Can I do this and survive three years in the Army?*

Before we reached the recruiter's office, Mom made the deciding statement that sealed my decision: "Go ahead, you're going to do it anyway." Mom knew me best of all people, and knew how strong-willed I could be.

Okay, maybe I will! I never spoke these thoughts to Mom, and never told her about my doubts. Had she known, her response may have been much different. As it happened, I can acknowledge now God's intervention during that decision of my life. But at that time, I could not have known that He was in this.

Mom and I had a good meeting with the recruiter. Before I graduated high school, I enlisted in the U.S. Army's Delayed Entry Program and was scheduled to leave that following November. The recruiter told me I could either choose my MOS, or where my permanent party station would be, but I couldn't choose both. I decided I would rather like the job I was doing, so I chose the track vehicle mechanic MOS for a three-year enlistment, versus the wheeled mechanic MOS for a four-year enlistment.

However, once I was in the Army, I came across many others who enlisted around the same time I did, but who were able to choose both their MOS and permanent party station. But again, I acknowledge this now as Divine intervention.

During my last year in high school and throughout that following summer, I was having some real close encounters with cops while I was high on pot. I don't understand why none of them ever realized that I was high; it should have been so obvious. One encounter almost ended in a tragedy for me.

It was the night of my high school graduation ceremony. Mom was in the hospital with an ulcer on her leg that was seriously infected, and she missed attending this special occasion. This was a big disappointment to both of us. Right after the ceremony, I visited Mom in the hospital wearing my graduation gown, and we had a tearful but nice visit. Afterward, I was pretty bummed out and drove around alone just getting high.

While driving around after midnight in the small town that I lived in, I started to really get into watching some headlights in the rearview mirror that were following me around. Then suddenly, the headlights turned into blue and red flashing lights. I then realized it had been a cop who was following me. By this time in my driving career, I was getting used to being pulled over by cops.

After I pulled over, the cop stopped his car behind mine, got out, walked up to my window, and asked me if I was in a hurry. I didn't know why he asked me this, but I was polite and replied that I was going to work that morning. As was normal procedure, he asked for my driver's license and owner's card.

Because of my Bronx experiences, I had made a leather pouch for my wallet that I would strap just below my knee hiding it under my bell-bottom blue jeans. I gave no thought as I reached down for my wallet to give this cop the cards he requested. With this innocent action that was normal procedure for me, this cop yelled, "STOP! WHAT'D YOU GOT DOWN THERE?"

But his command to stop did not register in my brain. As I continued getting out my wallet, I glanced back at this cop with an answer I thought he should have known: "It's my wallet."

I then found myself looking down into the barrel of his gun. This too didn't quite register in my brain, as I went right back to getting out my wallet.

He then asked another silly question he should have known the answer to: "What's it doing down there?"

Oblivious to the danger of a cop pointing his gun right at me, I answered innocently enough: "It's hiding."

By this time, a second cop car pulled onto the scene on the opposite side of the road. As the second cop got out of his car, the first cop quickly put his gun away.

Although I was pulled over because I ran through a stop sign that I didn't realize I ran through, I was allowed to leave with only a warning without getting a ticket. I was guessing the cop who pulled his gun out on me probably didn't want anyone to know that he did.

As I was driving off, it finally registered in my brain: *That cop had his gun pointed right at me!* Only God would have known how close I came to being shot that night.

The headlines at the local newspaper, maybe even national, could have read: "Cop Shoots Local Teenage Girl Dead Hours After High School Graduation."

Chapter 13
Army Beware

God had healed Mom and spared her the ordeal of losing her leg from the infected ulcer, and she was back home soon after my graduation. Had her leg been amputated during that hospital stay, my future would have been much different, as Mom would not have been able to take care of herself while I was in the Army.

But God had His purpose for leading me to enlist, and took care of all the details. I could not have known at that time how much this Almighty God was carefully orchestrating and nurturing my life journey.

The summer after graduation, I did get a part-time job at the dog kennel that bred German Shepherds. I also continued working at the hospital until my final days before going into the Army. At the hospital job, one of my teenage coworkers, who also got high on pot, had a mom who was a born-again Christian.

Mrs. V was a nice lady, and we had a few opportunities to speak alone about the Lord Jesus, about my pot habit, and about her daughter's drug habit, as she used other drugs in addition to smoking pot. I didn't have any desire to use other drugs at that time, but I started smoking cigarettes that summer.

I was convinced by then that pot as a plant really was a gift from God, and that He was okay with me getting high smoking it. I shared all this with Mrs. V during our conversations. Before I left for the Army, Mrs. V gave me a Good News translation Bible with a denim cover. She handwritten a special message inside: "Dear Angie. I pray someday you get high on the Lord. Love, Mrs. V."

She would never know how prophetic her words were, and how much I would appreciate that special Bible as her gift to me. I made sure this Bible came with me when I left for the Army.

About two weeks before I entered the Army, I found Michael waiting by Pegasus one night in the hospital parking lot after I got off work. Although it had been two years since he became a fugitive, Michael kept in contact with me and would often show up unexpectedly somewhere for short visits. We were always so close growing up, and our love for each other was always strong.

We drove around that night, smoked pot, and just talked. He was hitchhiking across the country, still a fugitive, and now a vagabond with no plans for his future. He knew I was leaving for the Army in two weeks with no address to give him for a follow-up contact; he didn't have an address to give me. I left Michael off holding a sign that he needed a ride heading south. As I drove away, I believed that at some time in the future, somehow and somewhere, Michael would show up unexpectedly again in my life. I never lost this hope all the years I spent in the Army.

Finally, my day to leave for the Army had arrived. This was a very emotional time for Mom and me. The recruiter picked me up early to take me to the federal building in Pittsburgh, where I would be going through tons of red tape paperwork that turned out to be an all-day process. After all the paperwork was complete, I was directed to a large room where many other wannabe soldiers waited. We would be swearing-in at the same time to join the Army before departing for the airport.

Soon, an Army guy came into the room and gave us one final warning before swearing us in. As I listened, red flags flew up: "If anyone has had any dealings with the police in any way that we don't know about, and the Army finds out after you get in, you could be court-martialed and thrown out of the Army."

Uh-oh! I had a quick thought that I needed to ask this Army guy, just in case. Trying hard to calm my fear of speaking in front of such a large group of wannabe soldiers I knew were listening, I raised my hand being very respectful, even while innocently thinking for sure this couldn't possibly also include traffic tickets: "Does that include traffic tickets?"

"Yep." His answer came without delay.

My tone betrayed my dismay: "Oh! You're kidding?"

A few little chuckles came from somewhere in this room full of wannabe soldiers after my response.

This Army guy's response sunk my heart just a bit: "Nope. Why? Do you have any?"

"Yep." I was honest but kept it short.

Now his tone betrayed he was concerned: "You're kidding?"

The chuckles got louder as a few more wannabe soldiers joined in. "Nope." *This conversation is not going in my favor!*

Almost demanding, he wanted facts: "How many do you have?"

It's not very good to answer a question with a question, but I did anyway: "Paid or unpaid?"

His demeanor and tone expressed alarm: "You're kidding?"

The chuckles turned into hearty laughter even before I answered, "Nope."

Now that this Army guy had the facts of my confession, he made a firm and authoritative decision: "Well then, you can't go in the Army."

My drawn-out response could not hide my disbelief and disappointment: "Awww! You're kidding?"

In the midst of hearing a final deep-down roar of laughter that seemed to come from every single wannabe soldier listening in that room—all at my expense—this Army guy's final answer smashed my heart as it sunk deeper: "Nope."

This wasn't good! Did my Army term end before it even got started? Good grief, it was only traffic tickets. It wasn't like I did something really bad. And only one was unpaid; the other three were already paid and taken care of. I was going to send money home to Mom with my first pay from the Army for the unpaid traffic ticket—really, I was. The due date to pay this ticket wasn't even close. Would this Army guy consider any of this? Nope! Not a fat chance! Before I was allowed to swear my life away for three years to Uncle Sam's Army, this traffic ticket needed paid.

Leaving the roomful of still laughing wannabe soldiers behind, I made the long journey downstairs from the federal building, and walked the long distance to the post office to get a money order to pay for this traffic ticket. And prior to this, I had to find a phone to call Mom for the address and information needed before I could send this money order. All this was taking place in a time zone of the last century without cell phones.

After getting all this done, I went right back to the federal building with receipt in hand to prove that all was completed as I was instructed to do. I believed that I could now be officially sworn into the Army, and leave for the airport.

I managed to find the same room I left the entire laughing wannabe soldiers behind, walked inside, and—*but wait! Where is everyone? The room is empty! Did I come to the wrong room? My sense of direction still stinks, but no, this is the right room.*

Had I been a born-again Christian at that time who believed in the pre-tribulation rapture, I would have thought for sure that everyone was raptured up out of this world, and only I was left behind—all for my unforgivable sin of trying to join the Army with one stupid unpaid traffic ticket to my name.

I couldn't find anyone. Not one wannabe Army soldier was left in that room. I couldn't even find the swearing-in Army guy.

Did they all leave me behind? They wouldn't leave behind, would they? Why would they leave me behind?

To my dismay, I was left behind, never given a second thought. I left the room despondent as I scoured around trying to find anyone who could tell me what I should do now. I thought all they had to do now was swear me in, take me to the airport, and off I would go to basic training to start my Army term. Simple, so I thought. But I was soon to learn that the Army does nothing simple, along with their motto of "hurry up and wait."

I wanted to go back home and come back the next day. But they weren't about to let that happen. Instead, I was put up in a nearby hotel, was given a meal ticket I used for a nice steak, had a great night's sleep after not sleeping the night before, and was all ready and raring to go in the Army the following morning. The only drawback was that I had to go through the entire red tape in-processing ordeal all over again, as all the paperwork had to show a different entry date. What a bummer! And such was life!

After arriving at basic training at Fort McClellan, Alabama, I learned that had I left the day before as planned, I would have been in a platoon that later proved to have some serious conflicts among the trainees. What I thought was a disadvantage in entering the Army, actually turned out for my best.

"And we know that God causes all things to work together for good to those who love God, to those who are called according to His purpose" (Romans 8:28). I was finding out just how much this God, to whom I had been praying to all these years, really loved me, and how He was constantly with me and watching over me, despite my own sins and shortcomings. I would learn this even more as my Army term continued.

Chapter 14
Basic Training

It was mid-November when I arrived at basic training. Someone from back home assured me that it would be warm at this time in Alabama. I guessed this person was never there in the winter. During our latter part of training, it got so cold that there were trainees carried off the field due to frostbite.

Once we got to our basic training unit, we had more red tape in-processing to go through. And then we were all given physical examines once again, and had our immunization shots given to us.

We all lined up for these shots and took our turn stopping between two medical technicians standing on either side of us. Each technician had a device that looked like a gun that shot needles in each arm at the same time. This experience reminded me of a herd of livestock getting their shots.

Each Army basic training company had about six platoons, with each platoon having forty female trainees. The barracks that housed us were open bays divided into four sections. Each section had eight double bunk beds and two single bunk beds. I was assigned one of the single bunks.

Mary, a thirty-five-year-old woman who was going to be an Army chaplain's assistant, had the bottom bunk right next to mine. How about that for coincidence? However, I don't believe in coincidences now, but it was different back then. Looking back, I can understand God was working in all areas of my life.

Mary and I had some great conversations about God and life many nights. During one of our conversations, I remember Mary asking God to "cancel that." Mary seemed to speak to God in such an intimate way that I truly admired her and her relationship with

God, and wondered if it were possible for anyone to have such an intimate relationship with such a faraway God. Very soon in the future, I would learn that God really wasn't far away after all.

As it often happens in Army life, there are those who end up with nicknames for one reason or another. One of my new friends in basic training gave me the nickname Mickie, which was derived from my last name, and followed me throughout the rest of my Army life. She wanted me to call her Kraut as her nickname, as she was of German ancestry.

I found it amazing being exposed to so many different types of women from different walks of life, and from so many different areas of our country. And we were all thrown together for one cause: serving our country. Most of those in our platoon were very nice, and just wanted to do their best and get through basic training without incident.

However, there were just a few who stuck together tight, with a couple of these women being bullies to others in our platoon in such a way that I had flashbacks from my Bronx days.

I was eating chow with Kraut when one of these bullies found her way to our table. While we were eating, I noticed she had nice table manners and told her so; I was sincerely trying to start up a friendly conversation. Apparently, she didn't think I was sincere, as she challenged me to a fight by responding in a mean tone: "If you can't back up your words, then don't say anything."

Wow! This threw me for a loop. I wasn't trying to pick a fight. However, my experiences while living in the South Bronx taught me a lot about life. There are times when a fight needs to be avoided at all costs. There are times when a fight cannot be avoided. And then there are those times when a fight should not be avoided, as doing so would never allow any peace going forward.

I knew I could not back down from this woman's challenge, or I would never hear the end of it. Now on the offensive, I assured this woman: "I'll back up anything I say."

The next thing I knew, without another word between us, she picked up her tray, I picked up my tray, and off we went heading outside for a real fistfight while my thoughts warned me of the outcome: *She is so big and fat and mean, she's gonna really beat me up good! How did she get in this Army being so big and fat?*

Although I had no doubt I was going to really get beat up during this fight, I knew I could not back down. As soon as we started heading out for this fight, Kraut ran and grabbed a drill sergeant and told her everything that was going down. Kraut didn't quite understand "survival of the fittest" jungle mentality, and believed she was doing the right thing.

This drill sergeant headed us off and stopped this fight before it even got started, and then chewed us both out. But boy, was I ever so glad she stopped the fight. Although I didn't have to fight this woman, the result of not backing down was the same. She and her "friends" never bothered me again for the rest of basic training, and this happened very early in our training.

Because of the time of year, the holiday breaks stretched out our training longer than normal, making it seem like basic training was never going to end. Most of us took our first borrowed leave (vacation time) and went home for Christmas. This was such a great break for me, and it was great seeing Mom, and Duke, who by then was showing his age.

On the bus heading back to basic training, I befriended Carly, who after all our training was over, without knowing it at that time, would end up at my permanent station in Georgia, where we became very good friends. This was just another plan from God.

Once everyone was back at basic, we jumped right into our last part of our basic training, which was bivouac training. During this training, each trainee had to qualify shooting with our M16 rifle. There were three available levels of qualification with each having their own distinct medal: marksman was the lowest, sharpshooter was the middle, and if you were really good at hitting the target you got the expert level as the highest.

On the day everyone zeroed in their weapon before this qualification shoot, which meant each weapon was adjusted according to each individual trainee, I was sick and made to stay in the barracks. When it came time for our qualifications the next day, my weapon was not zeroed in. I remembered praying to God this day that He would help me to at least get marksman as a qualification. There is an old cliché: "Be careful what you pray for; you may get it."

When my target holes were counted, twenty-two hit the mark. Number twenty-three was ever so close that I thought for sure it would be counted, but it wasn't. Twenty-three target holes needed to hit the mark for sharpshooter. This qualification incident may seem insignificant to even share now, but I can tell you, it was far from being insignificant at that time.

This whole scenario was the very first time I understood without a doubt, that God was speaking to me, and in the process, He was teaching me a very important lesson about prayer. Had I asked God to help me do my best, no doubt I would have had twenty-three hits on the target to qualify as sharpshooter.

God was also teaching me another significant truth in my life: He was with me and heard every prayer my heart offered up to His throne. Knowing these truths about such an Almighty God was to be very important in my near future.

Once we qualified with our M16 rifles, we had training with hand grenades. For part of this training, real and very dangerous live hand grenades were used—the ones that would blow up anyone nearby to smithereens.

To begin with, each female Army trainee had to throw two live hand grenades over a three-sided wall while two men stood on either side of her to be sure to deal with any blunders. We were told if anyone dropped their hand grenade, they were not to move at all, but to let one of the men grab it and throw it over the wall before it blew us all up. This exercise was not one of my favorites!

One female trainee just dropped her hand grenade over the wall instead of throwing it way out and over, which caused dirt to shoot several feet up in the air that landed on all of us. By the time my turn came around, the requirement was dropped down to throwing one live hand grenade each, which was fine with me. Surprisingly and thankfully, none of us female trainees blew up anyone during this exercise.

We also had to qualify with throwing hand grenades as close as possible to various targets. We were given fake ones to use for this training exercise. There were the same three qualification levels with the hand grenades, each having their own distinct medal. I was excited when I was able to secure an expert level for my hand grenade qualification. Yep, I was getting better but wasn't there yet. This cliché holds true: "Close only counts in horseshoes and hand grenades."

All of basic training was tough. But one of the worst training exercises we had to go through was running several hundred feet up a hill to attack a bunker, which was a small structure partially buried in the ground where in a combat zone would house the enemy. We wore all our combat gear for this exercise: fully loaded backpacks, winter parkas, combat boots, and helmets. We had our M16 rifles in hand, and wore heavy bulletproof vests, as we were given live ammo (real bullets) to shoot at the bunker.

We went out in pairs running up this hill that was full of mud while hiding behind boulders, bushes and trees. At the same time, we used hand signals to communicate with each other while shooting our live ammo at this bunker, and hoping we wouldn't shoot each other. As all our gear weighed us down, we went slipping and sliding and falling all the way up this hill. And with each piece of mud that accumulated on us as we went, our gear only got heavier.

While each team was taking their turn attacking the bunker with live ammo, following close behind all the way up this hill was this male drill sergeant (who was also wearing a bulletproof vest) screaming at the top of his lungs: "Move it, move it, MOVE IT! You need to move faster, faster, FASTER!"

I can still remember what I was thinking while going through this horrible training exercise: *What am I doing in this Army? Is this drill sergeant safe screaming at female trainees under these horrible conditions while we all have live ammo?*

We either passed with a "go," or had to do it all over again with a "no-go." I sincerely felt terrible for any team who had to do this all over again.

Then finally, after all the grueling training and exercises in the cold, waking up before dawn, dealing with mean drill sergeants and a barracks full of strangers, and going through all kinds of stupid inspections, it was time to graduate from basic training.

I was anxious and looking forward to AIT (advanced individual training) at Fort Knox, Kentucky, and learning all about being a track vehicle mechanic, and continuing my Army life now that the worst of my training was behind me. AIT had to be better than basic. After all, basic training was supposed to be the "make or break" training period of any military career. If you were able to get through basic training, you could get through anything in the military. Anyway, those were my thoughts at the time. I was to learn differently real soon.

Chapter 15
Advanced Individual Training

My AIT training was an interesting thirteen weeks of my life. During our in-processing at Fort Knox, Kentucky, all trainees arriving were instructed to surrender over all civilian clothes and was put on a thirty-day post (Army base) restriction, which meant we could not go off post. We were told that this was standard procedure. I managed to keep back some of my civilian clothes along with a jacket, as it was in the dead of winter when I arrived. Back then, Army personnel were not permitted to wear combat fatigues out in the civilian public, but could only wear dress uniforms.

Because there were so many Army trainees trying to get through this track vehicle mechanic course, the training classes were split into morning and afternoon shifts; my class was on the afternoon shift. This was not a bad schedule. We got off training after eleven at night, ate a late chow, partied, and then slept in some in the morning.

There were forty-three males and seven females in our class, the most females in any one class up until that time, so we were told. After a short orientation into the training course, we were given the opportunity to drive track vehicles in the snow, up and down hills, just slip-sliding away, which was a neat experience.

On the first day of actual training, I found myself in a room with other wannabe Army grease monkeys looking at a piece of machinery that almost filled the entire room; there was only enough room left to maneuver around as needed. *What is this thing?* There were complex wiring harnesses hanging from different parts of this strange piece of machinery. It wasn't long before our instructor came in and gave us some insight: "This is an M60A1 tank engine pack."

Really? But where's the rest of the tank? I kept my thoughts to myself as the instructor gave each of us an instruction book of our own to use: "Here is your instruction book. Read it and learn each lesson. When you feel you are ready, I will come back and give you a demonstration test. You will either get a 'go' for pass or a 'no-go' for failing. If you get a 'no-go', you will have to read more and test out again. If you have any questions or problems learning anything, I'll be around."

Then he was gone!

I may not have been too sure of what to expect from this training course, but for sure, I never expected it to be a self-paced learning program, and this was how the majority of the course was taught. I was also sure I wasn't the only one in this training who never saw a tank or tank engine pack before entering the Army.

I soon realized that choosing the track vehicle mechanic MOS for an enlistment of three years, versus the wheeled mechanic for four years, didn't make too much difference after all. I found out quick that Army grease monkeys were trained to work on almost anything that moved, whether they had tracks or wheels.

In addition to the different track vehicles, such as the tank and APC (Army personnel carrier), we were trained to work on wheeled vehicles that included the famous Deuce and a Half truck (known as a Deuce), Army Jeep, and the not so famous Gama Goat (six-wheel-drive semi-amphibious off-road vehicle).

Our CO (commanding officer, captain in rank) of our company had a powder-blue fastback Mustang exactly like Pegasus, and seeing it brought back a longing for the car that I left home until my Army training was over. I found myself standing in front of this captain on several occasions while at Fort Knox. Maybe it was my Bronx upbringing, or my strong-will, or just my rebellious disposition, but I managed to get three article fifteens during this training. Two of these were company grade (company level) while the last one was a field grade (battalion level).

An article fifteen is considered non-judicial punishment given at the sole discretion of commanders for minor misconducts or offenses, such as oversleeping or missing formation. Punishment for an article fifteen can consist of any or all of the following: restrictions, extra duty work, forfeit of pay, reduction in rank. Types of punishments were also at the discretion of commanders.

I don't remember now what my misconduct was, but there were others in our class platoon who also received article fifteens. Our captain issued the company grades, and our colonel (battalion commander) issued the field grade, which was more severe.

Because of these article fifteens, my restrictions were changed that confined me to the company area only, and lasted almost the entire duration of training. I also did extra duty work that mainly consisted of raking leaves in a nearby park on post, which I was positive had never been raked in years, and did other extra duty nonessential work just to keep me busy.

I managed to get out of doing any extra duty work for the field grade article fifteen, only because no one was keeping track of whether or not I was doing it. I never forfeited any pay, and I was already at the lowest rank, so I never had any reduction in rank for these article fifteens.

I also had frequent room inspections because of these article fifteens. Our females' barracks was a block building that had single-occupant rooms on several floor levels. With living in the Army barracks, there were many who had keys and free access to our rooms. I was able to move the locker in my room near the door in such a way that with the locker door open and up against the doorknob, anyone trying to open the door would jam it and not be able to enter. But of course, I had to be in the room for this to work.

While waiting for one of these inspections, I took a nap on my made-up bunk only to be awakened by the jammed door. This didn't make the captain too happy, who arrived with his sergeant. And if this wasn't bad enough, he was irate when he found my civilian jacket hiding under my mattress during his inspection.

After lifting this jacket out, this captain dropped it on the floor and told the sergeant: "Deal with this." He then walked out without saying a word to me, but the look on his face spoke volumes to his anger. My civilian jacket was confiscated until I was no longer on restrictions.

Soon after this inspection, I found myself standing in front of our colonel for the field grade article fifteen. During this meeting, this colonel told me that they knew I was breaking restrictions, and then gave me a warning I will never forget: "Mitikas, if I ever find out you broke restrictions again, I will crucify you!"

Just after this meeting, arrangements were made with the owner of a tattoo shop off post to open on a day he was normally closed so that our group of friends, six females, could all get tattoos at the same time.

After this colonel's warning, I remembered thinking that Jesus was crucified, and I remembered the circumstances when I inadvertently read Leviticus 19:28 for the first time opening a Bible while still in the Bronx. Although the Jewish laws do not bind Christians, God still shared His heart with me through this Scripture—He did not want His people getting tattoos. Maybe the colonel's warning was really from God that I should have taken more seriously?

However, I ignored the red flags that flew up. I was strong-willed and rebellious at the time, and gave little thought to challenging authorities in my life that I should have obeyed. Even knowing I would be breaking restrictions again, and knowing I would be considered AWOL (absent without official leave) while off post, and worst of all, even knowing God's heart regarding tattoos, I still made the defiant decision to go off post and get a tattoo with my friends.

I'm not sure how tattoos are done today, but back in those days, it was very painful as bunches of little needles ripped into my skin. I remember thinking: *I'll never do this again!* But because this tattoo guy did such a horrible job with my tattoo (and with everyone else's), and I felt lopsided with a tattoo on only one arm, I got another tattoo at my permanent station while my messed up one was fixed.

I also had to hide my tattoo from everyone except my friends who went with me. If anyone else had found out I had just gotten a tattoo (and no one did), it would have proved without any doubt that I broke restrictions again.

There were strong bonds of friendship made during this part of my Army term with some special people. Val was my get high buddy, and together, we played some pranks on unsuspecting people. Anna was a friend who also became my roommate when we went together to Ft. Benning, Georgia, after this training.

Another dating couple pretended to be a mom and dad to me. One weekend, the three of us went off post. Mom and dad went their way while I went my way for some adventurous excitement. We planned on regrouping later that evening. The colonel's last stern warning about breaking restrictions was still very fresh and active, but far from my concerns.

So off I went on my pursuit for adventurous excitement, hitchhiking around town, not knowing who would pick me up, where I would end up, or how I would be getting back. And really, I wasn't too concerned about knowing these little details.

It didn't take long as I stood on a street corner, thumb sticking out, looking young and innocent in a town near the Fort Knox Army post, before this young guy picked me up. As we drove away and talked, we found out that we both enjoyed smoking pot. So we decided to find a secluded area to smoke a joint and get high.

Naïve me only had thoughts of getting high, but looking back on that night, I could believe this guy had other thoughts in mind. He was driving, and I expected he knew the area, because I sure didn't know the area. And besides, my sense of direction still stunk.

This guy found a secluded spot somewhere and parked it. There were some lights in the area, but by this time, it was late at night and dark out. Before we lit up the joint, a vehicle showed up from out of nowhere and stopped behind us with headlights shining on our car.

My thoughts were flying through my mind. *This isn't looking too good!* Two guys got out of this vehicle and started approaching our car. *Yep, this is not good! Who are these guys barging in on our getting-high time?*

As one of these guys went over to the driver's side of our car, the other guy went to my side. Now I could see them more clearly. *Oh, you guys are MPs (military police)! This is bad!* My thoughts were confused now. *What are you guys doing so far off post?*

The expressions on the faces of these two MPs spoke volumes to their disgust and anger. *Yep, this is really bad!* The MP on the driver's side spoke first to the guy who drove us here while the second MP waited on my side: "You are parked unauthorized in a restricted area on the property of the United States Government."

Uh-oh! This is really, really bad! This MP proceeded to interrogate this guy extensively after demanding his license. Now I was really confused as to what happened. *Can it be possible that we somehow ended up back on Fort Knox?*

The MP on my side asked me if my father was in the Army. Up until now, I was guessing they assumed I was just an Army kid. With my short stature and long hair, I looked far too young to be in the Army myself.

At this point, I decided it was not wise to lie to this MP, especially with that look of disgust and anger plastered on his face. I fessed up that I was the one in the Army. After my confession, this MP demanded I surrender my military ID, and after I did, with an angry and authoritative demeanor ordered me out of the car. *This is getting worse than really, really bad!*

Because I was the one in the Army, it seemed that all attention was concentrated on me while the guy who drove us here was left alone and allowed to stay in the warm car. As these MPs kept me standing outside shivering—probably more from my nerves than the cold—the MP who ordered me out of the car started interrogating me extensively, and then chewed me out for other reasons as well as being unauthorized in a restricted area. I managed to hold my ground and not lie, but without telling him the whole truth.

As I endured this verbal beating from this MP, my thoughts flew into alarm mode: *Oh boy! If these MPs find out I'm AWOL, I'm done; it will be all over for me! They'll for sure haul me into the stockade. I will once again find myself in front of the colonel having to answer for being caught red-handed breaking restrictions and being unauthorized in a restricted area. He'll not only crucify me; he'll court-martial me and then throw me out of this Army! How do I manage to get into such messes?*

After what seemed like hours later, the interrogation and verbal beating ended with a final stern warning from this MP: "If you ever have any other involvement with the military police again while on this post, and I find out about it, I will come down hard on you."

After his warning, we were escorted out of this restricted area and off government property, and left to go our way.

By this time, the guy who picked me up hitchhiking was so scared and shook up, he said very little. I could tell that all he wanted to do was leave me off anywhere fast; it was as though I had some kind of plague. We never did smoke that joint. But he was nice enough to leave me off where he had picked me up.

My pursuit of adventurous excitement for that night out became more than what I had bargained for. This was the closest I ever came to being caught red-handed breaking restrictions. But thankfully, close only counts in horseshoes and hand grenades.

Someday, I believe it will be known just how often and how fierce the spiritual battles were raged in my defense and won by the angelic warriors, even in spite of my own stupid actions and sins. God alone would know what I was really spared that night. And to be sure, I was not only spared being hauled into the Army stockade. I believe those MPs were sent from God and used in a powerful way for my protection, and I am pretty sure they had no idea how God had used them.

Finally, as with basic training, the time came to graduate and move on with my Army term. This training ended with me doing very well in the self-paced mechanic course, having learned how to work on all sorts of track and wheeled vehicles, along with their complex wiring harnesses.

The same colonel, who had given me the severest warning while issuing the field grade article fifteen, took a personal interest in my progress in training, and turned out to be a really nice guy. He wanted to present my certificate for completing the track vehicle mechanic training course personally to me, as he admitted while doing so: "I never thought you were going to make it through the training."

As I stood in front of this colonel one final time as he presented this certificate, I saw a different man than I did before. This colonel was sincerely pleased that I had made it through the training and wished me well in my future serving in the Army. Maybe, just maybe, he too was really sent from God?

Chapter 16
Fort Benning, GA

My Army term proved to be the most transformative season of my life thus far. God's nurturing and protection over my life were manifested in powerful ways as He continued to draw me closer to Himself. During this time, God orchestrated many different people in and out of my life, and all according to His purpose.

Even after all these years have past, my heart is moved with fond and nostalgic memories of the lives that have touched mine, the friendships and love shared, and of all that transpired during my Army term.

I had joined the Army about two years after the Vietnam War had officially ended. The many years that followed were considered "peacetime" for the United States. I have the utmost respect for all honorable veterans, but especially those who have seen combat. I was one of the fortunate ones who never saw combat while serving my country.

Because of this peacetime period, and given the years that have past, I am sure there are many differences to when I served compared to those now in the military. In addition to not being permitted to wear combat fatigues (solid OD green color) out in public as they do today, random drug and alcohol testing also never happened while I was in, which I understand is standard practice now.

Before leaving Fort Knox, I was given orders to go to Fort Benning, Georgia, for my permanent party station, along with Anna, who became my roommate. Once at Fort Benning, as usual, I had a few days of in-processing to go through before arriving at my unit. It was during this time after meeting some interesting people that I realized—this Army was a society within a society.

During my in-processing, someone had offered me a white powder drug to try, which I refused. I wasn't into doing drugs other than smoking pot at that time. I was still convinced of my rationale that marijuana as a plant was a gift from God, justified me smoking it. I continued with my nightly prayer life, and acknowledged and loved God in my own way.

I was told many times while in training at Fort Knox that once I got to my permanent station, because I was a female, I would be put in an office working as a secretary or administrator of some sort. These instructors were adamant that there was no way I would be allowed to work as an Army grease monkey. Upon hearing this, I was even more determined that was not going to happen to me. I trained as a track vehicle mechanic; I was going to work my trained MOS.

As an overview, the Army unit of structure starts with divisions as the largest. Each division may consist of three brigades. Each brigade can have 2-5 battalions; each battalion can have 4-6 companies; each company can have 4-6 platoons; each platoon can have 16-40 soldiers assigned to it. Each platoon is divided up into squads of about 4-10 soldiers each, with each squad having their own sergeant as a squad leader.

I was assigned to Delta Company (Company D) in a direct support battalion that was part of one of the largest infantry brigades at that time; this brigade has since been dismantled. The Delta Company compound where we worked and where the enlisted males were housed, was located in an area known as Harmony Church. The enlisted females of Delta were housed on Kelly Hill, an area a few miles away from Harmony Church.

Kelly Hill had several newer brick buildings that all had air-conditioning. Most of these were barracks with several floor levels of double occupancy rooms. All the barracks were intermixed on each level with enlisted males and females from other companies of the same support battalion. The entire atmosphere of Kelly Hill reminded me of a university campus.

The Army didn't seem to care how we decorated our rooms in the barracks. While I was home on leave picking up Pegasus, I brought back many of my posters, and acquired more weird ones from a neat store off post. Anna and I had our lockers set up creating a hallway in our room so that anyone looking in from the main hallway was not able to see anything inside.

Although there was leniency on the décor, cleanliness was mandatory. There were more general inspections of our living quarters on Kelly Hill than what Delta had on Harmony Church. GI (general inspection) parties, which were designated times for everyone to clean everything, were also mandatory.

I never liked living on Kelly Hill, and with many higher-ranked personnel prowling about, it was more risky to smoke pot. The area itself had a known crime problem, which included sex offenders. One such sex offender made his way into my room one night while our door was unlocked. As he tried to look under my blanket as I slept, I woke up and caught a glimpse of him. When I looked over my top bunk and saw he was crouching, I yelled a few colorful metaphors at him before he ran out of my room.

There were some benefits with a few problems when the females of Delta lived on Kelly Hill while the rest of Delta worked and lived on Harmony Church. For a while, no one knew where or even if the females were doing PT (physical training); this was a benefit, at least to us females anyway. When this was discovered, no one could decide where we would do PT; this was a problem.

Getting to company formations on time at Harmony Church was another challenge for some of us. Company formations were mandatory to make, and required the entire company unit to line up in divisions of platoons and then squads for each soldier to be physically accounted for. Formations were held in the assigned areas of each company for PT, afterward before going to our jobs, after lunch before returning to our jobs, and at other times for special reasons.

Being late for formations or missing them all together was considered a minor infraction. Jackie was a female sergeant from Delta with a room across from mine, who seemed to have a real physical problem with waking up in the mornings. It seemed to be perfectly fine for Jackie to be late or miss formations without any consequences. Maybe working in the HQ (headquarters) office of Delta and in constant close contact with our CO (commanding officer, captain in rank) made the difference?

The actual Delta compound on Harmony Church was a few miles from Kelly Hill, several miles from Main Post, and located way out in the boondocks surrounded by miles of woods. In complete contrast to Kelly Hill, the overall atmosphere of Delta's compound reminded me of a camp settlement.

There were several old WWII era wooden barracks built on stilts that housed the enlisted males of Delta on this compound. These barracks were divided inside with thin walls making them into separate rooms from their original open-bay days, as they were used during WWII, and had no air conditioning.

The other buildings on Delta compound were of the same construction and era. Very little improvements other than the thin walls were ever made over the years to these WWII buildings. The barracks latrines (bathrooms) were open bays of sinks, toilets and showers, without dividers or curtains for privacy.

Our platoon mechanic shop building where we worked on this compound was huge, and it had to be. All sorts of Army vehicles, engine packs of track vehicles, and the heavy equipment needed to move these engine packs were housed in this building.

There was one large latrine available in this mechanic shop, which was also an open bay of sinks, toilets and showers, without dividers or curtains for privacy. On the latrine door was one flip-sign that spelled out "males" on one side, "females" on the other side, and was flipped according to the gender of who was occupying the latrine at the time. There were several females in our platoon working in our shop when I first arrived, much to my surprise. When we had to use the latrine, a real person was used as a door guard, as there were no locks on the latrine door.

Overall, those of Delta Company, both males and females, were a special group of folks, including our sergeants. But the real special bonds were between those from the rank and file, as we all worked, ate and lived in close quarters together, and we partied hard together. Many of my friends from back home thought this Army life was going to calm down my smoking pot; nothing was further from the truth.

With Delta compound being way out in the boondocks surrounded by woods, it was much easier getting high more often than on Kelly Hill. There was a community bong that was hidden in the nearby woods that our close-knit partying group of comrades knew about and used to smoke our pot with. As a community bong in the woods, no one could be busted with its ownership, unless you were actually caught using it. (A bong is a water pipe. Its construction allows the smoke to go through a glass globe filled with water that acts as a cooling chamber before inhaling the smoke into the lungs.)

I thoroughly enjoyed the Delta compound area and my Army grease monkey job. I felt a real sense of accomplishment with each piece of equipment I worked on, and never once felt I had to prove myself to my fellow comrade grease monkeys. I was also able to drive with great enjoyment many different Army vehicles, some even without training.

Such was the case when I was told to use a Gama Goat to chauffeur a sergeant and his group of detainees around post. I had never driven a Gama Goat before, but this didn't concern me. The only difference from a Gama Goat compared to other Army vehicles that I knew of was that it was a six-wheel-drive semi-amphibious vehicle. But I wasn't going in the water with this thing; I was just chauffeuring a bunch of men around post.

When I found this Gama Goat, I got inside and looked around the cabin. *Yep, just what I thought.* Gas pedal, brake pedal and clutch pedal were all in the same line-up as any other vehicle I had driven. The manual transmission and shifter were in the normal place, only the gears were a little tighter. After I ran through the gears a few times, I thought: *Yep, no big deal. After about thirty minutes with driving this thing around, I will be as comfortable driving this as any other Army vehicle.* There was only one small hurdle I saw that needed conquered before starting out. I looked around the cabin some more: *Yep, only one small hurdle.*

While I sat in the driver's seat, I got the attention of some innocent guy just walking around minding his own business and waved him over: "Hey, hey. Come here, come here."

This guy was nice enough to make a little detour in his stride and came over to where the Gama Goat was parked. I then asked him: "Do you know how to start this thing?"

He showed me where the starter was. I thanked him for this little bit of information, and off he went continuing on his journey. In my defense, the starter was in a totally different location than any other Army vehicle I had driven before.

I pushed in the clutch, pushed in the starter, engine started running, and presto—hurdle conquered. I carefully backed out of where it was parked being mindful of the pedestrians and trees that may jump in my way, and off I went to collect my guinea pigs—I mean passengers—for my maiden drive with a Gama Goat on this assignment.

Once I reached my destination, a nice sergeant situated his men in the back-cargo area, climbed in front with me, and then gave me a somewhat concerned expression—his first reaction to seeing a young female behind the wheel of this strange semi-amphibious vehicle that would be driving him and his detainees around post.

But that was okay. By then, I was getting used to males outside of Delta Company giving me strange looks while driving some of these Army vehicles around. I was humble as I asked this sergeant to bear with me while fessing up that this was my first time driving a Gama Goat; a confession that made him just about turn white as a ghost. He didn't say anything, but his expression spoke volumes to his thoughts of concern.

After thirty minutes of driving this sergeant and his detainees around, I was very comfortable handling this Gama Goat. When the assignment was over, and I drove these men back to their starting point, this sergeant bid me farewell with good wishes.

Remarkably, I never had any mishaps with any of the Army vehicles I drove; although I did come close a few times. While driving a Deuce on Main Post and making a turn, I saw the whites of a man's eyes with his horrified expression while the front end of the Deuce came within inches of his own beautiful truck. I wasn't too concerned myself with how close I came; after all, I wasn't dealing with horseshoes or hand grenades.

Chapter 17
Beginning of Drug Abuse

I came to Fort Benning using a string of profanity as my everyday language, more so than when I was in the Bronx. I could outdo the best of the best swearers. I'm not proud of this, just stating facts. Although my language was horrible, I made a concerted effort never to use God's name in vain as any part of my colorful metaphors. I had started smoking cigarettes just out of high school and continued this habit in the Army. It seemed that most military personnel smoked back then, and it made for a sure way to get breaks during our working hours.

While Kelly Hill was not the safest place, I had no fears being at Delta compound with my comrades, or anywhere else partying with them. There was a rented house just off post which was handed down through many different comrades. This house became a hub for parties with cookouts roasting deer, kegs of beer, and an abundance of marijuana. Although I didn't like beer, I drank it sparingly while fully indulging in smoking pot.

We also went to other places for our hardy parties as a group. While we all gathered at a rock quarry drinking beer and smoking pot, we went swimming in the nearby pond. We used a cliff that was umpteen feet high to jump off into this body of water. I too jumped off this cliff while trusting the guys who were in the water to keep me safe if I ran into problems. Looking back now, I realize that was a stupid and dangerous way to have fun. It was only by God's grace that none of us were hurt or killed.

I had some friends show up at Fort Benning from my other training posts besides my roommate Anna. Carly, who I met on the bus returning to basic training from our Christmas leave, showed up at Delta. Carly's MOS was wheeled vehicle mechanic with an enlistment of four years. Then Darla, who I knew from basic training, came to Fort Benning. Darla was assigned to a different battalion stationed on main post; her MOS was repairing eyeglasses. Darla had developed tendinitis in her foot, but because it wouldn't heal, the medical staff put a walking cast on it hoping that by keeping it from moving it would eventually heal.

For a while, Darla and I were getting high buddies. When we didn't have pot to smoke, we used an over-the-counter drug in pill form that caused us to hallucinate. As we continued using this drug, each time we had to take more pills for the same high effect.

During this time, Pegasus developed a major defect by the left engine mount where it rusted and was cracking apart that caused a constant pull to the left. Immediately after letting go of the steering wheel, Pegasus headed in the left lane.

On several different nights out driving around while doing this drug, I hallucinated and saw the front half of a Deuce stopped and parked across my side of the road. Each time I slammed on the brakes and swerved to miss this Deuce that wasn't there, Pegasus flew to the left and into the oncoming lane. When this would happen, Darla, who was also high on this drug, responded in the same way: "No, Mickie, we can't park here."

I was always too messed up to explain to her that I wasn't trying to park in the middle of the road, but that there was a Deuce on my side that I was trying to avoid hitting.

Then one day, while driving during daylight when I wasn't under the influence of anything, I came across the front half of a Deuce stopped and parked on my side of the road, and in the same spot and way each time I saw it when I was hallucinating.

Only this time, it was a real Deuce and not a hallucination. I was able to stop just before smashing into it. Only God knows whether I would have survived had I crashed into this real Deuce.

Once I understood about the spiritual warfare that goes on, I often wondered if that wasn't a setup by Satan in his attempts to destroy my life? And unfortunately, I was giving Satan all the ammunition he needed to continue his schemes to destroy my life through the drugs I abused.

I had one encounter with civilian cops while driving off post one night when Darla and I were high only on pot. The cop who pulled me over said I was staying in the lane, but because the car was swerving within the lane, he was sure I had been drinking alcohol. I didn't offer any explanation on the steering defect, but I assured him that I had not been drinking alcohol. But he didn't believe me.

This cop ordered me out of Pegasus to walk a line that I managed to do fine, but this didn't satisfy him. For another sobriety test, he questioned my education, and then told me to recite the alphabet. I rattled off the alphabet song all kids were taught but messed up royally when I got to LMNOP.

This cop then read me my rights and hauled me to the police station for a breath analyzer test. I expressed my concern of leaving Darla in Pegasus, but he assured me that another cop would stay parked behind as a guard. Darla was sleeping with her foot with the cast resting on the dashboard. When the breath analyzer test came back negative, he stated, "But that doesn't mean you're not on something else." He didn't push to find out what that "something else" was. Once back at Pegasus, I woke Darla up and told her everything that had happened.

Soon after this, Darla and I both realized that taking those hallucinating pills and driving around in a Mustang with a severely defective steering issue was not safe, for us or anyone else. I didn't stop using the hallucinating pills, but I was more careful not to drive too much while under the influence of that drug. I always felt capable of driving when I was just high from pot.

Soon it became obvious to many that I was doing more drugs than just smoking pot. Living on Kelly Hill in close quarters with so many others, it was harder to hide the drug abuse. Although I was never caught or drug tested, my CO ordered me to attend a drug and alcohol rehab facility for two meetings as an outpatient. Hank, another comrade in my squad and close to our Sarge, was also sent to this rehab facility at the same time with the excuse that he drank alcohol excessively.

But Hank did not have a drinking problem. It became obvious to me that his presence was for the sole purpose of keeping an eye on me to report back. In my defiant attitude over being ordered to this rehab facility, I went there while I was high on pot. I was at a point where it didn't matter to me who knew I smoked pot, when I was high, or what I was supposed to be doing while I was high.

During all this time while doing these hallucinating pills, smoking pot, partying with my comrades, jumping off cliffs, driving around in a defective Mustang, God still had His angelic warriors guarding me, even as they continued their spiritual battles in my defense—yet unbeknown to me at that time.

I continued praying each night to God, as I had been since I was a little girl, but with the exceptions of some nights when I was really messed up. Only now, my prayers were changing a bit.

I was hearing that gentle whisper echoing a warning: I was on a dead-end road to destruction. And with this whisper echoing in my heart, I cried out many times during my prayers to this same God, no longer asking Him if marijuana was right or wrong, but crying out for His help to stop the drugs that I knew were wrong.

Chapter 18
Conflicts With CO

When I first came to Delta, someone told me that as long as you did your work well, even if you missed formation or messed up in other ways, they would let things slide by and you wouldn't get in trouble. He didn't add that this only pertained to certain individuals, and was not the general rule.

I cannot pinpoint the reasons at the beginning for the conflict between my first CO at Fort Benning and me, but we didn't seem to hit it off well from the start. Maybe bringing along three article fifteens from AIT didn't help much? Or maybe parking Pegasus under the Delta Company wooden sign that irritated him so much was the cause? But that ended quick, so that couldn't have been it. I was also very outspoken, which again was something this CO didn't like. Whatever the reasons, while this captain was in charge of Delta, my Army term was—I'll just say for now—interesting.

This CO often singled me out and treated me differently than others who had similar infractions as mine. It was not unusual for some of our rank and file to be late for formations or miss them altogether, especially after a weekend. This was considered a minor infraction in the grand scheme of offenses possible, as anyone can oversleep. As this minor infraction was overlooked for some, it was never overlooked with me.

One weekend had the 4th of July on a Tuesday. Because of this holiday, we were given leave from our work duties for both Monday and Tuesday, but had to make formation each day in case there were emergency jobs that needed done. Several comrades missed formations one or both days, as I did. But I was the only one who received an article fifteen over the missed formation.

With this non-judicial punishment of an article fifteen given at the sole discretion of the CO, there was an appeal process involving a court-martial trial. In most cases, this route was never advisable; if you lost the appeal, you could end up court-martialed. The CO could also suspend the punishment of an article fifteen at his discretion, and then take it out of suspension at a later date; after which, there was no chance for an appeal.

My CO so much wanted to burn me on something significant enough to get me thrown out of the Army. His attempts and attitude towards me only fueled my defiance and determination to challenge his authority.

Because of this missed formation, he administered an article fifteen with the full intent to suspend the punishment. Many times, this captain had summoned me into his office for a one-on-one confrontation when he would berate me and express his disdain towards me.

During one such confrontation, he reiterated his authority to take out of suspension the article fifteen, but clearly stated he was going to wait around and give me another article fifteen so that he could get me thrown out of the Army.

On another day after being summoned into this captain's office, I came fully prepared and determined to do what I could to stop what I considered were his verbal harassments. As I stood at attention in front of his desk fully armed with my offensive weapon in full view and already using it, he took good notice. In his all too familiar mean tone, he demanded an answer: "What'd you got there with you, Mitikas?"

As if he didn't know what my weapon was, I respectfully answered, "It's a tape recorder, SIR." I really emphasized "sir."

After my answer, ooh, did he get irate! I never saw him so angry. His entire physical demeanor transformed before my eyes. His blood vessels went popping out of his neck. I could almost see steam coming out of his nostrils. His eyes were shooting daggers, but they didn't turn red—too bad, that would have been a sight to see. Although they could have turned red after I left his office.

I was trying so hard not to laugh or smirk in his face at his reaction to my tape recorder while still standing at attention, but couldn't hide the twinkle of laughter in my eyes. People tell me I always wear my emotions on my sleeve. He tried to control his anger but didn't succeed as he threw me out: "Get out of here, Mitikas. Close the door behind you and wait outside my office."

As I turned to leave, I saw he was reaching for his phone. I found great satisfaction and humor as I stood outside his office knowing he was scrambling around calling people to find out if I had the legal right to record our one-on-one confrontation. I knew I had the legal right, so long as it was in plain view and known I was recording our conversation. Apparently, though, he wasn't quite sure of my legal rights.

Finally, several minutes later, he ordered me back into his office but said nothing about the tape recorder I still had with me. But because he knew I was recording our conversation, he was careful in what he said and made this confrontation very short.

Not long after this meeting, another incident happened that also supported this CO's disdain for me. I was working outside on a fall afternoon in our maintenance yard on an engine, as I normally did. Because of the cool air, I did not take my fatigue shirt completely off but instead, rolled up the sleeves just enough so that they wouldn't get greased up while I worked. Before the day was up, my CO summoned me into his office for another one-on-one confrontation.

As I stood at attention in front of this captain's desk once again, he explained that he saw me working with my sleeves partially rolled up, and attributed it to my uniforms being too big. He then ordered me to buy new uniforms that would fit me better.

I tried explaining to him why I had my sleeves partially rolled up instead of taking the shirt completely off, but he didn't care what I had to say—he never did.

My CO then told me that he was canceling my leave of absence I had scheduled in just a few weeks without giving any reasons why. He had the authority to cancel this leave, but it was an abuse of his authority and supported his disdain for me.

I defiantly responded, "That's okay, Sir. I was going to cancel my leave anyway." This was the truth, but because I spoke with such defiance, I'm sure he didn't believe me—and it didn't matter to me that he didn't.

After my CO issued a second article fifteen for another minor infraction of oversleeping, I filed a complaint with the JAG (Judge Advocate General) office for help. The JAG was supposed to offer legal help in such cases when Army personnel felt they were being treated unfairly. It was becoming very obvious to many others by this time that I was singled out and treated differently than others with similar infractions, including Jackie, the sergeant who missed formations regularly herself due to her own chronic oversleeping. At one time, our superiors thought Jackie could keep tabs on me so I wouldn't oversleep, among other reasons. This would have been the blind leading the blind!

Although my CO and I had conflicts, and I knew he wanted me thrown out of the Army, I continued doing my grease monkey job to the best of my ability. I wanted to be sure I pulled my own weight with our workload. It also helped that we had a sergeant squad leader who was well-liked and respected by all of us, and who recognized and appreciated our hard work.

Chapter 19
Presence of God

During this same fall season, a white powder drug started circulating throughout Delta compound. This drug looked like the same drug that was offered to me when I first came to this post during my in-processing seven months earlier, but had refused to try it then.

Because I was comfortable with my getting-high comrades in our platoon—as they always respected me—I would spend time with them at the compound after work hours instead of being on Kelly Hill. One night, when this white powder drug was circulating and we were in someone's room partying, a strange guy showed up who was not from our company, and asked me out in the hallway so we could talk alone—or so he thought.

However, taking their turns one by one, my comrades were purposely making trips back and forth keeping an eye out for me while we talked. It was obvious they had concerns and didn't trust this guy to be alone with me. (The friendship and trust I shared with some of these guys was special.) I found out much later that this strange guy was the one who started circulating this white powder drug that he claimed was THC.

THC (tetrahydrocannabinol) is a concentrated derivative of marijuana. I was still believing that marijuana was okay with God for me to get high on. With my comrades doing this white powder drug, it wasn't long before I tried it too. But the high from this white powder was different than the high I got from pot. It was a strange high that felt so wrong, and made me feel totally incapable of thinking straight or doing anything. I tried it only a few times during this fall season.

It was just after the New Year when I received Mom's letter telling me that Duke was put to sleep the second week of December. She waited to tell me because she didn't want to ruin my Christmas. I was upset about losing Duke and not seeing him for a last time. I was also upset about not being there with Mom when this happened. My heart was saddened for her; now she was really alone without Duke.

With this heavy on my heart, we geared up to go on winter training maneuvers to Fort Drum, New York. Our equipment was shipped by the railroad while the personnel flew to New York. Although this training was only several weeks long, it proved to be grueling for us troops. We didn't go skiing like the officers did while we were there. To break some of the tension and stress, our guys built a very detailed snow-woman.

No one had pot or drugs during this training, but we drank on some nights after work hours. Even Jackie, the sergeant our superiors thought would keep tabs on me, got drunk to the point that others had to help her along. So much for keeping tabs on me!

We were all thrown into wooden barracks with open bays for our sleeping quarters during this training. One of our females went sleepwalking through the barracks one night and urinated on Jackie while she slept. Apparently, some animosity between the two was hidden and showed up during this sleepwalking episode. This incident became humorous to the rest of us.

It was while we were at Fort Drum that I received notice that my JAG complaint investigation against my CO was dismissed. My Sarge squad leader and others knew more of the ins and outs of this JAG investigation and our CO's attitude towards me than I would realize at the time, but their hands were tied.

With everything I was going through, I started reaching out to God even more, as I realized no one else was helping me. I knew using the hallucinating pills was wrong and caused the minor infraction of oversleeping, which fueled my CO's plan to use another article fifteen to get me thrown out of the Army. The JAG complaint only put a temporary delay to this captain's plans.

During this time, I promised God that I would not use the hallucinating pills again. I was still rationalizing that pot was okay for me to smoke. I didn't know back then how wrong it is to make promises to God. Once we do make a promise, we better keep our promise. I've learned since that God does not take lightly to broken promises made to Him.

Once JAG dismissed my case, my CO took out of suspension the punishment for the second article fifteen that was part of this JAG investigation. As an extra duty assignment, I was ordered on a Friday, to paint the floors of the offices in the wooden building that was occupied during our short stay at Fort Drum. But these floors didn't need painted. My guess was that by Monday, it was believed that the floors would have dried enough to walk on.

My Army MOS was a track vehicle mechanic, not a painter. For this paint job, I was given a few gallons of grey oil-based paint and one brush. *Okay; I won't argue. You guys want me to paint these floors? I'll paint the floors—no big deal.*

There were about four offices in this old wooden building. My painting process was about the same for each office, but with extra special care given to my CO's office.

I popped open the paint cans and saw all the oil sitting on top of the paint, and then went to town on my assignment. I poured the paint on the floors of each office making sure it was well dispersed until all the cans were emptied. I then used the only paintbrush they gave me to spread this paint all over the floors.

I painted around the legs of the desks and chairs, around the garbage cans, around my CO's skis that he had standing up against one corner of his office, and around his boots that were just sitting there. I painted around everything without moving anything. The paint was thick, gooey, and smelled really bad. It took several days for this paint to dry, if it ever dried.

A few days later, my CO came up to me and asked if I was ready to paint the floors again. I answered respectfully: "Sure, Sir; I'll paint the floors again."

He then showed me the bottom of his boots that were covered with grey paint, and asked with a smirk: "Are you going to give us another hard time with the paint job, Mitikas?"

I just smirked back and laughed to myself. *Do you suppose maybe, if I had mixed the paint first and not poured it on so thick, it would have dried better?* I wisely kept my thoughts to myself. That was one of the few times that I didn't do my best at a job I was given. This captain's disdain for me and my defiant attitude towards him gave me a good reason not to.

After this great paint job I did, I wasn't ordered to do any more extra duty during this winter training, or even afterward. In fact, that was also the last article fifteen I received during the rest of my Army term.

Finally, the training was over, and it was time for us to head back to Fort Benning. Once we arrived in Georgia, we were bused to our barracks. The males from Delta went to Harmony Church while the females went back to Kelly Hill with the rest of the infantry support battalion. While we were on the bus going to Kelly Hill, someone pointed out a deer on the side of the road. I couldn't see the deer and wondered: *Why can't I see the deer?* (There is a reason why I shared this that will be understood later.)

There were some incidents the following days that played a significant purpose in proving to me that God was present in my life, even though I was not deserving of His presence.

The barracks on Kelly Hill housed both male and female soldiers in the same building and on the same floors. As several of us were climbing the stairs going to our rooms late at night once back at our barracks, some guy unknowingly dropped his wallet out of his pocket. I saw it, grabbed it, got his attention and gave it back to him. Carly witnessed what I did and told me later I should have kept his wallet. I defended my actions: "Why should I keep it? It wasn't mine, and I knew who dropped it."

The next day, Carly and I were at a mall in downtown Columbus, Georgia. She was using a pay-phone at an open booth while someone behind her was impatiently waiting to also use the phone. (Remember those pay-phones in our last century?) When Carly got off the phone and left the booth, neither of us knew that she had left her wallet there in plain sight. But the woman who was impatiently waiting to use the phone knew. As it was, this woman could have alerted Carly that she had left her wallet and given it back to her, but instead, she kept the wallet for herself. There was a reason why these two incidents were important.

In the few days following our return from Fort Drum, for some reason I was being very mindful of the presence of God. I recognized God was teaching both Carly and me powerful lessons on honesty with what happened with both wallets, and at the same time, proving His presence. I shared all this with Carly, but I don't know whether she believed me or not. But I believed it, which proved very significant in the days to follow.

Around this same time, some of us were in a trailer that was converted into a bar, with another trailer connected that housed the restrooms. Between the two trailers was this vicious German Shepherd dog that was tied up and lunged at me when I went to the restroom; he reached the end of his leash just short of reaching me. I always loved German Shepherds, and thought someday I would love to own one.

With this dog almost reaching me for an attack, instead of leaving him alone like someone else with better common sense would have done, I decided to talk him out of his viciousness so I could pet him. I never said I learned lessons easy! The vicious dogs that attacked me at the junkyard when I was very young left me with no emotional scars or fear of dogs. I wasn't drinking like everyone else in our group was at the time.

As I was petting this dog as though we were always best of friends, someone from our group came out of the trailer bar, and seeing me petting the dog, he also tried approaching the dog. My warning that he wasn't friendly halted him while the dog proved it by viciously reaching the end of his leash for an attack. I believed that God had given me a gift with animals that I love so much, and believed this as another proof of His presence during that time.

Soon after this, the white powder drug began circulating again throughout Delta and on Kelly Hill. What really was this white powder stuff? The high from it was so strange and felt so wrong, even though it was labeled as THC.

I went for a walk around Kelly Hill one night while high on this white powder THC, really missing Mom, missing Duke, wondering about life and about what was going on with my life. During this walk, I thought I saw Duke walking around, and near him, two deer appeared from out of nowhere and just stood there looking at me. As I watched these animals, they quietly slipped away into the woods.

I wondered: *Was that Duke's spirit, or is this THC the cause of what I saw? What really is happening to me and around me? Why am I being so mindful of God's presence while getting more involved with this white powder THC?*

There were some very powerful spiritual forces all around me that I was not aware of during that time. The angelic warriors of the Most High God, who had been given charge by God Himself to protect me, were gearing up for the fiercest battle over me against the spiritual forces of evil and wickedness in the heavenly places. (Ephesians 6:12.)

While at the same time, Satan and his demons were gearing up for the complete destruction of everything I was and held dear and believed in, the complete destruction of my very soul.

And while these powerful spiritual forces were gearing up for this great battle over me, I too was raging a battle within myself between my heart and my flesh.

As I felt the special presence of God these past few days as never before, my heart that loved Him was longing for more of His presence, while my flesh was longing for a better high.

I still believed that this white powder drug was THC, a derivative of marijuana, which as a plant was a gift from God that He was okay with me getting high on.

Satan and his demons were deceptively using the very thing I believed was a gift from God to destroy me.

Meanwhile, God was profoundly making sure I was very aware that His presence was with me.

And the battles would rage on!

Chapter 20

My "D" Day

It was the Saturday after our return from Fort Drum, when Carly and I met with two guys on Kelly Hill who were friends with each other. I didn't know either of them well. Carly knew the one guy who was from Delta but was not from our platoon. The second guy, who I will call Dopey, was the one who had appeared at our Delta compound when this white powder drug first showed up, and who had spoken with me alone when my comrades became so watchful over me. I did not know when we first met that Dopey was the main supplier of this white powder drug that he claimed was THC. The four of us agreed to go on a double date the following day.

One method of using this powder THC was to snort it up your nose. Now that I was even more convinced that this stuff was THC, I felt safe using it. When Sunday morning came around, I snorted two long lines of this powder THC before we met for this double date. None of us had any pot at the start of this day; the only thing we had was this THC.

When the four of us met, Dopey and I went in the back seat of the car. Carly and her date were up front. While in the back seat, Dopey offered me more of this powder THC. I accepted his offer and snorted two more long lines that he prepared for me. I never believed anyone could overdose using pot, and since THC was a derivative of pot, I really didn't think taking more of this stuff would be any big deal. We ended up going to a car-racing event early that day.

Soon after arriving at this car event, I realized what I did before: My high from this THC was not the same high I was used to having with pot. Because of this strange high, I questioned Dopey about this white powder drug: "Is this stuff really THC?"

Dopey answered, "Yes, it's THC."

However, something was really wrong with this high.

During this entire day in the spiritual realm unbeknown to me, the angelic warriors were keeping their defensive guard over my life against the demons, who were also present and being so clever as they planned their schemes to destroy me and everything I held dear. There were a few scuffles between these powerful spiritual forces that caused swords to clash with sparks flying, but the fiercest battle was yet to be fought.

The angelic warriors were patiently waiting for the precise moment when they knew they had the commanded authority over these demons to render them powerless in their schemes to destroy me; that moment would come in God's perfect timing.

A few times during this day, Dopey attempted to get me alone to lie in the grass with him, which I adamantly refused to do, and for good reasons. As a counter to his attempts, I made sure I told Dopey about the moral conviction that I refused to compromise because of God in my life. But I was sure he knew all about my moral conviction, as some things were well known in an Army community lifestyle.

Dopey acted as if he never heard a word I said. He had his own intentions he was planning for the end of our date. My belief in God and making it clear I refused to violate my moral conviction meant nothing to him.

While I struggled this whole day feeling something was so very wrong with this high, I was also profoundly aware of God's presence, as though He really wanted me to know that He was with me, always. And because this high felt so wrong, several times throughout this day I would ask Dopey the same question: "Is this stuff really THC?"

He never once faltered with his response: "YES! IT IS THC!"

Dopey seemed irritated that I kept asking him the same question. He never caught on that I was more irritated with his behavior, his schemes, and his indifference as I shared about God in my life.

Once the car event ended, the four of us went to a restaurant for a meal. The baked potato I had was empty; the steak was as though it wasn't real. I was not sure how the others were feeling with their "highs." They may not have used as much of this powder THC as I did. Dopey may not have used any at all. I never saw him snort any that morning when I accepted what he offered. But for sure, my high was still going strong and still very wrong.

After dinner, we split up without me realizing this was pre-planned. Carly and her date went somewhere; I didn't know where and no one told me. Dopey and I ended up at some trailer home off post where another Army guy lived who Dopey said was an MP.

As I walked into this trailer home, the angelic warriors, who had been surrounding me this entire day, followed along while defensively ready to unsheathe their swords in a microsecond if needed to protect me. While the same demons that swished around and drooled their saliva on us all day long, and who had scuffled with some of these same angelic warriors, followed suit.

The resident demons who claimed this as their domain, put up a strong front against these angelic warriors who had dared to invade their turf. And as if the arrival of these angelic warriors weren't bad enough, within a few minutes later, several more angelic warriors arrived on the scene. Then all at once, all the demons started arguing and fighting among themselves while blaming each other for the presence of these angelic warriors.

Dopey introduced me to the MP and his wife or girlfriend; I didn't know which title she claimed, so I wasn't the only female present. I was offered a non-alcoholic drink that I accepted. As I sat in this home with these strange people I had never met before, the MP pulled out some pot, loaded a bong with it, and passed it around for all of us to hit on. (A hit is one long inhaled drag of smoke from the pot through the bong, which is a water pipe.) At this, I wondered: *An MP with pot! What is wrong with this picture? Is this guy to be trusted, or is this a set-up?*

This was the very first time during this whole day that Dopey and I smoked real pot. I was still so very high from the THC that I took that morning, which never diminished in its intensity; another sign that this high from the THC was so wrong.

When the bong reached me, I took my first hit and then sipped my drink. I then noticed the TV was playing but the sound was turned completely off. Weird head music blasted away on a stereo as the bong made its way around for the second time.

After my second hit, I sat there getting even more high, if that were possible, and then a thought came to me: *I'm too messed up to pray tonight.* Looking at the TV, I soon realized that everyone on that TV looked like they were high themselves. *Can those people also be high?* The weird head music continued blasting away as my mind started spinning fast.

Unbeknown to any of us, in the spiritual realm the Captain of the Host of God arrived, and with him another mass of angelic warriors converged in battle array. With this onslaught of angelic army present, the demons became frantic, and crying out for their own reinforcements, Satan himself arrived with another group of his demons prepared to battle for my very destruction.

But aside from small scuffles with a few swords clashing and sparks flying, these powerful angelic warriors just held their ground against these evil forces. They were still patiently waiting for the word from their Captain that they had the commanded authority needed for complete victory in this looming battle they were about to rage over me.

My "D" Day/20

The bong made its way around for the third time. I took another hit and just sat there. Unbeknown to me, my brain was being destroyed. The effects of smoking pot while having so much of that so-called THC already saturated in my brain could be compared to lighting a match to dynamite, and then just waiting for the explosion. I could not have known at that time the dangerous effect of combining the two.

The scuffles between the angelic warriors and the demons were increasing. Powerful blows with clashing swords sent up fiery sparks that caused smoke as though it came from hell itself. The sulfur breaths of these demons were heated, as vulgar threats were thrown in the faces of the angelic warriors while these demons claimed this domain for themselves and my very existence for destruction.

As the familiar sweet aroma of marijuana permeated the air, I sat there relishing the exhilarated high. The weird head music continued blasting away as I saw everyone on TV looked like they were really messed up in their own minds.

And then the explosion happened!

My thoughts were racing: *Was another drug put in my drink without my knowledge? Is the pot in the bong laced with this powder THC? Is the enormous amount of THC I took earlier finally hitting its climax? Is this white powder stuff really THC?*

With the presence of Satan and his reinforcements, the demons became even bolder as they claimed dominion over my life and soul, demanding my destruction, demanding my entrance into their hell. The angelic warriors held their ground defending me, as they were commanded to do by the Most High God, but uttered no threats or disputes against these demons.

Then I realized, as much as I tried, I could not move any part of my body. I could not even speak. My brain was being destroyed and was no longer functioning correctly. My heart was pounding out of my chest. And then I floated out of my body and hovered in the air looking down where my body sat, as though it was no longer my body I was looking at. Once back inside my body, I received a demonic revelation: I would die that night!

No one in the room was paying any attention to me. No one there had any idea what was going on. No one had any clue of the spiritual battle raging at that time over my very existence. No one knew I was going to die that night.

As the spiritual battle approached a fierce climax, this great fear filled my heart. I then realized: *I did this to myself! No one forced me to take so much of this THC. No one forced me to take those hits on the bong. But did someone put another drug in my drink? Never did I get high like this smoking pot, regardless of how much I smoked at any one time. But after coming here, after the drink, after smoking real pot in the bong, the high that was so wrong and never diminished in its intensity from all day long, just exploded!*

As I sat there knowing I did this to myself, unable to move, unable to speak, my heart pounding out of my chest, wondering what was happening to me, I realized the truth: *I really am going to die tonight!* Now I was paralyzed with fear that was indescribable!

In the midst of everything happening and being paralyzed with indescribable fear, from within my heart that knowledge of God's presence He had profoundly made known to me, came alive.

Without a shadow of a doubt, I knew the God to whom I had been praying to since I was a little girl was right there with me. In the midst everything, I voiced in my mind what deep within my heart I knew to be true: *God's here; He'll help me!*

No sooner did I finish acknowledging this truth, God manifested His presence with His overwhelming peace that rushed throughout my entire being instantly obliterating every trace of the indescribable fear within me. God's manifested presence assured me of His willingness to help me.

At the exact moment God manifested His presence, every angelic warrior instantly went into battle array with gleaming swords unsheathed. All the demons went into a bewildered frenzy at this sudden offensive stance by this angelic army.

As the fierce swords clashed, the demons continued with their vulgar sulfur breaths demanding their rights to destroy me. The angelic warriors kept silent as they continued defending me while powerfully holding these demons at bay.

As I sat there basking in God's presence and peace, I glanced around and realized—nothing had changed with these people. Still, no one in the room with me had any clue as to what was taking place, within my own heart or in the spiritual realm.

And then God's peace started to slowly dissipate as the fear slowly came back, a sure reminder that my life and everything I held dear was still in very grave danger of being destroyed. It was then that I understood: *Only God Himself is going to be able to save me from dying!*

With the fear now back in full force, still unable to move or speak, my heart pounding out of my chest again, a gentle whisper issued an authoritative command that only I heard: "Now, you must ask God for His help."

I know that whisper; it's so familiar to me!

I obeyed instantly and prayed, *"God, please help me! And please . . ."* (I cannot share the rest of my prayer.)

Microseconds even before I uttered my cry to God for His help, the precise moment all these angelic warriors had been patiently waiting for had finally arrived. God gave His word to His Captain, who gave His word to his angelic army. Now every angelic warrior present knew: They had God's commanded authority, and with this, their complete victory in this raging battle over my very existence was secured.

With God's commanded authority, the Captain of the Host of God instantly engaged Satan in battle, authoritatively invoking the name of Jesus as his final affirmative to victory: "The Lord Jesus Christ rebukes you, Satan! Angelika is not yours, and never will be; she belongs to God!"

With their swords flaming as lethal weapons, all the angelic warriors who had converged for this very purpose, now raged this battle with a fierceness that was out of this world, as they too authoritatively invoked the name of Jesus, as did their Captain.

Satan and his demons frantically swished around in a frenzy that proved to help destroy each other, no longer trying to defend their domain or destroy me, but trying hopelessly to survive this angelic army onslaught that was too powerful for them. At the same time, they were bewildered, wondering what went wrong with this whole scenario.

As the angelic warriors gained their victory, Satan and his demons limply swished away, wounded and defeated, whimpering as they went. Only the resident demons refused to leave, but hovered in the corner cowardly, whimpering in defeat, and staying far away from these angelic warriors.

After this fierce spiritual battle was won, God gave me the ability to speak again. I looked over at Dopey, who was just sitting there oblivious to everything that just transpired, and oblivious to the fact that I was dying from an overdose on what he vehemently claimed was THC.

With an authority that was not my own, and in a tone that left no room for debate, I demanded Dopey: "Take me back!"

Nothing more needed said; he knew exactly what I meant.

I was still in grave danger. The demons were defeated and could not destroy me, but physically, I was still dying from this overdose. I had snorted four very long lines of this white powder drug; an amount that far exceeded a normal get-high dose.

And who knew what else I took while at this MP's home? What was in the drink, or what was laced with the pot that I smoked in the bong? Something had caused the THC explosion.

Or was it God Himself who kept me alive this whole day until I reached out to Him? Was it God Himself who kept me alive until His army of powerful angelic warriors fought and won the victory in this fiercest battle over my very existence?

God had manifested His presence in such an extraordinary and powerful way to me, and by doing so, I believed He assured me that He was more than willing to save me from dying, and to completely heal me from this overdose.

I needed to get back to my barracks and to my room. I desperately needed to get alone with God, to cry out to Him for His forgiveness, for His help, and for His healing. On that night, I knew without any doubt that my life depended solely on God's mercy, power and willingness to save me from dying.

Chapter 21

God's Healing

Dopey and I left the trailer home, and as soon as we got into his car, he tried a few advances on me. But I pushed him away and adamantly refused to let him come near me or touch me. He took my refusal to heart and left me alone. If he was offended by my actions, I never gave that a thought.

I was still overdosing from Dopey's so-called THC and had only one thought: getting safely back to my barracks room and alone with God. But unfortunately, I had no idea where this trailer was in relation to Kelly Hill or even Fort Benning, and no idea which direction we needed to start towards. I was totally depending on God for His protection and in constant prayer during the drive back.

I started praying for God's help to get me back safely and not allow us to be pulled over by any cops or real MPs, as I was not in any condition to deal with any authorities right then. I also prayed that my roommate would be asleep when I got back to our room.

It took a while to get back to Kelly Hill, but as Dopey drove I kept silent, except for asking him one final time the same question I had been asking him all day long: "Is this stuff really THC?"

It was as if an angelic warrior held his fiery sword to Dopey's throat and demanded him to speak the truth this time: "No. It is not THC. It is really PCP."

Dopey had lied to me all this time about what this white powder drug really was. My mind was spinning now trying to grasp this new truth. I had no idea what this PCP drug was, and it was a good thing I didn't know right then while I was overdosing on it. It never once occurred to me to seek any medical help with this overdose, even after being told it was not THC, but a drug I knew nothing about. I just knew I needed to get alone with God, as I truly believed that God was the only One able to save me from this overdose, and I truly believed that He would.

When we finally arrived on Kelly Hill, I got out of Dopey's car, walked away, never looked back, and never saw him again. It was late at night as I walked alone on Kelly Hill. I found my barracks amongst all the others, walked past the barracks guard on duty, and climbed up the long flights of stairs to reach my room. The door was unlocked, so I quietly walked in and locked the door behind me. Anna was fast asleep in her bunk bed.

Now safe in my barracks room, I crawled on my bunk bed and sat up against the wall. Whereas earlier I had once thought I was too messed up to pray this night, I now started praying for my very life, desperately crying out to God to save my life and to forgive me for all my sins. I was crying out to God knowing full well that I did this to myself, and that I did not deserve for God to answer my cry and spare my life, but I desperately cried out to God anyway.

Then I felt God's presence and peace again in a powerful way. Without any doubt, I knew God was right there with me as I cried my heart out to Him. My tears flowed down my face like a flowing river as I was being cleansed, healed and saved by the only One who I knew could save me. I was being touched by God Almighty Himself in a powerful way.

In God's presence as He was healing me, He showed me flashbacks of my life. In these flashbacks, I saw God's presence in my life while yet in the womb, all during my life, and in some very special ways during the most difficult parts of my life. Even when I didn't know God was with me, He had always been there with me, protecting, guiding, teaching and disciplining me.

The radio was softly playing in the background all this time, and I was made aware of a special tune: The Music Box Dancer.

This tune went right along with God's presence and His Holy Spirit, as I felt such an overwhelming awareness of God's powerful love for me.

Then without giving it another thought, as though God's Holy Spirit took over my prayer, I started into my nightly prayer: *"Now I lay me down to sleep. I pray the Lord my soul to keep . . ."*

I continued praying the very same prayer that God's Holy Spirit taught me as a little girl. And this night, I ended my prayer with a very special "I love You, God."

After this nightly prayer, I sat there for a while being still in God's presence until eventually, I drifted off to sleep knowing that God Almighty was with me; I was now safe in His care.

When I woke up the next morning, the high from the PCP was still lingering to a very small degree, even after almost twenty-four hours later of taking this drug, but just enough to prove the seriousness of my overdose was real and was not to be taken lightly. Everything else seemed to be new, fresh and beautiful. I had been in the presence of God Almighty Himself in an extraordinary way, and His presence was still with me.

I also realized an amazing truth that I could not grasp in its entirety at that time, and still cannot even to this day: God loves me so very much that He was willing to save me from myself. I took that drug of my own free will. I should have died that night. I should have lost everything I held dear, or even worse, I could have been destroyed mentally for life. Neither of these scenarios happened only because God loves me so much, and was willing to heal me and save me when I cried my heart out to Him.

The morning after God had healed me, I told everyone who would listen what happened the night before, how I overdosed on this PCP that was labeled as THC, and how God Himself had saved me. Even though I still did not understand what PCP was, I wanted all my comrades to know how bad this white powder drug was. I don't believe this drug was ever used again by any of my comrades after what I told them I experienced.

It was much later that I learned the street name for this drug was angel dust. I had heard about angel dust before, but I didn't understand what it was. In preparation for sharing this PCP overdose experience in this book, I did some research on this drug. I learned that during the time frame of when I overdosed on it, it was one of the most dangerous drugs to hit the streets. Even today, there are no known antidotes for PCP overdoses.

I also learned that it was common practice for those selling this drug to label it as THC, so that people would not know exactly what it was, or how addicting and dangerous it was. Other things I learned about PCP brings chills to me knowing that this was the drug I overdosed on so many years ago.

I think often of that night when God first manifested His presence to me and saved me, and I am always in awe of God and His love for doing so. That was only the beginning of a much deeper spiritual journey with such a precious and loving Lord God.

Two days after God saved me, I saw my deer while driving with some friends to Kelly Hill. Actually, all of us witnessed an incredible phenomenon of a multitude of deer standing on both sides of the road that spanned for about a good half-mile long. It was as if God had commanded every deer that lived on Fort Benning to converge at this very same time and place just so I could see them.

"As the deer pants for the water brooks, so my soul pants for You, O God" (Psalm 42:1).

Chapter 22
My New Life

It was in March when God had saved me. About this same time, someone offered Mom a five-year-old miniature poodle for a pet named Buttons. It took some insistence on my part for Mom to finally agree to take this dog. My dream was always to have a German Shepherd someday, and planned to get one after getting out of the Army. Mom knew of my dream, but I knew she needed some company before then.

I flew home for a short visit around this same time. I always kept in close contact with Mom my entire time in the Army, no matter what was going on with me. Mom and I were always so close, and time and the Lord Jesus only proved to draw us closer.

I shared with Mom about my new relationship with God during this visit. I was comforted to learn how God was drawing Mom closer to Himself at the same time He was drawing me closer to Himself. In reading back some of her letters recently, which are priceless to me now, I can see how she reached out to God in prayer for so much, and in asking God to keep me safe. I too was asking God to keep her safe for me as well.

I would like to say that I totally gave up all thoughts of getting high again after God saved me from that PCP overdose, but that was not the case. I continued to believe that marijuana, as a plant, was a gift from God, and that He was okay with me smoking it, providing it was the only thing I got high on. At that point in my walk with God, I could believe that I was the worldliest Christian that would ever live. I wanted both the things of the world and the things of God. However, God was never going to be satisfied with being in second place in my heart or life.

I still had that Good News Bible that Mrs. V had given me just before entering the Army, which came along with me. It was this Bible that I started reading right after God saved me. I was anxious to learn more about this God who manifested His presence to me, and who loved me so very much.

One day I was speaking to God, and as was my habit, referring to God as just "God." He then gently reminded me of what the Scriptures reveal as to all He really is as the Triune God: God the Father; God the Son, Jesus Christ; God the Holy Spirit.

What a revelation for someone who had always referred to God as only "God." I understand now that this was not out of the ordinary as to how the Holy Spirit teaches God's children. But having never experienced this before, this was very special to me.

There weren't too many Christians available for me to talk to and learn from at the time. Going to church had never occurred to me yet, as it was never something I had practiced doing, or witnessed anyone else doing while growing up. My spiritual walk had only consisted of loving and acknowledging God, and praying every night. However, God was propelling me into a deeper relationship with Him as my Heavenly Father, with Jesus Christ my Lord and Savior, and with the Holy Spirit indwelling my heart.

It wasn't long after I was saved that my comrades began calling me Sister Mickie. I still had just over twenty months of my enlisted term to complete, and so much was happening fast during this time. The powers that be of our support battalion decided to move the Delta females off Kelly Hill and over to Delta's compound with the rest of our company. One entire wooden barracks was cleared out for the females.

Our CO wanted me to room with Jackie, that female sergeant he was convinced would keep me straight. Thankfully for both of us, Jackie made such a fuss about this arrangement that he backed off on his decision. I knew better than to say anything, as he never listened to anything I had to say anyway. Afterward, Jackie picked her room that was for a single occupant while the rest of us also had our pick of rooms.

These old WWII barracks had only two floors. I chose the room on the second floor that directly looked over our HQ building. I figured this way, I could be aware of anything that might be going on that I needed alerted to, such as—marijuana sniffing dogs showing up unexpectedly.

Since we were just a few females, we were allowed the double occupant rooms to ourselves if we wanted. We were also permitted to paint our rooms any color, but had to buy the paint ourselves. For my room, I chose purple for the walls, bright orange and yellow alternating for the two window trims and baseboards. Some of my close-knit comrades commented that my color scheme would not look right. They didn't know what I had in mind.

I decorated the purple walls with posters and other hippie-type décor. I used my lockers as a hallway with a cardboard sliding door between the two. (This cardboard came with the new lockers that I put together.) I painted bubble letters in different colors on this sliding door that spelled out: "Welcome 2 the Stoned House." I also painted the inside of my room door orange and yellow with bubble letters spelling out peace, love and freedom.

I finished it off with a beaded curtain at the end of my locker hallway that anyone entering had to walk through. It was a lot of work, but after I was all done decorating my room, these same comrades admitted that I knew what I was doing with my color scheme. They all thought the room turned out really nice.

These old WWII barracks suited me just fine out in the boondocks, even without air conditioning. I never did like living on Kelly Hill. And since I put Pegasus out of commission because of the defect by the engine mount, it made it that much easier getting to formations on time.

Fort Benning had a self-service car center where enlisted personnel could take their own vehicles and work on them using equipment provided by the Army, such as car lifts, mechanical tools, and other much needed equipment. This self-service car center also had technicians available to help while we worked on our vehicles. I took full advantage of this great benefit when I decided to rebuild my engine. Many of my comrades were more than willing to help me with this major task.

But before my engine could be rebuilt, I needed to get another Mustang body to put it in, since the original body was defective beyond repair. Once I removed my 351 Windsor engine and manual transmission from the defective body, I tore the engine apart, and stashed the different parts scattered throughout Delta compound in the rooms of my accommodating comrades; the engine block was in my room. I don't remember my reasoning for stashing my engine parts like this. Maybe I thought it would be less conspicuous if it weren't all congested in one barracks room?

It wasn't long after the females moved to Delta compound that our CO decided to do an inspection of our barracks. With being so newly saved by the Lord, I tried my best to do things right and to be the perfect soldier, and I worked hard on this inspection.

My extra combat boots were all spiffed up, shining so much you could see your face in them. My uniforms were all pressed and buttoned up in my lockers. My dressers were all organized perfectly. The floor was shining clean. Even my engine block stashed in my room, having just been bored out with new pistons put in, was perfect sitting in one corner on a red blanket so it wouldn't damage the floor. I left the sliding cardboard door in between my lockers open so my CO wouldn't have to slide it open as he came in. Yepperreo, everything was just perfect for this inspection—I was ready for this one!

My CO arrived at my room accompanied by one of his sergeants. He walked through the little locker hallway and parted the hanging beads to get into my room. I stood at attention and acknowledged his entrance. He gave me his stern look with his "at ease" command. He then walked around my room taking his time to look at every poster hanging on the purple walls, what was on my dressers, at my engine block sitting in the corner, all without saying another word.

My CO checked out my lockers with my uniforms hanging all buttoned up perfectly, just the way they were supposed to be. He checked out the shining floor, my shining boots, my perfectly made-up bunk bed. Everything was put in its place. Everything was just perfect.

He walked around my room for a second time looking at everything on the walls and dressers, and then stopped to look at my engine block again. I stood there watching his every move as he inspected my room, but he never showed any expressions or made any comments.

He walked slowly around my room for a final time taking everything in, and then stopped again to stare at my engine block as it sat there minding its own business.

This captain then walked over to where I stood and facing me, gave me his stern look. I snapped back at attention and waited, and as our eyes made contact, I wondered: *Is there hope this captain has a heart somewhere inside of him?*

He stood there a few more seconds before asking me one question: "Mitikas, when are you going to get your engine out of everyone's room?"

The answer should have been obvious, but I respectfully humored him: "When I find another '69 fastback Mustang body to put it in, Sir."

He turned and left without saying another word to me.

Chapter 23

Adventurous Joy Ride

"What's your name?"

I didn't know this guy, but he seemed nice at this party I was at with some of my comrades: "They call me Mickie."

He wasn't too satisfied with my answer: "What do YOU call yourself?"

I smiled at him with sincerity and told him truthfully: "I don't have to; I'm always here."

His smile spoke volumes. We were getting high just smoking pot at this party and were using my surgical clamps that served as a novelty roach clip. (A roach clip is any device used to clip on and hold the very end of a pot joint so that those smoking it would be able to smoke the pot to the very last without getting burned.) He started to put the clamps down by the ashtray as I thought: *Those are mine!* As if he heard my thoughts, he turned and gave me the clamps. *Did he just hear my thoughts?*

I thought that was pretty neat, and then decided to ask God for the gift of ESP. Extrasensory Perception is definitely not a gift from God. As a matter of fact, with what I understand now, I will go out on a limb and claim ESP as a demonic gift, something psychics would have and use. After asking for this ESP gift, it was as if someone whacked me on my head as a way of showing me how wrong I was to ask for such a thing.

While at this party, I made another conditional promise to God that was just as wrong, if not more so, than asking for ESP. My quest for another '69 fastback Mustang body proved to be a very difficult task. As I was putting out a cigarette, I promised God that I would stop smoking cigarettes if He would help me find a

Mustang body. I was getting bronchitis with smoking cigarettes, so to stop smoking them was only for my best. But I wanted to use it as leverage to get what I wanted from God while also stopping what was detrimental to my health.

Entertaining any of these thoughts was not something that God was pleased with. I still had not yet learned that it is so wrong to make promises or deals with God. Looking back now, I can see Satan being involved in his subtle, conniving ways of trying to draw me away from God with these thoughts. But because I did entertain these thoughts and made this promise "deal" with God, I was accountable to God—and to be sure, He held me accountable.

However, with God being Sovereign and in control of my life, He was not about to be manipulated in any way by any of my "deals." God was not going to help me find a Mustang body unless and until He was ready for me to find one, period. This was something else I did not understand at that time. But I was going to learn all this the hard way, as I normally learn lessons in life. It wasn't long after my promise deal was made to God that I broke it.

Throughout my Army life, strong bonds of friendships were formed. With some of my comrades in Delta, these bonds grew stronger as time went on, even as my prayers for them grew stronger. I did date a couple of guys, but after my experience with being in God's presence, after His healing and saving me, for some reason my desire to date was dissipating.

Most of my comrades were like brothers and sisters. I also befriended the wives of my married comrades and treasured their relationships like sisters. But Carly was my dearest sister to me. Because of my relationship with these comrades, I was comfortable with them coming to my room to get high smoking pot. I refused to let go of my belief that marijuana was God's gift, even to the point that I wondered if there was going to be marijuana in Heaven too?

Soon after making my promise to God, two of my brothers came to my room one night to get high while we played Monopoly, a board game that Michael and I always loved to play.

Tie Rod, so nicknamed because he wrecked his car and broke the tie rods, was a quiet kind of guy who observed everything. Ham, so nicknamed as part of his last name, was more outgoing. While the three of us were just having a good old time, playing honestly, getting high as we played, one of them lit up a cigarette. Forgetting all about my promise to God, I bummed a cigarette and smoked one, and it took only one to seal my fate.

As the smoke from my cigarette flew out the window, so did my promise to God. And while this window was open, Satan flew in with his stronghold. Soon after I broke my promise, dangerous and mischievous thoughts also came rushing in.

I saw him first, and throughout this evening, I had my eye on him each time I looked out my window, and each time I longed to use him. All throughout this evening as we played Monopoly, smoked cigarettes, got high smoking pot, I was watching him from my window as he sat outside of HQ. He was all by his lonesome self, looking so cute, just sitting there, just waiting for someone to come and take him for a ride. *What harm can it be if we take him just for a short joy ride? No one else is using him right now anyway. I'm sure no one will miss him.*

When we finished playing our game of Monopoly, and still very high on pot, I shared my longings with my two brothers as I again looked out my window watching him: "Hey, guys, let's take the Jeep and go for a joy ride."

Nothing more needed said; my brothers jumped on my adventurous idea.

Army vehicles didn't have keys to start the engines, but used push buttons located somewhere within the cabin of the vehicles. This Jeep was parked right in front of HQ, and was secured with a chain and padlock with the key somewhere in HQ. The sergeant on duty in HQ was Boo Boo, so nicknamed as he reminded all of us of Yogi Bear's constant companion. Boo Boo was short and chubby, and a great guy who would do just about anything for you; except, I was sure, let you take the Jeep for a joy ride.

With the Jeep locked and Boo Boo on duty in HQ, we needed to devise a good plan on how to commandeer this Jeep, go on our adventurous joy ride, and then bring the Jeep back without anyone knowing it was gone. I became the appointed ringleader: "Okay, guys, so here's our plan!"

Then off we went with our assignments to execute our plan on commandeering this Jeep. But as soon as we left my room, I forgot most of our plan. By then it was late at night, having spent a good bit of time playing Monopoly and getting high before deciding to go on our adventurous joy ride. Tie Rod, with a cast on his forearm from when he wrecked his car, went into HQ first; I followed suit just a few minutes later.

After I walked into HQ, Tie Rod and I made eye contact, and then only his eyes glanced down at his hands and quickly back up at me. I followed the trail of his eyes and saw he was twiddling the key, showing me he already had it. I quickly but smoothly looked away. *Wow! How'd he get the key so fast?* This was my cue.

To distract Boo Boo from Tie Rod, I decided to ask him if he had any extra toilet paper I could have. Boo Boo looked around, and without finding any to give me—being the nice guy that he was—offered on his own to go and fetch some rolls from one of the male barracks. This was a surprise to me, but was working out so well in getting Boo Boo out of HQ.

As Boo Boo left HQ to go for the toilet paper, I made eye contact again with Tie Rod without saying a word—this was now his cue. I then went bebopping after Boo Boo to the male barracks.

Again, I wondered in amazement: *How can this be working out so well just on its own?*

Boo Boo walked about sixty feet, made a left around the corner of the male barracks, and went inside; the entry door was out of sight of HQ. I followed along and waited for him outside.

Each wooden barracks was laid out the same. Just inside to the right of the entry door was the latrine. In less than a minute, Boo Boo was back outside the barracks with two rolls of toilet paper in hand that he seemed happy to give me. As I took the toilet paper from Boo Boo, I gave him a very appreciative thank you before we turned to go our separate ways.

With HQ in our sights again, Boo Boo glanced over to where the Jeep used to be parked as I followed his gaze. *Uh-oh! He noticed the Jeep is gone!* And at the same time, so did I. *Great job, Tie Rod; that was swift!*

I ignored Boo Boo's bewildered expression and headed over to the female barracks across the path to drop off the toilet paper while Boo Boo headed back to HQ at a fast pace.

After dropping off the toilet paper in my barracks latrine, I wasted no time heading back past HQ to get to where the Jeep was now, around another building and safely in Tie Rod's care. But as I was walking past the HQ open window, I overheard Boo Boo talking on the phone. As I quietly stood outside the window listening to his conversation, I realized what Boo Boo was talking about and with whom. *Awww, Boo Boo! Did you really have to call the MPs about the missing Jeep? This is not good!*

There was no way now we were going to be able to bring the Jeep back as originally planned; we would get busted for stealing the Jeep for sure. *What a bummer! This was only supposed to be an adventurous joy ride with no harm intended. Oh well! So much for the rest of Plan A. We'll just have to move on to Plan B.*

Chapter 24
Military Police Raid

Actually, we didn't have a Plan B. With forgetting most of Plan A after leaving my room as it was, I was still marveling at how well everything played out so sequentially perfect, as I believed it was happening just by chance while commandeering the Jeep.

I knew it was pretty obvious to Boo Boo that Tie Rod and I were involved, even though we never spoke in HQ. Ham was watching as he hid behind a barracks just waiting for us to get the Jeep. You would have thought that with the MPs notified, we would have had second thoughts, a different course of action:

Like maybe—abort our adventurous joy ride, bring the Jeep back right then, beg for forgiveness and hope for mercy?

Nope, that wasn't happening!

We were too far into this to turn back now. Besides, our hearts were set on going for our joy ride with this Jeep. We weren't about to let one sergeant and a few MPs deter us from our adventurous joy ride. Whereas Tie Rod and Ham stood a better chance of finding some mercy, if for nothing else, for a first offense. As for me—with our CO still looking to get me thrown out of the Army as it was—I would be a goner, literally.

After overhearing Boo Boo speaking with the MPs, I hurried over behind the barracks to where Tie Rod had our Jeep; he was still behind the wheel. Ham came from his hiding place and jumped in the back. I jumped in the front with Tie Rod and then gave them the bad news: "Let's get out of here fast; Boo Boo just called the MPs on us!"

Without hesitation, Tie Rod went speeding off with the Jeep even with his arm in a cast while Ham and I held on for dear life. He drove opposite Kelly Hill and Main Post going only where he knew he was going.

Once we were safely out of the area, we took turns driving our Jeep for miles on the back roads and wooded areas of Fort Benning, into the stillness of this warm summer night, with a full moon up above and a little mist in the air. We joked and laughed and had a good old time without a care in the world, until finally deciding it was time to get back to our barracks for the night:

"Okay, guys, so now what do we do with this Jeep? We can't just drive it back now that the MPs were alerted."

I parked the Jeep a few miles away from Delta compound just off the road, embedded in the woods, but sticking out enough that eventually, someone would come along and find it. Ham took his shirt off and used it to do a very thorough wipe down of the entire Jeep making sure none of our fingerprints could be found. Tie Rod took his good arm and threw the chain, padlock and key far enough into the woods so no one could find them. Once we were satisfied with how we were leaving the Jeep, off we went on the long hike several miles back to Delta compound.

As we were heading back, we saw no one; not one person was out looking for us. Before reaching our compound, the three of us made an agreement that we were not going to tell anyone, not even anyone from our getting-high comrade group, that it was us who took the Jeep. At this point, we were taking no chances on getting caught. No one was looking for us; maybe we wouldn't even be considered suspects.

Upon finally reaching Delta compound, we walked right into a welcoming committee of two MPs just waiting for us to come back, as they knew eventually, we had to come back. So much for the hope of not even being considered suspects!

These MPs started interrogating us right where they met us. In a mean, firm tone one of them demanded, "So where's the Jeep?"

We all played innocent: "Jeep? What Jeep?"

These MPs didn't seem too happy with our innocent response: "The Jeep that you three stole and drove out of here! Where did you leave the Jeep?"

Claiming the Fifth Amendment—mum was the word.

They decided to haul the three of us into their station down on Main Post, a few miles from Delta compound. Tie Rod and Ham sat in the open back of the MP pickup truck while I sat in the cab between the two. They purposely had a conversation back-and-forth in front of me as we rode:

"Yep, we know exactly where this Jeep is. All we have to do is follow the tracks."

"We'll have this settled in half an hour."

"We'll get the ones who stole this Jeep, no problem."

"Yep, once we get the Jeep and dust for prints, we've got 'em."

I was sure they thought they were intimidating me, but they could not have been more wrong. I sat there listening to these two smart alecks and laughed to myself knowing it would take them a real long time to find the Jeep. I knew the tracks they saw, and knew they were not going to lead them to the Jeep.

I was also confident that Ham did such a thorough job wiping down the Jeep, there was no way anyone's fingerprints, let alone ours, were left to be found even if they did find it. But hey, I wasn't going to tell them any of this. I was also confident they would find this all out for themselves—eventually.

Once at the MP station and after getting our fingerprints taken, they tried interrogating us some more. But claiming the Fifth Amendment again—mum was still the word. We waited there for a good while until finally, without finding the Jeep, without any evidence to pin this one on us, they took us back to our barracks. So much for their boasting in getting this settled in half an hour!

A few days later, with the Jeep still missing, a group from Delta was lined up around the wall of a room in a building on our compound. I don't remember now what the reason was for this waiting in line, but I cannot forget the bantering going on about the Jeep.

Someone who was not part of our getting-high comrade group, upon seeing our CO walking in, decided to holler across the room in his hearing: "Hey, Joe, what'd you do with the Jeep? We know you stole it."

Joe replied, "I didn't steal the Jeep. You stole the Jeep!"

Someone else chirped in: "No, Larry stole the Jeep. Where'd you hide the Jeep, Larry?"

And back-and-forth the bantering went on over the stolen and lost Jeep purposely in the hearing of our CO. I was listening to all this, as was Tie Rod and Ham from where they stood in line. I glanced over to my two accomplices while trying not to show any emotions, but laughing inside at the same time, and hoping they wouldn't show any emotions either. We all saw how this bantering was making our CO furious. It would seem everyone knew about the stolen and lost Jeep without a clue where to find it.

After we left this room, Tie Rod, Ham and I got together and reiterated our agreement not to say a word to anyone that we were the ones who took the Jeep. And we believed not even our getting-high comrade group of friends suspected us.

As we spoke among ourselves now, I was again marveling to my brothers how everything played out so sequentially perfect just on its own, as though everything happened just by chance. Even to how Boo Boo went on his own out of HQ to fetch the toilet paper. Then they told me what I did not remember about our plan after we left my room: "You planned it all out just the way it happened."

My response was disbelief: "Really? I don't remember that."

They assured me I did: "Yep. Even down to knowing there wasn't gonna be any toilet paper in HQ when you asked Boo Boo for it."

Now I was amazed, "Is that right? Wow!"

Ham continued, "You even had it all planned out how you were going to get Boo Boo out of HQ to fetch the toilet paper, so Tie Rod could drive away with the Jeep."

I finally accepted my ringleader role albeit humbly: "Wow! That is scary! And all this time, I thought it just happened the way it did all by chance."

Now that some of those in Delta ruffled the feathers of our CO by bantering in front of him, he was out for vengeance; there was no doubt with what he did next. I could almost imagine his embarrassment and berating from his own superior officer: "What do you mean a Jeep came up missing from your company compound? And now you can't find it?"

In the meantime, I had no doubts our CO knew who the culprits were who commandeered the Jeep. He was going to find something to burn us on, one way or another.

The following day after the bantering our CO endured by his troops in that room, he brought in the drug-sniffing dogs. Somehow, we were all alerted that the dogs were coming through our barracks just before they came. I had a small amount of pot in a bag, enough for a few joints, that I needed to stash somewhere and quick, before going out to PT formation. I looked around my room wondering: *Where can I hide this pot so no one can find it?*

As I had very little time to really think this out, I stuffed the bag of pot in the toe part of my right combat boot, and then off I went to make formation, hoping beyond hope that my pot would not be discovered. As we all stood outside in formation wearing sneakers as part of our PT uniforms, the MPs and their drug-sniffing dogs went through our barracks.

I was told that the dogs alerted at my room door, but I had my doubts. But it didn't matter. They were going to search my room regardless of whether or not the dogs alerted, if for no other reason, my CO would see to that. When I was called in for the room search, I was met by three MPs and one drug-sniffing dog standing in front of my door, but there was no female MP present, and no one searched my person.

After we all walked into my room, I went on my own and sat on my bunk to watch these MPs search my room just knowing eventually, they were going to find my pot. With the presence of this drug-sniffing dog right in the room with them, how could they not find my pot?

One MP began fussing with the dog and gave him a ball to play with, and after only a few chomps, he took it away from him. *A ball! Is that all you give your dog as a reward? He deserves better than that.* I so much wanted to pet this beautiful German Shepherd, but knew now was not the time.

As I watched these MPs thoroughly search my room, my thoughts expressed my resignation as to the outcome: *This is it! My CO is finally gonna get his wish and throw me out of the Army! I am a goner for sure!*

I glanced over at the dog. *Why isn't this dog alerting them to the pot in my boot?*

My boots were within arm's length right next to where I was sitting on my bunk, with the drug-sniffing dog quietly lying there just a few feet away. *Wow! Can the odor in my boots be that strong that it can mask the smell of pot? Gee whiz, I do change my socks every day.*

As I continued watching these MPs search my room, another powerful thought came rushing to me. Spontaneously, I nonchalantly and very quietly reached over, grabbed my boots, slipped off my sneakers, and slipped into my boots while trying hard to ignore the scream of pain coming from my toes as they protested sharing their space with my bag of pot. I laced up my boots, and then quietly placed my sneakers where my boots had just a moment ago occupied.

I glanced over at the dog quietly lying there looking my way: *There, now find the pot, doggie! If you couldn't smell it with my boots just sitting there, there's no way you're gonna smell it now with my stinky feet inside of them.*

Out of all the MPs searching my room, no one noticed me swapping my sneakers for my boots; not even the dog alerted. I watched as they continued their thorough search for drugs, all the while my pot was in my boot that I was now wearing, with the drug-sniffing dog still quietly lying there just a few feet away.

Without finding any drugs or paraphernalia related to drug use, the MPs finally left my room. I so much wanted to pet the dog before they left, but knew I better leave well enough alone. After they left, I went for breakfast. When I came back, there they were again, just waiting for me.

It must have been my CO wanting just one more try at finding something he could burn me on, as they now had a female MP who patted me down when I came back. I was still wearing my boots, with my bag of pot in my right boot, as I dared not take it out while they were still in the area. But by then, my toes were numb. And the dog was still not alerting to the pot in my stinky boots.

I would have loved to have been a fly on the wall just so I could see my CO's reaction when they informed him that they didn't find anything in my room or on my person that he could burn me on. I knew of only one guy that something small was found in his room during this drug raid, and I don't think he lost any rank over it. My

CO would have used anything they found in my room or on me to throw me out of the Army—without a doubt.

This was the closest I ever came to getting busted with pot during my entire life, not just while I was in the Army. And forget about not being horseshoes or hand grenades. This was way too close for comfort.

And had I not overheard Boo Boo speaking with the MPs before driving off with the Jeep, we would have driven the Jeep back and right into the MP welcoming committee.

I was never aware as to the particulars, but eventually, the Jeep was found with no harm or damage done to it while it patiently waited for someone to find it. To my knowledge, only those who branded us as suspects in the disappearance of the Jeep believed the three of us were involved.

Even if they had tortured me while asking where the Jeep was, I couldn't have told them anyway. My sense of direction stunk back then, as did my feet, and neither one has improved much over the years.

Chapter 25
Field Training

I was halfway through my Army term when everything happened with the Jeep and drug raid. I could argue that as Army grease monkeys, we did have use of many Army vehicles with some liberties. But even so, obviously, the way we commandeered the Jeep even for only a short joy ride was wrong. I have made my beliefs about smoking pot at that time well known, so I won't excuse away that action.

I knew of no real reason back then why I got away with all that I did and managed to stay in the Army, even with my CO knowing everything I was involved with. The only reason I can think of looking back years later, is that God still had plans for me while in the Army that He was going to make sure came to fruition.

Although I narrowly escaped being caught in possession of the Jeep and with pot, I could not escape the presence of God in my life and my accountability to Him. None of what I did pleased God, but to be sure, my broken promise to God to stop smoking cigarettes claimed the biggest wrong.

I have learned over the many years with my walk with God, that I am accountable to Him to such extremes that I cannot even begin to explain. God's discipline rod in my life started out gradually and gently. As the years went on and I became closer to the Lord, His discipline increased in severity. I can recognize God's discipline during that time when I broke my promise only years later, but back then, I could not.

After I broke my promise to God, I very clearly remember things were going wrong left and right. God will never bless anyone who has broken a covenant with Him, regardless of what that covenant may be. I remember asking myself one day in frustration: *Why is everything going wrong?*

The answer came immediately and clearly: "Because you broke your promise you made to God."

Ooh, now I remember! I had forgotten all about my conditional promise I made to God that I would quit smoking cigarettes. It didn't matter now whether or not I got a Mustang body to put my engine in. What was important was that I repent, ask for His forgiveness, and start keeping my promise I made to this Almighty God, who I was now accountable to in ways I was just beginning to understand. With this remembrance of my broken promise to God, I quit smoking cigarettes right then, cold turkey, and for all time.

Not long after this, I ended up at a junkyard while hitchhiking around looking for a Mustang body. I walked in and asked the guy in charge if he had a '69 fastback Mustang body I could buy. He answered me with a question: "You mean the white one?"

"I don't care what color it is!"

We walked to another part of the junkyard, and there it was, just sitting there the whole time I was looking for one. God was not going to let me find this Mustang body until He was ready for me to find it.

Actually, it turned out to be a Mach 1, which was even better than just a fastback. It was a little rough in the body, and had some rust even for being in Georgia. But there was no defect near the engine mount as Pegasus had. It originally had an automatic transmission instead of a manual, but with a little modification here and there, my three-speed manual transmission would work just fine. I bought the body, had it towed to Delta compound, and parked it right next to Pegasus.

Now that I finally found my Mustang body, I gathered up my engine parts that were still scattered in several different rooms across Delta compound, and got started rebuilding my 351 Windsor engine. Many of my comrades were more than willing to help me out with putting Pegasus II back together, and their help was very much appreciated.

I made my maiden drive back home to Pennsylvania right afterward for a special leave that Mom and I both enjoyed. With transportation this time, we had opportunities to go places we couldn't go on my last leave when I flew home.

During and after my leave, some of my getting-high comrades moved out of my life. Some went overseas while others were at their ETS (end term service) date. One comrade went home prematurely due to a brain tumor. When we heard Richard had passed away, it brought grief to our hearts and hit us hard.

After my return from leave, our unit geared up for another field training trip. Our destination was Eglin Air Force Base, Florida. Our vehicles weren't shipped by rails for this training, as they were to Fort Drum. Our convoy of military vehicles was miles long, and took several hours for the two-hundred-plus mile trip.

Pops, so nicknamed because he was really old at the age of twenty-six, was my partner driving a Gama Goat during this convoy. But Pops would not let me take my turn driving. His reason was based solely on the fact that a psychic woman using tarot cards predicted he was going to be in a vehicle accident with a woman with long hair. He claimed this same psychic predicted Richard would go home before Christmas. Because Richard had no intention of going home before Christmas, Pops took this as a sign that this psychic's predictions had merit. I didn't agree but took no offense to Pops trusting his driving above mine.

During the drive, Pops fell asleep, and had I not awakened him just before he crashed in the vehicle ahead of us, sure enough, this psychic's prediction would have happened. We also witnessed a car roll over alongside of us while driving in this convoy. No doubt, Satan tried his best to get us in an accident, which would have proved to Pops that this psychic's tarot card predictions were to be taken seriously.

At this time in my life, I was still ignorant that psychics and clairvoyants were people who received their knowledge from demonic influences. Engaging in their services is dangerous demonic dabbling. We survived this field trip without any accidents, but only by the grace and protection of God.

Once we reached Eglin Air Force Base, Pops and I became roommates while our Gama Goat was our "home." By then, I was the only female left in our company, as all the others had left for one reason or another. Sleeping in a Gama Goat with Pops was the best solution. Pops was always trustworthy and respectful towards me. He had his side of the Gama Goat; I had my side.

During the time we spent in field training, when our Gama Goat was not being used it had to remain camouflaged. This required our teamwork, putting netting all around it and on top, using tree branches and anything else we could find for camouflaging its location. If we didn't have to move this Gama Goat, this would have been an ideal little hideaway.

But not only was our Gama Goat our home, it also served as our traveling mechanic shop. For any on site jobs that we needed to be at, we drove our Gama Goat out of camouflage to where our services were needed to repair any broken-down equipment. Once back at our parking area, we camouflaged it again.

Most of our jobs required repairing broken equipment during the night so that they would be ready for the next day training maneuvers. Each time we came back from a job, our home was filthy with the red clay dirt that collected inside while driving around the woods in Florida. With being disgusted with the filth, I took on the self-appointed responsibility of cleaning our home prior to us getting any sleep. Pops would have been perfectly fine sleeping in a Gama Goat covered in red clay dirt, but because he never complained about my preference in sleeping in a cleaner area, I could only assume he too was glad for my cleaning efforts.

Few people knew anything about our night jobs Pops and I went on. This was obvious one day when we were all in company formation, and someone was needed to do some menial work. In front of this entire formation, our CO shouted out to the sergeant in charge and singled me out for this menial job: "Pick Mitikas. She hasn't done anything since she's been here."

I was really ticked off over his berating in front of everyone, and his obvious ignorance to what Pops and I were doing during this field training.

Not long after this berating from my CO, someone gave me a black snake that he had captured. I didn't learn anything from the black snake biting me at the age of seventeen while scouring junkyards for parts for my wrecked Mustang. I gladly accepted this snake and handled him as though he had been a long-time pet. I thought he was cute, and by the time he was given to me, had calmed down enough to accept my handling.

While I still had this pet snake, I had lost my helmet on the job site the night before. Since we were playing war games in the field, I thought there was some leniency to the dress code for military attire of keeping any hair off the collar, but knew it was still mandatory to wear headgear while outdoors.

The next day, I went hiking to the job site to find my helmet. I had no headgear on while my long hair flowed down my back as this five-foot black snake wrapped around my neck. My plan was to find a safe spot away from everyone to let my pet snake go free.

I found my helmet soon after I reached the job site. But it took much longer to find a good area to free my snake. Once I was satisfied with a good spot, I gently released my snake and watched him slither away and disappear in the tall grass to freedom.

The following day was Sunday, and I decided to attend a field church service while not caring what denomination it was. I was still fuming over my CO's berating me in front of everyone, believing that everything I had ever done pertaining to doing my best on any job while in this Army meant nothing to this captain.

During this church service, an Army chaplain gave a very interesting sermon on Colossians 3:23-24: "Whatever you do, do your work heartily, as for the Lord rather than for men, knowing that from the Lord you will receive the reward of the inheritance. It is the Lord Christ whom you serve."

This chaplain emphasized that when we worked, we were working for Jesus and not for men. He emphasized that it really didn't matter if anyone saw our hard work. Jesus knew everything, and His opinion was what really mattered. This gave me a whole new perspective going forward in my working career. I had always tried working conscientiously regardless of any job I worked. But now I understood that with Jesus as my Lord, I had a more worthy reason to do so. I never forgot his sermon and how God Himself spoke to me through this chaplain in a powerful way, and just when He knew I needed to hear this.

Right after this church service, two officers who had been attending the service came up to me and humorously confessed, "We saw you yesterday walking around with no headgear on and your long hair flowing down your back. But we also saw that black snake wrapped around your neck. So we decided we better leave you alone."

Chapter 26
The Lord's Command

I was always willing and ready to go into combat if called to do so while I served in the Army, but I am thankful to the Lord this never happened. However, we had to be "Ever Ready Support" (our support battalion insignia logo) for combat circumstances, and these field training maneuvers were for such a purpose.

One day, I found myself being the chauffeur of a "butter-bar" second lieutenant during this field training, so nicknamed due to the one gold bar rank insignia, which is the lowest rank of a newly commissioned officer. This butter-bar was a nice guy, had a strong foreign accent, and was as green as they come to Army life.

While living on Kelly Hill, I ran into this officer one day in the main hallway. When he saw me, he got my attention to tell me that my guinea pig I had in my room was not permitted in the barracks. But he was at a loss as to what this animal was called.

As this officer tried to be so authoritative, he stuttered trying to find the right name to describe this animal, and with his hands cupped to the size of my guinea pig, twirled them around while his eyes went back and forth between his hands and me with his puzzled expression: "And that thing . . . that . . . that . . . that thing . . ."

I felt so sorry for him struggling to name my guinea pig that I just had to help him out. Being the nice soldier that I was, I suggested, "Rabbit?"

He smiled and responded excitedly just like a kid discovering for the first time a treasure: "Yeah, rabbit. You can't keep that rabbit in the barracks."

"Okay, Sir." I was respectful, but walked away shaking my head and laughing at the same time thinking about my rabbit who was missing his long ears and bushy tail.

Now that we were in the field, this same officer wanted me to take him for a long joy ride around our wooded areas on this base. This was fine with me; I didn't mind at all humoring this butter-bar. But when he asked to drive the Jeep for himself, now I had to be authoritative but respectful: "Sorry, Sir. You are not permitted to drive this Jeep; it's my responsibility."

He was disappointed, I could just tell by his downcast expression. *Now if you want to commandeer this Jeep without me knowing about it and go for a joy ride yourself, who am I to judge? Been there—done that—didn't get caught.* I would have loved to have seen his reaction had I said this to him, but I knew better than to let him in on my thoughts.

Out of all the vehicles I drove while in the Army, the Jeep was my absolute favorite. That evening, we were scheduled to go on blackout night maneuvers driving in a convoy in the wooded areas using only our blackout lights. My vehicle was supposed to be this same Jeep that I had been driving around during most of the day chaffering this officer. I was so much looking forward to this night maneuver, as I thought it would be a great opportunity to see some nocturnal wildlife.

Late at night, I drove this Jeep to the assembly point for this blackout convoy. In the creepy dark wooded area of our temporary base, I got my Jeep in line with all the other vehicles, anxiously waiting for the word to start out. All vehicles had their engines idling, headlights off, blackout lights on, the Army being consistent in their "hurry up and wait" motto.

Finally, after what seemed like forever, we were given the command to move out. I got all excited—*Yepperreo! Blackout maneuvers, here I go!*

I waited my turn to start out, and then after just a few feet worth of driving, my Jeep died. No one stopped to assist me. They all just drove right past as if I wasn't even there. *What a bummer! Maybe I should have put diesel in this thing after driving that butter-bar around all day long—but who would think—after all, I'm only an Army grease monkey.*

Needless to say, I missed my golden opportunity to drive in this blackout night maneuver. And such was life! I could think of worse things that could have happened during this field training, like getting bit by that six-foot rattler snake that slithered a few feet in front and across my path. Overall, it was an exciting trip. I learned a lot and was glad for the experience.

Soon after returning to Fort Benning from this field training, I had my wisdom teeth pulled and was put on a medical restriction order to stay in my barracks room the following day. I made sure to give HQ a copy of this medical order as soon as I returned from the dentist.

However, this medical order did not fit in with my CO's plans. After almost twenty months of this captain being my CO, he was moving out of my life and on to another unit. With God's help, I managed to stay in the Army regardless of all his efforts to get me thrown out.

Prior to my CO exiting our unit, per procedure and for his replacement, everything had to be inventoried in our company, including all our mechanical tools that Army grease monkeys used and were responsible for. My CO ignored my medical restriction order, and the next day when I was to stay in my barracks, he ordered me to the mechanic shop building to inventory my toolbox. It just couldn't wait for one more day.

Violating a medical order was a serious offense in the Army. So my CO's order to me was unlawful. I voiced my protest on the grounds of my medical order, but this captain never did care what

I had to say. I would have been within my rights to disobey him without consequence, but chose not to.

Instead, on one of the coldest days in December, after just having my wisdom teeth pulled, I went to the mechanic shop that had very little heat and obliged my CO by laying out my toolbox for this inventory. Afterward, I went back to HQ at the request of the first sergeant, who serves as the CO's right hand, because he wanted to see my copy of the medical order again.

After reading my medical order for a second time in front of me, he pointed to the date of December seventh and justified my CO's unlawful order by saying he thought my restriction was for seven days and not just one day, as if that made a difference. Maybe it did to him, but a medical order was a medical order. This first sergeant was new to our company with no knowledge of the conflicts that had transpired during all this time between this current captain and me.

My CO was just coming into HQ, and upon seeing me there, I guessed that he assumed I came back there on my own accord. He spoke to me in his berating tone I was all too familiar with: "Did it really kill you, Mitikas, to go and inventory your toolbox?"

I confronted him on his statement: "That's not the point, Sir. I was on a medical order to stay in my barracks."

As he turned and stormed away towards his office, I hollered back to him: "I LOVE YOU TOO, SIR!"

As Christians, we are supposed to love everyone. However, my reaction to his was just as wrong. I was furious over his disregard for my medical order and his berating attitude towards me once again. Now it was my turn to storm out!

Back in my barracks room, I looked out my window over to HQ, and then went storming around my room. *This is his last straw! He was totally wrong to violate a medical order! After all these months of dealing with this captain and his attempts to get me thrown out of the Army, now I finally have him! Now it's gonna be my turn to burn him!*

As I continued fuming within my heart against this captain that I have been in constant conflict with for so long, I decided to ask the Lord Jesus what I should do. I'm not sure why. My mind was already made up. I now had my chance to burn this captain, and I was going to do it. And besides, I really didn't expect the Lord to answer me.

But the Lord did answer me. It wasn't an audible voice I heard, but His command was undeniable: "Let it go."

It sure wasn't the answer I wanted to hear: "But You don't understand, Jesus. Look at everything this captain has done to me! After all these months of trying to get me thrown out of this Army, this is my chance to burn him. Finally, this is my chance to get even, to get vengeance. I am justified in wanting to burn him, as he was so wrong. After all this time and all I have been through because of him, I can't let it go. I don't want to let it go."

I vented on the Lord Jesus my pretense that I was always the innocent victim, while purposely ignoring any of my own wrong actions that surely also played a role in this turbulent relationship with my CO. The Lord didn't respond to my venting. He didn't have to; He knew the outcome.

I walked back to my window still fuming and stared out at HQ again knowing this captain was in there. I still had the strong desire to burn him, as I still believed I was justified in doing so. But I could not ignore the Lord's command.

As I stared out my window at HQ, I wondered about this God that I was just beginning to really learn about, knowing His love for me, knowing His protection and nurturing from the time I was in the womb. And as I wondered, the anger I had against this captain slowly dissipated. The Lord Jesus came to me as my Savior; now I must obey Him as my Lord.

I had been growing closer to God in some powerful ways these past nine months since He saved me from overdosing. I had been reading through that Good News Bible ever since. My prayer life had been morphing again. I could not have known the blessings God had in store for me through my submission to obey His command. But He knew I would obey, and He knew it was only because of my love for Him.

I made sure the first sergeant knew I was not pursuing this unlawful order and injustice because God had told me not to. I don't know if he passed this along to my CO or not, but it didn't matter to me. The Lord gave me a command that I needed to obey. This CO was leaving my life for good. Maybe with my new CO things would be better.

Things seem to circulate fast around an Army compound. Even without telling anyone, this situation too became well known throughout our company. I was waiting in line for mail soon after this when some guy in front of me, who I didn't know very well, turned around and told me what I already knew: "You could burn 'em, you know!"

His demeanor told me that was exactly what he thought I should do. I responded, "But I'm not."

I didn't say anything more to this guy, and I didn't speak to anyone else about the situation. I needed to let it go. I knew God had spoken to me in a very clear way as I had never experienced before, and I wanted and needed to be obedient to Him.

However, very soon after this, I was going to experience such a blessing from the Lord for this simple act of obedience to His firm command to "let it go."

Chapter 27

Little Dukey

Out of the three Christmases during the time I was in the Army, I was home only for the first one. Mom never wanted me to travel in the winter months, and I honored her wishes. Now on my first Christmas Eve as a born-again Christian, I thought it would be nice to attend a church service for this special occasion celebrating the birth of my Lord Jesus.

Pegasus II was out of commission again, but I don't remember now why. I had bummed a ride from a friend to Main Post to attend the Catholic Church for a Christmas Eve service; it was the only church on post I knew of. I had intended to hitchhike back to Delta compound after services believing some Christian would pick me up and take me back. With the legitimate excuse of no transportation, I was at peace with this decision even knowing it would be way after midnight when I would need this ride back.

After services, and all dressed up in my best pair of blue jeans, out went my thumb in front of the church. It wasn't long before some nice guy picked me up, and as soon as I got in his car, he started lecturing me on the dangers of hitchhiking.

I thought about explaining to him how I believed God would protect me on this journey back from worshipping Him, but decided against it. I was sure he wouldn't have understood anyway. After asking me where I was going, he offered to take me all the way back to Delta compound. But first, he wanted to settle his family back home, all of whom were in the car just ahead of us.

After reaching his home on post, I waited in his car with the engine idling for a long time while he tended to his family. Finally, this nice man returned for my promised ride back with a bag of homemade Christmas candy that he gave me with a smile. My mom had always warned me never to take candy from strangers, but neglected to warn me of the dangers of hitchhiking around. I thanked him for the candy and accepted his gift in good faith.

Unbeknown to either of us at that time, God had a special purpose planned as a result of this meeting. It turned out that this man was a first lieutenant in training for six months at Fort Benning. His wife, two children, and his aging mom all lived with him in the officers' housing complex on post.

His son was eight months old, and his daughter was three years old. This couple and his mom were born-again, Holy Spirit filled Christians of the Catholic faith. In this special family, I witnessed the love of God as they lived out their lives honoring their Lord Jesus.

I shared with Isaac and Rebekah my experience of overdosing with PCP and how God had saved me. I was also open about my practice of still getting high, and of my belief that marijuana as a plant was a gift from God. They accepted me just as I was, and invited me to attend their prayer meetings of Charismatic Catholic Christians that met every Friday night on Fort Benning.

Around this same time, I was with an Army friend from Delta just driving around off post and getting high. We stopped at a convenience store and gas station to fill up. As I waited in the car, I saw this cute little mutt hanging around the station looking so lost. He was about 50 pounds, had a long thin coat of black fur with white underneath, his legs were white and tan feathered.

When I saw him, I got out of the car and went over to pet this cute little mutt, and as I was going back to get into my friend's car, he tried to follow me. I went back and petted him again as I gently spoke: "No, you can't come with me. You have to stay here."

As I started walking away again, this little mutt stood there looking at me with his little floppy ears pinned down in a dejected expression to my words, as if he understood everything I just said to him. I got back into my friend's car and looked sympathetically at this mutt: *Even though he's just a mutt and not a German Shepherd, he still needs love and care.* When my friend came back, we started to drive off as I remarked, "I wonder whose dog he is?"

She turned around and drove to the front of the store and suggested, "Go in and ask them."

And so, I did: "Do you know who this dog belongs to?"

They elaborated on their answer: "No. He's been hanging around for about two weeks now."

I thanked them for their answer and got back in the car. I left the door wide open and looked at this mutt. He was still standing there with his dejected expression watching me with his sad big brown eyes. Then I spoke to him again: "Well, come on!"

Nothing more needed said to lure this mutt to me. With my uplifted invitation, he ran and jumped on my lap, and as he rested his little head against my chest looking up at me, I could almost hear and feel his sigh of relief: "I got a new mommy!"

And then reality struck me: *What on Earth am I going to do now with this mutt while living in a barracks on an Army post?* I hadn't prayed about this before inviting this mutt into my life. But as time went on, I saw this as God's blessing.

I always lived in the barracks during my three-year term in the Army. I had a better chance of keeping this mutt while living at Delta compound than living on Kelly Hill. If I wasn't allowed to keep a guinea pig in the barracks on Kelly Hill, for sure, I wasn't going to get away with keeping a mutt. But at Delta, in WWII wooden barracks, with our compound nestled in the woods and out in the boondocks, the atmosphere was completely different.

I once had a parakeet in my Barracks at Delta. Then there was Oreo, a black and white cat that was our mascot who roamed around our compound. Oreo showed up frequently asking to come into my room. And as always, my door and heart were open for animals. I only had ten months left before getting out of this Army and heading home. *Well, no matter. This mutt is mine now, no doubts. I'll figure out something to do with him.*

I named this mutt Little Dukey, and he and Oreo got along great. As every responsible dog owner should do, I took him to a vet soon after I got him. It turned out that he had heartworms and ear mites. The heartworms could have been the cause of his dismiss from his previous owner, as the cost to get rid of these parasites was expensive.

The heartworms took two treatments to get rid of. The ear mites were not as bad to treat. But Little Dukey always limped with his front paw that showed a scar. Only God knew what this little mutt went through before I got him. This mutt sure wasn't my long-awaited German Shepherd, and would probably delay me getting one. But he was my lovable mutt now till death do us part. However, it wasn't easy keeping him while I served out the rest of my Army term.

It was about four weeks after the arrival of our new CO that Little Dukey showed up on the scene. This new captain and I had a mutual respect, and he didn't say much about me keeping a mutt in the barracks at the beginning. I believed our good relationship was the blessing from God because of my obedience to His command not to pursue what my previous CO had done by violating my medical order. Had I pushed the issue, this new CO would have been entangled in the mess since he was part of the inventory request. But I can say for sure, my former CO never would have allowed me to keep a mutt in my room, or anywhere else on our Delta compound.

Chapter 28
Deeper Walk With God

I   It was early in January when I started attending the prayer meetings. The Lord Himself was propelling me into a deeper and closer walk with Him, and He was using this special group of born-again Christians He had brought into my life for that purpose.

Everyone who attended these prayer meetings were connected to the Army in some way. Sister Jane, the nun who led these prayer meetings, was connected to the Army through the Catholic Church. I also met Naomi and Joshua, another dear couple that came to visit Sister Jane, and who just happened to live in Pennsylvania miles from my hometown. God brought us together at this time for when I would be back home. God always proved faithful in orchestrating my life journey for His purpose.

During my very first prayer meeting, I witnessed a type of worship that was foreign to me. As I sat there quietly, I took it all in while observing these people with their eyes closed, hands raised worshipping God, praying in a way that was so different to what I knew prayer was, and praying out loud, no less. *I never prayed out loud in front of anyone. Do I have to do that too?*

As I observed this group of Christians worshipping God, the Holy Spirit moved upon me with such a peace, even though all this was foreign to me, and led me right into this worship.

Then I heard some of them speaking in what I thought at the time was gibberish. I knew nothing about what speaking in tongues meant, which is only one of the many gifts from the Holy Spirit. (Acts 2.) To top it all off, some man spoke out in the first person, as though it was from God Himself, which I later learned was the gift of prophecy.

I had no idea what was happening at this prayer meeting. I had no idea that God's Holy Spirit was the Orchestrator while leading His people in worship. But I was so open to everything, and once everything was explained to me, I never doubted the gifts of the Holy Spirit of God.

It wasn't long after I started attending these prayer meetings that I was eager for this new life living in the fullness of God's Holy Spirit. But at the same time, I struggled with letting go of getting high smoking pot.

During one meeting, I asked these dear friends to pray over me to receive the baptism of the Holy Spirit, which is receiving the fullness of God's Spirit. As they prayed—and some prayed in tongues—someone received a word of knowledge, another gift of the Holy Spirit, revealing that there was a hindrance within my heart that I needed to surrender to God before He would baptize me with His Holy Spirit.

My only thought was that I was still getting high smoking pot. I openly confessed this ongoing practice to these dear friends. But they were all in agreement that this practice was not the hindrance.

After more prayer and seeking the Lord, through another word of knowledge, it was believed the hindrance had to do with my dad. Some of them did not know my dad had died so early in my life. Growing up and in my young adult years, I always longed for a father to a powerful degree. When God allowed my dad to be removed from my life so early, in essence, it was God's way of making sure He was my only Father I would ever know. In my own heart, I needed to acknowledge and surrender to God as my only Father. Once I did while being prayed over, I immediately felt God's peace and the baptism of the Holy Spirit.

This experience with my Christian friends praying over me and sharing words of knowledge taught me two things. The most important was the role that God wanted in my life as my only Father. The second is also important for everyone to understand: God accepts us right where we are, but loves us so much that He will not keep us there.

It was soon after being baptized in the Holy Spirit that I started speaking in tongues, also known as a prayer language. But I wanted to know for sure that this was really from God's Spirit.

Reuben, a sergeant who attended these prayer meetings with his wife, Roseanne, suggested I ask the Lord to change my prayer language to Greek as a sign to know if it was really from His Holy Spirit—so I did.

Although Reuben knew I was Greek, he didn't know how far removed from the Greek language I was at that time, and that I would not have known if God had changed my prayer language to Greek, other than knowing that He did change my prayer language. It was years later before I understood that God did change my prayer language to Greek, and why He used Reuben to lead me to ask that He would.

It is appropriate that I interject some Scriptural truths at this time regarding God's Holy Spirit. I received a prayer language, a special gift from the Holy Spirit of speaking in tongues as described in Acts and other parts of the Holy Scriptures.

However, just because someone does not have the gift of tongues, does not in any way mean they do not have God's Holy Spirit in the fullness. God's Holy Spirit is the only one who decides which gift(s) He wants to give to each of His children.

There are other Scriptural truths regarding the Holy Spirit: Once someone accepts Jesus Christ as their personal Lord and Savior, the Holy Spirit indwells their hearts; being baptized in the Holy Spirit is receiving the fullness of the power of God's Holy

Spirit; the Holy Spirit—the Third Godhead Person—should never be referred to as an "it"; the Holy Spirit always glorifies the Lord Jesus Christ.

Prior to attending these prayer meetings, I had no knowledge of any of the gifts of the Holy Spirit, such as speaking in tongues, words of knowledge, discerning of spirits, prophecy, or any other gift given by the will of God's Holy Spirit. (1 Corinthians 12:4-11.)

After learning about these gifts, I had no knowledge of the debate going on as to whether or not these gifts were still being manifested among Christians today, or if they were long gone with the first Christians. All I understood at that time was that these gifts of the Holy Spirit were being manifested at these prayer meetings that God had strategically propelled me into.

By the time I understood about the debates regarding these Holy Spirit gifts, God had already established some of these gifts in my walk with Him, and had firmly rooted me into His word regarding these gifts for His children for today. It is extremely difficult, if not impossible, to convince anyone that something is not true once they have experienced it for themselves.

During this time, I was spending weekends with Isaac and Rebekah after prayer meetings on Friday nights, and returning to my barracks after Sunday church services. They had opened their home and hearts to both Little Dukey and me. They also had a little brown mutt named Heidi, and except for one jealous action of Little Dukey upon seeing for the first time another dog come to me, these two mutts got along well.

I also had the privilege of helping with the kids, and learning about family life as a born-again Christian. My dream while growing up was always to get married and have my own kids.

Isaac and Rebekah and their family were a special part of my life until June, when God moved them on to another season in their lives.

At the end of June, I attended my first Christian seminar in Atlanta, Georgia, where I learned so much more about my relationship with this powerful, loving and jealous God. It was confirmed at this seminar that when a child loses their father at a young age, it is God's way of ensuring that He is their only Father. As the Scriptures declare in Psalm 68:5: "A father of the fatherless and a judge for the widows, is God in His holy habitation."

During this seminar, God began convicting me of getting high, and showing me that this practice was now becoming a hindrance to growing closer to Him. And I wanted to grow closer to the Lord. I wanted more of His Holy Spirit and His gifts, and all that God wanted for me. Although I did not understand at that time God's call on my life, nor His demands and costs peculiar to His call, I knew I didn't want any hindrance in my relationship with Him.

And so, after getting high on marijuana for over four years of my life, with the belief that as a plant it was God's gift, I put that part of my life aside. But as with quitting cigarettes, after about four weeks of not getting high, I smoked a joint again. I never made any promises to God regarding not smoking pot, as by then I understood fully how wrong it is to make promises to this Almighty God.

However, the conviction from God's Holy Spirit after I smoked another joint was overwhelming, and I knew I had no other choice but to put this practice behind me once and for all.

Soon after I stopped smoking pot, the powers that be of our support battalion decided to move the females of Delta back to Kelly Hill. I was guessing the main reason for this move back was due to a few new females coming into Delta Company, with some of them being very pregnant. Kelly Hill was more populated, had the newer buildings with air conditioning, and was closer to Main Post and the hospital. I still had a few months left to go before getting out of the Army, and would have preferred staying at Delta compound with the rest of my comrades. But as usual, no one asked for my opinion on this move back.

So, after sixteen months of enjoying my purple, orange and yellow room to myself, in the peaceful atmosphere of a camp settlement surrounded by woods, and keeping Little Dukey with me, I was forced to leave to go back to Kelly Hill, and share a room with someone I never met before. A Christian family with two young boys, who lived off post, were willing to keep Little Dukey until I could take him home.

Soon after moving back to Kelly Hill, I attended my first Charismatic Christian retreat with some of my friends from the prayer group. This was different from the teaching seminar I had recently attended. The atmosphere during that weekend was out of this world, literally. I felt as though I was in Heaven praising God with His children while experiencing a movement of God's Spirit that was powerful. I felt such a tremendous love from and for God's children there. I also felt a powerful presence of the Lord, and His overwhelming love and peace. During a time when I was on my knees praying with Roseanne, I experienced for the first time a physical and very special anointing from God's Holy Spirit.

When I returned to Kelly Hill, it was such a spiritual letdown. Little Dukey was off post. My Delta comrades were at Delta compound. I was now back in an Army barracks surrounded by so many people I didn't know since I had just moved back there. I felt such oppression upon my return while realizing for the first time the spiritual warfare that was going on.

I hadn't learned yet about the authority that Christians have in the name of Jesus for victory over such spiritual warfare. There was a lot I still needed to learn, and was going to learn in the years to come. As a matter of fact, I truly believe Christians never stop learning and growing in the Lord in this world. This is not a bad thing, so long as we continue to learn and grow, and learn to follow the Holy Spirit's leading with complete obedience.

Ah, yes, obedience! That was something else I really needed to learn. My obedience to the Lord in not pursuing anything against my first CO for his blatant disregard of a medical order, was not in any way an indication that I had learned obedience, which will be proven in the years ahead.

Soon after this retreat, I was given my first prophecy from the Lord that He wanted me to speak to the prayer meeting group. But I was very timid in speaking up in front of people. I wasn't one hundred percent positive it was from the Lord, and even if I was, I wasn't sure I really wanted to give His prophecy. As I waited on the Lord for some time, Roseanne spoke up and asked, "Mickie, do you have a prophecy?"

And so, the Holy Spirit squealed on me! Now what do I do? Where do I go? How do I hide? How do I get out of this? Yepperreo, obedience was something I really needed to learn. I finally realized I needed to answer her: "Well, I think so."

You'd have to know Roseanne back then. She was special and attuned to the Lord: "Well then, Mickie, you better give it."

And so, I did. I had no other choice. God is God. When God commands, we must obey Him whether we want to or not, period. I would learn this lesson the hard way in the years that followed.

This was just the beginning of learning obedience, and learning what prophecy was all about, and learning about God's prophetic call on my life.

Chapter 29
End Term Service

We had a term in the Army whenever someone's ETS was coming up: It was one simple word—short. Another unique way to convey this term was putting your thumb and index fingers close together showing a small space between; this space got smaller as the time got shorter.

When people knew you were short, inevitably you were asked the same big question: "So, what are you going to do when you get out of the Army?"

My answer never wavered, "Whatever God wants me to do."

Those who knew me just smiled in response. Those who didn't know me often asked again: "But what do YOU want to do?"

My answer was the same: "Whatever God wants me to do."

Their bewildered expressions spoke volumes to their thoughts. By this time, most of my getting-high comrades that had been here when I first came to Fort Benning were gone. Those who were left and others who came later all understood I was out of the getting-high scene now and into another season of my life. And although I didn't get high anymore, I still associated with my comrades who did, even as I prayed for them, even as I still do so many years later as the Lord brings them to remembrance.

Just before my ETS, I was spending the weekend with Roseanne and Reuben. We had planned a love feast with our prayer meeting group that Saturday at their home. I was making a Greek lasagna dish and baking a cake; others brought whatever they wanted to share for this feast.

Roseanne and I had decided to pray together that Friday night, a practice I had come to love. During this prayer time, Roseanne was led by the Lord to ask that He show me in a vision some of my future serving Him—and He did. What I doubted was from God, He gave that part of the vision at a different angle to Roseanne for confirmation. Through this vision, the Lord gave me a glimpse of my future, and taught me what a vision was from His Holy Spirit.

Ever since God first manifested His presence to me and healed me from that overdose, something began changing with my relationship with Him. While growing up, I always had a dream of getting married someday, having two kids, boy first then a girl, and being the best wife and mom I could be. But after experiencing God's manifested presence, and now after His vision of my future, my dream wasn't important to me anymore.

The very next morning, I spent time alone with the Lord and expressed that whatever His will was for my marital status in my life journey, I would accept and was sure I would be happy with. I didn't ask God to show me His will or expected that He would, but He did, and in a very special way that I will never forget.

As I was being still in God's presence, He showed me a vision where I was dressed as a bride standing next to Jesus. Then Jesus gently slipped a wedding band on my finger that melted on. I didn't see the face or form of God the Father, but I knew He was before us on His throne.

I shared this vision with Roseanne that morning. As we celebrated our love feast as though it was the wedding reception, a gentle shower was falling outside, a sign of God's blessings.

While still at Roseanne's home, that same evening during my quiet time with the Lord, I asked Him to confirm the vision and His will to me. In less than four weeks I was leaving the Army with a new season of my life beginning. I really wanted to know now God's will without any doubts so that I could put this part of my life behind me, and just concentrate on my relationship and calling from this Almighty God.

Alone in God's presence, the Lord gave me a second vision as confirmation to His first to live a celibate life. I was again dressed as a bride standing next to Jesus. Each of us had a crown on our heads as we stood in front of God the Father. In this second vision, it was God the Father who gently slipped the wedding band on my finger that melted on, as though it could never come off. Then the two crowns on each of our heads were crisscrossed three times. In a Greek Orthodox wedding ceremony, the person who sponsors the bride and groom performs the crisscrossing of the two crowns.

Through these two visions—at the tender age of twenty-one—the Lord God confirmed His call on my life to be celibate. However, as I grew closer to the Lord, He made it clearer to me that it was a marriage covenant of devotion, commitment and obedience He had called me into with the One-Triune God: God the Father, God the Son, and God the Holy Spirit—the Third Godhead Person who had crisscrossed the crowns in the second vision.

Over a year prior to these visions, I had put in for a Germany tour but was denied. Now that my ETS was near, I was called before my new CO on a rare occasion. This captain had recognized and appreciated my conscientious Army grease monkey work, and we continued with mutual respect.

Standing before my CO now, he wanted me to stay in the Army; another contrast to my first CO trying his best to get me thrown out. This captain offered me a deal: I could extend my current Army term or re-enlist, and then go for a Germany tour. I respectfully declined his offer but thanked him anyway. I knew this was not something God wanted me to do. By God's grace and help, I was about to complete my enlistment commitment with the Army. I can look back now and count it a privilege and honor to have served my country and God in that way.

I also knew my mom needed me. God had taken care of her while completing His purpose for leading me into the Army. But with her health declining, I needed and wanted to be home for her. But before going home, I was going to experience a strong lesson from the Lord.

God had been convicting me to obey the traffic laws. Just prior to getting out of the Army, I was driving around post one day proud to have a copy of my ETS orders plastered on the driver's side back window, with great big ETS letters in black marker that allowed anyone to see what they were without reading the small print. This was common practice for "short" soldiers.

While driving around this day going faster than what I should have been going, I ran over a rabbit. I felt bad about the rabbit, but I didn't slow down as I should have. I kept speeding on this road while fiddling with my radio trying to tune in a good station.

And then I spotted them! But it was just a little bit too late!

This entire company formation of two-hundred-plus soldiers was running in PT double-time right on the road I was flying on. As soon as I saw them, I slammed on my brakes leaving behind a trail of skid marks as the tires screeched their warning alerting everyone to imminent danger.

As I plowed into this company formation, every single soldier scattered as they ran every which way, any which way, while not knowing which way to run—trying to get away from me. These soldiers reminded me of how ants react running around in a frenzy after something falls on their covered anthill.

As I sat in Pegasus II at a dead stop in the middle of what was just a moment ago an organized formation of soldiers doing their routine PT, I saw their leader come running over at top speed to where I was with such an angry expression on his face, that if looks could kill, I would have been dead meat instantly!

I couldn't know his rank while in his PT uniform, but it didn't matter—there was no doubt he was in charge. He didn't mince any words as he chewed me out royally: "What do you think you're doing? You could have killed someone!"

Innocently and honestly enough, I replied, "Sorry! I didn't see you guys!"

This really set him off on me as he yelled louder: "Are you serious? You couldn't see an entire company formation? What were you doing? What were you thinking?"

And then he spotted my ETS orders plastered on my window with that great big "ETS" written in black marker. He spoke again, his demeanor even angrier: "You are so lucky, lady! Are you so lucky! You could have killed someone!"

He would have been justified to formally address this unsafe traffic violation. Seeing my ETS orders may have been the only thing that saved me—and the Lord. I endured his angry demeanor until he was done chewing me out, and then he walked away in disgust to gather up his troops.

I drove away very slowly while still in the midst of everyone in this company formation. As I drove past these soldiers still scattered around, they stared me down—some with angry expressions, some with bewildered expressions. But it was obvious they all had the same thoughts: I was some maniac woman they needed to avoid at all costs.

After all the close calls of getting caught doing something stupid that could have been used to get me prematurely thrown out of this Army, now that I was ready to get out, had I even just bumped one person, my ETS would have meant nothing. They would have thrown me in the stockade and extended my service time, and it would not have been on a Germany tour.

It was only by the grace of God that no one was killed or even hit. Unfortunately, I didn't learn my lesson of obeying traffic laws after this incident. I never seem to learn lessons in life easy!

Chapter 30

Going Home

Finally, the time came for me to get out of the Army. With leaving the Army with the rank of specialist four (yep, I made it to that rank), an honorable discharge, Little Dukey in tow, and all my belongings that weren't shipped, I headed home.

I had real aching feelings in my heart leaving this Army life behind. I realized just how much it really meant to me, especially the people whom God had strategically placed in my life during these past three years. My nostalgic memories of my Army life and the special people I shared this life with, will never go away.

Once I was back home, my life drastically changed. I also realized soon enough: I really didn't know what God wanted me to do, even as time went on. It was during this time of starting a new season in my life, that the Lord gave me that special Scripture verse in several different ways as confirmation of His constant nurturing during my life. This Scripture verse continues to hold special meaning in my spiritual walk with Jesus: "I will instruct you and teach you in the way which you should go; I will counsel you with My eye upon you" (Psalm 32:8).

As so often people take Scripture verses and apply them on their own merits, there are times we also need to read just beyond a word the Lord has given us. Psalm 32:9 continues with a word of admonishment: "Do not be as the horse or as the mule which have no understanding, whose trappings include bit and bridle to hold them in check, otherwise they will not come near to you."

With this word from the Lord, I just tried my best to follow God's leading one step at a time. And He was more faithful than I could have ever known He would be, and certainly more faithful than I was to Him. Those visions I received just before leaving the Army were to be further into my future than I would realize at the time. As the years have come and gone, I have learned one very important truth about God—His timing is never my own.

Mom was still living in that dilapidated house we rented so many years earlier. Once I was back home, so many adjustments needed made, more so between Mom and me living together again than civilian life itself. After all, my poor Mom missed out on the growing process between entering the Army as a staunch pothead, and leaving the Army as a born-again, Holy Spirit filled Christian.

For a long time after I came home, Mom held on tightly to her belief that it was okay to believe, but it was not good to be "too-too much into it." But as the Lord was faithful and as time went on, Mom witnessed a lot of my growing pains during my walk with this Almighty God.

I arrived home in mid-November. This first Christmas was going to be special for Mom and me, and we were both looking forward to spending this time together. But there was one member of our family that I still missed so very much.

I never forgot about Michael, my brother who I had always loved so much and was so close with growing up. I hadn't been in contact with him since that last time I saw him just before going into the Army, when I left him holding a sign that he was heading south. But he knew when I was getting out. I had been praying for him for so long, and believed he was going to do one of his out-of-nowhere appearances this first Christmas. I knew of no reason why Michael could not show up again.

I debated with Mom about not wanting to go to a family friend's home for Christmas as we had done in years past, claiming instead that I wanted to stay home for when Michael came. I bought and signed a nice Christmas card for a brother, wrapped up a couple of gifts I bought, and then I waited, as Mom finally agreed to stay home this first Christmas. But Christmas came and went, and Michael never showed up.

I prayed, and waited, and hoped that Michael would show up at some time, but he never did. My long-lost brother was really gone. I never thought that my last time seeing Michael was going to really be my last time. Had I known, I wonder if things would have transpired differently?

My heartbreak over losing Michael returned full-blown now that I knew he wasn't coming home. I had no way of contacting him, no way of knowing if he was even alive. Many nights I cried my heart out over the loss of my only brother, and to the only One who did know what happened to him.

Finally, as my tears over Michael touched God, He responded to my heartbreak with a word that I will never forget. Gently God spoke, even as I tried to quiet my heart from my tears: "Worry not, My little one, for he is in My hands."

I shared this word from God with Mom. She believed this meant Michael was no longer alive. I had already lost a dad while I was so young, I didn't want to believe my only brother was also gone for good. And I would argue then, the Lord didn't tell me he was dead, only that he was in His hands.

But as the many years went by, and Michael never showed up, I was little by little accepting that he was never coming home. Had he been alive, Michael would have contacted me somehow, I was so sure of this. I was never to have any real closure on what happened to my only brother. But for sure, Michael continues to be in God's hands, as I have His word on this, and continues to be in my heart. Only by the grace of God do I have His peace concerning Michael. (Philippians 4:7.)

Soon after I got home, I started attending faithfully the Greek Orthodox Church Mom was a member of. I also got in touch with Naomi and Joshua, the couple I met while still in the Army who had visited Sister Jane. This couple led a prayer meeting group that met every Friday that I started attending. God used these prayer meetings for the foundation of learning how He speaks through and to His children by the leading and anointing of His Holy Spirit.

Even during my own quiet time alone with God, I was learning from His Holy Spirit as He continued to morph my prayer life. As I would fellowship with God, and being still in His presence, even as I would awaken in the middle of the night to pray, the Holy Spirit would speak to me through visions, through God's written Holy Scriptures, and directly to my heart. The Lord God was also showing me some of what was to come yet far into the future.

I was learning, not only about this Almighty God to whom I had been praying to since I was a little girl, but I was learning about His prophetic call on my life.

As the Lord God was teaching me to recognize His voice, He was teaching me the importance of obeying His voice. I was also going to learn in powerful and severe ways, the consequences of disobeying God's voice.

Chapter 31
God's Refining

My first employment after getting out of the Army was a grease pit job, literally. I started working in a steel mill that manufactured different types and sizes of bands of steel piping that threads were cut into. These threaded bands of steel were used to screw over or inside the ends of longer steel pipes, depending on if they were male or female threaded, and protected the threads on the pipes from damage during shipment. The different types of rotary machines that were used to cut the threads into these bands of steel were very dangerous to operate.

Each machine had two heads with several steel blades that were several inches long, each head operating separately while rotating at thousands of RPM. A constant flow of dirty, stinky oil was poured on the blade heads to help the blades cut into the steel bands without burning out. After a work shift of operating these machines, I was soaked to the skin with this oil while chips of metal found its way inside my clothes, socks and boots. It didn't matter how long or what I used when I showered or bathed, as soon as I would sweat, I would smell like this stinky oil.

There was one machine that splashed oil in my face every time the heads were lifted to remove and replace the steel bands. To protect my face from this splashed oil, I operated this machine with a piece of cloth hanging in front of the blade heads. This cloth protected my face from the splashed oil, but also limited my view from the operation of lifting and lowering the blade heads.

One night while operating this particular machine, I didn't see the rotating blade head lowering back down on its own as my hand was positioned to grab the steel band. I felt someone grab my hand and pull it out, leaving the steel band where it was just as the blade head brushed ever so lightly over the back of my hand. I realized afterward that someone in the spiritual realm saved my right hand from being severely injured. (Psalm 91:11.)

This job lasted only ten months working the afternoon shift, six days a week, and then I was laid off, as most of the steel industry was crumbling at that time.

But before being laid off, God spoke to my heart a direct word of His impending refining process: "I am about to test you. I will refine you as one who refines gold and silver. I will take away from you all the things that are not of Me."

It was during this time that Mom's health started to decline further due to her diabetes. Then her left toes developed gangrene from a simple sore. She spent several days in the hospital, and being unable to do anything more for her, she was sent home with all her left toes black and dead. We were told that eventually, her toes would just shrivel up and fall off. This was not something we were looking forward to witnessing!

People from my prayer group had been praying for Mom, as I had been. Only my prayers weren't just for a healing of her toes. I wanted Mom to have a closer relationship with God, to understand my walk with God, and to believe in the Holy Spirit and His gifts He wanted to bestow on those who have accepted Jesus as Lord. The Lord spoke to me as I prayed for Mom in this way on different occasions during the years we lived together. His words of instruction and encouragement were similar each time.

God told me that I was not to speak to Mom about her faith. He assured me that He was drawing her closer to Himself in special ways, and that His Holy Spirit was within her. Over the years that came and went long afterward, God confirmed the truth of His promises concerning Mom in some very special and powerful ways that I am so grateful for.

After Mom came home from the hospital with black dead toes, I had the honor of helping her each day soak her foot in a pail of warm water. I believe this was supposed to help the toes shrivel up and fall off. It was Easter morning when I discovered the miracle happening. As I dried her foot with a towel after just being soaked, I cried out to Mom in excitement: "Look, Ma, they're turning pink!"

Aside from a small part of her big toe that the doctor had picked off, all of Mom's black dead toes gradually, in God's time, came alive again. They became as pink as they were before the gangrene had set in. Through this miracle, God confirmed His word spoken to me regarding Mom. God was also confirming His word spoken to me regarding His refining process. This too would be gradual, in God's time, but undeniable.

For several years after I came home from the Army, I was on a roller coaster ride in my walk with the Lord God. I never went back to smoking pot or using drugs, and I was always faithful to God's marriage covenant. But I was still falling short of God's expectations He demanded of me that were peculiar to His prophetic call on my life.

The Lord had graciously waited until His anger was diminished before revealing for the first time that I had angered Him, and He made it clear that my disobedience to the nudging's of His Holy Spirit was the cause. After this revelation from God, I really wanted someone to talk to about what I had just experienced with His anger. I reached out to those I believed were spiritual leaders in my life at the time for counsel.

I made an appointment with the Greek Orthodox priest and discussed experiencing God's anger. But he gently brushed me off as though I didn't know what I was talking about. I spoke with the leaders of my prayer group about God's anger that I had just experienced, but they didn't believe God would ever get angry with me, or anyone else for that matter. When I spoke with Mom about it hoping she would understand, she too would not believe that I could ever do anything that would cause God to become angry with me.

All these people who I thought I could speak with and receive counsel about this part of my walk with God, just didn't seem to understand. They were seeing the outward sign of my walk with God: living a celibate life, praying faithfully, taking communion, going to church and the prayer meetings. However, none of these people knew anything about God's call and expectations on my life, or how I was falling short.

After all my failed attempts to find even one person I could talk to about God's anger towards me during that time, I realized there were going to be areas of my walk with this powerful, holy and just God that I would not be able to share; at least not at that time and in the way I wanted to. Although it will seem like I shared my entire walk with the Lord for all to read in this book, there are still so many aspects between me and the Lord that can never be shared with others.

It was about this time that the Lord started dealing with my idols. While I was laid off from my job in the second summer after getting out of the Army, I went with a friend to see the second Star Trek movie at the theater: The Wrath of Kuhn. I had always enjoyed science fiction TV programs and movies, such as Star Trek, Star Wars, and many others. I shared earlier how Mom called the TV guide my bible during my younger life. I had gotten away from TV and movie watching for the most part while in the Army; although I did go to the theaters a few times.

Once I was back home, I did just a little more TV watching and going to the theaters. But after I saw this second Star Trek movie, I got back into watching these shows as though I was trying to make up for lost time. TV programs and movies were once again becoming entertainment idols in my life. Only now, these idols were becoming a major hindrance in my relationship with God.

Per God's recent word concerning His refining, God was making it very clear that He was not going to tolerate anyone or anything coming before Him, in my heart or in my life, ever. Unfortunately, I was far from being submissive to the Lord God's dealings and refining process.

Before I go on with this part of my walk with God, I need to emphasize that how the Lord deals with me may or may not be the same as He deals with others. Although there are definitely some TV programs and movies that Christians have no business watching, this form of entertainment in itself is not a sin, at least not for the majority of those who indulge in such entertainment. But for some, be it because of what they watch, or their abuse of the many hours watching such entertainment, or because of their calling or command from God, such a practice can become sin in their lives, a hindrance to their walk with God, and may become their idols.

God began dealing with me gently and patiently concerning my entertainment idols. As I was being anything but obedient to His demands and submissive to His dealings, as the many years went on, God's dealings progressively became stronger.

The Lord's gentle admonishing words became sterner. His dealings of refinement became His discipline rod. His anger, when at one time was hidden from me until it was diminished, became stronger while in His presence after each time I disobeyed the nudges of God's Holy Spirit.

At the same time, the Lord God continued wooing me closer to Himself as He faithfully dealt with me while sharing His heart: It is because of His love and prophetic call on my life that He will deal so severely with me when I sin against Him.

I never shared any of this with anyone at that time, having learned well from my first attempt to share with others God's anger towards me for my disobedience to Him. But the Lord made sure He confirmed everything in some very undeniable ways.

After watching the Star Wars movie, Return of the Jedi, several times, God spoke to me: "If you only understood fully what really lies ahead of you, you would not be wasting so much time in vain activities, but you would be spending more time with Me, and learning from My Spirit."

Even Christian movies that were Scripturally true I was gently admonished not to watch. I had a VHS tape ready to record the Jesus movie based on the Gospel of Luke. But when it started ahead of its scheduled time, I got angry because of missing the beginning. The Lord then spoke to me: "I am the real Jesus. If you want to learn about Me, come and spend time with Me."

After watching this same Jesus movie again sometime later, while in the Lord's presence during my quiet time, I felt His anger as He spoke a direct forewarning that would follow me all through the rest of my life journey: "I will punish you severely for what you fail to do."

This word from the Lord covered everything: I can fail to obey, and I can fail to do what I know is right. Many Christians would doubt God would ever speak such a word of warning to any of His children. Too often, God's children deny His righteous discipline. But to be sure, the absolute proof that God has spoken is the fulfillment of His word in His timing. In the years that follow, God fulfilled His word many times over and in many different ways.

As my rebellious heart struggled with God's demands, Mom's health continued to decline, even as my responsibilities in taking care of her increased.

Chapter 32

God's Tenderness

After my grease pit job, I was employed at a glass factory in my hometown for just a few months. This place of employment was known for laying people off, calling them back, then laying them off again. This on and off employment was not satisfactory for making a living. Meanwhile, the dog kennel I had worked at before going into the Army wanted me back for a part-time position. This eventually turned into full-time.

But I struggled with these employment decisions. When at one time I believed I made a wrong decision, God encouraged me when I needed it the most, as He was fond of doing, even in the midst of His severe dealings.

During such a time, God gently spoke to me: "My child, I have anointed you with My Spirit. My presence will always go with you. I will never leave you. I will always stay by your side, holding your right hand, and saying unto you, fear not. I have all things under control in your life. Know that all things will work out for good. Trust Me, and see the salvation of the Lord your God. You will see My promises unfold before your eyes. Promises that I have made before you were born, to cause good to come to My people, and to do only what is best for them."

As I left a higher paying factory job in my hometown, and accepted a lower paying part-time dog kennel job several miles away, I witnessed some of God's promises unfold.

Little Dukey had become a true house dog once home with me, and he always got along well with Buttons, the poodle who died only a few years after Mom got her. My desire to have a German Shepherd dog was always strong, but as long as I had Little Dukey,

I believed it was best to wait before getting one. But with working at the dog kennel again that bred and showed these beautiful German Shepherd dogs, things were about to change.

Deanna, the dog kennel owner, was raised in England, spoke with a strong accent, and had a difficult disposition. Megan, Deanna's mom, lived with her and was a sweet elderly lady who lived through the bombing in England during World War II. I truly loved Megan, and we always got along beautifully. Megan confided in me that she believed Deanna's difficult disposition was the result of a window falling on her head when she was a little girl.

A few months after I came back to work for Deanna, she offered me a puppy from one of her litters. The plan was to train this dog for obedience competition at dog show trials according to the AKC (American Kennel Club) rules, and get his CD title (companion dog). Once this dog got his CD title, I was going to start dog training classes at the kennel. I accepted her offer with delight. Each pup would have a name beginning with the letter "O" in following Deanna's alphabetically sequence for naming litters. I chose the name Olympus for my puppy before he was born.

Just before this litter was born, Mom went back into the hospital with her right toes this time showing signs of gangrene. Mom and I were always very close, and she would often tell me that I was her whole life. I could not think of anyone else in this world that I loved more than my mom. We had our arguments, as people who live together sometimes have. But the love we shared was special and so very strong.

With Mom's health declining even more, I cried out often to God and sought Him with my whole heart regarding her, but He already knew everything. I expressed to the Lord that I did not know how I would ever survive losing my mom, as I also expressed that I knew she would not be around for when God's ministry in my life according to His call would really begin.

As severe as God was dealing with me over the years in regards to His demands, to a more extreme was His love and tenderness in comforting me regarding my mom and our relationship, and her physical and spiritual well-being.

At the beginning of this new trial with Mom's declining health, God spoke to me some very tender words, and as always, His words did not return to Him void. (Isaiah 55:11.)

After praying about losing my mom while not knowing how I would ever be able to endure that grief, God spoke to me: "I will not let you suffer in the loss of your mom."

As I cried my heart out when I saw the gangrene spread to all her right toes, God again spoke to me: "My child, I have received your prayer. Your tears have reached my throne. Do not fear, for I am with you."

God always proved faithful to His promise of His presence in my life. Although things didn't turn out the way I had wanted and prayed concerning Mom, God's presence means just that: He will be with us always, even in the midst of some very fiery trials. And God's presence ensures our endurance through such trials.

After the surgery that lasted over eight hours while trying to use some of Mom's veins from her abdomen area for her leg area, hoping to gain some blood flow that would save the foot, the doctor came to me and said that my mom was a very sick lady. Mom spent several days in ICU after this surgery.

Mom had a lot of trust in her doctors, something I was struggling with. When her surgeon stated her right foot needed amputated, I told him I wanted a second opinion, which Mom didn't think she needed.

When this surgeon agreed to have another surgeon examine Mom's foot for this second opinion, I struggled with this too. How could there be an unbiased second opinion when each of these surgeons knew each other? I settled for requesting the current surgeon to examine the foot prior to amputation, and Mom told me he did. I was praying and hoping for another miracle as God had healed her left foot two years earlier. But that miracle never happened.

After the amputation of her right foot below the knee, Mom spent several weeks in a nursing home until her stump could heal enough for the prosthesis. Without Mom being able to walk or transfer herself without a lot of help, I was unable to care for her alone at home. This nursing home stay was very difficult for both of us. But God kept His word; He was with us and allowed Mom's stump to heal, which was a blessing. Some people with diabetes end up losing more of their leg due to the stump not healing.

Afterward, Mom spent several weeks at a rehab facility learning how to use her prosthesis. It was much easier visiting Mom in this facility since I knew it wouldn't be long before she was home again.

During this trial, the litter that I was promised a puppy from was born. Late at night, I watched as the first female pup came into this world, and before midnight, I watched as my puppy was born. Olympus was the only male pup born on my dad's birthday. He had a white upside-down "V" mark on his chest, so I was always able to easily tell him apart from his four brothers. There were seven live pups born in this litter.

Working at the kennel where Olympus was born was special, and gave me an advantage in raising this German Shepherd that many dog owners never have with their dogs. It was so obvious with how everything was playing out with this pup that God was in this with His blessings.

When the litter was only four weeks old, a family with kids came to look at the pups with the prospect of buying one. With a board put across the gate so the pups couldn't get out while the gate was open, six puppies ran up to the board jumping in excitement to see this family with kids. Instead of following his littermates in their excitement, Olympus sat down behind them and growled at this family, even at the young age of only four weeks old. I thought: *Boy, am I going to have my hands full with this dog when he grows up.*

The man from this family spotted Olympus. While being oblivious to his temperament he just displayed that would not have made a good family dog, he made a comment as he pointed to him: "Look at that big guy; I want him!"

Olympus was the biggest pup in his litter, the only male born on my dad's birthday, and the only male I watched being born. I truly believed God chose him from before he was born to be mine. And he was already showing signs of a temperament that was going to need a lot of attention to get under control.

At the comment by this man who was a prospective buyer, my possessive thought was known only between me and God: *You're not getting him; He's my puppy dog!*

Chapter 33

Obedience

Just before Mom came home from the rehab facility after learning to walk with her prosthesis, I took one of her friends to visit her, along with Little Dukey and Olympus. During this visit, I put Olympus on Mom's lap as she sat in a wheelchair, and even at only nine weeks old, he was so big he barely fit. This was a comical sight as Mom held on to him as I took their picture. Little Dukey was fine with the new pup all day long on this trip.

For a long time, it was only Little Dukey and me, and my only dog that I never needed to put on a leash; this was before the leash laws were in effect. Little Dukey was so well trained and obedient that he never went off the sidewalks until I commanded him to heel at my side. He had always got along well with Buttons, but then she was there when we first came home from the Army.

But when Olympus came home with us, Little Dukey once again displayed his jealous temperament. First, he jumped over our yard fence, something he never did before. Then to my grief, Little Dukey attacked Olympus when he just smelled his stuffed teddy bear, which sent the pup whimpering and running away across the kitchen. I called Mom crying that this wasn't going to work out. Mom was always supportive of me bringing a German Shepherd pup home, even while we had Little Dukey. She consoled me by saying that I just needed to give them time.

When Mom finally came home after several months of being away, it proved to be another big adjustment for both of us, since she could not do what she was able to do before her foot was amputated. This was due to her need to use a walker and not being as mobile. Not only did I have a puppy that needed cared for, but I also became the only much-needed caregiver for Mom.

The most difficult part of training Olympus was dealing with his temperament. I spent a lot of time socializing Olympus with different people to get his temperament under control. In order to receive the CD title per the AKC rules, Olympus had to allow strangers in the role as judges to run their hands all over him without growling, attacking, or even moving.

There were many other exercises Olympus had to do well for a qualifying score at the AKC dog trials, some of which included working off leash. He needed to qualify at three different dog trials to get his CD title, which was needed before I could start dog training classes at the kennel.

Olympus started out so well in his training, but then started to break off leash. He knew what I was asking of him as he ran around me in the dog ring in his playful manner. It took twelve dog trials to qualify at just three. Mom tried her best to encourage me each time I came home from a non-qualifying trial. She meant well as she asked me once: "Didn't he even win a dog biscuit?"

I responded gently: "No, Ma. They don't win dog biscuits at these dog trials. They either get a qualifying score or not." But when Olympus did qualify, he got second place twice and third place once.

While I was diligently training this very protective German Shepherd that God had given me, taking care of Mom, working full time, and doing everything else that needed done just for us to live, God was training me. My busy schedule and more responsibilities did not diminish God's expectations in my life. When I grumbled to the Lord asking why He would allow such a busy lifestyle at that time in my life, His response put me in my place: "It is enough to know it is My will."

I then started recognizing a correlation between my training Olympus, and the Lord training me. I too understood what the Lord was asking of me, but I was falling short. The only difference was, I never knew when Olympus was going to break off leash in the dog ring, which was a real frustration for me. The Lord God, however, always knew when I was going to disobey Him.

During all this time, my roller coaster ride with this Almighty God continued. Scriptures are true in stating God's character: "The Lord is compassionate and gracious, slow to anger and abounding in lovingkindness" (Psalm 103:8).

God was patient as He began dealing with my disobedience to His demands to forsake my entertainment idols, to obey the traffic laws, to spend more time in His presence and learn from His Spirit, and to obey His voice. But as time went on, it was undeniable that God's tolerance of my disobedience to Him was coming to an end.

After being convicted on several more occasions about obeying the speed limits—a few speeding tickets later confirming this—here I was speeding on a highway again just outside my hometown, as I was running late for a dog training class.

As big as Olympus was, weighing in at 110 pounds, he would always just walk in Pegasus II, wrap the back half of his body behind the driver's seat as the front half of his body rested on the console between the two front seats. Although he never caught his tail in the door, he always knew to tuck it in. No one could easily see I had a huge German Shepherd in my small Mustang until they approached my car.

As I flew on this highway, I spotted some crazy man standing in the middle of the road flagging me down. *He's gonna get hit! Who is this nut in the middle of this highway?* As I flew past him, I noticed too late. *Uh-Oh! He's a Pa state trooper! This isn't good!*

I barely missed him, and then saw in my rearview mirror that he was heading fast for his car. As he came speeding after me, I had another thought: *Maybe I could get off the next exit and try to outrun him?* I chided myself for having such thoughts and wisely aborted my idea. Besides knowing this was definitely not something God would have been pleased with, I knew there was no way I would get away with a stunt like that. I decided it was best to slow down and pull over, and just as I did, this state trooper pulled in front of Pegasus II. He got out of his car with a mean demeanor and headed towards my car yelling, "Get out of the car!"

Upon seeing him and hearing his voice, Olympus reared his huge body and went into his attack mode. *This really is not good!*

This state trooper stopped dead in his tracks when he heard and saw Olympus, and yelled again: "And keep the dog in the car!"

I spoke to Olympus a familiar command: "You wait; I'll be back." This settled him down as I left him in my car.

This state trooper ordered me into the front seat of his car, and then started back to the first car he had pulled over and left to come after me. I voiced my concerns about leaving my car with my dog inside. I tried assuring him that he could trust me to wait until he was done with the first guy he pulled over. I never mentioned my initial thoughts of wanting to outrun him in a police chase. But he wasn't budging on changing his mind. Pegasus II with Olympus inside was left alone until he brought me back.

As this state trooper drove us back to the first car he pulled off, he respectfully chewed me out. Afterward, he was nice enough to let me go with only a severe warning.

I should have been past this kind of rebellion by now in my life. I finally got the message from God: Traffic laws are to be obeyed, just as the Lord God is to be obeyed.

Chapter 34
Undeniable Message

My dog kennel job was fascinating. Deanna loved to bring all kinds of animals home for her employees to take care of. Besides breeding German Shepherd dogs, the kennel also boarded dogs and cats, had two horses, a flock of sheep, a goat, and a Jersey dwarf bull named Adam, who grew much larger than what was expected, and eventually became dangerous.

With all these animals to care for, it was the sheep that fascinated me the most. God refers to His children as sheep, with Jesus being the Good Shepherd. It would be a great learning experience for Christian leaders to take care of sheep for a time.

Sheep are dumb, and they need help with everything for their lives: from trimming and cleaning their hoofs, to shearing their wool, to helping them have their lambs.

I watched Deanna one time soak her arm in a pail of hot water and smear soap all over it before sticking it way inside a ewe to pull out the lamb that was stuck inside. *Yuck! I'll never do that! That's disgusting, sticking your arm inside a ewe with all that yucky gook and blood.*

The day came when I was at the kennel alone when a ewe started having difficulty lambing (term used for birthing lambs). I waited as long as I could without jeopardizing the lamb's life while hoping and praying this little guy would pop out on his own. But when I realized the lamb was stuck and would not come out, guess what? There I was with a pail of hot water, soaping up my arm, and yuck, in it went to save this little lamb's life. When you gotta do something, you gotta do it, and God gives you the grace to do it. The lamb survived his forced entry into this world.

There were many times after a ewe had a difficult lambing that she would refuse afterward to care for her baby. At these times, these little orphan lambs had to be hand-fed with a bottle; now this I really enjoyed doing. These baby lambs would be out in the field, and with just one call from me, they would come running at full speed for their bottle while baaing all the way.

There was also the ram with an attitude who thought it was his right to buck me, even while I fed them. When he bucked me one time too many, I had it in for him. The next time I went into the corral, I was ready. As this ram bowed his head to buck me, I bowed my head, my fits in front, and before he knew what was happening, I rammed into him with a human buck. He changed his mind fast about bucking me. Humans do have dominion over these animals; we just have to take charge of that authority. Although I doubt I would ever do this with a wild animal.

I loved all these animals I cared for, treated them as though they were my own, and did my job conscientiously. I bet I was the best doggie-poopie-picker-upper there ever was—but really, it was the wrist motion that made the difference.

Deanna, though, with her disposition was a difficult person to deal with, especially as an employer. She had another business in Pittsburgh, and therefore was not at the kennel during the daylight workweek. But when I would hear her coming in while working the evening shift or weekends, I would always pray that God would bless the meeting and let it go well, as I never knew what kind of a mood she would be in.

It was soon after my full-time employment there that the kennel started to get rundown. The roof always leaked no matter how they tried to fix it, which caused the suspended tile to fall down and land on some of the boarding dogs. The oil furnace never seemed to work right. There was other much needed maintenance that was pushed aside. I often complained about some of the conditions these dogs were being boarded under. Then the time came when my paychecks started to bounce.

Deanna's last litter of pups while I was there was a disaster. About half the litter died under six months old due to a digestive disorder. The pups that survived had chronic diarrhea that no amount of doctoring could get under control.

I wanted to move on from the kennel, and tried my best to find better employment elsewhere. But God had spoken to me making it clear that I was not going to move on to another job until He determined it was time to move on.

During the time God began dealing with my entertainment idols and I was looking for better employment, I again grumbled to Him about my whole life circumstances, and about His dealings that I believed were too severe. Yet, God proved to be ever so faithful, even to His grumbling and disobedient daughter, and kept the communications open between us. God continued to speak to my heart through His Holy Spirit and His written word, as well as through many other means.

God's words spoken were at times stern; at times, so tender and encouraging as He shared His heart and call on my life. God was more than willing to deal with my angry, grumbling and disobedient heart, even as He continued His refining process of conforming me more to the image and likeness of His Son, Jesus, and all according to His purpose and call on my life.

When I complained to the Lord about the speeding tickets that caused me to be bypassed for employment at a post office, He spoke gently but sternly: "Do not reject My discipline, nor despise Me when I rebuke you. For what I do, I do because I love you."

When I didn't get employment at a major airline after a job interview, even after receiving a letter of recommendation by one of their pilots who boarded his dog at the kennel, the Lord spoke to me with His encouragement: "Come here, My precious little one, for I have not forsaken you, nor will I ever forsake you. For I love you and I am always with you. Know that I have all things under control in your life."

I also went for a job interview at an industrial chemical manufacturing plant near where I lived, which would have been the better of the jobs. After I was bypassed for this job also, the Lord specifically let me know that He was with me in that job situation. Just a few years later, the Lord confirmed His word when I was finally hired into this chemical plant, but it was only in His timing.

The Lord God had once told me that He had been speaking to me from my youth, yet not obeying His voice was my normal practice. When I became a born-again Christian and more familiar with God's voice, He demanded my obedience. As I grew closer to the Lord God, even as He dealt with me in all areas of my life, heart and attitude, I became so much more accountable to Him for everything in my life.

Now, decades later, I can see clearly over the years, not only the leading of God in my life, but also the progression of His dealings. What years ago was permissible by God in my life, as time went on and I grew closer to Him, progressively became less permissible, and eventually came to the point of zero tolerance by such a jealous, righteous and just God.

Over the years, seeds were planted that all grew in God's time with each time He spoke and dealt with me, and for the purpose of nurturing my walk with Him. I was twenty-nine years old when the Lord made some of His most profound forewarnings very clear to me in different ways.

About a week apart, I was given messages in two different dreams. Before the first dream, I believed watching a TV program or movie once a week would be okay with God. That night, I had a dream where I believed I could get high again on marijuana once a week, and it would be okay with God. During this dream, I heard the clear forewarning: "You will be punished severely by God."

The correlation between the two was clear: Indulging in entertainment idols was one and the same as if I would get high again, and God was not permitting either one in my life any longer.

In the second dream, I was putting my key in the ignition of my car when I clearly heard another forewarning: "God will spank you for it. Four years ago, it would not have mattered. But now, you will be spanked by God."

After this second dream, that morning while starting my car I heard the following message on the radio: "When people sinned in the Old Testament, they were punished without delay; corporal for the lesser sins, and by death for the greater sins."

As I continued my day at the laundromat washing clothes, I conversed with a woman on how well behaved her son was. She shared that she did spank him, but that she really loved him.

This same day, I was looking forward to watching a movie that I had reserved for rental on VHS tape that evening. However, God was sending His clear forewarnings through all these avenues that I was purposely disregarding, and He wasn't pleased with my attitude, to say the least. All this was happening around Easter.

Every Easter, Mom and I had a tradition of baking her famous Greek Easter cookies. When Mom couldn't bake anymore, I continued with our tradition and enjoyed it immensely.

The recipe took hours to complete. After the dough was made, a small amount was meticulously rolled and braided to form each cookie. Once the cookie sheet was full, each cookie was brushed with beaten eggs to give them a nice shine once baked. As soon as these cookies were done baking, they could be removed immediately from the cookie sheet, and the process of rolling another batch to fill the cookie sheet could be started.

On this same day, I was baking these Easter cookies. As I worked on these cookies rotating with three cookie sheets, I realized it was working like clockwork. With two cookie sheets baking in the oven, just when another one was filled with these meticulously braided cookies and ready to go in the oven, one cookie sheet was ready to come out. This clockwork left no breather time to wait between cookie sheets. But I also recognized that this clockwork never happened before, and never happened since, and I have been baking these cookies for years.

About nine cookie sheets later, with each needing baked for at least twenty-five minutes, the clockwork came to an abrupt halt. One cookie sheet full of cookies was not baking, and I could not explain why.

After putting these cookies back in for more baking time, I finally had breather time to just sit still and wait. And in this stillness, the Lord God spoke in His stern voice I was becoming all too familiar with: "My daughter, why do you provoke Me to anger?"

My heart sunk!

The Lord God never speaks in vain; His words never return to Him void; His words are never to be taken lightly. And it is never good to anger such a powerful and just God. All the different ways God was speaking His messages, all came together as one!

I understood then very well that God had orchestrated this entire clockwork process in baking these cookies, and then put an abrupt halt to it for one reason: He wanted to make sure I could not deny His stern message. I rented the movie only out of obligation for reserving it for that night, but I dared not watch it.

In the many years to follow, as I grew closer to the Lord God, though my disobedience to Him became less, the severity of His dealings intensified with each time I did disobey Him. Yet, at the same time, His intimacy and love also intensified, and in some extraordinary ways that cannot be shared.

Chapter 35
My Mom

Less than three months from God's stern message, Mom went back into the hospital. Six months before this hospital stay, she went to her doctor to have a fatty tumor examined. During that visit, her doctor assured us that there was nothing to be concerned about regarding this fatty tumor. It was right after this doctor's visit that God spoke tenderly to me again regarding my mom, as I was still very concerned about this tumor: "Do not be worried or concerned about your mom, My daughter, for all will go well with her."

I had God's promise on this. God cared so much about my mom, and about my love for her and my desire that she would grow closer to Him. So often, God would allow me to see how He was drawing her closer to Himself in special ways, as confirmation of His word.

Mom had a hard time in the beginning when I first came home from the Army with my walk with the Lord, and with my quiet time I would spend with Him. I would be upstairs praying for a while, and then, out of her impatience, she would holler up: "Angelika, are you almost done yet?"

The answer was often the same: "No, not yet."

Then one day when I came down, I gently told Mom that whenever she would call up while I was praying, it would interrupt my time with God. Afterward, when I would pray and then come down, Mom would tell me: "See, I was good; I didn't bother you."

My mom was so special. One time after coming down from praying, Mom told me in jest, but she was being truthful: "God sure didn't give you a good singing voice."

I responded in jest, but also knew she was right: "Gee, thanks, Ma! Every kid wants to hear that from their mom."

I was unaware that Mom was able to hear me singing to God, and I was sure to be more careful afterward. A joyful noise to the Lord is not always well received by others who hear it.

As time went on, I was seeing how Mom was growing closer to God. We started having deeper conversations about God, even as she started to accept my walk with Him. Such was the time when I asked her: "Who do you love more, me or God?"

I was thrilled when Mom answered: "God."

Mom always told me I was her whole life. Knowing now that she loved God more than me, this was an answer to prayer.

A few times Mom caught me off guard by her questions: "Did God tell you anything about me?"

Where did that come from?

I realized not only were our conversations deepening, but Mom's understanding of God's call on my life was also growing. I was caught off guard myself by what I asked her one day, as I had no plan of asking her such a question: "Do you know why God called me?"

Her truthful answer surprised me, which only confirmed that she had heard from God Himself. I never felt led by God's Spirit to share with Mom, or anyone else at that time, God's prophetic call on my life. Yes, indeed, the Lord God was keeping His word He spoke to me concerning my mom: He was drawing her closer to Himself in special ways. If I had only one person in the whole world to choose who would understand God's call on my life, that person would be my mom. But I didn't have to choose; God chose for me. I just smiled at Mom when she answered me.

Mom and I were always very close, and I never doubted her love for me, ever. She was humble, and always appreciated anything I would do for her. At one point, she was so concerned that she was holding me back from getting married, believing it was because I was taking care of her that I remained single. I reminded Mom of God's call on my life to be celibate, and assured her that taking care of her was exactly what He wanted me to do. I tried my best to make sure Mom knew that she was not at all holding me back from anything.

Now she was in the hospital again because of that fatty tumor that became infected, the same tumor that only six months ago her doctor assured us was not something we needed to worry about. God didn't have to tell me; I knew this was my mom's last hospital stay. I was just so sure she was not coming home this time.

Because of this belief, I was visibly anxious each time I visited her. Until one day, God again spoke tenderly to me regarding my mom: "You will receive your mom back, My daughter, for I will heal her. Do not fear, for I am with you. Believe that I have spoken."

With God's assurance that He was going to heal my mom and I would receive her back, I was able to put aside my belief that she was going to die during this hospital stay. This allowed us some really great quality time with each other as I visited her.

While in the hospital, a team of three surgeons attended Mom, the same team who amputated her right foot four years earlier. When she first went into the hospital this time, one surgeon was on vacation; one surgeon had just broken his leg; the third surgeon was carrying the weight of responsibility for all three on his own. I am sure that this third surgeon was exhausted trying to take care of all the scheduled surgeries, along with any emergency surgeries that came up, including my mom's.

Mom was a bit out of it when she first went into the hospital due to the infection and fever. I visited her every day, but she and no one else thought to notify me until the very last minute for the first two emergency surgeries she had regarding the infected fatty tumor. I had more notice with the third surgery. After three surgeries in less than two weeks, Mom was unable to walk again, and no one could give me a reason as to why.

I was the only family member that Mom had. Deanna wasn't too happy with my extra responsibilities during this time, and would get annoyed each time I had to take off work to be there for Mom. This hospital stay was a few months long.

One day at work, Deanna phoned me from her office insistent that I use someone else's special dog food they had left at the kennel to feed one of her own dogs with the chronic diarrhea. This dog food was specially formulated for digestive problems, but was very expensive and only obtained through veterinarians, and it did not belong to Deanna.

In addition, I had just spoken to the client who had left this special dog food at the kennel, and booked another boarding stay for their dog in the next day or two. During our conversation, I assured this client that their special dog food they had left at the kennel would be available for their dog on this next boarding visit.

I explained all this to Deanna on the phone, but she insisted that I feed this special dog food to her dogs with no assurance that she was going to replace it for this client. I ended up quitting my job that day, but it was not the way I had wanted to leave. There was another person working, so I didn't have to worry about the care of the animals.

Mom saw an immediate sense of peace in me after leaving the kennel without that stress in my life, and commented on it. I had thought she would be upset, but instead, she seemed so at peace herself with my decision. Mom was so encouraging as I visited her without a job, even while she was laid up in the hospital. By then, Mom trusted more in God than I could have known at that time.

I had always believed after God spoke that He would heal my mom, October was going to be her homecoming; I'm not sure why.

We had planned to drive around enjoying the beautiful colors on the trees the fall seasons of Pennsylvania are known for.

It was a beautiful Saturday while visiting Mom when she related to me about the looming skin graft surgery needed to close her wound. It had been left open all this time to heal—and it was healing very well. I tried my best to encourage her as she was very despondent over this looming surgery. I emphasized that this skin graft would help her heal faster and she would be home soon.

During this visit, Mom asked me to organize her clothes in the drawers in her room. Her smile and delight after doing so warmed my heart. She asked that I cut her nails that were getting too long for her preference. I went to the cafeteria and brought her back some vanilla ice cream, which people with diabetes can have.

We had a nice visit with some great conversations between us that Saturday. I was so much longing for Mom to come home so I could take care of her once again. I wasn't sure how I would do this without her being able to walk yet, but something would work out, I was sure it would. Only one more surgery loomed, which would help her heal faster. I truly believed the end of Mom's hospital stay was soon.

I left this beautiful visit with Mom in such high spirits, as I believed God was keeping His word: He was healing her, and I was going to receive her back. I spoke to Mom again by phone just before retiring for the night, at which time she told me she wasn't feeling well. She seemed fine when I left her. We ended this conversation expressing our love for each other, as we always did.

Chapter 36
Mom's Homecoming

Just past seven o'clock the next morning, Sunday, the phone rang and woke me up. I was up earlier and should have stayed up for prayer, but as was my recent habit, I went back to sleep. A nurse from the hospital unit where Mom was staying at was calling. I barely registered what she was telling me: "Your mom stopped breathing, and her heart stopped. Can you come to the hospital? And bring a friend, don't come alone."

I hung up the phone and sat there numb. *Did she just tell me my mom died in a roundabout way? NO! My mom is not supposed to die! God promised me He was going to heal her, that I was going to receive her back!* I went into instant denial to what this nurse had just told me.

Jonathon and Molly lived just around the corner from where Mom and I lived. They were very close old-time friends of Mom's, with their friendship going back even before Mom had moved to New York in her twenties. I phoned Molly and told her what the nurse had said, and asked if she could meet me at the hospital. I made another phone call to Naomi, my dear friend from my prayer meeting group, and told her what the nurse had said and asked to be put on the prayer chain. I left right afterward without waiting for anyone to come with me.

In the twenty-minute or so ride to the hospital, my thoughts raced in prayer to the only One who knew my whole heart: *"Father, she cannot be dead! You told me You would heal her! Jesus, I know Your voice! You spoke to my heart! You promised me I would receive her back!"*

Finally at the hospital and walking at a fast pace to reach my mom's room, I vaguely heard someone call out my name as I passed the nurses' station. I refused to stop for anyone while my thoughts continued in prayer to God and claiming His promises.

After walking into the private room that Mom had stayed in for several weeks, I found her on her back with a tube sticking out of her mouth. *Ma never liked lying on her back!* Several medical technicians were there wrapping up their equipment, sober and ignoring my mom. After a quick glance at Mom and around the room at all these people, I had only one thought: *These people need to get out of this room! NOW!*

What I thought was a polite request for everyone to exit the room, apparently was more of a firm demand. I could not have known what my demeanor was at the time. I'm sure God's angelic beings were helping by gently pushing these people out, knowing that this time was to be special, that I needed to be alone with my mom, and alone with God.

Without a word of protest from anyone, everyone dropped what they were doing without hesitation and exited the room upon my demand to do so. I followed behind making sure to close the door behind them.

Now alone with my mom, I touched her still warm arm and started talking to God once again, as I had been the whole time driving to the hospital: "Abba, please! She was not supposed to die. You gave me Your word. You said You would heal her. You promised I would receive her back. She is all I have. I have no one else. You can bring her back. Please raise her up again. How can I ever believe anything You will ever speak to me again?"

This was not supposed to happen! How could this happen? Why did this happen? I wanted my mom back, but she was not coming back. I wanted answers, but could not still my heart to listen. The Lord God was silent, engulfing me in His arms, letting His peace rush over me, knowing I would understand soon enough.

At the very same moment I was grieving the loss of my mom and pleaded for her return, the Lord Jesus was embracing her in His arms, even as she was experiencing a blissful peace she had never experienced before. Being in the Lord's presence and in His Paradise of Heaven for the very first time, if given the choice, my mom would not have wanted to come back. My mom was with the One she loved the most in this world, the same precious Lord God who had been drawing her closer to Himself.

My mom suffered so much during her life in this world. For the last several years of her life after her foot was amputated, she was a shut-in, going out of the house only a handful of times because she was so afraid of falling outside. Being in God's presence, in God's Paradise of Heaven, my mom will never again suffer. She will never again fear for her future or mine. Finally, my mom had no more questions about God and about why things happened in her life.

My mom had shared with me often that when it was her time to go, she wanted to die in her sleep—and so it happened. I rejoice greatly in how much God loved my mom in His special way.

I lost all track of time in the room alone with my mom and in God's presence. I would have continued being there alone had it not been for Molly coming in, and right behind her came the medical technicians who had exited the room following my demand to do so. They had been waiting just outside the door for this opportunity to come back in and retrieve their medical equipment. And just moments later, my friends from my prayer meeting group showed up. Unbeknown to me, they had decided to come. Isn't it beautiful how God surrounds us with His people when He knows we need them the most?

Mom's Homecoming/36

I managed to make the arrangements for the wake and funeral. I asked the Greek Orthodox priest to affiliate the service. I felt led by the Lord to leave the Greek Orthodox Church some years earlier after faithfully attending for my first few years out of the Army. Mom, though, was still a member of this church.

A married couple who I had never met before, showed up at my mom's wake. Matilda and Joseph had a ministry visiting people in hospitals and nursing facilities before becoming missionaries in South Africa. Matilda shared with me that she had spoken with my mom just a week before the Lord took her, and during that time she accepted Jesus into her heart to be her personal Lord and Savior. I didn't have the opportunity to question them further during my mom's wake.

As I saw my mom in the coffin, I realized something was different about her that was so unlike others I had seen in coffins in the past, and now with several years later, even afterward. My mom was so beautiful, so natural, so peaceful, like she was just sleeping and not at all dead. This was a unique blessing and comfort from God.

Although God was showing me in some very powerful ways that He was still with me, this entire ordeal of losing my mom so unexpectedly was very difficult to deal with. I still believed I heard from God that He was going to heal her, and that I would indeed receive her back, which gave me the peace to visit her without the constant anxiety of believing she was going to die during that hospital stay. *Why did God speak to me as He did? Or did I hear Him wrong? How can I ever again believe anything God would speak to me in the future?*

In less than two weeks' time, I found myself without a job and without my mom. *What else will God allow to happen in my life?* I was not yet at the point in my walk with God to trust and believe, regardless of what He allows to happen in my life, He knows best and is still very much in control. But I couldn't find this trust back then. It was soon after my mom's passing that I no longer wondered what God was going to allow to happen in my life next; I lived in fear of what He was going to allow to happen.

However, in God's tenderness and compassion in dealing with my relationship with my mom, as always, He did keep His word. I would understand all this more as time went by. The Lord knew I needed some time without the stress of employment to help heal during this grieving process. He knows everything, even the deepest hurts and fears of my heart. And I did need healing, not only in my grief over losing my mom, but also in my relationship with such an Almighty God.

My mom had always told me, if anything happened to her, I should know that I was the best daughter anyone could ever have. Again, my mom was so special. But for several weeks of being despondent over my mom's passing, I was also fretting that I should have done things differently during our time together, especially regarding our last visit. Of course, I didn't know it was going to be the last time I would see my mom alive—but God knew.

After a few weeks of being despondent and fretting, God gave me a dream about my mom. In the dream, God made it clear that there was nothing that I should have done differently, even on my last visit with my mom. God also showed me in this same dream that He was holding me so close to Him, there was no way I was going to move to the right or to the left apart from Him.

On my mom's birthday, one month and two days after she went to be with the Lord Jesus, my Aunt Katrina phoned to check up on me, as she is fond of doing. After our conversation, for some reason, I sat down and wrote a poem about my mom. I had never written a poem prior to this one, and so far, never since.

As I started writing out this poem, the words flowed from God's Spirit to my heart as I wrote them verbatim—none of this poem came from me. The poem represents God's truth in my life:

The Lord's Consolation

I cried out in my grief and pain;
and in my anger, I did complain.
"Why did You take her?" to the Lord I cried.
"You said You would heal her, why did You lie?
Within my own heart, Your voice I heard.
Why is she gone, when You gave me Your word?
I loved her and took care of her, she was my own.
Together we had talked and laughed, now I'm all alone.
Your love and Your faith, we had always shared.
I believed that You were with us, I trusted that You cared."
The Lord then responded to my sad complaint.
He came into my heart and acknowledged my pain.
"I care for you more than you will ever know;
for I have called you by name, you are My very own.
My voice you had heard and My word you did receive;
but your understanding was clouded in your heart of grief.
I did heal your mom, in more ways than one;
for now she is made whole and is one in My Son.
Her pain is gone, her suffering has ceased;
she lives now in Paradise, enjoying My peace.
Her road had ended, her purpose on Earth fulfilled;
she gave you life and love, so that you might do My will.
Her greatest desire for your life now,
is to fulfill your purpose, and to Me avow.
Your road ahead will be hard and long;
but trust in My Spirit, and you will be strong.

> The return of My Son, you will proclaim;
> for this you were chosen, for this you were claimed.
> Believe and know, My daughter, that you were never alone;
> for My Son gave His life for you, in Him you are My own.
> And because you cherish My love in your heart,
> your mom is not gone, you were never apart."
> Though I still grieve and bear my pain,
> I know now, what is my loss, is my mom's gain.

YES! The Lord God fulfilled all His words spoken to me regarding my mom. Although I grieved, the Lord did not allow me to suffer during her loss, as He took her home peacefully and suddenly, but only after drawing her closer to Himself. The Lord had also healed her, but in His way and for His purpose, and I know I will receive her back in His timing.

Several years after my mom went to be with the Lord, I was speaking with Matilda while she was home from South Africa, and I picked her brain concerning her last conversation with my mom:

"So tell me, please, what all did you and my mom talk about when she accepted Jesus into her heart before she went to be with the Lord?"

Matilda took her time and was very willing to share with me her last conversation she had with my mom: "We were talking about you and your walk with Jesus. Your mom shared with me that she heard you praising God in Greek. Your mom told me, 'But my daughter cannot speak Greek. She was never able to speak Greek, even from the time she was a little girl. But I heard her praising God in Greek.' I asked your mom if she wanted what you had with Jesus. She said yes, and then accepted Jesus into her heart as her Lord and Savior."

Matilda had discerned that my mom heard my prayer language, the Holy Spirit's gift of tongues, when she heard me praising God in Greek. When I asked God to change my prayer language to Greek while I was in the Army as a sign that it was from His Holy Spirit, unbeknown to me at that time, He did.

My mom never shared with me how or when she heard me praising God in Greek; how I so much wish she would have. Perhaps it was that time when she jested that God didn't give me a good singing voice? The joy I felt upon hearing this testimony was indescribable.

This confirms that the gifts of the Holy Spirit, including speaking in tongues, are still very alive and active today, and with a very real and meaningful purpose.

Yes, indeed, over and over again, God confirmed He really did draw my mom closer to Himself. To know that God loved my mom so very much, that He would allow her the blessings of hearing me praising Him in her ancestral language of Greek that she spoke fluently, yet knew I could never speak, continues to bring overwhelming joy to my heart. (Acts 2:1-12.)

Chapter 37

Darkly

It was about four weeks after Mom passed that I found employment at a nearby bakery. I rarely worked forty hours a week making minimum wage, and the schedule was weird, but it was something for the time being. On Saturdays, when I would be leaving my house at two in the morning to go to work, I had a very strong urge to yell out in my small-town neighborhood for all to hear: "Wake up, everybody! Gotta make the donuts!"

I continued to explore other available employment options that would offer a better income with a guarantee of forty work hours a week. But without a college degree, I was limited to where I could apply.

When I was getting ready for a job interview at a tile manufacturing facility, I gave a lot of thought as to what I should wear. I really needed this job, and wanted to make a great first impression at this interview. Not having a business suit, I wore a pretty dress; it was the best I could do right then.

On my drive home on this hot summer day from this job interview, which I thought went fairly well, I wriggled around in this dress thinking how uncomfortable it was. While waiting for a traffic light to turn, I wriggled around some more, looked down at this dress that was becoming increasingly uncomfortable, and then burst into a hearty laugh. *Dummy me! No wonder this dress is so uncomfortable; I'm wearing it backwards. I'm sure that made a great first impression on this job interview.*

I didn't get the job, but didn't go in despair. God had other plans for my employment career. Two job interviews, two physical exams, and about three years after my first interview, I was finally offered employment at that industrial chemical plant near where I lived. This was the same chemical manufacturing plant that years earlier just after my first interview, the Lord had given me His word that He was with me in this job situation.

In the timing of my employment, I witnessed firsthand the providence of God in strategically planning out my career at this chemical plant. This was evident as I met those who interviewed and had physical exams around the same time I did over the years, but were hired prior to my hire date. These people progressed throughout the plant site due to their seniority in a much different path than what God had planned out for me.

This chemical plant was originally built on behalf of our government to produce rubber for the WWII war efforts. Over seventy years and several different owners later, this chemical plant still exists, though it has since become much smaller in number of employees and production. At the time I was hired, there were many different departments in operation that were spread out over the 420 acres of land this chemical plant was located on.

In order to work at this plant, hourly employees had to join the local labor union and pay union dues. I was hired into an entry-level plant pool position called material packager, and assigned to work in the Darkly Department. I was going to be working shifts of midnight, afternoon and daylight, respectively rotating on a seven-seven-six work schedule.

My first work shift after a full week of orientation was the midnight shift. Bud, the foreman who was working, took me on my first tour of the Darkly packaging area that would be part of my responsibilities and work area.

As Bud led me through a strange building he called the blender structure, I obediently followed. As we went up several flights of metal grated steps, through multi-levels with metal grated floors, through an intricate maze I was sure I would never learn my way around, I kept talking to myself: *Just keep going up and don't look down. I really need this job.* Looking down through the metal grating made me feel like I was going to fall straight down to the bottom floor. I never realized before this night how afraid of heights I was. This was not a good start for me!

After finally reaching the top level, Bud led me through a door to an outside platform, also made of metal grating, that formed around the building. Bud then climbed a metal ladder that hung on the side of this building up to the roof, and once there, he directed me to follow; I fearfully obeyed. Bud then explained the equipment located on this roof that I needed to know about.

At the highest point of this entire plant site, umpteen feet up from ground level, Bud pointed out the wind cone on the roof of Darkly. He then explained that in case of an emergency when we needed to evacuate the plant, we were to use this wind cone to determine the direction the wind was blowing, and then meet for our designated evacuation assembling area upwind. All this was great to know. *What am I doing here, Lord Jesus?*

While outside on this roof, overlooking a potential great fall, on my very first midnight shift during a freezing winter month, Bud shared his thoughts with me. I then realized, he had more than one reason for leading me all the way up to peanut heaven. Bud wanted to be sure he was out of earshot of anyone else before giving me his word of warning.

After Bud leaned over the railing and looked down, he turned back to me and calmly spoke as though he knew me well: "The guy that you are going to be working with, Sweeny, is really bad news. He's mean, arrogant, lazy, and cannot be trusted. No one else wanted to work with him, so they decided to put you with him. Nathan, the last foreman who is temporarily assigned out of the department, will be back soon. Sweeney hates Nathan because he wrote him up. When Nathan comes back to Darkly, Sweeney's gonna make trouble. Just be careful and watch yourself, but don't give up. Sweeney is supposed to retire in a few months, so just hang in there."

Bud asked me not to repeat what he just told me. Having just met Bud and being so new on the job, I was at a loss as to how to respond to him. By that time in my life, I knew it was best to hold off making judgment calls on people. I wisely kept all this to myself and tried to store everything Bud said into that never-to-forget part of my brain.

After Bud finally got me back on safe ground level, someone else took me for another tour through Darkly's production process explaining how the actual Darkly pellets were made. There was a very distinct odor that came with Darkly, a department that produced small round rubber or crystal pellets. The other production departments at this industrial chemical plant produced different types of small expandable polystyrene beads.

Finally, I was taken to meet my shift partner, who seemed irritated at my last tour guide for taking so long with me on his tour. I tried my best not to have a first opinion of Sweeney, who was a burly man, well over six feet tall, twice my age, of Slovak descent, who mumbled when he spoke, and loved to flip his false teeth around in his mouth while making sure to catch them just before they fell out.

Looking around the "L" shaped packagers' control room office that I found myself in and was part of my work area, I saw that covering the walls were several control panels the height of which went from the floor to the ceiling. On these panels were switches and knobs following long, curving lines going somewhere, with red and green light indicators below these lines—some of which worked, and some didn't. There were other panels that were

227

weight scales with their own set of switches and knobs, and red and green lights.

Outside this office door were several air operated control valves that were part of the two blenders and two upper hold-bins that I just saw going up to the roof with Bud. The blenders and attached hold-bins could each hold over 45,000 pounds of Darkly pellets. These blenders were huge vessels that were tumbled around full circle for several minutes, mixing and blending the pellets that were put into them for each order that had to be packaged out. All this was only part of the process and equipment that I was supposed to learn about to succeed on this job!

I don't believe to be easily given to intimidation, either by people or situations. But I need to confess, after everything I had thus far seen on my first-midnight shift on this great job I desperately needed, while knowing it was an industrial chemical plant I was going to be working at, I had some major concerns with alarming thoughts that would not stop racing: *Where did you put me now, Lord Jesus? How am I ever gonna learn all this and succeed in this job?*

Chapter 38
Darkly Pancakes

The production process at Darkly was unique from all the other departments on this plant site, and so was the responsibility of their material packagers. Unlike every other department, the Darkly packagers needed to be available at a moment's notice to assist the chem techs (chemical technicians), who were responsible for producing Darkly, whenever there was an upset in their production process that produced what was called "pancakes," minus maple syrup.

For this assistance, each Darkly packager was issued a full-face respirator much like the gas masks I used while in the Army. All employees also had to wear hard hats, safety glasses, hearing protection, steel-toed shoes, and Nomex clothing that were fire retardant. I was told there was always a possibility of flash fires working in this chemical plant. *I really hate fires!*

Darkly had two very similar production lines simply called Line One and Line Two. Each line included one of each: mix tank, feed tank, reactor, extruder, and hotcutter. The small round rubber or crystal pellets produced at Darkly was used as a feed product for different customers. These customers would then melt down the pellets and mold them to use in their applications, such as automotive instrument panels.

The Darkly production process was continuous. It started off as a liquid chemical called styrene. During the mixing process, several 75-pound rubber bales were cut down by a powerful machine and then added to the styrene. Maleic anhydride, another liquid chemical, was added just before transferring the polymer feed into the reactors.

While the polymer feed continuously moved into the reactor from the bottom, and then out of the reactor from the top, it would thicken as catalyst was continuously added. From the reactors, the polymer feed went through the extruder where most of the styrene was sucked off the polymer making it firmer but still pliable.

At the end of this extruder was a hotcutter, a piece of machinery that had several sharp blades up against the back of the faceplate that had several small holes. As the polymer squeezed through these holes in the faceplate, these steel blades would spin at the rate of over twenty-two-thousand RPM cutting the polymer into small round pellets.

Steam pressured to seven-hundred-pounds kept the faceplate hot enough to cut the pellets without smearing the polymer on the faceplate. The water that carried the pellets from this hotcutter chamber through the intricate piping going up several floor levels, and then through the drying system, was heated to 199.4°F. Almost every piece of equipment in Darkly was extremely hot.

Because the production process was continuous, it took much more than just turning a switch to shut-down or start-up a production line in Darkly. This was one reason why it was completely different than all the other production departments at this chemical plant, which produced their products in reactors one batch at a time.

Any slight glitch in Darkly's continuous production process in any way or with any equipment needed an immediate response to mitigate the consequences. Otherwise, a literal catastrophe could happen, causing the production line to be down for days, even weeks. When these glitches happened, or for start-ups or shut-downs of the lines, or for changing the hotcutter blades, the polymer feed moving through the extruder through the hotcutter was diverted to flow out of the extruder on a metal plate on the floor just before the hotcutter. As this polymer dropped down on this metal plate, it would form what was called "pancakes." Once the task was completed that caused the need to produce pancakes, the polymer feed was diverted back through the hotcutter.

Handling these pancakes when I first came to Darkly was a nightmare in itself. When pancakes were made in Darkly, the two material packagers were needed to assist with handling and moving these pancakes from the metal plate to the outside area for cooling. Once these pancakes started coming out of the extruder, the material packagers had no control in stopping the flow or regulating the rate of speed these pancakes came out.

Once each pancake got to be about eight to twelve inches diameter on the metal plate, someone had to be there with a shovel cutting it off from the feed that continued dropping, and get it outside for cooling. Each shift crew had three chem techs, two material packagers, and one shift foreman working.

The majority of material packagers preferred one person to stay at the metal plate and throw out the pancakes to the person outside. But Sweeney preferred each person to take their own pancake from the metal plate and walk it outside for cooling.

This meant that each of us took our turn pushing an extremely hot blob of pliable rubber while billowing smoke that stunk from dangerous chemicals (thus the need for a respirator) through a narrow doorway to position it outside for cooling, and then hurry back inside for another one. The pancake polymer was so high in temperature, when one landed on my boot one day that I couldn't get off quick enough, it caused a second-degree burn on my foot through my leather boot.

All this information about my new chemical job with the production of Darkly and pancakes was explained to me on my first-midnight shift working when normally I would have been sleeping. I tried to grasp everything I was told, but it was a lot to take in just coming off the street with no experience.

Working with Sweeney my first week was Jethro, an extra relief chem tech who was there to help for my training purposes. His relief job title meant he also covered vacancies in both the chem tech and material packager job positions.

On my second-midnight shift in Darkly, as the three of us were walking back to the material packagers' control room office, an ear-piercing alarm started blaring. *What's going on? Do we evacuate the plant now?*

I never got a chance to voice my questions as Sweeney flew into the office, grabbed his respirator and yelled as he ran out: "They're going down! Grab your mask and let's go!"

Who's going down? Too late; he was gone!

Donning my respirator to use for the very first time, I ran after Sweeney without knowing what to expect, but whatever it was, apparently it seemed pretty urgent.

And then I saw them!

Darkly's famous pancakes were being perfectly formed as they fell on the metal plate beneath them. Water splashed on the metal plate to keep the pancakes from sticking to it. Someone had a water hose splashing the ground around the metal plate and outside, in the middle of winter, no less. (The water was used to help slide the pancakes to the outside area for cooling.)

I watched Sweeney grab a shovel, and using it to cut off the flowing polymer feed dropping on the metal plate, he expertly pulled out the pancake, flipped around and started pushing it with the shovel to go outside through the narrow doorway.

I needed to learn fast! I grabbed another shovel and mimicked what I just saw Sweeney do. Just as I headed outside pushing my pancake, Sweeney passed me heading back inside for another pancake. I positioned my pancake as I thought it should be outside for cooling, but what did I know, I was just a new hire. By now,

Sweeney was heading back outside with his second pancake. I hurried back inside for my second. *Where's Jethro for help?*

Each pancake had to be cut at just the right size. Too small, the next one got too big for the next person. Too big, it was harder to handle and to push outside. If the shovel stayed on the pancake too long as you were pushing it, a hotspot formed on the shovel that made the pancake gook stick on the shovel. To get this gook off, the gook needed to be cooled off using the water, then the shovel needed banged on the ground and hopefully, the gook got off before you needed to grab your next pancake. Otherwise, the stuck-on gook on the shovel just kept accumulating and growing with each pancake it touched thereafter, and then the shovel would not let go of the pancake.

The metal plate could also get hotspots that caused the pancakes to stick to it. If this hotspot was not immediately scraped off, the gook accumulated and grew with each pancake that fell on it, making it nearly impossible to pull off the next pancake. I had to learn all this the hard way while on the job training, doing it for the first time on my second midnight shift.

After my third trip for a pancake, I started to hyperventilate, which fogged up my respirator mask. Then my shovel got a hotspot that kept growing with each pancake it touched. I did not know that I needed to or even how to bang this gook off yet. And then the ice formed from the water that was splashed on the ground outside to help slide the pancakes.

As I was barely succeeding in catching myself from falling on the ice, hardly able to see between my foggy mask and the billows of smoke from the pancakes, my hardhat kept falling off, even as I tried my best to keep it on over the respirator straps. While all at the same time, I fought with my shovel that wouldn't let go of the pancakes as I continued going back and forth, inside and outside, through that narrow doorway with a hot blob of stinking rubber.

As I desperately tried to keep up with my turn of pulling these pancakes out, I kept wondering: *Am I gonna survive this night? Are these pancakes ever gonna stop coming out?*

Several pancakes later, Jethro finally showed up for help. He was with his chem tech buddies helping on their end. *But what about me, the new hire, who never did this before in my life?*

Next thing I knew, a flying pancake came out the doorway about the size of a Frisbee. And then another flying pancake came out, and then another. *Wow, these pancakes can really fly!* Aside from having to dodge these flying pancakes, this process of handling the pancakes was much easier, at least for me anyway. Now the pancakes were slipping on the ice instead of me. It seemed Jethro preferred to throw them out versus going back and forth as Sweeney preferred.

A few pancakes later, Jethro disappeared again. Sweeney and I were back to each grabbing our own pancakes, walking them out, and then back in again for another one.

Then this big, fat guy started jumping around in a panic screaming "fire, fire," as I saw flames, to my horror, coming off a piece of machinery just before I reached for another pancake. Someone else nonchalantly walked around and reached for a fire extinguisher, as though this was a normal procedure.

The foreman screamed at him: "NO! NO! Don't use the extinguisher! I'll have to write a report! Just put it out with water!"

Too late! The fire extinguisher did its job.

I grabbed my pancake, and then Sweeney came in for his next pancake. On my next trip back in, someone stopped me in the doorway from going in for another pancake. I heard a loud bang, then another loud bang, and then it was all over.

One little pancake was left drooling itself on the metal plate. *Are we finally done with these pancakes? What am I doing here, Lord Jesus? Where did You put me now?*

Chapter 39
True to His Word

I could not have known at the very beginning of my employment the pivotal role this chemical job career would play in God's ongoing nurturing and refining process, even as He continued conforming me more to the image and likeness of His Son, Jesus. The trials and storms I endured were at times so intense, that I really could have gone in despair had it not been for the Lord Jesus in my life. But then again, God allowed them for His purpose, and through them He drew me closer to Himself.

The spiritual battles raged on as the evil forces tried their best to discourage me enough to quit this job. The angelic warriors were given charge by God Himself concerning me, and were determined that God's plan for placing me where He did was going to come to fruition. True to His word spoken to me, God was with me in this job situation, and in more ways than I could ever know.

The material packagers in the other departments in this chemical plant packaged their product beads in 1,000-pound boxes during their entire shift similar to an assembling line type job. The material packagers working in Darkly not only packaged our product pellets in the same size boxes, but also packaged the pellets in 50-pound bags. We also loaded the pellets into bulk railcars, bulk trailer trucks, and seabulk containers that were shipped overseas. Any number of these packaging methods were done each shift, and rotated depending on the orders. This made for a less monotonous job much more to my liking.

Darkly's material packagers were also responsible for moving our own product feed pellets per our orders, which again was different than the other material packagers' responsibilities. The amount of feed pellets that were moved was mostly in batches of 38,000 to 45,000 pounds for each order.

Using huge blowers and an intricate piping system that was connected to the outside silo vessels that stored the different types of Darkly pellets, these pellets were brought into one of our two blender systems. When loading railcars, the feed pellets went directly from the silos into the railcars using another blower system and intricate piping that was several hundred feet in length. If someone was not paying attention to what they were doing, it was easy to cross-contaminate the different types of product pellets into the different containers, or overfill the upper hold-bins to the point that the piping got plugged.

Everything pertaining to this Darkly entry-level job had to be mastered to perform it proficiently. This included all the different containers' packaging equipment, upper hold-bins, blenders, silos; and all the blowers, valves and intricate piping systems connected with these. All the different control panels and weight scales in the packagers' control room office, and all the control panels and air operated hydraulic valves connected to the railcar loading rack, also needed mastered. The complexity of this job only added to my thankfulness to God for helping me learn it well in such a short time, before Sweeney flip-flopped on me.

Once Sweeney learned that Nathan was coming back as our shift foreman, he turned against me with a vengeance, as though it was all my fault. I made sure Sweeney knew that he needed to leave me out of his war with Nathan. I was only on this job six weeks by then, and I needed to get my hundred-twenty-day probation period in before I was officially a permanent employee.

But Sweeney didn't care about me. He had such a hateful grudge against Nathan that overflowed into our working relationship, which I thought was going well up until then. I continued to work conscientiously doing my best to get the work done, often without Sweeney's help. This only fueled Sweeney's harassment towards me.

Our railcar loading station was secluded; it was two city blocks away from the Darkly production area and near the river. This loading station had a long flight of metal grated steps going up to the loading rack, which had a movable platform that was lowered and raised onto and connecting to the top of the railcar using a valve-controlled hydraulic system. The platform and loading rack were also made of metal grating.

One midnight shift, Sweeney and I were finishing up loading a railcar. While I was still on the platform closest to the railcar, Sweeney raised the platform using the hydraulic system. This was a major safety infraction that put me in a dangerous situation while I was still on the platform. I turned to Sweeney and spoke in a firm tone: "You mind waiting till I get off?"

I was angry and fearful at the same time by his actions, and his mean, mumbled response only intensified my emotions: "You got a problem?"

I gave him a glare that shot daggers at him and spoke volumes: *Yeah; I got a big problem! YOU!*

But there is a time to speak, and a time to refrain from speaking. I wisely decided that was a time to refrain. We were alone down at the railcar loading rack and secluded for me to challenge him. Anything could have happened, and who would have known whether it was accidental or intentional.

I never told anyone what Sweeney did to me on the railcar platform. I learned all too soon: No one wanted to deal with Sweeney or his harassment towards me. Throughout this time, I trusted God for His help, protection and wisdom. But I will admit, there were times when I wasn't wise in dealing with Sweeney, and took matters into my own hands.

During the summer months, this chemical plant would employ college kids of permanent employees to help them out with a job and to cover vacations. We had a sweet young girl, Tammy, working with us the only summer I worked with Sweeney.

One hot summer afternoon shift, Sweeney and Tammy were working on the bagging system line filling 50-pound bags. The bagging system was notorious for breaking the bags or missing the spout, which spilled the pellets on the floor. An empty 1,000-pound box was needed to put the pellets into from the broken bags.

On this night, I was working by myself on another packaging piping line filling these 1,000-pound boxes one at a time with Darkly pellets. Before each box was filled with pellets, whether off a packaging line or from broken bags, a wooden pallet skid needed placed under it so that when these boxes were full, each one could be moved elsewhere for storage using a forklift.

I had just enough of these skids near where I was working to finish my order. Sweeney, though, needed a skid for another empty box for the pellets coming from the broken bags on the line he was working on with Tammy. Sweeney, being the lazy guy that he was, would not go outside to get himself a skid.

As I saw Sweeney coming after one of my skids, I informed him that all my skids were counted and would be used. Ignoring me, he grabbed a skid for his own use mumbling, "I'll get you another one."

By this time in my employment, with my probation period over and being well fed up with Sweeney, his harassment, and everyone's nonchalant attitude towards what I was enduring with this mean old man, I decided the war was on. I knew Sweeney was going to laugh at me as I made my way outside going after one last skid that I needed to finish my order. The skids were stacked in an area that was a good distance away from the building where we were working.

As Sweeney walked away dragging my skid with him, I angrily followed behind. After he dropped the skid on the ground and turned his back to get his box to place on top of it, I saw my chance. Without hesitation, I grabbed my stolen skid and stomped back to my workstation. Turning around to place his box on my skid that was now gone, he angrily dropped his box and stomped back to where my pile of skids waited to be used.

And the war raged on!

Sweeney grabbed for a second time the very same skid mumbling again in a meaner tone: "I told you I'll get you another one." He then stomped back to where his box was and dropped the skid in place.

Once again, I followed him and went after my skid. Grabbing it now as Sweeney watched, I swept it away quickly letting him know again before I stomped back to my workstation: "And I told you all my skids were counted."

Sweeney stomped back a third time, grabbed the same skid as I watched him from where I was making a box, then stomped back to his box while keeping his eye on me as he went along.

The war should have ended now, but it didn't!

I angrily stomped back to where Sweeney was as he defiantly dropped my skid on the ground glaring back at me, daring me to pick it up again. I instantly reached to grab my skid again and as I did, Sweeney was ready and grabbed the other end.

And the tug of war raged on!

On one end of the skid was a short young woman defiantly tugging away; on the other end of the skid was a burly mean old man tugging away. Sweeney and I went back and forth tugging on this skid with neither one of us willing to let go of their end. I yelled at him once again: "I told you all my skids were counted."

He yelled back, "I told you I'll get you another one."

What a great example we were for this sweet summer-help girl to witness. Here we were, two adults fighting a tug of war over a skid! I could only imagine God's angelic warriors shaking their heads and chuckling as they unsheathed their swords to block the blows of the demons.

Our eyes glared at each other, his arm raised slightly, I realized his intention and defiantly challenged him: "What are you gonna do now, strike me?"

With my defiant challenge, Sweeney instantly let go of his end of my skid. As I walked away in victory with my skid in tow, I heard Sweeney order Tammy to go outside to get him another skid.

That battle was won, but my witness for Jesus was lost!

I realize today that the Christian action in a situation like that should have been to just let the mean old man have my skid. But I wasn't there yet in my walk with the Lord Jesus to just let this go.

It was the principle of the issue while my stubborn Greek temper got the best of me. Or was it my South Bronx demeanor rearing its ugly head again? I wouldn't let that mob of kids have my twelve cents. Why should I let Sweeny, a mean old man who had been harassing me for so long to no end, get away with stealing my skid that I needed?

And the war raged on!

Because of being conscientious with my job, I had a good working relationship with Nathan; this also fueled Sweeney's harassment towards me. But neither Nathan nor anyone else made any attempts to address Sweeney's harassment of which I was victim, not even the union reps. Everyone's consoling advice to "just hang in there, he's gonna retire soon," just didn't seem to help me much. This work environment was emotionally very upsetting to me, even off the job.

Nathan approached me one day concerned—but not for me—that those who knew what was happening did not want me to take

Sweeney's harassment issue to human resource to get it addressed. Had I felt that was what God wanted me to do, I would have.

But while in prayer one day over this situation with Sweeney, I saw a very clear vision of the right hand of God going through our packaging area. This message from God that He was with me in this difficult job situation didn't change the situation. God used everything to teach me of my real need to trust Him for what He allows to happen in my life, where He allows me to be, and His reasons for allowing it, even though I may not always understand His reasons.

After working with Sweeney for almost ten months, he finally retired. My next material packager partner was a new hire, a man from West Virginia who believed women should be kept barefooted and pregnant.

I knew as a woman in a man's world doing a man's job, there were going to be men working with me who felt I had no business in the job I was in, and would treat me accordingly. But thankfully, I did have a few coworkers who understood that I needed this job as a self-supporter, and acknowledged my attempts to be a conscientious worker.

I continued my career believing it was really the Lord Jesus whom I was working for, as I never forgot that Army Chaplain's sermon on Colossians 3:23-24: "Whatever you do, do your work heartily, as for the Lord rather than for men, knowing that from the Lord you will receive the reward of the inheritance. It is the Lord Christ whom you serve."

Chapter 40
My Home

Going on in my life during this time was my desperate need to find another place to live. I was still living in that dilapidated house that Mom and I had moved into years earlier. We had wanted to move into something better before she passed away. But we were never able to afford to buy a house for ourselves, and with our dogs to consider, many options for other rented houses were eliminated.

My landlord, who was born and raised in Greece, owned many other rental houses in the area, but hated putting any money into his rental properties. Mom and this man had words on many occasions over our poor living conditions; the conversations were always in Greek.

Little Dukey had to be put to sleep about a month before I started my chemical job due to cancer. I had ten great years with that little mutt I found while in the Army. Despite the aggressive welcome Little Dukey gave Olympus upon first coming into "his" home, these dogs were more compatible than I could have ever hoped for. Mom was right; they only needed some time to adjust. Now that Olympus was alone for the first time in his life, he seemed to really miss his little buddy. Still having a huge German Shepherd to consider, I prayed about and started looking for a house to buy that was sure to have a big yard for Olympus.

With Olympus in tow on a cool fall day, I went scouring the area around near where I worked and came across a realtor sign in a neighborhood that seemed a bit secluded for my liking, but decided to take a look anyway. Upon leaving Olympus in Pegasus II—I still had that rust bucket—I approached the house that was connected with the sign. When I knocked on the door, an older man answered and invited me in for a tour. This was the first house I looked at during my long quest to find a house.

After this man gave me a short tour of his house, I spotted them! Lining up in several rows as though they were soldiers themselves as part of a private army—looking very sharp—they proudly laid there almost chuckling at their potential evil intent. *Is my imagination getting the best of me?*

Catching a glimpse of this army of knives that were spread out so uniformly on the kitchen table, an eerie feeling came over me. I looked away quickly but smoothly, hoping not to bring any attention to the fear that I was sure was now plastered on my face—not to mention in my heart—and then chided myself: *What am I doing in this house all by myself with this man I know nothing about, and without anyone knowing where I am? I'm from the South Bronx, for crying out loud! I should know better than to put myself in a situation like this.* Accepting the situation I put myself in, my thoughts continued trying to figure out how to get out of this house safely.

The man seemed nice enough, and if he noticed my fearful glance at all his knives, he didn't let on. But when he offered to show me the basement, I calmly but politely declined, "Thank you, but no thank you. I need to get back to my dog I left in my car."

After my getaway out the door I had come in, I was gone and for good. The headlines could have read: "Woman's Body Found Dismembered in Secluded House for Sale."

My quest for what I believed was a desperate need to locate and purchase a house turned out to be a real lesson from God in waiting on His timing.

That dilapidated house I lived in was literally falling apart. With "knob and tube" for electrical wiring, almost the entire house ran on one fuse. The bathroom that was built long after the house was had no heat, and had a window that was rotting away. Along with the termites having a feast eating away at this house, there was mold and mildew galore that made their home in the basement, which was lined with cinder blocks that crumbled just looking at them. The last straw was the roof leaking causing a huge bulge right above my bed.

When I complained about the termites to my landlord's employee who overlooked the care of his rental properties, he asked me, "Do the termites bother you?"

My response was obvious, at least to me: "Well, I think when I fall through the floor they're gonna bother me."

When I complained about the leaking roof, this same employee came over to inspect the bulging ceiling above my bed. After pushing this bulge up several inches, he assured me that the ceiling was not going to fall on me while I slept.

As my diligent quest for a house continued, some of my well-meaning friends were getting very upset with me in my refusal to take their advice to hurry up and buy something better to live in. They gently reminded me of the falling apart house I was living in, of the lower interest rates, and of the market for buyers going on. My response was also gentle, but adamant and never wavered, "I can't just buy a house just to buy a house. I have to buy the house that God wants me to buy."

I would find houses that I liked and could have lived in, but I kept relying on God's Holy Spirit to speak to my heart as to whether it was "the house" that God wanted me to buy. God speaks to us many times and in many ways, but we need to be attuned and discerning to the voice and leading of the Holy Spirit. A lack of peace regarding any decision I am trying to make is one sure indication that the Holy Spirit is putting a check on my intentions. But I also rely on other ways that God's Spirit speaks to me, and not just on His lack of peace.

My Home/40

During my long quest to find a house, God had spoken to my heart letting me know that He had just the right house for me, but only in His timing would I receive it. And I really needed to follow God's direction as to which house and where He wanted to plant me to live.

Then one year at the end of August, during my quiet time with the Lord while my thoughts were on something other than buying a house, He spoke to me a specific time frame for when I would have my house: "Before the grass stops growing and the leaves change their colors, you will have your house."

I've learned that the Lord has a sense of humor. He knew my spontaneous lighthearted response to His definite time frame of getting my house after diligently looking for almost four years by this time, was without irreverence: "I don't know, Lord. You better hurry up then. Cause all this stuff is gonna happen in just four weeks, and it takes eight weeks to close on a house, and I haven't even found a house yet."

One absolute proof that the Lord God has spoken a word is the fulfillment of His word in His timing. Two days later, my realtor agent phoned about a house that was up for sale. We had a good working relationship. She would inform me of houses that went up for sale, and after looking at them around the outside first by myself, I would let her know if I was interested in seeing the inside. This would save her time as well as my time in locating the right house.

Upon hearing the description of this house with an integral garage—which I thought was part of the basement—I didn't want to see this house. However, since some of the houses I didn't want to see before I ended up liking, I decided to give it a chance.

When I saw this house for my look around outside, I saw that the garage was attached to the side of the house and not underneath. I went around to check out the backyard and found it huge with lots of trees that reminded me of a private park I knew Olympus would love. I contacted my agent asking to see the inside of this house. And then I prayed, "Please, Lord, tell me the first time I see the inside of this house if this is it."

When I walked inside this house, I entered a time zone of the 1950s. The house was not abused, but in the thirty-six years since it was built, everything original of that era was untouched, including the famous pink bathroom. This wasn't a bad thing per se, as the price reflected the need for updating, and gave me the opportunity to remodel per my taste. As I went through this house, I knew without any doubt when God spoke to my heart. *Yepperreo, this is my "home" that God ordained for me!* I jokingly tell people that my house was being built the same time I was.

However, it took some doing convincing my realtor agent that this was it. She asked me four different times the same question: "Are you sure this is it?"

My answer never wavered, "Yeah, I'm sure. This is the house God wants for me."

I was the very first buyer being tried out on a new accelerated home mortgage closing program that was supposed to only take four weeks or less, instead of the normal eight weeks; everything was verbally approved instead of waiting for it in writing. I had the closing of my house with the garage door opener in my hands before the grass stopped growing and the leaves changed their colors. Once again, God was true to His word, even with my lighthearted response to Him.

Even though it took almost four years of diligently looking and waiting on God for the exact house He wanted me to have, it was well worth the wait. I have never been disappointed after waiting on God's timing for anything.

Chapter 41

Irreverence

Way too often, the Lord's righteous judgments are denied or misunderstood, even by some of God's own children. The Lord Jesus did not go through such agony, and shed His precious and holy blood to issue anyone a license to sin. The sacrifice of Jesus as the atonement for our sins was meant to reconcile us with His Holy Father to become His children. God's grace is amazing, but we must never abuse it.

God customizes His nurturing and discipline for each of His children who love Him, and according to His purpose and call on their lives, although there may be some similarities. The severity in which God deals with some may or may not be the same as He deals with others. This truth needed re-emphasized before I share God's dealings with me in the next few chapters.

I always remained faithful with God's marriage covenant He had called me into. However, the Lord God has made it very clear to me many times over, that embracing my entertainment idols was just as though I had committed adultery against Him, with my disobedience to Him being just as wrong.

As the many years moved on, the Lord God proved to be unrelenting in pursuing my complete surrender and perfect obedience to Him in all areas of my life, while also dealing with my heart's attitude towards Him during His dealings. During all this time, the Lord was also teaching me what a holy and reverent fear of God really meant.

As the Lord continued drawing me closer to Himself during His severe dealings, my disobedience to Him became less and further apart. However, the severity of God's dealings intensified with each time I did disobey Him.

There were times when I would come into the presence of God during my quiet time only to experience His righteous anger towards me. But in the midst of it all, God kept reaffirming that it was because of His love and call on my life that His dealings and refining process were so intense.

Now with a new home of my own to move into, along came my idols. I had a vast array of VHS tape recordings of Star Trek, Star Wars, and other TV programs and movies that I knew the Lord would not allow me to watch, but nevertheless, I refused to let go. So why was I keeping these idols? They sat in a closet in my spare bedroom where I kept my guinea pigs and birds that I loved.

One night during my quiet time while in God's presence, I requested that He allow a hedge of angels to surround my home for protection. His response to my request was undeniable. Before this could happen, all my idols had to leave my home, and for good. I didn't want to deal with what the Lord was directing me during that time. So instead of surrendering to His will, I pushed aside what I knew He was speaking, and continued my time with Him by praying for others. To say that my response to God's direction that night was displeasing to Him would be an understatement.

I didn't have a home church at that time. My attendance at the prayer meeting group I loved was cut down because of my rotating shift work, not to mention all the overtime I also worked. I really had no one to share with about any of God's dealings within my life, nor did I want to.

In the workplace, I was known as an overly conscientious worker with a perfect work attendance that got along well with the bosses. Because of this, I was often looked upon as more of a salaried employee than union employee; this was not popular in a union shop. I was also known as a single Christian woman living out her calling to a celibate life faithfully. I may have appeared to many the good Christian, but no one is good except God alone. (Luke 18:19.)

The reality, though, was a different story. I was falling short of God's demands peculiar to His call on my life, which meant so much more than anything and everything else.

Many times, God will use Scripture to confirm what He has spoken to me. When I pushed away God's direction to cleanse my home from my idols, He confirmed His word with Isaiah 57:12-13: "I will declare your righteousness and your deeds, but they will not profit you. When you cry out, let your collection of idols deliver you. But the wind will carry all of them up, and a breath will take them away."

It took a few days to totally surrender to God's will, but eventually, I got rid of these idols in my life; I really had no other choice. When my heart is not right with God, there is absolutely nothing in my life that is right.

Two years after this idol cleansing from my home, and several years into this chemical job, the company was sold to another chemical company. This turned out well for everyone involved. Soon after this, the new company purchased a slew of computers and placed them within the different departments throughout the plant site for all their employees to use.

Installed on these new computers was a complex computer program used to keep track of all that went on with this chemical company. In addition to training their new employees on this complex program, we received training on using their email system as a new way of communicating throughout the plant site.

And along with all these computers floating around came the computer games. Mind Sweep, Solitaire, Free Cell, and many others, including access to the Internet, were readily available to everyone. I didn't have a PC of my own during that time, but with access to these computers in my workplace, I found myself getting very addicted to the card game Free Cell.

Any addiction in the life of a child of God is wrong; it consumes us and draws us away from the Lord. To the degree that God deals with it depends on many factors, the most important being God's call on the life of His child who has the addiction.

I knew I was getting addicted to Free Cell, and I knew it was wrong in my walk with the Lord God. However, I purposely ignored the nudging of the Holy Spirit dealing with me on this addiction, and in doing so, I grieved Him.

I was coming into work one midnight shift and looking forward to my break from work to play Free Cell. After playing a few games and before going back to work, my thoughts revealed the irreverent sin of my heart's attitude; the consequence from which would cost me dearly: *God didn't actually tell me I couldn't play Free Cell. So, I'll just keep playing it until He does.*

God is holy, righteous and just; He always has been, and always will be. God is not only able to judge the thoughts and intentions of everyone's heart (Hebrews 4:12), He will do so with those He has called for any purpose, and His judgment will either be in this world, or in the world to come.

The next time I started playing Free Cell on that midnight shift, I was overwhelmed with God's anger towards me, and to such a powerful extreme that I cannot fully describe. Although I stopped playing and told the Lord I was sorry, His powerful anger towards me did not abate for a very long time afterward.

After working my midnights, I would normally have a four-day weekend off. But after this weekend, I was also scheduled for a week of vacation. I planned on visiting friends my first day off, and then staying around home the rest of the week. As was my practice before leaving my home to go anywhere, I asked the Lord to please, bless my home, my dog, and my pets. The Lord's stern response was unexpected and pierced my heart: "Why should I?"

He was still very angry with me!

During that entire week of vacation, I was despondent knowing my relationship with God was not right, in addition to having so many other things go wrong. Through it all, I knew God was punishing me for my heart's attitude regarding ignoring the nudging of His Holy Spirit.

One evening during that week, I was very fearful to come into the presence of God during my quiet time, but knew I could not avoid my time with the Lord. In God's presence that evening, I searched the Lord's heart concerning why I was fearful. The Lord expressed that He was still very angry with me.

Why would God get so angry with me over a computer card game? There was more to God's righteous anger and my heart's attitude that I was going to learn, but only in His timing.

Several months after all this happened, I had to put Olympus to sleep at the ripe old age of thirteen and a half years. He had so many health problems during his lifetime, but each time God pulled him through. The Lord had spoken to me once assuring me that He had no desire to take Olympus from me prematurely.

When his organs were shutting down, I called a vet who had promised that he would come to my home to put Olympus to sleep when it was time. And the vet came, even between the scheduled surgeries he had that day. I held Olympus in my arms when he was first born, and I held him in my arms as his life slipped away.

But this was not the way that I prayed he would go! I didn't want to make the decision to put him to sleep. I had wanted him to die peacefully in his own backyard. I am ashamed to share that as I cried over losing Olympus in this way, I told the Lord I hated Him because He did not answer my prayer my way, as I wanted Him to. The Lord knew that with the vet coming over and taking care of everything, including his body, it was the easiest way for me, as He also knew what my response to Him would be.

The Lord did not show any anger or displeasure because of my attitude towards Him as I cried over losing Olympus in this way. He was compassionate and patient, as He understood very well that I could never hate Him, and that what I spoke to Him was only because of my grief. But He also understood what this dog meant to me, and perhaps meant too much.

Once I calmed down, I told the Lord I was sorry for what I said. The Lord then spoke a firm direction in His commanding voice: "I do not want you to get another one."

Several months later, the Lord gave me several warnings over a period of time letting me know, that the next time I disobeyed Him, I would regret my disobedience for the rest of my life. I had been contemplating watching a sequel to a movie that I had seen years earlier that I really loved. I am still not always able to understand God's restrictions in my walk with Him, but that does not give me an excuse to defy them.

A few months after God's severe warnings, and living over a year without a dog, I entertained the thoughts of getting another German Shepherd. With these thoughts, I ordered, received and watched a video from a dog kennel that bred these beautiful dogs. I ignored the conviction of the Holy Spirit while ordering this video, that doing so and entertaining getting another dog was a willful act of disobedience to the Lord. The irreverent sin of my heart's attitude once again grieved God's Holy Spirit!

I watched the video, but was so convicted afterward, that I repented and confessed my sin to God, returned the video, and gave up all thoughts of getting another dog of any kind.

Scriptures bear the truth: "If we confess our sins, He is faithful and righteous to forgive us our sins and to cleanse us from all unrighteousness" (1 John 1:9). However, this Scripture truth does not indicate that there are no consequences left to deal with after sinning against such a holy, righteous and just God, even with God's forgiveness.

For the next couple of months, I knew my relationship with the Lord was not right. I continued to search the Lord's heart concerning our relationship during this time, as I also did off and on for almost two years as to why, really, did He get so angry with me regarding Free Cell.

Now, in God's time, and during my quiet time in His presence, after almost two years of His silence regarding His anger with Free Cell, He gave me only one word for His response: insolence. I asked the Lord for His definition of insolence: contempt. Afterward, I researched these words while just opening the dictionary to the correct page for insolence. There are no coincidences with God.

Not only did I willfully disobey the Lord regarding playing Free Cell, it was my irreverent heart towards Him that was dangerously wrong. The Lord God also made it clear to me, that had it not been for the sacrifice of Jesus on the cross for my sins, I would have forfeited my life that night after such an irreverence towards such a holy, righteous and just God.

The following morning after what the Lord made clear to me, I woke up feeling what a dark and ugly heart I really had. How could I treat such a loving God in such a horrible way? The Lord God loved me so much that He sacrificed His only begotten Son for my sins, even as Jesus gave up His life for all the sins of the world. And I can never forget how God had saved me from that PCP overdose.

I finished my daylight shifts Thursday very remorseful over everything the Lord had shown me. With barely a full day off between changing shifts, I was gearing up to go into my seven midnight shifts the next evening. As was my practice, I spent time with the Lord before going out to work that first midnight shift.

While in God's presence, He reminded me of my insolence towards Him regarding Free Cell, and then made it profoundly clear: My attitude and disobedience to Him in regards to the dog video and entertaining getting another dog was another act of insolence towards Him.

After God exposed the magnitude of the sins of my irreverent heart, the Lord Jesus expressed that He was going to judge me for both acts of irreverence towards such a holy God, either in this world, or on the day of His judgment—He gave me the choice.

The Lord Jesus gave me His word: If I submitted to Him in dealing with my irreverent heart in this world, He would remove the hindrance these sins had caused in my relationship with such a holy and righteous God, and draw me closer to Himself.

I love my Lord and my God with every essence of my whole being. My relationship with Him is so precious to me, and will always mean so much more than anything or anyone else could ever mean in my life. I trusted the Lord's love for me and believed His word.

I submitted to my Lord Jesus and His dealings as only He knew I would. But to be sure, I was totally unprepared for His response to my submission.

The Lord Jesus spoke in His stern voice that I knew all too well by then: "When I spank you, you will know it."

Chapter 42

God's Spanking

The Lord God had given me ample forewarnings over many years, that He will deal severely with me when I sin against Him. During when my rebellious heart struggled the most with God's demands peculiar to His call, one day in His presence, I saw a vision of God's hand holding a crown that burst into flames. The Lord God then spoke in His commanding voice: "In the fire of affliction and judgment will your heart be broken."

Psalm 119:75 declares it well: "I know, O Lord, that Your judgments are righteous, and that in faithfulness You have afflicted me." Hebrews 12:5-13 also confirms the truth of God's discipline with any child He has called His own.

As God's severity increased in a gradual progression through the years, He was drawing me closer to Himself. At the same time, God was sharing with me in an equal gradual progression and in some very special ways, His prophetic call on my life. The Lord also revealed in undeniable ways that knowing His rod intimately was an aspect of His call that was unavoidable.

So to receive such a direct word from the Lord God who is omniscient, omnipotent and omnipresent, of His impending spanking just before starting my seven days of midnight shifts, working in an industrial chemical plant where mishaps can easily happen, was more than a little unsettling to me, to say the least.

Truthfully, there are no words to fully describe how I felt afterward. I tried my best to believe that the Lord really didn't mean what He said. But with years of forewarnings gone past, with years of His severe dealings, the Lord's word of His impending spanking loomed constantly as I worked out my midnight shifts.

I managed to work five midnights without a mishap. During my quiet time with my Lord before my sixth midnight, I found myself basking in God's presence and peace in an extraordinary way. Then all at once, I became overwhelmed by God's love for me.

While still in God's presence, I heard a familiar tune playing somewhere outside the window that was so special between me and the Lord Jesus: "That's our tune, Jesus."

The Music Box Dancer, the same tune that played in the background when God was healing me from overdosing on PCP over twenty years earlier, was being played by an ice cream truck driving on my cul-de-sac road. I never knew of any ice cream truck driving in my neighborhood the several years I lived there prior to that night.

The Lord then spoke in His commanding voice resonating His love: "I love you, My daughter. With your whole heart you know this is true."

The Music Box Dancer continued playing in the background, even as I continued basking in God's presence, peace and love. The Lord knew I needed a powerful affirmation of His love before leaving for work that night.

The new company that bought our chemical plant a few years earlier decided to reduce our workforce across the site during this time; after which, Darkly had only one material packager per shift crew. One less person in Darkly was definitely not the best and safest scenario to work in. During an upset situation when pancakes were made, four people needed to be out there handling the situation. This left no one available in the control room to watch or attend the second production line while the first production line was being taken care of.

To alleviate the concerns working with one less crew member, the company installed "dummy alarms" in the tune of Westminster Chimes to alert the chem techs of critical alarms, which when blaring, could be heard way beyond the boundaries of Darkly. An immediate response to any critical alarm was needed to mitigate the consequences from what caused the alarm. But without anyone being in the control room to check the DCS (distributed control system) computers as to what was alarming, these dummy alarms were not a satisfactory replacement for the extra person needed.

However, the new company wasn't satisfied with this reduced crew number. For whatever reason, they didn't like Darkly from the beginning, so they decided to put Darkly up for sale. Some new prospective buyers were scheduled to come and inspect Darkly this following morning from when the Lord affirmed His love to me. Because of this inspection and pending sale, I wanted to make extra sure that the packaging area was spotless clean. If our current company didn't want Darkly, maybe this new company would buy us and keep us running.

The bagger system line that filled 50-pound bags and was notorious for dumping several hundred pounds of pellets on the ground during operation, was no longer in service by this time. But all the conveyors to this complex system and the carton filling part of this line were still intact.

As was my habit in cleaning this area, I would go on top of the conveyor lines to make sure I could blow out every last pellet from underneath all the steel legs and connecting conveyors with an air hose. This took a considerable amount of effort and care, but I had done this so many times before in the nine-plus years working in Darkly; this was a normal cleaning procedure for me.

The two corner turntables connected to this conveyor system could turn powerfully without warning even with the electrical power off. There were electronic cross-eyes that if the beams were broken, an air operated hydraulic power system would slam the turntable around. If a person's limb happened to be in the wrong place at the wrong time when these turntables turned, it could easily get snapped off. I was aware of all this, so in addition to turning off the electrical power source before cleaning this area, I always turned off the air power source as well. I always tried my best to work safely.

With all the energy sources off, air hose in hand as a blower broom, I climbed on top of the conveyors. Once I was done blowing out all the pellets from around the conveyors, I would always ease off to the ground one leg at a time. I've done it this way so many times before without any mishaps.

This night, as I eased off the conveyor that was about two feet high from the ground, my left foot got stuck on the edge of the conveyor while my right leg and body kept going in a twisting motion heading for the ground. I lost my balance and landed full force on my right leg, and then fell backwards on the ground. Instant excruciating pain in my right knee told me I just received more than a little boo-boo injury that I could easily hide away, another practice that was unofficial normal procedure, at least for us union workers.

My very first thought after landing in a sitting position on the ground was that I needed to get up out of embarrassment before anyone saw I just fell. It's embarrassing to fall, let's face it; our pride is always hurt the most. With it being a midnight shift and about 1:30 in the morning, with everyone else busy about their own business, I was glad no one else was around to see me fall.

My second thought was that I needed to hide this injury. Although we were supposed to report all injuries, I really didn't want to report it with all the red tape, hassles, and again, the embarrassment that went with it.

Walking into the newer Darkly control room where the packagers also occupied now along with the chem techs (we also had our own DCS computer that replaced the outdated control panels), I decided to let only my crewmembers know that I hurt my knee; that should suffice the need of reporting it.

Their response was typical for men: "Well, you're walking on it okay. You must not have hurt it that bad."

I really wasn't expecting their sympathy! By then in my chemical job career, I was the only woman out of twenty-four union workers in Darkly, and I got along well with these crewmembers.

Going back outside to my area to finish my cleaning, I discovered that I was able to walk on it without limping, but only if I walked very slowly. Before the shift was over, one crewmember convinced me to report my injury. The knee had started to swell up almost immediately after it was injured, and close to the end of the shift, I could not bend it at all.

There were no longer shift foremen on each crew by this time; they were the first to go on these job cuts. Instead, there were only two supervisors on plant site, trained in first aid, and were called shift coaches, with each having responsibility for their half of the plant. The shift coach I called to report this injury that night also knew something about sports injuries, and recommended a surgeon in Pittsburgh, a good distance from where I lived. *Surgery? I'm not thinking surgery. It's only a small knee injury. After my long weekend off with some rest, it'll be just fine.*

I humored this guy, though, and listened to what he had to say about Dr. Rite, this terrific orthopedic surgeon he knew about.

I had to come back in that morning during when I should have been sleeping to see the on-site company doctor. He never told me his thoughts of a ligament tear. I never told him about the huge hidden bruise that came with the fall.

I was willing to work my last midnight while hoping that by the time I came back to work four days later, it would be fine. The doctor was more than willing to let me work my last midnight, thus keeping this from becoming a loss-time injury. But he wanted to see me back on Monday during my scheduled day off.

During my weekend off, I cried out to the Lord Jesus over this knee injury and searched His heart. In His presence, the Lord made me profoundly aware that through His loving hand and for His purpose, He orchestrated this knee injury as His spanking—something I already believed but wanted to deny.

On Monday, the company doctor took me off my material packager job position and put me on medical work restrictions. I was then put on the daylight shifts until my knee healed. There was a guy scheduled to be bumped out of Darkly because of the packager job cuts, but was able to stay working on my shift until I was able to go back on my old job. This guy was very happy about this arrangement, which also kept my material packager position readily available for when I was ready to come back to full duty.

On the daylight shift once a week, a few workers from different areas of the plant had a Bible study that I started attending. During one of these Bible studies, some guy told a story about the old-fashioned sheep shepherds. He stated that when a shepherd had a lamb that continually went astray, which was a detriment to the lamb's well-being, the shepherd would break the lamb's leg, mend it afterward, and would then keep this lamb close to him during the healing process. This practice bonded the lamb closer to the shepherd, and once healed, the lamb would not go astray again.

I did some recent research on this story in relating it now. There seems to be a debate as to whether this practice was truth or myth. But it didn't matter at that time. Through this guy, the Lord spoke to me and confirmed why He orchestrated this injury in the first place.

Chapter 43
Beginning of Workers' Comp

The stories are familiar to most of us with a twist here and there to some degree. The man with a claimed work-related back injury is videoed on top of his house replacing the roof. The person with a bad leg from a work-related injury is seen mowing the grass. And so goes the stories of those who have abused the workers' comp system. All these stories depict the injured worker as a scammer, someone who is too lazy to work for a living. Now with the Internet, some of these stories would go viral. This abuse of workers' comp has caused a very dangerous stigma that makes it difficult for those who are truly injured to get professional medical help.

There are those who do abuse the workers' comp system, I do not deny this, and those who abuse it make it bad for the majority who do not. But what is never told, never videoed, and never documented is the fraud and deception the insurance companies, employers, and even some in the medical profession commit against injured workers. Committing insurance fraud to any extent is a criminal offense punishable according to the law, regardless of who is committing insurance fraud.

My employer was self-insured with workers' comp. There were some regulations in the Workers' Comp Act of Pennsylvania that they purposely were not in compliance with. But for the most part, they took care of their injured workers. It was a different story with their third-party insurance administrators, who in one instance actually falsified a medical report document in my case.

Each state has its own workers' comp laws and regulations. With a work-related knee injury, I was propelled in the intriguing web of workers' comp, and into an arena that proved to change the course of my working career, as well as my life.

From the very beginning of reporting this knee injury, I made sure to get copies for myself of all accident reports, medical reports, diagnostic reports, and everything and anything else that was generated and related to my injury. I was also very careful as to what I signed or didn't sign regarding my workers' comp case. Because our local union had no one knowledgeable in workers' comp, I realized early in this nightmare, that I had better learn my legal rights for myself, because no one else was going to help me.

I first realized this when Theodore, the HR (human resource) leader at the time, and Jezebel, his associate, visited me one day while I was working daylights in Darkly. With these two people sitting in front of me, I informed them that I was now the least paid person in Darkly because of my injury.

Because I had a "loss of earning power," meaning I could not earn what I did before my injury because of my injury, I was entitled to a partial pay benefit making up some of the difference per the workers' comp law. These two HR people understood this benefit very well, especially being a self-insured employer in workers' comp. However, their ongoing practice was to never pay this benefit unless the injured worker acknowledged they had this partial pay coming to them.

After making this loss of earning power acknowledgment known to these two HR people, Theodore stated, as though this was his cue: "It's time to leave."

Then they were gone without addressing this benefit. I didn't push the issue then. I wasn't expecting to stay on medical work restrictions and on daylight shift for too long while losing out on earnings by not being able to work overtime, and not getting shift differential. My knee was going to heal soon, and all this would be over. This was wishful thinking at best on my part.

Not too long after this injury, I was sent for an MRI that showed an ACL (anterior cruciate ligament) tear. The company doctor was pushing for surgery while I was not. According to the Workers' Comp Act of Pennsylvania at that time, I had to treat with a doctor who was on the panel list of physicians supplied by my employer for the first ninety days. I found out after the fact that the orthopedic surgeon I chose on the panel list was not the best to do ACL reconstructive surgeries.

In fact, according to several other people, this doctor was not very good even in other areas of his so-called expertise. I found this out firsthand when this surgeon reinforced all this by his actions, or lack of, in dealing with my knee injury. With the company doctor pushing for surgery, he agreed along with HR to let me go off their panel list and consult with that "terrific" orthopedic surgeon that the shift coach, who I had reported the injury to, had recommended.

After several weeks of therapy trying to avoid surgery, I finally agreed to have this new orthopedic surgeon, Dr. Rite, perform an ACL reconstructive procedure on my knee. I did my homework well on my injury and what was involved in the surgery and rehab.

This surgery involved using screws to secure another piece of a ligament in place of my original ACL. I was adamant that biodegradable screws were used, and adamant that only part of my own hamstring was used to reconstruct the ligament. And I did not want morphine, an addictive drug, for a painkiller. Dr. Rite agreed to my wishes—or so I thought.

After doing my homework regarding my upcoming surgery, I had more homework to do regarding the Workers' Comp Act of Pennsylvania, which outlines the laws and regulations of workers' comp. I went to the county courthouse library looking up key information in the Act itself, and made copies of the pertinent information I thought I was going to need. In addition, I ordered the entire Workers' Comp Act book from the Pennsylvania State Book Store, which was available at that time to anyone for a price.

Three months after my injury, and four weeks before the scheduled date of surgery, I grumbled to the Lord Jesus over all this. I expressed that He was too severe in allowing this to happen. He was too severe in how He dealt with me—and I grumbled on . . .

I hated being on medical work restrictions. I hated the therapy. I hated dealing with the doctors. And I really hated the thought that I was going to be totally out of it while a bunch of strangers—who I will never know—were going to be gawking at and making all sorts of jokes about my body while tearing out part of my hamstring to piece together another ACL. I was going in and out of despair during all this time with this knee injury. I was so sure that the Lord was going to allow something to go wrong with the surgery that would leave me crippled for the rest of my life.

When the Lord Jesus had enough of my grumblings I threw at Him, in His presence, I felt His strong anger towards me. He then reminded me of a vision He had given me years ago of a future event where I saw myself walking. Through this vision, the Lord assured me that I would not be crippled the rest of my life. The Lord also made sure to remind me that I had submitted to His dealings, and that it was my actions that justified His spanking.

The Lord Jesus also made it clear that He did not spank me in His anger or in His wrath; He was not out to destroy me or be cruel to me. The Lord profoundly made me aware that He spanked me because of His great love for me, to remove the hindrance my irreverent sins caused in our relationship, to ensure I learned perfect obedience to Him, and to draw me closer to Himself. Through His spanking, the Lord Jesus began engraving in my heart a reverent fear of God, without which, I cannot grow in intimacy with the Almighty Lord God of the Universe.

Once I repented and asked for forgiveness for provoking the Lord to anger with my grumblings, I felt His overwhelming love and reassurance that He was still in control. The Lord God knew exactly His plans on using His spanking rod to achieve His purpose for my career and life, to demonstrate His grace and power, and all for His praise, honor and glory.

After I submitted to the Lord again in all this and resigned myself to having this surgery, I went into this with a good attitude. It was right before the scary Y2K turnover event. People all over the world were apprehensive during that time, stockpiling food, batteries, and all sorts of other survival paraphernalia for this projected tragic event that was supposed to stop the world from turning—so to speak—all because the computer systems were not supposed to recognize the new millennium turnover.

I had a very different reason for stockpiling goods at that time. I supplied myself with enough groceries and things that I thought I was going to need for the six weeks of being grounded at home without being able to drive. Surgery was scheduled for the middle of December, so I also prepared for Christmas and all the doings for that special occasion.

I picked up my brace that I was going to live in for several weeks after surgery, making sure it was the correct size. I made the arrangements for my physical therapy before surgery so there would be no delay. It was going to be a long haul to recoup from this surgery, and rehab was going to be difficult. But I was determined from the start that I was going to do absolutely everything I was supposed to do, told to do, could do, and even more, if possible, to ensure a full recovery from this surgery so that I could return to my normal shift and job as soon as possible.

I had all my ducks in a row, as they say. However, I had no clue that by doing so would make all these ducks that much easier to shoot all at once; I would find this out soon enough.

Chapter 44
Surgery

My surgery was the first one scheduled for that day. I remembered little about the surgery preps, except to notice that everyone in the operating room seemed to know exactly what they were supposed to be doing as each worked on their responsibility, and then I was out of it. The doctor had ordered morphine as a painkiller, which I did not know until after the fact. I distinctly remembered telling this doctor I did not want morphine; I thought he agreed to abide by my wishes!

Once in the recovery room, I started having difficulty breathing. The nurse who was attending me seemed indifferent to my concern that I couldn't breathe by her response, "Well, your oxygen is at ninety-eight percent. You're fine."

I did not know at that time that I was allergic to morphine. My response to her indifference was a little firmer: "I don't care what my oxygen level shows; I'm telling you I cannot breathe."

Again, she seemed indifferent: "So long as you're not breaking out in hives, you'll be fine."

As I continued having difficulty breathing, I wondered: *What is with her attitude towards my concern? Breathing is a vital part of being able to stay alive. Is it because this is a workers' comp case? Oh, I know! They were probably gawking at my body while I was out of it and making fun of my tattoos. She probably has a poor opinion of me thinking I'm a pothead. But that was a very long time ago. And these people don't know me from Adam. Or should I say Eve? Surely that can't be her reasoning for being indifferent to my concern of not being able to breathe?*

I was guessing these folks had not seen too many tattoos of a marijuana leaf with a mouse running up the stem during their profession (the mouse represented me as Mickie for my nickname in the Army). I couldn't think of any other reason for this nurse's indifference to my difficulty in breathing.

Once I found out that it was morphine I was given, I didn't let them give me any more. I left the recovery room and headed home breathing a little easier, but I still did not know I was allergic to morphine. And I did not know the pills prescribed for pain also had a derivative of morphine.

That evening after surgery, two very dear friends of mine, an older couple who were like parents, came to sleep overnight at my home to make sure I was okay after this surgery. Marie and Wayne wanted to help by bringing their own bedding, which I appreciated. But the fuzzy orange blanket they brought, though never used and still in the bag it came in, was so old that once out of the bag, it disintegrated into hundreds of tiny orange fuzz-balls that immediately went airborne, flying all over my living room where the couch was open for them to sleep on.

I took a pain pill before going to bed that night that did nothing to lessen the pain. With having a full brace on my leg, dealing with unbearable pain, having another allergic reaction with the pain pill that this time was causing me to itch all over, and having nightmares all night of tiny orange fuzz-balls attacking me—needless to say—my first night after surgery was not good.

In the morning, I begged Wayne to please, vacuum my living room and try to capture all these fuzz-balls that seemed to still be flying around, which he gladly did. Marie and Wayne knew the Lord Jesus, and their love and care towards me showed it.

The day after surgery, my entire leg, from the top of my thigh to my foot, was a complete mass of bruises of black and blue and purple, and every color in between. I had no way of knowing this much bruising was not normal after an ACL reconstructive surgery, at least not until after the post-op doctor's appointment. Then my big toe became extremely painful, which sent me into a panic mode that caused me to cry hysterically. *Mom's gangrene started with her toes! Am I going to lose my leg also?*

That morning, I spoke with the surgeon, Dr. Rite, and told him of my allergic reaction to morphine. He prescribed another painkiller and told me that my first day would be my worst with the pain. As time went on, he proved to be very wrong.

Dr. Rite was on vacation for my first post-op appointment ten days after surgery, so I saw his associate, who I had never met before. The leg from my thigh to my foot was still very visibly bruised. In the examining room, I expressed concern that my big toe was becoming very painful, as was the rest of my foot. This doctor ignored my concern and spoke over me to his accompanied nurse concerning my next appointment: "Don't schedule her back for at least four weeks. I don't want Rite to see the leg while it's this bad."

That wasn't very comforting to hear! You mean all legs don't look this bad after an ACL reconstruction? And this is ten days after the surgery. You should have seen it the day after. But I didn't voice any of my thoughts. I really didn't have a chance to speak much at all. He finally turned and spoke to me: "Everything looks good. Keep wearing the brace and doing the therapy, and come back in four weeks."

I asked him again, "But what about the pain in my big toe?"

Too late; he was gone!

I hobbled out of the examining room to the waiting area where another dear friend of mine was sitting, who also knew the Lord and who brought me to this appointment. I expressed to her my concerns and what this doctor said. I knew my dear friend was a prayer warrior and was praying for me, as I knew others were.

As time went on, I kept wearing the brace and faithfully doing all the therapy I was told to do, but the pain only increased in intensity. My next appointment was with Dr. Rite, but by then, the leg showed no signs of bruising. I expressed my concern to Dr. Rite that my big toe and foot was still very painful, as well as the knee and the entire leg by this time. Dr. Rite took his index finger and trailed it over my big toe, but said nothing about the pain: "Wear the brace two to three more weeks, don't drive during that time, and come back in six weeks."

"But what about all the pain I'm dealing with?"

Too late again; he was gone!

I sat there wondering: *Don't these doctors care about what I have to say?* Then it dawned on me. *Oh, I forgot! It's that workers' comp stigma!*

After this appointment, my knee started moving on me, and popping, and becoming increasingly painful. It wasn't only the pain that concerned me; it was the thought that something had gone wrong with the ACL graft. The knee was so much worse now than before the surgery. Something had to be wrong to be causing all this. My physical therapist told me the pain and movement of my knee was in my head. *That wasn't very comforting to be told! Oh, I forgot again! It's that workers' comp stigma!*

While dealing with all this pain and trying to get someone to believe me, I had to deal with the hassles of workers' comp. There were forms that I should have received within ten days of reporting my injury that were never sent, which I did not realize at that time. Now that I was off work, these forms and others, including multiple copies of some, were being sent requesting my signature. I was still due that partial pay benefit I was denied from before I went off work. My employer also overpaid me for three weeks, which I wanted to promptly repay. But Theodore would not allow me to repay this overpayment until I was back to work.

I had to do more homework well and quick learning for myself. I needed to understand what I should or should not be signing with these forms, how I was supposed to be paid while on workers' comp, and what my legal rights were. I needed to safeguard myself in what was the beginning of a real workers' comp nightmare.

I went back-and-forth with Theodore and HR while I was off work, quoting the Workers' Comp Act as to my understanding how the system was supposed to work, and quoting our union's contract agreement with management. They should know the law and how this system works better than I should! They've been through this before with many other injured workers. How could all of this have gotten into such a mess?

Finally, in getting Theodore to understand what was out of compliance with the Workers' Comp Act, what was incorrectly done per our union's contract agreement, and what needed done now to correct everything, I calmly but firmly told him while on the phone: "It's not my job to make sure your people do their jobs correctly." He took my comment well; I'm sure he knew the truth in what I just stated.

In the midst of all this, as though this were not enough, the company hired a new nurse for their plant Medical Department, who made my life very difficult, and who acted as though she was the doctor. Soon afterward, they also hired a new plant doctor, who acted as though he was the nurse. For some reason, the previous doctor was let go while I was off.

From the very beginning, this knee injury was to be a real lesson and training ground in my life, and in more ways than I understood at that time. With God's help, I was learning everything well, though I was learning the hardest way possible—in the midst of a fiery furnace.

Chapter 45

Second Opinion

It was a few months into this nightmare when I started losing confidence in Dr. Rite. After trying a prednisone pack and then a cortisone shot, I started looking for another orthopedic surgeon for a second opinion. I needed to know what was causing me so much pain.

Dr. Rite released me back to work on sedentary duty after four months, but I asked to include using the forklift as well. I wanted to carry my own weight by doing meaningful work, and found plenty to do within my medical work restrictions, including work that was not supposed to be mine to do. I even worked part-time in a salaried position helping with the material packagers' work order schedules. All this was significant to be able to do in a union shop, but it also reinforced to many coworkers their thoughts that I was anti-union. No one, including me, knew where God was going to lead me from here in this labor union.

Even though I was kept on the daylight shift and doing meaningful work, what I really wanted was to go back on my normal shift schedule, do my normal material packager job, and put all this behind me. But that wasn't happening anytime soon.

While on steady daylight, I rotated through all the crews when they worked on their daylight shifts. Some coworkers, who were not from my normal crew, thought I was milking (prolonging) this injury, and to show this, they put a stool (as used to milk a cow) in the women's restroom for me to find.

When I found this stool, I took it with me, walked into the control room filled with these men, held it up high for all to see, and then asked in a no-nonsense tone of voice loud enough for everyone to hear: "So, what happened to our employer's anti-harassment policy?" You could have heard a pin drop.

I put the stool back in the restroom—it proved useful in there—but never heard another peep from anyone about milking this injury. No one had any idea what I was going through with this injury or with this workers' comp nightmare.

About five months post-op and still dealing with so much pain, I'm in the examining room once again with Dr. Rite. I insisted on another MRI, as I needed to know for sure what was wrong—and he agreed. Before leaving his office building, I told one of the nurses that I wanted a copy of the MRI report as soon as she received a copy—and she agreed.

It was a few days after the MRI when Dr. Rite called me personally and left a message on my answering machine: "The MRI report states nothing is wrong with the knee, everything is fine. We'll talk when you come in for your appointment."

I sensed he was lying to me; he was holding back some truth that he did not want me to know. A copy of the MRI report was never sent to me per my earlier instructions. I contacted the hospital myself for a copy, and after two attempts was told I could stop by and get a copy. I had intended to do just that, until the Lord directed me differently. I didn't know why, but I didn't need to understand why. I followed God's leading and did not force the issue with getting the report before my next appointment with Dr. Rite. By this time, I had another orthopedic surgeon picked out for a second opinion.

At my next appointment, I handed a nurse at the nurses' station a copy of my MRI films I was told to bring. In the examining room with Dr. Rite, he adamantly stated, "The MRI report states the ACL graft is fine. There is nothing wrong with the knee. Everything is the way it should be post-op. You'll be fine. Eventually, the pain will just go away on its own."

I just stared at him after he spoke. *That's a smirk on his face. Oh, I get it! It's that workers' comp stigma rearing its ugly head again! He doesn't believe me, as he hasn't all along.*

I made eye contact with Dr. Rite while pointing to the knee and told him in a firm, calm and deliberate tone: "I cannot be in this much pain and nothing be wrong."

Again, Dr. Rite was adamant: "I'm telling you the MRI showed nothing is wrong. The pain will eventually go away."

Why didn't he just say what he was really thinking: "You have no pain, you liar. You're just lazy and trying to get out of work."

Maybe he would have thought differently had he known I was doing more work at that time than even on my old job? Maybe he would have thought differently had he known my relationship and accountability to the Lord God of the Universe? But what did he know? The workers' comp stigma was just too powerful for him to believe anything else could be wrong.

I stopped by the nurses' station on my way out and requested again for a copy of the MRI report. The nurse who I had requested this from over two weeks earlier, got up and left upon hearing my request. Another nurse finally supplied me with a copy of my own.

Once outside the building, I started reading the MRI report while walking to the garage; I didn't want to wait another minute to read it. After reading that the report stated a screw might be protruding into the joint space, I became furious. *So, Dr. Rite, the report does state something could be wrong after all! Who is the real liar in this workers' comp case?*

I realized I was no doctor, but a screw, however it was protruding, could seem to be the cause of some pain. I made an abrupt about-face and headed straight back into the medical building. I walked past the receptionist station and headed straight for the nurses' station, and once there, almost demanded, "I want my MRI films back."

My demeanor left no room for discussion. Someone handed them back to me: "Thank you. I will bring them back when I'm done with them."

And out I went for my long drive home with a lot to think about, and a lot to talk about with the Lord.

Had Dr. Rite told me the truth about what the MRI report stated, I would have accepted it with a sigh of relief that at least there was a possible cause of pain that eventually would go away, as these screws were supposed to be biodegradable that dissolve.

But he lied to me, which really upset me. I understood now the Lord's direction in not obtaining the report for myself before this appointment. Had I read the report and had an opportunity to discuss with Dr. Rite what it stated, I may not have pursued a second opinion. The Lord knew it was time I moved on to another doctor to find out the real cause of the pain, which apparently was more than just a screw protruding into the joint space.

Once home from this appointment, I found Dr. Ortho's phone number where I had left it on my dining room table just waiting for me to call. He was part of the orthopedic surgeon group who took care of the professional athletes in the city of Pittsburgh.

My first appointment with Dr. Ortho went well. He seemed to know what he was talking about. He was nice to me and treated me with respect. Now that I had the ears of a totally different orthopedic surgeon who had no history of my case, I laid it on him: "My big toe is really painful, and my foot, and my whole leg."

He was listening. And on I went with all my complaints and weird sensations I had been experiencing: "When I touch this part of my knee, I feel it over here. When I touch this part, I feel it over here. And this part of my leg doesn't even have any feelings when I touch it."

He caught on that I had nerve damage but didn't elaborate. He also didn't think the screw protruding was the cause of the pain.

An x-ray taken at his office that day showed osteopenia in the knee area. He talked about getting a bone scan but then never ordered one. I was careful not to say anything negative about Dr. Rite, only that he was the one who did the surgery, and that I wanted a second opinion as to why I was having so much pain.

I was in compliance with the workers' comp regulations in seeing another orthopedic surgeon. Although my employers' Medical Department was being difficult to deal with, they accepted that it was time for a second opinion.

After seeing Dr. Ortho, I went back to see Dr. Rite a few weeks later. He said the screw protruding in the joint was dissolved by then, and that osteopenia was not uncommon after knee surgery. He also said that he didn't think I needed a bone scan, and then added, "And I don't think you have RSD."

I had no idea what RSD was or why he mentioned it, but decided not to even bother to ask him; he would probably lie to me anyway. As a matter of fact—I realized too late—I made a mistake seeing him again. It was time Dr. Rite got totally out of the picture.

Once I obtained Dr. Ortho's report, I read that he stated, "She has some signs of reflex sympathetic dystrophy." I then noticed it indicated that Dr. Rite was sent a copy before my last visit with him. No wonder Dr. Rite had a lot to say, and a lot to disagree with.

Was the reflex sympathetic dystrophy the "RSD" Dr. Rite mentioned he didn't think I had? I had more homework to do. I did extensive research on this RSD, and I didn't like what I was learning. I recognized the correlation of the progressions of my symptoms to what I was learning were the symptoms of RSD. *Can I really have this off-the-wall neurological pain disorder? And if I do, what do I do now? Where do I go from here?*

After much thought and prayer, I decided to go back to Dr. Ortho. Since he was the first who thought I had symptoms of RSD, I was sure he would help and guide me in what I should do next.

Chapter 46

The Plague

Dr. Ortho stated that my next follow-up with him should be in three months. After what I was learning about RSD, I didn't wait till then. Within two weeks of my last visit with Dr. Rite, I was back to see Dr. Ortho, who seemed irritated that I had come back so soon. While I was on the examining table, he started examining the knee, holding the leg up, and telling me that the surgery was done well. I told him, "I never said the surgery was not done well. I want to know about the RSD."

With this, he abruptly tossed my leg on the table and walked over to the counter where an intern was standing; she was present for training. I wondered what she thought of his actions he just displayed? Dr. Ortho's demeanor was totally different than from my first visit with him. I was very upset with this and thought: *What is his problem, and why the change in his demeanor? Oh, yeah! The workers' comp stigma strikes again!*

After Dr. Rite read Dr. Ortho's comments on RSD in his report, I was sure the two of them had a long discussion about my case. I could only imagine what was said, but God knew. The actions of Dr. Ortho now told me that he no longer believed I was truthful in describing how much pain I was dealing with.

Dr. Ortho came back to the table where he had left me and handed me a written referral to a neurologist without saying much else. I left his presence extremely upset. Once in my car, I burst out crying to the Lord: "What do I do now? Where do I go from here? No one believes me. No one wants to help me. I am in so much pain. Is there not one person out there, anywhere, who believes me and is willing to help me?"

As the Lord comforted me, He brought to mind the bone scan Dr. Ortho neglected to order for me. I thought the bone scan had to do with the osteopenia in my knee. I was to find out later why this bone scan was so important to have. With remembering the bone scan, I called Dr. Ortho's office on my cell phone. Darren, the medical secretary, answered. I told him: "Dr. Ortho mentioned getting a bone scan before but never ordered one."

Darren was nice and asked me to hold on while he looked into this. Once he came back on the phone, he said he would mail me a prescription for a bone scan that could be used at any hospital.

After I had the bone scan done, I made sure to get a copy of the report myself, and asked for the actual films. Once I knew the report was sent to Dr. Ortho, I contacted his office. I was told that the asymmetric increased activity in the right knee and tibia plateau was suggestive of RSD. I found out later that in the early stages of RSD, a bone scan was the only diagnostic test that supported RSD; at least that was the belief at the time. Now with the bone scan results, Dr. Ortho was able to confirm his belief that I had RSD to the neurologist prior to my visit with her.

By this time, my whole right leg was feeling like needles were pricking it, and not too long after this, my whole body was feeling these pricking needles that became painful. Then I started getting jerked out of my sleep with a hot burning pain in my left thigh, as if someone had put a hot poker on it; although it was my right knee that had the surgery. To alleviate this burning pain, I would get out of bed and start walking around my home in the middle of the night to calm it down. There were even times that light touches on my leg with a bed sheet caused excruciating pain.

It was going to be over four weeks before I could get in to see the neurologist. I was going in and out of despair over all the weird excruciating pain I was dealing with. I needed to talk to someone about what this RSD was, and if I really had it.

I found an RSD support group over the Internet with a phone number inviting anyone who needed help to call. Although a little reluctant, I called the number. I was nice and explained why I was calling: "Hi. I got your name off the Internet offering support for those with RSD. I have some questions I thought maybe you could help me with. I'm not sure but I think I may have RSD."

The woman who answered was anything but nice: "Why are you calling on a holiday? You should not be bothering me today."

Wow! Was I taken aback! The Fourth of July was Tuesday. I was calling on Monday. I responded, "Today is not the holiday. Tomorrow is the holiday. You know what—never mind—sorry I bothered you."

I hung up and immediately burst out crying to the Lord in total brokenness: "I don't want this RSD! I don't want to deal with this pain for the rest of my life! I want this nightmare to end! I am so tired of dealing with people who don't believe me, who are mean to me only because I am trying to get help!"

From the time I injured this knee, only once did I feel the Lord's anger, which was the night four weeks prior to surgery when I grumbled to Him that He was too severe with His dealings. Other than that one time, throughout this entire nightmare ordeal, I felt the Lord's overwhelming love.

The woman from the RSD support group called me back a few days later apologizing for her response. She explained that her service dog was sick and close to being put to sleep. I expressed my sympathy and understanding on how she felt about her dog. We talked a while as I explained what my symptoms were and asked if she thought I had RSD. She wouldn't give me a firm answer. We ended this conversation on a much better note then we did on our first one.

Until I saw the neurologist, I was on my own researching and learning about this RSD that I now believed without any doubt I had. RSD is short for reflex sympathetic dystrophy, and is also known as complex regional pain syndrome, or CRPS for short. To make it simple to understand: RSD is a neurological pain disorder.

Anyone can develop RSD from the trauma of an injury or surgery. The nerves get so damaged from the trauma that they never heal. But instead, these damaged nerves go berserk and send pain signals to the trauma site even after the site itself may have healed, and may also send pain signals to other parts of the body not initially affected by the trauma. These damaged nerves also affect the blood flow, which causes extremities to become cold, blue, and more painful, with irreversible deformities occurring in the worst cases. Each person's RSD condition and pain are individualized and unpredictable. Becoming totally disabled from RSD is not uncommon.

The best treatment for RSD is to get the affected limb moving and functioning as soon and as much as possible, to try to get the nerves to understand that there is no longer an injury or cause to send pain signals. However, neither too much activity or too much inactivity is good; there needs to be a happy medium. Once I understood all this and realized the ACL graft was fine, I stopped babying my leg and started using it as normal as I could while trying to ignore all the pain it was still causing me.

When my employer's Medical Department, and their third-party insurance claim person, Jerry, got a whiff I may have RSD, red flags flew up. The rules of workers' comp were about to change. RSD plus workers' comp equals the plague, both with physicians and insurance companies. There really isn't any cure for RSD, which makes it a lifelong painful condition with treatments that are very expensive.

Finally, after weeks of waiting, I found myself sitting in the waiting room for my visit with Dr. Donna, the woman neurologist Dr. Ortho had referred me to. As I waited, I was given a slew of forms to fill out. One of these forms had diagrams of what I can only describe as a more fuller and rounded version of the stick art form of naked-genderless people. I was instructed to circle every part on these "naked people" that corresponded to where on my body I was experiencing pain.

I glanced around at the other people waiting to be seen. I wondered: *Where are these people from? What kind of pain are they dealing with? What landed them here?* Some of these people looked scared and nervous, while others didn't seem to care one way or another that they were there. A few looked like they were strung out on drugs. I was guessing painkillers grabbed a hold on some of these people and were controlling their lives now.

There was a coffee station in the waiting room available for anyone wishing to help themselves to a cup; one woman decided to do just that. As I watched her empty several packages of sugar in her coffee cup, I noticed that she seemed the most strung out. I made a resolve in my heart: *I am not going down that same route. I will not allow drugs of any kind to control my life again.*

When I met Dr. Donna, she seemed nice and knowledgeable about RSD. She gave me a prescription for Neurontin, a drug that was supposed to help with the RSD nerve pain. She also explained about lumbar sympathetic nerve block injections that were given in the back to numb the nerves to stop the pain signals. She then wrote out a prescription for these nerve blocks, and referred me to a pain clinic on the other side of Pittsburgh—further from my home—to have these done.

The treatment plan was for a series of five of these nerve blocks to start with. After each nerve block injection was given, I would need a designated driver to get me back home. I learned that the treatment for RSD needed to start no later than three months from the onset of symptoms for the best prognosis. It was now seven months past from my very first symptom. I was concerned with this delay, but it wasn't my fault no one believed I was dealing with so much pain.

Getting these nerve blocks was a nightmare in itself. Unbeknown to me at the beginning of this treatment plan, the pain clinic Dr. Donna referred me to was a well-known training facility for anesthesiologists, the doctors who administered these nerve block injections. I understood well that there was a need for doctors to have hands-on training to get proficient with procedures they were learning. But there needed to be a rotation through their guinea pigs. People are not pincushions!

There were foreign doctors in training from many different countries sticking needles in my back that were six inches or more in length. An x-ray machine was used to guide the needle to the precise spot that was needed to numb the nerve. The first nerve block injection was administered without incident, but they missed the mark; it didn't help at all. After experiencing the first injection, I knew a little of what to expect with the second.

While lying on my stomach and unable to see what was going on, a foreign doctor tried injecting the second nerve block. But after several pricks, and feeling the needle going in and out and moving about, and with this second procedure taking so much longer than the first one took, I finally said something in total frustration: "Are you guys almost done yet?"

No answer. I wanted to say more, but I was really not in any position—literally—to complain too much. After a few more pricks, and feeling the needle moving in and out and around in the back some more, finally, I was told it was all over.

Once back in the preparation area, Dr. Scope, the woman doctor in charge, came in to see how I was doing. I wasted no time expressing my complaint to her: "How many times did you guys stick me with the needle?"

I was furious being a guinea pig pincushion again, and even more furious with her answer: "Well, we had to find the right spot."

Really? I kept my thoughts and anger under control. They sure found the right spot all right on this second nerve block. It helped the pain the most out of all five blocks that I had. However, in the process of finding the right spot, they poked a hole, or maybe more, in my spine. The next day after this injection, I became so nauseous, vomited, and had a headache that felt like my head was about to explode. Marie, my dear friend, finally convinced me to go to the hospital emergency room.

During my next appointment, I complained to the nurse who was putting in an IV—with someone else's blood on her ungloved hands—that the last injection administered landed me in the emergency room with a hole poked in my spine. I related the excruciating headache with lying down helping to ease the pain, and the nausea and vomiting I experienced. She seemed indignant that I would dare complain, and then wasn't very gentle with the IV needle. *Maybe I should have waited till after she was done with the IV before I complained?* She didn't seem to believe me, and why should she? Silly me, this was a workers' comp case.

I felt totally helpless believing I had absolutely no other choice, but to get these nerve blocks at this facility that used me as their guinea pig pincushion for their doctors in training. With the time delay in receiving treatments for the RSD, it was imperative that these nerve block injections were administered correctly.

Out of five nerve block injections, only two were administered correctly and helped relieve the pain. But even then, after only a few days, the pain came back with a vengeance. It was as if the nerves wanted to send me a message: "You mess with us and we'll get you back."

Only those who suffer from this weird RSD condition can understand the unpredictable and excruciating pain it can cause.

Chapter 47

Conspiracy

It's almost one year now from the initial date of my knee injury. Four doctors have confirmed that I have RSD. With the bills coming in for these expensive nerve block injections, my employer's Medical Department, and Jerry, were getting concerned with this diagnosis and the medical expense.

For whatever reason I don't remember now, I requested Jerry to send me copies of my medical records he had been receiving during all this time. Jerry obliged, but with a notice that in the future, I was to get these records directly from my treating physicians and not from him, and this was fine with me.

While reading the initial report of Dr. Ortho that Jerry had sent me, I realized something was different. Getting out my earlier copy of the same report I received from Dr. Ortho's office, I did a comparison between my copy and Jerry's copy.

Wow! I could not believe what Jerry had done! He actually did a manual cut and paste. Three-quarters of Dr. Ortho's second page of his initial report that included stating I had symptoms of RSD were missing. The before and after paragraphs were put together in a way that no one could tell anything was ever between them. On the bottom of the page, I could see a fraction of what was cut out. This was a workers' comp insurance claim representative falsifying documentation, and it took a significant effort on Jerry's part in doing so, as the report was his faxed copy and not an electronic copy.

After receiving Dr. Ortho's altered report from Jerry, I also received a medical authorization release form from him with instructions for me to sign it and send it back. Once signed, this authorization release form would have given Jerry—and anyone else with a copy—the legal authorization for the following: to obtain any and all medical records from anyone who had ever treated me, at any time, for any reason; to interview these medical physicians and attendants; and to interview and correspond with any and all current and past employers.

I had nothing to hide. I rarely saw a doctor over the years, and never claimed a work-related injury with any other employer. But it was the principle that was involved. I read this medical authorization release form a few times, and after just receiving Jerry's altered report of Dr. Ortho, I made a firm and defiant decision: *I'm not signing and returning this form! You've got to be kidding me! Do they really think I'm that stupid?*

There is nothing confidential in a workers' comp case. All this time they have been receiving everything and anything they wanted regarding this work-related injury without any signed authorization from me to do so. Anything else regarding my past life—they didn't need to know about.

My employer's Medical Department claimed they knew nothing about this release form sent from Jerry. However, while reviewing my records in HR, I saw a note from the medical secretary stating I had not returned this release form yet with my signature. After Jerry's altered report of Dr. Ortho, and with my employer's medical department and HR getting so involved and lying to me also, I trusted everyone even less than before—if that were possible. I ignored this release form and just put it aside.

By this time, the local union officers recognized my self-taught knowledge of workers' comp from when I got them involved as witnesses over some issues since my return to work, and any thoughts that I was anti-union had dissipated. With the knowledge that I had learned, they decided to appoint me as a workers' comp rep for our union members, without pay. With this appointment, I jumped at their offer to attend a workers' comp training seminar to learn more about this intriguing web of workers' comp.

A group of lawyers conducted the training and added to my knowledge, which became very beneficial for me and others in our union. At this seminar, I received copies of all the different forms that the Department of Labor and Industry for Pa used for workers' comp, and learned the ins and outs of these forms. And I was correct regarding that medical authorization release form; it was definitely not a form that I needed to sign.

After I returned from this seminar, my employer's Medical Department decided to bring me in for a physical by their own new company doctor. And I was ready for this one! I went armed with a signed letter that I wrote up myself, revoking any and all authority from my employer for releasing or obtaining any medical records from any of my personal physicians, and stated they were not to have any contact with my personal physicians.

The new Ms. Nurse had a conniption when I gave her my letter, claiming they had the right to any information pertaining to my work-related injury, and of course, I understood that. My letter was not going to change any of their rights to receive any of my work-related medical information. But by now in this workers' comp nightmare, I about had it with everyone involved!

I told Ms. Nurse in a firm tone that only reinforced I knew what I was talking about: "I know your rights, and I know my rights, and I want that letter kept in my medical file." She wasn't happy with me, but at that point, I really didn't care.

After this meeting with Ms. Nurse, Jerry sent again the same medical authorization release form certified. I guessed he thought that would intimidate me into signing it, but that didn't happen. I countered his certified letter with my own letter reiterating his authority to receive only the medical information pertaining to my injury and related RSD condition. I also stated for the record, that he had no legal authority to contact any of my personal physicians.

The situation was getting heated from all fronts. I became elusive with my employer's Medical Department and their Ms. Nurse, who thought she was the doctor, and who seemed obsessed with the fact that I was diagnosed with RSD. I relied on God's help and direction, and having learned my legal rights, I was confident through His strength in exercising them.

From the very beginning of this nightmare, I always made the final decision regarding any medication I was given. The morning after taking Neurontin for the first time, it took over twenty minutes for my blaring alarm clock to finally wake me up. That morning at work, while still feeling the effects of that drug, I came within inches of smashing with the forklift a very expensive and hard to replace piece of machinery stored in the warehouse while the production line was down for maintenance. I realized then that I could not work safely while taking Neurontin; one or the other had to be eliminated. I decided the Neurontin needed to go.

But the time came that I realized I needed to make more medical decisions for myself in this workers' comp nightmare. Someone had shot all my ducks I had in a row long ago. Something needed done to change the course I was on.

After five nerve block injections with so many different anesthesiologists administering them with varying results, I canceled the appointment for the sixth injection. My firm decision was to never again be a guinea pig pincushion for their doctors in training. My plan was to try for another series of nerve blocks administered by someone competent. A friend had given me the name of an anesthesiologist that she had received nerve blocks from for another condition, who was nearer to where I lived.

At my next visit with Dr. Donna, I noticed a sign at her facility with the names of the doctors she originally sent me to for these injections. A foreign woman doctor who was at my last nerve block appointment, walked in with Dr. Donna for this visit. I started adding everything together, and I didn't care for the answer. But it didn't matter! I was taking control of my treatments from here on. I had done everything I was told to do and thought I needed to do to heal from this nightmare, but so far, nothing was working.

I explained to Dr. Donna that the nerve blocks needed to be administered by someone closer to my home, and that I was going to see another anesthesiologist for further treatment. I also told her I was dissatisfied with the facility she originally recommended with so many different doctors administering the injections.

I then spoke to the foreign woman doctor and asked her directly, "Were you the one who gave me the last shot?"

This doctor just stared at me without answering.

I had made it clear to Dr. Scope that I wanted her to give the injection at my last appointment, and not one of her doctors in training. Being on my stomach while these were administered left me with no ability to verify who was really giving the injection.

Dr. Donna had tried to get me to see their psychologist during my first visit with her, but I firmly refused. Now she was adamant I see their psychologist stating that was part of the treatment for RSD; I was just as adamant in refusing. With absolutely nothing confidential in a workers' comp case, I wasn't about to give someone else the opportunity to interrogate me in this nightmare regarding the weird pain I was dealing with, and to generate more reports for anyone to read. I left this appointment with Dr. Donna with a course of action of my own.

It was time I saw Dr. Delano, who was supposed to be a competent doctor in administering nerve blocks according to my friend. I gave his office all the workers' comp information they requested prior to my appointment, but never told my employer's Medical Department I was going to this doctor. I had five business days to inform my employer of this visit per the Workers' Comp Act for this doctor to get paid. I was using everything I learned over the course of this past year regarding workers' comp to my greatest advantage.

Dr. Delano and Jerry had contact with each other before my appointment. I'm not sure who made the initial contact, but it didn't matter, the results would have been the same regardless. There seemed to have been a concerted agreement between these two, that the objective for this appointment was for Dr. Delano to convince me and my other doctors that I did not have RSD.

Jerry had sent Dr. Delano the bone scan report and other reports from my doctors before my appointment, and without my prior consent or knowledge. He really didn't need that medical authorization release form signed from me for anything, other than obtaining what he did not legally have the right to obtain.

As I sat in the waiting room unaware of the conspiracy going on between Dr. Delano and Jerry, I was given a bunch of forms to fill out similar to all the other forms I have many times before painstakingly completed at the other pain clinics. By this time, I was so sick and tired of these forms and the paperwork. Someone, somewhere, had made thousands of dollars with the copyright of these naked-genderless-people forms, I was sure of it.

Dr. Delano was very arrogant with me during his exam. When I told him I was feeling the pricking needle pain throughout my body, he asked, "Even in your eyeballs?"

He then adamantly told me that I did not have complex regional pain syndrome, using the newer name given to RSD, and stated I needed to have another bone scan done and some other nerve conductive tests.

Dr. Delano became downright mean when he realized that I refused to believe what he was telling me. He wasn't living with my pain 24/7 as I was. He left the room in an angry huff with the plan of coming back in. I didn't wait for his return. I got dressed and left his office building without even stopping at the front desk. On my way out the door, I glanced down the hallway and saw him sitting in his office with his side turned. He was on the phone, most likely speaking to Jerry.

Once inside my car, I sat there and burst out crying to the Lord again. I was hitting a brick wall every which way I turned trying to get help dealing with this RSD. It's no wonder people with chronic pain disorders have such a hard time dealing with their pain. When no one believes you are dealing with pain and will not help you, it just aggravates the pain. It becomes a vicious cycle that cannot be broken.

I called Jerry for some reason after this horrible appointment, and was told that his last day of employment there was the same day that I saw Dr. Delano. I often wondered if their conversation was recorded and he was terminated? God would know, and I could only have my own gut feelings as to what happened.

Dr. Delano had sent Dr. Donna his report before my next appointment with her. While in her waiting room again, I glanced around at what seemed like the same people I had seen before. *They still seem strung out. Does this vicious cycle of pain, drugs, doctors who don't know how to help, and more pain ever end?*

By this time, I had tried numerous pain medications that included a variety of narcotics and anti-depressants. Some of these drugs didn't help at all. Some had such weird side effects and made me feel high again that I refused to take them.

While speaking with Dr. Donna in her examining room, I realized that she so readily accepted the conclusion of Dr. Delano's report when he adamantly claimed that I did not have RSD. She justified her flip-flopped diagnosis by stating, "But you're so functional. You're really not that bad yet."

I stared at her for a few moments before I spoke, "I thought the goal was to treat this thing so that I didn't get disabled or irreversible deformities. Because I can still function does not mean I am not dealing with an awful lot of pain I rather not deal with." *The workers' comp stigma is rearing its ugly head again!*

I then firmly stated regarding the nerve blocks: "It was not fair to me to be their guinea pig pincushion for all those doctors in training. With the time delay before these treatments, it was imperative that these injections were administered correctly."

Dr. Donna's only response was to try again to convince me to meet with their psychologist. Once again, I adamantly refused. Before leaving her office, I made the firm decision that Dr. Donna was not going to dictate my medical treatment for the RSD any longer. I was going to keep her as my RSD doctor on paper only to keep my employer's Medical Department off my back, but only until I sought the Lord on what I should be doing next.

After this appointment with Dr. Donna, that night I woke up every twenty to thirty minutes from literal nightmares of demons and people beating on me and trying to kill me. All this stress of trying to get help with this RSD aggravated the condition more.

During all this time, I kept Dr. Ortho as the orthopedic doctor who was overseeing my medical work restrictions. After he read the bone scan report and realized I wasn't another workers' comp stigma case he was led to believe, we had a good relationship going forward. I never told him about my dissatisfaction with his referral, Dr. Donna, or my plans on weaning away from her care.

I started on my own swimming for therapy, which helped once the water stopped hurting my legs, and took calcium for the osteopenia. I saw a gradual improvement without medication and nerve blocks, and realized that the Lord was still in control over my situation. He knew that it was best I did not get any more nerve blocks; although I did not know this at the time.

Chapter 48
Independent Medical Exam

I first got wind that I was scheduled for an IME (independent medical exam) while leaving after my last appointment with Dr. Donna. Her receptionist desk found the appointment on their computer system and spoke about it in my hearing. It was some time after this that I received a certified letter from Sandra, who I didn't know, regarding this IME.

These IMEs are not unusual for workers' comp cases, and are ordered and paid for by the workers' comp insurance company, or in my case, a workers' comp self-insured employer. Too often, these IME doctors favor those who pay for these exams without regards to what the actual exam verifies as a diagnosis.

I was determined not to submit to this IME. Per the Workers' Comp Act, I believed I had language in the regulations to support such a refusal after just having the company doctor examine me; all this was based on my employer being self-insured with workers' comp. After what I just went through with Jerry's interference with Dr. Delano's exam, I did not want to submit to another doctor paid by the insurance company or my employer, as I believed such a doctor would not be truthful in his diagnosis.

However, the Lord made it clear to me that He wanted me to submit to this IME—so I did. This IME proved very beneficial not just for that time in my life, but also many years later.

I had contacted a group of lawyers once I was diagnosed with RSD, believing that I needed their help. These lawyers assured me they would be available should I have any questions in the future. With an upcoming IME scheduled, I contacted them for some advice. Their advice was not to bring any medical reports of any kind that I had of my own to this IME appointment, and like a dummy, I listened to them.

Now that I found myself sitting in yet another doctors' office, with the same stupid naked-genderless-people form that I was asked to fill out, I noticed an older woman walking in. When she reached the front receptionist station near where I was sitting, I heard her announce who she was and that she was there for the IME case. I perked up at attention upon hearing my last name slaughtered in pronunciation, but no worse than how I slaughter the English language.

This older woman, Sandra, took a seat just as I was called into the examining room. As I went in, I asked the accompanying nurse: "Who is that woman?"

This nurse answered my abrupt question in a nice manner: "She's a field nurse."

I defiantly responded, "Well, she's not my nurse, and she's not coming in with me."

This nurse ignored my comment as she spoke in Sandra's defense some positive remarks about her, trying to assure me in a roundabout statement that Sandra was a woman that could be trusted. I processed all this but with much reserve.

With this same nurse in the room, Dr. Saul, the IME doctor, started his interrogation and asked me to relate everything from the beginning. I did so thoroughly and truthfully, as I have always tried to do with all these doctors' interrogations. By now, having related my story so many times, it was imprinted in my brain.

I started at the beginning with the knee injury, went through the surgery, through my journey trying to find out what was causing so much pain, until I got to the part of seeing Dr. Ortho and having a bone scan done. At the mention of the bone scan, Dr. Saul interrupted me with a surprised, almost excited question: "You had a bone scan done?"

My response was one of disbelief that he did not know: "Yes. Didn't they send you the report?"

Silly question on my part! Of course they didn't send him the bone scan report. It was the only diagnostic test that would have supported the diagnosis of RSD. And dummy me, I listened to the lawyers and didn't bring anything of what I had. Mindy, the new insurance claim person who replaced Jerry, had sent Dr. Saul every report from the doctors and diagnostic tests that they had, except the bone scan report and Dr. Delano's report.

Dr. Saul asked me what the bone scan report stated. I told him: "Asymmetric increased activity in the right knee and tibia plateau. They didn't scan the foot." *Sounds impressive using the medical terms from the report. Maybe he will believe me.*

He wrote all this down, as did his accompanying nurse, and then asked that I continue with my story. I told him all about being a guinea pig pincushion at Saint Mary's Hospital for their foreign doctors in training, and related my failed attempt with Dr. Delano to get another series of nerve block injections. I even told him that Dr. Delano did not believe I had RSD. There was no reason to mention the conspiracy between Dr. Delano and Jerry. I had no documents to prove that really happened, just my gut belief, which normally proved pretty accurate.

Dr. Saul noticed the changes in my right leg and foot that were suggestive of RSD, and confirmed this diagnosis to his nurse in my presence, but he didn't speak directly to me on this. As I was leaving his office, I saw Sandra go in to speak with Dr. Saul about my case, which was her main purpose for coming.

To have an IME doctor confirm a diagnosis of RSD in a workers' comp case was rare in those days. Maybe things have changed since. I very much appreciated Dr. Saul's honesty. I understood afterward why the Lord wanted me to submit to this exam. I also understood the importance of having an unaltered copy of this IME report for my own records. I was told that I could not receive this report directly from the IME doctor; I never believed the truth in that. However, I expected to receive a copy of this report without any problems. But it turned out to be more difficult than I thought.

After Sandra spoke with Dr. Saul, her next obligation was relating this conversation to Mindy. I was sure my employers' Medical Department—Ms. Nurse in particular—was privy to what Dr. Saul said. Along with Dr. Saul's diagnosis, he authoritatively recommended a detailed treatment path forward, part of which included another series of nerve block injections administered by a competent anesthesiologist.

Now there was a concerted effort by everyone involved to get me to have more needles stabbed in my back, with more possibilities of poking holes in my spine. Where were these people months ago when I tried to get another series of nerve blocks from Dr. Delano? Ms. Nurse claimed she knew nothing about my appointment with Dr. Delano. Her ties with Jerry were too strong. I did not believe she was being truthful.

Just after this IME appointment, I was walking through the gatehouse into work when the guard on duty grabbed my attention. Holding a phone receiver in the air, he informed me that I had a phone call. *Great timing, or is this a coincidence?* I don't believe in coincidences, and with cameras all over the grounds, I was sure I was viewed when I pulled into the parking lot.

I took the phone from the guard, said hello, and heard Mindy on the other end. She didn't ask how I was doing, but started right into her reason for the phone call: "Angelika, Dr. Saul confirmed you have RSD and recommended you get another series of nerve blocks. So are you going back to Dr. Scope at Saint Mary's for more nerve blocks?"

I was on guard and very careful with how I responded. Not because the guard was listening, but because this was a work phone. I did not trust Mindy at all, or anyone else at this point, and with good reason. I did not know exactly how Dr. Saul worded his recommendation in his report, as I was still waiting for a copy, and apparently, so was everyone else. They only received his diagnosis and treatment recommendations verbally from Sandra.

I respectfully responded to Mindy: "I'm not going back to Saint Mary's for more nerve blocks. They were practicing on me, and I didn't appreciate that."

Mindy wanted my path forward: "So where are you going to go now for these nerve blocks?"

I instantly realized the leverage needed that would ensure I received Dr. Saul's IME report for myself.

I stated my firm path forward to Mindy: "When I get the IME report for myself, I will discuss it with my physician, and then make a decision as to what I should be doing next." *That sounded really great. Now you will all know that I will not move forward until I get the IME report.*

I was truthful, although I really didn't have in mind the doctor I was referring to. No one knew of my plans of never returning to Dr. Donna, or finding another doctor to oversee my RSD medical care. But I needed that IME report, and if they knew I was waiting until I received it before moving forward with further treatments, I was sure to receive a copy, and hopefully soon.

I spoke with Sandra myself later about this IME appointment. During our conversation, I realized that she was one person I could trust, which spoke volumes about her character. And no wonder, I found out while speaking with her that she was a Christian woman. Now that the same Lord Jesus knitted us together, she spoke about her granddaughter and asked me to pray for her. In remembering Sandra now as I relate this story so many years later, I said a prayer again for her granddaughter. As Sandra was older back then, I can only think that she is with the Lord Jesus now.

Sandra confided to me that Dr. Saul stated he was not going to complete his IME report until he had a copy of the bone scan report for himself to read. Why didn't anyone send Dr. Saul a copy along with everything else they sent him prior to my appointment? And why wasn't anyone supplying Dr. Saul with the bone scan report now in order for him to complete his IME report? None of these people really cared about getting in writing that I had RSD. I was the one who needed this in writing from this IME doctor more than they did.

So, I came up with a good plan. I sent Dr. Saul the bone scan report myself with a nice cover letter so that he would complete his IME report, believing I would get this report soon afterward.

A few days later, I received my letter and the bone scan report back with a letter from someone at his office stating that Dr. Saul had never seen me, and that I sent the report to the wrong doctor.

I could not believe this just happened!

Frustrated and disgusted over everything that was happening, I sent Sandra a copy of the bone scan report so she could ensure Dr. Saul received it in order to complete his report.

In the meantime, I was diligently searching for another doctor who I could trust to treat this RSD, as at that point, I believed that I had no other choice in the matter. I needed to be under the medical care of someone while dealing with this off-the-wall, lifelong neurological pain disorder.

Chapter 49

Taking Control

It was over eight weeks from the IME appointment before I finally received a copy of Dr. Saul's report. His treatment recommendations seemed urgent in his report, but apparently, not urgent enough to get his report out sooner.

Dr. Saul advised referring me to an anesthesiologist who was competent in performing lumbar sympathetic nerve blocks, as he suggested I could have at least six more of these injections. He believed that if I didn't improve considerably with these fluoroscopically guided blocks, it would be reasonable for me to undergo a continuous epidural catheter infusion (a device inserted in my back to control injection of a drug). He also suggested some different types of medication and physical therapy. As he stated in his opinion, I had a fair to good prognosis, and then sealed it with his authoritative advice: "I would not delay her treatment. I would encourage you to have her involved with an anesthesiologist who will perform the treatment plan which I have outlined."

This report was all Ms. Nurse needed. She was obsessed with my diagnosis of RSD from the beginning. Knowing now that it had been over two months since my IME appointment and going untreated—according to her—well, this was just too much for her to deal with.

As much as I tried to be elusive with Ms. Nurse, she was a bothersome presence in my life, and I'm being nice describing her in this way. She wanted to personally go over the IME report with me. However, I really didn't need nor especially want her help understanding this report. By then, I thought I was capable of reading and understanding a doctor's report for myself. If there were words used that I didn't understand, I knew how to use a dictionary; I learned at least that much in the South Bronx school system. There was a recent time when no one wanted to believe I had RSD, or that I was dealing with so much pain. The workers' comp stigma was just too powerful for these people to get past. The story changed now that "their" IME doctor confirmed the diagnosis and added an elaborate treatment plan. Now the pressure was on from Ms. Nurse, and Theodore, the HR leader who some had nicknamed "Doctor" because of his involvement with people's medical situations.

No one knew how diligently I was looking for a doctor I could be comfortable with, and perhaps get another series of nerve blocks. I was doing everything I could to get past this RSD trauma to gain a normal life again. But it wasn't easy, to say the least. I continued hitting a brick wall trying to get help with this workers' comp "plague."

I contacted Dr. Saul's office now that I had the IME report to prove that yes, he did see me at one time, asking that he take me on as a patient. He was an anesthesiologist who administered lumbar sympathetic nerve blocks; I was sure he thought himself to be competent.

However, Dr. Saul laid out an elaborate treatment plan that he was capable of administering, but then refused to take me on as a patient. His excuse for refusing—he did the IME. He also refused to recommend anyone else to take me as a patient. Sandra also tried hard to find a doctor to continue my treatment but with no success. As she put it: "I'm pulling my hair out trying to find someone to treat you." (Sandra really did turn out to be a unique person I trusted, and I thanked God many times over for bringing her into my life during that time.)

As I have often done throughout this situation, I sought the Lord's direction more diligently than I was looking for a treating doctor: "Lord, why are You not telling me what to do now? I really need a doctor to treat this RSD."

The Lord God never speaks in vain; His words never return to Him void; His words are never to be taken lightly. (Isaiah 55:11.) When God speaks, He has a perfectly good reason to speak and brings home His message: "If I tell you now what to do, you would go and do it now. And now is not the time to do it."

So, I waited on the Lord for His further direction in His timing.

I was still taking the calcium for the osteopenia and swimming for therapy, which seemed to help. I was still working on medical work restrictions, but made sure I was doing anything and everything I could do within my restrictions to carry my own weight in Darkly, including some work that normally, a salaried employee should have been doing.

Lucas, upper management boss of Darkly, often expressed appreciation for the work I did while on medical work restrictions. I always got along well with Lucas and the other bosses in Darkly, at least up until that time in our working relationship.

So when Lucas showed up at the warehouse shanty office that had windows all around to speak to me alone (which was not advisable practice in a union shop), I didn't give it much thought; that was until he blindsided me with his comments about my medical condition: "Angelika, I just read the entire IME report. The prognosis is good. But you are being perceived as refusing treatment. They really want you to have another series of nerve blocks. I'm not sure how much longer we can find work for you in Darkly while on medical work restrictions."

With this, I turned my back to Lucas and tried to compose my emotions while processing everything he just told me. He could not have confronted me at a worse time. This man had no clue what I have been going through all this time in this nightmare, and diligently trying so hard to find someone willing to treat this plague that I now had to live with for the rest of my life.

Apparently, Ms. Nurse was beside herself with obsession when I refused to meet with her about the IME report and my ongoing medical treatments. She gathered up her troops and had a meeting about me, without me. Not only was Lucas present, but also another Darkly upper management boss, and doctor Theodore himself. This meeting was all about the IME report concerning my medical condition and getting more nerve blocks. *Oh, I forgot! Nothing is confidential in a workers' comp case!*

I was given a copy of Ms. Nurse's progress notes outlining her involvement in my case after the fact, so I have the documentation regarding this meeting. There was no legal avenue to address this gross injustice of allowing other than the medical personnel the privilege of reading an IME doctor's report regarding my medical condition. My privacy should have been respected, but it was not.

How many other doctors' reports did Theodore and these bosses have access to and read? There was some very personal information in those reports that I would have never wanted anyone else to know, let alone my male bosses. Good grief, what would have happened had I signed that blanket form authorizing the release of all my other personal health information?

Theodore, as the HR leader, was above Lucas, and it was obvious in observing Lucas' nervous demeanor in this shanty office relating all this to me that he was out to protect his own job. Everyone's concerted effort now to try and intimidate me into receiving another series of nerve blocks, only made me more determined to take control over my own medical situation.

We ended our conversation in the warehouse abruptly, as I told Lucas I needed to take care of the truck driver waiting for my services. The following morning after the department meeting in the Darkly control room, Lucas called me into one of the offices for another confrontation. As he closed the door behind us, I went into my offensive mode. He wasted no time asking his direct question: "Did you find a doctor yet for more nerve blocks?"

Deliberately, and in a tone that was confident more from my relationship with the Almighty God than my own ability, not caring who heard me through the thin walls, I responded, "I am not going to be pushed or intimidated! I am not going to again allow just any doctor to stab me in my back with a six-inch needle to poke holes in my spine! IT'S JUST NOT GOING TO HAPPEN! You people need to back off from me right now and leave me alone. When I find a doctor for further treatment, I will make it known."

Without my prior knowledge or approval, Lucas sent emails documenting what I said during his confrontation. As I was copied, I replied and copied everyone he did expressing the inappropriate mishandling of my medical information and workers' comp case from the beginning that resulted in my mistrust of everyone. As a result, a meeting was scheduled with those involved from medical and management to discuss everything that went on, with union reps present as witnesses.

I left nothing uncovered during this meeting as the cause of my mistrust of everyone up to that point, including showing Jerry's altered report from Dr. Ortho that he sent me compared to the original. The facts were well presented, and my current position was well known to everyone: I was going to handle my own medical care from now on without anyone's interference.

Finally, the Lord led me to Dr. Renwick, a neurologist near where I lived. I handled making this appointment totally different than Dr. Delano's. I wanted to ensure I received a totally unbiased exam and determination for further treatments with this RSD, and to know whether or not I should be receiving more nerve blocks. I wanted no interference by Ms. Nurse, Theodore, or Mindy with this doctor prior to my appointment.

To ensure this, I made the appointment for the very last one of the day, knowing if they called the insurance company or my employer's Medical Department, they would not likely contact anyone to discuss my case, as they would have all gone home for the day. This doctor's office never asked, and I never offered any information that this was a workers' comp case when I made the appointment. And my plan worked! By the time I gave them the information that this was a workers' comp case while waiting for my appointment, it was too late to even think about calling anyone.

So here I was again, sitting in yet another doctor's office, filling out another naked-genderless-people form with the same instructions to circle every part on them corresponding to where I was experiencing pain. By now, I was sure the copyright owner of these forms had made tens of thousands of dollars for his artwork.

I brought with me the IME report, the bone scan report, and some other doctors' reports for Dr. Renwick's review. I was totally upfront with this doctor, who seemed like a really nice guy.

Dr. Renwick was pleasant as he asked the same million-dollar question so many other doctors have asked me in the past: "So, where are you experiencing your pain?"

Obviously, no one ever really reviews the naked-genderless-people forms that I so painstakingly fill out!

Dr. Renwick read in the reports I gave him that I carried a diagnosis of reflex sympathetic dystrophy. However, he was reluctant to agree to this diagnosis, and explained to me why during this visit, and noted it in his report: "RSD does not advance to other parts of the body as her symptoms have, such as the opposite leg, right arm, or entire body."

He even stated in his report that he had never heard of complex regional pain syndrome, but that I explained to him it was the newer name for RSD.

It sure didn't take me long to realize that Dr. Renwick was definitely not up-to-date on RSD. The fact that my symptoms had advanced to other parts of my body was indicative of RSD.

But I didn't argue with this doctor. I was done arguing with doctors, and nurses, and therapists, about whether or not I had pain, whether my pain was from RSD, in my head, or whether I was just another case of the workers' comp stigma striking again. I was so done with everyone and everything, period!

In my car now after yet another appointment with a doctor who did not believe I had RSD, I once again burst out crying to the Lord believing I wasn't clear on His direction: "Now what do I do, Lord? Either these doctors don't believe me, don't know how to help me, or don't want to help me. Where do I go from here? What do I do now? I need to be under the care of some doctor, somewhere, somehow dealing with this RSD."

OR DO I REALLY?

I had five business days to notify my employer of this appointment in order for Dr. Renwick to get paid according to the Workers' Comp Act. I sent my letter to Theodore certified. I gave two copies personally to the union's chief shop steward (a union representative who was the local union president's right hand) with instructions to hand-deliver a second copy to Theodore. The other copy was for the union to keep. I wanted to make sure everyone had a copy of this letter of notification of this last doctor's appointment. It was short and to the point: "I am notifying you that on this date, I saw Dr. Renwick for further treatment of my RSD condition. This notification is in compliance with Section 306 of the Pa Workers' Compensation Act."

I explained in the letter that Dr. Renwick's professional determination was that I would not benefit by having more nerve blocks, but instead, he prescribed another medication that I was going to start taking. This didn't make Theodore or Ms. Nurse very happy. But I really didn't care at that point.

The medication Dr. Renwick had prescribed to treat the pain was something that was used to treat RSD. As was my practice, I researched all prescribed medications thoroughly before taking anything. This medication also had the potential of negatively affecting my white blood cell count; this didn't appeal to me. But until I received another direction from the Lord, I decided to try this medication. This would at least get Ms. Nurse and Theodore off my back for the time being.

The chief shop steward related to me Theodore's response upon hand-delivering a second copy of my letter to him: "We wanted her to have more nerve blocks."

Sure, they wanted complete control over my medical care and condition, and add in there my life, not just my employment. But they weren't getting it!

The chief shop steward's response back to Theodore was great: "But her doctor doesn't think she needs more nerve blocks."

Sometime later, I read Ms. Nurse's notes in my medical file that she contacted a lawyer to try and force me to have more nerve blocks. The lawyers' comeback according to her notes was also great: "A workers' comp judge may perceive a needle in the back as invasive. It would not be cost-beneficial to pursue this."

I realized that seeing Dr. Renwick was God's leading after all. As I also concluded that it was the Lord who kept me from having more nerve blocks after so many failed attempts to get another series. The Lord knew more nerve blocks would do me more harm than good. How could I forget? God was still in control. The Lord had orchestrated a grand scheme from the beginning for why He allowed this to happen. I needed to trust my Lord above and beyond and completely for the outcome of all this.

Chapter 50

End of Nightmare

God's timing is always perfect, and almost never our own timing. Three weeks after everyone received notice that I was not going to have another series of nerve blocks, a chem tech job in Darkly came open. There were two chem tech title positions related to the process of Darkly: the mixologist and lead operator. The two mixologists on each crew worked their own production line and made the mixes for the process, which involved a lot of physical work. The one lead operator on each crew was responsible for operating the reactors and overseeing the entire production process, which involved less physical work, but had much more responsibilities. This job bid was for the mixologist position. It was posted while upper management and union officials were in negotiations for the current contract that was soon to expire, and off plant site.

For whatever reasons—I never asked—God wanted me to bid on this mixologist position after passing it up at His direction several times over the past eleven years working in Darkly. In fact, I knew without a doubt, not bidding on this job would have been disobedience to the Lord. Since I've been there, done that, and didn't want to go there again, I obeyed the Lord. It was never God's will for me to return to my original material packager job position from when I initially injured my knee.

With negotiations going on and so many higher-ups out of the plant, when I was awarded the job per my contractual rights, and the announcement was posted throughout the plant by Adrianne (HR secretary), there wasn't much anyone said at the time.

I wasted no time on my own initiative to start the training on the mixologist position within my medical work restrictions. I was not covering an official "job" shift position, so I was able to do so, and no one questioned me.

My second appointment with Dr. Renwick was just after this job award. Afterward, I weaned myself off the medication he prescribed without anyone's knowledge, including his. I didn't like the potential side effects of this drug. Besides affecting white blood cells, it could also give people suicidal thoughts. I wasn't planning on returning for a third appointment with this doctor. But I kept everything I was planning on doing to myself, as I was exclusively following God's directions now.

At my next appointment with Dr. Ortho, I requested he release me to full duty, and he did, without hesitation. I believed he was glad to be done with Ms. Nurse, who continued to bombard him with a slew of paperwork to fill out on my behalf. I sent Theodore another certified letter that informed him of my release to full duty, and expressed that I was in full agreement with this release. But I made sure to state for my own protection, that I was still dealing with the RSD condition.

After I had received the IME report, I had again contacted the lawyers and sent them a copy, as I believed their help was much needed. But when I received their paperwork asking that I sign over all power of attorney to them, with many other stipulations and binding agreements, this didn't sit well with me and I told them so. Their response, "Well then, we can't help you unless you sign the paperwork. But if you need us in the future, just give us a call, we'll be here to help."

So, I gave these lawyers a call weeks before seeing Dr. Ortho for the final time. I left a voice message stating that I was expecting to be released to full duty in a few weeks, and I wanted their advice to be sure I knew what forms I should or should not be signing.

It was over six weeks later, the day after Theodore received notification of my release to full duty, when they finally returned my call. It was their turn to leave their voice message. They acknowledged my release to full duty and were now offering their assistance. I had believed for some time that these lawyers had contact with my employer without my knowledge. My mistrust of these lawyers was now sealed, as I don't believe in coincidences. I ignored their voice message, as they initially ignored mine.

The chief shop steward, who knew about my case from when I returned to work, left his employment due to a nice severance package offered during these last contract negotiations. Marshall was appointed to fill the vacancy of his unexpired term.

Now without a physician overseeing my care with the RSD, without an orthopedic physician overseeing my return to full duty, without any lawyers for legal advice, and without a union rep familiar with my situation, it was just me and the Lord God.

In obeying God in His direction to go out on my own, I landed at the place where He wanted me all along: I had no other choice but to totally trust Him for absolutely every aspect of my life. And during all this time in this nightmare, God had proven faithful to me while orchestrating all this in the first place for His purpose. (Romans 8:28.)

However, Ms. Nurse and Theodore weren't quite ready for me to return to full duty. I was now a liability that they didn't want. RSD is a lifelong condition that can go berserk with the slightest trauma of another injury, or even emotional stress. The possibility of becoming disabled with RSD always exists, and if that ever happened, all the time spent training me for this new mixologist position would be wasted.

Who really contacted the lawyers once Theodore received my notice that I was released to full duty? Would everyone have preferred I settle this and terminate my employment? But that wasn't going to happen! God still had some major plans He was going to make sure came to fruition in this career He had chosen for me at that very time in my life.

Per plant policy, I had to be released by the company doctor before my release to full duty would be accepted. I knew that this was only going to be an interrogation by this doctor, and that I would not be examined. To ensure there was a witness to what was said, I asked Marshall, as the appointed chief shop steward, to be present. It was awkward going into a doctor's examining room with a man who was not in the medical profession. But hey, what can I say! Sometimes, you gotta do what you gotta do.

With being new in his union rep position, Marshall had no previous knowledge of my medical condition, my workers' comp case, or what has been transpiring all this time. So I didn't think he would believe me if I told him that this so-called physical for release to full duty was going to be a way by which they would try to label me unfit for my new job. Ms. Nurse knew enough not to object to a union reps' presence after everything else that went on up until this time.

I was spiritually prepared for this battle by God's grace, with His armor on and holding tight to His shield. (Ephesians 6:11-17.) I was totally relying on God's Holy Spirit to give me in that very hour what He wanted me to say. I was going in there, not as an injured worker fighting for my job, but as the daughter of the King of the Universe.

Someone once told me while dealing with all this: "You're fighting a really big company, and you're not going to win."

My response: "But my God is so much more bigger, and He is in complete control."

Once I was in the examining room, Dr. Puppet wasted no time starting his interrogation: "So, I understand that you are going to bid on a mixologist job."

BINGO! That was their foremost concern on their minds, as I suspected. I corrected him calmly, letting him know they were too late: "I have already bid on, got the bid, and have started training for this mixologist job."

He was caught off guard and stared at me with his confused eyes wondering what to ask next. He zeroed in exposing their true motives: "I understand you've been released by Dr. Ortho to return to full duty. We have some concerns with this work release. Maybe we should send Dr. Ortho some forms explaining what is involved with your mixologist job for confirmation whether you are capable of doing these new duties."

This doctor was irritating me. Imagine that! I replied calmly in a deliberate tone: "Please leave Dr. Ortho alone. You guys have bombarded him enough with your forms to fill out concerning my condition. What more do you want from him? He has other patients he needs to be concerned about besides me."

Dr. Puppet continued, "We have concerns that you may have some problems with doing the duties of this mixologist job."

Marshall jumped in at my defense: "If there is anything she has difficulty doing, others are willing to help with the task. She's been doing the training well so far."

Dr. Puppet continued his interrogation and twisted around the million-dollar question, and to my benefit: "So, what causes you more pain?"

I gave him one word for my answer: "Aggravation."

He got my point. I later read in his notes that he added, but which was not something I said, "Like what you people are giving me." I always believed that patients should have the opportunity to write reports on their version of an office visit with a doctor. But of course, no one ever asked me, and that never happens. And I was being truthful. Stress and aggravation have been proven to flare-up pain from RSD.

It was so obvious that Dr. Puppet goofed by not asking me the million-dollar question so many other doctors dealing with this RSD had asked: "So, where are you experiencing your pain?"

Was it possible there were some in the medical profession who did not know about the naked-genderless-people forms? But this didn't get past Ms. Nurse, who seemed dissatisfied with Dr. Puppet's interrogation.

Ms. Nurse jumped in with her question. She wanted to hear the answer to the million-dollar question directly from me, but used a deceptive way of asking: "Why does Dr. Renwick believe you do not have RSD?"

Ms. Nurse knew why, as she read his report. The indicative nature of RSD advancing to other parts of the body was the very reason Dr. Renwick stated in his report that he did not believe I had RSD. I caught on; she wanted me to admit that the RSD had advanced. I wasn't about to give these people any ammunition to claim I was physically unfit for my new job.

I was truthful but didn't give her the answer she wanted: "Dr. Renwick's knowledge of RSD is not up-to-date. He did not even know they changed the name to complex regional pain syndrome."

Touché, Ms. Nurse! Her downcast expression told me she was disappointed with my answer.

Dr. Puppet seemed more lost and confused now. Ms. Nurse's question caught him off guard. *Maybe you guys should have rehearsed this better?*

By this time, with their motive clearly exposed, my anger level maxed out. Very calmly and deliberately—with my blood boiling—I made eye contact with Dr. Puppet and let him have it: "All I want is for you people to leave . . . me . . . alone . . . Can I make it any clearer than that?"

Dr. Puppet stared at me and paused a few seconds as he processed what I just told him before responding, "No . . . No . . . You've made it very clear."

Now it was my turn to ask my million-dollar question: "So what's your final decision?"

Dr. Puppet ignored my question and instead, extended his hand for a shake. I took his hand but determined not to deviate from my demand for an answer: "So what's your final decision?"

As I was still speaking, Dr. Puppet got up from his stool, gave me a final look, let go of my hand, and started walking away from me without a response. On his way out the opposite door I had come in and heading towards his desk, I called out again in a firmer and louder voice: "EXCUSE ME! DO YOU MIND TELLING ME WHAT YOUR FINAL DECISION IS?"

It was as though an angelic warrior put his sword to Dr. Puppet's throat, demanding he return to give me his final decision. Dr. Puppet made an abrupt about-face and headed straight back into the doorway he had just exited. He stood there with his right elbow on the doorframe, right hand holding his head, and acted like a little kid that just got caught red-handed doing a naughty act.

"Well," he hesitated as he moved his head back and forth rubbing it with his hand, trying to find the right words to say that would not get him in trouble with Ms. Nurse, who was helplessly watching the scene unfold. "I suppose," he hesitated again as he continued moving his head back and forth in a nervous twitch.

I wanted to scream at him: *JUST SPIT IT OUT, MAN!*

Finally, he declared his final decision: "Since your coworkers are willing to help you with your job if you need it, I suppose I can release you to full duty."

Now the patient scolded the doctor: "That was really rude of you and unprofessional to walk away from me while I was asking you a question."

Circling his hand around his head as he moved it back and forth in another nervous twitch, he confessed, "Well, I just wanted to mull it around in my head first."

I glanced over to Ms. Nurse, who was still standing in the examining room, and made eye contact. She quickly lowered her head in resignation and left the room without saying another word.

But the truth was, he needed to consult with Ms. Nurse and her troops before making his final decision while they met again over my medical care, my career, and my life. With the chief shop steward as a witness to Dr. Puppet's final decision, there wasn't much anyone could do to keep me from my new mixologist job.

Discussing this later with Marshall, I asked his opinion as to how I did. He responded, "You were a perfect example on how to control anger and still stay calm."

I admit that staying calm with anger was not always the case. My Greek temper was very capable of getting the best of me. But for that time, God took control as I submitted to His Holy Spirit.

However, this workers' comp nightmare was not over until the paperwork was signed. I knew I needed to protect my future, medically and with my employment, so I was extremely careful with what I signed. With God's help, I learned the legal intriguing web of workers' comp pretty well. Without a lawyer for advice, I relied on God's wisdom and what I learned regarding the forms I had copies of supplied through the workers' comp seminar offered by different lawyers than those I tried dealing with.

I informed Theodore that I would only sign the "supplemental agreement" form, and only if it read suspending my benefits. I made it crystal clear that I would not sign anything terminating my benefits. I emphasized the unpredictable nature of RSD, and the possibility of this condition going berserk at any time. He told me he understood. And I understood, how these forms and agreements were worded was so important.

Mindy, while still the claim person, sent out three copies of the same supplemental agreement forms deceptively abbreviating terminating my benefits, with a letter stating I needed to sign these forms and return them. Whether Theodore was privy to Mindy's intention in how she worded this form, I cannot say. I told Theodore why I was refusing to sign these forms, and then gave him in writing what the wording needed to state before I would sign off on this case. It wasn't long after this that Theodore left his HR role for another position in the company.

After receiving the second set of supplemental agreement forms again deceptively abbreviating terminating my benefits, and with an addition by Ms. Nurse to control my medical care, I was furious. I was going to write them a letter explaining why I was refusing to sign these forms again, until God directed me to let it go—so I did. I waited on the Lord before doing anything else.

Four weeks later, a new claim person came on the scene, along with Jezebel, the new HR leader and former assistant to Theodore. Jezebel questioned me why I didn't sign the forms yet. I again explained what the wording on this supplemental agreement form needed to state for my own protection before I would sign it.

A few days later, Jezebel admitted that the new claim person took my side stating she didn't blame me for not signing the supplemental agreement forms before, as she wouldn't have signed them either the way they were worded.

Soon after this, the supplemental agreement form came with the revised wording I requested for my protection. I signed off on three copies ending for now my nightmare with workers' comp, and ending all medical care dealing with this off-the-wall, lifelong neurological pain disorder that could go berserk at any time.

Chapter 51
Another Hard Lesson

I was forty years old when I injured my knee, and spent almost two years dealing with my workers' comp nightmare. Although the Lord orchestrated this knee injury as His spanking and knowing the lifelong consequences, He had a grand scheme planned from the very beginning of using it as a catalyst to prepare and propel me into arenas as His training grounds, and all according to His purpose. However, the Lord was going to be sure I understood well before entering these arenas, that He will always demand first place in my heart and life.

Although I followed the Lord's leading in bidding on the mixologist position, I had real concerns that I would be able to learn and do this job. It was so much more complicated and dangerous than what the material packager's job entailed. I also had concerns dealing with the constant RSD pain, and the unexpected flare-up burning pain that was so intense and would happen without warning. I wondered often how I would deal with this flare-up pain should it happen at a time when I was doing a difficult or dangerous job task, such as changing blades on one of the hotcutters? However, I knew I had to keep all these concerns to myself. But God was faithful, and with His help I learned my mixologist job well after a few months of training.

It was just after being fully trained as a mixologist when the Lord led me into another submission to His Lordship over my life. The Lord wanted me to submit to His discipline when it was only in my heart to disobey Him, before I disobey, so that I would not disobey Him. God is able to judge the thoughts and intentions of the heart. (Hebrews 4:12.)

But this was not by any means foolproof in ensuring my obedience to the Lord. I've learned in my walk with God that there is a sharp distinction between His discipline, His punishments, and His spankings. The Lord's discipline in my life is the least severe of His dealings; His spankings are the most severe.

The response from the Lord Jesus for such a submission was overwhelmingly the most precious He has ever spoken, and instantly engraved in my heart for all time. In the midst of all the severity that I have experienced in my walk with God thus far, and have been led to openly share, so much more overwhelmingly is His love and tenderness towards me.

Now as a mixologist, I went back to the same shift as before, but the roles had changed. My buddy, Jethro, was now the lead operator. Barney was my mixologist partner, who had a reputation of not being very attentive to his job duties. The lead operator had more responsibilities and depended a lot on his two mixologists, and not just for making the mixes correctly.

There were four DCS (distributed control system) computers on our console, which controlled most of our equipment outside the control room. Jethro had two computers, and each mixologist had their own; all our computer screens and controls were interchangeable. I sat in the middle of the three of us, which gave me full view of each computer overseeing the entire Darkly production process, and made for some very interesting shifts.

Jethro, on my right, taught me a lot about the lead operator job on his DCS computers, and allowed me to help him with his other responsibilities out in the field process area. Barney, on my left, taught me a lot of what I should not be doing as I watched him closely monitoring him on his DCS computer. It was always easier to stop a major blunder than dealing with the repercussions.

There were two similar production lines in Darkly. I worked Line Two, and Barney worked Line One. Whosever line went down

315

had to help Jethro on his end getting it started back up, while the other mixologist helped our lone packager with the pancakes that were produced during these procedures.

There were several tasks that needed done to start up or shut down a line, or change blades on the hotcutters when chunks were being thrown from a smeared faceplate. Everything had to be done in a precisely timed sequence. If anything was not done according to this sequence, catastrophes could happen.

I had worked with Jethro while he was the lead operator for a few years, and we always worked well together. Whenever we had to change blades and restart the hotcutter, we each knew exactly what we needed to do in this precisely timed sequence in order to successfully complete this dangerous task without incidents.

On one particular day, though, Jethro knew something was not quite right. We successfully changed the blades and restarted the hotcutter without incidents. But once we were back in the control room, Jethro made a comment to me that I also knew was true: "What happened out there? You acted like you didn't know what you were doing."

This was an isolated incident, but I knew what happened. I didn't elaborate with Jethro, as he would not have understood. God had disciplined me for purposely not spending any time with Him that morning before leaving for work. When God disciplines me, I just can't seem to do anything right.

A year and a half later, Jethro had retired and Barney became the lead operator. I was working a Saturday daylight shift when the Lord disciplined me again to get my attention regarding not spending time with Him, but I didn't quite get it.

That same Saturday evening, I had spent a great deal of time working on my duties as the workers' comp rep. Because of this, I went into my quiet time with the Lord much later than usual for a

Another Hard Lesson / 51

daylight shift, cut my quiet time short, and went to bed late, but not before He spoke to my heart.

During my quiet time and in His presence, the Lord reiterated what He had shown me many times over the years: my time with Him must be a priority in my life, my relationship with Him must come before anyone and anything else in my life, I cannot do anything well without His help. The Lord also warned me that any disobedience to Him going forward would affect many more lives than just mine alone.

The next morning while trying to wake up, I kept hitting my alarm snooze. This caused me to run late, and I left for work without spending any time with the Lord. For most of God's children, this missed prayer time would not have been a big deal. But in my walk with this holy God, though it was not premeditated disobedience, the Lord still held me accountable for my negligence.

As mentioned before, it took very little for a catastrophic event to happen in Darkly. One seemingly little glitch in our process, or one little hiccup in a critical pump, a line could go down for days, even weeks. There was an expression the guys used for Darkly's mishaps or blunders—SHAD. I will clean up the acronym by substituting the first word: stuff happens at Darkly.

The group of guys working at Darkly during my first several years as a chem tech tried our best to cover each other's mistakes, if at all possible. This kind of comradeship reminded me of my Army days. I couldn't always say the same in the latter years. But there were times when a blunder just could not get covered up.

With Darkly being a continuous production process, it was critical that the pumps used during this process were always operable. Each production line had two pumps readily available for use for each of the pumping systems. Should a pump that was running malfunction, the spare pump next to the running pump would need to be in most cases, immediately put into service to replace the malfunctioned pump to hopefully mitigate any consequences to the process. During the process of switching pumps, valves on the piping had to also be switched over, which made the process of changing pumps more involved.

During the Sunday daylight shifts, which rotated once each month for each crew, each spare pump for each pumping system had to be bump started and then shut off to make sure they were operational. This daylight Sunday, it was my turn to check these pumps for operational readiness while Noah, my new mixologist partner, monitored the DCS computers.

When the spare water pump on Line One did not bump-start—being the conscientious worker that I was—I decided to troubleshoot the cause, which would give our maintenance guys a better understanding of what needed done to repair the pump.

These water pumps were critical, as they took the cut pellets from the hotcutter through an intricate piping system that went up through several floor levels to the top dryer system, and then to the hold-bins. If the pump being used failed, someone needed to respond immediately by switching the valves of the spare pump and start it up, or get to the hotcutter to divert the polymer feed to the metal plate just before the hotcutter; otherwise, plugging up this intricate piping system was inevitable.

My first step of troubleshooting was to check that the breaker for this pump was on and not tripped off. So, off I went climbing up several flights of early 1940s cement-poured stairs to the breaker rooms, a considerable distance away from the water pumps and the Line One hotcutter. As I entered the breaker room full of several electrical cabinets, each controlling several breakers, I found them peacefully purring away with their humdrum noise while emitting a distinct odor all their own.

Each Line One water pump had their own breaker on a different electrical cabinet that was labeled. I located the breaker of what I thought was the spare water pump.

It took only a few seconds to switch this breaker off, push the reset button, switch the breaker back on—the Westminster Chimes alarm blared—my heart sunk!

I knew instantly what had happened!

I had inadvertently turned off and reset the breaker on the running pump instead of the spare pump. There was no way to turn this pump back on from where I was, and no one was able to get to it fast enough to avoid the catastrophe my blunder had caused, which happened immediately after the running pump shut down.

Each crewmember carried radios everywhere we went for safety reasons and allowed for instant contact. Our security guards and shift coaches also monitored these radio communications. No one answered my radio calls as I flew down several flights of cement stairs and straight to Line One hotcutter. No one showed up for help, not even Barney as the lead operator.

When I reached the hotcutter, I slammed the dump valve to divert the polymer feed to the metal plate on the floor so the line wouldn't plug beyond the hotcutter—only to realize—with the dump valve and another control valve next to each other, I slammed the wrong valve in my OH-SHAD mode. *This is turning out to be a major blunder on my part!*

But it didn't matter at that point. All the safety interlocks that were put in place to shut down our production process during such a malfunction of a critical pump triggered, and immediately shut down everything else, including the feed pump feeding polymer into the reactor. Unfortunately, though, these safety interlocks weren't quite fast enough to avoid plugging up the piping going to the dryer system, as they were designed to do.

With our feed pump also shut down due to the interlocks, I then had to hurry outside to restart the feed pump going into the reactor to cool it down. Otherwise, without polymer feed moving into the reactor, we would have had a runaway reactor to contend with, in addition to everything else my blunder had caused. It was several minutes later before Barney finally showed up.

My blunder of turning off the running pump caused the line to be down for days, and just when our product was needed the most. All the intricate piping that went up several floor levels to the dryer system had to be taken apart and unplugged from the pellets that fused together and became hardened polymer. Some of the piping had to be put in the burn-ovens to burn out the polymer inside. I was very upset with all the extra hard work my blunder had caused everyone involved. This was the only major blunder I ever made in the years working as a chem tech in Darkly.

That evening during my quiet time and in the Lord's presence, He reminded me that His discipline the day before was His forewarning; this major blunder was His punishment.

The Lord God is a very jealous God, a consuming fire, and absolutely demands first place in my heart and life. The Lord knew He was about to propel me deeper into the intrigue arenas of this union for His purpose. But before doing so, He wanted to be sure this hard lesson was learned: Not even my union responsibilities were to come before Him. And with everything the Lord was calling me into, He wanted to make sure I also knew: I needed His help to do everything well.

During the investigative meeting for my blunder, it was discovered that the electrical breakers were not labeled as clearly as they could have been. Therefore, I received no other consequences, and no one was the wiser as to why this really happened. But I never forgot the Lord's hard lesson in all this moving forward.

Chapter 52
Workers' Comp Rep

Our local union was part of an international labor union organization, and under their leadership. Within our local union, there were several representative roles, with almost all of them elected by the union membership. However, my workers' comp rep role initiated from my self-taught knowledge of the intriguing web of workers' comp after my knee injury, was an appointment by each local union president, and was part of God's grand scheme. Daryl, the third president who kept me in this role, supported me more than his predecessors.

I always took my union responsibilities very seriously. For years, I coached in the background with helping anyone who needed and wanted my help dealing with their workers' comp case. I was sure management knew that I was the one responsible for why many refused to sign medical authorization release forms, except for releasing "information pertaining to their current work-related disabling condition."

By this time in history, OSHA was well established and well respected as a federal agency for over thirty years. During one summer, I was sent by our local union to another training seminar for certification in OSHA.

At this seminar, I related to an OSHA agent giving a class that it took almost eight weeks to obtain copies of my medical records I had requested from my employers' Medical Department, with no one contacting me regarding this delay. This OSHA rep encouraged me to file a formal OSHA complaint against my employer, as this was way beyond the mandatory time limit of fifteen working days for receiving such requested information. In quoting him: "If they did it to you, they will do it to someone else."

No one else was hurt by this OSHA violation, and I believed it would not happen again to anyone else since I brought it up to upper management. I also knew filing OSHA complaints were drastic actions, and without God's direction to file this, I did not.

I learned invaluable information during this seminar, including information on the OSHA 300 logs. These logs kept a detailed account of injured employees, and whether their injuries resulted in any medical work restrictions, which would entitle them to the partial benefit under the Workers' Comp Act due to a loss of earning power. I also learned that it was an OSHA mandated regulation for management to report all injuries on these logs, and to comply with any employees' request for complete copies of their 300 logs, and both within certain time limits. I tucked away all this information I learned for future use.

Just two months after this seminar came the rash of injured union members in our plant site. Lisa was just hired as the new HR leader, as Jezebel moved up the ladder in our company.

With many of these injured workers on a medical work restriction with a loss of earning power, they were entitled to the partial pay benefit from workers' comp. Management's practice of refusing to initiate this partial benefit unless the injured worker acknowledged they had this coming, and neglecting to ensure it was paid within the time limits per the Workers' Comp Act, were still ongoing and violations of the Act.

Because of this, I decided it was time I came out from behind the scenes to address these violations to Lisa, Adrianne (HR secretary), and Ms. Nurse, all of whom were involved in processing these workers' comp forms, along with their new third-party insurance claim person.

My email addressing this was courteous, well written and to the point. I explained what the Workers' Comp Act stated was proper procedure, the time limit for this benefit to be paid, and explained what forms should have already been sent to these injured workers that were not sent. I was not requesting any pay or other confidential information regarding these injured workers. I only exposed their non-compliance with the Workers' Comp Act, and requested that these issues be resolved and not happen again in the future. I signed the email as the union's workers' comp rep, and copied the injured workers and union reps. I didn't ask for any discussion on the matter, nor requested or expected a response.

Lisa responded two days later with an email that was a bit aggressive and threatening, and not at all courteous as mine was. Lisa outlined her demands of my compliance with the company's email system, and the limitations on using it only for "legitimate company matters." She expressed that my title of "workers' comp rep" was not a recognized company title, and therefore, I was not permitted to use it as part of my email signature. She even claimed that my subject matter was "confidential, and cannot and will not be discussed" with me. She threatened discipline should I not comply with her demands, and copied everyone I copied on my email, and added two of my supervisors.

Apparently, I hit some nerves by exposing their ongoing non-compliance with the Workers' Comp Act. But that was okay! Never one to be easily intimidated, I had a plan moving forward.

I always got along well with Daryl, our local union president. But I was to find out soon enough, Cain, our International Union staff rep, didn't quite care for me as the workers' comp rep. Cain was above Daryl, and as our staff rep was supposed to help support our local union officers when needed.

I was told later, Cain had informed Lisa and the rest of management that they didn't have to recognize my role as the workers' comp rep because I was appointed by the local president, and not elected by our membership. I was sure Cain didn't clue management in on the fact that he wasn't an "elected" union official either, as staff reps were appointed by the International Union district directors, and not elected by our membership.

This marked the beginning of a significant arena in my life that would go on for many years involving Cain's refusal to support my efforts to represent our union members. The Lord would know all about this, and would be right there with me during these fierce battles while demonstrating His grace and power when I am weakest. But for now, I still had that plan, which I believed was by God's leading.

It was time to use that information I learned about the OSHA 300 logs. After Lisa's email, I requested complete copies of these logs of the past three years. According to the Workers' Comp Act, any injured employee who was not paid a benefit, had three years to reclaim that benefit. The plan was to use this information from the logs, trace back three years, contact those who were on medical work restrictions, and find out who didn't get this partial benefit paid. I could then work on getting their benefits paid to them, as well as the recent injured workers.

While being very compliant with Lisa's email usage demands, I made sure to send my letter requesting the OSHA 300 logs certified, and not through the company's email system. And per OSHA regulations at that time, the company had until the end of the next business day after receiving my request to comply.

Daryl knew beforehand of my request for the 300 logs and supported me. But the chief shop steward elected with Daryl really panicked when he found out what I requested. You would have thought I committed some hideous crime. But that was okay too! No one knew at the time, but this chief shop steward was in negotiations for a salaried position with the company, which explained his panicked response upon hearing of my request.

Management's response the day after receiving my request for these OSHA logs was to send me for a random drug and alcohol test. I knew they weren't going to find anything in my system, but they were hoping to. Ms. Nurse, who also received a copy of my request, had the nerve to ask me while administering this test: "Did you ever have a random drug and alcohol test done before?"

My response revealed I knew what they were up to: "If you want to call this random."

Ms. Nurse just turned around and walked away without saying another word. Her response only confirmed that this was not random. Our relationship never improved once out of her grip with my medical care.

Over six days later, I finally received copies of the OSHA 300 logs. Management did their best to find a way not to comply with my request, as they did not want me to have this information, but realized they had no choice. Their purposeful delay in complying with my request was a violation of an OSHA mandated regulation.

Everyone must have forgotten the prior violation of another OSHA mandated regulation when it took almost eight weeks to receive copies of my requested medical records, which happened just months prior to this last request for the OSHA logs. My good-faith gesture in not filing a formal OSHA complaint against that violation flew out the window. It found company as time went on when other good-faith gestures I made also flew out the windows.

Once I received the logs, I learned of others who were not paid their partial pay benefit. Because the company refused to rectify these injured workers' benefits, with God's leading and Daryl's prior approval, I filed a formal OSHA complaint for management's non-compliance in supplying my request of the OSHA logs in the time limit set forth per OSHA regulation.

I knew this complaint would not cause an OSHA inspection of our chemical plant facility, but only an inspection of our company's record-keeping procedures. I wasn't in the plant when this OSHA complaint investigation was going on. But it was relayed to me how things transpired. The woman agent from OSHA simply asked Monica, the safety person at the plant, to bring up the OSHA 300 logs on her computer. When she did so within a minute, this agent simply asked, "Why did it take over a week to give the logs to this employee upon her request?"

The end goal was accomplished. Our injured workers were paid their due partial benefits, and this practice of neglecting to pay this benefit, and within the time limit it was supposed to be paid, was stopped.

Trout, a trustee officer on the union e-board who worked at Darkly, commented to me regarding Lisa's aggressive email response and my actions that followed, as it didn't take long before everyone knew what had transpired: "Lisa's email was meant to intimidate you. But instead, it just ticked you off and made you more determined."

He used a more colorful metaphor in his wording, but the point is made. There was no vindictiveness on my part. I was only trying to get these injured workers their paid benefit that by law, they had coming to them.

And I didn't stop with our company. As an amalgamated union with members from three companies, I sent requests for copies of the OSHA 300 logs to the management of the other two companies, as each employer maintained their own OSHA logs.

In following up from what I learned from these logs, one company was also out of compliance with workers' comp by neglecting to initiate this partial pay benefit to their injured workers. With my intervention and God's help, three union members were paid a considerable amount of money that they were rightfully owed under the Workers' Comp Act, and without having to pay a lawyer's fee.

Soon after this, the union's chief shop steward jumped the fence and became a salaried supervisor before his union rep term was up. There are several officers' positions on a local union's e-board (executive board), which included trustees. One trustee was appointed to fill this chief shop steward's unexpired term. This left an opening for another trustee position that was offered to me. The reasoning was that it would provide me with more authority as the workers' comp rep being on the union's e-board. I had God's direction in accepting this trustee position, which was to be for just under a year. Elections for all local union officers were going to take place that following November, which happened every three years.

However, being the workers' comp rep who was now a trustee union officer did not go over well with management or with Cain. But this didn't discourage me at all. I continued doing my work as a Darkly mixologist, as well as my union roles, conscientiously. I was still working for the Lord Jesus in all that I was doing.

My workers' comp role for all three company groups, and my short trustee appointment, was used significantly by the Lord for His training and preparation before He propelled me into yet another arena in my career. No one understood any of this at that time, including me.

God always has His own timing for what He does, and for when and if He decides to reveal what He is doing. Since God is Sovereign and has all things under His control, His children need only to obey His directions one step at a time. I was learning this valuable lesson firsthand.

Chapter 53

New Arena

A few months after my OSHA complaint and my Darkly blunder, management and union officials were preparing for negotiations for our soon-to-expire contract. Our employer was self-insured with their healthcare benefits while a third-party health insurance administrator handled the claims on their behalf. Thinking back now, I'm not sure how or why, but I was led by the Lord to get involved and address this medical benefit that many of our union members had issues with.

Daryl supported my desire to contact several different health insurance companies asking for competitive quotes on insuring our union members. I initiated another information request for management to send census information directly to these health insurance companies for accurate quotes. When they didn't comply with my request timely, I contacted Gremlin directly, their corporate lawyer, and politely asked him what the holdup was in sending this information.

Gremlin seemed nice enough to me while on the phone, but apparently, I violated some sort of protocol by contacting him. I believe Cain's toes were the ones that got stepped on. Gremlin then contacted Cain, who then contacted Daryl and told him to confront me about this so-called protocol that I violated.

Daryl was nice to me: "You contacted the company's lawyer!"

I believe it was a statement more than a question. I responded innocently enough, as I didn't think I did anything wrong: "Yeah, I had to. How else was I gonna find out about when this census information was going to be sent to these insurance companies?"

These healthcare insurance quotes were needed within a certain time frame to present them during negotiations for the best chance of being accepted. And they weren't getting done without the requested census information. I saw no big deal in contacting Gremlin, who was just a man in my way of getting these quotes. Daryl was still nice when he told me not to contact Gremlin again. (Only God knew then my future dealings with Gremlin.)

After getting the healthcare insurance quotes, I made the arrangements for these insurance representatives to present their information to management and the union during negotiations. Much to the dismay of management and Cain, Daryl supported my presence at negotiations to ensure that what these representatives presented to me was presented to everyone else. This was my first exposure to an atmosphere of contract negotiations.

The healthcare insurance quotes were great with premium coverage. However, both management and union negotiating teams agreed that they would not negotiate for new healthcare. This was very upsetting to me, especially after all the hard work and time I personally put into this. But my hard work was not totally in vain. As compensation, our union members were offered a bonus each year they filled out a lifestyle questionnaire connected to our healthcare, which lasted for several years.

Although my initial goal for getting these quotes did not materialize, God had another goal unbeknown to me that came to fruition. The Lord God had given me a special word not too long into my chemical job career. I cannot share everything the Lord spoke, but I can share a small part: "Your name will be spread in the workplace as one who is steadfast in your commitment to a celibate life, and in your commitment in serving Me. No weapon formed against you will ever prosper." (Isaiah 54:17.)

With it being well over sixteen years working at this plant site—the last six years as the workers' comp rep—less than a year as a union trustee—with my recent and well-known involvement with management, the union, and our union membership, the Lord was about to fulfill His word.

It was in May that our negotiated contract was accepted. Elections for new union officers were scheduled the following November, and would be sworn in during our December union meeting. With a taste of being a union rep, I was praying and seeking God about what union position, if any, I should run for during these next elections.

Our local union consisted of predominantly men with fewer than ten percent women, and was amalgamated with members working in three separate company groups; my company group had the most union members. This decision was major, as I really wanted to discern what the Lord wanted for me, and not my own desire. However, I found out soon enough, I wasn't quite ready for what the Lord was leading me into.

I made a mental run through of my "wannabe list" for when I grew up. On the list I found zoologist, Seeing Eye Dog trainer, and Army enlistment term. Even employment at some zoo found its way on the list. Somehow, though, I couldn't find local union president anywhere on my "wannabe list."

The Lord God speaks and leads in many different ways. Sometimes God speaks within our hearts in such a soft voice that if we are not listening attentively, we can miss His message. Sometimes God speaks and leads gradually, giving precious time to adjust to His will while knowing exactly when time of adjustment is needed. The Lord was speaking and leading me the past several months, but I was in denial. Until one day at work, I was overcome all at once by the Lord's clear revelation: I was going to be the next union president for our local union.

As I was driving home after this revelation and stopped at a red light, I went into a panic mode as I realized, as the elected union president, I was going to be the chairperson conducting union meetings in front of predominantly men. I've witnessed some real heated battles go on at some of these union meetings. I still had some real problems speaking in front of groups of people, regardless of whom they were. Flashbacks of my very first time I tried speaking in front of a group of kids I didn't know came flooding back. I lost my voice then, and couldn't speak to tell anyone I couldn't speak. In addition to all this, my English still hadn't improved much in the forty-seven-plus years I'd been on this Earth. What was I going to do chairing a local union membership meeting during one of those heated battles? What was I going to do about all the other meetings with groups of people I was going to have to speak in front of?

There were also some major responsibilities that came with this union president position. It was also one of the most thankless positions anyone could ever hold in a union. I was so unprepared and inadequate to succeed in this position, at least on my own. And really, union president wasn't even on my wannabe list! *What is the Lord thinking leading me into the office of union president?*

Once I was home and focused on the Lord, He calmed my fears as He spoke without a doubt once again: It was His will that I be the next union president. God wasn't concerned that I felt inadequate for this position, or fearful of speaking in front of people, or concerned of being in a thankless position spending so much time and energy helping people who one day would be my best of friends, and the next day would do a real flip-flop and become my enemies.

The Lord showed me that this wasn't about me or my abilities or what I wanted. This was all about what the Lord wanted to do through this position to teach and train and prepare me for His next ministry years later. And if I wanted to be obedient to Him fully, I knew I didn't have a choice in the matter.

I've learned in my walk with this Almighty God, that when God calls me, or anyone for that matter, to do anything, He is expecting obedience and not ability. God's Holy Spirit is very capable of equipping His children with what is needed to accomplish and succeed in what the Lord has called them to do.

By this time, with everything I had been involved with in recent years, my assertive and tenacious personality was well known to management and others at my place of employment. Someone in Darkly made a comment while we were discussing me running for union president: "Ange, if you get elected union president, there would be an audible groan from the company."

As though this was his cue, the shift coach walked into our control room after this statement was made, yet he was nowhere near to hear our conversation. This same man asked the shift coach: "What do you think about Angelika being elected our next union president?"

This shift coach made an abrupt about-face, let out such a loud audible groan while shaking his head as he walked right back out of the control room without speaking a word. I was sure he had no clue to the real reason the rest of us spontaneously gave a hardy laugh at his response.

Trout was also running for union president against me, along with two other men, and tried to dissuade me from running. His reasoning was that if I ran along with the others, the votes would be split and another man would get elected instead.

My response revealed my determination: "It doesn't matter, Trout. I'm supposed to run."

I gave Trout credit. After working in Darkly with me for over sixteen years and witnessing my walk with the Lord, he knew enough to let the issue go; he never said another word about it.

I made up my flyers for my campaign using some nice scroll parchment paper, and in doing so, I wanted to be sure everyone knew that if they elected me as union president, they were getting a packaged deal. My flyers stated plainly: "If elected President, I will do my very best to do what is RIGHT, with the LORD'S help."

Daryl commented on my statement about the Lord: "You shouldn't have put that in there. I wanted you to win."

Daryl was a Christian but not as vocal about it as I was. He was sincere, and by then had retired on an early severance package that came from the last contract negotiations, but was still acting as union president until his term was up after this next election.

My response was just as sincere: "Daryl, if God wants me elected as union president, it doesn't matter who doesn't."

In all sincerity, I was just following God's direction. I could remember thinking I'd have a huge sigh of relief if I did not get elected. But as the days moved closer towards election day, I was looking forward to this new arena from the Lord's hand. I was going to be the first and probably only woman union president elected at our local union. It had always been the good-old-boys club of union leadership with very few women ever getting involved. After I got elected, I accepted this position as a ministry from God, serving first and foremost as servant to my Lord Jesus; second, as servant to the membership of our local union.

With the Lord's last strong message through His punishment with my blunder in Darkly still fresh in my heart, I understood His timing and purpose for such a hard lesson. The Lord will always demand first place in my heart and life, and I will always need His help to succeed in anything I do. As I grow closer to the Lord and into His ministry, He has shown me that my obedience to Him will be even more crucial, as so many lives will be affected by my relationship with this Almighty God.

I was not a perfect union president by any means, and made my share of mistakes. But I always tried my best to do what was right, and encouraged others to do the same. Because I understood my legal rights and authority in this elected union president role, I displayed an assertiveness that I tried my best to rely on the Holy Spirit to direct. I was outspoken and at times very confrontational. I never liked being taken advantage of, nor liked it when others were taken advantage of. I had a Greek temper that would at times flare-up with the need of God's Spirit to control, while other times my strong anger was purposefully manifested.

God proved faithful in using this union president position to fine-tune these characteristics for His call and purpose. But most importantly, the Lord God taught me that truth must be spoken, convictions must be maintained, integrity must be honored, even knowing there will be tough consequences to pay.

There were many issues I sought the Lord's leading on so sincerely and intensely, through prayer and fasting, only God and I would know. And even in those times, the outcome was not always what I had prayed for or wanted. But there was never a time that I did not see God working.

Even in situations when things seemed to go all wrong, and I stood alone—being pounded on all fronts—God proved more than faithful in standing right by my side, softly speaking unto me "fear not." (Isaiah 41:9-13.)

The purpose in sharing this turbulent arena of my life is not to vindicate any actions of my own, nor to put anyone else in a negative profile. The purpose is to testify of the demonstration of God's grace and power at work in one ordinary life.

As the Scriptures clearly state: "And He (Jesus) has said to me, 'My grace is sufficient for you, for (My) power is perfected in weakness.' Most gladly, therefore, I will rather boast about my weaknesses, so that the power of Christ may dwell in me. Therefore I am well content with weaknesses, with insults, with distresses, with persecutions, with difficulties, for Christ's sake; for when I am weak, then I am strong" (2 Corinthians 12:9-10).

Chapter 54
Union Overview

Local unions are under their respective national or international unions' directed leadership. During my years of employment, our International Union merged twice with other larger international unions. Although our local union officers had the opportunity to attend the International Union's convention in Las Vegas to voice their approval or objection to this last merger, it proved only to be a formality; the powers that be had already decided on the merger. This last merger happened about a year and a half before I was elected union president.

There were agreements in place as to how and when all the local unions would be fully transitioned into the new International Union, which was a multi-million-dollar organization. Part of the agreements included a gradual transition over several years of local union officers' positions and elections schedule, policies, and union dues pay structure. There were some policies and by-laws the newly merged local unions had to abide by from the beginning.

Cain was with our local union for many years prior to this last merger, and was kept on afterward as our staff rep. Since the district directors appointed staff reps, the local unions had no say in choosing their staff reps. I always believed this was an injustice to each of the local unions' membership.

At one time, everyone in our local union worked for the same chemical company. Years before I was hired, this chemical company was split up and sold to three different companies, which was how our local union became amalgamated.

There were several different elected officers on our e-board (executive board) that represented all three company groups.

Union president and vice president were just two of them. Each company group had their own trustees, and the other two company groups each had their own group chairmen. My company group had a chief shop steward, who was my right-hand helper. Shop stewards were elected as first-line reps in each of their respective department areas, but were not on the union's e-board. Each union officer was elected on their own merits. A union president never got to pick a running mate, nor anyone else to be on their e-board.

In addition to having an International Union by-laws for amalgamated unions, our local union also had our own adopted by-laws that were approved by the International Union that we also followed. These by-laws governed pertinent practices for our local union, including our meeting schedules. As the union president, I was the chairperson for these meetings, which had to strictly abide by the Robert's Rules of Order guidelines. Each month, the first Tuesday was our e-board meeting, and the second Thursday was our membership meeting.

The responsibilities of local union officers are to enforce and police their contract, represent their membership in other areas, and are the mediators between management and their local union membership. Our contract agreement and the labor laws made our elected local union officials the exclusive representatives of our local membership.

Union officials are placed on the same playing level as their employers' management because of the labor laws in the United States, with protected rights and authority to speak and give opinions in ways that rank-and-file union members do not have. This was something management strongly disliked, but which I took full advantage of.

There were several management personnel that directly dealt with union leadership. At the time of my election, a new plant manager, Caleb, was just coming on board. Caleb turned out to be a really nice guy who genuinely cared for those working at his plant, and seemed to want to work with the union leadership for the most part.

Lisa, HR leader, wasn't too bad to begin with, considering our initial conflict with the workers' comp email, and my subsequent OSHA complaint for her non-compliance with my request for the OSHA logs; all this took place a little over a year before I took office as president. Later on, Jezebel returned to her previous role as the HR leader replacing Lisa. (Management was never able to manage their personnel well.)

Ferengi, another salaried employee, worked in Darkly as a cadet engineer when I was first hired in this chemical plant. From this entry-level position, he eventually became a boss in Darkly. After a few years, he left for a position at another plant site with the same company; I was sincerely sorry to see him leave. When he returned and became the manufacturer leader of the plant while I was union president, our relationship changed drastically.

Nathan was my foreman when I first came to Darkly, and we had a good working relationship. However, conflicts are bound to happen when two people are on very different sides of a fence. He moved up the ladder to be Darkly's general foremen while I was president; after which, things were never the same between us.

Adrianne was the HR secretary who processed and recorded the grievances, scheduled the meetings, and took care of the union's bidding process and job awards. She was a very nice person, honest, and as Italian as they come. She sincerely did her job to the best of her ability, with any mistakes (and she made many) easily and patiently overlooked because of her genial personality and sincere smiles. I had a soft spot for Adrianne. There were times she was caught in the crossfire, and I felt for her.

Sabrina was another HR consultant, but with her husband, Jason, as a union member, this caused a lot of conflict of interests.

For any who are unfamiliar with union and management relationships, here is a synopsis of the process used to address most differences between the two parties:

When there is an alleged violation of our contract (also called the collective bargaining agreement, or CBA) or disagreement between the union and management, a grievance is filed to address the issue to try and resolve it between the parties. There are usually three steps to a grievance process.

First step is the first-line supervisors' chance to resolve the issue with the shop steward as the first-line rep on behalf of the union. If this doesn't work, it can move up to second and third steps with the HR leader and plant manager getting involved with higher union reps. If the grievance is not settled satisfactory, the union can choose to take the grievance to arbitration, where an unbiased arbitrator hears the grievance and makes the final judgment. The arbitrator's ruling is supposed to be binding. During arbitration, each side presents their arguments and documentations with certain people testifying at the hearing.

Our contract had specific time limits for each step of the grievance process; any side who was not compliant with these time limits forfeited their rights to settle the grievance in their favor.

Another avenue to address grievances is to file a National Labor Relations Board charge. The NLRB is an independent federal agency that assists labor unions and employers when there are alleged unfair labor practices, grievances regarding contract violations, and issues with obtaining requested information connected with addressing grievances. NLRB charges can be filed against employers or unions.

Chapter 55
First Major Issue

I never received training for any elected union officer role before being elected union president. The only training I received was the workers' comp training at the seminar (in addition to my self-taught knowledge) and the OSHA training. In contrast, International Union staff reps receive excessive training prior to being put into these roles, and then periodically to help them with their responsibilities.

Once I was in office, Cain dumped my very first major issue in my lap that he neglected to take care of months earlier. There were less than a handful of job positions that our contract dictated were awarded using an inner job interview panel that consisted of management and union employees. All other contractual jobs were awarded per seniority.

Prior to our last contract negotiations, our local union was almost sued for discrimination from the outcome of these job interview panels, and this was not the first time a lawsuit almost happened. Union employees were not supposed to be involved in any way with promoting other union employees. Management knew this liability and realized that as long as our union members were also on these interview panels, management alone could not be sued for discrimination in job awards as a result of these inner job interviews without implicating the union as well. Management wanted to keep this union shield for their own protection.

Contract language needed changed to get our local union members off these interview panels to safeguard our union from future lawsuits. Now that I was the president, Cain directed me to address this issue through a "letter of agreement" that was to change the contract language regarding these interview panels. I really wanted to confront Cain on his negligence in addressing this issue when he should have done so during our last contract negotiations months earlier when he knew this liability existed, and when contract language changes were supposed to be made.

But being new in my president position, I didn't want to cause any waves with Cain, so I kept my thoughts to myself. I already knew he didn't particularly want me elected as president, and neither did some of management, excluding Caleb. I brought along a lot of baggage with me in this role by way of my assertive and tenacious personality that was by then well known, with the Holy Spirit as my driving force.

This was also a very controversial issue and sore spot for our membership. I didn't appreciate at all that Cain dumped this issue in my lap first thing in office, but now that he did, I wanted to handle this delicately and make sure our membership understood fully why this contract language needed changed before they voted on the issue. Any letter of agreement changing contract language outside of contract negotiations required a membership vote agreeing to it before it was officially agreed upon and signed, which was the correct way to handle it.

I brought this issue up at three membership meetings, and sent out an email explaining this in detail. Cain accused me in front of everyone at the third meeting that I was dragging my feet on the issue; he purposely ignored his own negligence in addressing this during contract negotiations when he should have addressed it. But I was following God's direction in dealing with this. If Cain believed I was dragging my feet, so be it; it didn't matter to me!

The membership vote was in favor of signing this letter of agreement and getting our members off these interview panels.

At the beginning of all this, management was agreeable to changing this contract language with a letter of agreement. Now that it passed a membership vote, management reneged on their word. It took several more weeks dealing with management trying to get them to honor their original agreement to sign this letter.

Now the Lord brought Theodore back into my life. But our roles had changed. He was no longer the HR leader but was still in management, and I was the elected union president.

Upon walking into Darkly one afternoon, Harry, the union's newly elected chief shop steward who also worked in Darkly, handed me the letter of agreement with his and Theodore's signature on it, and informed me that I could now sign this letter also. He then walked out the door for the day.

Shame on Theodore for not remembering way back when dealing with my own workers' comp case, that I don't just sign documents without carefully reading them and knowing the full implications of what I am signing. (How documents are worded is so important, and signatures on them are significant.)

When management realized I was holding them to honor their agreement to sign the letter, they tried to take advantage of the situation for their benefit. They had revised the original letter to include more contract language changes that our membership did not vote on nor agreed to change. Obviously, once I read the letter, I didn't sign it. The following day, I approached Harry and asked if he even read the letter before he signed it, and sure enough, he had not.

I spent the next several weeks going back-and-forth with management, copying our union e-board and Cain, trying to get this letter of agreement worded once again to the basic objective of just getting our membership off these interview panels and get it signed. But management was adamant they were not going to honor their original agreement without getting more of what they wanted from the union for their benefit by way of contract language changes.

Finally, while Harry and I were at a labor and management meeting, I brought up the letter of agreement one final time in the presence of Caleb, Lisa and Theodore. In a very calm but deliberate tone, I made my position very clear:

"I have been going back-and-forth for several weeks now trying to get this letter of agreement worded and signed, as we all agreed we would do prior to our membership voting on this issue. But you know what! I really don't care now if this letter of agreement ever gets signed. I am telling you all right now, the members of this local union are not going to participate on interview panels again. So whether we sign this letter of agreement or not makes no difference to me at all at this point."

All that baggage I brought along with me to this union president position added weight to my demeanor.

After my asserted statement, all three of these management representatives glanced at each other with bewildered expressions. Caleb then asked Harry and me to leave the room so they could have a caucus without us. This was a good sign!

When Harry and I returned, Theodore stated on behalf of management: "We'll make three copies of the original letter of agreement and sign it."

The Lord directed me to come prepared. I replied, "You don't have to make copies. I have three copies of the original we agreed upon with me that we can all sign right now."

They all looked at each other as I saw their resignation. They couldn't back out now; they knew I had them. And so, my first major issue was successfully resolved with the Lord's help. I'm not sure they ever realized how God's Holy Spirit was my driving force. But He was, to be sure, and for His purpose. I could never have done any of this without God helping me.

Chapter 56
Making Waves

It always takes time to adjust to new positions and people that are placed in our lives. There were just a few on my e-board who didn't care that I was now the union president; our financial secretary was on the top of the list. Be it because I was a woman, or a Christian, or both, or they just didn't like me personally, the reasons didn't make a difference. My actions of trying to change some long-standing practices that I believed were wrong on the union's side seemed to only fuel these negative attitudes towards me.

Some thought they were being nice in warning me that if I continued addressing issues and causing waves, I wouldn't get re-elected. My unwavering response was always the same: "I'm not concerned with being re-elected. I am concerned with seeing that things are done right."

The main practice that caused the most contention was our union officers clouding their minds by drinking beer during our e-board meetings while we discussed difficult decisions regarding the livelihoods of our membership. I said nothing about this practice while I was a trustee on the e-board, even as I witnessed intense arguments over issues that could have been resolved in a more reasonable way had the beer not been involved.

I always believed our union members deserved the best representation we could offer them. After all, our members elected us into these positions, and with their hard-earned wages, paid our union salaries and paid for the beer their reps drank during these meetings.

As the president now, I tried explaining this to these e-board officers, some of whom were newly elected and just getting started in these positions. I would have had no complaints had these officers waited till after our meetings to drink their beer, as I was requesting. This request also carried over to our membership during our membership meetings. This became a real source of contention among us.

Cain made it clear from the beginning that he was not about to support me trying to address this beer issue, as he showed strong anger towards me each time I brought it up. After a few attempts at addressing the beer drinking during meetings, I backed off for a time. We had other issues that we needed to address as a union, and we needed unity to do it.

There were other practices I did manage to calmly change. One was the abuse of paying lost time wages on a regular basis to some of our officers. I believed it was wrong to pay out eight hours of lost time wages so someone could miss their work schedule to attend a thirty-minute union meeting, when some of these same officers didn't always make a commitment to attend these meetings when it fell on their scheduled days off.

Another abuse of our local funds involved spending thousands of dollars on our annual union-family picnic. I witnessed in the past years how so many cases of beer and extra food went to supply private camps after the picnics. Now that I was in a position to curtail this abuse, with God's help I managed to do so. These changes didn't earn me any brownie points with some of my e-board officers. But I believed we had to be good stewards with how we used our members' union dues money.

There were so many issues going on at the same time. While some were enormous, others were confidential and dealt with members who became disabled and needed help dealing with their medical and disability benefits.

I recognized that the Lord gave me unique wisdom dealing with medical and many other benefits, and the many forms and agreements that accompanied these benefits. (How documents and agreements are worded is so important.)

Early in my term as president, it was brought to my attention during a membership meeting, that our union members were being required to sign a medical release form authorizing our plant Medical Department to obtain private health information from their personal physicians. This private health information was used to replace our contractual annual physicals performed by a company doctor, and was used to determine the employees' fitness to work. By this time, there was no longer a company doctor on site, and Ms. Nurse, who was part of my workers' comp nightmare, was also replaced with another nurse.

During this meeting, some of our members stated that they were extremely upset that they had already signed this medical release form authorizing the release of their private health information, as they believed there was no way to revoke it after it was signed. With the wisdom and assertiveness the Lord had given me, I assured them that they could revoke any previously signed authorization to release medical information.

After this meeting, I sent out a plant-wide email to our union members letting everyone know that they did not have to sign this medical release form, and attached a letter anyone could print and sign for their use revoking any previously signed authorization to obtain and/or release private health information.

Many of our members took advantage of this letter and returned it to our plant Medical Department, while others refused to sign this medical release form after reading my email. I knew this email and my involvement would get back to management. After Caleb and Lisa confronted me on my involvement, the issue was quickly resolved between us in favor of the union.

As the elected union president now, I had no qualms using the company email system for union communications, as I believed I had the legal right to do so. But I was always careful not to divulge anything detrimental to our union.

From the very beginning in my president role, management was habitual in contacting Cain over how I dealt with issues. When Cain confronted me claiming I was wrong to use the company email system for union communications, I informed him that I had in my possession, an NLRB case won by another union president in defense of using his employer's email system for union communications. I knew this too would get back to management. After making this known to Cain, I never heard anything more about using the company email system for union communications. (The NLRB reversed this ruling years later.)

There were times I had support from others on our e-board, but there were also times when I had to reinforce to some of our union officers our own obligations to follow our contract language. And when push came to shove, I also found out that the position of union president had a dual role: It also served as the union scapegoat. It didn't matter who was part of making a decision in this union, all fingers pointed to the union president. And there was always someone, somewhere, somehow, who wasn't happy with a decision made.

Knowing all this only solidified my resolve to try my best in doing what was right, according to the Lord's standards and not according to anyone else's. This was my personal agenda, as Cain always accused me of having one. However, this resolve was at times a real tough challenge that came with many negative consequences. I was learning, though, to trust God for His help in dealing with these consequences.

Chapter 57
Cain's First Tirade

It wasn't too long in my term as president that Cain made his lack of support towards me well known. Management was also aware of his lack of support even before I was elected into this role. Soon afterward, I found out just how much Cain really didn't like me.

Cain was directly above me, and the only link to the International Union; at least that was what I was told at the beginning. Staff reps are supposed to support the local union officers and help them when needed. There were times when Cain supported me on some issues, but would often do a real flip-flop afterward, and decide to support management or others instead.

Very early in my term, Cain insisted that as a local union, we should allow our International Union representatives to bring in instructors to conduct a shop steward training session for all three company groups. Cain also directed our local to pay from our own funds the lost time wages for all these stewards to attend this training, and to supply food for everyone present. This was my first exposure to Joab, our International Union district director, and their representatives. I need to say that I wasn't impressed with the training or these men. Cain even admitted afterward that this shop steward training was very poorly presented compared to our former international's shop steward training.

This training had cost our local a great deal of money and was something I always regretted, as no one benefited at all. Everyone could have learned so much more by just reading the shop stewards' handbooks made available to the local unions.

After paying for this training, our funds went below the normal range needed to operate the local union. I had requested our financial secretary on several occasions for the opportunity to go over his books together, as I had the authority to do, but he kept avoiding my requests.

During one of our e-board meetings, it was voted on and agreed to move some of our funds from a money market type account into our savings account to help during this time, and from there, into CDs. Our financial secretary should have handled this fund transfer, even though as the union president, I had the legal authority to handle this as well.

Our money market fund advisor contacted me when the check had arrived at his office. When I called our financial secretary to let him know, he answered his cell phone while on top of someone's house replacing a roof, at which time he instructed me to handle the check—so I did. I deposited this whole check into our savings account at our credit union. I then informed our financial secretary what I did, and told him he could transfer what he needed into the checking account for bills, and then put the rest in CDs when he had the time. This happened on a Friday.

On Monday, this financial secretary ranted and raved on the phone at me while accusing me of infringing on his job and transferring funds without the authority to do so. He threatened that he was going to turn me into the International Union for this wrongful act, and then resign from his position. He was so upset because he wanted the whole check deposited in the checking account and not the savings account. I had emails from him previously when he was instructing me in a demanding tone to make sure these funds were moved as soon as possible, or he was going to resign his financial secretary position.

I have experienced many people during my life that cannot be reasoned with no matter how patient or gently I would try; this man was one of them. I tried my best to calm him down as I reminded him that he asked me to handle the check, and that all he had to do was move some of the money into the checking account to pay the bills. But no amount of patient reasoning would calm him down.

As he ranted and raved over and over the same accusations and threats without much of a chance for me to speak, I finally had enough and told him, "If you want to turn me into the International, go ahead. If you want to resign from your position, go ahead. This conversation has now ended." Click.

I didn't need this aggravation with everything else going on at that time. It was just announced that there would be a workforce reduction at our plant site. I was still working rotating shifts at Darkly as a chem tech while also taking care of my responsibilities as union president. This week, I was working my midnight shifts, and found myself in meetings with management during the days over these workforce reductions and getting very little sleep.

On a difficult day during this week, Cain sent an email asking if I was going to be available the following day to meet with him. When I requested why, his answer came back short without a real reason: "Issues I would rather not discuss over the phone."

With all that I was dealing with that week on so little sleep, I was in no condition to meet with him and told him so. But while speaking with him on the phone later, he said it was about my financial secretary filing a complaint against me with the International Union for wrongfully transferring these funds. Cain said he was going on vacation for three weeks and would not be available during that time to settle this, and that he was going to be in the area anyway. Cain lived over a two-hour drive away.

So, I relented and agreed to meet with him. At this time, I trusted Cain to handle whatever my financial secretary told the International about me, believing Cain knew my integrity and relationship with God would not allow me to do anything in a wrongful manner regarding our union's funds. I should have prayed about this meeting, but I was vulnerable with so little sleep and my concerns with all the workforce reductions. Satan also knew when I was most vulnerable and played it well against me.

The meeting was just the two of us at the union office off plant site. I walked into a real trap that day I still regret agreeing to. But I also felt I had no choice given what Cain said it was supposedly about. Had I known Cain's real motive for this meeting, it never would have happened, at least not without a witness.

This man had a real tirade session berating me on issues he embellished or fabricated. He did not have one good word to say about me. Some of my e-board officers had contacted him before this complaining about my attempts to address the beer drinking at meetings, but this wasn't brought up until the end.

Cain also fabricated a claim that I was sending out emails to people warning them not to contact him about me or for any other reasons. I challenged him for evidence of these emails while knowing none existed, but he ignored my challenge.

Cain brought up my financial secretary's complaint filed against me to the International for improperly handling funds that he claimed I had no authority to handle. I tried showing Cain the previous emails I had in my possession from this same financial secretary demanding I ensure these funds were moved, but he refused to even acknowledge these emails. Cain knew I had the legal authority to handle this fund transfer, and that I didn't do anything unlawful or wrong. But he recognized an opportunity to use this complaint to lure me into this meeting for his own personal agenda against me.

Finally, Cain brought up the beer drinking issue. BINGO! He didn't like my attempts to change the good-old-boys club long-standing practice of drinking beer during meetings. He never liked me as the workers' comp rep, and he didn't like me as the union president. As a matter of fact, I was convinced as time went on that he had a real hatred for me. I truly believe that had Cain thought he could have gotten away with physically beating me during this meeting instead of verbally, he would not have hesitated to do so.

I realize in my walk with God, the battles in the spiritual realm continue to rage on, even often as a result of my obedience to the Lord. God's angelic warriors came in with me to this meeting with swords unsheathed and ready for battle against the demons, who swished around drooling saliva as their sulfur breaths spurred their hatred, hoping for their own victory in destroying me.

I had many thoughts during this meeting of just getting up and walking out and leaving Cain alone with his demon buddies. I was sure he did not know how Satan and his demons were using him as a pawn to undermine God's will for my life. But by the grace of God, and with the strength from His Holy Spirit, I held my ground, defended my position, and kept my emotions under control, which was not easy. But when I am weakest, God's power is demonstrated strongest. (2 Corinthians 12:9.)

There are no words to describe what I felt when this meeting was finally over almost fifty minutes later. Cain's main goal, and Satan's, was to break me down and get me to resign from this union president position. But what Cain didn't know even as the spiritual battle raged on, was that God was the One who put me in this position in the first place, and I wasn't going anywhere until the Lord was ready for me to move on.

Cain left a message that evening on my answering machine. He had spoken to my financial secretary, and asked me to give him a call back when I had an opportunity so that he could discuss with me what was said between the two of them. The following day was the beginning of Cain's three-week vacation and my reprieve from dealing with this man. I didn't care at all what these two men had to say about my supposedly unauthorized handling of funds that I had the legal right to handle. I knew I didn't do anything wrongful, and I knew what this was all about. I never returned his call. I never told anyone in the union about this tirade meeting with Cain.

A few days later, my financial secretary resigned from his position. Once he was out of the picture, I was able to go over his books as I had requested to do many times before but was denied. It was then that I discovered his honest mistake of double paying to the International Union their share of our union dues that they required each month, which was the main reason we were short on funds. It took me several weeks of a lot of hard work and aggravation, and going back-and-forth with the International Union dues account people, before this mistake was made right and our local was reimbursed our share of the union dues.

At that meeting, the battle raged and the victory was won, as neither Cain nor Satan reached their goal. But the wounds I came away with took several years to heal, and then left some painful scars. This proved not to be the last tirade session I would endure from this man who was supposed to support our local union, and me as their union president.

Chapter 58
Darkly's Blunders

The Darkly production process had equipment and reactors that were very expensive, unpredictable, dangerous, and had extremely high temperatures and pressures. Factor into this dangerous equation human error or someone not paying attention to their job duties, literal catastrophes, serious injuries, or even loss of lives could result.

I witnessed some serious incidents during my time in Darkly: a ten-inch metal flex line blown apart (with near misses of serious injuries), process flash fires, dangerous chemical spills, and some serious second and third-degree burn injuries. Because of the dangers and complexity of the Darkly process, many chem techs would not take on the responsibility of the lead operator role, not even for the higher pay this position offered.

In all the years of the existence of Darkly, I knew of only two reactor "set-ups" ever happening, which meant the polymer inside the reactor got so thick that it could no longer be moved out of the reactor by any means, while also creating high pressures and high temperatures within the reactor.

These reactors were huge round vessels that held 20,000 pounds of Darkly polymer feed that was continuously moving in the reactor from the bottom, and out from the top. Inside the middle of each reactor was an agitator: a shaft that went from the top to the bottom of the reactor, with paddle-type blades attached at several different heights. This agitator had to constantly rotate to keep the polymer inside moving as it reacted to the temperatures and chemicals. From these reactors, the polymer feed went into extruders and continued through the hotcutters, creating Darkly pellets as the finished product.

Reactor set-ups could happen for many different reasons: loss of a feed pump moving the polymer feed in and out the reactor, loss of a reactor agitator, or any number of other glitches in the Darkly process could cause reactor set-ups. A reactor could also "run-away," a term for getting dangerously out of control due to high temperatures or high pressures, which could also cause catastrophes.

All available means to save a reactor were always exhausted before dumping the contents to the Darkly reactor dump box. Any dumped reactor involved a lot of paperwork and reporting to special environmental agencies because of the release of emissions from the contents. However, if a decision to dump a reactor's contents was not made while the polymer in the reactor could still be dumped, the result was a set-up reactor.

Both these reactor set-ups happened within months of each other and on my crew with Barney as lead operator. In defense of Barney, Line Two reactor set-up was due to a plant-wide power outage. Because we were running our highest rubber content product in this reactor during this power outage, when the plant emergency backup power did not come on, and our Darkly emergency reactor dump system also failed, this reactor was doomed. Without the agitator running due to the power outage, the response time to dump this reactor before it was beyond dumping was only about twenty minutes.

It took several weeks with men going into the reactor—a very dangerous task—to break up the polymer and clean it out before it could be put back into service. Line One reactor was out of service for scheduled maintenance during this power outage.

Line One reactor set-up happened a few months later, but was avoidable. The product running during this time was our crystal

Darkly product that had no rubber content, because of which permitted a much longer decision-making time and response of about two hours before the reactor was beyond dumping. During this night, we lost both feed pumps, and were unable to get either of the emergency styrene pumps running to add styrene into the reactor to help cool it down. With nothing going into the reactor, it was only a matter of time before the feed inside would set-up. The agitator was still running at the start of this fiasco.

Barney had called Lucas about the situation, who came in that evening to help save this reactor without having to dump it. As the amps on the agitator were slowly going up, an indication that the polymer feed was getting dangerously thick, there was plenty of time to make the decision to dump the reactor way before it had a chance to set-up. However, Lucas and Barney ignored my advice to dump the reactor before it was too late to dump it.

After two hours of doing everything we could to get either feed or styrene into the reactor, the agitator kicked out, a sure sign the polymer was set-up beyond dumping. I understood the reactor was doomed. But when Lucas requested for someone to reset the agitator breaker and start it again, I realized that these two men still did not understand the fatality of this reactor. The agitator immediately kicked out again after it was turned back on.

Harry came in as the next lead operator to relieve Barney. When we told him Line One reactor was set-up, he responded in disbelief: "What do you mean Line One reactor is set-up? You can't set-up a reactor running crystal; it's impossible." When he realized we told him the truth, his expression spoke volumes.

These set-up reactors were not the only incidents on our crew with Barney as lead operator. Some mishaps or blunders could be fixed before anything serious happened. Some occurred that it was only by the grace and protection of God that no one was seriously hurt or killed. Another fiasco that involved Barney caused a major fire in Darkly.

It was a Sunday daylight shift when the Westminster Chimes critical alarm blared. Line Two hotcutter was throwing chunks from the smeared polymer on the faceplate. Someone needed to reach the hotcutter immediately to divert the polymer feed to the floor before the line plugged. Small fiber drums were now used to collect the pancakes instead of dropping them on the metal plate to be pushed outside one at a time for cooling as was done before.

Changing the hotcutter blades after throwing chunks had several tasks that had to be done in a precisely timed sequence. It was vital that the timed sequence in diverting the polymer feed and the scalding water back through the hotcutter to restart it was perfect; if it wasn't, the polymer feed would smear the faceplate and throw chunks again, with the whole process of changing blades having to be done all over again.

Barney was the one responsible for diverting the polymer feed and scalding water back through the hotcutter, but he didn't get it just right. After a few unsuccessful attempts by Barney to restart the hotcutter, with each time smearing the faceplate and throwing chunks, our dryer system plugged up.

Ollie was my new mixologist partner. Together, we made at least three different trips up several flights of metal grating stairs to physically unplug the dryer system from the chunks that were caused by Barney's unsuccessful attempts to restart the hotcutter.

This dryer equipment could not be de-energized while unplugging it; it was interlocked with other equipment that needed to keep running. In addition, the 199.4°F heated water that went through this dryer system had only a butterfly valve holding it back at the hotcutter, which could easily be bumped open allowing the scalding water to reach us and cause severe burns. This made for a very dangerous task that normally was never done during a routine blade change.

During the second and third trips of running up to unplug our dryer system, I pleaded with Barney over our radio to shut the line down so that we could clean this system out safely. But as usual, he ignored me, as he did not want to answer for why the line went down. The shift coach and others, who monitored the radio communications throughout the plant site, never interjected. No one showed up at Darkly to check on us or help us out.

Meanwhile, the polymer pancakes continued coming out of the extruder filling up these fiber drums. But with so many fiber drums being filled that needed dragged outside for cooling, our lone packager had no time to hose these drums down to cool them off once outside. These fiber drums sat there with their smoke billowing away while the inside of them continued heating up.

Then the interior of one of these fiber drums burst into flames. With this drum close to our silos that stored the finished Darkly product, the fire swooped up the side of the silo.

When I saw this fire, my heart sunk. Trying to keep calm, I quickly headed for the fire alarm while calling on the radio pleading for help: "Fire at Darkly! Someone please, come help us!"

No response from anyone on the plant site. I reached the fire alarm box, pulled it, and waited for the blasts that when counted would announce to everyone an emergency situation was going on at Darkly. But no blasts came from this alarm. Trying not to panic, I continued calling on the radio: "Fire at Darkly! Help! Help! Fire at Darkly! PLEASE, SOMEONE COME HELP US!"

Again, no response. By now, Barney realized he had no choice but to shut the line down while his crew tried desperately to put out this fire. Ollie reached for the fire hose and went outside to the fire, but when I turned it on inside, no water came out. As I watched the fire lick up the side of the silo—no means to put it out—no alarm sounding—no help coming—I thought for sure we were doomed. Darkly was going to be no more!

Finally, for what seemed like forever, Gertrude, the only woman shift coach, showed up. She contacted our skeleton fire brigade crew who showed up with their trucks. The silo was salvaged with just the outside burned. Barney stayed inside the Darkly control room during this time dealing with the process of cooling down the reactor, or we would have had a set-up or run-away reactor to also contend with.

Someone could have been seriously hurt or killed during this fiasco. But thank God, as I often did, no one was. Silos and equipment can be replaced. Injuries cannot be reversed, and lives lost are lost forever.

Per procedure, Gertrude should have had all of us drug and alcohol tested after such a serious incident, but she did not. On many occasions, I confronted Barney on his bad work habits with what proved to be a prophetic warning: "If you don't straighten yourself up, you're gonna get fired. I'll fight to get your job back because it's my job to do so. But I'm also gonna bid on your lead operator position."

Soon after this, Barney went out on sick leave, something he did often. While Barney was off, our crew had several different lead operators covering his vacant schedule. Noah was newly trained as a lead operator and working with me on our midnight shifts. We always had a good working relationship while he was my mixologist partner—now was no different. During this time, Line One was scheduled for a controlled maintenance shutdown. Nothing needed done in a hurry. We had the time to make sure everything was done safely.

After the line was down, I turned off the hotcutter, opened the drain valve leaving the 199.4°F heated water to drain on its own, and went to take care of some other duties that needed done for this shutdown. When I came back to the hotcutter, I didn't think the water was drained yet from the chamber. I left it alone again for more draining time while I did other work.

The Line Two hotcutter had a safety green-light that turned on when the chamber was drained of water, indicating that it was safe to unclamp the collar and separate the hotcutter from the chamber. The Line One hotcutter did not have this safety green-light feature.

When Noah came to help me with the hotcutter, I informed him that I didn't think the water was drained. He checked the sight glass on the piping and decided the water was drained, but I was unable to see that it was. Before unclamping the hotcutter from the chamber, I looked again at the sight glass myself, and I asked him once again making sure he knew I had my doubts: "Are you sure? I really don't think it's drained yet."

He looked at the sight glass a second time, and was more confident: "Yeah, it's drained."

With Noah's second and confident opinion that the water was drained, we prepared to disconnect the hotcutter. The hotcutter was a very heavy piece of equipment. It was put on wheels and a track to help manually move it from the chamber once it was unclamped and disconnected. It took a split second from when I unclamped the collar of the hotcutter from the chamber, that it flew backwards on the track with a powerful force from the water that was not drained. Instantly, the scalding water that was still in the chamber splashed my face, as I was in the direct line of fire, and splashed Noah's stomach and arms. This was a classic cliché example: I trusted him and got burned.

Only one certified lead operator was scheduled to work per shift in Darkly, even though it was the only continuous production process and the most dangerous on our plant site. None of the other departments would operate unless there were two certified lead operators on the shift. Noah refused to go to the hospital because there was no one qualified to take his place. The shift coach didn't push the issue for the same reason. I tried convincing Noah he should go to the hospital, but again, he flat out refused. Neither did I go to the hospital.

Ollie, with his worried expression that I can still see, gave me a cold compress for my face. Throughout the entire rest of the midnight shift, I kept up with the cold compresses.

Noah and I had a conversation during this shift when I reminded him: "I didn't think the water was drained."

He looked at me with a shocked expression, as though he was hearing me say this for the first time, and replied with an accusing tone: "Then why didn't you say something?"

I told him the truth: "I did. But you didn't listen to me."

I then dropped the issue. No point rehashing the truth; nothing was going to change what happened.

Noah ended up with second and third-degree burns on his arms and stomach, which caused him to spend several weeks off work. I was burned on my face with the same scalding water that burned Noah, and had I not been wearing my safety glasses and hardhat with its bill over my eyes, my eyes would have been burned as well.

During the course of several years working in Darkly, I witnessed many chem techs burned by the same scalding water that left ugly scars. This should have been a very serious and painful injury to my face leaving me with ugly scars. But the Lord had healed me. I had no lingering painful effects once this shift was over, and no blisters or scars afterward.

But for several days after this trauma, I kept reliving this accident over and over again, with the emotional trauma taking much longer to heal.

Chapter 59
Performance Reviews

Barney returned from his sick leave working on our last afternoon shift, but was not covering his job his first day back; someone else was covering the lead position. At the end of this shift, Barney mentioned to some of the guys that he tried cocaine while he was off. One of these guys turned him in to management with concerns. Barney's next shift was daylight. As he was coming in, he was stopped at the gatehouse and sent to medical for a drug and alcohol test. He was not allowed back into the plant until the results came back. When they came back positive for cocaine, he was immediately terminated.

Our employer had a self-referral drug and alcohol program that allowed any employee with a problem to turn themselves in to medical for help, with the promise they would not lose their employment. But they had to turn themselves in prior to a positive test result.

There were many stipulations on this self-referral program, including frequent random drug and alcohol testing, with any infractions resulting in immediate termination. While on this self-referral program, these employees remained on their present bid jobs, even safety-critical jobs such as chem techs.

At any time, those on this self-referral program could have a relapse, come to work under the influence, and medical could miss this between testing. This was a safety issue our employer never took into account. It was confidential who was on this self-referral program. The union leadership only got involved when there was a termination, an infraction, or the employee requested the union to get involved.

There were obvious concerns with anyone using drugs or alcohol in our safety-critical work environment, and concerns with this self-referral program. I brought up some of these concerns to Cain and others in the International Union very early in my president term. As a result, I was cautioned in dealing with anyone suspected of drug and/or alcohol use in a union shop. I was told that the union could easily be sued if any union officer wrongly accused someone, or turned them in for being on drugs or alcohol and afterward, it was discovered that this person was clean. Many people never understood the complications dealing with this issue.

With Barney terminated, I really didn't want to bid on his lead operator job, even though I had told him I would. I found it very difficult working rotating shifts as a Darkly chem tech while being the union president. Adding into this equation working mandatory overtime each week, there were days that I was worn out. I was hanging on during this time only with God's help.

I remembered being a little intimidated when I first came to this industrial chemical plant—over seventeen years ago—wondering if I could learn the material packager job. Then came the Lord's leading to bid on a mixologist chem tech, another job position I had doubts I could learn and do, especially while dealing and learning to live with the RSD condition. Then the Lord moved me into the union president role, another position I had to completely rely on God's strength and wisdom to deal with.

But really, it was all about obeying the Holy Spirit's leading once again. So, I obeyed and bid on the lead operator position. Once I received the bid, my responsibilities at my place of employment increased drastically. The time frame was just over a year into my union president term.

Soon after Barney was terminated, management called a meeting with Harry and me to announce a new documented performance review process with one-on-one meetings between a supervisor and union member. Ferengi, Lisa, Caleb, and another management woman, Loraine, were present at this meeting. It was a cold January day with the meeting down front in the gatehouse conference room, a long-distance walk from Darkly.

As Harry and I sat there listening, Caleb explained about this new performance review process they planned on implementing immediately. They wanted to make sure the union knew about this in their hopes that we would agree. So often, management would come to union leadership wanting us to agree to something that they knew from the get-go was a violation of our contract. If they could get us to agree, they would then be able to invoke their long-standing, well-rehearsed defense to our union members when they complained about it: "But your union agreed to it." And so it was now with this new performance review process.

I understood exactly what the goal was behind these reviews: Management wanted a means to document poor work habits in an ongoing effort to build negative profiles on certain targeted employees to support their termination. At the same time Barney was terminated, another woman, Tracy, was terminated.

Tracy had some disposition and work issues that I was well aware of, as she worked in Darkly earlier in her employment. She had received a discipline letter over the past year that Harry and I were unaware of at the time, yet the letter indicated we both received copies; I viewed this as falsifying documentation. Union reps were always to be notified and present whenever a discipline letter was issued to one of our members. Because Tracy saw we were copied, she never bothered to contact us, as she believed we just didn't care about her situation.

Ferengi's excuses for Tracy's termination were lame at best. I was sincerely concerned when she was overwhelmingly distraught over losing her job. Instead of filing a grievance to address her termination, I was able to negotiate a retirement deal for Tracy that both parties were satisfied with. When she thanked me for how I was able to help her, I expressed it was only through God's help that the outcome ended so well. Yep, I understood very well management's motives behind these performance reviews.

Caleb was a nice guy and sincerely cared about the success of the plant site. We had a good relationship up until recently. But I had a job to do of enforcing our contract, and I always tried doing any job to the best of my ability.

During this meeting, I gave Caleb ample time to explain their proposal for these reviews while I remained silent. As I patiently waited until he was completely done speaking, I was praying for God's help to control my anger, as I could feel my blood boiling.

Once Caleb was done speaking, I spoke to him in a deliberate but calm demeanor: "There are provisions in our contract to have annual performance reviews for just very few certain job positions, which this union negotiated before my time. To implement these performance reviews for every union employee one-on-one with their supervisors, or even with union reps present, would be a direct violation of our contract that I will not allow."

Harry didn't speak at this meeting, at least not when I was there, but he watched and listened to everything. Caleb was adamant that management was going to implement these performance reviews. As Caleb spoke again on the benefits of such reviews, he emphasized that this would not turn into any discipline for individuals. I heard this story before.

There was another ILP process (investigative learning process) that was implemented years before, which at the time of its infancy was clearly expressed would never result in any disciplinary action for any of those involved. The sole purpose of this ILP process was to thoroughly investigate the cause for all incidents that happened in our plant site, whether from equipment failures or human errors, and then devise a corrective action for future prevention. Over the years, this ILP process morphed into a direct means to desperately find fault with union employees, regardless of the cause for these incidents. This often resulted in severe disciplinary action for these union members, while any participation of salaried personnel who were also proven at fault was purposely ignored.

About twenty minutes into this meeting, I decided it was going on far too long. Once again in my deliberate demeanor, I stated for a final time: "These performance reviews are a direct violation of our contract. If you insist on implementing this process, I will do everything I can to stop it. I am asking you, please, just drop the whole issue. Do not implement these performance reviews."

Caleb looked at me, then looked around quickly at the others, and after glancing at Harry at the far end of the table who still had not spoken, turned back to speak to me. Caleb was just as deliberate: "No! We are not going to drop the issue! We are going to implement these performance reviews immediately, and the union can do what they have to."

Harry kept silent. By this time, I was done with these people. I was determined this was now going to be a major battle, if not a full-blown-out war. As God's Holy Spirit took control of my anger, I said nothing more as I calmly gathered my pen and notebook, placed them within my briefcase, and then stood up from the table. All eyes were upon me as I carefully and slowly put on my parka, zipped it up, grabbed my hardhat and gloves, swung my briefcase over my shoulder, and gently pushed the chair back into the table. No one said a word as they watched me.

While I stood at the chair, I looked around the table at everyone and made one final deliberate statement that was more of a command than anything else: "Have a nice day!"

I walked out calmly but in hot anger, and gently closed the door behind me.

Now alone in the hallway, I became even more furious, if that were possible. *Harry missed his cue! How can he do such a thing? Where is my right-hand union chief shop steward?* Anytime a union president walks out of a meeting like the one we just had, every union member is supposed to follow suit, especially the next in command. But unfortunately, Harry hadn't learned this yet. *Or did he just not care?*

The long walk back to Darkly out in the cold didn't cool off my anger any. When Harry finally returned to Darkly, I told him he missed his cue. What was he doing in there all by himself? Did he not at all get what went on? Harry tried to defuse my anger as he told me his discussion with Caleb and the rest of management after I left: "I just told them you were going to do everything you can to stop this. And you will."

"Well, that's what I told them!" *No matter!* I had my vice president have a talk with Harry about the unspoken code of conduct of never remaining in a meeting when the union president walks out. Harry then understood, or so I thought.

Harry was a great guy, but full of pride to be sure. He demonstrated this every day working in Darkly as a lead operator. Now that he was the second in command as union chief shop steward, his pride ruled his role well. But he also had a soft spot in his heart that he didn't want people to see.

Someone shared with me what Harry once told a few people while referring to me dealing with another major issue as the president, as he emphasized my ability to deal with it: "But you never saw her in action."

The reality—I don't believe anyone really understood that God's Holy Spirit was my driving force of all I did in that union president role, even though I always gave Him the credit.

Chapter 60

First Board Charge

Management continued their habitual contact with Cain regarding my actions, which made my role as president very difficult. Cain often sided with management even after indicating he would support me on an issue. I was not always privy to the communications between these parties, but there were times it was made known to me; such was the case after that last meeting announcing the performance review process.

After I found out that management had contacted Cain, I contacted him for advice on dealing with the performance review process. Cain gave some invaluable advice when he wanted to. It took me a while to learn to sift through when I should heed his advice, or when I should not, as I knew there were many times he favored management, and to the detriment of our union.

This time, Cain did more than advise me on what to do; he was adamant I listen to him: "Take a day off on union business, go to the NLRB and file board charges against the company regarding the performance review process."

I had already filed a grievance on the issue. I hated taking any time off for union business at the local's expense, and Cain knew this. But he was adamant that I follow his direction.

Just a few months before this time, I had contacted the NLRB office regarding a grievance information request Lisa denied, which pertained to receiving proof that a union member received his vacation pay that I had filed a grievance for him to receive prior to him passing away from cancer. It just so happened that his mother attended the same church I had started to attend, and I was working with this member's son to wrap up his father's employee benefits now that he passed away.

The NLRB agent I had spoken to regarding this told me I was entitled to receive this proof of vacation payout, and if the company did not supply this information request, it was a violation of a labor law that I should file a board charge on. However, God did not lead me to file this board charge at that time.

I had told Cain about this conversation with this board agent just after it took place, but he didn't believe that this agent stated I was entitled to this requested grievance information on behalf of someone who had passed away. Cain asked me for the agent's name that I spoke with so he could speak with him and find out the truth on his own. I never heard back on the result of this contact. Cain always hated it when he found out I was right!

Now that Cain was adamant I file board charges on the performance review process, I decided to bundle the charges and included this previously denied request for information violation, and a second denied request for information for another grievance, as they were both still within the six-month time limit for filing board charges.

Once at the NLRB office, the agent on duty took all my information for the complaint, and completed all the forms needed to file these charges. When he asked me to sign the forms, I had a real lack of peace. I needed more time to think and pray about this now that I went this far before deciding if this was the route I should be taking. I took the complaint forms home with me. I was told I could sign these anytime and mail them back in.

For several days after this during different opportunities, I spoke with Caleb and expressed that there was nothing personal, but I was going to pursue this issue outside the company if management insisted on implementing the performance review process. I wanted to give him a heads-up, hoping beyond hope that

First Board Charge/60

this whole ridiculous issue would be dropped once and for all without taking such drastic actions with filing NLRB charges. I don't believe Caleb was taking me seriously. It was unfortunate that he found out differently when I hand-delivered him the board charges a few days after our last conversation. I really didn't want to file board charges, but after giving it several days of thought and prayer, and without resolution, I felt there was no other choice.

Not long into this, I found out that filing board charges was no easy task, and this first time around turned out to be a horrible experience for me.

Clyde, the board agent assigned to my case, was not the one who initially took my complaint, but he was the same board agent I spoke with months earlier regarding my denied request for proof on the vacation payout grievance; the same denied request that was now part of these bundled board charges.

Clyde was a mean burly man who was not at all professional when he spoke with me concerning these charges. He used such profanity that was downright disgusting. He expressed that he would be a real "BLANK-BLANK" to me when taking my affidavit.

As Clyde spoke, I thought: *And this man is a federal government employee! How can he talk to anyone like that, let alone a woman? Did he think I also spoke that way because I am a union president?* I was horrified when I left there the first time we met, and decided then I was not going to meet him alone for the affidavit.

Because Cain was the one adamant I file these board charges (he also agreed with the bundle charges), he needed to be there when I gave the affidavit. He always supported other locals and went with their officers when they filed board charges. I wasn't so sure this was a good idea, but I couldn't think of anything else to do with Clyde. Cain agreed to be present when I gave the affidavit.

Afterward, Clyde asked to speak to me alone without Cain, which didn't happen. Unfortunately, I had to go back alone dealing with Clyde regarding these board charges.

During this next visit alone with Clyde, he asked me out to lunch, which I flatly but politely refused. A few days after this, Clyde called my home three times in one night. When I saw on my caller ID that it was Clyde calling after work hours, I refused to answer the phone. He left three recorded messages on my answering machine, which I transferred to a cassette tape for evidence if needed at a later date.

On the first message, Clyde stated he wanted to come to my home stating my address, and if I could call him back within an hour, he could still come that evening. His excuse was that he wanted me to sign papers separating the charges for the denied requests for information for the grievances from the performance review charge before he could process these. His second message stated he wished he had my cell phone number. His third message stated he was calling from his home, which my caller ID verified. Just hearing his voice on my answering machine gave me chills.

I told Cain that Clyde was making advances on me, and what he said on his three voice messages left on my home answering machine, thinking Cain would help me address this. Cain told me not to say anything to anyone until after the board charges were over with, at which time he promised to help me address the issue formally. I believed him and kept all this to myself.

Meanwhile, Caleb started going around the plant site to the different departments and shifts having his propaganda meetings with union members, and complaining about the board charges and arbitration the union was pursuing for someone who tested positive for cocaine.

As it has always been our local union's practice, Barney's termination case was discussed and voted on for arbitration first by the union e-board, and then at the membership meeting. As union president, I only vote on such issues as the tiebreaker. To protect our local union from lawsuits, almost all terminations went to arbitration, albeit some would agree reluctantly.

None of us condoned drugs in the workplace. Our defense was that Barney deserved a second chance, as others were given after testing positive for drugs. I only discovered this during my investigation preparing for Barney's termination grievance.

When Caleb showed up at Darkly, he seemed surprised I was present during that shift. I confronted him about his propaganda meetings and his disparagement of the union officers, which was the sole purpose of his meetings.

I expressed that the union had the legal right and obligation to pursue someone's termination case, and the legal right to file board charges for management's intent on violating our contract. Up until recently, Caleb and I had a good rapport with each other.

With my confrontation came a heated argument between the two of us over everything going on. I then blurted out in the presence of everyone: "I should not have had to fight for a dying man to receive his vacation pay."

Caleb exploded after this statement, and then stormed out in hot anger.

When Harry and I boycotted our next monthly labor and management meeting, Caleb showed up at Darkly again asking to speak to us alone over the issues. Things were not going well between management and the union. But personal feelings needed to stay out of this. It was understood that each of us had a job to do that we were going to do. Harry and I agreed to attend the next labor and management meeting.

Chapter 61
Good-Faith Gesture

Many times during my years as union president, I was profoundly aware that one of the main purposes God had in placing me in this role was to use the fierce opposition He knew I would be exposed to and have to endure, to teach me to rely solely on His wisdom and direction and strength to get me through. This training would be used to prepare me for the ministry He would later call me into.

The Darkly union members were bitterly divided over the termination of Barney. Some were so angry that a union member would dare turn in another union member, regardless of who this person was or any circumstances involved. Others were angry that the union would dare represent Barney in such a termination case.

I endured such fierce opposition from both union and management people over the decision to arbitrate Barney's termination, a decision I had no vote on. That union scapegoat role kicked in again, but by this time, I was getting used to this.

This was my first exposure to an arbitration hearing and to Gremlin, management's lawyer. Gremlin had subpoenaed all the witnesses to appear for this arbitration, including me.

The witness chair was in the middle of a "U" shaped formation of tables and chairs. Management and their Gremlin sat to the left of the witness chair. I sat to the right with Cain, other local union reps, and Barney. The arbitrator sat in front of the witness chair behind a table.

There was ample space between the witness chair and the rest of the people present. I assumed this set-up was normal for an arbitration hearing. After being at other arbitration hearings, I realized it was not. I guessed this set-up was a precaution: Just in case someone went berserk, the others had time to get out of the way. This arbitration was not held at any company premises as others were, but was held at a nearby hotel conference room.

All the witnesses waited in a separate room, and were called in one at a time. After testifying, each witness was directed back to the waiting room. Ollie came walking in with an obvious confident and prideful demeanor. It was believed that Ollie was the one who turned Barney in to management.

Cain had questioned Ollie if he would have a problem with another employee working with him while on the self-referral drug and alcohol program; Ollie said he would. Cain had to drop it then because of the confidentiality involved. I would never know if Ollie knew that his most trusted relief chem tech partner, who covered the lead position, was on the self-referral program.

While I was being questioned as a witness, Cain had said something that Gremlin thought was funny that caused him to call out across the room in the hearing of everyone: "I love you, Cain."

Cain responded with spontaneous laughter and seemed pretty proud of himself. I pondered all this to myself. As the years went on, I found myself in strong competition with Gremlin for Cain's support. I confronted Cain more than once concerning his conflict of allegiance. Gremlin almost always won this competition.

I prayed to the Lord before this hearing, as I often did before meetings, that I would only speak what He wanted me to speak and in the way He wanted. After the hearing, Cain really criticized my testimony. And as often as he berated me up to that point in our union relationship, I was still not callused to his remarks.

During my quiet time with the Lord that evening, while feeling bad about my testimony in believing Cain that I blew it, the Lord confirmed that I said exactly what He wanted me to say. The Lord also reinforced my need to keep my eyes upon Him only, and not to worry about pleasing anyone else except Him. With this encouraging word from the Lord, I quickly got over this feeling that I blew it. I tried my best to help Barney. I also realized that I was never going to do anything that Cain would be satisfied with, and the sooner I accepted this, the better off I would be.

When we lost the arbitration, Barney's termination was final. With the arbitration over, the performance review grievance and board charges were the major issues left to deal with. When I told Clyde that I was working with management on these issues, he was furious with me. He stated he did not want me contacting management, Caleb in particular, at all with these issues. Clyde wanted to deal with it his way, and forget about me as the president trying to resolve this and heal our broken union and management relationship.

Clyde had contacted Gremlin, who was handling the board charges, and informed him that the NLRB decided management had two violations regarding the information requests for grievances. Gremlin then became furious and contacted his buddy, Cain, to vent on him. Making a full circle around, Cain was furious at me for filing the board charges now that his buddy was furious with having to deal with violations. I was guessing Cain forgot his adamant direction for me to file the board charges to begin with. *The union scapegoat gets beat up again!*

While Cain berated me over the board charges, he did another flip-flop and told me that many people spoke so highly of Clyde, that he just knew I fabricated his advances. Cain was adamant stating, "There's no way a board agent would ever volunteer to go to a private home for someone to sign board charge papers."

I held my ground and countered, "I have his messages on cassette tape. Would you like to hear them?"

No response! So much for Cain helping me to address dealing with such an unprofessional NLRB agent who made advances on me when this was all over, as he promised he would. I should have seen this coming with the fondness between Cain and Gremlin. It took some months later before I found out just how belligerent Clyde also dealt with Gremlin. Of course, Cain was not the one to tell me this; although I'm sure Gremlin had told him.

This performance review saga dragged on for several months. I rallied our troops for support to not back off until management completely dropped the whole issue. I dealt with a lot of hassles and hard work with the NLRB, and went back-and-forth with management through the grievance process just before having to decide to arbitrate before the issue was finally resolved.

When management finally relented and dropped the whole issue, I told Caleb that in addition to withdrawing the performance review board charge, I would withdraw the other two board charges that were violations for the company. Caleb assured me it was not necessary to withdraw the two violation charges; they would deal with them as best they could.

But as usual, the Lord always had the final word on my actions. Following God's leading, in a good-faith gesture with the hopes of building a better relationship between the union and management, I found real pleasure emailing Clyde informing him that I was withdrawing the performance review board charge and the two violation charges he so aggressively wanted to deal with.

The Lord taught me so much in this trial. First and foremost, I always need to keep my eyes on Him, especially in the midst of such fierce opposition. Second, I always need His wisdom, direction and strength to help me through all situations. Others will fail me to some degree, regardless of who these people may be, their good intentions, or my relationship with them. Humans are fallible, unpredictable and untrustworthy at times. But the Lord Jesus will never leave me nor forsake me. He is the same yesterday, today and forever. (Hebrews 13:5, 13:8.)

Chapter 62
Contracting Out

For several months, and during the entire ordeal of the performance review grievance, termination arbitration and board charges, I was in training for the lead operator chem tech position. After getting my lead certification, I was back on my same shift schedule as the lead operator. I was working with Ollie and Stanley as my two mixologists. I knew these two men did not at all care for the union, or me as president.

Ollie and I had a good working relationship at one time. However, Ollie developed strong ill feelings towards me because of some of my decisions as president, including arbitrating Barney's termination case, that he never got over.

Stanley was a relief operator who also covered the lead position, but was covering on my crew on an open mixologist schedule. I got Cain involved when Stanley asked me to stop what he believed was harassment with frequent drug and alcohol tests while he was on the self-referral program. When we couldn't help him, Stanley and Cain almost came to blows in a heated argument.

This crew situation was distressing for me. I needed to depend on these two mixologists in order to do my own lead operator job well. But the Lord proved faithful, and He supplied me with all that I needed to oversee such an unpredictable process while operating expensive and dangerous equipment successfully, even in the midst of a difficult situation dealing with men and their ill feelings towards the union and me.

The next major issue I challenged was the contracting out of our union maintenance work that our own union craftsmen were capable of doing. For several years, management had been diminishing our Maintenance Department through attrition. Several severance packages had been offered over the years targeting our maintenance positions. Management's intentions were always to use the resident contractors they kept on the plant site to supplement this workload.

The last reduction in our Maintenance Department happened just seven months into my union president term. No one was forced into involuntary layoff, but several maintenance craftsmen were bumped out of their department, and were still bumped out during this time of challenging this contracting out of union work that was an ongoing abuse by management.

During management's campaign to erode our Maintenance Department, they sold most of their heavy equipment to the resident contractors during my predecessor's term as president. This offered management what they considered another legitimate excuse for contracting out the union's work: They did not own the necessary equipment for our own maintenance craftsmen to do the work.

For every contracting out job, the union president and chief shop steward received a contracting out notice explaining certain aspects of the job, with a brief explanation justifying why this work was contracted out versus having our own maintenance craftsmen do the work. On so many of these notices sent by maintenance supervisors, they clearly admitted in one way or another that there just wasn't enough union maintenance personnel to meet all the operational needs of the plant; the cause was management's deliberate attrition of our maintenance workforce.

As a union, we were losing job positions over this contracting out abuse that management was getting away with. But what really aggravated me was the justification on some of these contracting out notices that stated the union craftsmen were consulted, and they were the ones who determined they could not do the work.

These contracting out notifications would come to the union via email. Just as I was reading one stating the craftsmen were consulted and determined they could not do the work, Marshall, one of these craftsmen, was just walking through Darkly's control room. Roles in life change often, and in the process, people and their responsibilities also change. Now I was the union rep and Marshall, once the appointed chief shop steward at the end of my workers' comp nightmare, was just a union member.

I took full advantage of this opportunity. I called Marshall over to where I was, and while pointing to the contracting out notification still up on the computer screen, I confronted him: "So tell me, why can't you guys do this work?"

Marshall gave a lame excuse I can't recall now, but I cannot forget how ticked off I was at his excuse. Here I was, trying so hard to stop these contracting out jobs so we could keep our own work for our union maintenance and not lose any more job positions, and people like this lazy man were going against everything I was trying to accomplish. It was his sub-group craftsmen who eventually were eliminated. But he didn't care; he was retiring.

I filed a grievance for the contracting out abuse, and then put in a contractor cost information request. I wanted to do a comparison of the cost of using these resident contractors versus our own union maintenance craftsmen. My recent good-faith gesture in withdrawing the two board charges that were violations for management's refusal to supply requested information relative to resolving grievances, just flew out the window. I waited for a rebound, but it never happened. I was sure it found its way to the first good-faith gesture of not filing an OSHA complaint for taking almost eight weeks for my requested copies of my medical records, which also flew out the window.

I patiently waited for this contractor cost information that I legally knew I had the right to request and receive, but when I finally got it, it was incomplete. Consequent requests were being ignored several weeks following. Cain had agreed for me to file another board charge for these denied requests. Following God's direction, I did so.

With another board charge filed for the contractor cost information Gremlin had to deal with, Cain did another flip-flop with his lack of support after the fact, and became furious with me for filing the charge. And Cain sure didn't want anyone else supporting me.

Up until this time, my e-board gave me full support dealing with this whole contracting out grievance and board charge. However, my next meeting with the e-board after Cain's flip-flop turned into a vicious ambush on me. Now they all did a flip-flop concerning their support, a sure sign Cain had spoken to them. But at this point, I was still not realizing everything that was happening behind the scenes.

Soon after this e-board ambush, Cain phoned me, and by his own admission, related all the derogatory comments he made about me to Daisy, the board agent assigned to this new board charge. After this conversation with Cain, the equation was just beginning to form.

The following week was the membership meeting. Cain called me aside just before the start and tried to assure me: "No one is doing anything behind your back."

By now, I was doing my best to avoid any confrontation with this man as much as possible. So why did he call me aside to make such a statement? Was his conscience bothering him? Or was he trying to make sure I didn't have these thoughts?

After what Cain just told me, his derogatory comments to Daisy, the e-board's vicious ambush, the equation was becoming complete; everything seemed to add up to one culprit against me.

I didn't need this confrontation and getting all upset right before a union meeting. I was still having difficulty at times speaking in front of these people as the chairperson. This was a local union meeting that didn't need Cain to be present. So why did he choose to sit up front on the platform next to me, when he sat with the membership on the floor during other meetings?

At the start of every union meeting, after thanking everyone for coming, I would ask everyone to stand, say the pledge of allegiance to our Flag, and to please remain standing for a moment of silence for all our departed brothers and sisters. At every single union meeting I led—I only missed one all my years as president—during our moment of silence I would say a silent prayer: *Lord, please bless this meeting and let it go well. Please don't let me say anything I should not say, but only what I should say and in the way I should say it.*

When I was done praying, I would ask everyone to please be seated, and would start the meeting. Cain wasn't happy that I cut short his confrontation before this meeting. Sitting up front next to me, he tried to continue it right after the meeting was over. But by then, I was done with this man.

The next time I spoke with Daisy, I let her know that Cain told me all the derogatory comments he told her about me. My next statement to Daisy echoed what I now knew was always the case with Cain: "All I can say is, this man has a very low opinion of me."

I let it go at that. I was determined not to lower myself to Cain's standards by saying anything negative about him. Thankfully, the conversation between Cain and Daisy did not negatively affect her assessment of this case.

Once I received the entire contractor cost information, Daisy wanted to facilitate a meeting between Caleb, Gremlin and me regarding the board charge. This meeting took place at the company's corporate office building several miles away from our plant site. Cain always wanted to be involved whenever Gremlin was involved in anything. But I never informed Cain of this meeting. His flip-flopping support and derogatory remarks made to Daisy concerning me, justified my decision to exclude him. And besides, Daisy never mentioned she wanted his presence.

The purpose of our meeting with Daisy was to agree upon and sign a letter indicating management would cooperate with the union regarding information requests and questions on other matters. Gremlin, after commenting that he noticed Lisa's habitual practice of not responding to my emails, asked to add wording in this letter before we signed it, that management or their representatives would respond within two business days after receipt of such requests or questions from the union.

I once saw a message during that time that my "M" drive was being accessed when I couldn't log onto my work email. This message appeared many times afterward during when the union was dealing with significant issues, such as board charges or arbitrations. It was their computers and email system. I could only guess that was how Gremlin knew of Lisa's habitual delays in responding to my emails.

It was during this meeting that Gremlin also remarked to Daisy that it was a pleasure dealing with her versus the last board agent, referring to Clyde.

Cain never mentioned this meeting to me. But by his increased aggressiveness towards me in the weeks following, I knew he was told of his exclusion as our International Union staff rep and resented me for it.

Chapter 63

Vindictiveness

About two weeks after this meeting with Daisy, while I was going over the contractor cost information with a salaried employee, the union e-board was called into a last-minute meeting. The purpose was to announce that the plant site was going idle. One hundred and thirty union members were going to be laid off, supposedly only temporarily, which was almost our entire union workforce. No salaried personnel were going to be laid off during this idle period. This layoff was only for the company group I worked for, and did not involve the other two company groups from our amalgamated local union.

Caleb was not present at this meeting. During this meeting, I confronted Ferengi with a direct question: "So tell me, how much money is the company saving by having all these layoffs?"

Ferengi at times could be honest; although his honestly often displayed his contempt towards the union: "This was not a cost savings business decision."

I responded, "Really? Then what was it?"

Lisa did a quick backpedal in their defense: "Well, we are not making product. So if nothing is going out, nothing is coming in."

Some of these same management people were present when Caleb justified the contracting out of union work by stating they contract out so when the work is not there, they wouldn't have to lay off our own union maintenance craftsmen. Caleb had tried to reiterate management's long-standing practice of avoiding layoffs. So much for that rationale now!

Lisa previously worked in management at the glass factory that I worked at when I first came home from the Army. This factory had a revolving door policy of laying people off and calling them back, giving absolutely no regards to how that type of on and off employment played havoc with people's lives. Now that she was HR leader at our chemical plant, she brought along with her the same revolving door.

Just over a week after this initial announcement of this massive layoff, the union e-board was called into another meeting. Present from management during this meeting was Ferengi, Lisa and Theodore. Theodore's role had changed from being the HR leader during my workers' comp nightmare, to being the head of Beady, another production department.

Theodore announced that the layoff for his department needed to be delayed. The reason was that our customers of Beady heard about the layoffs, and were highly concerned that they were not going to be getting our product they needed. Imagine that! All this was taking place towards the end of November. Trying to start up any production department in the middle of winter posed significant challenges due to the cold weather.

With this new revelation, as union president on the same playing level as these management people, I made a statement to them without hiding my strong anger: "If we lose customers because we cannot supply them with the product they need, all because of a layoff that was not a cost savings business decision, I'm going to be extremely angry." (Not that I wasn't angry already with these layoffs.)

Lisa left the meeting crying hysterically after my statement, which I had no regret for making. Management made the decision to layoff our union workforce; let them each deal with their own conscience now.

Soon after this, Ferengi called another meeting with the union e-board concerning how these layoffs were going to happen. According to our seniority contract language, personnel in plant pool job classifications were laid off first, even if they had more seniority in overall employment. Personnel in job classifications not in the plant pool were laid off according to their departmental seniority, and would be able to bump into the plant pool job positions if they had the seniority to do so.

Ferengi was habitual in his blatant disregard of contract language whenever it interfered with his personal agendas, especially when it came to managing the union workforce, and had no qualms disregarding contractual seniority rights in the process. This next meeting regarding how these layoffs were going to play out was just one example.

By this time, Ferengi knew me well as president. Knowing I would never agree to his blatant disregard of contract seniority language, he would play on the sympathies of other union leadership hoping for their agreement, and this time, it almost worked. And Ferengi always had only one reason why he wanted agreement from the union before implementing his personal agenda against our contract. He wanted to be able to invoke his long-standing defense should anyone question his actions: "But your union agreed to it."

Present at this last layoff meeting was also Lisa and Caleb. Ferengi wanted the e-board's agreement in keeping only lead operators working as fire watch in each of the shutdown departments during the layoffs, one per shift working the four-shift rotation schedule, regardless of contractual seniority rights.

There were a couple of e-board officers that this directly affected. As lead operators, they would have stayed working while others in their department with more seniority were forced into layoff status. Ferengi knew this, and he was also looking out for a few of his other favored employees who were lead operators. He used the excuse that lead operators had more knowledge than other chem tech positions while reiterating this as only a temporary layoff.

Working as fire watch meant only manning the idle departments and making rounds while ensuring no dangerous incidents happened, such as fires. Any chem tech job position had enough knowledge to work as fire watch.

I had to call our e-board officers out three different times during this meeting for a caucus—as they were caving in—to reiterate our responsibility to enforce our contract language: Seniority must rule for layoffs.

Ferengi's badgering when he wasn't getting his way would at times lead me to exasperation. But I also knew him well; he rarely got his way, at least with me. Coming back in from our last caucus, Ferengi still badgering over keeping the lead operators regardless of seniority, I finally told him: "If you want to keep only lead operators working during this layoff, go ahead, that's your decision. But we are not going to agree to it, and I will be filing a grievance over the contract violation."

As I knew he would, Ferengi finally backed off, stating he didn't want a grievance filed over the layoff issue. At the end of all this, our contract for layoff seniority was honored, and we gained one additional chem tech remaining in each department, with the extra more senior chem tech working daylight for any other issues that may arise.

Just after the announcement of this massive layoff, I met with Cain one-on-one, which he initiated. Because of everything going on, and with him directly above me, once again, I felt I had no choice in the matter. But this time, I was on guard and prepared to walk out on him if needed.

During this meeting, I confronted Cain boldly and asked him why he hated me so much. Of course, he denied my accusation. I responded to what I had come to know was true: "Yeah, you do.

You are out to destroy me! Why? I have been in competition for your support with management and Gremlin all this time."

Cain never responded. Instead, he told me that corporate, from the company I was employed with, was blaming me as the union president for the cause of this massive layoff.

Was this management's vindictiveness against me for exercising my legal rights in addressing the contracting out abuse, and filing the board charge to get the contractor cost information to fight this issue? Ferengi did admit that this massive layoff was not a cost savings business decision.

The timing was obvious, and I don't believe in coincidences. I was getting to know management pretty well and would not put anything past them. This was happening just a few months before we were going to negotiate a very difficult contract.

How did Cain find out about this? Was he part of and in agreement with their decision to layoff almost our entire union workforce? But I had a much bigger question that I would never know the real answer: Was what Cain just told me true, that corporate was blaming me for this massive layoff?

This was not the first time I left a meeting with Cain in extreme turmoil. I could only guess that one or more of the demons that were battling God's angelic warriors during that meeting, latched on for a ride afterward.

After this meeting with Cain, everything behind the scenes added up for a final sum. My math was always better than my English. This equation finally revealed the real culprit for all the turmoil I was dealing with—Cain!

Chapter 64

Victory

I have come to learn in my walk with God, if there is something He wants me to know about, He will always bring this knowledge to my attention in His timing, and at times, in unique ways.

During the time of the contracting out grievance, board charge and layoffs, I just happened to discover an International Union policy specifically stating that alcoholic beverages at establishments owned or rented by local unions were not allowed, with the exception for occasional social affairs sponsored for members and their families. This exception was needed for their own protection. Every International Union function I attended had plenty of alcoholic beverages available.

There was also an amalgamated local union by-laws manual that the International Union dictated local unions were to follow that clearly stated: "The local union president shall enforce the provisions of the International constitution, and of these by-laws, and the policies and manuals of the International Union."

So, there you have it! I had every legal right to enforce this policy dictating that there be no alcoholic beverages at our union hall that as a local union, we rented for our use.

I showed Cain a copy of this policy, hoping he would now support waiting till after meetings before our officers and members consumed their beer while claiming this time as a social event. But instead, he went absolutely berserk on me. When Cain told me later that he contacted Joab, our International Union district director, to complain that I was addressing the beer issue—

although he never told me what he said—I also emailed Joab, but was sure to copy Cain.

In my email, I quoted some key language of the policies, manuals and by-laws, and asked my questions. Joab never responded. Instead, another International Union representative, Alfred, contacted me via email asking me to call him regarding my questions on the policies of the International Union. I attempted to contact Alfred several times per his request, but he too never responded. And so, the buck was passed around without ever getting any answers as to why the International Union had policies they refused to enforce, and refused to support any other officer wanting to enforce these policies.

After approaching Cain with the policy on beer, he requested I give him the date and time of our next monthly e-board meeting. He said he wanted to address "issues" with all of us. But I knew what Cain's intentions were going to be during this meeting. By now, I was fully trusting God for everything. I knew the One to whom I was really accountable to. And to be sure, it wasn't our e-board, nor Cain, nor an International Union.

Cain made sure to contact everyone on the e-board prior to this meeting regarding his intentions. Some e-board officers purposely did not attend this meeting. One member showed up only after Cain had left.

Cain ranted and raved at me during this meeting about what he claimed was my vindictiveness against management, and claimed that I was a dictator with a personal agenda who had no authority to try to control the beer drinking. I endured Cain's tirade in front of my e-board officers as I watched them guzzle down several bottles of beer each in as little as twenty minutes.

I had asked Cain on numerous occasions what he thought my personal agenda was without ever getting an answer. Cain never mentioned he knew corporate was blaming me for the layoffs, a sure indication of who really was vindictive, and a sure admission of his involvement with management on his own without any of our knowledge.

The demons swished around while drooling their saliva, enjoying their freedom during this meeting, until the angelic warriors appeared. Clashing swords now with these demons, the angelic warriors raged this spiritual battle in my defense, as I said nothing while enduring Cain's tirade against my character as a union president in front of my e-board officers.

Once Cain had left and his demon buddies were defeated, I continued the meeting with the e-board as though nothing had happened. But I saw no point in having a real meeting now that these union officers, who our membership elected and trusted to represent them, were full of so much beer in such a short period of time.

As long as I kept my eyes on my Lord Jesus during this meeting, I was able to continue on while disregarding what this mean-tempered man thought about me. Afterward, though, I became very distraught, believing God had let me down, but this only lasted a short time.

In the Lord's presence during my fellowship with Him that evening, He reminded me that His grace was sufficient, and that His power would always be demonstrated best when I am weakest. (2 Corinthians 12:9.) God also reminded me of the many members of this local He had used me to help, and of the many times I requested input and supported decisions others were more in favor of while I also sought His direction.

But the most important of all that the Lord reminded me, was that I was serving Him in this position: the Lord God who is omniscient, omnipotent, omnipresent, and able to judge the thoughts and intentions of everyone's heart. (Hebrews 4:12-13.) I am so fond of the Scriptures that appear four times in one way or another in the Gospels with the same promise: Everything secret will someday all be known. (Matthew 10:26; Mark 4:22; Luke 8:17 & 12:2.) This was only one battle. I knew more were coming.

Cain's attempt to beat me down in front of my e-board officers hoping this would at last stop all attempts on my part to address the beer issue, backfired on him royally. I became all the more determined to address a practice that I truly believed was so wrong. Cain proved he really did not know me, nor did he know my walk with such an Almighty God. And apparently, neither did so many others. However, everyone was going to witness the One who was really supporting and protecting me.

Our next membership meeting was nine days later. Cain's derogatory tirade against me at the e-board meeting was still fresh, and by then, well known by many others in our union. I had a plan that was supported by lots of prayer and fasting, and I was prepared to put my plan into action at this next meeting, knowing that with the upcoming layoffs, this meeting was going to be well attended by our membership.

I was always told that there was no higher authority in a union than the local membership. At the start of this meeting, Cain decided on his own to sit up front and right next to me. I was getting used to his arrogance towards me.

In the spiritual realm, the demons were swishing around laughing and drooling their saliva, breathing their evil intent as everyone walked in and took their seats. These demons were confident of their victory tonight. They were totally unprepared for the onslaught of God's angelic warriors converging in battle array, with swords unsheathed and ready to fight this battle in my defense at the command of their Captain.

I went through the formalities of our pledge of allegiance, a moment of silence for all our departed brothers and sisters while saying my usual prayer to myself, and then commenced in addressing union business. It was a lively meeting and well attended with lots of questions about the layoffs and upcoming arbitration for the contracting out grievance.

After I was sure everything was addressed of importance to our membership, ignoring Cain next to me, I read and explained to our membership the International Union policy concerning alcoholic beverages not being allowed at any facility that the local union would rent for use, with the exception of social affairs.

I was clear to explain that the time after union meetings would be considered our social affair for our officers and members, and that by refraining from drinking beer until that time, we would still be in compliance with this policy. I reiterated that it was the responsibility of the local union president to enforce all policies and by-laws of the International Union.

I also expressed my opinion, that it was inappropriate that some of our e-board officers would drink beer while trying to make important decisions regarding our members' livelihoods, the same members who elected these union reps.

Surprisingly, up until now, Cain said nothing. But I could feel his eyes boring into me with his hatred, while the demons swished around laughing their heads off believing they were going to have the victory. Someone on the floor displayed his annoyance that I would dare bring up such an issue with everything else going on. I ignored him too and went on with my plan.

I had intended on presenting a motion to the membership at this meeting, requesting that we follow this International Union policy by waiting till after all union business was conducted before anyone consumed beer that was provided. Having said everything on the beer policy issue that I wanted, I then announced, "I want to entertain a motion . . ."

Before I could state my motion, Cain, just waiting for his opportunity to attack, stated, "Your motion is out of order."

I confronted Cain in the hearing of everyone: "You can't call my motion out of order; I didn't even state it yet!"

By this time, the demons and angelic warriors were clashing their swords in a fierce battle, with the angelic warriors gaining the upper hand. As everyone was watching this spectacle between Cain and me up front, I heard a voice shouting out loud and clear from the floor: "I want to make a motion that we follow that policy you just read."

Upon hearing this motion and ignoring Cain, I jumped into action: "Is there a second to the motion?"

Someone else raised his voice loud and clear: "I second the motion."

I was moving fast: "Are there any questions to the motion?"

There were no questions. Without hesitation, I called for a vote: "All those in favor of the motion signify by saying aye."

Resounding ayes were heard throughout the union hall.

"All those opposed signify by saying no."

Just a few feeble noes were heard. With a strong proclamation, I announced, "Motion carried," and down went the gavel.

I called for a motion to adjourn, and the meeting was over.

By this time, the demons were subdued and whimpered in defeat, wondering what had happened. The Captain of the Host and a few of his angelic warriors stuck around for my protection, as I ignored Cain seething at the teeth at the outcome of all this.

As an act of vengeance afterward, Cain wrote a libelous letter to me, and sent it to Joab and all our e-board officers. In the letter, Cain accused me of disrespecting him and the International Union, and going against our membership during this meeting. Cain also stated many other lies regarding me in his letter. This was Cain's habitual personal agenda against me: destroy me with his poison of slander and derogatory comments he fed others about me.

However, the vote to follow this International Union policy regarding the use of alcoholic beverages at the facility we rented was clearly supported by our union membership. And with so many in attendance, they were well represented. But apparently, Cain felt he needed to do something to save face with our e-board officers, especially after his tirade against me in front of them while meeting with us, and then losing this battle.

After receiving Cain's letter, I contacted Alfred once again via email, the same International Union representative who was supposed to contact me prior to all this on the issue. I made sure to attach Cain's letter:

"I called you three times and sent you an email; you responded to none. Does the Internationals' e-board officers drink beer while making important decisions regarding our union? My dealings with this International Union and their representatives have been very discouraging and disappointing experiences. I understood that the International Union was there to help and support the local unions. Where did I go wrong believing this?"

Now this got Alfred's attention. We had a positive discussion when he called after receiving this email. Alfred also believed it was inappropriate for union officers and members to drink beer while conducting union business. He said he had wanted to be at the last union meeting, but Cain told him not to come.

The good-old-boys club code of conduct strikes again: Don't step on anyone's toes—right, wrong, or indifferent! But it didn't matter. The Lord God had everything under control, and He wasn't about to share His glory with anyone!

Chapter 65

Contracting Out Arbitration

All the layoffs and everything that went with it kept me busy. I was one of the fire watch senior employees that kept working. I remember thinking that Ferengi and his management friends ruined this Christmas season for everyone in our union at our company group. Those who were laid off were left wondering if they were going to have a job the following year. Some of those who had the seniority to stay working had their vacations canceled. And all of us were left wondering what was going to happen next with our lives and our jobs. All this for what Ferengi stated was "not a cost savings business decision."

I'm not sure how other union presidents handled layoff status for their members, but this time was very upsetting to me. I was determined not to forget those who were laid off.

What we were told originally was to be just a few weeks of temporary layoffs, turned out to be much longer. I sent out letters every four to six weeks to everyone on layoff status with an update of what was going on. Because of such a large number of our members being laid off at once, I worked with the unemployment office in our state setting up meetings to get everyone settled and getting checks.

During this time, someone from the unemployment office encouraged me to file a petition for TAA (Trade Adjustment Assistant) for our members. If approved, this TAA would offer federally funded training for anyone deciding to seek alternate employment. As I always tried to do, I followed God's direction that this was not the time to file this TAA petition. I have never been disappointed when I've waited on God's direction and timing before moving forward on such important decisions. I would understand God's direction just six months later.

Our members trickled back to work from this layoff over a period of a few months, but without concrete contract language for bumping back into the plant pool job positions. Some of those recalled had previous "bid" plant pool jobs with preferred daylight schedules that others were occupying. All this caused a lot of contentions before everyone was eventually back to their pre-layoff job positions. This was definitely not a good time to be a union president.

Prior to the layoffs, our e-board and union membership voted to take the contracting out grievance to arbitration. While researching for information that would help us win this arbitration, I found a contracting out arbitration award from years earlier that the union won, which covered the identical attrition scenario of management reducing our maintenance workforce while supplementing the workload with resident contractors.

I gave this prize arbitration award to Cain to use as an exhibit example in our defense, since he was going to lead the arbitration. Unfortunately, this was a major mistake on my part. (Any past arbitrations or grievances won by the union were always of great value in the union's defense for any similar issues being grieved.)

I also had documented comparisons of the cost between our union craftsmen and contractors (thanks to the contractor cost information I requested), which proved it was more cost-effective to use our own union workforce for this work; I even factored in the cost of our union benefits. I also found documentation that spanned over the course of several years detailing the purposeful attrition by management of the Maintenance Department union personnel on several different occasions.

In addition to all this great documentation, I had all the contracting out notifications that were sent from different salaried maintenance supervisors that clearly stated in one way or another, that their rationale for contracting out union maintenance work was due to the company no longer having a sufficient number of our own union craftsmen to do the work.

With all this great documented information, I was sure we could win this contracting out arbitration. However, before the arbitration hearing date, Cain did another one of his flip-flops: He decided on his own not to go through with the arbitration. (Who was the dictator?)

I was furious as I watched Cain give Ferengi our prize past arbitration award blatantly in front of me during a meeting, as he stated, "I'm giving you a copy of this past arbitration award so that you can know we can win this arbitration."

His actions betrayed all of our union members working at this chemical plant facility. I said nothing during the time, but watched Ferengi gleaming as he took our prize document from Cain.

It was no wonder management had such disrespect for our local union, particularly me as their president. Management knew they had the support of our staff rep, even as they knew Cain went against my authority and the direction of our union membership. His betrayal to our local union had in the past been mostly behind my back, but now he blatantly showed his betrayal in front of me. I was fighting a losing battle trying to save jobs by keeping our maintenance work for our own union maintenance craftsmen.

I could have fought Cain's refusal to go to arbitration over such a wrongful contract violation. But with so many of our union members still on layoff waiting to be recalled, God's direction was that this was not a battle I should fight right then. Not too far into the future, there would be other battles over Cain's betrayal that the Lord would lead me to challenge.

But for this time, I tried mending this rift by requesting our membership at our next union meeting to vote agreeing to cancel the arbitration. The purpose was to show management that we, as a local union, though we did not agree with our staff rep, would support his efforts dealing with management to find another way to resolve this contracting out issue without arbitration. And once again, I had the membership support with this vote.

I never told anyone in our union about Cain's blatant betrayal. I was learning that too many thought highly of Cain as our staff rep. To prove everything that Cain was responsible for doing against our local union would have been near impossible. It took time, but eventually, others found out the truth about his betrayals.

An agreement was drafted as a good-faith gesture, outlining what turned out to be management's lame efforts to show they were going to reduce the contracting out of our union's work. As with previous good-faith gestures, out the window this agreement flew with no rebound in sight!

Three months later, another maintenance reduction forced another bump-back of these craftsmen into plant pool positions, even while I was receiving the contracting out notifications with the same rationale as their excuse for contracting out: insufficient union craftsmen to do the work.

Another grievance was filed for this current reduction stating the violation was "ongoing." A second arbitration was scheduled several months later. It was always a setback waiting so long for these arbitration hearings. Cain had phoned me with his desire to also cancel this second arbitration. As we argued back-and-forth, I told him that this had been going on far too long, and enough was enough; now we have to address it. He finally agreed for arbitration. No one ever really knew all the personal battles I had with Cain trying to convince him to support our local union, as he was being paid with our union dues money to do.

During this arbitration hearing, between Cain and Gremlin, I was interrogated for well over two-and-a-half hours. A few maintenance guys were present who also testified. Gremlin did not like me at all, and did his best to push my buttons in an attempt to provoke me into an outburst of anger. It almost worked—but the Lord intervened and kept me calm. I saw Gremlin's disappointment that he didn't get the response from me he so much desired.

After everything was said and done, even with all the documents supporting the attrition defense and cost benefits of our own maintenance union workforce doing the work, we still lost the arbitration. Gremlin had submitted as part of his post-brief, our prize past arbitration award that Cain had given to Ferengi, and distorted it in a way that was used against the union in favor of management.

The arbitrator never took into consideration the union's attempt to resolve this in good faith when the last arbitration was canceled, but instead, also used that against the union. In the arbitrator's post-hearing brief, he claimed he denied the grievance because the union did not address the contracting out issue in a timely fashion due to the last arbitration being canceled, and because we did not file more grievances for each and every contracting out occurrence. The blanket grievance of this violation being "ongoing" didn't convince him that it needed to be stopped.

Although we lost the arbitration, the union benefited with language from the arbitrator's award referencing two particular job duties that were once contracted out, which management used in their defense were given back to our union workforce. These jobs included building scaffolding, and pumping out gook from a water lagoon. This may not seem significant, but in the months to follow, it proved to save two more plant pool jobs during the final permanent reduction of our workforce. The announcement of this permanent layoff would be in the very near future.

Chapter 66
Our Contract

With only two months from the announcement of our last "temporary" personnel layoff, and just prior to our contract negotiations for our contract soon to expire, management informed the union that by the end of that year, there was going to be a fifty percent permanent reduction in the union workforce at this plant site. They wanted to create a smaller workforce "footprint," as they explained it, to try and generate a reliable profit. The only way this reduction could happen and still keep the plant running was that one of our departments would have to permanently shutdown.

As the local union president, I was part of contract negotiations for each of the three company groups in our amalgamated union. The other two company groups already had their contracts negotiated earlier during this president term. Our contract was going to be my third.

The first contract negotiated was for Company A. It was very difficult and a real eye-opener for me. Cain always got along well with Barry, their group chairman. When the management of Company A proposed eliminating the union's defined pension plan, I heard no objections from Barry when Cain stated in our caucus that he was going to offer a counterproposal that only new hires would not receive a pension. This was a huge benefit loss to new hires. Cain never asked for a discussion on the issue from anyone on the union's negotiating team. (Who was the dictator?)

This didn't sit well with me, but I was so new on the block with only three months into this president position, and being told repeatedly by Cain that this wasn't the contract of my company group, I held my peace and said nothing. But this sure opened my eyes as to why Barry and Cain got along so well. Cain never liked anyone challenging him on any issues.

The second contract negotiated was for Company B. In contrast to Company A's contract, the plant manager for Company B agreed to just about all of the union's proposals. Now, two-and-a-half years into my term as president, it was time to prepare for the contract negotiations for the company I worked for.

Over the course of my years of employment—being the very curious person that I am—I would often dig deep into our intranet (internal company website) looking for something that maybe, I would benefit from or needed to know about. This was a normal practice of mine even prior to being elected union president.

In doing some of this curious research, I found some of our union benefits' plan documents that clearly stated these benefits can be terminated at the sole discretion of our employer. This disturbed me, and I questioned, but only to myself: *Why did the union agree to such wording? Or do they not know that our benefits' plan documents contained language that these benefits can be terminated at any time?*

Fast-forward: Our contract had language that clearly stated some of these union benefits were offered "under the provisions of the plan." Knowing our contract language and what some of these benefits' plan documents stated, as the union president now, I was in a position during these next negotiations to address this major concern of our benefits being terminated at the sole discretion of our employer. How these documents and agreements were worded was so very important.

Prior to negotiations, we would prepare proposals for consideration for contract addition, language change, and requesting more benefits. Management also prepared contract proposals for what they wanted changed in our contract.

Both management and union negotiating teams would exchange their contract proposals simultaneously on the first day of our negotiations. It often took several weeks of negotiation meetings before both sides could agree on a tentative agreement to present to our membership for their vote to ratify (accept) or reject the contract.

Since Cain blatantly handed over our prize arbitration award won in favor of the union that I was saving for our contracting out arbitration, in addition to his habitual contact with management—and vice versa—I kept our proposals from him until the very last possible minute. This was my attempt to ensure management did not get them before our simultaneous exchange.

One of our prize proposals was meant to safeguard our union's benefits, asking that they not change for the duration of our current contract, unless such change was of greater benefit to the union. I believed that this proposal would protect our benefits from management unilaterally eliminating them "under their provisions of the plan" clause. However, it was believed that certain benefits were safeguarded by the labor laws labeling them as mandatory subjects of bargaining, such as retirement benefits, and therefore, could not be changed or eliminated without good faith bargaining by both parties. Our defined pension plan had very strong language right in our contract that safeguarded it from any changes without the union's agreement.

Just before our first meeting in negotiations, our entire chemical company was purchased by a very wealthy foreign government. We all had hopes of getting new management with this sale, but nothing changed, not even our name. At this same time, the Darkly business alone was again on the selling block pending another separate foreign company purchase.

Negotiating for management was Caleb, Ferengi, Lisa, two other management personnel, and Norman, who was a lawyer representing our new wealthy owners. Negotiating for the union was Cain, Harry, Marvin (recording secretary), two other union members just elected for this negotiating team, and me. When Cain was questioned by one of these elected members as to why we didn't have a lawyer, he proudly stated we didn't need one; he was our "lawyer."

Management's intent to create for themselves an advantage against the union during negotiations by announcing that our workforce would be permanently reduced by fifty percent by the end of the year, backfired on them royally. This announcement gave the union the best advantage that was not anticipated, and could not be reversed.

Management was told that these same fifty percent union employees, who would be without jobs, were going to have the opportunity to vote on our tentative agreement for our new contract. If this new contract was voted down, there would be a labor showdown that our current management did not want to show our new wealthy owners. When management realized that their preconceived advantage backfired, I saw each of their countenances immediately fall.

Our plant site business was just a very small fraction of the overall business these new owners acquired during this sale, and in comparison, was insignificant to the overall business purchase (other plant sites of our company produced a different chemical product). At the end of every labor strike, though the principles may have the victory, often there are no real winners. The possibility of a strike loomed over me with a force that I could not reckon with apart from my utmost trust in the Lord God for His help and intervention to avert a strike.

During one of the meetings in negotiations, Caleb announced that the pending sale of Darkly to another buyer fell through. He was very visibly upset about this, which in hindsight indicated he knew the fate of Darkly, the department known as the unwanted "red-headed stepchild" of the company. As the union president and a lead operator in Darkly, this announcement should have concerned me as well. But upon hearing this, God's peace, which surpasses all comprehension, powerfully rushed throughout my entire being with His assurance that He was still God, He was still in control, and all things were going to work out for the best. (Philippians 4:7, Romans 8:28.)

The union negotiated a very difficult contract in the best of good faith with concessions of three years of pay freezes, while some of our plant pool jobs were scheduled to reduce their wages in two-and-a-half years. This was the union's sacrifice in the attempt to keep the plant running during one of the most recent difficult times in our country's economy. Over the course of the next years until our next contract negotiations, it would be proven that only the union workforce sacrificed their wage increases, while salaried personnel received wage increases and bonuses during these same years. Another good-faith gesture flew out the window with no rebound!

Management would not budge on our prize proposal safeguarding the union's benefits while asking that they not change for the duration of our current contract. No one from management mentioned our 401(k) benefit to any of the six union officials present during these negotiations. This benefit included a company match with a percent cap to any union employee who also contributed from their paycheck to their 401(k) account.

This 401(k) was a major monetary retirement benefit that was supposed to be safeguarded as a mandatory subject of bargaining per the labor laws. Cain illustrated to management that they would save financially by not increasing what they contributed to these 401(k) accounts and to our defined pension plan benefits because of the union's willingness to agree to pay freezes.

After several grueling weeks of negotiations, we had a tentative agreement that we presented to our membership through two meetings for explanations, questions and answers. Cain and I agreed beforehand to a systematic way for which part we would each cover. It was a great show of how two people, who were almost constantly at odds, were able to work together for the benefit of our membership. One of my friends even mentioned to me afterward that we seemed to work well together. No one ever knew everything that went on between me and Cain.

The membership had over thirty-six hours to digest this tentative agreement before voting on it, a courtesy dear to my heart that I initiated as union president. The practice in years past was that it was only presented to our membership the very same hour it was to be voted on.

Our best-selling point for a contract that contained pay concessions was being able to keep all of our other benefits whole, specifically mentioning our 401(k) with company matching contributions. Another great-selling point was the negotiated severance package for those willing to leave on a volunteer separation, or those unfortunate to be forced into permanent layoffs by the end of the year.

When all was said and done, we had great support for a favorable vote to accept our concessional contract. This was a real victory for our union, and a true blessing from God, who I trusted the most for help to avert a strike.

However, our victory was marred on the very first day of our new ratified contract with a phone call from my agitated and very angry financial secretary, Ford:

"I was just in HR seeing Adrianne (HR secretary) when Lisa pulled me aside and told me, 'By the way, the company is eliminating our contribution match to the union's 401(k) benefit.'

I said, oh really? And then Lisa told me, 'Yes, we told the union we were eliminating our contributions during negotiations.' "

Listening to Ford, I was imagining his angry and surprised expression as he related his response to Lisa: "REALLY? IS THAT RIGHT?"

I believed what Ford had told me, but there's nothing like hearing it straight from the horse's mouth. I immediately phoned Ferengi: "Ford just called to tell me that Lisa told him, the company is eliminating their match to our 401(k)?"

His response was his arrogant norm: "Yes. We mentioned it twice to the union during negotiations that we were eliminating our company match contributions."

My response was more angrily articulated than even Ford's: "You never mentioned our 401(k) in negotiations!"

Ferengi was adamant he was telling the truth: "Yes, we did. When we told the union that we were eliminating our company match, the union never challenged it."

I was furious with this arrogant little man as I responded, "Had you told us the company's intentions on eliminating their match to our 401(k), things would have turned out much differently!"

Ferengi's arrogance reared again: "Well, I'm sorry to hear that."

My next response said it all: "REALLY?!" Click.

I was done with these people! We convinced our membership to vote for a concessional contract with the best-selling points that we kept whole all of our other benefits, especially our company match to our 401(k). These good-faith gestures just never stopped flying out the windows, never to rebound. I was sure they were meeting up with each other for a mockery party.

Chapter 67
New War

I phoned Cain right after speaking with Ferengi and relayed what was said. His initial response was also outrage. The union's negotiating team took the strong position that this was a gross act of bad faith bargaining and an unfair labor practice by management, because of their premeditated decision to not put their intentions to eliminate such a huge monetary retirement benefit on the negotiating table.

After it was known that management was eliminating their company match contributions to the union's 401(k), there was an outrage among our union membership, especially after voting in favor for a concessional contract. Matters were made even worse when management personnel told some of our membership that during negotiations, the union was told about this huge monetary benefit being eliminated, yet did not challenge it.

Before learning about our loss with our 401(k), a meeting was scheduled with the union's negotiating team and management to go over some finer details of our contract agreement. We met with Cain before this meeting and discussed everything that went on. Cain told us during our caucus, that after we address the issues this meeting was scheduled to address, he was going to feign anger over management's bad faith bargaining over the 401(k), and then walk out of the meeting; he told us we were to follow suit.

And it happened just as Cain planned. When the union walked out of this meeting, we left a very bewildered and upset management team behind. That evening was our regular union membership meeting. Everyone applauded as we related what transpired, and how we all walked out of this meeting with management over their unilateral elimination of their company match contributions to our 401(k).

Cain followed up our meeting with management with a strong letter to Caleb and other upper management, and sent me a copy. In his letter, Cain let it be known that he was offended that management told our membership that the elimination of their company match was discussed with the union during negotiations, and made it appear that he did not raise any objection. As he stated in his letter:

"Local labor-management relations have always been a priority focus of mine. While it is normal in the course of business for an occasional genuine difference of opinion, this is an insult to me personally, and has caused serious deterioration of ongoing labor relations with management. I have ten (10) other facilities in your area. Can you even imagine the impact this is going to have on the membership when they hear that I withheld information to get a contract ratified?"

Cain's letter spelled it out clearly without reading between the lines. I understood what the rest of our union negotiating team did not understand during our meeting with management and Cain's feigned anger. Cain expressed more concern about his bruised reputation than our membership losing such a huge monetary benefit without good faith bargaining. And in the next few days to follow, it was obvious to me that Ferengi, Caleb and Lisa were more concerned about their deteriorating relationship with Cain than unilaterally taking away such a huge benefit that should have been a mandatory subject of bargaining for the union. Now I was faced with another war to deal with, and behind the scenes privy to no one else, another fierce battle with Cain.

Cain had contacted two union lawyers: Amelia, from the International Union; and Jesse, our local union lawyer, who we kept on retainer for thirty-five plus years. Without conferring with each other, both lawyers gave us the same advice over the 401(k) unilateral elimination of the company match: File a grievance and NLRB charges.

After receiving the lawyers' responses, Cain asked me if I wanted to speak with Caleb to see if the company would leave our 401(k) plan as it was, or if I wanted him to speak with Caleb. I emailed Cain and told him that the company needed to know we were in this together. I offered to arrange a meeting for all of us, including Harry, the union's chief shop steward, to try to resolve this without a grievance or board charges. Cain agreed for me to arrange this meeting that he would also attend.

When I told Ferengi that Cain requested a meeting to resolve the 401(k) issue, his eyes lit up with enthusiasm. Management always held Cain, as the International staff rep, in the highest esteem, which was a stark contrast to their obvious disdain for me as the lowly local union president. No matter. I cared more about what my Lord Jesus thought about me than anyone else anyway.

Cain had a two-hour drive from his home to our chemical plant, so he requested I schedule this meeting prior to another appointment he had at another facility in our area. I was always more than willing to accommodate his schedule, and did so for this meeting.

Caleb had tried previously on numerous occasions to contact Cain via phone to smooth out their relationship after receiving his strong letter, but Cain ignored his contact. It was the morning of this meeting when Cain finally took Caleb's phone call. Cain phoned me afterward to tell me that he had just spoken with Caleb regarding the 401(k) issue, and as a result of their conversation, our afternoon meeting that I had scheduled was canceled. Cain cut our conversation short without any explanation as to why it was canceled, or what was said between him and Caleb. I was furious with him and sent him an email that evening expressing this. The email synopsis expressed my sentiment:

"I set this meeting up at the last minute because it was important that you be present when I spoke with Caleb and Ferengi about the elimination of the company match. Just your support alone would have been able to resolve this easily, since both Caleb and Ferengi really cared what you thought and wanted your favor. Both our lawyers were on the same page with the same advice. You talk to Caleb, and then everything changes. This meeting was supposed to do so much good in resolving this issue without a grievance and without board charges for the benefit of our local membership. Instead, everything backfired."

Cain's response was feigned ignorance: "I have no idea what you are talking about, as usual. You're on your own. Do as you please."

Yep, I've been on my own all along without your support! Did he miss my whole point? I could not have made it any clearer than I did. I wanted and needed his support to resolve such a big issue. But no, he didn't miss my point. Something was said between Caleb and Cain about this whole issue that I would never know. And without the knowledge of anyone else in this union, my private war to address this major issue raged on.

Just hours after Cain responded to my email, his conscience must have gotten the best of him. He sent another email asking if I was willing for a phone conference, which would include Caleb, Ferengi, Gremlin, and Jesse as our lawyer representing our local union. Cain left the final decision up to me, and I agreed. If there was a chance to resolve this without legal hassles, then that was always the best route for everyone involved.

I basically listened in on the phone conference and took great notes. It wasn't too long into the call that Gremlin recommended "we separate at this point."

Jesse stated at the end: "We'll assume the company will get back to us and let us know what they plan on doing."

Gremlin was very direct: "No. We've clearly decided to eliminate the company match contributions. Not before July. There are technicalities on how this will play down. We haven't landed on when."

The phone conference ended with the direct and clear stated decision that management was going through with their intentions to unilaterally eliminate their match contributions to our 401(k).

Management canceled our labor and management meeting for the following day. Two days after our phone conference, informational meetings went on throughout the plant site by management personnel making sure every crew was covered. I just happened to walk in on one of these meetings at Beady, another production department, with no previous knowledge that these meetings were going on and for what purpose.

Ferengi was leading this meeting and explaining the business outlook for our plant site. At the end of the meeting, I was surprised to hear Ferengi discuss the 401(k) issue, and then state that the company was "considering" eliminating their company match to this benefit. This statement was a complete contradiction to what Gremlin directly stated to the union at the end of our phone conference just two days earlier.

I was never afraid to confront Ferengi, either one-on-one or in front of anyone; today was no different: "So tell me, Ferengi, did something change from just two days ago when Gremlin stated at the end of our phone conference, that the company clearly decided to eliminate the company match contribution?"

His response was as lame as they come: "That was just talk from our attorney and not from the company."

Ferengi should have known I wasn't stupid. I countered, "And your attorney represents the company!"

As far as I was concerned, any statement coming from the company's lawyer was more validated than coming from anyone else from management. I knew that these weren't genuine informational meetings, as they were labeled, but another round of propaganda meetings that roused the anger from a majority of our membership for no reason. I had several union members come to me, even weeks later, furious with what management said about our 401(k) benefit. One e-board member almost came to blows with someone in management giving some of these propaganda meetings over his disparaging remarks of the union officials.

I wondered if Cain endorsed these meetings in an attempt to heal his bruised reputation that he seemed so concerned about? Management completely changing their original story that the union was told in negotiations of such a huge monetary loss, to now telling our membership they were only "considering" eliminating their company match, would reverse any thoughts that Cain withheld information to get a contract ratified. And once again, I would never know. But I do know what transpired afterward trying to sweep this gross act of bad faith bargaining under the carpet.

Less than two weeks from our phone conference, less than four weeks from our ratified contract, Cain and I finally received the letter from Caleb officially stating management was going to "amend" our 401(k) plan in the form of eliminating their company match contributions. The start date of this new amendment was the following January first. Cain and I received this letter in June. Management also offered, as stated in this letter, to meet with the union to "discuss this change to the 401(k) plan."

Cain was adamant that Jesse was going to be the only one to handle this whole issue with the 401(k) on the union's behalf while eliminating any and all of his involvement. Normally, Cain would never have allowed anyone to handle what was supposed to be his job responsibility.

So, what was going on here? What did Caleb and Cain agree to when they finally spoke and then canceled that first meeting I worked so hard to arrange over this 401(k) issue? I wasn't convinced that letting Jesse solely handle this was a good idea. My phone conversation with Jesse the day after he received Caleb's letter confirmed this.

I was at work when Jesse called my cell phone: "Angelika, I received the company's letter stating the elimination of their contributions was not going to go into effect until January first of next year. So, we are not going to address this issue until then."

On guard with my mistrust I've had all along of this lawyer and his conferring with Cain, I expressed my opinion as deliberate yet as calm as I could: "I am not at all comfortable waiting till January, six months from now, to address this issue."

He was adamant: "We are not going to deal with this until January. There are going to be new legislation and new NLRB members appointed soon, and it's best if we wait till all this has taken place before addressing this issue."

Jesse's excuse had no merit. This man was going to blow our chances to even challenge this properly by not dealing with this in a timely fashion. I tried again convincing him waiting was not a good idea: "If we wait till January, six months from when management gave the union official notice in writing of their intent to eliminate their match contributions to our 401(k), it will be too late to file a grievance, and too late to file board charges."

Jesse wasn't hearing anything I was saying to him. His conversation told me he had conferred once again with Cain before he called me. In hearing him speak, it was as though I was hearing Cain: "NO! We are going to wait until January to deal with this. I want you to do absolutely nothing right now, except write a letter to management telling them that from now on, they are only to deal with me on this issue. And I want you to send me a copy of that letter."

I was getting irate to the max as Jesse continued, "And if you don't do exactly what I am telling you to do, you can find someone else to represent you."

Jesse's last threat sealed his fate, and sealed my resolve that I was not waiting till January to address this issue. I kept calm in the midst of strong anger and ended our conversation at this point: "I have to go now; I'm at work." Click.

I may not be college educated, but I look in the mirror at least a few times each day, and I have yet to see "stupid" stamped on my forehead. Maybe this was only visible to a select few?

Did this so-called lawyer really think I was going to write a letter to management relinquishing my responsibility in dealing with this issue to only him, and send him a copy? If this union had lost our chance to even attempt to fight this and gain back this huge monetary benefit because of waiting six months to address it, even at the advice of our lawyer, I was going to be the one blamed. Not Jesse. Not Cain. But me—the only union scapegoat. And by this time, I was tired of running around as the scapegoat.

What was this all about anyway, trying to sweep this under the carpet? What deals were made with management behind my union president back, and who was benefitting by these deals? Surely, it wasn't our local union membership. And it sure wasn't the union scapegoat!

Chapter 68
Another Tirade

*I*t didn't take Jesse long to realize that I wasn't sending him a copy of the letter that he demanded I write to management giving him exclusive authority to deal with this 401(k) issue. When we finally spoke on the phone again, I confronted him on his threat that I would have to find someone else for representation if I didn't do exactly as he demanded. He vehemently denied ever saying such a thing. This proved one of two things to me: Either he was a boldfaced liar, or he was way beyond his mental capability to continue being an attorney. He was way up there in years, far beyond normal retirement age. Neither of these excuses were acceptable to me.

I realized that if this union was going to at least have a fighting chance to salvage our 401(k) company match benefit, I would have to take matters into my own hands. It was obvious that neither Jesse nor Cain had any intentions on addressing this issue before January, if even then. But I needed to do this creatively to minimize any tirades from Cain.

I filed a grievance just within the time limits to do so per our contract. I used the date of management's official notice in writing to the union of their intent to eliminate their matching contributions. I knew waiting for the effective date of six months later to challenge this would totally forfeit all our chances to even address this issue. The very first thing an arbitrator looks at even before hearing a case is whether the grievance was filed timely, and if not, why wasn't it.

I then arranged for a second time, another meeting with management per their request in their official letter to meet with the union to "discuss this change to the 401(k) plan," which would be outside the grievance process. Jesse initially said if he were available, he would attend this second scheduled meeting. I tried reaching Jesse twice while leaving voice messages on his phone asking for his confirmation of his attendance at this meeting, but he never responded. I followed up with an email to Jesse and copied Cain, documenting my two voice messages, and letting Jesse know that I filed a grievance over the issue. I made sure to reference "per your advice to file a grievance," referring to his initial direction given to Cain at the beginning of all this for the union to file a grievance and board charges.

On a Sunday evening, Cain phoned Lisa and had a private conversation over the entire subject matter without conferring with me prior to. Cain's follow-up email sent that evening to Lisa confirmed their phone conversation and reiterated what was agreed upon between the two of them. Cain stated in this email that the second meeting that I had arranged was also going to be canceled. He disclosed that since a grievance had been filed over the issue, they (Cain and Lisa) had agreed to extend the time limits of the grievance until another meeting could be scheduled. Cain also made sure to state that since lawyers were representing both parties, Gremlin and Jesse would be the ones to schedule the next meeting between them to "discuss this change to the 401(k) plan," which would be outside of the grievance process.

Cain had copied Gremlin, Jesse and me on his email to Lisa, confirming to all copied that I was to be pushed totally out of the way, and that only Jesse was going to deal with this major issue on behalf of our local union.

Something was going on here that I did not at all appreciate. However, no one knew the One who was the real driving force of my actions. With much prayer and direction from the Lord, I moved forward on my own.

At this point, the grievance was only processed at the first step per our contract, and only I had a copy after Nathan, now Darkly's Department head supervisor, denied the grievance and signed it.

As usual, I always tried to cover all my bases; this was for my own protection as well as the union's. In doing so, I sent Jesse an email and copied Cain, explaining that because management and Gremlin were now aware that a grievance was filed (thanks to Cain's disclosure in his email to Lisa), I felt obligated to process it further and would do so.

Because Nathan noted on the grievance that this was a higher management issue and not a departmental issue, I contractually bypassed the second step of the grievance process. I explained to Jesse and Cain that there would still be plenty of time prior to the third-step grievance meeting to reschedule that meeting requested by management in their official letter announcing their company match elimination, to "discuss this change to the 401(k) plan," and that this meeting would include Gremlin and Jesse.

I took this email opportunity to make it clear to both Jesse and Cain that I wanted to be informed of the progress going forward with this 401(k) issue, and I wanted to attend the meeting that was rescheduled with Gremlin. I reiterated again in this email that I was not at all comfortable with waiting until January to address this issue. I also asked Jesse where our local was in regards to our retainer fee, and what other fees we were looking at for his services. I was still uneasy about Cain's insistence that our local use Jesse, or any lawyer, to deal with this 401(k) issue.

I didn't wait for a reply from either of these men before further processing the grievance. After I sent this email, I went to see Adrianne and had her stamp and move the grievance for third step, now giving management a copy for the first time. I followed up with an email to Adrianne identifying the grievance, and asking her to please, make sure that the third-step grievance meeting was scheduled within the thirty-day time limit as set forth in our contract; it was her responsibility to schedule grievance meetings. Thirty days excluding weekends and holidays would also put the pressure on Gremlin and Jesse to schedule their meeting with management if they wanted to "discuss this change to the 401(k) plan" outside the grievance process.

Later that same day, I received another email from Cain referencing his previous email and mutual agreement with Lisa that the time limits for the grievance filed were extended, and that there was no need for me to further process the grievance at that time; he was sure to copy Jesse on this email as well.

I learned in so many ways, timing is everything. And such is life! Cain sent his instructions too late. I saw no point in responding to his email. I knew Lisa would contact him once she knew the grievance was stamped and moved to third step.

I received another email from Cain the following morning: "Call me at your first opportunity. Cain."

Although this was a one-liner, I read between the words; contact from Lisa had been made. I was never able to understand what Cain was gaining with all his meddling with management behind the scenes. But apparently, it was something worthwhile.

It didn't matter that the grievance was processed further, or that one was even filed. It was my legal right to file grievances on behalf of our local union. And it was my legal right—although very difficult—to see to it that this issue with the 401(k) was addressed timely on behalf of our membership: the ones who were losing out on such a huge monetary retirement benefit without any good faith bargaining. Retirement benefits were supposed to be protected under the mandatory subject of bargaining clause per the labor laws.

Since Cain was directly above me in the chain of command in this union, I respected his position and called him that evening per his request, which was a major mistake on my part. My second major mistake was not ending the conversation sooner than I did.

Cain's raging anger towards me was unmerited, and his accusations hurled were unfounded, all because I processed a grievance! He ranted and raved at me: "I told you not to process the grievance further. I need to rein you in. You're going to screw it up for everyone. You need to stay out of it and let Jesse do his job. He's the professional. LET HIM DO HIS JOB!"

I tried my best to reason with Cain and calm him down, but found it was like reasoning with a wild animal in an angry frenzy. After about twenty minutes, I abruptly ended our conversation. I was so very upset, to say the least.

This same evening, I had planned a visit with my dear friend, Marie, who was like another mom to me. Marie had worked in a manufacturing facility dealing with this same union for over thirty-five years. I was always able to confide in her on so many issues that I was faced with as union president, in addition to sharing our walk with the Lord. Marie knew all about Cain and his verbal beatings of which I was victim.

After just entering the door of Marie's home for this visit, she took one look at me and asked, "What's wrong?"

My response spoke volumes: "I just got off the phone with Cain."

Nothing more needed said until I was ready to confide in her everything that went on. I thank God for those who He places in our lives just when we need them the most. These special people become an extension of God's love and care.

Chapter 69

Going Over Heads

When God has placed a determination within me, any kind of intimidation from others in their attempt to discourage or stop me only makes me more determined. Cain hadn't figured this out yet.

I tried several times after Cain's last tirade to mend our union relationship, but he would have none of it. So onward I went dealing with this 401(k) issue as God led.

The main reason Cain said he was adamant that Jesse, as a lawyer, needed to deal with the 401(k) issue was because of the ERISA laws (Employee Retirement Income Security Act). When Jesse sent our local union his current charges for what he had researched thus far in connection with this issue, the charges were excessive—over thousands of dollars excessive.

When I requested copies of what he researched for our own records since we were paying for this, I was more outraged when I learned that his research only surrounded the NLRB laws to determine if there was a valid board charge. We didn't need to pay a lawyer for this type of research! It is the responsibility of the NLRB agent once a union files a board charge to determine the validity of the charge, and if there is a violation of the labor law.

And so, as they say, enough was enough. It was time Jesse was removed from the scene. With his excessive bill in hand, I had no problems convincing our e-board officers to fire this lawyer. Since Cain did not want to deal with this 401(k) grievance, I went over his head and tried contacting Amelia, the International Union lawyer who initially also advised us to file a grievance and board charges at the beginning of all this. But when Amelia wasn't available, I went even higher up the chain and contacted her boss, Matthew. I was on the roll and wasn't stopping for anyone.

Matthew was considerate and spoke at length with me on the whole issue. I tried not to put Cain in a bad light but instead, I spoke around his lack of support, trying to convince Matthew that our local needed more help in dealing with this than what was happening. Because of this, Matthew wanted to give the reins back to Cain in leading this issue. And so, the buck was passed again!

Even with Matthew involved, Cain was adamant that he was not going to deal with this 401(k) grievance. I could only guess that it was because of an agreement he made with management. By this time, though I did not know all that went on behind the scenes, I knew Cain's main reason for wanting a lawyer involved had nothing to do with ERISA.

I asked Matthew about getting an International Union lawyer to handle this case. He stated that the International could not supply lawyers to all local unions requesting one. My response echoed my exasperation with how this whole issue was being handled by these so-called International Union representatives that our union dues were paying: "So, how does the International pick and choose who they will support with a lawyer?"

Matthew gave me no definitive answer.

However, in my correspondence with Matthew, I did get some documented satisfaction that my direction in filing a grievance was correct. Not that I doubted my actions in doing so, but getting it documented from an International Union lawyer who copied Cain, proved that I really didn't have that "stupid" stamped on my forehead that only a select few could see.

After doing my own research using Elkouri, Elkouri, How Arbitration Works (an invaluable resource manual for labor unions and anyone dealing with arbitrations), I quoted the exact section to Matthew and explained my concern:

"My understanding is that if we meet with management per their request in their official letter that announced their match elimination, to 'discuss this change to the 401(k) plan' outside the protection of the grievance procedure, they can then come back to us and claim impasse. At which time, they would have the legal right to unilaterally eliminate their match contributions, and we would have forfeited our right to challenge this."

Matthew responded through email and agreed with my interpretation of this quoted Elkouri section. Cain gave no reaction or response, though he too was copied. Cain always hated it when I was right!

Or was that the plan all along? Was Cain and management in cahoots hoping to achieve impasse dealing with this issue, so the union would forfeit our legal rights to challenge this? That was not happening, thanks to God's leading.

For the third time, I scheduled another meeting with management to deal with this 401(k) issue. Only this time, I put in writing that this meeting was going to be under the third-step grievance procedure, and would also satisfy management's request to meet with the union to "discuss this change to the 401(k) plan."

Lisa hadn't been made aware of my ongoing attempts to continue addressing this issue by going over Cain's head. As far as she and management knew, this issue was dead in the water. It was obvious to me that no one had any intentions on scheduling another meeting after they canceled the second meeting I scheduled almost four weeks earlier.

When Lisa received my third-step grievance meeting notice (I also went over Adrianne's head in scheduling this grievance meeting), she went crying to Cain, as usual. Lisa wanted to know from Cain what was going on, instead of asking me as the local president who initiated this grievance and scheduled the meeting.

Lisa forwarded my meeting notice to Cain, along with his initial email reiterating that they (Cain and Lisa) had an agreement that the grievance time limits were extended, and reiterated Cain's instructions that the next meeting to "discuss this change to the 401(k) plan" was to be scheduled between Gremlin and Jesse outside the grievance process. Lisa also copied Cain's buddy, Gremlin, on her email.

So often, I wished I could have been a little fly on the wall when some of these people opened these email messages. Cain's response to Lisa was one of those times: "The local has taken a new direction concerning the 401(k) plan grievance. Please confer with Angelika for further explanation. Cain."

Lisa saw that Cain copied me on his response to her. She responded that she would discuss this with Gremlin. I never heard the outcome, and she never conferred with me. Knowing how these people speak among themselves without my knowledge, I was guessing Gremlin had a long conversation with Cain over this whole issue.

Our third-step grievance meeting on this issue was less than five minutes. Cain didn't show up for this meeting, even though contractually, he should have been present. Lisa's handwritten answer on the grievance form was simple: "The company does not believe this is arbitral." So much for trying to resolve this issue among ourselves!

Management had no intentions of working with the union to resolve this grievance on the 401(k) issue. Their minds had already been made up. They were going to eliminate their company match contributions to our 401(k), which represented hundreds of thousands of dollars loss benefit to our union members, without good faith bargaining per the labor laws—and Cain was doing all that he could to support them.

Matthew had advised Cain that this grievance needed to go to arbitration even before we received Lisa's third-step grievance answer. I wasted no time informing Lisa of our intentions to arbitrate this grievance. Matthew had recommended another lawyer to handle this case outside of the International Union group of lawyers, as Cain was still adamant that he was not handling this grievance issue. The fees for this new lawyer would also be paid for by our local union.

However, to not challenge such a gross act of bad faith bargaining by management would have been so wrong. The time frame was now three months from when we ratified our contract in May. Arbitration wasn't scheduled until November. It seemed arbitrations were never timely scheduled.

This would not be the last fierce private war I would fight alone against Cain while trying to stop his betrayal of our local union through his willingness to support management instead.

By God's help and with the Holy Spirit as my driving force, I won this war and thwarted the attempts of both management and Cain to sweep this gross act of bad faith bargaining under the carpet; although I would never know what their private agreement was for trying.

Chapter 70
Darkly's Fate

I saw the handwriting on the wall the previous January when I was fire watch during the "temporary" layoff. Caleb's somber demeanor as he announced during negotiations that the sale of Darkly fell through told me he knew the fate of Darkly back then. The formal announcement to end commercial production of Darkly and shutdown the department did not come until June, the same month official announcement in writing came regarding the elimination of our 401(k) company match.

After the announcement of Darkly's shutdown, I went on a long mission trying everything I knew to reverse this decision. The initial shutdown date was delayed several times due to our customers desperately needing our product. Imagine that!

I began my mission by writing overseas to Mr. Barrett, a CEO on our new board of directors from that foreign government who bought our chemical company, asking for his help to reverse the decision to shutdown Darkly. Mr. Barrett replied that he was not part of the business decisions of our chemical plant. Soon after this, I found the corporate announcement on our intranet: After some legal filings with a foreign union overseas, Mr. Barrett and other CEOs on the board of directors would share information and cooperate on all aspects of the businesses. This announcement was dated before Mr. Barrett received my letter.

Continuing on my mission to save Darkly, I had meetings with our Pennsylvania county commissioners, and contacted a vice president of our International Union. But no one was able to help. Absolutely nothing was going to save Darkly.

Ferengi was habitual in direct dealing with our rank-and-file union members, and sharing with them even in writing what he would not share with union leadership. Such was the case when he responded to a maintenance union employee questioning the Darkly shutdown. This maintenance employee gave me a hard copy of Ferengi's response in email.

The main excuse Ferengi gave this man for shutting down Darkly was claiming that the auto industry was falling apart. But as so many people pointed out during that difficult economy, eventually, the auto industry had to come back. No one could envision a world without cars.

Darkly was the preferred choice for many auto manufacturers for instrument panels and other uses. Per Ferengi's email, the decision to shutdown Darkly also put these customers in a financial hardship, as Darkly was already tooled for use in model cars for several years ahead. These auto manufacturers would have to buy enough of Darkly resin feed to get them through these years, or remake molds and tool in alternative materials to be used.

There were other applications for the use of Darkly. A food-grade application was successful over the years. Darkly was also being trialed for use in solar panels, as the high maleic anhydride content made it highly resistant to heat. One month after announcing Darkly's shutdown, our company received a patent to combine the Darkly resin with wood fibers to produce a floatable wood product. Darkly was made nowhere else in the world. There were similar products, but there was only one authentic Darkly resin that our customers seemed to favor.

For years, Darkly carried this chemical plant making multi-million dollars of profits each year, while the rest of the plant limped along for the ride with their financial losses. So why make a business decision to permanently shutdown a business that proved to be so profitable, and had so much potential to grow in other applications, and while there were still plenty of needs for our product? Only God knew the real reasons behind this business decision to shutdown Darkly.

But to put in place a smaller footprint at this plant, Darkly, always the unwanted red-headed stepchild of the company, was the sacrificial department. It took only a little more than a year after Darkly shutdown to hear Ferengi and other management responsible for this business decision to admit shutting down Darkly was a major mistake. I was surprised they admitted it, but it was too late by then to reverse their decision.

To the surprise of many (and herself), Lisa was also asked to leave before this fall season. Jezebel returned to her previous role as HR leader to replace Lisa. Caleb announced during negotiations that he would also be leaving sometime after our contract was ratified. Ferengi related to many that he told corporate they didn't need to replace Caleb's position as plant manager; he was capable and willing to assume his responsibilities. Thus, Ferengi became the first self-appointed plant manager.

During the same time of the announcement of the permanent shutdown of Darkly, and while I was still in this private war trying to get the 401(k) issue addressed timely, further behind the scenes was my responsibility of ensuring that the enhanced severance agreement was worded correctly and represented truthfully all that was negotiated. Sabrina, the wife of Jason in the union, was the HR consultant handling these documents. Sabrina initially sent out agreements and documents from a previous enhanced severance package that contained stipulations that were not discussed nor agreed to for this current severance package.

Sabrina could be as strong-willed as I was at times. However, the difference between us was that I never relied on my own ability, but relied on the Holy Spirit, and His strength and guidance to deal with issues. This difference proved all that was needed to succeed beyond my own ability to do so.

It took a lot of back-and-forth persistent emails, copying wording from documents, and adding changes that needed incorporated, before I was satisfied with how these documents were worded. (How documents and agreements were worded was so very important.) Since the union was still employing Jesse at the time, as an added precaution, I asked for his review of the documents when they were finally completed. His response was to encourage each member wishing to consider leaving employment to consult their own lawyer before signing any agreements.

With Darkly shutting down and my position as a lead operator eliminated—in my own heart—I too was contemplating accepting the severance package and leaving employment. The timing seemed good, as my commitment as president would have been fulfilled by the end of the year. I wasn't old enough to take an early retirement yet, but the prospect of working anywhere else in the plant didn't appeal to me.

By that time in my career, I had the most seniority for first choice of plant pool positions to bump into per our contract for a workforce reduction scenario. But the only position I was really interested in was in the Liquid Handler Department as a handler. This was not a plant pool position, and had a preferred daylight schedule. Another more senior Darkly native had bid for this position just after the shutdown announcement, so this position was not available, and only the Lord knew when it would be.

However, the Lord wasn't ready for me to leave employment at this industrial chemical plant just yet. Had I known what the next few years would be like for me personally, I would have debated with the Lord on His direction to stay employed. I have yet to win a debate with the Lord, but it would have been animated on my part at best.

Chapter 71
Ferengi's Agenda

Most of the seniority contract language was agreed upon many years before my term as president. It was very complicated and contingent on having plant pool job positions available for older employees to bump into.

There were different levels and types of seniorities with different job classifications; plant pool jobs were in the lowest job classifications with the least job security. When there was a department workforce reduction or a department shutdown like Darkly, those with enough seniority would bump into the plant pool. This created a domino effect that could cause less senior plant pool employees to be forced into layoff while the older employees remained working in the plant pool.

Adding to all these complications was Ferengi's adamant desire to manage the personnel at this plant site according to his personal agenda while disregarding contract seniority language. There was so much conflict going on during this plant workforce reduction time, all of which created a very hostile environment, especially in Darkly and for the union scapegoat.

It started with Jason, whose material packager trainer job (a plant pool position) was supposed to be eliminated along with the fifty-percent cutbacks of the union workforce. Before Sabrina married Jason years ago, she and Jezebel, who was the HR leader at the time, originally created this daylight preferred "trainer" title just for him while paying him slightly more than a material packager wage, which the union agreed to.

Ferengi and Lisa relentlessly badgered me for several months prior to the final reduction in workforce, and at every possible opportunity, trying to get me to agree that Jason had the contractual right to bump a Beady chem tech out of their job position, which would have given Jason the more secure job out of the plant pool. Contractually, plant pool employees could not bump chem techs out of their higher job classification positions.

I always believed there were real conflicts of interest when union employees were paired in some way with management employees. This combination brought a lot of strife to our union, and to me personally. Regardless of Jason's favoritism with higher management, I could not allow such a gross violation of our seniority contract language. My adamant refusal in allowing Jason to bump a chem tech only added fuel to management's disdain they already had for me.

But none of this mattered in the long run. Ferengi, and Lisa's replacement, Jezebel, kept Jason in his material packager trainer position way beyond the date it was slated to be eliminated, another contentious scenario I had to deal with.

The hostility continued full force from the gossip of how these personnel bumps into the plant pool from the Darkly shutdown was going to happen. I walked into Darkly one day to hear that the plan was for older chem techs to leave Darkly and train for their new plant pool positions, while younger chem techs would be allowed to continue working as chem techs until they were laid off from the plant. This was another gross violation of our contract seniority language I could not allow to happen. This gossip went on for several weeks, with even shift coaches and other salaried personnel coming to Darkly just to talk about this personnel transition plan.

Nathan was one of the originators spreading this gossip. I had known Nathan for almost twenty years by this time, most of which was as my supervisor. We always had a good working relationship, until I became the union president. Nathan was not at all happy about leaving his own employment earlier then he planned, and blamed me for everything, including the shutdown of Darkly. I'm sure he believed there was merit to his accusations. Nathan's alternative to leaving employment was to go back working rotating shifts as a shift coach supervisor, but he refused the offer; he always hated working shifts.

Nathan's main objective in circulating this personnel transition plan was to rile up the troops against me so that I would eventually agree to such a gross violation of our contract seniority language. Had I agreed to this plan, Nathan would have worked longer in his current supervisory position, as well as the younger chem techs working longer while they decommissioned Darkly.

I directly confronted Nathan about starting this gossip and informed him that it needed to stop, as I was not going to agree to it. This turned into an extremely heated confrontation when he angrily accused me of violating our contract with the severance packages our union members were offered for these layoffs. After I told him everything in the severance packages were negotiated and agreed to during our last contract negotiations, he changed his tune. But it was too late! The wounds made during this difficult time took their toll on our relationship.

But the real culprit behind this personnel transition plan circulation was Ferengi. On several occasions and over the course of several weeks, I confronted Ferengi in person and through email warning him that I was not going to agree to his personnel transition plan, as it was a gross violation of our contract. I told him the gossip his salaried personnel were circulating about "his" plan needed to stop, that it was causing a hostile environment for everyone in Darkly, especially against me.

And Ferengi knew better than to purposely allow such a gross violation of our contract to circulate among the Darkly union rank and file before it was presented to union leadership for approval.

But for a long time, Ferengi had a real disdain for me as president that was obvious to many. He ignored everything I said and continued pursuing his personal agenda with his personnel transition plan, even knowing all the hostility it was causing.

Ferengi called his meeting to present his plan in writing to the union e-board, once again with hopes that they would agree to his plan when he already knew I would not. It was now the first part of November. This was my first meeting with Jezebel present after her return (personnel were never managed well at this company). Harry had been out of work on sick leave for several weeks by this time, leaving me alone to deal with everything going on with Darkly and the shutdown hostility. But in reality, I was never alone, as my Lord Jesus was always by my side.

Ferengi's personnel transition plan was very detailed. He had dates for when everyone was going to move and what jobs each person would be working, all without any consideration for canvassing people for their choice of plant pool jobs for bump-backs, per seniority, per our contract. He had also planned on moving out some other people from their bid plant pool positions that were not part of the domino effect moves of Darkly shutting down, just because he wanted others working in those positions.

Ferengi's plan outlined that the younger chem techs of Darkly, who were slated for permanent layoff, would stay working in Darkly longer, even after the shutdown, when it should have been older chem techs staying to work in their department for decommissioning. In addition, his plan showed that for a third time during my term as president, the Maintenance Department was having their personnel numbers reduced.

Ferengi's audacity to present his personnel transition plan in writing at this meeting while believing we would even entertain such a gross violation of our contract, infuriated me.

The Lord had used many situations in this president position to teach me to control anger. I wasn't perfect yet, but I had come a long way. But I didn't have a chance to say anything before my vice president and acting chief shop steward instantly blew up in anger on Ferengi after reading his plan, and then they walked out of the meeting. The other e-board officers followed suit.

Before I walked out, I reminded Ferengi that I had warned him: His plan was a gross violation of our contract that this union would not agree to—and now he knew. Ferengi and Jezebel were visibly angry because of the reaction of the union's e-board. Too bad for them! It all came with the territory.

No one wanted to see Darkly shutdown. But Ferengi was just making matters so much worse with his audacity and his personal agendas. There were even crews split into older and younger chem techs feuding with each other. By this time, I hated coming to work, as each day I had to deal with several hostile confrontations, even from some people who did not work in Darkly.

My next shift at work after Ferengi's meeting with the e-board was midnight. The demons had the upper hand. They swished all around the Darkly Department, seething with anger and hatred as they formed trails with their sulfur breaths, even as they swung their worn-out rusty swords: the result of numerous lost battles with God's angelic warriors over the life that was now approaching. These demons drooled their saliva as they fed on the hostile atmosphere. They were confident that tonight was going to be their victory; tonight, they would reach their ultimate goal of destroying me.

I walked into Darkly's control room my first midnight right into what I perceived as a lynch-mob; a group of angry men were just waiting for me. As soon as I walked in, these men attacked me as they hurled angry and hateful words at me, waving hard copies

FERENGI'S AGENDA/71

of Ferengi's transition plan in my face with the words on top of the page: "The Union Turned It Down."

Posted on several walls and bulletin boards around Darkly's building were several more copies of Ferengi's plan with the same words written on top.

God's angelic warriors were well aware of this battle, and well prepared. The Captain of the Host summoned his army in battle array at just the right moment for the best element of surprise. The forces of evil fought in a frenzy against the very same angelic warriors who had been given charge over my life by the command of Almighty God many years before.

Ollie and Stanley were among these angry men present. I had seen Stanley react in hot anger before over what seemed like an insignificant incident, and with his own confession of having bipolar, I knew this was not a normal "let's beat up the president" confrontation.

It didn't matter that the whole e-board also refused to agree to this plan at the meeting—I was the union scapegoat. I tried not to provoke anyone as I reiterated to this angry mob that I could not have agreed to such a gross violation of our contract, even though it would have allowed them to stay working longer. But these men heard nothing I said. They just continued with their angry confrontation. This night was one of the very few times as union president that I believed I was in danger.

After all my attempts to reason with these angry men, and seeing Stanley so much more visibly angry than the rest, I walked out of the Darkly building and radioed the shift coach asking him to come to Darkly as soon as possible. I gave the shift coach no hint as to why I asked him to come, but since we all carried radios, I knew Stanley and everyone else were aware of this contact.

The departments on our plant site were spread out far apart over 420 acres, and it took about fifteen to twenty minutes for the shift coach to finally arrive at Darkly. As I stood outside waiting on the shift coach, Stanley came outside after me. He spoke a little calmer now that he knew the shift coach was alerted. Stanley asked me if I was afraid of him? He seemed remorseful of his behavior and tried to convince me that he would never hurt me. I've had many conversations with Stanley in the past, each time trying my best to be patient and understanding in dealing with him, knowing how quickly someone with his disposition issues could be provoked to anger. I told him truthfully: "Yes, because of your anger, I am afraid of you right now!"

Before the shift coach showed up, Stanley left me alone and went back inside Darkly. I spoke with the shift coach about the situation and let him know I was fearful that I was in danger, but I did not give him any names. I told him that as of then, I thought everything was under control and that I would be okay. He honored my wishes to let it go, but also told me that he would be around, and to call him if things changed for the worse again. I thanked him for coming before he left.

Meanwhile, in the spiritual realm, the angelic warriors gained the victory over the demons. I walked back inside Darkly's control room into a very thick and dark atmosphere of silence. The men who were present from the previous shift had left by this time by a back way. I would be working the entire midnight shift with angry men on my crew.

Stanley wasn't a bad guy, and even claimed to be a Christian. But his anger with such disposition issues was a concern, as well as his past on the self-referral program. Ollie never did get over his ill feelings towards me over some of my decisions as president.

I understood that this was a difficult time for everyone, especially those working in Darkly. But no one seemed to remember that my responsibility was to enforce our contract. There were going to be people on both sides of the fence who were not going to be happy no matter what decision I made. But I was not going to let anyone, by way of intimidation or in any other way, to dissuade me from fulfilling my responsibilities as president.

The hostility didn't end on lynch-mob night. The propaganda continued by some salaried personnel fueling the hostility, as they went throughout the plant site bragging about how the Darkly people were in such a feud over the bump-back moves and the department shutdown.

I confronted Ferengi, again, over this hostile environment that he and his salaried personnel were fueling, especially against me. Ferengi adamantly denied any responsibility by him or his salaried personnel for this hostile environment, and denied any wrongdoing in how his personnel transition plan was exposed. Someone had circulated the hard copies of the transition plan throughout the plant site to others. Some union members advised me to file a lawsuit against management over their involvement in promoting this hostile environment against me. But this was not the direction the Lord was giving me.

I tried arranging a meeting with the e-board and Darkly's union members on plant site hoping to calm things down. I also asked Cain to be present to help while letting him know about the hostility, and that there were many wanting to decertify from the union because of refusing to agree to Ferengi's personnel transition plan. But as usual, Cain refused to help me, either with this meeting or otherwise.

Ferengi, on the other hand, insisted on being present should we have a meeting, even though it was only to be union members.

Because of all this, I scratched the whole idea of this meeting. I decided I would deal with everything on my own with God's help, as I have done over the years with so many other issues.

435

Chapter 72
Another Term

When things were going well at this chemical plant and people were being hired, when the economy was growing and profits were being made, that was a good time to be a union president. But with everything going on during this time, the morale at this plant was at an all-time low. This was definitely one of the worst of times to be a union president.

I really didn't ask for this president position. I would have been very happy just being a union trustee, or something else, or nothing else. I would share with people that it was the Lord God who led me to run for union president, and then jokingly add: "But I ran in the wrong direction."

So, what was the Lord thinking leading me into another term? After much prayer and seeking, I had no doubts—whatever His reasons—God wanted me as union president again. So much for contemplating the severance package!

The Darkly shutdown was rescheduled several times because our customers needed our product. The final scheduled date was at the end of December. Just ten days after Ferengi's personnel transition plan meeting, and less than a week from the dreadful lynch-mob nightmare, it was election day for new union officers with the biggest turnout ever for voters.

News traveled fast at that plant site. A great guy from Beady approached me in the parking lot of the union hall where the voting was taking place, and expressed his concerns about what happened on lynch-mob night at Darkly. He said if that ever happened again, just give his department a call and someone would be right there to help. I thought that was very nice of him and his coworkers, and expressed my thanks to them all for their concern and willingness to help me.

I didn't need to be told; I knew many people were hoping and banking that I would not get re-elected as president. Salaried personnel were on top and weighing heavy on the list. The union's recording secretary, Marvin, who ran a few times before without ever being elected president, thought now was his chance.

With the low morale of our members, a recent concessional contract, announcement of the loss of our 401(k) company match, a department shutting down, people permanently being laid off throughout the plant, Marvin had it in the bag—so to speak—to win this time. Two others were also on the ballot for president.

Marvin was Ferengi's confidant, and I was sure would have been his puppet had he won. Working in Ariel (Ferengi's favorite department) as a lead operator, he was instrumental in the union losing all the plant pool positions there. (More on this will come later.) Marvin was so confident of his win for president that he sat in the voting booth area promoting himself. This was not legally permitted if your name was on any official election ballot, and not just for unions. Marvin had an air of pride while addressing those coming in to vote. I never protested his presence in the area. I believed that Ferengi timed his personnel transition plan meeting when he did to ensure I didn't get re-elected.

But the Lord's will prevailed! I had almost a brand-new e-board to work with from my company group for my second term as president. The only problem was that some of these new union reps were in cahoots with Jezebel and Ferengi big time, and with other salaried personnel. I would not know the full extent of this at the very beginning of this new term in office. But it didn't take me long to realize that this next e-board was going to be difficult because of these conflicting allegiance relationships.

I had great hopes that Jezebel was going to be different to deal with than Lisa. And she was different, but not for the better. We just didn't seem to hit it off good from the start. That first meeting when we rejected so aggressively Ferengi's personnel transition plan, seemed to seal the fate of our ongoing turbulent relationship.

It was only after I was re-elected as president that Jezebel tried to document her lame attempts to deal with lynch-mob night. Many people knew that I blamed management as the culprit in promoting this hostile work environment against me through Ferengi's obsessions with his personal agendas. Jezebel sent her email to my home email address while acknowledging I was on vacation. She said it was brought to her attention that I felt threatened while at work, and she wanted to talk about this after I returned from vacation. I wisely ignored her email.

Over two weeks later, she followed up with another email sent again to my home email address. This one was shorter, more direct, and ended with two questions: "Is there any follow up required? If not, can I assume that this is not an issue?"

There are times when the Lord makes the motives of others transparent to me. I knew what Jezebel was doing through her emails. She was always obsessed with making sure everything was well documented to her advantage, which at times backfired on her to my advantage. I always labeled her as the "Document Queen" of our company. But in all honesty and the first to admit, I wasn't too far behind her in this area as the "Document Princess."

I also knew by now that not addressing some issues when presented, would be assumed that it was agreed upon. I guessed that my response was totally unexpected to Jezebel, as I threw the blame back on management, and exposed her motives through her emails of trying to dissolve management's responsibility for this hostile environment I endured. My ending statement left an open door: I expressed that I would deal with this on my own without her involvement, but was sure to thank her for her concern anyway. Jezebel never responded.

Once again, I was following God's direction to let this lynch-mob incident go. Stanley was leaving on the layoff soon and was to start training for a new career with the TAA that he so much was looking forward to. I didn't want anything to mess this up for him or anyone else by pursuing that incident.

This same November, we finally received approval for the TAA (Trade Adjustment Assistant) that I filed earlier in May, and the timing could not have been more perfect. Had I not waited on the Lord's direction on this, and filed for this TAA when advised to do so by the unemployment office rep that previous January, everyone would have missed out on the enhanced program offered only for those petitions filed after a certain date in May. Even salaried personnel leaving employment during that time were able to take advantage of this TAA. I have never regretted waiting on the Lord for His direction and timing before making decisions.

I emailed all the TAA information to everyone just before they were laid off. My email contained hopes and prayers that everyone taking advantage of this benefit and training would find a rewarding and sustainable career outside of our current employment. And my prayers went beyond what I stated in this email. Many nights I cried out to the Lord God, as I was more concerned for those working at this plant site and their welfare than my own.

I remember walking around Darkly just before the shutdown: *What should I do now? All my efforts to save Darkly failed!*

The Lord interrupted my thoughts with a familiar Scripture: "Trust in the Lord with all your heart and do not lean on your own understanding. In all your ways acknowledge Him, and He will make your paths straight" (Proverbs 3:5-6).

Chapter 73
Warehouse Job

With having the most plant seniority being bumped into the plant pool, I was the first to choose my job position. Dwayne, the union's elected sergeant of arms, received a bid into another department, which made his Logistic Department warehouse job available. Any plant pool position was a pay cut, but the warehouse was steady daylight. After almost twenty years of grueling rotating shifts, working daylight was the only plus.

Working in this warehouse in the union was Samson, Marty and Tara. Marty was a newly elected e-board trustee, and Tara was an elected union shop steward. Both Marty and Tara also worked in mark-up salaried positions quite often, which gave them extra wages, but which I believed was a conflict of interest. While in these salaried positions, they were temporally transferred out of the union. I always spoke against this conflict of interest, but never took any action to stop it at the beginning.

Henry was my first-line boss in the warehouse, and the best boss I ever worked for at this chemical plant. We had a great working relationship and system going. Although contractually I was permitted time away from my job duties for union business, often I would work through my breaks and my unpaid lunch to make sure the work was done before taking care of union business. I made sure I carried my share of the workload. Tara didn't like my conscientiousness, and used it to cause strife between us.

I found out early on, there were union coworkers tattling on fellow union coworkers to higher management in this warehouse. I was often the victim of this tattling, and was called on the carpet numerous times for what proved to be false accusations. Although

I knew those responsible for this tattling practice, I could never prove it. All of this made for a very difficult environment for me while working in the warehouse.

This warehouse position had many different aspects to the job that I needed to learn. Some of my new job duties dealt with several types of semi-tractor-trailer trucks. While some of these trucks needed loaded with the product that was produced at this plant according to each order from our customers, other trucks came in with supplies that needed unloaded.

There was also the yard-truck (semi-trailer cab) that I had to learn to use proficiently for backing in and pulling out most of these semi-trailers and shorter seabulk trailers in the warehouse dock doors. I found out the hard way, the shorter the trailer, the harder it was to spot (put in place) correctly. I never drove a tractor-trailer before. Tara showed me twice how to use the yard-truck, and then left me on my own. It took some time, but I finally mastered it. I always believed that the Lord knew I would need that experience sometime in my future.

The Ariel Department, located a good driving distance away from the warehouse, was also part of my new area of responsibility for loading trailer trucks. The Ariel product was boxed out into thousand-pound boxes that were stored in a large freezer, and then it was transported in freezer-trucks to our customers. The cold from these freezers always aggravated my RSD condition.

To remedy this RSD aggravation, when weather permitted, I drove the warehouse-covered forklift with a heater to Ariel, a practice many frowned upon, and used it going into the freezer for the boxes to load into the freezer-trucks. But I knew I had to keep the real reason for using this covered forklift to myself. I had managed to keep my RSD condition under a tight lid, and those currently in management were far removed from my nightmare dealing with this off-the-wall neurological pain disorder.

When I first came to the warehouse, I noticed this same covered forklift had missing side mirrors. It didn't take me long to discover that the design of how these mirrors were mounted on this forklift caused them to get ripped off while driving through any hard-plastic curtain, such as those in the warehouse doorways and Ariel's freezer. In the near future, I would get blamed for every side mirror that came up missing on this forklift.

Another warehouse job duty involved moving railcars throughout the plant site. I always had a healthy fear of being around railcars and railroad tracks. Now with being over half a century old, I had to learn to work with these monsters and around railroad tracks. The Lord has a real sense of humor as He directs my life!

This railcar job was by far the most difficult to learn, the most physically demanding, and the most dangerous. It required two people working well together; I cannot emphasize enough the importance of working well together. Any communication barrier between the two, any bad attitudes, any inattentiveness, any number of other distractions, someone could get seriously hurt or killed, or have a serious incident happen.

The locomotive driver could not see beyond the connected railcars hooked to the locomotive. Because of this, depending on whether these railcars were being pulled or pushed, the second person working as the ground-person, walked alongside the rail tracks a few feet ahead of the moving railcars and became the eyes of the locomotive driver. It was imperative that the locomotive driver followed the directions of the ground-person with only one exception: if there was a hazard unknown to the ground-person.

The main responsibility of the ground-person was to ensure the safety of the plant site while moving these railcars. With 420 acres of land and the areas spread out, all employees, contractors, and others were permitted to drive their own vehicles and company vehicles around the plant site. There were also plenty of bicycles and pedestrians moving about the plant, and other workers around the rail tracks loading and unloading railcars. The ground-person had to be constantly vigilant to ensure that no one got in harm's way, and to alert and stop vehicle and pedestrian traffic when needed while these railcars were being moved.

The ground-person communicated through a radio and/or hand signals to give directions to the locomotive driver when to slow down, stop, start out, and in describing the distance to hook-up to the railcar ahead. The ground-person worked the couplers, which connects the railcars, when unhooking and hooking railcars together, and at times, had to go in between the railcars to do this.

The ground-person had to ensure that the end railcar of each string of connecting railcars left on the tracks had their hand brakes properly applied. This involved climbing on and off the railcars to manually engage or disengage hand brakes.

In addition, the ground-person was responsible for making sure each railroad track switch was in the right position for each track the railcars were being moved on. These track switches were heavy and awkward to operate, and were used to switch from one track to another track. Flags on these track switches indicated the position they were locked in. If these track switches were in the wrong position as railcars moved over them, it could cause a derailment. Thus, the ground-person had the most physically demanding and the most responsibility of the job.

I started this job in January, not the best time of the year to be learning how to move railcars for the first time. But I was working for the Lord, and I always tried to do my best on any job I worked.

I was just starting to learn the intricate network of the rail tracks and their switches when one morning, I went out on the rails and discovered something phenomenon had happened—all the rail tracks had disappeared! They were all gone, just like magic. Only the very top of the flags on the track switches could be seen sticking out from all the snow that was dumped the night before.

Dwayne worked with me until I was trained before he was moved to his new job position. Together, or so I thought, we were supposed to use shovels to dig out the track switches from all the snow and ice before we could make rail moves. Dwayne got the Kubota, a four-wheel-drive vehicle we used to get around the plant, and drove us to the first track switch to dig out. When we arrived at the track switch, I saw only one shovel in the back of the Kubota. *Well, that's not going to work with two people!*

I knew Dwayne from being on the e-board and from our union activities for many years by this time. Dwayne was a great guy, and great at disappearing when there was work to be done. Now that I was working on the job with him, well, some things about people never change. I looked at the lone shovel and innocently asked, "You only brought one shovel?"

As though this was his cue with everything planned out, without hesitation, he announced, "I'll go get another one," and before I could say anything else, he jumped back in the Kubota and was gone.

Okay. I'll start digging out this first track switch and he'll be back soon, and we can move on to the next switch. After about twenty minutes, I was done with this track switch and walked on to the next, barreling through knee-high snow as I went. With each track switch I dug out, my irritation grew. I kept looking out for Dwayne to come back, and all I saw was more snow, as I was now in the middle of no-man's-land, alone.

When Dwayne finally came back to where I was, I asked him a stupid question: "Where've you been all this time?"

I can still see his face as he replied, "I had to look for a shovel?"

My tone exposed my disbelief to his excuse: "All this time?"

Someone told me later he was in the smoke-hut smoking his cigarettes and keeping warm.

We had an abundance of snow that winter. At the beginning, I thought it was only because of the snow that I was falling so often. Samson always got a good laugh at me while we worked the rails together, as he described it: "First I see you, and then I don't. You get hidden in all the snow."

Once all the snow was gone, I realized that the snow was only one of several culprits causing me to stumble and fall. As the ground-person on this rail job, I was hiking over rough terrain: navigating and stumbling over big rocks, little stones, mounds of dirt, sinking sand hills, all sorts of vegetation sticking out of the ground. At times I stumbled over what appeared to be nothing at all. I worked this rail job in all types of weather while trying to be sure I didn't fall on the rail tracks and get squashed in the process. This rail job was going to prove to take its toll on me in many ways in the years to follow.

While hiking miles along the rails with these monsters and dealing with everything this new job entailed, I often spoke to the Lord Jesus. I would gently remind Him how old I was—as if He didn't remember—and then would ask Him: "Is this REALLY what You want me to do for the rest of my working career?"

The Lord never answered me. I was sure He just chuckled away my question while knowing exactly what my future held, knowing He was working on His plan and purpose for my life. I just continued working this job doing my best while trying to ignore the pain from the aggravated RSD condition.

All I have just shared regarding my new warehouse job was instrumental in the turmoil I was to endure in my near future. However, God's grace proved sufficient to ensure my endurance.

Chapter 74

Assertiveness

With a new job, another term as president, a new chief shop steward who I will name Chief, and a new union e-board, along came new and difficult challenges. With the recent loss of our contracting out grievance arbitration, it was very disappointing that we also lost our 401(k) grievance arbitration. As a retirement benefit, this should have been governed under the mandatory subject of bargaining clause per the labor laws, and never allowed to be unilaterally taken away from the union.

This 401(k) arbitration had cost our local union thousands of dollars in lawyers' fees. With Cain insisting a lawyer should handle this case, the International Union could have and should have assigned one of their lawyers to help our local union, but they did not—we were on our own. I never told anyone about my private war trying to get this issue addressed timely so that we did not forfeit our rights to challenge this. I also filed NLRB charges, but their decision was to defer to the arbitrator's decision.

I sent out an email to our union members regarding this lost arbitration. Here is a synopsis:

"Management's premeditated decision to not put on the negotiating table their plans to eliminate such a major monetary retirement benefit this union has had for years, but instead, waited to inform us after our current contract was ratified, was a gross act of bad faith bargaining on their part, which can only be viewed as an unfair labor practice. That justice in this case on behalf of the union was denied does not by any means justify management's wrong in their actions nor make it right; it merely serves to soothe their consciences."

I toned it down from my original draft and waited a few days before sending it. Soon afterward, the union and management had our monthly meeting with the e-board present. Management had originally asked at one time, and the union agreed, that we would not discuss grievances or arbitrations at these meetings. Yet, Ferengi insisted that he wanted to give his side of what happened with the 401(k) issue. Out of common courtesy, I agreed, which was a major mistake on my part.

I listened as Ferengi addressed a brand-new e-board with no experience in these positions. They did not know the labor laws, and were never in any contract negotiations. They knew nothing about how management and Cain tried to sweep this gross act of bad faith bargaining under the carpet. They were not privy to my private war trying to get this issue addressed timely to ensure we did not forfeit our rights to challenge such a huge monetary retirement loss. And they did not know that our local union spent thousands of dollars trying to address this while Cain and our International Union officials refused to help us.

Ferengi began his story by stating that arbitrations and board charges were very serious, and that the union should not be going to arbitration or filing board charges. This could very well have been perceived as a threat or scare tactic while addressing an inexperienced union e-board, especially while some of them were in co-hoots with management to begin with.

Ferengi continued by stating that right before the original temporary layoffs in December, management told the union of their plan of eliminating their company match to our 401(k). Ferengi's bald-faced lie infuriated me. He just proved that management had already decided to eliminate their company match long before our contract negotiations, and purposely did not notify the union leadership until after our concessional contract was ratified.

When I confronted Ferengi on his lie, he backpedaled and stated that they had "intended" on telling the union about it before the temporary layoffs. All that Ferengi just stated only proved my claim that management's premeditated decision was a gross act of bad faith bargaining.

Ferengi continued disparaging the union officials when he insisted that management told us during negotiations of their intent to eliminate their company match to our 401(k). But Ferengi's last statement was the breaking point: He claimed management believed the union's silence after informing us of their elimination of their company match, indicated that we were glad the company was not touching our defined pension plan.

These statements made it appear that all the union officials at negotiations were negligent in our responsibilities to safeguard all of the union's retirement benefits, especially by not challenging such a huge monetary retirement loss.

Marty, warehouse e-board member riding the fence while working mark-up to a salaried position, responded to Ferengi innocently enough: "Well, I didn't know all this. Thank you for telling us."

I finally told Ferengi he had said enough, and then I left in hot anger, but without my new e-board officers. With some of them in cahoots with management, including Marty, I knew they would not have followed me out even if they knew the unspoken code of conduct for such meetings: When the union president walks out, all other union reps follow suit. The union's newly elected vice president, who was also in negotiations as an elected negotiating team member, was not present at this meeting.

This was Ferengi's touché against me for the arbitration announcement email I sent, but it backfired on him. I let some time pass—I learned this wisdom—before I confronted Ferengi in an email with what he stated at this meeting. By this time in my president experience, I knew copying Gremlin for his knowledge would be leverage in getting the seriousness of my point across.

I expressed to Ferengi that I was sure no one in that room understood his attempts to disparage union officials, and his perceived threat to a brand-new e-board that the union should not be going to arbitration or filing board charges, were all unfair labor practices that would justify another board charge. Gremlin would know all about unfair labor practices, and just the mention of another board charge in itself would arouse Gremlin's attention.

Ferengi backpedaled again, and copied Gremlin in his email. He denied his comments about arbitrations or filing board charges, and added, "If others in the meeting believe that I stated that, please feel free to pass along this message to clarify that that was not my intentions."

Had I not copied Gremlin, I knew Ferengi's response would have been much different.

During this time, there were still several union members on layoff status, with more scheduled for layoff in the near future, including four operators in Beady, a department that produced an expandable foam bead product used for different applications.

However, the great managing skills of those in charge delayed four different times at monthly intervals, these next scheduled layoffs. The last delay left these employees in limbo without notification of their job status. Management was never able to manage their workforce personnel well.

There were also many who took advantage of the severance package and went into early retirement, which caused numerous vacancies in Beady without enough properly trained operators to fill them. This caused unsafe working conditions with so many older chem techs being bombarded with overtime filling open schedules, while so many "trainees" were trying to learn a job that was going to take months to learn. Everything was in chaos.

In the midst of this mismanagement culprit, the union was told that the technology for making a Beady product that was the most profitable and superior to other manufacturers of the same product, was sold to a manufacturer in China for one million dollars. Selling our technology was viewed as a betrayal to our plant site and our union workers. Soon after this announcement, management announced that this company was sending visitors to our facility to better learn our process for their own benefit. It was bad enough that our technology was sold. But now our union workers were expected to help these visitors learn their process!

I was invited to the initial meeting at Beady announcing these visitors, with many chem techs in the department also present; I was sure management regretted this invitation afterward. Kirk, a salaried employee, was leading this meeting.

Kirk made it very clear to our chem techs that management wanted only the technology that was sold to these visitors exposed, without exposing technology concerning the other product produced at Beady. I had some real concerns with this warning, especially with repercussions from management towards our union chem techs should something inadvertently be exposed that wasn't supposed to be exposed.

Kirk also knew of the outrage of the Beady chem techs over these "visitors" coming to their department to learn their production process. He tried to defuse their anger by stating to them at this meeting, that "there would be no requirements" on the part of our own chem techs regarding these visitors during the time they were in the department or on our plant site.

As soon as Kirk stated this, I fired back: "I will hold you to your word!"

My assertiveness as president was well established by that time, thanks to the driving force of God's Holy Spirit. Everyone present knew I meant what I said, including Ferengi. I intended to follow up afterward on this meeting, but was held back by God's leading from initiating an email to Ferengi; I understood why after I received Ferengi's email.

Specifically referencing Kirk's comment that the chem techs had "no requirements," Ferengi clarified his own expectations. He stated these visitors would be spending time in the control rooms and operating areas, and although a salaried technical person should be available to help, he made sure to state his expectations were that the Beady chem techs would be courteous, professional, cooperative and responsive to these visitors.

Ferengi then tried justifying this betrayal of our technology by adding, "I know that you and others have some concerns about this arrangement. But I really do believe that it will actually turn out to be beneficial to the business and to our plant site."

Selling our technology and having these buyers come and learn our process, so that they can produce our products and take away our jobs, could not benefit our plant site!

I was sure my response was not appreciated. I defended our chem techs, as I assured Ferengi that they would be courteous and professional to these visitors, but reiterated that I would hold Kirk to his word: "Beyond that, there are no requirements."

I then emphasized the difficult state of the Beady Department due to the mismanagement of personnel at this plant site. I reminded Ferengi that our Beady chem techs had their own "trainees" they were responsible for, and their safety was their priority. I strongly suggested that while these visitors were on the plant site and in the Beady area, that at all times a responsible salaried employee should be accompanying them. I made sure to emphasize why:

"This would ensure that these visitors' questions and concerns are addressed, ensure their safety while in a chemical operating facility totally unfamiliar to them, and ensure that they only receive information on our prime production process, and nothing on our secondary production process, which management seemed very concerned about safeguarding."

I ended my assertive email with another strong statement I knew would not be appreciated, but legally, I had the right to say:

"Please be aware that the union will not assume any liability with regards to these visitors during this visit or any time in the future. If you have any further concerns or questions, please let me know. Thank you."

Ferengi never responded. But it didn't matter. I had a whole department up in arms over these visitors coming, and my utmost concern was their safety and jobs, not visitors from China coming to learn our technology. I sent the email to several chem techs in Beady, including Chief who worked there, with my permission to print it out as a reference.

And someone did print it out, and left copies floating all around the control rooms and other areas for anyone to pick up and read, including management and their soon to come visitors. The result was that this scheduled visit by these visitors was canceled. Instead, a few technical salaried personnel went to their facility overseas to teach them our technology.

None of what I did as president endeared me to management. I was soon to learn that I had a huge target on my front and back for management's campaign against me. And they managed to recruit for their campaign force some e-board officers, and Darkly natives, who still resented and blamed me for the Darkly shutdown. But God always kept His word spoken to me so many years earlier: "No weapon formed against you will ever prosper." (Isaiah 54:17.)

Chapter 75
Flex Job

There are some union and contractual specifics that are connected with several issues that presented fierce trials in my terms as union president. It is of benefit to explain these in a clear way for a better understanding of why some of these were the main cause of such fierce opposition. Explaining job descriptions is one of these specifics.

Every job classification in the union workforce at this plant site had a specific job description that governed the duties and responsibilities of that job. There was a designated article in our contract describing in detail how these jobs and job descriptions were managed, which included how they were changed in some way, re-evaluated for a higher wage, or created for new job positions. As the union president, it was my responsibility to police these job descriptions, and contractually, I could agree to any changes proposed by management, or propose changes myself for the union or individual jobs.

This contract designated article regarding job descriptions had limitations on how changes could be proposed and agreed upon, and a grievance process to address any disagreements with any requested proposed changes coming from either management or the union.

Although I utilized my authority to review job descriptions (with the input of those working the jobs), there were times when I felt the need to bring in the union e-board for their input, especially when any job description involved the addition and/or drastic changes of different positions in our union workforce. This was the case with the Beady flex operator job description.

Going back in history: A union president had agreed to a job description for a flex operator to be used in Ariel only. This flex operator job was in the classification of chem tech, and was not a plant pool position. However, it also allowed those in this position to perform the duties of plant pool material packagers daily, but only in their Ariel Department.

Marvin was the union's recording secretary during my first term as president, and was a lead operator in Ariel. While working as fire watch during the last temporary layoff, he convinced Ferengi without my knowledge, to eliminate all the material packagers in Ariel, and make everyone either a flex or lead chem tech operator. This action dwindled the number of plant pool positions used for contractual bump-backs during layoffs. Due to the flex operator job description already in place and the layoff status of that department, when this was finally brought to my attention, although I did not agree with it, I wisely discerned by God's Spirit that this was not a battle for that time.

Fast forward to our last contract negotiations: Ferengi brought proposals for several job description changes, including flex operator jobs to be used in Beady and Darkly. No one knew an entire department was going to shutdown at that time. These flex jobs would have eliminated all of our plant pool material packager positions. With Ferengi bringing these into negotiations, he wanted to circumvent my contractual responsibility dealing with job descriptions, hoping that Cain would be more favorable to agree with these and his personal agendas, as he knew I would not.

With our complicated seniority contract language that had been in place for the past several contracts by that time, I knew it would be detrimental for our union workforce to lose any more plant pool positions. Our bump-back contract language for layoffs was contingent that there were plant pool positions available for more senior employees to bump into and remain employed, which also gave them bidding rights for job advancements.

Using the fifty percent reduction of the union workforce announcement that was planned for the end of that year, but not yet knowing who these people would be, and with the material packager positions being the largest plant pool group, I was able to convince our negotiating team that the union could not afford to lose any more plant pool positions.

Cain never had any qualms going against my wishes, but would balk when the whole negotiating team was in unity—this was my hope—and it worked. Ferengi did not succeed in getting his flex operator job descriptions agreed to during negotiations that would have eliminated all plant pool material packager positions in our plant site.

Fast forward to ten months after our contract ratification: Jezebel, on behalf of Ferengi, sent a meeting notice to Chief and me to discuss a Beady flex operator job description, and attached the exact flex operator job description that was presented for the union's agreement during negotiations, with the same wording that these operators would be able to perform the plant pool material packager's job responsibilities in Beady. (How these job descriptions were worded was so very important.) Jezebel asked that we keep this confidential until we can meet and discuss it, and then added, "Rest assured that this job description will not result in reducing the number of plant pool positions."

With visions of previous good-faith gestures the union had made over the years flying out the windows with no rebound still fresh in my mind, could I believe this? Not a fat chance! Down the road, I knew our last existing plant pool material packager positions would be gone, just like it happened in Ariel.

During this meeting, Ferengi and Jezebel took full advantage of their mismanagement skills that were by this time perfected, and declared that if we agreed to this new flex operator job description, it would add four more union jobs to the headcount in the Beady Department. I needed to admit that this was not a bad angle of approach on their part.

However, with my experience knowing Ferengi well by then, I understood he was manifesting his horse-trade mentality while at the same time, indirectly admitting that Beady could not run efficiently with his initial restructuring plan of reducing the department by four union employees still scheduled for layoff, but at some undetermined future date.

Ferengi was also trying to circumvent our contract indirectly with these flex operator positions, as he also admitted that he did not have the flexibility in our contract to use the Beady personnel fully as he wanted for this department. With these four union positions already existing in Beady as sweco operators (also non-plant pool positions), Ferengi was only adding responsibilities with his flex job description, yet was calling these four positions "new" positions.

Chief, who was working in Beady as a lead chem tech, while being new on the block in his higher union rep position and was not part of our last negotiations, thought I was overreacting over Jezebel's initial email presenting this flex job description and after this meeting discussing it. His initial response, "You're just mad because this was brought up in negotiations. Maybe we need to take a look at this?"

Alvin, one of the four Beady sweco operators scheduled for the layoff, though not currently a union rep, was elected as a union team member in negotiations and had more past experience as a previous union rep. Alvin was willing to call Ferengi's bluff and take the chance of layoff, instead of agreeing to a job description that might potentially eliminate our last existing plant pool material packager positions. It didn't take long for Alvin and me to convince Chief that Ferengi's flex operator job description agenda was detrimental to our union workforce.

Now that our confidential meeting had taken place, I emailed this job description to the chem techs in Beady for their knowledge and input, and copied our e-board officers. Marty, warehouse new e-board member riding the fence, questioned my actions: "Isn't Ferengi and Jezebel gonna get mad that you sent that email to the people in Beady?"

I just looked at him. His response to my expression and silence spoke volumes: "You don't care, do you?" *He's learning.*

Behind the scenes were some of the former Darkly chem techs now working as Beady material packagers, who had their own agendas and private discussions with Ferengi over these new flex job positions. While thinking only of themselves, they had hopes that if the union would agree to these flex jobs, eventually, and perhaps real soon, they would all become flex operators when Ferengi decided to eliminate all the Beady material packagers, as he did in Ariel. This type of direct dealing between management and union rank and file went against the labor laws and our contract, and only served to undermine the union's responsibility to preserve everyone's job.

I tried explaining to these Darkly natives, that had the union agreed to these flex job descriptions and the elimination of plant pool material packager positions while in negotiations, these same Darkly guys would now be out of the plant on layoff directly from Darkly without a job, and without any chance for bidding rights for higher and more secure positions, per our seniority contract language. But as much as I tried, I could not get through to these Darkly natives. They were still hostile and resentful towards me while still blaming me for the Darkly shutdown.

Jezebel was also working behind the scenes to undermine the union, and in her position and what she did was a more serious violation of the labor laws. Andrew, one of the sweco guys working in Beady scheduled for layoff, had a salaried fiancée, Wendy, working in administration with Jezebel.

I ran into Wendy in a restaurant during this Beady flex job saga. Wendy approached me to say that Jezebel had directly told her if the union did not agree to these flex operator jobs, Andrew would lose his job. Jezebel encouraged Wendy to inform Andrew of what she said. Wendy warned me to be careful dealing with Jezebel, claiming she can be vicious and cannot be trusted, and confided that there were many working with Jezebel who wanted to collectively turn her in to their own boss. I don't know if this ever happened. I never saw Wendy afterward.

After hearing what Jezebel had said to Wendy, I was furious to the max. This was a direct attempt to undermine and blackmail the union into agreeing to these Beady flex jobs. I understood later that Jezebel had a more personal agenda that involved securing Jason's job on behalf of Sabrina. Had I been able to prove what Jezebel had said without implicating Wendy, I would have legally addressed her actions to the fullest extent possible.

I discussed this flex job description with the union e-board at length and explained why we should not agree to it. The e-board voted to support my position. When I emailed Ferengi and Jezebel with our decision, I began on a positive note. I stated that the union appreciated their recognition that Beady did indeed need the four sweco operators, who were scheduled for layoff, in order to run the department efficiently. I then expressed that the e-board was not in favor of agreeing to the flex job description.

However, in the spirit of a good-faith gesture to work together, I revised the existing sweco job description (which was to be replaced by the new flex job description), and attached it as a counterproposal with the hopes that it would be something we could all agree with. Ferengi countered back with a modified flex job description with some wording change that he said would alleviate some—not all—of our concerns of losing the plant pool material packager positions.

Too much of what was going on during our e-board and membership meetings was getting back to management. This was obvious when management confronted me asking why all of the union's e-board voted on this flex job issue, instead of only those working at our company. Although our company group held the majority on the e-board, all issues were discussed with the whole e-board with everyone having a vote. Since we were amalgamated, any arbitration costs came out of our collective funds. I only voted as the tiebreaker.

When I presented this modified flex job description at our next e-board meeting, I spoke in favor of a serious consideration, and then made sure only those from our company group voted this time. I didn't like the modified version, but I was hoping to resolve this issue and make sure these four sweco guys were not laid off. However, the vote was again to reject Ferengi's modified version.

After I emailed Ferengi the union's decision to reject his modified version, he sent his response: "As the union has also rejected the modified flex job description, the company will therefore, move forward and post the new positions using the original Beady flex operator job description."

Ferengi's actions went against past practice and violated our contract that prohibited such a unilateral job posting using a job description that the union would not agree to. His actions were also to spite the union, and demonstrated no consideration for the union's concern that our last plant pool material packager positions were safeguarded. Otherwise, he would have posted the modified flex job description that he said would alleviate some— but not all—of our concerns to safeguard these positions. But instead, he posted the original flex job description.

After this email from Ferengi of his unilateral posting of these four flex jobs, Chief exploded in anger and finally understood somewhat of the temperaments of Ferengi and Jezebel that we were up against; I already knew from past experience.

I emailed the entire Beady Department again and explained that the union was going to challenge the unilateral posting of the original flex job description with a grievance and to the full extent possible. But I also advised anyone who wanted to bid on these jobs to do so, as I stated: "No one ever knows the outcome of such a challenge."

I didn't want anyone to lose out on a job opportunity without knowing for certain we were going to win this challenge.

Jason received one of the four flex operator job bids, which was another contract violation; incumbents were to receive job bid awards first. Now with two counts of contract violations, Jason was finally getting out of his plant pool position.

I questioned Jezebel for justification of Jason's job bid award. She claimed through email that these were new positions. I understood then of Jezebel's personal reason to undermine and blackmail the union by what she directly told Wendy. This email backfired royally on the Document Queen when I used it against her while challenging this flex job description.

Had Ferengi posted the modified version instead of displaying his vindictiveness by posting the original version, maybe the route we took would have been different. But we could not take any chances of losing our last material packager plant pool positions.

I was now facing another war with management and with Cain. But God was still very much in control, working on His nurturing for my life, and for His purpose of demonstrating His grace and power when I am weakest. However, I would still be left with severe wounds to deal with.

Chapter 76

Counterproposal

The familiar cliché, "read the small print," has a wealth of meaning, and also covers large print. It is imperative that important documents and agreements are worded just right. This also holds true to union grievances.

In understanding this, when I filed the grievance over Ferengi's unilateral posting of the flex jobs using the original flex job description that violated our contract, I wasn't taking any chances, and gave the wording much thought and prayer. I made sure to include a very clear requested remedy on the union's part to "expunge the Beady flex operator job posting and job description, and continue to retain the sweco/area operator job and job description."

If we won the grievance, or arbitration should we go that route, I wanted to make sure management had no excuse to layoff the four union operators, who were originally scheduled to get laid off prior to the presentation of this flex job description, with a remedy that only requested "expunge" without a clear "retain" included.

Cain didn't approve of my wording for the remedy. His advice was to just state "expunge the flex job." But it didn't matter to me what Cain advised I should do at this point in our union relationship. I was exclusively following God's leading.

At the third-step grievance meeting, Ferengi admitted it was a trust issue with the risk existing to eliminate our last plant pool material packager positions. Cain was at this grievance meeting and repeated the same statement to Ferengi and Jezebel several times: "You cannot get through the grievance and arbitration process what you could not get in negotiations."

Ferengi did his habitual backpedaling: "My recollection, we shared the flex job description. It was not something we proposed."

The grievance was not settled, so the whole e-board and local union membership voted to take it to arbitration.

The arbitration hearing date was almost eight months from when this flex operator job description was first presented to the union. As our International staff rep, Cain was supposed to handle all our arbitrations. Cain had told me once that it was not unusual right after an arbitration hearing, and in the presence of the arbitrator, that he and Gremlin would meet and then make a deal to settle the grievance apart from intervention and waiting on the arbitrator's decision.

When I first heard this, I questioned him: "Then why even go through with arbitration? That is such a waste of time and the local union's money to go through arbitration only to settle it without waiting on his ruling."

His response was lame: "That's just the way we do it at times."

I was sure these side-deal settlements only happened if Gremlin believed management lost the arbitration.

I had several past practice dealings with job descriptions, along with accompanying emails from Ferengi and Sabrina, all supporting scenarios when new job positions were not posted for job bidding until the union agreed to the job description. I had no doubts we could win this arbitration. My doubts were with Cain and his willingness to support our local union.

Time was moving fast while I waited on Cain to send me his available dates for a meeting with our union reps who were going to testify at the arbitration. We all needed to prepare well and win this time. As a matter of fact, I realized Cain wasn't sending me anything regarding this arbitration, not even payment information, as he had done with past arbitrations. *What is going on? Is their side-deal settlement already in progress?*

Finally, I emailed Cain and clearly confronted him on his lack of information for this arbitration that was not supporting his past practice. He sent me a snippy response. My next email was a bit more direct. I reminded Cain that he gave Ferengi the past arbitration case won by the union, which we were going to use as a precedent setting for our benefit at our maintenance contracting out arbitration; the same arbitration that Cain initially refused to do. After agreeing for a second time to arbitrate the contracting out grievance, Gremlin had submitted this past arbitration case won by the union with his brief, and was able to twist it around so that he and the arbitrator used it against the union.

I tried being as nice as possible dealing with Cain via email as I pleaded, "Please, we need to win this flex job arbitration, and we can, if we work together."

He gave his normal response when blowing me off: "I have no idea what you're babbling about. I never enter into an arbitration case with the intent to lose."

Did I believe him? Of course not! He was forgetting that he told me about his side-deal settlements afterward with his buddy Gremlin to settle grievances before the arbitrator's ruling.

I tried a much softer approach after his snippy responses: "I was trying in a roundabout as nice as possible way to ask you to please, do not disclose anything to Gremlin that we are going over for the flex arbitration."

He got my message, but it didn't matter to him. I knew Cain well enough by then and his ways. I had no doubts his side-deal settlement was already in progress with his buddy Gremlin. Following God's leading, I knew I needed to take matters into my own hands once again. Otherwise, we were going to lose this arbitration, if we even had at all.

At this same time, we were working on trying to stop the plant pool reduction in wages scheduled the following month of May, that was agreed upon during our last contract negotiations. The time now was November. Ferengi and Jezebel had presented the union with a letter of agreement keeping everyone currently in these plant pool positions whole in wages until our current contract expiration, thus temporally avoiding the wage reduction scheduled. Anyone entering these positions would be at the lower wages. However, they also wanted to reduce the wages of the warehouse plant pool positions with the same stipulations, although these were not originally included for a wage reduction. This was not agreeable with the union e-board.

Knowing Cain's plan on making a side-deal settlement just after our flex job arbitration hearing, I prepared a counterproposal that would avoid arbitration altogether, and in the process, gain wages for every union member working at our company group.

I discussed my counterproposal with Chief and my vice president before drafting it up, and they were in full agreement. My counterproposal on behalf of the union not only requested keeping all plant pool positions whole in wages, but included a request for a three percent wage increase for everyone beginning the following first of the year. I believed this pay increase was fair, since all this time while the union was in a pay freeze, salaried personnel were getting their wage increases and bonuses.

The incentive for management to agree to this union counterproposal was that the union would agree to accept the modified version only of the flex operator job description, and then cancel the arbitration. We really did not want to agree to the modified version, but agreed it would be worth it if we could get something for everyone while keeping plant pool positions whole in wages, and with the same pay increase. And with the wording in this modified version, our last existing plant pool material packager positions were somewhat—but not totally—safeguarded.

My counterproposal covered all bases for our protection, as I stated in a "non-precedent setting and without any prejudice or repercussion towards the union in regards to any current or future grievances or arbitrations."

I drafted up a nice email to Ferengi and Jezebel explaining in detail the union's counterproposal, with an attached letter of agreement with everything in simple terms for their consideration. I made it clear in this email, if management was not willing to accept our counterproposal, the union would give our response to their last letter of agreement proposal to only keep those affected by the wage reduction whole, along with their extra stipulations concerning warehouse plant pool jobs, and we would proceed to arbitration for the original flex job description grievance.

Before I sent this email to Ferengi and Jezebel, I sent everything to Cain for his review before meeting with him on another grievance, so that we could discuss everything in person—and we did. I followed up our conversation that evening with another email (Document Princess) letting Cain know that I thought a lot about what we discussed earlier, and believed we should send this counterproposal to management for their consideration. Cain's reply in writing was his clear agreement with sending the counterproposal: "That's fine with me."

Others on our e-board also had a chance to review this counterproposal. I never told anyone on the union e-board that the reason I was pushing for this union counterproposal, was because Cain had agreed to a side-deal settlement with Gremlin apart from arbitration right afterward, and that we were going to have the flex operator job description shoved on us anyway at the end of all this. I decided this was on a need-to-know basis. And besides, I was sure no one would have believed me had I told them.

Once I received Cain's approval, I sent everything to Ferengi, Jezebel and other management involved, and copied Cain and Gremlin. I added a closing statement to the final email:

"Please, let us start out the New Year, not by waiting for a pending arbitration ruling, but with a letter of agreement that proves to everyone at our plant site, that the union and management have made a huge step forward in mending what has become obvious to many as a turbulent relationship. Thank you."

I also sent a copy of this same counterproposal email to Alvin, whose opinion I respected. Alvin had taken my advice to bid on the flex job just in case we lost this challenge. His job was one of the four sweco positions scheduled for layoff. He was also part of the union's negotiating team last contract when this flex job description was presented and rejected, and would be testifying at the upcoming arbitration challenging this violation of our contract.

With much more union rep experience than many on the current e-board, Alvin's response was encouraging: "I think everything in your proposal is fair and reasonable. Let's hope they're (management) smart enough to realize this and act accordingly. Good Luck."

Alvin believed in luck, good or bad. I believed in Divine intervention. I was following God's lead in everything, and praying all would work out for the best.

Chapter 77
Turning in Cain

Within hours of sending the union's counterproposal, Jezebel responded on behalf of management after their workday hours: "We have reviewed the union's new counterproposal as outlined and cannot accept it. Additionally, we are withdrawing the company's letter of agreement proposal for stopping the scheduled wage reductions. We will continue to comply with the contract as it is written for the wage reductions."

Until the point of sending the union's counterproposal, there was an open dialogue between union and management trying to keep whole in wages those working in the plant pool positions scheduled for wage reductions several months in the future.

I was upset, to say the least. There were no reasons given for the abrupt end of all dialogue because of a counterproposal sent to avoid arbitration while giving management something they once requested: the modified version of the flex operator job description. Pulling everything off the table in this way spoke volumes to me, if not to anyone else involved. It was obviously an act of disdain for the union scapegoat, and only supported management's ongoing campaign to undermine the union by causing strife among our rank and file against union leadership—me in particular.

I knew more was going on behind the scenes. It was out of character for Ferengi not to jump at the chance to at least talk about getting the union to agree to the modified flex job description to avoid arbitration, unless he had assurance from Cain for another settlement. I also knew Ferengi had a fondness for the former Darkly chem techs now Beady packagers, who were scheduled for the wage reductions in their plant pool positions.

It didn't take me long before I understood everything: Ferengi rejecting this counterproposal was a win-win scenario for him and management. They would be getting what they wanted anyway at the end, which was the flex job, while making sure to create another round of hostilities against the union scapegoat for sending out the counterproposal that ended all dialogue on stopping the wage reductions. Ferengi knew there would be plenty of time in the months ahead to work out another deal for his favored Darkly natives.

The following morning after receiving management's response to our counterproposal, I had another conversation on cell phone with Cain. I told him we needed to set dates for our union reps to meet with him and go over what was needed for our arbitration for the flex operator job grievance. This conversation did not go very well. *So, what else is new!*

As we spoke, it became obvious to me that Cain had intended to blow off the arbitration altogether. But I wouldn't let on that I knew this. I tried being as calm and as nice as possible, knowing that on the other end of this phone was a volatile mean-tempered man who did not at all like me.

I tried again while reminding Cain we had less than two weeks to prepare for this arbitration, and we really needed to win this one. His response was anything but calm and nice: "NO LOCAL UNION PRESIDENT IS GOING TO TELL ME HOW TO PREPARE FOR ARBITRATION!"

I abruptly ended our conversation. I was so done with this man! I started crying and talking to my Lord, which was more of a desperate pleading: "Please, Lord Jesus, remove this man from my life! I am so tired of his raging anger and hurting words hurled me! What am I going to do now?"

The Lord then gave me His direction!

For the past year or so, I attended monthly meetings with other local union presidents that were arranged by Newbie, who was a union president of another manufacturing plant down the road from where I worked. Newbie also worked part-time for the International Union with hopes of becoming full-time. Newbie had once requested I sign political letters supplied by the International Union encouraging our members to vote for that current democratic presidential candidate, but I had refused. This didn't win me any brownie points with the International Union, but that was okay with me. These union presidents' meetings were to get to know and help each other in our president positions. Although Newbie would encourage me to attend these meetings, something was not right with him, but I couldn't put my finger on what that was at the time.

During some of these meetings, I rubbed shoulders with other International Union reps and shared what I thought was in confidence, some of my difficult adventures dealing with Cain. Some of these reps advised me to turn Cain in to his boss, our District Director Joab, and even offered their support should I choose to go that route. But I never acted on their advice. I knew it would only cause more turmoil between Cain and me. Up to this point, I was able to continue representing our membership despite Cain's attempts to the contrary with his private side deals, and some that weren't so private.

But now things had changed. Cain was blowing off this flex job arbitration; just as he blew off the first contracting out maintenance arbitration; just as he tried blowing off addressing our 401(k) issue and then refused to do that arbitration—today was the last straw. And Ferengi and Jezebel just proved they could not be trusted even if we did agree now to the modified version of the flex job description. Our union needed to win this arbitration to preserve our last existing plant pool material packager positions.

Following the abrupt end of my conversation with Cain, and after my crying spell with Jesus, I went into action. I wrote up a letter to Joab stating our local would like to request that Cain, our current staff rep, be replaced. I also stated that we would like to request that the International Union supply our local with a staff rep or lawyer who would be willing to conduct our upcoming arbitration scheduled to take place on December first. I typed in the names of our e-board officers who I had contacted prior to and knew would be willing to sign this letter with me. I had three original letters signed.

Rayman, the Company B group chairman, also signed the letter as a member of our union e-board. By then, there were a few who were finally learning about Cain's lack of support with our local, yet some were still reluctant to take any actions against him. When staff reps are appointed by district directors and not elected officials, this is an injustice to the memberships that are forced with a staff rep who may not want to support their local union.

I had Joab's cell phone number and called him asking for a meeting to present the letter to him personally. Joab responded with what I believed was his normal reply when receiving calls from lowly local union presidents. It was the same response I received the last time I called him: "I can't hear you on my cell phone. You need to call my office tomorrow when I am there, and we can talk then."

Right! I remembered the last time I called him back at his office the day after his same lame excuse, and never did speak to him. I decided to call his office right then to speak with his secretary to find out about when he would be there the next day for a visit. Sue, his secretary, told me she didn't have Joab's schedule, and didn't know if he would even be in the office the following day. Her instructions were to call first before coming.

During this time, I enlisted our prayer warriors at the church I had been faithfully attending for their prayer coverage with all that was going on. Since I had been on daylights from when Darkly shutdown, my Christian family was growing.

With needing to win this arbitration weighing heavy on my heart, and with the leading of God's Holy Spirit, instead of calling Joab back the next day hoping he would take my call, I decided to make the ninety-minute drive from my home over to his office. I managed to find the place without getting lost—a miracle in itself.

I parked my car, but wasn't quite satisfied with my park job. As I went back to my car for a normal re-park, I spotted Joab and his assistant, Abner, as they were just pulling into the parking lot. *Wow! Divine appointment!*

As I watched them, Joab and Abner got out of their respective cars and headed towards the back of the building. I then went bebopping into the front entrance. Sue spotted me as I entered the building with a bewildered expression on her face and asked, "May I help you?"

We had never met before this day. Innocent me forgetting Sue didn't know my tenacious personality, and thinking nothing of going against her instructions to call before coming, I simply announced, "Hi. My name is Angelika Mitikas, local union president of 8-70. I came to . . ."

Ah, she remembered! I didn't get to finish my sentence before Sue admonished me. Her demeanor now was anything but polite: "I told you to call before coming. I don't know the director's schedule for the day, or if he will even be in at all today."

I wasn't going to be intimidated by this woman at this point in my mission: "I just saw the director and his assistant pull up in the parking lot and heading for the back door."

I could almost see her indignant demeanor deflating as she thought for a few seconds before deciding on a response: "Oh!" She thought again for a few seconds: "Well, have a seat, and I'll see if the director has time to meet with you."

It was a long trip from home. Some things were more of a priority than others. With Sue's instructions to just sit and wait, I took this opportunity to take care of one demanding priority: "Is there a restroom I can use?"

Sue was nice, and being a woman herself, directed me to the back of the building. Walking back there and almost reaching the restroom, as Divine appointment would have it, I bumped right into Joab and Abner as they were making their way through the back door. Never one to miss such opportunities, I instantly held out my hand towards Joab. As he obliged my offered handshake, I announced, "Hi. My name is Angelika Mitikas."

While shaking his hand, I continued, "Local union president of 8-70. I spoke with you yesterday, but you couldn't hear me on your cell phone. You asked me to give you a call today. Giving it much thought, I decided I would just take the chance and drive down here to meet with you face to face."

Joab didn't know what to say. After a few moments of silence, he asked me to give him a few minutes to settle in before meeting with me. I responded, "Okay. I have to use the restroom anyway."

I'll refrain from any description of my activities while in the restroom, only to say this much—I was singing praises to the Lord as I was laughing to myself—there was no way all this was happening apart from Divine intervention. I could just imagine the spiritual warfare going on right then. Now that I saw Joab and Abner in person, I was sure they would not try slipping out the back door that they just came in without meeting with me.

By the time I was done with the restroom, I didn't need to go far before Joab asked me into his office. His assistant Abner was present as his sidekick. I had very little respect for either of these men, but knew their intervention was needed to ensure this arbitration took place, and to ensure a win.

I presented the letter signed by some of our e-board officers asking that Cain be replaced as our staff rep. I explained about our upcoming arbitration and stated that Cain didn't want to conduct it. Joab gave Cain a call while I was right there. *The good-old-boys club strikes again!*

Joab didn't want to step over Cain, so he decided that he would meet with our e-board with Cain present so he could give his own defense to our letter and concerns for this arbitration. Naïve me thought that this meeting was only for the opportunity for each party to be heard for an unbiased judgment call.

Now in my second term as a local union president, I was sure my name was well known with this International Union district for several reasons: my first financial secretary's accusations of my alleged mishandling of our local funds; my attempts to address the beer-drinking; my refusal to sign those politically charged letters supplied by the International Union; my standing vote against any member dues increase at the International Union's convention (along with another delegate, we stood and honored the direction of our local membership in voting against this dues increase); not to mention how my name sticks out like a sore thumb to begin with. And thanks to Cain's poison of slander and derogatory comments he fed others about me, I could believe my name was also blackballed.

I had left voice messages in an attempt at contacting two of the International Union reps that had promised their support if I ever decided to turn Cain in to Joab. No one responded in time for help in dealing with this upcoming meeting. So much for their support! It didn't matter. I knew I had the Lord on my side. I saw Him in this situation, but without knowing the outcome.

After my meeting with Joab and Abner, Cain emailed me that management wanted to re-open talks on the counterproposal I had sent. I wondered: *What is up with this?* Trying to find out from the horse's mouth, I emailed Jezebel asking her about this without implicating Cain in any way. Her response did not support what Cain had told me. I sent Cain her response and questioned the contradiction. His response was short but spoke volumes: "Gremlin offered to meet with me on the issue."

BINGO! Cain sent his response after knowing I turned him in to his superiors for not wanting to do the arbitration. Was that really smart on his part? Was Cain really expecting that the outcome of our meeting with the e-board and his superiors was going to allow him the freedom to follow through with his side-deal settlement with Gremlin outside of arbitration? After all this time working with Cain in our union relationship, it was apparent that he never grasped that God's Holy Spirit was my driving force.

There are times that the Lord's direction in my life lands me in a fierce warzone that leaves me severely wounded. But it is always best to be in God's perfect will in a fierce war zone, then be outside His perfect will in a peace zone. God is very capable of healing any wounds I may receive in the process.

The Lord always has a greater purpose for what He does and allows in my life that I cannot always understand at the time. But I don't need to understand everything the Lord is doing. I need only to obey Him one step at a time.

Chapter 78
Vicious Meeting

I contacted every e-board officer from our company group notifying them of this meeting with Cain and his superiors. Cain had his own contact with everyone, including his buddy, Barry, the Company A group chairman.

Less than half of the e-board officers showed up for this meeting. Barry showed up at the beginning for a few minutes as a character witness for Cain, and then left. Judas, e-board member in cahoots the most with management, was present and ready to prepare his detailed report to give to Ferengi and Jezebel when this was all over.

In the spiritual realm, a slew of demons were swishing around everyone, drooling their saliva, spurring their hatred for me with sulfur breaths, swinging their worn-out rusty swords, relishing what they believed were their rights to be present and expecting their victory. Then an army of God's angelic warriors converged with gleaming swords unsheathed, ready to bust apart these demons' inflated pride.

I came well prepared for this meeting, spiritually and physically. On top of a pile of emails I had in hand was the one Cain sent agreeing to the union's counterproposal dated prior to when I sent it to management. Also included in this pile were many other pertinent emails clearly showing Cain's lack of support over the course of several years, including his refusal to support me dealing with the hostility from the Darkly union members. I also had a picture of the derogatory remark about the union someone wrote on the whiteboard in Darkly before the shutdown. I made two copies of everything with plans to present these to Joab and Abner. But without knowing what to expect from this meeting, I held back these documents and relied on the leading of God's Spirit before submitting anything.

Abner, sidekick and assistant director for Joab, sported a large cross hung around his neck. But his words and actions did not demonstrate any of the fruits of the Holy Spirit that would support he was a Christian.

Joab sported his normal prideful and superior demeanor after being in his position of district director unchallenged for far too many terms. During the most recent nominations for the International Union's election for officers (district directors are elected officials), two other men attempted to run against Joab for his position. However, these men were persuaded that it was in their best interests to withdraw their nominations. Thus, Joab went unchallenged and retained his position for yet another term.

Cain started the meeting with his normal hurtful words hurled at me, displaying in front of everyone present what I have been dealing with all this time at the mercy of this mean-tempered man. Several times in this meeting, Cain added his demeaning comment of "she's wacko" along with his lame accusations.

While Joab and Abner witnessed their subordinate display such unprofessional name-calling and vicious verbal abuses against another union officer, they said nothing in protest to Cain. Neither did any of the other men present say anything in protest to Cain's vicious verbal attacks. And these men called themselves professional union officers!

Cain began his accusations by bringing up my concerns when I had confided in him regarding the advances from Clyde, the first board agent I dealt with. I thought: *What does that have to do with the arbitration this meeting is supposed to address?* I said nothing as Cain continued complaining that I asked him to be present for my first affidavit with Clyde, and then added, "I liked his style." He ended with his demeaning comment of "she's wacko."

Cain then brought up the local union's practice of voting on arbitration cases instead of the staff rep making the decision, claiming he explained to me that this was not the practice of our new merged union. I defended myself by exposing the total truth of our conversation regarding this practice: I was the one who brought up the question of this practice to Cain with our new merged union. Cain's response was warning me not to change what had been the long-standing practice of our local union. Cain's superiors made no comment to what I stated in my defense.

Cain finally brought up the arbitration. But it was only to complain that I called him once while he was eating dinner—as if I knew when he was eating—to ask about the arbitration. In Cain's next breath, he complained that I sent him emails instead of calling him about the arbitration. If anyone understood the conflicting statements Cain was making, no one led on.

I patiently waited for my opportunity to speak and defend the request for a new staff rep. I brought up Cain's lack of support while refusing to help with the hostility during the Darkly shutdown, and when the Darkly union members wanted to decertify from the union because of rejecting the transitional personnel plan proposal. I then gave Joab and Abner each a picture of the derogatory comment about our union that someone wrote on the Darkly whiteboard, but they never even looked at it. Instead, they gave me blank stares with no comments.

Judas then spoke up in Cain's defense, claiming only one person in Darkly wrote that on the whiteboard, and that the Darkly union members did not want to decertify from the union. I refuted Judas' claims stating he never worked at Darkly, nor was he a union rep during when all this hostility was happening.

Judas continued as he fired back another round of attacks, including feigning to be offended because he knew nothing about the signed letter against Cain. Judas then made his accusation that I had no authority to send out the union's counterproposal that ended all talks with management trying to keep whole those looking at wage reductions per our contract.

Abner took his cue and responded in a reprimanding tone towards me: "You should not have sent out the counterproposal without first going through your staff rep."

It was time to present to Joab and Abner, Cain's email spelling out his clear approval of the counterproposal dated prior to sending it out to management, with my email below explaining the proposal to Cain in detail. I responded to Abner's reprimand respectfully: "I did go through my staff rep first. I sent Cain the counterproposal prior to discussing it with him in person, and followed up with another email later. Cain responded back through email and gave me his approval before I sent the counterproposal out to management. Here's the email with Cain's approval response."

Neither Joab nor Abner paid any attention to the copies of the email I just placed in front of each of them, and acted like they didn't hear anything I had just said. Instead, Abner called me vindictive and went through his own demeaning name-calling that sounded as though they came straight out of Cain's mouth.

I just stared at Abner. *Where did all that come from? He doesn't know me from Adam. Ah, the blackball game! The unspoken code of conduct in the good-old-boys club strikes again!* These three International Union reps had their own private conversation about me, and heard only Cain's biased and fabricated stories. *And I thought this meeting was arranged so that all sides could be heard fairly?*

The attacks from Cain started again: "She's wacko. She screwed it up for everyone. Management was so ticked off over the counterproposal that they didn't want any more talks with the union."

Cain was taking no responsibility for giving his approval for me to send out the counterproposal before I sent it. So how did Cain learn management was so ticked off over this? Cain had a Bat-phone to management that no one ever knew about, which included an autodial to Gremlin. Cain's own confession in writing that Gremlin had offered to meet with him over the issue only confirmed his connections.

After hearing from Cain how I screwed it all up for everyone, Joab, while again ignoring Cain's verbal abuse he threw at me, mimicked Abner's words that were well rehearsed prior to this meeting. With having no other basis for a reprimand in defense of all the other unmerited accusations hurled at me, Joab told me again: "You should not have sent out the counterproposal without first going through your staff rep."

What is wrong with these so-called professional union officers representing a huge multi-million-dollar union? What am I doing in this role as local union president dealing with such biased and mean-tempered men?

I was getting discouraged trying to get through to these men. I tried not to let my discouragement reflect in my tone as I responded to Joab's reprimand, hoping to somehow get through their biased demeanor: "I did go through my staff rep first, and received Cain's approval to send out the counterproposal BEFORE I sent out the counterproposal. It's right there in front of you."

Pointing to the email right in front of him, I continued, "Please read the email. Cain told me it was fine with him."

Joab and Abner ignored me again, never once taking notice of the documented confirmation of what I just said that was right in front of each of them.

The demons were getting bold, perceiving the arrows thrown from all fronts, they poked at these men, agitating them on, making sure their vicious arrows were aimed straight for my heart.

Werner was present at this meeting, a man hired in with me over twenty years earlier, who at one time I considered a friend. Now a trustee on our e-board, Werner followed suit with the others throwing some of his own arrows at me, stating he was angry because he did not see the counterproposal prior to management getting their copy. Werner knew he was on vacation when I sent this out, which I reiterated at this meeting for all to hear. But no one seemed to hear anything I was saying. It was as if these demons held their slimy claws over everyone's ears whenever I spoke.

Marty, union trustee fence-rider, was present and took his turn throwing arrows at me. Marty never mentioned that he had the opportunity to review the counterproposal and voice his opinions prior to when I sent it out. That would have been in my favor, and nothing in my favor could be known at this vicious meeting against me.

Also present at this meeting was the union's vice president, who signed the letter against Cain, and who also approved the counterproposal prior to sending it to management. This man's silence during this whole meeting was more hurtful to me than all the vicious accusations coming from everyone else.

Everyone seemed to forget one thing: I was elected in this position with every legal right to send out that counterproposal, and even more so because Cain approved it first. But no one was blaming Cain for his role in agreeing to this counterproposal.

No one was blaming management for their vindictiveness to end all talks regarding stopping the wage reductions, all because of the counterproposal sent to avert arbitration. This whole scenario was a concerted opportunity to personally attack me while knowing I was going to take the full brunt of the blame for all talks that ended.

After all these arrows pierced my heart, Abner once again threw their well-rehearsed reprimand for the third time: "You should not have sent out the counterproposal without first going through your staff rep."

How many times are they going to tell me this? I tried again, exasperated, but made sure my tone was softer, thinking maybe that would get through their biased demeanors: "I did go through my staff rep first. Cain sent me his approval before I sent out the counterproposal. There it is in the email in front of you. Please read the email for yourself."

Blank stares. No one was catching on. No one in that room was hearing anything I was saying. Or were they purposely ignoring the documented facts right in front of them?

And with this, the angelic warriors went into a raging onslaught against these demons, knowing the outcome God had commanded and were bound to fulfilling God's will.

Cain now requested the e-board present to vote to accept the modified version of the flex operator job description and cancel the arbitration.

BINGO! By now, my discouragement turned into irritation. As the chairperson of our e-board and membership meetings, with an authoritative tone I knew was not going to be appreciated by these men, I refused to allow the vote to take place. I referenced key facts in Robert's Rules of Order that I knew these higher union officers, if not the e-board officers, knew well:

"There is no quorum now present of our e-board, and no pre-announcement of such a vote taking place at this special meeting that was called. In addition, our local union membership voted to take this grievance to arbitration. It doesn't matter that this is not the practice of our union now. They still voted, and with no higher authority than our union membership, the vote stands. Therefore, another vote on the issue cannot happen at this meeting."

With these demons now experiencing an onslaught from these angelic warriors that was out of this world, these men finally heard what I just said. I turned to Joab now, ignoring Cain and his hurtful remarks: "We need a staff rep willing to do this arbitration. Cain does not want to do it."

As the angelic warriors were gaining the upper hand in this spiritual battle raging in my defense, a few of the demons clutched on Judas as their final hope of victory; he started another wave of attacks. With all the other grumblings as unmerited accusations now thrown at the wayside, with Joab and Abner obviously having no grounds to act in their defense, Judas focused again on my sin in sending out the counterproposal. I held my ground and kept calm while knowing the victory was already determined.

All eyes and ears were attentive on Judas as he declared his exaggerated claim that the entire union membership was outraged at the counterproposal, and that I would hear all about this at the next union membership meeting.

The truth was, only a few former Darkly natives now Beady packagers knew anything about this counterproposal, having received their information from Judas. Or could it have been straight from the horse's mouth, Ferengi? As Ferengi continued with his little direct dealing practices with our rank and file rather than dealing with the union's leadership, either culprit could have been responsible, or both.

Without any obvious actions against me in defense of all these unmerited accusations, Joab took this opportunity to reprimand me for a fourth and final time: "You should not have sent out the counterproposal without first going through your staff rep."

Okay! Are these men purposely being ignorant and mean towards me? Or are they just playing the good-old-boys club to the max? My irritation turned into climaxed anger. Between the disrespectful name-calling, verbal and vicious attacks, and all other unmerited accusations hurled at me, what little respect I may have had for any of these men was completely gone by this time, never to return.

For one last time, I tried to get through to these biased men. I made sure my speech was clear and deliberate, but calm, even though I wanted to scream at them: "I did go through my staff rep first. I discussed it with Cain, and then received his approval to send the counterproposal BEFORE I sent out the counterproposal. It's right there in front of you in the email. Cain said it was fine with him. He was just as responsible, if not more so, for sending out the counterproposal as I was."

This didn't calm my anger, but I was on the roll. All these men just stared at me. Ignoring everyone's blank stares, without hesitation, I continued. With a tone I knew was not going to go over well with these men—which I really didn't care—I pointed to the email and told them one final time: "READ THE EMAIL IN FRONT OF YOU! WHAT PART OF THIS DO YOU NOT UNDERSTAND?"

With all the vicious attacks and reprimands hurled at me, the attempts to distract from the real purpose of this meeting almost went undetected. Finally, the angelic warriors gained the victory. With the demons bound and subdued, as I still commanded the floor and now everyone's attention, I continued on with a determination not my own:

"This flex operator job and job description was unilaterally posted by management against the union's approval, and is a direct violation of our contract. During our last negotiations, it was presented to the union as a company proposal, but we refused to agree to it. It contains wording that would allow our last plant pool material packager positions to be eliminated. Our contract language for layoffs and bump-backs are contingent on having plant pool positions, and we cannot afford to lose any more of these positions. Cain does not want to take this flex operator grievance to arbitration. We need someone who is willing to arbitrate this and win."

I would have done the arbitration myself, but there would have been no way these men would have let a lowly woman local union president arbitrate such a sure-to-win grievance. Finally, with these demons subdued and their slimy claws removed from covering all the ears of these men, Joab heard what I just said.

Looking over to where Cain was sitting, across the table and diagonal to where he was, Joab spoke to Cain authoritatively about the arbitration: "If they requested this in negotiations and did not get it, you can win this arbitration. They cannot get through the grievance or arbitration process what they could not get in negotiations. You can win this without any problems."

I watched Cain carefully as he listened to his superior, and saw his countenance fall instantly, and his arrogant demeanor deflated. I've seen this expression before on Cain's face. I knew Cain was now resigned to not only doing this arbitration, but also winning it. Cain's agreement for a side-deal settlement with Gremlin apart from arbitration just flew out the window. Maybe it will meet up with all the past good-faith gestures I've made with management over the years that also flew out the windows, never to rebound. The meeting ended after this.

My quiet time with my Lord Jesus that evening was difficult, until in His presence, He brought to remembrance His words spoken to me: "My grace is sufficient for you. For My power is perfected in your weakness." (2 Corinthians 12:9.) There were times I would ask the Lord: "How much weaker can I get?"

I had no doubt that I was obedient to the Lord by sending out that counterproposal, and with turning Cain in to his superiors. The meeting didn't turn out as I wanted, but I knew God had a plan and purpose for everything, which He allowed me to understand much later in time. God was also teaching me to leave all consequences resulting from my obedience to Him, committed to Him.

What I experienced at that vicious meeting at the mercies of such mean-tempered men, for any reason let alone for doing something I had the approval from my superior and legally every right to do, was so wrong. Eventually, though, I saw the Lord's vindication on my part.

Newbie called me the following day. He was not one of those I tried to contact for help prior to all this. My guess was Cain called him to relay what happened. I expressed to Newbie that I had no respect for anyone at that meeting, including his favored District Director Joab.

Although we did not get a new staff rep as requested, I knew we were going to have the arbitration. I was also confident that Cain would do his best to win, and would not make his side-deal settlement that he had planned with Gremlin outside of the arbitrator's ruling. I knew Cain well enough by then, and I knew his reputation meant more to him than anything else. Cain would not want to lose face now with Joab or Abner, his superiors, by blowing this arbitration.

Chapter 79

Flex Job Arbitration

Arbitration was set for December first. Two days prior, Cain finally met with the union reps who were going to testify during the hearing to prepare. I met again with him the night before. I presented to Cain all our documents I had prepared that would help us win this arbitration. And we were set to win; I had no doubts about it.

This hearing was at the company's corporate building thirty minutes from the plant site, where most arbitration hearings were held. The union had a little room on the first floor just inside the building for us to meet for a final discussion before the hearing. We had to wait for someone to escort us upstairs where the actual hearing would take place.

During the arbitration hearing, my four prize exhibits of past practice over the years dealing with job descriptions for new positions were presented. These were accompanied with documents and emails from Ferengi and Sabrina that supported these new positions were only posted for job bidding after agreement was made between both sides, and supported those that did not receive agreement were not posted.

There were also many notes from our negotiations showing the original flex job description as presented during negotiations, and supported the union clearly rejected this proposal. I also presented Jezebel's reply email justifying Jason's job award claiming these were "new" positions, which backfired on her when it was used in favor by the union.

Gremlin was representing the company and tried his usual tactics of trying to rattle the union reps into a display of anger with his interrogations. I've seen him in action before, and if he succeeded, he would glance over at the arbitrator to be sure he noticed it as well. None of us gave in to his tricks. As a matter of fact, there were a few times when Gremlin displayed anger and was rattled. I noticed he didn't seem prepared at all for this arbitration compared to many others, and I was sure he realized this too.

At the conclusion of this hearing, as most everyone started to leave the room, I was the last one heading for the door along with Cain. Gremlin and the arbitrator never budged, but sat there as though they had a pre-arranged meeting afterward. Just as I was ready to exit through the door, Gremlin stopped me and spoke while trying to be respectful of my position as the union president in front of the arbitrator: "Angelika, if you don't mind, I would like to speak with Cain alone for a few minutes."

They weren't going to be alone; the arbitrator was sticking around for this meeting. I responded, "Sure."

What did he expect me to say, I did mind? I continued out the door and closed it behind me as my respect for their privacy.

Catching up with the other union reps by the elevator, I informed them that we should continue downstairs and wait for Cain, as he and Gremlin had some things they wanted to discuss. I knew what this meeting was all about, but kept that to myself, as I was sure no one else would have believed me.

The union was so well prepared with great documentation supporting our position. Gremlin knew he lost the arbitration. Now he was expecting Cain to keep his word on that side deal they had planned as a settlement without waiting on the arbitrator's ruling. And apparently, the arbitrator also knew.

I didn't concern myself with what was going on at this pre-arranged meeting. The victory was already won at that vicious meeting; although I came away with many wounds. I had since committed all this and the outcome to my Lord Jesus.

We waited for Cain in the little room assigned to us when we first came to this corporate building on the ground floor, and not long afterward, Cain showed up. His countenance was so obviously downcast with a solemn demeanor that Alvin asked him if anything was wrong. He blew off the concern and just told us we all did well, and left it at that.

It was obvious after the arbitration hearing that Gremlin and management knew they lost. Because of my direct interference with this side-deal settlement outside of arbitration between Cain and Gremlin, that target management had already placed on me while in this union president role just got bigger. With this, the vindictive retaliation and harassment that I had been enduring from management, especially coming from Ferengi and Jezebel, intensified after this arbitration.

Jezebel, the company Document Queen, was obsessed with documenting her fabricated wrongful actions she claimed I was responsible for as president, all in her attempts to defame my character and create more hostility against me from my e-board officers. And unfortunately, to my harm, she was succeeding.

Jezebel must have been stewing after the arbitration over what she could fabricate next, and then decided to reference something I had done several weeks earlier.

In her email she sent out the next day after arbitration, and copying the entire union e-board, she accused me of giving out false information to some of our union members, who were still on layoff status from the Darkly shutdown, concerning possible recalls back to work. By then, the mismanagement culprit realized that any further layoffs of the union workforce would not allow the plant to continue to run the business productively and safely.

Jezebel stated that because of my false information—according to her—that I sent out, she would no longer inform the e-board officers of their intentions to recall employees.

Copying everyone as well, I replied that her information was incorrect, and if she had issues with anything I conveyed to anyone in this union, she should do so with me face to face, and not through the email system.

But it was too late! It wouldn't have mattered anyway!

Judas and Marty were at the warehouse first thing that morning. Walking at a fast pace towards me while I was loading a truck, with angry looks throwing daggers with their eyes, they started another round of vicious attacks once they reached me, accusing me of playing the role of human resource representative.

I contacted Gremlin regarding this email from Jezebel with her fabricated information in her latest attempt to cause strife between e-board officers and me. I expressed my total disgust over all the vindictive retaliation and harassment I've been enduring all along, which he had been made aware of as it was happening. I made sure Gremlin knew that if he didn't put a stop to it, I was going to get my own lawyer to deal with it.

I have always believed and still do, that if God wants me to know something, He always manages to inform me, somehow and someway. Gremlin responded to my email almost two weeks later. He apologized for his delay, and then explained what happened.

At the conclusion of the arbitration hearing, he felt ill, as his pulse rate had suddenly dropped to a dangerous level. He was taken to the emergency room and had a heart pacemaker put in. I knew Gremlin had to be so angry because Cain refused to follow through with their agreement for a side-deal settlement after the arbitration hearing, and in front of the arbitrator. Gremlin also knew that I was the cause. By this time, I believed Gremlin hated me just as much as Cain did.

Not everyone understands how anger, resentment and bitterness can cause harm to those who harbor such feelings in so many ways, including physically, while at times excludes harm to those to whom it was projected against.

The union membership meeting was the following week from the arbitration hearing. As I have always done before every union meeting during our moment of silence for all our departed union brothers and sisters, I prayed for God's blessings, and to *"please, don't let me say anything I should not say, but only what I should say and in the way I should say it."*

Judas' claim that the entire union membership was outraged because of the counterproposal and would show up at this meeting was exaggerated just a bit. I looked out on the floor and saw only a few Darkly natives now Beady packagers, with angry stares as they waited till new business was announced before they threw their accusations and daggers at me. I had worked for years with these same guys, and trained Jared to the best of my ability for his chem tech job in Darkly; none of that mattered now. Judas was also present to give his report to Ferengi and Jezebel.

Jared started the round of vicious attacks, as he claimed I had no right to send the counterproposal that ended all talks regarding stopping their scheduled reduction of wages for their positions. The others, including Ollie, and Noah, the son of my predecessor Daryl, followed suit with vicious attacks. Judas then stood up and told everyone that Joab reprimanded me for sending out the counterproposal without Cain's approval. Judas was still denying Cain's role in all this, as was everyone else who knew the truth.

During this whole meeting, Cain sat there on the floor with the membership relishing all these vicious attacks while never once admitting to his prior approval of the counterproposal and of my actions of sending it out to management.

Chief was sitting right next to me on the platform up front, along with the union's vice president. Both these men approved the counterproposal before I sent it, but neither one offered any words in my defense.

In fact, no union officer present who had approved this counterproposal before I sent it out, said anything in my defense. I was there on my own, enduring these vicious attacks for something I legally had every right to do, and with my superior's approval. I allowed these guys to vent their anger and throw their daggers until I had enough.

Responding as led by God's Spirit, I finally hit the gavel and spoke in my own defense: "I take full responsibility for sending out that counterproposal, even though I had Cain's approval before doing so. But I will not take the responsibility for Ferengi's vindictive actions in withdrawing their letter of agreement proposal because of it. You can blame your buddy Ferengi for ending all communications and throwing everything off the table regarding addressing the scheduled reduction in wages. There will be no further comments on this topic, and if anyone ignores this call, they will be declared out of order and asked to leave."

I took a motion to adjourn, down went the gavel, and the meeting ended.

Some of these Darkly guys, along with Marty, Werner and Judas, approached Cain while still in the union hall after this meeting, with their desire to modify our local union by-laws to include language that would prevent a union president from making such proposals. I found it incredible that no one was blaming Cain at all for his role in approving this counterproposal before I sent it. Talk about selective hearing! This was a bad case of selective blaming!

All these men also wanted to file formal charges to remove me from being the union president. It didn't matter to me at that point.

I knew no weapon formed against me would prosper. And as time went on, nothing came to fruition from any of these threats.

The annual Christmas party sponsored by the union for kids of both union and salaried personnel was two days after this union meeting. I always loved this event, as I saw it as a great way to bridge the divide between union and salaried personnel through innocent kids. I always enjoyed seeing the kids and their parents, and would marvel at the resemblance, even in personalities.

While I was sitting at the front table checking in those coming in, Jared came in with his boys. Upon seeing his entrance, Ferengi came over, and they greeted each other with a manly embrace and exchanged warm smiles. They made sure to display this right in front of me. I heard through their actions a message between the two: "Well done, friend."

Apparently, no one was blaming Ferengi for his vindictive role in ending all communications over the wage reductions that would also affect Jared. All anger, blame and resentment were hurled at the union scapegoat, which was the plan all along behind the scenes. Seeing this display of affection from these two men, who obviously had a plan in place for my harm, poured salt into my still bleeding wounds after such a fierce battle. But I showed no emotions and said nothing. My Lord Jesus was very capable of healing these wounds, if only I would let Him.

Less than a week later, I had an interesting conversation with Ferengi in his office about the counterproposal and arbitration. Ferengi confessed that he was the one who was really ticked off with the counterproposal. As he put it: "I was angry because you requested a three percent wage increase for everyone."

Really? After everything you have done and tried to do against this union, even unilaterally taking away our 401(k) company match? I kept these thoughts to myself. Instead, I countered, "All you had to do was say no. But don't just cut off all communications!"

Ferengi just looked at me as I continued, "That was so unprofessional, and really sent out a message throughout this plant site of your disdain towards me."

As I knew Ferengi well, I saw he was in deep thought. I continued, "I thought I was giving you something you really wanted by offering the modified version of the flex operator job description."

Ferengi seemed remorseful and confessed, "I thought we had a good chance of winning the arbitration. I'm not so sure now."

Ferengi continued with what I already knew were his thoughts: "I thought we would settle this outside of arbitration."

I calmly threw it up in Ferengi's face my intention was the same, but without reiterating my added goal to gain something for everyone: "I tried!"

But why would he deal with a lowly local union president, and one he so much disdained, when he believed the International Union staff rep was going to make a side-deal settlement with Gremlin apart from arbitration? I didn't let on that I knew what settlement he was referring to.

Ferengi then told me: "If the union wins the arbitration, you will be losing four union job positions, as we will expunge the four flex job positions and layoff the four sweco operators."

Ferengi thought for a few seconds before he continued his confession, "I don't know how we can run the Beady Department with four less people."

I responded to Ferengi's assertion with my own that I knew was safeguarded by God's leading: "No, Ferengi. We won't lose four jobs. The arbitrator will use the remedy requested, which also stated to retain the sweco/area job and job description."

It wasn't until New Year's Eve when I received the email from Cain with the arbitrator's decision. I didn't open it until after church services that evening; I didn't want anything to ruin that night. When I opened it later, I rejoiced in the Lord for His vindication.

The arbitrator's final ruling: "Based on the specific facts of this case, the company violated the agreement (contract) when it created a new job, flex operator in the Beady Department. The grievance is granted. The company is directed to expunge the Beady flex operator job posting and job description, and continue to retain the sweco/area operator job and job description."

The arbitrator granted the union's remedy word for word, just as God had directed me to write it on the grievance. (How documents and agreements are worded is so important.)

Had I taken Cain's advice instead to only write "expunge the flex job," we may have lost four union jobs, if for no other reason other than vindictive retaliation, which had been the long-standing practice from this management over the recent years, and to which I would soon be the victim of again in full brunt force.

This entire saga proved to be one of those fierce warzones I would never forget. However, God was still on His throne, nurturing and protecting me according to His purpose.

Chapter 80

Unpardonable Sin

I always look forward to the start of a new year. This one was starting with a great victory for the union: winning the flex job arbitration and safeguarding our last existing material packager positions. Going on in my personal life was another huge victory with my commitment to my Lord Jesus.

After church service one day, a dear sister in the Lord approached me with a great question that I knew did not come from her: "Have you ever been baptized as an adult?"

With her question came the conviction of the Holy Spirit. Being baptized as a baby meant something to my parents. But the spiritual truth is that each born-again Christian must decide on their own to obediently follow Jesus into baptism. Once the Lord brought this to my attention, I was now accountable to Him.

It was only a few months since our church had called a new pastor in his late seventies, who had a lovely wife as his partner in ministry. It just proves the Lord is always ready to use us, no matter our ages. This pastor was delighted that my dear sister and I wanted to be baptized with him conducting the ceremony.

My obedience to follow Jesus into baptism was my public announcement of my allegiance to Him as my Lord and Savior. I have no doubts that this decision played a significant role in provoking the onslaught of demonic rages while I was being attacked on all fronts, and for my convictions to continue doing my best and what I believed was the right things to do.

I fasted often during this year, sought God's will intensely, and grew closer to Him during this most difficult time of my life. Often while in God's presence during that time, the Lord would assure me that He was still in control, intricately and intimately working through every aspect of my life. I was sure no one in my secular arena understood any of this.

Now just over one year from when I came to this warehouse, I was saddened to learn that Henry, the best boss I ever had, was terminated from employment. They said it was because of major mistakes that Henry made in processing shipping documents. I often wondered if part of the reason was that we got along so well working together?

Max was another warehouse salaried employee who took Henry's position. Max was in his early thirties, but somehow, wasn't quite matured yet. This was evident by his refusal to wear his jeans on his waistline. I repeatedly confronted Max about this practice while reminding him that he was a now supervisor and not a teenager, and asked him to please, not wear his jeans showing off his underwear. When he kept ignoring me, I sent an email with the same request (Document Princess). He then started wearing a lab coat when I was around to hide his underwear, but still refused to wear his jeans on his waistline.

Just a few months into this year, another significant event happened: Our recording secretary resigned her position on her own accord. She was never committed to this position, and rarely showed up to perform her job duties. Normally, the union e-board would have appointed another recording secretary for this unexpired term. But I suggested having a union membership vote to decide on this replacement, which was not acceptable with some on our e-board.

However, with the recording secretary's position being automatically part of all contract negotiations for all three company groups, I believed this position was too important not to have our membership decide who would fill this unexpired term.

My church family prayer warriors covered me on this issue, as they were always faithful to do upon my request.

I covered all my bases when I called a special e-board meeting with plenty of advance notice, and scheduled it conveniently just before our monthly membership meeting. I made it clear that the purpose of this meeting was voting to allow a membership vote to decide on our new recording secretary. I also made it clear that if the outcome of this vote was against a membership vote, the e-board would appoint someone to fill this unexpired term at this same meeting.

The e-board voted with everyone present except Barry, but only after I waited as long as possible for him to show up. The vote was a tie, and my vote was the tiebreaker; our membership would vote and decide who their new recording secretary would be. Barry showed up after the monthly union meeting had started. He told me afterward that he was stuck in traffic due to an accident, and had he been there, our membership would not be voting on this position. I saw this as another Divine intervention!

Tara and Alvin were the two nominated for their names to be on the election ballot. When Alvin won this election, matters were made worse for me working with Tara in the warehouse. Although I was out of the voting area, Tara blamed me for interfering with the election because I endorsed Alvin to some of the people. I was guessing she didn't remember Marvin was in the actual voting booth area endorsing his own wannabe union president dreams during our last officers' election. But it didn't matter. Tara would have found some other reason to blame me for her loss. She wanted to pursue charges against me for this so-called election interference. But once again, the Lord safeguarded me from yet another round of allegations that never came to fruition.

Around this same time, it came to my attention that the Darkly natives now Beady packagers were direct dealing with management, again, regarding their scheduled wage reductions. Soon after this, these guys approached me on the issue. For one final time, and with the whole e-board in agreement, I approached Ferengi and Jezebel with the simple request to rescind the wage reductions scheduled to happen in just a couple of months.

We were so close this time in getting this simple request agreed to. However, Ferengi contacted Cain over the issue and got him involved, knowing that whatever he wanted, Cain would agree and support him. Ferengi never wanted to give anything without getting something back in return, which was his normal horse-trade mentality. With Cain involved, Ferengi went after the other two plant pool positions that were not included in the original scheduled wage reductions: the warehouse positions, and the only maintenance plant pool storeroom position.

Cain and the entire e-board were present at the meeting called to discuss this. Ferengi, Jezebel and a few other salaried personnel were present on management's side. While Ferengi was displaying his badgering temperament desperately trying to get his way, I was getting a pounding headache. I tried my best to stop these talks and get the union out for a caucus before agreeing to something we would later regret. But Cain took over the meeting on behalf of the union, and refused to have a caucus with us. With Cain supporting his buddy Ferengi, we were doomed.

The result was agreeing to a letter of agreement until the current contract expired. This letter stipulated that all union members already working in these plant pool positions would be "frozen" in these higher wages, as well as anyone who would bid into these positions before the cutoff date of the original wage reductions. Anyone bidding these jobs after the cutoff date would earn the reduced wages. The other two plant pool positions not originally slated for wage reductions were also reduced in wages with the same stipulations.

Also included in this letter of agreement was the opportunity for those bumped into plant pool positions from any department workforce reductions to start accruing departmental seniority after twelve months in these positions, if they so desired, even without bidding into these positions.

Ferengi covered everything his favored Darkly natives wanted. Not accruing seniority in these bumped into roles was another contention I endured for months from these guys, and another cause for their vicious attacks at union meetings. Their ongoing direct dealings with Ferengi were evident when during these vicious attacks, they admitted management was putting the blame on "their" union leadership for refusing to allow them to accrue seniority in these bumped into plant pool positions. This was just another example of management's campaign to undermine the union. I, too, wasn't accruing seniority in my bumped into role in the warehouse, but I accepted this as part of our contract language.

Judas had claimed our union membership was outraged over my original counterproposal just months earlier when I tried getting something for everyone. In contrast, this letter of agreement that Ferengi and Cain managed to get agreement for tore our union apart, literally. With two other preferred daylight plant pool positions now targeted for wage reductions, this letter of agreement became my "unpardonable sin."

It didn't matter that Cain took over the meeting and agreed to this, along with the e-board. And it sure didn't matter that I tried my best to stop all talks before agreeing to something we would later regret. The union scapegoat once again took the full brunt of the angry blame for this agreement across the plant site. And such was life! I knew this came with the territory.

Since this agreement was a change to our current contract, I presented this to our union membership via email prior to a vote to accept or reject this agreement. This email began as follows:

"Attached is a copy, two pages, of the letter of agreement proposed by the company to union leadership as a result of our simple request to please, rescind the contractual wage cuts due to take effect this coming May."

Reading back over the email as I relive this scenario now, I sounded just like Aaron did in his lame excuse he gave Mosses for his golden calf sin: "Then they gave me the gold, and I threw it into the fire, and out came this calf!" (Exodus 32:24, NIV).

Less than half the membership showed up to vote on this letter of agreement, and it only passed by three votes. No one wanted to see anyone lose wages, even when agreed upon during negotiations. Unions are supposed to try their best to keep everyone in a higher wage and whole if at all possible. But targeting our two preferred daylight plant pool positions not originally slated for a wage reduction was the killer.

Cain was adamant that he would be the one to sign this letter of agreement on behalf of our local, along with Jezebel. In the past, it was always the union president and chief shop steward who signed these. Ever since I turned Cain into Joab, it was obvious that he was taking over the leadership of our local union. Although our membership could not realize this, those on the e-board should have.

Cain and Jezebel had decided to change the wording on the letter of agreement after our membership voted to accept it. Not only was this wrong, but they also added wording that gave the union no chance during our next contract negotiations to reverse these reductions in wages. Now came another battle with Cain!

When Cain refused to listen to me in keeping the wording as our membership voted on it, I roused our e-board officers to finally speak up to Cain—which no one ever seemed to want to do—as their protest of the changed and added wording. Cain was furious that I was making such a big deal about the wording.

However, as stated before, it was imperative that these documents and agreements were worded just right. I was viewing this language change after what we had agreed upon, as another bad faith bargaining practice of management, and Cain's direct interference on his own that went against the direction of our e-board and union membership through their vote.

Finally, I challenged Cain on my own and told him, if the letter of agreement wasn't going to be signed exactly as worded and presented to our membership for their vote, I was going to have another membership vote showing the changed and added language. It almost didn't pass the first time; I was sure it wouldn't pass a second vote. By then in our union relationship, Cain knew I meant what I said.

I endured more angry and hurtful words hurled at me from Cain through the process, but the result was a letter of agreement worded just as it was presented to our membership. I don't believe anyone ever really knew the personal battles I fought against Cain on behalf of our union membership.

I was now allowed to start accruing seniority in the warehouse as a bumped into position because of this letter of agreement, and secure my warehouse daylight position. But I turned down this opportunity. My decision was not only a matter of being sure I did not take advantage of a letter of agreement as president I was part of, but more importantly, I was being obedient to the Lord. I also knew my obedience in turning down this opportunity could eventually cause me to lose my warehouse position in the future.

However, I was leaving the consequences of my obedience for the Lord to handle, as my future was in God's hands and no one else's. Although I regretted the stipulations in this letter of agreement and the vote to accept it, God used it for my benefit in the future that was unbeknown to me at the time.

Chapter 81
Standing Alone

A   Around the same time as my unpardonable-sin letter of agreement, management realized that not only was the company business unable to run without the personnel who were scheduled for layoffs, which never did happen, they needed to recall those who were laid off from the Darkly shutdown. The mismanagement culprit strikes again, but it was in the union's favor this time. It was unfortunate that some union members took their severance package after being told their layoff would be permanent, thus eliminating their chances for this recall.

There was new contract language added during our last negotiations that was meant to address the chaos that went on during the last recall from the supposedly temporary layoff. This added recall language allowed a less senior employee returning from layoff, and who held a previous "bid" plant pool position before layoff, to return to this bid position.

However, the intent was that this was only allowed when there was a position open. It was never the intent for the less senior employee to bump out an existing more senior employee currently working the plant pool position as a bumped into role.

Cain, Chief and I were present during a meeting when Jezebel and Ferengi brought up questions regarding this added recall language, while keeping it to themselves that this scenario would play out soon. Cain understood the intent of this language, as he negotiated this during our last contract, and had years of formal training and experience dealing with negotiations and contract language. Cain offered no interpretation during this meeting, while I explained the intent of the language, and what was not the intent. Everyone at this meeting understood and accepted my interpretation, or so they said.

Just two weeks later, Alvin, as the newly elected recording secretary, offered a different interpretation of the same added recall language. Alvin was also present during negotiations and should have understood the intent, and what was not the intent.

Any opportunity for Cain to go against me and support others was an enjoyment for him. What everyone collectively agreed with two weeks earlier was the correct interpretation, flew out the window (my past good-faith gestures would never be lonely). Now they all did a flip-flop on me with Cain taking the lead, and rejected my interpretation of the intent of this contract language.

Soon after this flip-flop, this scenario was being played out. A less senior employee with a previous bid as a Beady material packager was being recalled from layoff. Everyone, except me, adamantly supported his right to bump out Ollie, who had more seniority and was currently working the material packager plant pool job as a bumped into role.

Ollie requested I file the grievance over his bump-out, and did not want any shop stewards involved due to the controversy over this added recall language—so I did. Bypassing the shop steward and Chief didn't make either of them happy. Cain had informed Jezebel that he would not support the grievance, thus enforcing his dictatorship role even further. Cain was still bearing a grudge over my interference with his side-deal settlement with Gremlin for the last arbitration. Our flex job arbitration win meant nothing to Cain.

This saga went on for several weeks, and became well known that I was enduring such hostility from Cain and the union's e-board opposing my interpretation of this added recall language, and opposing my willingness to pursue Ollie's grievance, which caused me so much grief.

Unions are stronger when there is solidarity. When a union president stands alone on an issue, it is not only unpopular, but very difficult, especially for the president. But I had to stand my ground; for me to do otherwise would have been wrong.

One day, Jared came to me and spoke in defense of his buddy Ollie, asking if I was still going to fight his bump-out grievance. I told Jared I was, but I was standing alone on this issue. Jared acknowledged that he knew this.

The wounds of just a few months earlier from when Jared and Ollie attacked me so viciously at the union meeting over the counterproposal I had sent were scarred over by this time. Both these guys were now asking and expecting my unbiased and professional help. I thanked God for His grace to continue in the ministry and role He had placed me in, even in the midst of such well known ill feelings towards me.

Now there was a grievance I filed and was adamant had merit, yet Cain refused to support. By then, everyone knew me well enough to know I was going to pursue this grievance regardless of Cain or anyone else on the e-board, one way or another.

Jezebel decided to post a Beady material packager job for bid before the cutoff date for the higher wage, hoping that Ollie would get the bid so that his grievance would get settled through the bidding process and just go away.

However, Ollie did not get the Beady material packager job bid. James, nephew of Marty, the e-board trustee fence-rider, was awarded this job bid. James was also in the material packager position through his own department workforce reduction, and was older than Ollie.

When Jezebel realized James got the job bid, she initiated a little deal with him, but was sure to get Chief's agreement before presenting it to James. Jezebel wanted to be able to invoke their long-standing, well-rehearsed defense should anyone learn about this little deal and question it: "But your union agreed to it."

Jezebel promised James that he would be recalled back into his previous department six months in the future while paying his higher chem tech wage during this waiting period, even though he would still be working in the material packager position that paid a lower wage. But there was one condition to this deal: James had to turn down his awarded Beady packager bid so that Ollie would get it. Jezebel really wanted Ollie to get this bid so that his grievance would just go away.

James was the one who approached me with Jezebel's "little deal," and asked if it was contractually permitted, as he wanted to do what was right himself. When I explained to James why it was not permitted, he accepted my explanation without question.

I then contacted Chief and questioned him on this little deal. Chief was a nice guy but had a very short fuse, and never liked me questioning him on anything. With his strong disagreement with me over filing Ollie's grievance, and knowing I was going to pursue it, his fuse with me was even shorter.

While speaking with Chief on the phone, he expressed strong anger towards me with hurtful words for my interference with his agreement for this little deal. After receiving his nasty email later with more angry and hurtful words, he claimed that he didn't make a little deal, but that he was only doing "his" job. I believed Chief knew my interpretation of the added recall language was correct, and that he also wanted Ollie's grievance to just go away.

I read Chief's email a few times, and each time, I walked away from it. I was so very hurt and angry over this entire saga while trying my best to do what was right according to our contract and for all involved. I waited for some time to pass before I responded to Chief's nasty email: "So, what's 'my' job? The union scapegoat?"

It took some doing and more grief, but I finally convinced Chief of the detriment of agreeing to violate our contract by favoring one employee above another in a blackmail-type private deal; we had to undo his agreement for this little deal with James.

I arranged a meeting with Chief, Jezebel and Ferengi, and told them we could not agree to the deal offered to James. I explained to them that the contractually correct way was to recall James back into his previous department now, not six months from now, for him to rightfully receive his higher chem tech wage. I was so sure that they would agree to this. I knew that Jezebel and Ferengi wanted Ollie's grievance to just go away, as they also knew I would pursue this grievance on my own if it wasn't settled.

They agreed, and recalled James back into his previous department as a chem tech earning his higher wage, which made him happy. This gave Ollie the material packager job bid, so his grievance was settled through the bidding process. The recalled employee from layoff went back to his plant pool material packager bid position, as it was open once James was recalled to his previous department.

After all the hostility and grief I endured from so many over this entire saga for several weeks, yet I refused to give up any ground, in the end, everyone was happy. I was the only one who came away with wounds again.

Just a few weeks later, those who strongly opposed my interpretation of this added recall contract language, even from management—except Cain—admitted that they understood my interpretation of the true intent was correct.

But the damage was done and could not be undone. Standing alone against so many in this union leadership and proving their lack of support to management was going to prove harmful to me in many ways in the near future.

Chapter 82
Morphed Campaign

Without a doubt, this year was not turning out well at all. Unbeknown to me at this time, the worst was yet to happen. Cain's ongoing lack of support for me was now in full force and out in the open. Add to all this the lack of support from the e-board officers over the disagreement with the added recall language and my willingness to pursue Ollie's grievance, along with my warehouse coworkers who were constantly turning me into management with their fabricated drama, that target on my front and back was getting much bigger.

With management believing I was out on my own without the backing of my so-called union brothers and sisters, their campaign for my harm morphed into a campaign to terminate my employment, and was amply fueled. They just wanted me to go away with their desire becoming ever so obvious to many.

Then there was Darkly being demolished building by building, with slabs of concrete from the buildings ground to smithereens by a huge machine, and dispersed all over the area that at one time was a multi-million-dollar profitable manufacturing business.

Gone forever was the banging sound of the blue door leading to the reactor area, the poured concrete steps that existed since the era of WWII, and the smell of Darkly pancakes permeating throughout the plant site. And gone forever was the Westminster Chimes alarm announcing to all that a critical situation in Darkly was in progress. The only remaining building of Darkly that was left intact was the storage warehouse still bearing the name Darkly on the sign on front. But after a short time, even that sign was torn down, eliminating all remembrance of the existence of Darkly.

In the midst of everything else that was happening thus far, Audrey, the head supervisor of the Logistic Department, asked for a meeting to "chat" with me, as she put it, about some issues, but specifically stated that this was not disciplinary in nature. Max, the new warehouse boss, was at this meeting, along with our vice president as my union rep. It gets pretty bad when a union president needs union representation!

The issues that were brought up turned out to amount to nothing. Audrey referenced the missing mirrors on the covered forklift that continued to get torn off going through any hard-plastic curtains, and she blamed me for every missing mirror. I distinctly remembered these mirrors were missing upon my arrival at the warehouse. *Who was blamed before I came around?* Audrey referenced conduit at a dock door that was already broken, but somehow, my name was also earmarked for the blame. Audrey also stated that I was turned in for talking on my cell phone while stopped on a forklift; she didn't acknowledge it was in a safe area. Everyone in the warehouse was guilty of this practice.

It was obvious that some of my coworkers were turning me in for what they thought could be used against me. I was sure the culprits were Tara and Marty, but I had no concrete proof of this. Marty worked mark-up to a salaried position even more during this year because of Henry's vacant position. And when Marty wasn't available, Tara worked this mark-up. I continued speaking out against this conflict of interest with these union reps working mark-up salaried positions, which only agitated an already hostile work environment against me in the warehouse.

When Tara went beyond her job duties by authorizing outside contractors for a union maintenance job, I spoke to her about it, letting her know that crossed the line and was not her job. Tara turned on me with angry words, called me a female dog, and told me that she only did what she was told to do. Max stood in the break-room doorway and witnessed this entire exchange between us, but said nothing. Had I been the aggressive one, I was sure something would have been done against me to address it.

Tara just didn't seem to like me very much, and displayed this more so since she lost the election for recording secretary. I believed there were other underlining issues, including jealousy, as she once ran for union president a few years before I did but wasn't elected.

Marty was unstable in his feelings towards me, as one moment he was a friend, and the next he could turn on me. Marty confided to me years before what his disposition issues were, so I tried to be patient with him.

Samson and I worked well together; although some of his work habits concerned me regarding safety, especially working the rails. Samson also proved to be a man who didn't want to own up to any of his mistakes, but would blame others instead.

A few weeks from Audrey's first meeting to chat, she called me in for another meeting. Just the day before, Marty, while working his mark-up salaried position, was seeking advice from Samson and me on how to direct the workflow. As we discussed among ourselves as we normally did, who would be going out on the rails versus staying inside loading trailer trucks, someone spoke up stating that Tara had medical work restrictions. The conversation then went to a question: How do we decide on the workflow when we didn't know what Tara could or could not do?

Tara, as the warehouse trainer, had other work opportunities the rest of us did not have, but she also worked the rails and loaded trailer trucks. Tara found out about our conversation questioning her medical restrictions from one of the others, as she was not involved. Out of the three in this conversation, Tara singled me out and turned me in for harassment because of this conversation questioning her medical work restrictions. Audrey's second meeting was about Tara's so-called harassment charge.

Jezebel, Max, and Chief as my union rep, were present for this second meeting. At the close of this meeting, it was decided that Max would direct the workflow in the warehouse even when Marty was on mark-up. In this way, Tara's medical work restrictions would be honored without the rest of us knowing anything about her medically.

As Chief and I walked away from this second meeting, he turned and spoke to me: "They're trying to document enough on you to get you fired. And I don't know if I could get your job back."

Both were obvious truths to me also, but hearing it from Chief increased my own concerns. The following day proved this.

The next day, Marty took the lead with another group discussion on the workflow. With the previous meeting fresh in my thoughts, I told Marty that Max needed to direct the workflow. With this, Marty blew up on me: "What changed since yesterday? Is there something I need to know about? Because if I lose mark-up opportunities because of you, I'm going to sue the union."

I dropped the issue and without getting Max involved, Samson and I decided to work the rails that day.

Just after I came inside from working the rails for a couple hours, hiking in the heat, jumping up and down on these railcars, and hurting as I normally did after working as the ground-person, Chief came walking in the break room with his angry demeanor asking me what was going on.

What did I know? I went out to work on the rails without waiting for Max to direct the workflow because my coworkers didn't know he was supposed to. I responded to Chief: "What'd you mean what's going on? Who called you here?"

Chief became visibly angrier by my questions. Just about this time, in came Jezebel breathing fire and hate and directed me into the office; Chief followed suit. Obviously, they had spoken prior to this meeting about me with someone alerting them to when I had returned from the rails. This did not go over well with me!

In the office where everyone could hear everything and see everything through the windows, Jezebel raised her voice in anger while warning me, if I didn't stop my defiance, she was going to discipline me. I was at a loss now. I just looked at her trying to figure out what I did to deserve this angry outburst from her?

Jezebel continued with a second warning: "I am not going to put up with any more of your defiance. You are causing complete disruption in this warehouse among all the workers."

Jezebel never once explained to me what she was referring to, what had happened that brought her here, or who spoke to her. She gave me no opportunity to speak in my own defense before throwing her angry words and threats at me. Chief never interjected on my behalf.

I finally asked Jezebel: "What are you talking about?"

Jezebel continued in her anger: "When Marty is on mark-up, you are to listen to him just as though he was the supervisor, and follow his direction for the workflow. I am not going to put up with your defiance any longer."

Now things were starting to clear up. Now I was the one getting angry: at Marty, for once again turning me in to management; at Jezebel, for handling this so unprofessionally with her biased hatred towards me, and never giving me an opportunity to explain my side of the story; at Chief, for not giving me a heads-up to this ambush meeting.

I told Jezebel truthfully: "I understood at the close of the meeting yesterday, because of Tara's medical work restrictions, Max was going to direct the workflow from now on, not Marty."

I then turned to Chief while believing since he was at the same meeting, he would remember this and confirm what I just stated: "Tell her, Chief."

Chief just stared at me with his own angry demeanor.

Jezebel would not let up on her ranting and raging. While witnessing such a display of biased contempt towards me, I wondered: *What really is wrong with this woman? How can she be the head of HR with such outbursts of anger and such biased hatred?* As Jezebel continued with the same angry words, I responded more firmly. *Maybe she didn't get it the first time:* "I just told you that I understood at the close of the meeting yesterday, because of Tara's medical restrictions, Max was going to direct the workflow."

I turned to face Chief again and asked, "Chief, are you going to tell her?"

Again, Chief stared back at me, and then in his angry tone he finally spoke, "You don't want to know what I have to say!"

Wow! What was that all about?

One last round of Jezebel's outburst of anger and threats now fueled with more confidence after Chief's response, and I had enough. Taking my position as union president on the level with Jezebel—as it was clear Chief was not going to speak in my defense—I ended this meeting with an authoritative demeanor: "Okay, Jezebel. You've made your point several times. You can drop it now."

Outside the warehouse area, Chief attacked me with his anger I was becoming all too familiar with: "I don't care if you are the union president, I will never lie for you."

I was horrified. I was devastated. I could not believe what he had just said and implied. We all misspeak at times. However, I do not purposely lie, for me or for anyone else, nor would I ever ask anyone to lie for me.

Unfortunately, this was not the first time Chief and I had different interpretations from meetings, emails, or contract language, and it would not be the last. Whatever the cause for the misunderstanding, Chief and I didn't come out of the meeting the day before with the same thoughts that Max was going to direct the workflow from now on. Or was Jezebel able to manipulate him with her habitual fabricated drama of events?

Whatever Jezebel had said to Chief prior to her raging confrontation with me was enough for Chief to believe her side of the story while never even caring to hear my side.

Max approached me later that day expressing he was sorry for what happened: "I should have told the warehouse folks this morning that I would be directing the workflow from now on."

I responded, "And now you're saying this only to me? Why didn't you speak up when you heard Jezebel raging at me?"

Max didn't respond to my questions, but offered another confession: "I told Marty afterward that he had no business harassing you. And I told Judas that he was not to come to the warehouse anymore harassing you."

I thanked Max for what he told me—even though it was after the fact. I understood his position for not wanting to confront Jezebel. Salaried personnel were afraid of her. There were a few other salaried personnel in the warehouse that had their employment terminated in recent months. And to be sure, no one wanted to show Jezebel they were even remotely on a union president's side, especially when that union president was me.

Chapter 83
Cannot Be Bought

This year was the International Union's convention in Las Vegas, an event that happens every three years. We had contract language that made it mandatory for management to allow the union president time off for union business without pay to attend this convention. Each of the two other company groups were going to have their group chairmen also attend per our by-laws for our local union. I made arrangements with Penny, my friend from New York, to meet me in Las Vegas with a planned visit to the Grand Canyon for that weekend after the convention.

The rail job needed two certified rail workers to perform the job. I had given Audrey notice with almost five months leeway to cover my job for this union business time off. Samson had the last two days of that same week scheduled off as vacation days for his trip to Las Vegas. The first three days of that week were still open. I had more employment seniority for contractual preference in requesting time off than Samson, but I didn't see the need to push that issue nor wanted to.

Marty had been a union warehouse worker for years, but as of that time, was still not fully trained on the rail job portion of the warehouse duties due to his own medical work restrictions. This was one reason Ferengi wanted Marty put out of the warehouse when Darkly shutdown through his personnel transition plan proposal that was adamantly rejected. Marty never knew how close he came to losing his warehouse daylight job.

In our contract was a job classification called the AST (area support technician), a fancy name for labor group. This AST group was the lowest paying plant pool job classification, and moved about the plant working different plant pool jobs on mark-up for the higher pay that particular job was paying. This mark-up was different than salaried position mark-up.

Management had tried for several years to convince me that the AST group needed to train and certify on the rail job portion of the warehouse job duties, as they worked other warehouse jobs. As union president, I could have easily agreed to this added job duty for the AST job description, but believed this was not the right thing to do. Although all jobs at that time in the warehouse were plant pool positions, the rail job was in a class of its own.

I had many good reasons for my adamant refusal to include the rail job in the AST job description. This rail job was very dangerous, and involved a much higher skill level with more training needed than all other plant pool jobs. There needed to be good concentration and communication with a two-person team that worked well together to do the rail job safely.

The AST group normally had two to four employees at any given time, and was mostly an entry-level type position with frequent turnover of new employees. As jobs in the plant came open with bids, new hires would often move out of the AST group. Even those ASTs who were there for some time were constantly moving in and out of different plant pool jobs. Because of this, no one in the AST group would be doing the rail job frequently enough to maintain proficiency for safety reasons.

In addition, with this rail job vital to the operational needs of the entire plant site and kept excluded from the AST job duties, I held hopes that the union could get this recognized for a higher wage in the future. But more importantly, I was following God's direction in my steadfast refusal to allow the AST group to work the rail job.

All these reasons were solidified after I started working the rail job and understood it better for myself. However, my working this job now also gave management a blackmail opportunity to convince me to change my adamant refusal to allow the AST group to work the rail job.

After giving Audrey almost five-months of advance notice for my union business time off request, I requested up-dates on this several times. It was a few weeks before the convention when I was called in for a meeting concerning my requested time off. As was habitual when management knew I would not agree to something, they also invited the e-board to be present.

Since the last two days of that week already had one certified rail worker off (Samson), and since two certified rail workers were needed to do the rail moves for the plant site, I was presented with a blackmail ultimatum at this meeting: I could either agree to allow the AST to train on my rail job, or I would not be permitted time off to attend the International Union's convention.

Jezebel and Audrey waited to give me their ultimatum until they thought there was just enough time to train an AST for my rail job, but not enough time to process a grievance to arbitration or NLRB charges before the convention. There were other options available to cover those two days for rail moves, as was done in the past, but everyone refused to even consider them.

Jezebel, Audrey and Ferengi believed this was another win-win scenario for them, as another vindictive act against me. Either I would agree to this addition of the rail job to the AST job description, something they had wanted me to agree to for the past several years, or they would prevent me from going to the convention. A win-win for them, but either way, a loss for me.

Once again, Cain had his own interpretation of the contract language regarding union business time off for this convention, and supported management in their belief that this was not contractually mandatory. Once again, Cain convinced the e-board of his interpretation of this contract language and gained their support against me. And once again, I was holding my ground standing alone both with my interpretation of this contract language, and with my adamant refusal to allow the AST group to train and work the rail job. But the Lord would vindicate me in the very near future.

I went over Cain's head and contacted Matthew, the International Union lawyer I dealt with before. Matthew agreed with my interpretation of the contract language: It was mandatory that Management allowed me union business unpaid time off to attend the International Union's convention. Matthew contacted Cain via email and copied me, and advised him to file a grievance and arbitrate this before the convention. However, management planned their timing well; there was not enough time to do this.

Even after Cain received direction from Matthew on the issue, he continued to support management against me in refusing this mandatory union business time off. When I sought the Lord's direction on how to deal with this, His direction was for me to do nothing; He was going to handle everything. And so, I did nothing.

Although I was standing alone once again, I held my ground. I was adamant that I was not going to agree to something for a personal gain that I would not agree to all these years. The rail job was not going to be included in the AST job description, period. I was prepared instead to cancel the trip.

I would have thought that by then, everyone would have known that the Holy Spirit was my driving force, and as a union president, I could not be bought with a personal gain under any circumstances. But apparently, they thought differently.

Chapter 84

Retaliation

This industrial chemical manufacturing plant had rules and procedures governing just about every job task and situation you could think of. It was just over a year since I had volunteered for the plant-wide procedure committee designed to review and modify the plant-wide procedures periodically and when necessary. Each department had their own procedures that those working in the related department would review and modify.

My main purpose for wanting to be on this committee was to have input on these procedures to ensure that they were compatible with our union workforce, as only salaried personnel were on this committee. How these documents were worded was so very important. Ferengi was in charge of this plant-wide procedure committee.

Existing as part of the process to discipline employees for any infraction or incident, especially in regards to these rules and procedures, was management's "corrective action policy." This policy could have easily been called the "termination process policy," as it outlined exactly the documented steps needed to ensure any employee terminated as a result of going through this discipline policy would be justified, whether the last infraction or incident was justifiable for termination or not.

There were actually four steps to this corrective action policy before termination, but only three were numbered as steps. This process started with the counseling session, when an employee was guilty of a very small infraction or incident. Following this counseling session was the actual step-one, a documented verbal discipline letter that was always kept in the supervisor's file. Step-two was a written discipline letter. Step-three was called a DML (decision-making leave) discipline letter, which consisted of one to three days off without pay. The documents for steps two and three were kept in the employee's HR personnel file indefinitely; this changed the following contract. If another infraction or incident followed the DML discipline letter, the employee was terminated from employment. Any arbitrator would be hard-pressed to reverse a termination case that had a documented trail through these discipline steps.

Although these steps were normally followed, any discipline step could be bypassed depending on the severity of the infraction or incident. This corrective action policy was strictly adhered to for those targeted and on management's most-wanted list. For more favored employees not targeted, even major infractions or incidents were at times overlooked.

Within one week, two significant incidents happened on the rails. Tara and Samson were responsible for a railcar jumping on top of a track-end stopper (a huge triangle of metal secured at the end of a rail track used to stop railcars). And Marty, though not yet fully trained on the rails, was responsible for a railcar running through a track switch the wrong way.

The track-end stopper incident had a huge cost for repairs to both the stopper and the railcar. The track switch repair was not as costly, but it did put the track out of commission for a few days. Neither of these employees received any discipline letters. I was sure their tattling on me secured their exemption from being held accountable even to major incidents.

Right about the same time I was given the ultimatum decision to either agree to add the rail job into the AST job description, or be refused time off for the convention, I had an insignificant incident while working as ground-person on the rails. I had a misstep along the tracks due to a low spot that caused a very sharp instant pain in my knee, and then the pain was gone. Since I was so used to dealing with the rough terrain and the pain it caused while working the rails, I never gave it another thought. This happened about an hour before our workday had ended.

That evening, I experienced an intense aggravation of the RSD pain in my knee. Thinking back through the day as to what could have triggered this, I remembered the misstep incident. RSD is so unpredictable that any triggered event causing an aggravation may have a delayed reaction from when the actual event occurred.

Because there was an actual misstep incident that caused the aggravation of the RSD, I reported the incident as soon as possible the next morning. There was never any indication of how bad any given aggravation of RSD would become, and I didn't want to take any chances should this RSD go berserk. I only told Abby, the plant nurse, that my concern of the RSD was why I reported the incident. The RSD ended up settling down, which had I known was going to happen, this incident would have gone unreported.

Abby wanted me to see Dr. Willy, who was contracted as their company doctor off plant site, due to her concern with the RSD. Dr. Willy knew enough about RSD to know that inactivity of an area that had been aggravated with pain was not good, just as too much activity was not good. Abby had a hard time understanding this characteristic of RSD. Dr. Willy had to convince Abby that it was best I use the leg versus babying it. So I continued working my job, and nothing else became of the incident, yet.

As the time got closer to the convention, Samson's pool league lost the opportunity for the tournament he was going to Las Vegas for. Because of this, he canceled his two days off. This left no excuse for management to deny my time off for union business for the entire week to attend the convention. And so, God handled everything. I have never been disappointed when following God's direction to wait on Him and allow Him to work.

I emailed Ferengi that same morning I found out about the full week becoming available for my time off to let him know. The retaliatory response from Ferengi was to give me a step-one documented verbal discipline letter that same afternoon for not reporting the knee misstep incident immediately. He purposely bypassed the counseling session.

Per plant-wide procedure, all incidents were supposed to be reported immediately. Reporting my misstep the following morning, which was less than two hours of actual work time, was not soon enough for Ferengi. I don't believe in coincidences. It was almost three weeks from when the actual misstep incident was reported before I was given the discipline letter.

Jezebel, Audrey and Ferengi's attempts at a win-win scenario for themselves backfired on them. They did not get my agreement to add the rail job into the AST job description, and they could not deny my time off to keep me from going to the convention. I accepted this discipline letter from what I knew so well by this time as their normal vindictive personalities.

In this step-one discipline letter, they stated that they had concerns about whether I could perform my job safely and effectively day in and day out. Noted in this discipline letter were incidents they believed supported their allegations. Most of the referenced incidents were the ones Audrey had already met with me on just a few weeks earlier when she specifically told me her "chat" was not disciplinary. These incidents were ruled out at that time as not being my fault. Also noted in this discipline letter was another insignificant injury that I reported per procedure, even though I knew it was not going to amount to anything. This injury was proved to be caused by faulty equipment.

Another incident I was earmarked for the blame noted in this discipline letter was leaving the yard-truck running in the dead of winter after going home for the day. This yard-truck was used to shuttle semi-trailers and the shorter sea bulk trailers in and out of loading dock doors. Samson was responsible for leaving this yard-truck running and hooked to a trailer, as he was trying to unfreeze the brakes of the semi-trailer. No one told me there was an investigation over this incident, or that I was being blamed for it—not until I saw it noted in this step-one discipline letter that I was given in July.

This was only the beginning of management's campaign to process me through their "termination process policy" to justify terminating my employment. Twelve days after receiving this step-one discipline letter, I received a step-two discipline letter for loading a trailer truck one bag short of the customer's order. These bags were fifteen-hundred pounds each and filled with Beady's product. Several of them were loaded one at a time on each trailer truck using a forklift.

After I loaded this truck, it stayed in the loading dock overnight before the driver picked it up, in view and accessible to anyone walking through or working in the Beady packagers' area during the afternoon and midnight shifts. I always had doubts that this was an honest mistake on my part.

After the second discipline letter, I had a conversation with Ferengi while expressing anger over what I believed was vindictive retaliation by management. Ferengi defended himself by saying that these were discipline letters meant to help improve my work performance, and not to terminate my employment. *Right!* He then added, "We'll wait and see what your union representatives have to say about them."

Ferengi knew I was at odds with the union e-board the last few months due to our disagreements on the added recall and union business time off contract languages, on my willingness to pursue Ollie's grievance no one else believed had merit, and on my refusal to agree to add the rail job into the AST job description.

Ferengi was also well aware of Cain's lack of support towards me over the years, which had escalated during this year since the flex operator arbitration saga. All this was giving Ferengi and management hope that they were going to succeed with their campaign to terminate my employment.

Ferengi knew that Cain was scheduled to retire following his vacation in September, after the International Union's convention in August. These discipline letters were both given in July. Ferengi was so anxious that I file grievances on these discipline letters in time for Cain to have the third-step grievance meetings. I was not as anxious, and for obvious reasons.

I purposely prolonged filing the grievances to just under the time limits, and then delayed the grievance meetings while using the contractual excuse that the shop steward, as the first-line rep, was on vacation. Max relayed a message to me that "they" wanted me to schedule my first-step grievance meetings to rush along the process of addressing these discipline letters. But I wasn't about to let them rush this along for their own agendas. And my timing worked out perfectly. Cain was long gone before these grievances were heard in third step.

After receiving two discipline letters in less than two weeks, I became distraught, and more so because Jezebel fabricated her dramatized defamation of my character while also being sure to document a negative profile on me. I was so stressed out working while trying so hard to make sure another infraction, whether my fault or not, did not happen for an excuse to continue me through their "termination process policy."

I really had a hard time allowing the Lord to handle this situation now, even after seeing how He worked out everything else thus far in my union president's role and throughout my life. When you know you are targeted for harm, it takes so much more to trust in the Lord God to protect you and get you through.

I was at a point where I hated everything about this job, this union, and being the union president. But I was too young to retire, and too committed to fulfilling my obligations as president for the current term that I knew nothing about my circumstances were going to change anytime soon.

The Lord had spoken to me during this intensive turbulent season of my career through Scripture. The Lord's profound messages became engraved in my heart. The first message was through Psalm 56, which described all I was going through, and made it undeniably clear to me that I needed to put my trust only in the Lord God.

The second message was also undeniably clear: "Your God has commanded your strength" (Psalm 68:28). I was going to survive this morphed campaign against me to terminate my employment only through the Lord's strength, and not my own.

Max approached me one day and referencing everything I was enduring during this same time frame, expressed that it was no wonder I may lose focus when being attacked by so many people at all angles. I was surprised to learn he understood what was going on better than I believed he did.

Upon my return from Las Vegas (for the record, I didn't gamble one-cent), Marty finally jumped the fence and accepted Max's vacant salaried position. Ollie was awarded the job bid for Marty's union warehouse position. Because of the wage reduction that resulted from my unpardonable-sin letter of agreement, those older than Ollie refused the job. Marty then worked almost five months on mark-up while training for his salaried position until he was officially moved out of the union, while Ollie trained for his warehouse position.

Once Marty jumped the fence, I wasted no time requesting his resignation in writing as a union trustee on the e-board. I then went through the proper procedure to add in our local union by-laws language that prohibited any union representative while in that position to work mark-up to salaried positions, as during such time they are temporarily transferred out of the union. This needed to pass by a two-thirds majority, and with the full support of the union membership, it passed with no problems.

With the convention over, Cain was scheduled for a vacation that would take him into retirement. I emailed only Cain and asked him who would be covering for him while on vacation, or if he knew who his replacement would be. Cain copied his normal nasty response for the other two group chairmen to read, letting the three of us know even while on vacation, he was still going to be our staff rep.

This man was never going to like me! I wondered if these two group chairmen understood anything of what I had been going through all these years dealing with this mean-tempered man?

But Cain was wrong after all. He sent another email soon afterward notifying us that Newbie was his replacement. Unbeknown to me at the time, Cain had been grooming Newbie to be his replacement for a long time.

During all my interactions with Newbie in the past at the presidents' meetings, there was always something about him that I was uncomfortable with that I just couldn't put my finger on. But even so, I expected things to be different with Newbie. I expected that there would be no more dealings with management behind my union president back, or lack of support from a staff rep whose main job was to support the local union officers.

Chapter 85
Union Representation

Just after Newbie became our staff rep, Company B was getting ready for their contract negotiations. This was my fourth contract negotiating as president, and my first with Newbie. My position as union president was always well respected by the management at Company B; a complete contrast compared with the management of the company I worked for.

Although this contract was very difficult compared to the one negotiated three years earlier with the union having to take a strong stand on many issues, it turned out well under the circumstances. It wasn't until we started negotiating that the union was told this coal-fired power plant was going to shutdown in the near future. We were able to get an enhanced severance package for our members because of this shutdown.

I could have been more involved as president with our other two company groups, but decided I would only get involved if I was asked. But when it came to workers' comp issues, there was no question: I was the go-to rep for our local.

I was often involved with Company B that employed only men. Their plant was located in the backyard on the property of my company, and supplied the steam power we used. I was always supported and treated with the utmost respect by these men. When they heard how the management at my company was trying to terminate my employment, they had real concerns. They told Newbie he needed to stop this, as no union president should be targeted as I was. With a new staff rep, I had hopes that things would change for the better.

The grievance meeting for my two discipline letters was the first with Newbie when heard in third step of the grievance process. After this meeting, Newbie expressed excitement believing he could win in arbitration the step-one discipline letter dealing with not reporting my misstep immediately. I confided in him how it aggravated the RSD, which was the only reason I reported it. Newbie then shared that his mother also developed RSD through an injury at her workplace. I believed with Newbie having some knowledge of RSD, this was in my favor.

Soon after this grievance meeting while meeting with Jezebel and Ferengi over another issue, another union employee, Kendra, was discussed at the end of the meeting. Bringing up issues when our staff rep was present continued to be habitual for Jezebel and Ferengi while hoping to get a more favorable response to their side than what I would offer—and often, they succeeded.

Kendra's infractions were excessive absenteeism, and with the employees' responsibility to enter all exception time in the company's time management computer program, she failed to enter some of her days missed for work. This resulted in her being paid for being at work when she was not. There wasn't a normal punch-in clock that recorded an employee's presence for a true pay system to be enforced. While going through the gate into the plant, a card was swiped that was only used to register the time and presence. Shift-work relief times varied greatly in each department, and some people came in the plant outside their normal work hours for other reasons.

Just a few weeks before this meeting discussing Kendra, I was in Adrianne's office and noticed a timesheet printout on the front side of her desk that anyone visiting her would be able to read. I glanced at this report and noticed Kendra's name on it, but didn't read it in detail. I didn't want to be guilty of reading what was on someone's desk. I had wondered often afterward if Adrianne left that where she did so it would get my attention knowing I was coming to visit her, and in the hopes that I would contact Kendra asking questions about her time entries?

Now in the meeting discussing Kendra, another employee with a target on the most-wanted list, Jezebel and Ferengi stated that they were going to terminate her employment because of these infractions.

When Newbie heard this, without asking my opinion, he suggested issuing a last-chance agreement letter to Kendra instead of terminating her employment. Jezebel and Ferengi jumped on the idea, as they knew what this letter meant.

A last-chance agreement letter was signed by the employee with the understanding that the employee was relinquishing all rights to union representation should they violate this agreement with another infraction. If they had another infraction, they would automatically be terminated without the option to file a grievance to challenge the termination.

However, Newbie did not know with being so new to our particular contract that there was language management was well aware of but failed to honor with regards to Kendra. This contract language stated that any employee who had accumulated six unexcused absences within a rolling twelve-month period, would be notified by management in writing with a copy to the chief shop steward of such circumstances, and warned if they were absent more than two additional times within the specified period they would be terminated.

In addition to Jezebel and Ferengi blatantly violating this contract language in this case with Kendra, no one seemed to care at all about hearing her side of the story before offering a last-chance agreement letter. Was her missed time entry just an honest mistake? Was she given the opportunity to correct this mistake? I guessed management was aware for a few weeks that she did not enter her missed time adding up the reason for the printout on Adriane's desk, who was the HR secretary.

When Newbie put it in the heads of Jezebel and Ferengi to offer Kendra a last-chance agreement letter, I spoke up and told him that we could not agree to this letter without first consulting with Kendra; after which, he was highly annoyed that I would dare make such a statement. I ignored Newbie's annoyance and asked Chief if he had received notification in writing per our contract while copying Kendra, when she missed six days in the twelve-month period. He answered, "No."

My next question was directed to Jezebel and Ferengi: "Why wasn't our contract honored in this case by notifying Kendra and Chief in writing with a warning, that if she had two more absences she would be terminated? But instead, you come to us now ready to terminate her employment?"

Jezebel had a "dumb expression" while tilting her head just slightly that I was so used to by then when she didn't know or want to give an answer. She just gave me her dumb expression. I never condoned missing work unless there was an absolutely good reason for it. Working at this plant site for well over twenty-one years by this time, I maintained a perfect attendance record with no unexcused absences. However, I believed that as union reps, it was not our right to govern disciplining employees for any reason. I was to find out personally and real soon, Newbie did not have this same conviction.

On our own after this meeting, I expressed to Newbie and Chief: "This is so wrong! They violated our contract and want to get away with it while setting up Kendra for termination. We cannot let her get a last-chance agreement letter over this. We need to hear her side of the story and represent her better."

Newbie didn't appreciate me stepping on his toes in the meeting in front of Jezebel and Ferengi, and bringing this up again annoyed him even more. Newbie had no consideration for Kendra, what she had to say for herself, or whether she was willing to work under a last-chance agreement letter.

That afternoon after this meeting, I contacted the guard at the gatehouse asking for report-off logs and gate entry/exit time reports for Kendra, which I was legally permitted to receive for investigating her grievance. Sabrina had already given me a recent printout of Kendra's timesheet. I wanted to compare these reports with the timesheet to verify that Kendra did have missed workdays, but failed to enter her time in the computer program correctly.

After work that same day, I returned to HR for a visit to Adrianne with the purpose of asking for Kendra's timesheet that was printed out and on her desk prior to when all this was brought before union leadership. I wanted to prove by the date on the original printout I saw that management knew she didn't record her time, but purposely did not let her know to give her an opportunity to correct the error as they have in the past for other employees, which I knew was past practice. I was viewing everything that management conveniently neglected doing while dealing with Kendra as a purposeful set-up for her termination.

When I arrived at Adrianne's office at a time I have in the past visited her, she was gone for the day, much earlier than she normally would have left. I looked around in the hallway wondering what to do next, thinking I really needed that previous timesheet printout to prove my point.

And then I spotted a pretty blue paper recycle bin. This bin was nothing more than a clean garbage bin as far as I was concerned. With all this injustice heavy on my heart and a strong desire to help Kendra, this recycle bin got my attention.

Giving no thought to my actions being wrong, even knowing I wasn't alone in the HR area, on impulse I looked inside this paper recycle bin hoping that maybe, that earlier timesheet printout might be in there. Trish was the secretarial salaried employee I knew was walking about in the area. While I was going through the recycle bin, Trish walked over to the copy machine to use it, which was right next to the recycle bin, and then asked me what I was doing.

I answered truthfully: "Just looking for something."

I didn't find the timesheet, and didn't take anything from the recycle bin away with me. It had never occurred to me that Trish would think anything of my actions to report it to Sabrina.

Right at this same time, another employee was terminated for an alleged infraction of his self-referral drug and alcohol program agreement. I witnessed Newbie flat out telling Jezebel that if there was ever an employee terminated for drugs or alcohol, don't even bother calling him. Newbie's strong position he made clear to Jezebel didn't sit well with me. He just told her he was willing to refuse his representation for union members on certain cases, even without hearing their case or their side of the story for himself. There are other possibilities for positive test results from drugs other than drug abuse, such as prescription medication, or even consuming poppyseeds before a drug test.

I never confronted Newbie on what he told Jezebel. I was trying my best not to make waves with Newbie. I still held hopes that he was going to turn out to be a better staff rep than Cain.

Chapter 86

Unethical Crime

I met with Kendra in the plant site union office the following morning to let her know what was happening before another meeting with Jezebel and Ferengi. Newbie and Chief were to be present at both meetings. I was still so irritated over Jezebel and Ferengi violating our contract, and then setting up this woman with a last-chance agreement letter now in the progress of being implemented without hearing her side of the story. I was not too happy with Newbie either over this issue.

Newbie showed up a little later and also met with Kendra at the union office. During Newbie's presence, I had said something to Kendra that Newbie again was very annoyed about, displaying contempt for me that I had hints of at some of the local presidents' meetings he organized before being our staff rep. Something was there that I just couldn't yet put my finger on, but I shrugged it off and ignored his demeanor.

Before meeting with management in the HR conference room, I approached Adrianne while in her office about the earlier timesheet printout. Adrianne told me that normally, she would always double check report-off logs with employees' computer timesheets, and notified them if they neglected to enter their missed time. I countered, "Why wasn't Kendra notified that she didn't enter her time in the computer timesheet program?"

You really get to know people after a while. Adrianne never answered my question, but instead gave me her "I can't tell you" sheepish smile, which told me everything.

While in the meeting with Jezebel, she confessed that they knew Kendra didn't record her time correctly in the computer program, but they didn't tell her to correct it because this had happened before. Had I known this, I would not have felt the need to search the paper recycle bin for that earlier timesheet printout to prove this point.

Kendra now present, she stated she remembered entering her missed days, but the computer program must not have saved it for some reason, which happened to her before. (The computer programs this company used were very complex.) This was not a side of the story even I thought of. But none of this mattered to Jezebel and Ferengi, nor to Newbie.

These people could not understand the stressful situation that employees were put in when they knew they were targeted, which in itself could cause infractions from the lack of focus on their jobs. Or did they just not care?

Kendra was so distraught and wanted to just quit her job because of all this. She did remain working under the last chance agreement letter. But I believed union leadership really let her down. As stated before, I didn't condone such behavior, but I would not govern the discipline of union members.

At the end of this meeting, Jezebel announced in front of Newbie how unacceptable it was that I would dare rummage through the HR paper recycle bin the night before after hours. I didn't know then that Trish had emailed Sabrina informing her that I went through the recycle bin, who reported it to Jezebel. When I finally got to read Trish's initial email over this incident weeks later, the time it was sent supported that I was in to see Adrianne when she normally would have still been working.

Without giving me an opportunity to speak before judging my actions, Jezebel made it out to sound like I purposely went to the HR office area after work hours for such a purpose. Jezebel dramatized my actions as such a horrible, unethical crime that I committed. I never offered any defense for my actions during that meeting. I accepted this as just another opportunity Jezebel took to defame my character in front of our new staff rep.

In the hallway after this meeting, Newbie opened his mouth loud enough for Sabrina to hear from her office, claiming how wrong I was to go through the HR paper recycle bin, and that this was something I could get fired for. I said nothing in response, especially knowing who was listening.

Jezebel was always obsessed with anything she could dramatize and document as a defamation of my character or any so-called wrongful actions on my part as a union president. I was sure she would lay awake some nights just thinking about what she could conjure up next against me.

Later this same day, after bringing it up at this meeting, Jezebel sent her email documenting my unethical crime—Document Queen strikes again—and claimed that I was wrong to request the reports from the guard, which I legally had the right to request and obtain. It seemed that Jezebel was going to let all this go with just documenting my unethical crime.

Once we were among ourselves, I defended my actions to Newbie, Chief and Alvin while letting them know what exactly I was looking for and why. These guys did not at all seem concerned that Jezebel and Ferengi violated our contract in their action against Kendra. Everyone was just focused on my unethical crime.

Good grief, it was a paper garbage bin for crying out loud! If I thought I was doing something that was wrong, I would not have done it, period, let alone knowingly while a salaried employee was present in the area.

Alvin suggested that I take the position I was looking for something I left lying around that could have inadvertently ended up in the paper recycle bin. But I would not lie about what I was looking for and why, not even to get out of what everyone now believed was an awful unethical crime on my part. I was more accountable to the Lord, who I knew understood everything.

All this was happening during the time my two discipline letters were being grieved. Jezebel and Ferengi had agreed to reduce the step-two discipline letter down to a step-one discipline letter, which will always remain in my supervisor's file, but would not budge on the first discipline letter asking to reduce it to a counseling session, which was a very reasonable request that should have been honored.

Any discipline letter that had merit for the union to challenge and was not, would be used detrimentally against the employee in the future. Knowing the morphed campaign now going on by management to terminate my employment, I knew this first discipline letter needed addressed. Newbie had already made it known in the presence of Chief and Alvin that he believed he could win an arbitration for this first discipline letter. When I presented this for a vote to the e-board and membership, all agreed to take this to arbitration.

The next day after I sent notice for this arbitration, and three days after the paper recycle bin incident, Jezebel emailed Newbie requesting a meeting with him and Joab—Newbie's favored district director—regarding filing a formal complaint against me for what she claimed was my "unethical behavior."

With agreement from Ferengi and Gremlin, as they were copied on her email, I accepted this formal complaint as another act of vindictive retaliation with coming the day after notification of arbitration for my first discipline letter. At this point, Ferengi, Jezebel and Gremlin did not believe they had grounds to issue another discipline letter to me for what they claimed was unethical behavior to rummage through the HR paper recycle bin; otherwise, no doubt, they would have jumped on the opportunity.

Prior to this recycle bin incident, Newbie had warned me about being careful how I obtained information to use for grievances. While speaking with Newbie regarding this formal complaint against me, he reminded me of his warning and again told me how wrong I was to go through the HR paper recycle bin.

After this conversation with Newbie, it was apparent that he and Jezebel were in constant communication over several weeks concerning my unethical behavior. When Newbie told me that Jezebel wanted to actually meet with him alone over this issue, I insisted on being present to speak on my own behalf. When Jezebel heard this, she refused to have the meeting at all. It took one email from me copying Gremlin, and she had the meeting while I was present.

During this meeting, Jezebel read from emails that were supposedly sent by Trish, who witnessed my unethical behavior, and Nancy, the guard who supplied me with the gatehouse reports. I was not permitted to read these emails for myself at this meeting, and was refused copies when I requested them afterward. No one seemed to care at all for what I had to say in my own defense. After this meeting, Newbie remarked that things were not looking good for me while referencing what was read from these emails.

I don't believe in coincidences. Newbie was governing behind the scenes. What started out as being only a request from Jezebel to file a formal complaint with Newbie and Joab regarding my unethical behavior, morphed into another discipline letter, almost five weeks from when I rummaged through the HR recycle bin.

Jezebel tried to renege on their grievance answer to reduce the step-two discipline letter down to step-one, while wanting this next discipline letter to be put at step-three, the step just before termination of employment. But Jezebel did not get her way. This next discipline letter for my infraction of unethical behavior was another one at step-two in the corrective action policy, leaving me with just one step to go before termination.

With over twenty-one years working in that industrial chemical plant by this time, up until that year, I had never received any discipline letters. With management's morphed campaign to terminate my employment now, I received three discipline letters in less than six months.

After this last discipline letter, I had another conversation with Ferengi that was very short and to the point. I did not try to hide my strong anger: "When is this vindictive harassment and defamation of my character going to stop? I am so disgusted right now with everything you people are doing to me!"

Ferengi's response was indicative of his familiar disdain towards me: "I can understand that you are feeling frustrated right now."

I threw some daggers at him with my eyes and stated firmly: "No, Ferengi! You have no idea what I am feeling right now!"

After throwing a few more daggers at him, I turned and stormed away in hot anger.

Chapter 87
Newbie's Canary

There were times when Newbie was willing to support me in my role as local union president. There were times he would govern situations behind the scenes while trying his best to hide this from me. Newbie had a very distinct demeanor about him when he was being deceptive, or whenever he thought his behind-the-scene contacts or deals were discovered: He resembled a cat that ate a canary but then tried to hide it. "Who, me? I didn't eat that canary; he just foo away!"

While all along a little feather was sticking out of his mouth!

Now that I received my third discipline letter, I did what I normally would do for any grievance: I requested information needed to help fight the grievance. With this thought, I emailed Jezebel requesting that the "hearsay" emails that she read at the meeting prior to issuing the discipline letter be sent to me. Since it was agreed that this grievance would be moved directly to third step in the grievance process that Newbie would attend, I copied him so he would know what I was requesting.

Newbie's email response only to me was his rebuke for requesting the information on my own behalf: "You cannot represent yourself! We spoke about this numerous times. Someone else should have made these requests on your behalf."

Newbie always took the position that union officials could not represent themselves, which was a claim I never believed and never bothered to research for myself.

Jezebel sent me the emails I requested as attachments to another email and copied Newbie. Never one to let an opportunity go by that she could use to cause conflict between union officers and me, Jezebel attached one of the emails that had her note to Newbie. By doing this, she wanted me to know that he already had these hearsay emails way before the last meeting that she wanted to have with him but without me, while also referencing their conversation about me. Now I understood Newbie's angry rebuke when I requested these emails, and it had nothing to do with his claim that I could not represent myself.

With the referenced emails to read for myself, I understood that Jezebel and Ferengi had lied to me during the meeting when she read these. I also saw that Sabrina took the lead in these emails after Trish's initial notification of my actions. Sabrina attempted to document my unethical behavior through these emails, which I was sure Jezebel had instigated. However, Sabrina's attempts at documenting what transpired and my interactions with Trish, and Nancy, the guard who gave me Kendra's reports, were not correct.

By the dates of Sabrina's emails taking the lead to document my actions, I saw that they were not initiated, along with the request for filing a formal complaint with Joab for my so-called unethical behavior, until the day after I had given notification of the union's intent to take my first discipline letter to arbitration, which was three days after the incident was known. Yep, I had no doubt this was vindictive retaliation for the arbitration decision.

Newbie once refused to use an email sent from another employee to me in defense of my first discipline letter that we were taking to arbitration, stating such emails were considered only hearsay. In contrast, he readily accepted Sabrina's hearsay emails as valid evidence against me while warning me that because of them it was not looking good for me.

After I received the emails from Jezebel while copying Newbie, he called my cell phone; the timing indicated he just ate that canary. I didn't want to hear his excuses, and since he never left a message, I ignored his call. Newbie purposely withheld his knowledge of these emails knowing I could have used them prior to that meeting that he and Jezebel wanted to have without me. I never confronted Newbie on his betrayal now that he was exposed, thanks to his newly found ally, Jezebel. My distrusting wall with Newbie was now securely in place. What was there all along that I just couldn't put my finger on was slowly being revealed.

Just two weeks after receiving these emails I requested, Marty was finally officially moved into his salaried supervisory position; the time frame was just after the New Year. Contractually, Marty had twenty days to jump over the fence again back into his union warehouse position, even though he had been working mark-up and training for his salaried position for almost five months by this time. I had just recently shared with Chief the scenario that was going to happen once Marty jumped back over the fence, as I was sure he would.

Because I refused to accept seniority in my warehouse position that the letter of agreement permitted, with Ollie now working there on a job bid award from when Marty accepted the salaried job, I was going to be the one bumped out. Unbeknown to me at the time, Jezebel had already emailed Chief and Newbie with this same scenario asking for their agreement.

Neither Chief nor Newbie had the courtesy to contact me for a heads-up that this scenario was going to play out, even though I just spoke with Chief about it. It wasn't until months later while I was putting files away in the plant union office, that I happened to run across a copy of this email that Jezebel had sent to Chief and Newbie. So much for union solidarity! Jezebel had justified her reluctance to copy me on her email claiming, "Due to the sensitivity of this issue, I did not copy Angelika on this note."

It was the afternoon of my birthday when Jezebel phoned to inform me that I was going to be bumped out of the warehouse because Marty wanted back into his union warehouse job position.

Jezebel followed up this conversation with an email (Document Queen strikes again) and was sure to copy everyone on the e-board, including Newbie, of this great news. She must have gotten over her concern about the sensitivity of the issue!

Just two hours earlier from when Jezebel had called, Max surprised me with a birthday cake for all of us in the warehouse to enjoy. I was never sure if Max knew of Jezebel's timing of her announcement that I was being bumped out. Maybe my birthday cake was really my goodbye cake?

Ollie came up to me to express, "Just so you know, I find no pleasure in knowing you are being bumped out the warehouse."

After working with Ollie for a few years in Darkly and since, I knew his demeanor spoke a different message. Things never got any better between us, even after I took the lone stand to represent him with his bumped-out grievance over the added recall contract language disagreement.

But by this time, it didn't matter to me. I was getting so used to people treating me with contempt, doing things behind my back, and discussing my issues without my knowledge or input, even though I was the union president.

Had Jezebel asked for my input, I would have told her the truth. She had no need to email my fellow union officers behind my back for their agreement. But Jezebel never portrayed professionalism in her HR leadership role. This was again evident when she copied everyone, e-board and Newbie included, sharing about another union member's medical condition with work restrictions. When this union member found out what Jezebel shared that should have been kept confidential, he was irate over the breach.

Once I was officially bumped out of the warehouse to become a lowly AST, though I stayed for a short time still working the plant pool jobs there, I informed Max that I could no longer perform the rail job portion of the warehouse job duties, as it was not in my current AST job description. He wasn't too happy about this but understood—that was life.

My obedience to the Lord in refusing to start accruing seniority in the warehouse per my unpardonable-sin letter of agreement turned out to be a real blessing, and was part of God's will for my career and life. As an AST, I was given a break from the warehouse tattlers, and the physical demands and stress of the rail job, and moved into a much less stressful position that afforded me more freedom throughout the plant site.

Jezebel continued her habitual contact with Newbie on every local union business, and copied him on every email that she sent to our local union officers. Newbie's job was to assist the local officers, not take over their responsibilities. Newbie's involvement with our local union in the short time he was our staff rep, almost five months by this time, by far exceeded Cain's involvement throughout the many years he was our staff rep.

I confronted Newbie on his persistence in being involved with our local when I saw he was attending every e-board meeting. I asked him if he attended all e-board meetings of every local union in his assignment? He ate another canary without answering me.

It wasn't too long after this that Newbie announced his best man at his wedding was hired at our company. By that time, all of our union members were called back from layoff with the need to hire more employees, thanks to the mismanagement culprit.

Around this same time, I had arranged a meeting with others at the union hall to go over our contract proposals for negotiations that were soon to happen. I was the last to leave after this meeting. As I was coming out of the union office, Newbie was just coming into the union hall for a meeting with another group. He was surprised when he spotted me, and asked what I was doing there?

When I told him, he responded, "I didn't know you were having this meeting."

I was becoming well-guarded with Newbie and didn't voice my thoughts: *Do you need to know everything?*

Newbie then asked if I had a few minutes to talk. Reluctantly, I went back into the office to oblige, but with flashbacks of meetings with Cain in this same union office causing some uneasy feelings. The timing was just a few weeks after Jezebel sent me the emails concerning my unethical behavior while exposing Newbie's prior knowledge of these, and two weeks before my first discipline letter arbitration. Newbie had ignored my recent emails regarding the arbitration, and I confronted him on his desire to back out. I wondered if this was why he wanted to speak with me now?

Newbie didn't quite seem to know where to begin, so he started out with small talk about his knee that he just hurt. I listened out of courtesy but saw he was eating another canary.

When he was done with his small talk, I took the lead and confronted him on his behind the scene deals and constant contact with Jezebel: "What is going on and why? Do you get every HR correspondence from every other company of those in your assignment that are sent to local union reps? Local union reps are the ones elected by their membership to represent those in their units, not staff reps."

He's having a hard time swallowing that canary! I ended this conversation with the expectation that never came to fruition: "It was supposed to be different with a new staff rep!"

Once again, things were slowly being revealed. Cain had done well in grooming Newbie for his replacement.

Chapter 88
My Arbitration

About seven months later from the actual incident, we had the arbitration hearing for the first discipline letter for not reporting immediately my misstep that aggravated the RSD. I made it clear to Newbie on several occasions that I did not want the RSD brought up during the hearing.

Gremlin used his usual tactics to ruffle the feathers of those he was interrogating. The Lord had been doing a great job teaching me to stay calm. I did not succumb to Gremlin's tricks; Chief didn't fare as well. When Chief pointed his finger at Gremlin and demanded he stop his accusations while showing strong anger, Gremlin sat back and looked over at the arbitrator, hoping he too saw the outburst.

While interrogating me, Newbie did not honor my request to keep the RSD confidential, but instead, in front of everyone asked, "Do you have a neurological pain disorder?"

I had no choice but to answer Newbie. When I stated I did, I was told to explain what it was. The arbitrator wanted to know what the initialism of RSD was. I noticed that he and Gremlin made a careful note as I stated, "Reflex Sympathetic Dystrophy."

No doubt, they did their own research afterward.

At the end of the hearing, Abby, the nurse, expressed concern that a medical condition was just revealed, and asked that all present would keep this confidential. But I had no expectations that would happen.

It had been well over a decade since I had developed RSD, and I was confident that this current management was far removed from that knowledge. I never wanted it brought up again, especially during that time, as I expected it would be used as another avenue to terminate my employment. They were going to get rid of me one way or another, this I was sure of. None of these people seemed to like me very much at that point of my career. And there was no doubt this went far outside of the boundaries of our plant site even to Gremlin, especially knowing he blew another arbitration that I was again the instigator.

Our contract expiration and officer elections were just around the corner from this arbitration. While preparing for our last contract negotiations almost three years earlier, I recognized that the transitional period with our merged union would end before our next contract expiration. This meant that our officer election month of November would be moved up to April to coincide with the by-laws of our new merged union. The new officers would be sworn in during our membership meeting in May.

By God's leading and wisdom, I had the foresight to recognize all this and understood that elections for new officers in April would be a disadvantage for the union with a contract expiration date in mid-May. I did not know at the time who would be in office for our next contract, or that I would be running and elected again for union president. Our other two company groups of our amalgamated union had different contract expiration dates that were not affected by this change in election month.

To eliminate this disadvantage, I had put in a proposal during the last contract negotiations to change the contract expiration month to March, just before elections of new officers in April. This gave incumbent union officers the best advantage to negotiate a new contract, especially after almost two-and-a-half years of dealing with management and the issues that came up. That time had come, and it was all part of God's plan for my career and life.

Soon after the arbitration, a meeting was scheduled prior to our contract negotiations with management. Newbie never told me he was advised what this meeting was about, or that there would be an expectation for a spokesperson for the union. When I prayed about this meeting, God had shown me that I needed to be prepared to give the union's position going into these negotiations. Unbeknown to anyone else, I did my homework and came well prepared with undeniable facts.

Present at this meeting for the union was our entire negotiating team of six members. This team consisted of four standing members: myself, as president; Newbie, our staff rep; Chief, our chief shop steward; and Alvin, our recording secretary. Our union's vice president and another shop steward, Bentley, were recently elected just for this negotiating team. Present for management was Jezebel, Ferengi, and Herschel, who was the company's vice president. On speakerphone listening to this meeting was my nemesis, Gremlin.

During this meeting, Herschel, as the company spokesperson, gave the usual picture of a struggling business that needed to keep the cost down and make a decent profit within a safe working environment in order to survive the current troubling economy. We all politely listened as he continued with his gloom and doom presentation; par for the course prior to contract negotiations.

After Herschel gave his speech, Newbie turned to me as if expecting me to now speak on behalf of the union. I took his cue, and with God's help from years of experience as the union president, I spoke clearly but deliberately with my prepared presentation that no one expected I would have:

"The union members at this company have not had a pay increase in almost four years. We lost over three-hundred-seventy-five-thousand dollars due to management unilaterally eliminating their match to our 401(k). Our entry-level AST group for new hires are now being paid less than what our material packagers were paid seventeen years ago. In comparison to others in the same job classifications in our amalgamated union at Company A, our higher job classifications and maintenance employees are at seven percent lower in wages, while our warehouse employees are at sixteen percent lower wages.

"This union did everything we could to ensure this plant site became profitable and survived over these past years since our last contract. Salaried personnel did not share this sacrifice, as they received their wage increases and bonuses during all this time.

"This union will negotiate and bargain in good faith, just as we did our last contract. We are going to be up-front, honest, and work with management. But we will also expect a fair contract with compensation for our losses. We want the end result to be a contract that we can be proud to recommend to our members for a favorable ratification vote."

After a few seconds of pause, I made my last statement even clearer and more deliberate, so as not to be taken lightly: "We have made our share of sacrifices. We are not making any more."

I looked over at our negotiating team and received approvals with smiles and nods.

It was Herschel's turn to respond. Herschel had always reminded me of an innocent little boy just trying to do what was right. I don't think he knew what to take of my presentation. With several seconds of thought before he spoke, while making eye contact with me, Herschel articulated every syllable of his statement clearly and slowly to make sure his profoundness was not missed: "O . . . KAY . . ."

During this meeting, knowing that Sabrina, wife of union member Jason, would be part of management's negotiating team, two guys from the union's negotiating team voiced concerns with this arrangement. It was too much of a conflict of interest, and as one guy pointed out, there was also a concern for what Jason may endure from his union coworkers.

Now Gremlin spoke up from the speakerphone, expressing that if there were any harassment towards any employees, those employees responsible for the harassment would be disciplined.

The next day after this meeting, I emailed Gremlin over his statement regarding harassment: "I am confused by your remark yesterday regarding disciplining union employees who are harassing other employees. You and others in the company seem to have made it clear to me that the company's anti-harassment policy defines harassment based on an individual's race, ethnic background, gender, age, disability, etc., per the law. I believe this was the reason you and others have always refused to help me with management's harassment towards me. Is there a different standard for union employees than there are for management?"

Gremlin's response sent from his cell phone was a simple "no."

I was positive Gremlin regretted his response after he received my response, "Then why was I refused help through the company's anti-harassment policy the several times I have asked for help dealing with management's harassment towards me?"

He never responded. It didn't matter; he got my point. I attempted several times to address the harassment from management over the years to no avail. Gremlin had just changed the rules to benefit them.

Chapter 89
Contract Negotiations

Soon after that last meeting, we prepared for contract negotiations, which was my fifth as union president. Newbie had once suggested that we could ask management to settle outstanding grievances while negotiating a new contract. With this thought in mind, I emailed Ferengi with an innocent enough request to expunge my unethical-behavior discipline letter. I didn't copy Jezebel, but I made sure to let Newbie know I was going to ask Ferengi to reconsider his position on this discipline letter before I did, and then sent him a copy. Newbie never commented nor dissuaded me from this course of action.

Ferengi forwarded my request to Gremlin, who took full advantage of the opportunity to throw a touché at me for my involvement in recent events he was not pleased with, including another lost arbitration under his belt, and getting his reaction in writing to my harassment definition that I was sure he was still beating himself over.

It was five days after Ferengi received my email, and the night before our first meeting for negotiations when Gremlin decided to respond. I believed there was a premeditated purpose for his timing. In Gremlin's response, he labeled my innocent enough request to be literally a federal crime. Quoting an LMRA (Labor Management Relations Act) section, Gremlin claimed that it was a "Federal crime for union officials to request, demand, receive or accept anything of value to influence him/her with respect to actions, decisions, or duties as a representative of employees."

Gremlin further stated that management read my email as my request to grant expunging a personal discipline letter as a thing

549

of value in exchange for influencing the positions taken by the union in negotiations. Gremlin knew better, as did everyone else copied, which included Newbie. It was well established by then that I was a union president who could not be bought.

Gremlin further threatened to refer my email to the attorney general for investigation if I did not withdraw my request. He then made the arbitrary decision that my discipline letter grievance would not be processed until after negotiations, now that I was guilty of another unethical crime.

After receiving Gremlin's email, I contacted Newbie, and speaking with him regarding my new alleged "federal crime," I had an uneasy feeling that he was part of this. With recent evidence that Newbie was contacted on a regular basis and involved in everything that involved me, I tried, but I could not find any reasons to believe differently.

Newbie offered to cancel the opening of negotiations scheduled the next day because of Gremlin's email. I perceived his offer to cancel as part of the premeditated purpose in the timing of all this. But I was determined that was not going to happen.

Newbie referred Gremlin's federal-crime email to an International Union attorney. Amelia responded that it was a bit of a stretch to read the LMRA section as suggested by Gremlin, and a further stretch to read my email in a way that would suggest I violated that statute. Amelia drafted up a response to Gremlin and waited for my approval before sending it. I asked Amelia to make her letter stronger by addressing the harassment I believed fueled Gremlin's response, but she wanted to leave it as is.

After receiving Amelia's response, Gremlin wrote up a lengthy defense of their interpretation of my federal crime request. The company's Document King, Gremlin, referenced the main reason was that the grievance involved a personal discipline letter, and I was the union's spokesperson at the communications meeting for negotiations the previous week. Apparently, I hit some nerves at that meeting that had not yet settled down.

Gremlin's lengthy defense ended reiterating his arbitrary decision to refuse to allow management to process my discipline letter grievance until after negotiations. I informed Newbie that Gremlin's arbitrary decision was a direct violation of our contract. Any delay in hearing a grievance within the time limits as set forth in our contract must be mutually agreed upon by both parties. Instead of speaking in my defense, Newbie's response to Gremlin was meant to nullify his contract violation: "We will grant the extension and postpone the grievance until negotiations are concluded."

Gremlin responded: "Thank you, Newbie. So that there is no future misunderstanding, the company has not requested an extension, but for the reasons previously stated will not further process this grievance until negotiations have concluded."

Gremlin's response documenting his arbitrary decision that violated our contract while ignoring Newbie's attempt to nullify it, would have secured the union's win in an arbitration hearing; he knew that. But he also knew he had Newbie's support against me.

I was so angry at Newbie's lack of support and attempt to nullify Gremlin's contract violation. I told him that I intended on speaking in my own defense. Up until then, I was letting Newbie and Amelia handle Gremlin's federal crime allegations. But when Newbie told me to let it go, I did, but only for the time being. I knew we had a difficult contract to negotiate right then. All this would have to wait. But I also knew I would get my say before this was all over while following the Lord's direction.

This was still going on the first few days into negotiations. But before contract negotiations were over, Newbie told me I would eat my unethical-behavior discipline letter. My strong belief that Newbie was governing behind the scene on this discipline letter was now solidified by his predetermination; everything that transpired so far supported this:

Newbie's personal judgment that I was wrong to go through the HR recycle bin from the very beginning; management's request to file a formal complaint with Joab that morphed into a third discipline letter; Newbie's prior knowledge of hearsay emails he so readily accepted without my knowledge, and without giving me any opportunity to read them and speak on the discrepancies in my own defense; Gremlin's timing claiming my innocent enough request was a federal crime; Newbie's attempt to nullify Gremlin's contract violation.

But the real killer: Newbie's predetermination that I would eat this discipline letter even before having the grievance meeting. Newbie never intended to represent me at all in this grievance. And Gremlin and management knew this very well.

Yep, Newbie was governing behind the scenes. I couldn't prove it, but that didn't matter; it was solidified within my heart. I continued with negotiations while committing all this to the Lord.

Jezebel and Newbie had put on a great show of exchanging cell phone numbers at our first negotiation meeting in front of our union's negotiating team, as if neither one had the information before then. I glanced over at Newbie during this exchange and saw he ate another canary. I was so disheartened by this premeditated deceptive show, which again only reinforced my distrusting wall that would now never come down.

Who did they think they were fooling? Maybe the others thought this exchange never happened before, but I knew better. I had been a witness of cell phone conversations between these two in the past. But I was more concerned for the rest of our union team than myself, as these men, who were going to be negotiating a difficult contract with our new staff rep, trusted him completely.

With the deceptive formalities of contact out of the way, we exchanged our proposals. The one company proposal that got our attention and concern was freezing the union's retirement defined pension plan with no alternative replacement presented at this time of exchange.

It was past practice when negotiating a new contract that everything that went on during these meetings were kept confidential between everyone present; although this was not reinforced during these negotiations. As dear to my heart was sharing the tentative agreement with plenty of time for our membership to digest before voting on it, it was just as dear to my heart in keeping our membership informed to certain negotiating discussions that I believed they had every right to know about.

With having our 401(k) company match contributions just taken away from the union unilaterally since our last contract, this proposal to freeze our pension plan was something I strongly believed needed shared with our membership, especially if we were to have any hopes of securing our pension.

After our first meeting exchanging proposals, I made sure everyone on our team knew I had no qualms about sharing this pension freeze proposal with our membership, and everyone agreed. Once this was shared within the plant among our union members, Judas came to my work area to express his disapproval that this pension freeze proposal had been shared. I responded that I believed it was perfectly fine to let our membership know about something that was so highly prized as our defined pension plan. Judas didn't like my response, but it made no difference to me. I answer to the Lord God first and foremost with all that I do, and I knew I had His approval for sharing this information.

Our negotiating meetings were not scheduled consecutively. When we returned to negotiations, management expressed outrage that our team would dare share such a proposal of freezing our defined pension plan before our negotiations were over, and was sure to throw the full blame on the union scapegoat for instigating what they believed was a breach of confidentiality. I had no problems with taking full responsibility for this action. No one knew at that time that I had plans to share this information with our membership in a more direct way if I felt the need. That was on a need-to-know basis and still in the near future.

But in order to get ready for how I was going to share this information, I had put in an information request to Adrianne for updated home addresses of all those in our union. Adrianne had supplied me with this information a few years earlier during the first temporary layoff, but now I needed an updated version.

When I paid her a visit concerning her delay in supplying these addresses, she was just leaving to smoke a cigarette. It was not unusual for us to talk in the smoke hut, so she asked me to follow her out. We continued our conversation outside in front of the HR building where anyone walking by could see us. Adrianne told me that Newbie informed her that she did not have to supply me with my requested union members' addresses, and offered to send me his email supporting this.

I paid Adrianne another visit after my work hours that same day when she didn't send me Newbie's email as she had offered to. Upon arriving at her office, I realized I just walked into a trap: Jezebel was sitting there with Adrianne waiting for me. I ignored Jezebel and spoke with Adrianne, but made sure not to mention Newbie's name: "Are you going to send me that email?"

Adrianne gave me her sheepish smile, but this time added a slight "no" nod. Jezebel then spoke, "Angelika, if you have issues with something Newbie sent, then you need to take it up with him and not with Adrianne."

I turned to Jezebel when she started speaking, then turned and walked out without saying another word.

Newbie always hated it immensely when caught eating that canary. Jezebel contacted him, and that evening right on schedule he called me. We had a heated conversation, and while he used profanity complained that it really ticked him off when I would question his support with my beliefs that he went behind my back. He must have been one of those select few who saw that "stupid" stamped on my forehead. I offered Newbie the perfect solution: "Then just stop doing it!"

It was soon after this that Adrianne sent me the updated addresses I requested.

Newbie's deceptive support went beyond dealing with me. During some time in negotiations, Newbie requested permission from our team to speak with Jezebel on his own for some innocent enough reason, but it was definitely not about the pension freeze proposal. I never voiced my mistrust to this conversation with Jezebel without us; I knew these men would not have understood.

Afterward, as we were walking to lunch, Newbie asked if we were willing to consider the International Union's pension fund as a counterproposal, since management seemed persistent on freezing our pension. We agreed, but clearly stated that we wanted to see this plan before agreeing to present this to management.

During lunch, Newbie received this plan document upon his request from the International Union through his iPhone email. When he received it, he asked if any of us had Jezebel's email address to forward it to her. Someone confronted Newbie on our agreed terms: "I thought we were going to go over it first ourselves before sending it to management?"

Another canary got ate! Newbie backpedaled quickly: "Oh, yeah; I forgot."

He let it go, and so did I.

Back from lunch with the management team present, Jezebel stated to Newbie in front of all of us: "We discussed among ourselves and decided that we have no interest in the International Union's pension fund."

Newbie turned to me with his "I ate the canary look" while writing a big question mark on a piece of paper for only me to see, as if he didn't know how she found out about this pension fund. Afterward, he expressed his dismay to our team: "How did she know about the International Union's pension fund?"

Someone suggested maybe he mentioned it when he spoke to her alone before leaving for lunch. This was another disheartening display of Newbie's lack of integrity with men who trusted him completely. I knew what happened, but wisely chose not to bring it up. We had a contract to negotiate, and confronting Newbie now wouldn't do any good for any of us. We needed to stay focused and united for a good end to all this.

During any negotiations with a union and management contract, there is always give and take on both sides while trying to get contract language added or changed that both sides can agree with. Without consensual agreement, additions or changes do not happen, or I should say, should not happen. Each side had their own proposals they were hoping to get agreement for.

Ferengi and Jezebel tried again to get the union to agree to add the rail job duties to the AST job description. They just didn't want to give up on this one. However, having had some months gone by since their blackmail attempt for me to agree to this, I was able to convince our union negotiating team that this was still a bad idea to agree to, and they followed my advice. The rail job did not get included in the AST job description.

Jezebel proposed changes to the article in the contract that addressed how job descriptions were managed and re-evaluated. I reminded her and everyone else, the union just won the flex job arbitration using that same article. Therefore, the union had no interest in changing any of the language regarding this article in any way. Jezebel had a conniption after I stated our position. But that was okay with me. Changes to contract language after such a win, or after several years of the same language that was proven strong, could prove detrimental to the union in the future. This article in our contract was never brought up again.

I had a proposal in to address the language concerning mark-up to salaried positions, and made it tighter for those riding the fence that management agreed with, surprisingly, but with a few tweaks. The union agreed to management's request for their corrective action policy (termination process) to be included in our contract, but with stipulations that any changes to this policy would be mutually agreed to by management and the union.

Along with agreeing to this inclusion of the discipline policy, the union requested and received agreement for a time limit of only fifteen days from when an incident and/or infraction becomes known for disciplining an employee; after which the window closes. The union also gained agreement that discipline letters would be removed from record after three years, with those letters two years old not being taken into consideration for further steps in the discipline process.

The union also gained language that allowed report-offs up to three days per year to be converted to vacation days upon the employee's request, and would not be considered as unexcused absences for purposes of their absence management process. This language change was a great benefit for our union members in many ways.

Chapter 90
Finishing Well

It was now less than two weeks before the expiration date for our contract. Management had yet to budge or given us any alternative replacement for their pension plan freeze proposal. Now was the time to execute my plan on sending this information more directly to our membership (thus the need for updated addresses). I drafted up a letter that I wanted to mail to every union member's home address. This letter was something that I truly believed was led by God, and to my knowledge was never done during any past contract negotiations.

I let everyone know in this letter that as of the date this was sent out, management's proposal to freeze our defined pension plan was still on the table, and they had yet to offer any alternative replacement for our pension for us to even consider.

I gave every member of our negotiating team the opportunity to read this letter for their input and approval before I sent it. Newbie was the only one who offered some changes. Some of his changes I agreed with, some of which I could not agree with.

One such change he proposed was to state that as a negotiating team, "we" would fight to keep our pension intact. The message I wanted to convey to all our members was that only if "we, as a union," conveyed "a strong message to the company that we are serious, that we are united, and that we are in agreement as 'one' in our goals to keep our current benefits," would we secure our pension and get a fair contract.

In this letter, I gave everyone a heads-up and stated clearly that the union may be taking actions in the days ahead to show our solidarity and commitment to achieve our goals, and should we go that route, I encouraged everyone to do their part in showing their support by participating.

At the bottom of this letter was going to be my signature as the union president taking full responsibility for the contents, so I was sure to have God's peace with the final version. I sent this letter to every union member in our company group including Ollie, with a salaried wife, and Jason, even knowing his wife Sabrina was part of management's negotiating team. So in essence, everyone, including management, received a copy of this letter and understood that the union was prepared to do whatever was necessary to keep our defined pension plan intact.

A few days after everyone received this letter, we were on our final day of negotiations. By God's wisdom, I understood our benefits in a way that was beyond most and my own limited ability. I tried again during these contract negotiations for another proposal trying to stop management from being able to reduce any of our benefits to a lesser value under their so-called "provisions of the plan" clause they dearly held on to. They offered these benefits but wanted to retain their rights to change, modify or otherwise eliminate them at their sole discretion, yet only clearly stated this in the actual benefits' plan documents, and not in our contract language. However, management again would not budge on this proposal. But the final blow was to management!

I had just returned to our team from a priority trip when Newbie announced to me that they had agreed and would present a contract language change that was supposed to be stronger in protecting our pension than what we had. I didn't question what this change was; I was trusting that this was going to be a good change. This was a major mistake on my part!

It was soon afterward that Ferengi, Jezebel, and the rest of management's team came in for what was to be our final meeting. Newbie, as the spokesperson, offered our pension plan language change proposal. I was hearing this for the first time along with management: "We would like to propose a pension plan language change as follows: The union's defined pension plan will not change for the duration of our current contract."

Wow, I cannot believe what I just heard! Instantly, I responded to Newbie in the hearing of everyone: "Hold on! We need to talk about this first!"

He did not hide his annoyance towards me and countered, "We don't need to talk about this."

I was not going to be intimidated by this man or his annoyance. I was determined that our pension was not going to be tied into this contract and at risk after this contract expired. I responded more firmly: "Yes, we need to talk about this now!"

With this announcement I got up to leave the meeting, and without hesitation our union team followed suit right on my heels. The unspoken code of conduct finally played out perfectly: When the union president walks out of a meeting, all union reps follow suit! This was an awesome show of solidarity, and just when we needed it the most!

There was a breaker room by the stairwell that we used for our breakout caucuses during meetings when we wanted to speak without fear of management overhearing our conversation. I waited until Newbie, as the last one to leave the meeting, to finally show up before speaking on the proposed pension language change. I was addressing mostly him, but wanted everyone to understand my concern: "We cannot tie our pension into this contract with that language change. We have very strong language protecting our pension in our contract as it is right now. Do not change it."

Newbie listened and thought, and then spoke, "We are just trying to make it stronger."

I knew it would have been detrimental to our defined pension plan in the future if this proposed language change was made. I was adamant it was not changing, and everyone needed to understand why. I responded, "NO! We are putting our pension at risk by tying it into this contract with that language change."

I emphasized it again for good measure: "We have very strong language protecting our pension as it is right now. Do not change it! Leave it as it is!" I trusted the Lord that I made myself clear.

Alvin made a confession that I will never forget. He turned to Newbie first as he spoke, "I understand what you are saying."

Turning to me and back to Newbie, Alvin continued, "I understand what Angelika is saying."

Now Alvin admitted he was confused, "I don't know which way we should go."

By now, I wanted to believe that these men understood the wisdom God had given me in this position and in knowing, how documents were worded was so very important, and the detriment in changing long-standing and strong contract language.

Newbie looked around at everyone, and without saying another word, he headed out of this room and back into the meeting; we all followed suit.

We all sat there as Newbie asked Ferengi a question that floored me: "Do you think with our pension plan contract language as it is now, you can just take the union's pension away?"

Ferengi's contempt and arrogance for the union reared its ugly head again with his answer: "If I thought that I could just take the union's defined pension plan away without their approval, I would have done so."

BINGO! That was exactly what he did with our 401(k) company match benefit. I could only thank the Lord God that our pension plan contract language was not changed at all, but stayed exactly as it had been for many years of past contracts, which also outlined exactly how this benefit was calculated and paid.

I knew Ferengi well. I watched him leave this last meeting very visibly angry and agitated as the final blow, as he was not able to take away from this union what he so much desired—our defined pension plan. I thanked the Lord God for His touché.

Finally, we had a tentative agreement to recommend for a favorable ratification vote. I would like to believe that the informational contract letter that God had led me to write and send to all our union members asking for their support, made all the difference in keeping our pension intact. Our team knew we had their support, as did management while also receiving their copy of the letter through Jason.

During the union's tentative agreement meetings prior to our membership voting on ratifying our contract, I made sure to thank all our membership for their show of support while letting them know that without which, the outcome with our pension and our contract would have been much different. As much as my unpardonable-sin letter of agreement tore this union apart, this contract, along with the letter I sent, did the exact opposite. If ever I was proud in this union president position, it was then towards our membership for such an awesome show of solidarity. Our contract was overwhelmingly accepted by our membership. And again, I thanked God for everything.

It was during negotiations when we received the arbitrator's decision that my first discipline letter was going to be expunged from record as a win for the union. With negotiations over, we had the grievance meeting for my unethical-behavior discipline letter.

I had requested but was denied any opportunity to speak with Nancy or Trish myself as my accusers regarding the discrepancies of information presented in those hearsay emails, which everyone knew Sabrina took the lead on. The injustice continued with

Gremlin's arbitrary decision that violated our contract. There was no consideration given for my own defense for my action that I still believed was not wrong. Nothing was going to make a difference as to the outcome of this grievance.

By the arrogant demeanor of Ferengi and Jezebel at this grievance meeting, it was obvious this was only a formality with no intentions to move on their positions. And why should they when Newbie was governing behind the scenes supporting them? This was obvious with his predetermined decision several weeks earlier that I would be eating this discipline letter, something I was sure Ferengi and Jezebel also knew.

I had plenty of time to push for arbitration before this grievance meeting and once the grievance was officially denied. I had marked particular sections of Elkouri, Elkouri, How Arbitration Works, that could have been used for a favorable arbitration. Gremlin's arbitrary decision to violate our contractual time limits for hearing this grievance also made it a sure-to-win arbitration. It never seemed to bother Newbie that his newly trusted allies had no qualms about violating our contract in their disciplinary actions. I would experience this again before my career would end.

However, I knew that the Lord didn't want me to push for arbitration. I needed to be obedient and trust God in His direction, as He knew my future better than anyone else. The Lord God was still in control, and He knew in the grand scheme of His plan for my career and life, He would be working everything out for my best. (Romans 8:28.)

It wasn't long after this grievance meeting that elections for new union officers were scheduled. With a moved-up election month due to the completion of the transition of the new union merger, everyone's term in office was cut short by seven months. I knew I would be losing this election and did not want my name on the ballot. But it was never about what I wanted, but only about what the Lord God wanted. The Lord had another message to send out through all this—I was not the quitter.

My vice president, who I will name from this point forward as Pres, won the election for the next union president. He was one of the guys who lost when I was first elected union president in what seemed so long ago by this time. Chief won a second term as union chief shop steward, and Alvin won as vice president. Newbie was going to stay on as our staff rep.

For the most part, I was okay with being voted out. We just had a very successful contract with an awesome show of solidarity from our membership. I also had another life outside of this union and workplace that no one here knew about. And being put out of the warehouse and into the AST group with so much less work stress proved to be a special blessing. There were many, mostly the Darkly natives, who gloated at what they perceived as my misfortune with being bumped out of the warehouse. Yet, God had used everything in a powerful way for my best and according to His purpose.

I finished all my union president duties to the best of my ability. It took over six weeks to sort out all the paperwork I was always too busy to properly file in the plant union office, which was a mold-infested dump with crumbling walls in a warehouse that had seen better days many years ago. I will admit that there were times while going through all this paperwork that I just wanted to throw it all out and forget about everything. But I needed to finish well to the very end. Once I was satisfied with sorting everything, labeling the files, making a list of everything I labeled and where I was putting it in the union office, I was so glad to be done with it all.

But there were still two very important issues that needed addressed while still in this union president role before I swore in the new officers in May and handed over the gavel to Pres. I told Newbie that I was going to be the one to send out the union's response to my grievance answer for my unethical-behavior discipline letter for going through the HR recycle bin. I gave this response much prayer and time going over what I truly believed was led by God to send. I addressed my email to Ferengi, Jezebel and Gremlin, and copied Newbie.

In my response, I made sure everyone knew that not pursuing this grievance to arbitration was not an admittance of my guilt. I reiterated that my action to go through the HR paper recycle bin was fueled by the injustice of management, as they themselves violated our contract in their actions against another union member who I was legally obligated to represent.

I made it clear that over the years, I was not the one who was unethical or dishonest during my terms as union president while dealing with management or anyone else. I again protested the attached documents to defame my character, and reiterated I was denied the opportunity to address my accusers face to face over the discrepancies of the information in the hearsay emails used against me.

I stated that the vindictive harassment I had experienced by management over the years went beyond the boundaries of those at our plant site when Gremlin, senior company counsel and compliance officer, labeled my simple request to expunge the discipline letter prior to negotiations to be literally a federal crime.

I reiterated what everyone who was honest could not deny: My conviction to never receive nor expect any personal gain as union president was never compromised—I could never be bought.

I closed my email by stating that should this vindictive harassment and campaign to defame my character and terminate my employment not end, but continue even after I was out of the office of union president, I would deal with it through all legal avenues available. This proved to be a prophetic warning that would be reiterated in the near future before it came to pass.

No one responded, but I didn't expect them to. Document Princess had my final say while yet the union president. Afterward, I knew I could not get away with such an assertive email.

The last issue that needed taken care of was giving explicit instructions for my future protection to those who would be my union reps. This email was sent to Pres, Chief and Newbie. The subject matter was titled: "Future Request, Please Remember." The email went as follows:

"I am going to ask each of you that if at any time in the future, management approaches any of you saying they are going to terminate my employment, issue any other discipline letters to me, or throw me out of the plant for any reason, please, do not even discuss with them any plea bargains, or last-chance agreement letters, or anything else until we have a chance to talk first ourselves. This is only a 'just in case' request. I would really appreciate it if you would all remember this. Thanks."

My main purpose for sending out these explicit instructions to these union reps was obvious. I wanted the opportunity to have my side of the story heard before these union reps made any final judgment calls based only on what management would relay to them; recent past scenarios justified my concerns. I was just being vigilant, as I knew that target on me was not going away anytime soon—if it ever would. This email also proved more prophetic than I could have known or wanted.

However, as clear and as nice as I made these instructions, when they were needed, they were still misunderstood, and even used against me.

Chapter 91
Critical Safety Concern

Roles in life change often, even as circumstances change. This is true in families, businesses, unions—the list goes on. However, God never changes. God's purpose for those He has called will also never change, unless we willfully disobey His will through our own free will that He has so graciously given us.

Although I was no longer a union rep in any capacity, God had planned on using everything He had taught me through all those years since my knee injury, to accomplish His grand scheme for my career and life, as was proven at the end.

Anyone who had such strong assertiveness while utilizing the full legal authority offered to a labor union official, and then continued in the same work environment while no longer being legally protected through the labor laws from past concerted union activities, work could turn out to be downright hazardous.

After I was no longer president, I saw a real change in some salaried personnel who once showed me respect hoping for a good relationship with "the union president." There were some who never showed me respect but only tolerated my president role because they had to. And then there were the few who always showed me respect regardless of anything.

I stayed working as an AST for almost a full year. There were several different job duties as an AST, but the main duty was pumping black gook that was thick and stinky, out of the lagoon located on the far end of our plant site, and then into a nearby holding tank. This job duty was very important! The gook was constantly generated from the coal-fired power plant in our backyard. If the gook was not pumped out, it would find its way into another lagoon, and from there into the nearby river. If that happened it was not environmentally good.

Once this gook was pumped into the holding tank, other operators pressed out the water using special equipment, and then piled the solid gook in a mound to be hauled away later. This pumping task was always a two-person job that was secured for our own union workforce through the contracting out arbitrator's award language.

In the award brief, in management's defense, the arbitrator noted that management claimed this pumping task was once a contracting out job that they gave back to the union workforce. With this in writing in an arbitrator's award, management knew better than to contract this job out again. Although we lost the arbitration as a whole, I had satisfaction that we at least saved two jobs in the process.

The original Stone Age wooden raft that floated out in the middle of the lagoon was equipped with a pump and hose. While one AST stayed on the raft to operate the pump, a second AST monitored the flow by the tank. By the time I was an AST, this wooden raft was replaced with a more sophisticated and very expensive 21st-century remote control boat called the "flumper." This flumper could be operated safely from the shore or tank area while pumping the gook into the tank. Any kid would love playing with this remote-control boat!

With his new flumper toy, Dominic, the company's prized AST and Darkly native, would do this pumping task on his own, thus giving management the impression that it should only be done with one AST. When I came on the scene, I repeatedly emphasized the still existing safety concerns with only one person being there alone, but no one seemed to care. Thus, another union member was responsible for the union losing another job position.

Virgil was the supervisor in charge of the flumper lagoon area and activities, and often tried to blame me for any malfunctions of the flumper boat, even when Dominic was the last to use it. Virgil would also accuse me of not being diligent with my flumper duties; although I was very conscientious in my effort to be the best flumper-operator there ever was.

As a matter of fact, Virgil always seemed to go out of his way to find fault with any job I did. He was a salaried supervisor who never showed me any respect as union president, and now seemed more intent on showing his disdain for me. (Virgil's wife, Loraine, was part of the performance review saga during my first term as president.) Virgil was also a supervisor in charge of different projects throughout the plant site, and was well known for putting completion of his projects ahead of any safety concerns.

Although another AST job duty was assisting on plant-wide projects that Virgil was often in charge of, Rita was the direct supervisor of the AST group, and would send out our job duties via email. When Rita emailed Virgil's request for an AST to be "hole-watch attendant" the following day on a project, she specifically asked that I be the one to assist him.

The duties of hole-watch attendant were safety-critical with the responsibility for someone else's life while they worked in a confined space hole, such as inside a reactor or other confined space hole. I had the hole-watch attendant computer safety training, but never remembered performing this job in the field.

In preparation for this assignment, I printed off the plant-wide procedure for "confined space entry" (which was way overdue for review) that consisted of thirteen pages, which also outlined the responsibilities for hole-watch attendant—and I was so glad I did.

OSHA, as a federal agency, also had mandated procedures and regulations regarding confined space entry work that our plant-wide procedures were supposed to abide by to ensure the safety of all the workers involved and who worked in the areas.

I reviewed this confined space entry plant procedure thoroughly, and made sure I understood everything that I was going to be responsible for while working as hole-watch attendant. With the timing being less than four weeks out from no longer being union president, and being sure that target on me had not gone away just yet, I was taking no chances. Any infraction or deviation from following a safety-critical procedure to the letter justified immediate termination of employment. But more of a concern than my employment was my responsibility for someone else's life while they worked in a confined space hole.

Prior to any worker (entrant) entering the confined space hole, the air inside the hole was tested at different levels with a special monitoring device to ensure there was a safe oxygen level, and to ensure there were no atmosphere hazards from chemicals or combustible gases. During the entire time the entrant(s) were working in the confined space hole, the air was constantly monitored using the same monitoring device. Should this monitoring device alarm, the entrant(s) were to immediately exit the confined space hole.

The primary task of the hole-watch attendant was to "ensure the well-being of those inside the confined space." This included "maintaining visual and/or verbal communications with the entrant(s)" at all times while inside the confined space hole. Should there be any emergencies, the hole-watch attendant was to immediately notify the entrant(s) to exit the confined space hole.

The confined space entry procedure also made it very clear that the hole-watch attendant was "required to perform non-entry rescue" should the entrant need to be pulled out of the confined space hole. This non-entry rescue was done using a retrieval device that was attached to the entrant(s) by way of a harness and lanyard worn by the entrant(s) during the entire time they were working in the confined space hole. With this retrieval device, if a worker became unconscious or disabled, they could be immediately pulled out of the confined space hole without danger to the hole-watch attendant.

It was management's responsibility to ensure each hole-watch attendant was trained and familiar with using the retrieval device to safely perform this non-entry rescue. Only specially trained personnel were permitted to actually enter the confined space to physically rescue entrant(s) should there be a need. There have been fatalities in workplaces when one worker entered a confined space to rescue another unconscious worker, and after entering was overcome by what affected the unconscious worker.

After reviewing the OSHA regulation and the plant confined space entry procedure outlining everything I just shared, with all this responsibility for someone else's life heavy on my heart, I had a really hard time sleeping the night before. My main concern was that I needed to know how to use this retrieval device. I knew I would not be able to live with myself should my negligence be the cause of someone losing their life.

I went to my new assigned area for my duties as hole-watch attendant the following morning as I was supposed to. Present inside the department's control room where this area belonged were two union members working: Jerome, a former e-board member and one of the initiators of the work permit; and Rick, who just happened to be the area union shop steward. The two outside contractors, who were going to be doing the actual work, were also present.

For every job assignment, a work permit was issued outlining pertinent information for both the workers doing the job and those in the areas, which had to be signed. These work permits had OSHA mandated requirements to list all equipment that would otherwise pose a hazard to workers working on or around them, and to indicate all their energy sources that were locked out and/or tagged out. This was to ensure that no equipment could inadvertently be operated and by doing so, harm someone. (This OSHA lockout/tagout requirement did not exist when my dad was killed working his safety critical job.) Other pertinent information mandated to be on work permits for confined space entry outlined the requirements for the hole-watch attendant, including the retrieval device for non-entry rescue.

It wasn't long before Virgil showed up at the control room to get everyone signed off on the work permit, including me. When I saw the retrieval device checked off on the permit, I didn't want to sign this permit until I was trained using this device. This training was another OSHA mandated requirement. Not only was it very important how these work permits were worded, signatures on these were significant.

I approached Virgil with my concerns about the responsibility for non-entry rescue: "I need hands-on training with the retrieval device for non-entry rescue."

Virgil's response was his usual nonchalant concern for safety: "You don't need to worry about non-entry rescue."

I wondered: *Does he not know how the procedure is worded? Does he not know OSHA's mandated requirements?*

I tried again making it clearer this time: "The confined space entry procedure specifically states that it is my responsibility as hole-watch attendant to perform non-entry rescue, and in order to do that I need trained on this retrieval device."

Virgil got visibly agitated and stated in an angry demeanor with his voice raised, "I told you that you do not need to worry about non-entry rescue."

Virgil wasn't getting it! As a matter of fact, I started thinking he just didn't care about what this procedure stated. I knew if push came to shove, Virgil would never admit to telling me that I didn't need to worry about non-entry rescue should any entrant(s) need rescued out of the confined space hole while on my watch.

Jerome and Rick quickly vacated the control room when they witnessed this conversation turning into a confrontation; they didn't want involved as witnesses.

I stood my ground against Virgil. I was not going to sign this work permit until my concerns were addressed. If Virgil insisted that I did not need to worry about non-entry rescue, then I wanted that in writing for my own protection and told him so: "Then we need a variance."

A variance was another document that would need drafted and signed by several higher supervisors, including Ferengi as the plant manager, explaining why a deviation from a safety-critical procedure was being permitted. As soon as I mentioned this variance, Virgil turned away in hot anger, walked around the desk to the phone, and contacted Monica, the plant safety supervisor.

I had dealings with Monica before. Ever since I filed that OSHA complaint when I was refused copies of the OSHA 300 logs in the time limit required while being the workers' comp rep, she always showed me a lot of respect; today was to prove the same. Calling Monica was the correct avenue to address my concerns. Once Monica was contacted, no further discussion with Virgil on the issue should have happened—but it did.

After contacting Monica, Virgil went to the control room door and holding it open, spoke in a commanding and mean tone: "Angelika, come out here; I want to talk to you."

By now, my defense mode was on full alert. I knew better and held my ground again. I had done nothing wrong, and this man was not intimidating me. Without hesitation, I refused his unlawful order to leave the control room to be alone with him: "I'm not going out there one-on-one with you."

Virgil came back into the control room still visibly angry and started berating me in front of the contractors: "I want you to be professional and courteous. I do not want you to deliberately delay the start of this project."

I responded, "Tell me how I have not been professional or courteous? I am not trying to delay this project. The confined space entry procedure clearly states that I am responsible for non-entry rescue. And I have every right to request and expect training on this retrieval device to safely perform my duties as hole-watch attendant."

This ended our confrontation.

During all this time, the two contractors, which included the man whose life I was going to be responsible for out in the field working in the confined space hole, were witnessing this exchange between Virgil and me; neither one said a word.

Once Monica met me in the field, she addressed my concerns to where I was satisfied, and only then did I sign the work permit.

However, Virgil's anger while trying to resolve a major safety concern was disconcerting. I wasn't concerned so much for myself with his behavior. My major concern was for new employees who would be put into the AST group, and who may be intimidated by such anger from Virgil or any supervisor that they may not bring up safety concerns that they should with job duties they would be unfamiliar with.

Since I was still on the plant-wide procedure committee that Ferengi was in charge of, I contacted him with my concerns that a safety-critical procedure was so overdue for review, and also requested a meeting with Virgil to address his actions. I made a direct request that I did not want Jezebel to be part of this meeting. I wanted Virgil present because it was important that he heard what I had to say, and had the opportunity to speak in his own defense—a courtesy that I was often denied.

Chapter 92
Mockery Meeting

There were many personnel issues that had come up that needed dealt with while I was union president. According to specific contract language: "The union agrees that it will cooperate with the company in its efforts to promote harmony among all the employees in the plant."

Through the years, I found that management took this language one-sided. While they expected the union's cooperation, many times management was the cause of the conflict.

One particular department had union members in constant conflict with each other. The instigator was Ferengi and his insistence that each department's trainer/production tech job classifications were in the same category as salaried supervisors. This only caused conflict among union employees, as Ferengi insisted that those in these roles were responsible for the work of the other union employees in their departments. I tried in vain several times to address this wrong expectation with Ferengi.

When Ferengi and Jezebel escorted a union employee from this same department out of the plant as a fear tactic, I made it clear that at no time should management escort any union member out of the plant without a union rep present. This was for their own protection, as well as for the protection of the employee and the union.

The company also had a "conflict resolution" process that was used for trying to resolve personnel issues between employees who couldn't seem to get along, but each employee had to agree to this process. During this process, meetings were held between the employees involved with each being allowed to have a "coach" of their choosing to be present as a witness.

When I requested the issue with Virgil be addressed, Jezebel sent out a meeting notice under the guise of this conflict resolution process. When I protested stating that this was management intimidation and not a personnel conflict, Jezebel just blew me off while stating we needed to provide an opportunity to hear both sides. That was my reasoning when I requested Virgil be present. But I just couldn't seem to remember Jezebel ever caring to hear my side of a story when it was against me!

Jezebel was a different person than anyone I ever met. There were a few times she would boast during meetings about her "tough" upbringing in the inner city of Pittsburgh. I wanted to challenge her to compare stories with my South Bronx upbringing. But she was never someone I felt comfortable with sharing anything apart from what was needed in our respective roles.

During this meeting, Jezebel was present against my request that she not be present, stating in a mockery tone that she was there as Virgil's coach. Chief was present as my union rep—not as my coach. Sabrina was officiating the meeting on behalf of HR.

Jezebel and Virgil were focusing on making this out to be a personnel conflict, which was Jezebel's goal all along. I brought up my concern of intimidation by Virgil while trying to address a major safety concern, expressing this needed addressed so it did not happen again with anyone else at the plant site, especially with new employees. But as usual, everyone just blew me off.

Jezebel then went into her HR leader role with a different approach: She tried making it out to be a poor work performance issue on my part. Chief wasn't willing to say anything, let alone in my defense.

I then spoke more firmly, as my former union president role came out automatically: "Jezebel, do not make this out to be a work performance issue on my part. It was a supervisor trying to intimidate an employee, who was trying to address a major safety concern. Virgil had absolutely no right to order me out of the control room for a one-on-one confrontation. Once Monica was contacted, there should have been no further discussions with Virgil on the issue."

At the end of the meeting, Sabrina asked me if I had any assurance that Virgil would not put anyone else in harm's way. I answered truthfully: "NO! I do not have any assurance that he will not put someone else in harm's way."

I referenced another major incident when Virgil ignored the safety of employees while focusing only on getting his project completed. Chief never said a word during this entire meeting. Maybe Jezebel had him convinced this really was a conflict resolution meeting, and he was just the coach instead of a union rep? It may not have made any difference either way.

When we left there, I was more upset with Chief's silence than anything else at that point and told him so: "Why didn't you say anything, not even in my defense?"

He gave his lame excuse: "You were speaking well for yourself. You didn't need me to say anything."

I was exasperated with this man! I had always tried my best over the years to be patient with him, even as much as he had hurt me, and to help and encourage him to be a good union rep. I responded hoping my tone was soft enough not to light his fuse, but I also wanted to make my point: "But I am not the union president anymore! Do you think it was appropriate for Virgil to order me out of the control room for a one-on-one confrontation?"

He was sheepish now: "No."

"Then you could have said so."

I then explained what I knew he did not understand of the situation: "I was a woman who would not back down from a male supervisor trying to intimidate me in front of other men. And Virgil did not like that at all."

This was the end of the conversation, but not the end of the issue. No one properly addressed this major safety concern and management intimidation issue to my satisfaction that this would not happen to anyone else. I emailed Jezebel and asked for the outcome of our meeting. Her response only showed her contempt towards me was still very much alive: "You and Virgil told two very different versions of the incident, and it was clear that we would NOT be able to reach agreement on the events that took place."

Again, I thought back to several years of dealing with Jezebel, and I just could not seem to remember her ever letting an issue go that was against me because of two different versions of a story. Management often changed the rules to suit them, especially when it involved an employee with a target on the most-wanted list.

As a result of everyone's nonchalant attitude toward this whole incident, I wrote to Herschel (still the VP of our company) explaining the entire situation and what my concerns were for others, especially new employees who may end up dealing with such management intimidation when trying to address valid safety concerns. It was three days later before Herschel responded.

In Herschel's email, he expressed that he spent several hours over the last two days investigating the issue, and believes everything that could have been done to address this was done. He further suggested that if I have ongoing concerns, I should raise the issues with my International Union leadership, Newbie.

He then forwarded his email with a note to Newbie while copying Pres, Chief, Ferengi, and Jezebel: "Dear Newbie. Following up on discussions you had with Jezebel, the following is my reply to Angelika Mitikas."

I always liked Herschel. At least he replied and copied me on his email to Newbie. But I was so angry reading his confirmation that Jezebel and Newbie once again had their conversations about me—without me. It was long after this issue was over when Chief finally confided to me: Jezebel told Newbie that I initially refused to do the hole-watch attendant duties. Just another example of her fabricated dramas to defame my character. And apparently, Newbie never cared enough to hear my side of the story, as he ignored my attempt to contact him.

While I was so angry over my union reps' lack of support in dealing with such a major safety concern, I wanted to write another email just to Newbie confronting him on his reneged offer he once gave me, that I could contact him at any time for his help.

However, when the Lord directed me to let it go—I let it go. Unbeknown to me at the time, the Lord had a touché response that He would lead me to send, but only in His timing.

Two days later during my morning quiet time, the Lord gave me the perfect response back vindicating my actions in this whole saga. I typed it out and sent it to Herschel and everyone he had copied on his email. Attached to my email was a scanned document that was posted all over the plant site of the safety mission statement. On this document were the signatures of Ferengi, Loraine (Virgil's wife), and Herschel with their invitation to not hesitate to contact any of them or a supervisor with any safety concerns. I wanted everyone to read and reference this document as justification that my contact with Herschel was at his invitation. My email was as follows:

"Dear Mr. Herschel: I would be remiss if I did not acknowledge with grateful appreciation your time and attention to this issue, honoring your commitment to safety, and honoring your invitation per the safety mission statement attached to contact you for any safety concerns anyone may have.

"It is unfortunate that the contractor, whose life I was responsible for, was not contacted to get his perspective as to the events that took place the morning of this incident, as he would not have had any pre-judgments on anyone involved; he would not have had any reasons to lie; and he would not have had any fear of speaking the truth.

"No one was grasping the seriousness of this incident. I believe that my main goal in contacting you was accomplished, which was having more assurance that this type of management intimidation was not going to happen again to anyone else who would be trying to bring forward a safety concern. My sincere concern for the safety and well-being of everyone at this plant site always ran deep, and was never connected to any union 'title'. Thank you again for all you have done. Please take care."

By copying everyone that Herschel had copied on his email to me, it was a touché that I knew was from the Lord God. I've never regretted waiting on God's timing and direction before moving forward on an issue. I never heard back from anyone. It took a long time before Chief would even speak to me after he read this email.

This major safety concern would not be the last one I would have that was not addressed properly, either by management or my union reps.

While still on the plant-wide procedure committee, I was part of the review and revision of the confined space entry procedure, and I made sure that the wording addressed my concerns of training for any retrieval device that any future hole-watch attendants may need. How these documents for procedures were worded was so very important.

Chapter 93
Work Goes On

I I really wanted to continue my employment peacefully by just going to work, doing any job conscientiously, and then go home leaving everything behind. This was not always possible just coming out of spending two terms as union president. I realized soon after I was voted out, Newbie considered me an annoyance he hoped would go away with many indications of this.

At one time, I had asked Newbie and Chief to address the actions of Jezebel purposely circulating a document that was clearly a draft, yet implied that I had agreed to it while president when I had not. Chief and Newbie refused to address this upon my request. So, I addressed it by sending a very respectful email to Jezebel. I politely asked that she and other HR salaried personnel to "please, be more ethically responsible in the future when handling sensitive documents" that they have been entrusted with that concerned the union, or me as past president.

Newbie and Chief had a heated conversation with me after Jezebel sent them my email. Newbie rebuked me again for speaking for myself, and then angrily added while referring to Jezebel: "You will not be satisfied until you have her job."

That was a real biased judgment call against me! Who was in the position to fire whom? And whose side was paying him with union dues for representation anyway? Good grief, Document Queen had a ton of documents that involved me. Someone had to address her unethical and unprofessional actions; my union reps sure didn't want to. This was only one example, and would not be the last time these union reps opposed me in favor of management.

As I continued working my lowly AST job, my break room and lunch area were in a run-down old building that housed the Liquid Handler Department. This department handled most of the dangerous liquid chemicals coming into the plant site, such as styrene and pentane, with responsibilities to unload these from railcars, tanker trucks and river barges.

There were two union employees working in this department. Lucinda was in this department for years, while Arnold, a Darkly native, had bid into this department before the shutdown. Arnold initially trained me as a Darkly chem tech, and we got along well. But now, he too had strong ill feelings towards me while blaming me for the shutdown. Some things were never forgotten!

For years, styrene was brought into the plant via river barges that were unloaded into field tanks two to three times a month. It took three handlers one full shift to unload styrene from one river barge. This was changed when those in this department no longer wanted the responsibility of being certified with the Coast Guard for unloading river barges. This was another example of union employees giving away their own work. After this change, two handlers unloaded styrene river barges, while a sub-contractor certified with the Coast Guard was called in to be the third person.

I had asked Lucinda at one time while I was president, if she needed or wanted me to try to get more people in this department. She was adamant that the two of them were handling everything well. Going back many years, this department was supplemented with our labor group as helpers. Then years later, this labor group was replaced with the AST job description.

When I became an AST, this group was still helping this department—only as needed—with a menial but very important task as the second person with monitoring the styrene going into the field tank while these river barges were unloaded. With me now being in the same building and helping with the river barge unloading, I got to know Lucinda so much better.

Lucinda was a Christian sister who I respected and cared for. There were conflicts over the years in this department involving Lucinda and different other employees, as well as supervisors, that I was part of resolving as president per our contract harmony agreement. I always tried to be neutral, and gave everyone an opportunity to share his or her side of the story. People are different, and some you just never get to know until you really get to know them.

It was the summer after the union officers' election that management approached the union wanting to add all the rail job duties of the warehouse into the Liquid Handler Department. This decision was based on the new styrene-railcar unloading project, which was a huge undertaking, very expensive, and drastically changed how styrene was handled on the plant site. Instead of styrene being shipped into the plant via river barges, it was shipped via railcars. This lessened the amount of time for a turnover on the funds for a more profitable way to buy styrene.

But in order to keep up with the demands of styrene, four railcars needed unloaded each day, as compared to two to three barges each month. The best benefit was that it allowed for the warehouse rail job duties to be moved into a higher wage job classification, and added two more positions in the Liquid Handler Department paying these higher wages. The handler job was also considered the cream-of-the-crop job in our plant. It was not a plant pool position, and had the preferred daylight schedule.

My adamant refusal as president over the years, and during our last contract negotiations, to add the rail job duties into the AST job description while hoping to gain a higher wage in the future for such a skilled safety-critical job, finally paid off. Only God would have known while I was only following His direction!

I understood then the providential timing of God in allowing the terms for union officers to be cut short. Had I still been the president, I would have been reluctant to agree to the addition of the rail job duties into this department, and for only one reason: It was very probable that I would be awarded one of these job positions through the job bidding process. God knew I never wanted any personal gain, or anything remotely perceived as a personal gain, through my role as president, and He avoided me being part of this decision. God is so faithful in orchestrating everything in my life for my best, and according to His purpose.

While the union and management negotiated this decision all summer, it wasn't until November that an agreement was finalized. Just afterward, there was an incident that involved Jezebel throwing Lucinda out of the plant. I heard Lucinda's side of the story, spoke some with Chief, and knew enough about Jezebel. But there were some particulars I knew were still unknown to me.

Lucinda and I kept in contact after she reported off on sick leave due to this incident, and I tried my best to help her while she was so upset. During this time, Lucinda said she would consider bidding on the handler job added to her department to get out of her current role as trainer/production tech. She confided in me that she believed it was her job responsibilities that caused her so much trouble through the years. This was not the first significant incident that resulted with her being disciplined.

It was in December when the two handler job bids were posted. The added rail job duties deterred most from bidding on these positions. I was the oldest who received the first job award. Samson from the warehouse was awarded the second job.

While Lucinda was still off, I told her that if she decided to take the handler position when she returned, I would consider bidding on her job. I confided that I didn't think I was capable of working the rails for the long-term. Most of Lucinda's job responsibilities involved less physical work. Unbeknown to me at that time, I inadvertently planted a seed in Lucinda's mind that grew to agitate some inner struggles I later understood she had. Had I known about her inner struggles, I never would have spoken to her at all about the job bids, let alone bidding on her job.

Audrey was the head of both the Logistic Department and the Liquid Handler Department. Nabal was the Liquid Handler Department's first-line supervisor. As great as Henry was as a first-line boss in the warehouse and how well we got along, Nabal was the complete opposite, and loved to flex his muscles showing he was the big boss. With having the former union president in his department, he seemed to flex his muscles even more.

From the very beginning, there were major training issues with everyone in this department. My advice given to Pres, Chief, and Newbie, when he later got involved, to speak to those currently working in both departments on these jobs for their input before agreeing to this was ignored. Chief told me later that the union was sworn to secrecy over negotiating this; although he kept me somewhat in the loop behind the scenes. My suggestion to post these jobs for bidding earlier that would have alleviated most of the training issues was also ignored.

Lucinda and Arnold knew the handler jobs, but had no experience on the rails. Samson was certified on the rails, but knew nothing about the handler jobs. I needed re-certified on the rails since I hadn't worked that job for over a year, and knew only part of the river barge unloading of the handler jobs. However, my experience working in Darkly while dealing with pumps and valves and piping configurations proved to be of great advantage to me in the handler job.

It was very chaotic and stressful in that department during this time. This was just another example of the mismanagement culprit that existed at this industrial chemical plant site.

Chapter 94
Initial Issues

The union had agreed with management that Tara, the warehouse trainer/production tech, would be part of the rail job training for at least two more years; neither she nor Lucinda were very happy about this arrangement. Lucinda was anxious to get Tara away from training people in her department, and anxious I get re-certified on the rails to achieve this. As the Liquid Handler Department trainer/production tech, Lucinda was possessive with her job duties. I was also anxious to get re-certified on the rails, but for the reason to be available for the handler training that I needed more.

While training on the rails for this re-certification, Tara watched me almost make a major blunder that would have been a significant incident. I was sure Tara would have stopped me before making this blunder had I not realized it first. Afterward, I apologized to Tara for trying to rush my re-certification.

It wasn't too long after this that Lucinda accused me of stalling on my re-certification and threatened me: "It will not go well with you if you don't re-certify on the rails soon."

Wow, I didn't at all care for that threat! I responded, "What do you mean it won't go well with me?"

Arnold instantly took Lucinda by the arm and practically dragged her out of the handler building without allowing her to answer my question, leaving me there dumbfounded and angry.

I had prayed for and really wanted a position in this department ever since the announcement of the Darkly shutdown. When I was finally awarded this handler job, I was so excited and looking forward to working my last several years with a Christian sister that I respected and cared about. The threat that Lucinda just threw at me was not the Lucinda I knew. This was only a glimpse of the revelation of her inner struggles, and the beginning of our working struggles.

Going back in history: In my first year as union president, I did a re-evaluation of Lucinda's job description and title, and after a considerable effort on my part, I was able to get recognition of her responsibilities to justify the higher trainer/production tech wage. Ferengi's position that these trainer/production tech roles were in the same category as salaried supervisors never changed.

I maintained and voiced my objection, even out of the office of president, that union employees were not to be in roles as salaried supervisors, nor take any responsibility for those in their department for how work was done or not done. I tried in vain several times to get Ferengi and others to understand this.

It was this very issue that caused personnel conflicts within the one department that Ferengi and Jezebel decided as a scare tactic to escort out of the plant a union employee. When I found out what they did after the fact, I made it clear to them while still president with Chief as witness, that at no time should a union employee be asked to leave the plant without a union rep present.

Now, several years after getting Lucinda's role recognized as a union trainer/production tech, I was dealing with her attitude in what her job titled morphed into. Only Lucinda took her role to more extremes. There were times that she would give work direction that was in direct conflict with what Nabal was directing, and I was caught in the crossfire. Any initiative on my part in getting training or doing my jobs on or off the rails was squashed by both Lucinda and Nabal, as they both believed everything must be channeled through Lucinda first, even regardless of her own inexperience with the rail job.

I also discovered early on after I came into this department, Lucinda was habitual with speaking with Nabal and supervisors one-on-one about issues she had with others, particularly me. I walked in on her conversations more than once without purposely meaning to while she told her one-sided stories.

When I realized I was not getting the handler training opportunities that should have been available, I approached Lucinda about it. Her suggestion was for me to speak with Nabal regarding my training issues. While knowing her attitude only aggravated the training issues, I told her it was not my practice to speak to supervisors on such matters. I realized soon enough that Lucinda just didn't want to train me on this job, even though that was her main responsibility.

This became so obvious when we were all supposed to meet at the new styrene-railcar unloading rack for training to learn the process as it was being put into service. Lucinda and Arnold had already received some training prior to this day. I arrived on the platform before anyone else had and waited for the others to show up. Lucinda saw me standing on the platform as she was walking towards the rack. When I saw her, I radioed with a light heart that I was just waiting for her expertise in showing me how to unhook the piping.

She radioed back: "Ange, I'm not training you on the styrene-railcar unloading rack. This is Arnold's and my area."

I didn't respond. I didn't know what to say. This was now my area too. Soon Samson, Nabal and Virgil showed up, as Virgil was also in charge of this project. When I saw Samson go on the actual railcar to be shown the unhooking, I just followed along ignoring Lucinda, who by then was on the platform and gave me some dirty looks as I walked past her. But I was determined to learn this job with or without her help.

Nabal monitored this radio conversation between us, as he did all our radio conversations, as did everyone else present. When he reached the platform, he asked me if anything was wrong. I just looked at him and kept my thoughts to myself. *Why are you asking me anything when you heard everything?*

Nabal had a bad habit of instigating an already bad situation, when he could have very easily addressed the issue as he was supposed to without my input against Lucinda. But he wasn't that type of supervisor. As a matter of fact, his supervisory position was only a stepping stone to move up the ladder in the company, but he was smashing his stepping stone to smithereens. I wasn't going to speak to Nabal about what he just heard and already knew. However, things changed drastically once a major safety issue happened later on.

It was obvious that Samson was given preferential handler training while I was pushed aside. After a few months in this department, he took his test for the next level and higher wage the last day he worked before going out for sick leave for surgery, which gave him the higher pay while he was off work. Now I understood his preferential training. No one told me about this. No one was telling me anything. While Samson was gone, we worked with one less person in the department, which caused the brunt of the ground-person rail job responsibilities to fall on me.

Tara tried training Lucinda for the ground-person duties for only a short time at the beginning of when the rail job was added to this department. This came to an abrupt halt when Lucinda decided the ground-person duties was not a job she wanted to do.

The ground-person was the eyes of the locomotive driver. The only time a locomotive driver should disobey the direction of the ground-person was if there was a hazard unknown to the ground-person. For years, the ground-person made the priorities as to how railcars were moved while taking into consideration the needs of the plant. This always worked well, and with good reasons.

One railcar move could take well over an hour to complete depending on where the railcar was in the plant. Factors involved how many railcars needed moved while shuffling back and forth on different tracks to dig out the one needed. Each railcar left on another track to shuffle one out needed their hand brakes applied on and off while doing this shuffling. If these railcar moves were not done in a good thought-out order, it could easily cause more physical work for the ground-person, and a longer time to make the move.

Samson and I always worked well together on the rails. While I was the ground-person, he would make suggestions on the moves that I would often take to heart. I recognized he had more experience on the rails than I did. The final decision was always left to the ground-person.

Lucinda and I started out working well together on the rails. I understood her learning curve and was patient. But as the weeks went on, she started to get an attitude against me for some reason, and then started to refuse to follow my directions when I was the ground-person. This was a major safety concern of mine.

If Lucinda didn't follow my directions, someone could get seriously injured or killed, or a serious incident could happen. My life was in jeopardy the most, as I was the one going in between these railcars dealing with the couplers, connecting the air hoses in a precarious position, jumping on and off while engaging and disengaging hand brakes, and walking alongside the rail tracks.

Lucinda was never able to understand that it was imperative she followed the directions of the ground-person while she was driving the locomotive, or just didn't want to understand. With her attitude, my safety concerns grew, and I knew at some point they were going to need addressed.

Chapter 95

Tormented Heart

The unsafe issues while working in this handler job just compounded on top of each other. It was not only while working the rails that I had some major safety concerns.

Pentane was a dangerous liquid chemical that was used throughout the plant site in the manufacturing processes. The pentane-railcar unloading process was primitive compared to the new styrene-railcar unloading process. While unloading pentane-railcars, disconnecting the piping afterward with the way they were attached would cause a significant amount of pentane to spill over the railcar and on the ground. This was always a major safety concern of mine.

When I questioned this process during my training, it was blown off from being a safety concern with the explanation that it didn't matter; pentane eventually evaporates, so there was no safety concern. *But what about before it evaporates?*

Pentane and its vapors are very flammable. One spark and you were gone. This happened once years ago at this plant. There was almost nothing left to the worker who was unloading the pentane-railcar after it burst into flames with him on top.

Even while sampling a pentane-railcar after unhooking the sample tube, there was a small amount of pentane left there with nowhere to go. When Arnold first showed me how to sample a pentane-railcar, he took the sample bottle after filling it and just swished out the extra pentane that was left in the sample hole—over the railcar and on the ground it went.

I did bring this sampling procedure to the attention of a safety person, hoping that the piping would be replaced with the same newer sampling process like the styrene-railcars had to avoid this spillage, but this backfired. The result of bringing up this spillage was to cause everyone more work by soaking the amount left in the sample hole with rags. Now we had a different safety concern with more work while dealing with rags soaked with pentane. Arnold and Lucinda liked me even less—if that were possible—after bringing up this sample spillage safety concern.

When it was time for my first solo for certification for unloading a tanker truck with another liquid chemical, I had a traumatizing incident. With being excited and nervous just a little with doing this by myself, I wanted to make sure everything was done perfectly. I wanted no incidents at all, especially with that target still on me.

After telling the truck driver to wait till I came back before doing anything, I made the long journey to Beady to sign the area permit log, which informed them that I was in their area, and signed on my work permit for unloading the truck. Signing these documents were mandated plant-wide procedures required for anyone involved with unloading a liquid chemical truck in any department area.

When I came back to the truck, Arnold was there and had started the unloading process without my knowledge. I almost always appreciated help from coworkers, but this was my solo. And besides, Arnold didn't sign the department area permit log or the work permit.

In addition, Arnold purposely bypassed the air regulator valve that was supposed to control the air pressure going into the truck that was used to push out the chemical. He also told the truck driver to connect the pressured air to his truck before hooking up his own hoses for unloading. Everything Arnold did thus far were safety infractions that violated our safety procedures, and if they became known, would get him fired.

When I saw everything that Arnold had already done, I was very upset. But because I didn't want to get into a confrontation with Arnold for helping, and I didn't want him fired, I just continued with the unloading. As I geared up with my protective chemical suit that included face shield, rubber boots and gloves while my back was facing the truck a few feet away, I heard a loud explosive noise.

Turning to the truck, I saw the driver splashed all over with this dangerous chemical due to having the pressured air put on the truck without being regulated. Thankfully, this driver was also wearing his protective chemical suit. I directed him to the safety shower so he could shower off the chemical from his suit. *This solo is not turning out well at all!*

Per plant procedure, all incidents must be reported as soon as possible. If I didn't report this and it became known, I could be fired for not reporting it. *But how can I report this incident without lying, and without getting Arnold in trouble for all his safety infractions?* I was traumatized over this whole incident!

Lucinda, who should have been watching my solo, finally came around to check on me. When she saw Arnold was helping and that he bypassed the air regulator valve, she too was upset.

When I finished unloading this truck, I sent an email to Nabal afterward without elaborating, but also without lying. I told Nabal that the driver was splashed with the chemical, but since he was wearing his chemical suit, he was able to shower off without any negative effects. No questions were asked later. I believed that because Arnold was involved, Lucinda didn't push the issue.

I was finding myself constantly vigilant over everything I was doing, trying to make sure I didn't do anything that could be used detrimentally against me, which made my job very difficult and stressful. I was constantly tormented with everything going on and my safety concerns, believing that something bad was going to happen while working this job—I was so sure of it.

I was also very disappointed that things were not going well between Lucinda and me. My expectations of working with a fellow sister in Christ were blown apart. I brought all this to the Lord Jesus in prayer: "Lord, what am I doing wrong, or what can I do differently to make this working relationship work?"

Soon after this prayer, the Lord gave me an understanding of the inner struggles Lucinda was having with my presence and being told she must train me to learn "her" job. Remembering over the years when I was the union president with situations involving Lucinda and personnel issues, at least two of them involved other employees needing training or helping her with her job. Lucinda had told me once years ago, that it was to her benefit to know things about her job that others did not know.

Lucinda was possessive with her knowledge, and always reluctant to share her knowledge with others, even when supervision told her to do so. She also seemed convinced that I was a threat to her, her job and "her" department. This was evident by some of the things she said and did to me. There were other deeper inner struggles she was dealing with that I do not feel the Lord would have me share.

With what the Lord had shown me, I knew I needed to be more patient and understanding with Lucinda, and asked for His help to do this. However, I wasn't always patient with Lucinda, I will admit this. There were times that she would not stop arguing long enough to hear my side of reason, but I was trying.

I tried speaking to Lucinda about how I prayed to the Lord and shared my prayer with her concerning our working relationship. I told her it was between her and Jesus whether she prayed the same. She just seemed to close herself up from hearing anything I was saying.

I so much wanted to learn all I could about this new job. While training in Darkly, I learned that there were times you just have to go along with the older folks and watch to learn. With this thought in mind, I tried to follow Lucinda when she went out to do some of the handler jobs when I wasn't busy on the rails.

When I showed up one day while she was doing something that was part of our job, I saw she became visibly upset by my presence. Trying to be patient with her, I told her I didn't mean to upset her with my presence, but I just wanted to learn what she was doing. She explained that she thought I was on the rails. I left not too long after this.

Another incident happened when Nabal gave me permission to watch Lucinda unload a chemical truck that rarely came in. When I showed up, she again became visibly upset with my presence, even knowing I was coming with Nabal's permission. Before starting the unloading process, Lucinda took off in the department pickup truck. After waiting for some time, I decided to radio her asking if she was coming back for the unloading. Arnold answered for her: "Yes, and Arnold's coming with her."

I couldn't wait too much longer, as I needed to get to the other two trucks that I knew how to unload by that time. Nabal came to me later and asked if I saw the unloading with Lucinda. He monitored our radio conversations! My response was short: "No." When he asked me why, I made it short again and to the point: "She left and I couldn't wait any longer. I had other trucks to take care of."

On another work delay, Nabal questioned me as to why a department had to shut down because of a rail move that wasn't made. I explained the entire situation in the best way I knew how while knowing this one was of no fault of ours. Nabal made matters worse when he later questioned Lucinda as well.

It was shortly after this that Nabal told me he knew there were issues between Lucinda and me, and offered for Chief or HR to get involved. I realized by then how he instigated issues and was making matters worse. So I finally spoke to him about Lucinda:

"I was dealing with Lucinda on my own and was doing well, until you questioned her about the rail move that didn't get done, even after I already explained to you what happened. She doesn't have as much experience on the rails as I do, and you should have just accepted what I told you. Now she is all upset about her job and thinking she has to write a statement defending herself. Please don't aggravate an already difficult situation."

All during this time, Samson was still out of work. It was shortly after he left that Lucinda was able to get a medical work restriction that prohibited her from working as the ground-person, but was allowed to drive the locomotive, which she preferred doing. I was the only ground-person doing the brunt of the rail job in our department. Arnold was never going to work the rails, as he was physically unable to; although he did not have a medical work restriction that supported this. Tara helped on occasions on the rails, but she too only wanted to drive the locomotive. There were a few times that I begged Tara to please, take a turn working as the ground-person.

I was getting worn out doing all the hiking over rough terrain, jumping on and off these railcars while applying and releasing handbrakes, and connecting air hoses. I found myself conversing with the Lord a similar concern while working as the ground-person as I did over three years ago when I first started working the rails. But now, He knew it was not lighthearted as before, but a grave concern: "I don't know, Lord, how much longer I can work this job. I am getting so worn out, and I am hurting so much."

It was obvious to me by this time, that the more I learned about this handler job, the more Lucinda's inner struggles were compounded. This only caused deeper issues with her while working with me on the rails, which was a portion of our handler job she was still learning herself.

I could not make Lucinda understand that it was imperative she followed my directions as the ground-person while she was driving the locomotive, as a major incident could occur if she did not, including injuring me.

A former plant manager once related to me how several years ago, a man was caught in the couplers of two railcars while they were being hooked together and was killed. I didn't want to be the next one killed on the rails because of the negligence of a coworker, even as my dad was killed by the negligence of his coworker.

I was constantly being tormented while working in the most perilous, hostile and physically demanding work environment I have ever worked in my entire working career, not just at this chemical plant. And what I feared concerning my RSD condition was happening: It was becoming increasingly aggravated.

I spoke with Chief on different occasions concerning Lucinda, expressing my safety concerns and the training issues with her attitude. I didn't relate to Chief what I believed her inner struggles were. But I did ask him to please, speak with her in the hopes that things could settle down.

Chief related to me the outcome of his conversation with Lucinda: She closed herself up and walked away, as was her habit when not wanting to deal with a situation. Matters proved only to be made worse while trying to address them.

Chapter 96
Enough Was Enough

Just after making the final decision to add the rail job into the Liquid Handler Department, Ferengi and Pres met with those in this department. I was present while being the AST in the building. Ferengi informed all of us of the job changes going on across the plant site.

During this meeting, Ferengi stated that the union wanted a re-evaluation of the handler job for a higher wage due to adding the rail job, and stated both parties agreed to a mediation process for this decision. Ferengi made it clear in front of all of us that management would honor the mediator's decision concerning this wage re-evaluation. That specific article in our contract dealing with job descriptions that governed in detail how these were managed and re-evaluated was still unchanged from when the union used it for the flex job arbitration win. This higher wage re-evaluation of the handler job should have fallen under this same contract article, and not the mediation process.

However, it wasn't long after the rail job was added that Ferengi and management went back on their word—imagine that—and stated they would not honor the mediator's decision on this re-evaluation for a higher wage. Management and the union then agreed to go through binding arbitration instead of the congenial mediation process. Chief was keeping me in the loop on some of the issues surrounding this whole ordeal. I had expressed to Chief at the beginning to just leave the wages as they were. The rail job moved into a higher wage classification just by adding it to the Liquid Handler Department. But Chief said the union wanted to try for a higher wage regardless.

After arbitration was voted on and decided, I told Chief that he needed to file a grievance and make sure all bases were covered. This was the process outlined in this particular contract article for re-evaluating job descriptions for a higher wage. The very first thing an arbitrator wants to know is whether the grievance process was contractually followed. I emailed Newbie about this, and he agreed that a grievance should be filed.

I wrote up a grievance for Chief that was very descriptive of everything that had taken place, which also implied I was kept in the loop, and signed it as the grievant being in the department for this higher wage re-evaluation. When I gave this grievance to Chief, I asked him to read it, and then speak to Newbie about it first before deciding to file it.

When I saw Chief in passing later that day, he informed me that he had filed the grievance with Adrianne, but he never spoke to Newbie about it. That was not what I asked him to do, but since it was done, I saw no point making an issue of it. It wasn't the first time Chief misunderstood something I had said to him.

Jezebel sent the scanned grievance to Newbie, Pres and Chief with her usual questions. According to Chief, Newbie chewed him out royally for filing the grievance.

Main issue—my name was on it!

There's an old cliché that surfaced here that held true: guilty by association. I hadn't gone away yet! This grievance only proved to Newbie and management that I was kept in the loop and still coaching in the background, and this didn't go over well with either of them. I was to find out soon enough that all this grievance did was widen that target on me. Newbie used another grievance for the arbitration, but was soon trying to back out of his agreement to arbitrate for this higher wage re-evaluation.

About a week after Chief filed this grievance with my name on it, Lucinda and I had a disagreement on the rails; this was not our first disagreement. I was the ground-person, again, while she was the locomotive driver. We had to move fully loaded styrene-railcars and spot them under the styrene unloading rack.

The first railcar in this string of connecting railcars had a damaged coupler. The couplers are hooked together to each railcar for connecting a string of railcars. In order to get to the styrene unloading rack, railcars had to be moved the longest distance through the most congested pedestrian and vehicle traffic areas of the plant site. We had enough full railcars without having to use this particular railcar, and I didn't want to move it through these congested areas with a damaged coupler. I instructed Lucinda to move this railcar to a yard track until someone who had more experience with railcars could inspect the coupler to determine if it needed repaired, or if it was safe to move as it was.

Lucinda didn't want to follow my directions. She argued with me on the radio that it was her job to determine if anything was wrong with a piece of equipment and if it needed maintenance. However, our procedures make it clear that it is all of our jobs to make sure our equipment was in safe working order. And it was my responsibility as the ground-person to ensure railcars were moved safely throughout the plant site.

I told Lucinda that by all means, go ahead and inspect the coupler. She didn't know what she was inspecting any more than I wanted to trust my judgment that this railcar was safe to move, and I had more experience on the rails than she did. The end result: I was adamant that this railcar with a damaged coupler was not going to be moved to the styrene unloading rack at that time. It took a lot of debating between us, but she finally followed my directions and moved this railcar to a yard track for a later date.

Did anyone in the entire plant site who monitored this conversation on radio, including Nabal and Audrey, understand the major safety concern I had with moving a railcar with a damaged coupler through the most congested pedestrian and vehicle traffic areas of the plant site? Apparently not! All this happened in the morning.

After this incident, I contacted a salaried maintenance employee who I knew could inspect this coupler before any decisions were made to move it, and to make arrangements for any repairs if needed. This contact was made via email while copying Lucinda and Nabal. I wanted to be sure this damaged coupler was properly addressed.

That afternoon, Lucinda refused to answer her radio when I tried three times to contact her. When I caught up with her while she was driving our department Kubota, I asked her to help me make more needed rail moves that afternoon, including moving a pentane-railcar for Beady. But Lucinda refused to go back on the rails with me. I never told anyone that Lucinda refused to help me move the pentane-railcar that afternoon and the next day, after we had another disagreement while hooking up the Rail Prince.

The company had just bought a very expensive but small locomotive called the Rail Prince that was used to help with the new styrene-railcar unloading operations, which mostly stayed at the unloading rack. The following morning, while hooking up the Rail Prince to the railcars to be bumped under the styrene unloading rack, Lucinda and I got into another debate on whether the coupler should be raised or left lowered while connecting the air hoses for the air brakes system. Since I was the one under the coupler making the connection, I felt very unsafe with it in the raised position, as at any time while I was in this precarious position, it could come down on me. This procedure debate was the last straw, and enough was enough.

Because so many people monitored our radio conversations, I didn't think it would be considered turning in a union member if I addressed these safety concerns now. Someone needed to get through to Lucinda to make her understand the dangers of working with this equipment and out on the rails, especially when she did not follow the directions of the ground-person.

I only wanted to meet with Chief and Nabal over the issue to ask them to please, talk with Lucinda in the hopes that they could get her to understand that it was imperative she followed the directions of the ground-person while working the rails.

Pres and Audrey decided to be present during this meeting, even though I didn't want them there, but no one cared to ask me. When I knew they would be present, I asked for Lucinda to be present also so that she could hear everything that was said and understand that my main concern was safety, but no one else wanted her present. *But I was the one who originally asked for this meeting!*

During this meeting, I expressed my safety concerns with hooking up the air hoses on the Rail Prince that morning, and with moving a railcar with a damaged coupler through the most congested areas of the plant site the day before. I clearly reminded everyone that it was my responsibility as the ground-person to move these railcars safely. I stated that all I wanted was for someone to speak to Lucinda and explain to her the importance of following the directions of the ground-person, regardless of who this ground-person may be. I did not tell anyone at this meeting that Lucinda refused to help me spot the pentane-railcar for Beady.

Nabal and Audrey wanted a personnel conflict resolution meeting between Lucinda and me. Chief was also adamant that I agree to this conflict resolution. Chief always knew how to play the union rep well when he was showing his authority over me, something he often failed to do while dealing with others. So, against my better judgment, I agreed to this conflict resolution meeting, even knowing just the mention of this to Lucinda would make matters so much worse—and it did.

On Friday the next morning, I read an email Nabal sent the night before stating the pentane-railcar should have been spotted (placed at the rack) that day for Beady. He stated their level of pentane was down to fourteen percent in the tank, and Beady cannot run their process below ten percent. Nabal made it clear this pentane-railcar must be the priority move for that morning.

I started the primitive locomotive so it could build up air pressure, and then went back to the handler building and told Lucinda that we needed to make this pentane-railcar our first move that morning and soon, per Nabal's email that she was also copied on. This set her off in one of her arrogant attitudes insisting she was the scheduler, it was her job to prioritize rail moves, and we were doing the outbound railcars as our first move and not the pentane-railcar move. The outbound railcar move would have taken up a considerable amount of time. This turned into a heated argument, as I reiterated that the pentane-railcar move was the quickest and needed done first per Nabal's email.

She responded, "Go in your office and time out, baby doll."

My anger took over as I responded in a firm tone: "Do not ever call me baby doll again!"

I left on this bad note and waited by the locomotive for Lucinda, who never showed up. Time was wasting. The pentane-railcar also needed sampled once at the rack, and lab test results needed to come back to confirm it was good before it could be unloaded into Beady's pentane tank to use. I was not going to get fired due to a department shutting down because they ran out of pentane. The fact that Lucinda was the one not cooperating with this move would not have made any difference in my defense, this I knew well. Once again, I felt I had no choice but to bring this forward. Nabal was not at the plant on this day, only Audrey was.

I contacted Chief by text letting him know that I needed a union rep as soon as possible. Even though we met the day before, only now did he text me saying that he was really ticked off at me because I lied to him about the grievance that he filed for the higher-wage arbitration. He was so sure I told him that Newbie was okay with filing my particular grievance, even though I only asked him to read it and speak to Newbie about it first.

This was not the time to text all this calling me a liar when I needed to get on the rails and move a pentane-railcar before his department shut down, and while I was dealing with a coworker who insisted I disregard the instructions from our first-line supervisor, but instead follow her instructions.

At almost every turn on this job, I was encountering hostility, misunderstanding, stress, even while dealing with major safety concerns working such a dangerous job with a coworker who just could not understand the dangers.

It took a while, but eventually, Chief showed up along with Pres, and soon afterward, Audrey showed up. We had a very short meeting as I explained Nabal's email and his instructions, and that I needed someone to help me make this pentane-railcar move before Beady shut down. Now they decided to call in Lucinda, who came in with her arrogant attitude she displayed with me earlier.

Lucinda sat down at the table and while only addressing Audrey, arrogantly proclaimed, "I'm the scheduler. It's my job to prioritize rail moves, not hers. I have information that she is not privy to because I'm the scheduler. It's my job, not hers."

She then got up to leave, but just before going out the door, she turned and in a provocative tone called me "baby doll" again in front of everyone, and then left.

No one present made any attempts to correct her, even knowing she was making decisions against what our first-line supervisor had given. *Did anything click in any of these brains here that just witnessed what transpired?* If Lucinda was willing to display such an arrogant attitude in the presence of a supervisor and union reps, didn't anyone wonder what has been going on when it was just she and I alone?

Audrey tried telling me that Nabal understood what was going on. I just looked at her without saying a word. I was trying so hard to control my own emotions, which were about to explode in tears. Was Audrey that naïve? Sure, Nabal knew what was going on. So did everyone else. But Nabal only proved to be an instigator and never addressed anything in a professional manner that would have alleviated the problem. Lucinda had Nabal's ear on all issues relating her one-sided stories while I remained in the background knowing this, yet choosing to say nothing in my own defense, until recently when enough was enough.

I still needed someone to help with that pentane-railcar move. Chief confirmed that pentane below ten percent in the tank would cause his department to shut down. Tara wasn't around, so the only thing I could think of was suggesting Ollie to be reassigned to help for just this day on the rails. He had worked the rails while it was a warehouse job, and it hadn't been that long since it was moved into the Liquid Handler Department. Pres and Chief left the room to discuss this before agreeing.

When they returned, Chief said they just spoke with Newbie, who said this reassignment for Ollie for this one day was okay since it was an emergency. I thought: *Wow! You guys are not rookies by now as union reps. Couldn't you guys make this decision on your own without Newbie's approval? Is Newbie still controlling this local union?*

Ollie and I spotted the pentane-railcar in about fifteen minutes. It was the easiest move with the pentane-railcar on the end of the string of connecting railcars it was hooked up to, and the pentane unloading rack was already empty. I radioed Arnold and Lucinda announcing the pentane was spotted and ready for one of them to sample. I received no response.

Chapter 97

Meltdown

The air was so thick on Monday. I felt so alone in this department and in this battle. Unbeknown to everyone, the spiritual warfare was going full blast. The demons were using everyone and anyone they could for my destruction. However, the angelic warriors had the command and authority from God, and would win this battle in the end; although I would once again come away with wounds that only God could heal.

No one was telling me anything about that conflict resolution meeting between Lucinda and me that Audrey, Nabal and these union reps were adamant happen against my better judgment. When Chief finally texted back on my question asking if he heard anything on this meeting, he only said Sabrina thought it was going to happen the next day.

Later that day, after walking in on Nabal speaking with Arnold in the handler building, Nabal turned before leaving and asked me, "Is anything wrong? You don't look happy."

Really? I just looked at him and never responded. This man was not supervisory material. He continued to instigate when he could have very well addressed everything prior to this climax. I guessed later that it was then that Nabal informed Arnold of the upcoming meeting that everyone seemed unwilling to clue me in on. It was much later before I was told that I needed to be present at this meeting. I wanted a union rep present, and the only one available but reluctant to come was Pres.

I walked into this meeting that everyone else knew why it was happening, and realized it was a trap: There were five against me. Arnold was sitting next to Lucinda. Nabal and Audrey sat opposite across the table from me. Pres was on the end to my right with his normal sour demeanor while being reluctantly present. Audrey made the opening statement: "We are not going to rehash anything of the past."

Audrey's statement spoke volumes to me, and confirmed that it was predetermined I was going to be denied the opportunity to speak in my own defense of any past issues that escalated the turmoil between Lucinda and me to this climax. I was going to be denied the opportunity to refute or even know what anyone else had said about me. No one had any plans on addressing my safety concerns or lack of handler training that I've been dealing with now for several months.

However, Audrey was sure to make it very clear during this meeting that I was expected to share my knowledge of the rail job with Lucinda. When I said very little, Audrey commented she didn't like my silence and accused me of shutting myself off. When I calmly agreed with something Nabal said, Audrey commented she didn't like my tone. This meeting was so biased against me it was devastating. I saw the meeting was ending without addressing my safety concerns, and I didn't want that to happen. So, I spoke up: "What about my safety concerns?"

This ignited Lucinda into one of her arrogant outbursts: "She's bringing up safety concerns? And she's my sister in Christ! And she was a union president! She confuses me on the rails when she gives me directions!"

When Lucinda admitted she was confused on the rails with my directions, red-danger flags flew up that only intensified my safety concerns. Lucinda then descriptively went through the sequence of directions that confused her: the exact directions any ground-person as the eyes of the locomotive driver would use. I then realized I was justified in bringing up my safety concerns that escalated to this meeting; although they were not going to be addressed. It would seem that no one caught on to the dangers of Lucinda getting confused while driving the locomotive. Or was everyone purposely ignoring these red-danger flags? I may be telling her one direction, and then she goes the opposite direction, which can result in me being harmed and not just equipment.

The meeting ended without any of my safety or other concerns addressed or even acknowledged. When Arnold and Lucinda left, I was about to leave too but then had an afterthought. Going back to where Audrey, Nabal and Pres were sitting, I asked them: "So, what happened to the conflict resolution meeting I was supposed to have with Lucinda?"

Audrey answered, "We decided the issue was not only with Lucinda."

Earlier that day, I had seen Ollie and Arnold speaking just outside the warehouse building. Although Ollie and I worked well together the Friday before, I could still sense his ill feelings towards me. I wondered now what did anyone else say about me that I would never know or have the opportunity to refute? I responded to Audrey: "Oh, I get it now."

Pres never said a word during this meeting, but spoke up now while berating me with his demeaning comments, and related an interaction with two maintenance union workers as his support: "You're the one with the problem. You were even mean to a couple of maintenance guys just the other day."

I knew the two guys Pres was talking about, and I knew that what he just stated was not at all true, as so many other biased comments spoken against me during this meeting were not true.

Audrey spoke again: "Pres said he was tired of wasting his time on this issue."

After she said this, I just stood there, unable to speak. This issue began with the damaged coupler as a major safety concern that involved the entire plant site in how these railcars were moved, and then morphed into exposing some real underlining issues that no one seemed to want to address. And Pres was tired of wasting his time on this issue! I was in his union president position, and I can say for sure, I never would have considered addressing such major issues as a waste of my time.

As I just stood there speechless after what Audrey just told me, Pres gave the final blow that ended it: "Chief didn't even want to be here for this meeting."

With this, I turned and walked out without saying another word. As I left, I realized I just put my job in more jeopardy while trying to address major safety concerns working with dangerous railcars with a coworker whose negligence just may be the cause of my harm.

I was heading towards the women's locker room beaten, and just wanted to die. In passing the maintenance building, I ran into the two maintenance guys who I knew Pres was referring to in the meeting. At one time, these same guys were staunch supporters of mine while I was the union president. Without another thought, I asked them a direct question: "Did either of you guys tell Pres I was mean to you the other day?"

One of them spoke up and seemed concerned that I would bring this up: "I was only joking with Pres."

I responded, "He just brought it up in a meeting against me stating that I was mean to you both."

He became defensive on my behalf: "Pres never should have brought that up in a meeting. I was only joking with him."

With this, I thought: *So, what else was said against me and by whom that was not true?*

Pres spotted us from afar and started towards us at a fast pace. When he reached the three of us, he went into one of his hissy fits and started berating me in front of these two guys without asking anything as to what we were discussing between us. His biased anger towards me only exposed his own inability to professionally deal with issues his union president role required of him: "I knew you would go and talk to these guys. You just cannot leave things alone."

Pres went on and on yelling at the top of his lungs and using profanity that he never used in my presence when I was president, while at the same time doing his normal war dance of jumping back and forth, and side to side—I'm not exaggerating. I needed to get away from this man! I turned and walked away without saying another word to him or anyone else.

Once I was alone in the women's locker room that no one else used, I locked the door and had an emotional meltdown. The devastation I felt after all I had been enduring these past several months with the escalation these last few days, overpowered my emotions. I could not catch my breath from crying so hard.

I thought of everything I went through these past several months trying to deal with this on my own. I thought of all my major safety concerns and the near misses on the rails, the biased comments from everyone, the hostility and angry attitudes of all these people pointing fingers at me as the only one at fault. These past few days were only the climax.

I thought back on all the years I served as a union rep. I remembered so many people I went out of my way to help, some at the risk of my own job, even those who were hostile towards me at one time. Now that I was the one in need of unbiased and professional union representation, I was being denied this right.

The writing was on the wall. My days at this job were numbered. It was only a matter of time before I lost my job, or a limb, or my life—and the sad part—I believed there were some people working at this plant site who would not have cared one way or another!

Chapter 98
God's Spiritual Healing

Since it was near the end of the shift by the time the meeting was over, I stayed alone in the locker room until it was time to leave for home. But I wasn't really alone. My Lord Jesus was engulfing me with His presence, even as I cried my heart out to Him. I felt His peace and knew everything I have been going through was well known to my Heavenly Father and Lord Jesus. I knew my Lord God would see me through all this, somehow. I left with no one disturbing me.

It was the first week of June. I was scheduled for a vacation the following week with previous plans of going to our church denominational general council as a lay delegate. I had grown close to my church family, and shared often the turmoil I went through during my terms as union president, and now with this new job.

Once I was home, I called my pastor to ask for prayers. While being the union president, I had called him often right before an unscheduled meeting, or when something else unexpected came up, knowing he would always be available and willing to pray with me. He had never let me down, and this day was no different.

I shared with him everything that happened and how upset I was. After praying with me, he asked if it were possible for me to take the rest of the week off from work to be sure I would make it to the council. At that point, I didn't know what to do, and told him I would pray and seek God's direction. There were too many days involved to just report off without getting fired.

My RSD condition had been progressively aggravated with all the previous stress and physical demands over the last several months, which I tried ignoring to continue working. With my emotional meltdown, the RSD became more aggravated to an alarming degree as the night went on. Without being able to sleep, and by God's leading without knowing the outcome of my actions, I reported off on sick leave in the middle of the night. If my doctor would not sign the paperwork, I knew I would lose my job. I only saw this doctor once the previous year for the first time. I had gone all those years since the end of my workers' comp nightmare without a personal care doctor of my own.

However, through God's grace, the paperwork was signed and this sick leave was approved. At least for the short term, my job was secured; although the aggravated RSD condition gave me concerns of ever being able to return to my full job duties.

I was so distraught with everything that happened, and with my union reps' lack of willingness to address any of my concerns. And these were the same guys I worked with while I was union president! I contacted Newbie the first day I was off, asking that he facilitate a meeting with Chief, Pres and me, and he agreed. But he reneged on this meeting, and it never happened.

Soon after, I tried again via email asking these reps to address my safety concerns on the rails, and my concerns over Lucinda admitting to getting confused with my directions as the groundperson. The email that Chief sent in response expressed his anger, was so very hurtful, and aggravated my emotional turmoil and the RSD even more. Chief's email was also damaging to these union reps: It clearly supported their lack of intentions and willingness to address any of my concerns or to protect my job.

I wanted to respond to Chief's email that he sent in response to mine, but the Lord held me back from doing so. Instead, the Lord led me into an extended fast as I earnestly sought His direction in all this.

I tried to put all this behind me as I went to my first general council for my church, along with my pastor and his lovely wife. As the three of us walked into the first session at council, the main speaker was just beginning to address the audience. He was a pastor from another denomination, which caused me to think it strange that he was speaking at our general council. It wasn't long into his sermon that I realized God's purpose for having this pastor speak at such a time as this.

As I listened to his sermon, God ministered to my own heart and started the healing process. This pastor spoke about the importance of speaking what God puts on our hearts to speak, regardless of the negative consequences that may come our way. He spoke about how the harvest of olives involved beating the tree all around to knock down the olives, and once they were harvested, how the olives needed beaten to produce the olive oil that was used for anointing and healing.

I understood God's correlation between my life of trials and hardships with the harvest of olives, and with the process of producing the olive oil for God's anointing and nurturing purposes in my life. I listened intently as this pastor finished by sharing the importance of not being ashamed of the name of Jesus, and how we must witness to His grace and power and glory.

After this pastor finished his sermon, the outgoing president of our denomination spoke on his terms of presidency, and humbly confessed that there were times he should have spoken up but did not, and he regretted those times.

I thought of my own union presidency then. I may not have been the best union president, but I can honestly say I did my best, and I had always tried to follow God's leading, even when standing all alone, often through earnest prayer and fasting.

After this assembly was over, I continued to be still in God's presence as He continued to minister to my broken heart. God gently reaffirmed through His peace and healing, His approval of my past and outspokenness to stand up for what I believed was right, and in defense of many people I was responsible for as their union president. God brought to mind how I was not ashamed to proclaim Jesus as Lord of my life, and to acknowledge His help openly and without apology. God also reaffirmed that I was not wrong to be concerned for my own safety now and that of others at the plant site; the consequence of which was putting my job in jeopardy. There were those who just wanted me to go away!

But I've learned, what people mean for evil against me, God means for good. (Genesis 50:20, Romans 8:28.) God used that time at council to reaffirm that He allowed everything that had happened as His preparation for His call and purpose for my life.

The Lord God continued ministering to me throughout the entire general council in powerful ways. Even as God was healing my broken heart, He was allowing the RSD condition to worsen. My feet were going numb while just sitting attending the council. Just short walks to restaurants proved to cause excruciating pain. I had no idea how I was ever going to return to my job.

So why would God start healing my broken heart but not the RSD condition? Because God is always more concerned for our spiritual well-being than our physical well-being. The RSD was also the direct result of the Lord's spanking through His love for my disobedience and irreverence towards Him; even though it was many years ago; even though He has long since forgiven me.

The Lord has also made it clear to me: He will not heal me from the RSD condition. It will always be a constant reminder that the Lord God will not tolerate any disobedience or irreverence from me because of His prophetic call on my life.

My Lord God was going to continue orchestrating my life journey according to His purpose, and was going to use this neurological pain disorder as a catalyst to that end. And because

God is Sovereign, whatever He wants to do, He does, end of story, period. (Psalms 103:19, 115:3 and 135:6.)

I had shared with Abby, the company nurse, my plans on going to the general council after I reported off on sick leave. I phoned Abby at the airport to let her know I was coming home and would return to work the following workday, though I was still concerned about my ability to do my job. She reminded me that I needed to clear my return to work with Dr. Willy, the contracted company doctor whose office was several miles from the plant site. Dr. Willy and I always had a good rapport, and he understood RSD to some extent.

During my appointment with Dr. Willy, I had shared what happened at work with the stressful situation and physical demands of my job, both of which aggravated the RSD, and he understood. Dr. Willy was just getting into Qigong (pronounced chee-gung), and he was so excited that I understood the negative effects stress could cause on the physical body. I had no idea what Qigong was, but agreed to get the book he recommended and read up on it. Dr. Willy also shared that he was going to a Qigong seminar in October. It would be much later before I understood that this Qigong was a holistic practice to heal yourself.

With everything said, Dr. Willy wanted me to take a few more weeks off from work. I asked to cut this short to only one more week. I knew Tara was scheduled off soon and didn't want to leave the plant without rail workers available. He agreed to split the difference. I still had concerns, but I knew God wanted me back to work sooner rather than later.

Chapter 99
Prophetic Warning

Before I move on with this saga of my life, I need to explain a brief history on the use of train air brakes, as it played a significant role at the end. When the company purchased the Rail Prince, it became known to management that the use of train air brakes was mandatory with this smaller locomotive. Because of this, Audrey contacted the company's other site located in a different state, and questioned their use of train air brakes while they shuttled railcars. She then obtained and reviewed their General rail operations manual for reference.

With the use of train air brakes, each railcar in the connected string that was hooked to the locomotive, would have a braking system of their own controlled by the locomotive air brakes cylinder. With the greater number of fully loaded styrene-railcars being moved at one time, train air brakes would greatly reduce the stopping distance and help control the string of railcars. Without the use of train air brakes, the locomotive brakes alone would have to stop all these railcars, which proved less effective to reduce the stopping distance and control such an increased force of so many fully loaded railcars.

Another significant safety feature when using train air brakes was that if a railcar disconnected from another railcar while being moved, any disconnection of the air hoses, which had quick-release connection ends, would instantly apply the train air brakes to each railcar and stop the runaway railcars. But even in such emergency instances, runaway railcars will continue traveling dangerously for a long distance before coming to a complete halt.

Using train air brakes was complicated and dangerous, as it involved high-pressured air, and required the cooperation of both the ground-person and locomotive driver working together. The connection was done by the ground-person, and involved stooping down in the between two railcars in a precarious position while connecting the air hoses together to each railcar in the connected string. Each railcar had two cock valves that controlled the pressured air, one on each end, that also needed to be in the correct operating positions while using the train air brakes.

It was normal to have to walk down the entire string of railcars several times to get the train air connected and charged up. The locomotive driver was the one responsible for applying the train air brakes to the moving railcars using the air brakes cylinder in the cabin. If this was not done or done incorrectly, the train air brakes on the moving string of railcars were not functional.

Train air brakes could also be applied automatically once the string of railcars was stopped. This was done by allowing the air hose on the first railcar hooked to the locomotive to disconnect on its own when the locomotive pulled away. But the cock valve on this first railcar had to be left open before the disconnect in order to apply the train air brakes to each railcar connected in the string.

For many years past, our primitive locomotive that was used for shuttling railcars on our plant site, did not have an operational train air brakes cylinder and system. The locomotive brake system alone was used to stop all of the connected string of railcars that were hooked to the moving locomotive. Audrey was unaware of this until she held a meeting with the rail workers questioning our use and knowledge of train air brakes.

During this meeting, Tara and Samson were adamant that train air brakes did not need to be used while shuttling railcars on our plant site. I said nothing at this meeting on the use of train air brakes, as Tara and Samson had more experience working the rails than I did at that time. Arnold and Lucinda had no experience working the rails and made no comments. But with the new styrene-railcar unloading project coming into play, we were going to be moving a greater number of fully loaded railcars at one time as never before.

Once Audrey and other management fully understood the safety benefits of using train air brakes, they contracted outside railcar mechanics to overhaul the entire train air brakes cylinder and system on our primitive locomotive for operational use. This overhaul was very expensive. They then contracted an outside trainer to come into the plant to give Tara and the four union workers in the Liquid Handler Department training on how to use this train air brakes system while shuttling railcars.

Once everyone was trained, Audrey and management were adamant that the use of train air brakes would be incorporated in the Liquid Handler railcar procedures manual, and made it mandatory that train air brakes would be used while moving more than four fully loaded railcars at one time. Lucinda was the one responsible for revising the Liquid Handler railcar procedures manual to include the use of train air brakes.

Audrey also made it mandatory that the General rail operations manual obtained from the other plant site, which included train air brakes procedures, was to be used along with our own Liquid Handler rail procedures manual. There were some significant discrepancies between these two manuals that caused a huge safety concern on my part that I was never able to get addressed. All this needed explained to understand the events soon to happen.

My first day back after my meltdown, I learned that Lucinda was on sick leave; she reported off two days after I did. During my time off, only Arnold was working in the department. Samson was going on three months being off work from his surgery.

Audrey and Nabal met with me first thing that morning to inform me that Marty and Ollie were now working the rail job portion of the handler jobs, even while they worked in the warehouse. I am sure Pres and Chief needed Newbie's approval before agreeing to this, as they couldn't agree before on their own for Ollie to cover the rails for only one day.

I had some real concerns with Marty and Ollie working the rails now, and not only because it was my job. My main concern was their safety with being unfamiliar with the use of train air brakes. When Ollie helped me on that one Friday, train air brakes were not needed.

When Audrey and Nabal left after our meeting, I checked my emails. And there they were waiting for my return! Audrey had sent two emails the same night of the June meeting while summarizing the meeting and the personnel issues, and making it clear that any ongoing issues would be managed through the corrective action policy with an HR representative involved. Believing that I put my job in more jeopardy by bringing forward my major safety concerns working the rails with Lucinda was true.

Audrey never had a past practice of sending out emails such as these, as she always preferred to just chat. I saw Document Queen coaching in the background. Jezebel wanted to make sure everything was well documented in order to justify their termination process against me. Those who Audrey copied on these emails proved this: Jezebel; Ferengi; Nabal; union reps; Audrey's own higher boss, Myer. Not one union rep copied gave me a heads-up that these were sent.

I believed my name on that grievance for the higher-wage arbitration that Chief filed without speaking with Newbie first, widened that target on me. I worded that grievance in detail, which implied I was kept in the loop behind the scenes and still involved with the union, at least with Chief.

Everything changed after Newbie chewed out Chief royally for filing that grievance, which caused a rift between Chief and me that was not going to mend anytime in the near future.

Later that same morning, on my first day back to work, I made a trip to the warehouse to hand deliver some paperwork and to inform Ollie that empty styrene-railcars needed moved out of the unloading rack. I took this opportunity to ask if he and Marty had any training with using the train air brakes system. Ollie gave me no definitive answer. While having to use the complicated and dangerous air brakes system, their safety was my utmost concern. Later that same afternoon, when I saw Ollie was having problems connecting the train air brakes system on the styrene-railcars, I helped him twice without hesitation.

The following day, I received another email from Audrey stating she received communications from union personnel that I was visiting other departments inquiring about their training, and if they were capable of performing their work duties. She stated that these union personnel felt interrogated by my questioning, and would prefer I come see her with my questions. Audrey claimed my interactions with these union personnel were unmerited and would not be tolerated again. Audrey never mentioned who these union personnel were.

Ollie never got over his ill feelings with me as union president. Although we worked well together on the rails that Friday he helped, I could still feel the tension between us. But he seemed appreciative each time I helped him with his problems with the train air brakes system. Ollie and Marty were getting a higher wage while doing the rail job now that it was in the Liquid Handler Department. It was obvious they wanted to keep doing this job for the higher pay, regardless of jeopardizing themselves or anyone else in the plant because of their lack of training and knowledge using train air brakes.

During several days afterward, Audrey came around a few times while I was unloading styrene-railcars to speak one-on-one with me. At one time, she asked me to trust her and to know she was sincere and honest. I then tried justifying my interaction with Ollie for safety reasons, stating he was the only one I spoke with, and he could have just told me to stop asking questions. Audrey got defensive, accused me of trying to intimidate her, and then threatened again to get HR involved; her response had no merit.

Myer also came around alone while I was performing my duties unloading styrene-railcars, claiming he just wanted to see the process in action. It was unusual for anyone in management as high up as Myer to go about the field process areas of the plant on his own, and I never had any interactions with him in the past. Needless to say, I was leery of his true motive.

While Lucinda was off work, just working with Arnold was more tolerable, as he understood my competence and initiative from training and working with me in Darkly. But the constant stress of losing my job loomed over me. I was also sure that no one knew just how much that June meeting with the biased attitudes while ignoring all my safety concerns adversely affected me emotionally, or physically with the RSD.

I started really feeling harassed with Audrey's threats to get HR involved, with her one-on-one meetings, with her subsequent threatening emails since my return to work, and with so much more that went on than what I shared here. In all her emails, Audrey made sure to copy those she did on her June emails, including the union reps. The Lord would know what was said among them all without my knowledge.

The lack of support and silence from these union reps told me what I knew from experience: They were supporting management against me while governing behind the scenes, and I was on my own once again.

I finally decided it was time I spoke on my own behalf. The Lord led me to specifically address this assertive email "To Whom It May Concern," and not just to Audrey, as I initially thought it should be addressed. When I sent this out from my home email address, I copied everyone Audrey had been copying on her emails. I said in this email what I was denied the opportunity to say during that June meeting. Here is a synopsis:

"Ever since the June meeting, I have been struggling with the comments made, the biased attitudes against me, and all that transpired during that meeting by those who attended. It was obvious that the focus was directed against me as the main one at fault. Audrey's opening comment stating, 'we are not going to rehash anything from the past,' made it clear to me that it was predetermined that I was purposely and concertedly going to be denied the opportunity to speak in my defense of anything of the past issues that caused the escalation to this level, and be denied the opportunity to refute or even know what others have said about me.

"I have been scrutinized and criticized over the past few months over my job performance and initiative both on and off the rails, over trying to get the handler training I should have, and over my attempts to address my safety concerns. I am constantly looking over my shoulders, on guard with who I speak with and what I say, trying to make sure I don't do anything at any time that can be used detrimentally against me. All this creates a very difficult and stressful work environment that no one should have to work in, not even a former union president. I have always tried to perform any job I had conscientiously and with initiative, and to work in this type of environment disturbs me greatly."

I reiterated what they all knew was the recent past of this current management trying their best to progress me through their corrective action policy during my terms as union president, with their goal of justifying my termination from employment.

I expressed that I was not taking lightly Audrey's threat to continue with this same pattern of using the corrective action policy as the result of my attempts to address my safety concerns working the rails, to address my disagreement with another union employee over their work direction given to me that conflicted with the direction of my first-line supervisor, and my initial attempts of trying to address these in a more reasonable way that was meant to avoid negative consequences to those involved.

I made it clear that I understood everything that Audrey outlined in her emails after the June meeting, along with her threat to continue through the corrective action policy, was the result of the collaboration of several individuals copied (including union reps). Thus, I claimed my address: "To Whom It May Concern" was appropriate.

I acknowledged everyone's lack of ability to address any issue involving me objectively and impartially, regardless of who was also involved, and claimed the aftermath of my terms of union president was the cause. I gave everyone a heads-up: I would address any future discipline for bringing forth safety concerns or for any unjust reasons through all legal avenues, outside the company as well as within.

This email proved to be another prophetic warning that reiterated my previous stated resolve prior to leaving as union president. I knew my union reps would never support my fight against management's campaign to terminate my employment.

The Lord knew I would be following His direction going forward and before taking any actions. I believe that the events that followed were destined to happen regardless of anything. God was orchestrating His grand scheme for the end of everything that He was going to allow to happen.

623

Chapter 100

Safety Regression

Just two days after my interaction with Ollie about the use of train air brakes, Nabal sent out an email to Arnold, Ollie, Marty and me, letting us know there was a hazard risk meeting reviewing the need and use of train air brakes.

Per Nabal's email, effective immediately, using train air brakes with the primitive locomotive was no longer mandatory when moving any railcars in the plant site, regardless of the quantity of railcars being moved at one time. Train air brakes continued to be mandatory using the Rail Prince locomotive.

However, Nabal made it clear that "train air brakes may be used if desired by the operators (rail workers)," such as when the "operator feels the quantity of cars is sufficient enough that the stopping distance may be compromised." Nabal stated that this procedure change regarding the use of train air brakes was the outcome of the hazard risk meeting.

I responded to Nabal's email and copied Audrey, letting him know that I was unaware of this hazard risk meeting to review the use of train air brakes, and requested to see this review and who were involved. I expressed my safety concerns and disagreement with the decision of not requiring the use of train air brakes with our primitive locomotive. I stated that with my recent experience, I now understood fully the safety hazards when not using train air brakes to stop these fully loaded railcars once moving, and the momentum of such a force should a string of railcars get disconnected from the locomotive would be disastrous. My safety concerns and disagreement with this regressed safety procedure change were now well known.

The next day, Audrey gave me a hard copy of the minutes of this hazard risk meeting, which I saw took place just after I went out on sick leave. Tara and Lucinda were the only ones from among those who worked the rails who attended this meeting. I was doubtful Lucinda would ever be trained as the ground-person, and in her current job position would only work the rails when others were not available. Tara would never be working the rails after the two-year agreement for her training assistance ends.

So why didn't this meeting wait until those who worked the rails full time were available to be present and consulted? Who really wanted this procedure changed to no longer mandate the use of train air brakes and why? Apparently, no one cared what the rest of us thought, or should I say, what I thought? After everything I have brought up recently regarding my safety concerns working the rails, I was taking this very personally.

All during this time, I was still on the plant-wide procedure committee that Ferengi was in charge of which reviewed plant-wide procedures periodically. There was a plant-wide procedure that clearly stated, until everyone currently working the actual job signed off on the procedure-change form acknowledging any change in a procedure, the procedure change could not be implemented.

This procedure-change form was not presented to anyone before Nabal gave those currently working the job permission through email to move forward with no longer using train air brakes. This was a major infraction on Nabal's part of a safety procedure rule with full knowledge of Audrey. But I learned well over the years: It was okay for management personnel and some special union employees to ignore safety rules and procedures, and to violate contract language without consequences.

About three weeks from my return to work, Lucinda returned from her sick leave. This was the first time we met since the June meeting. I tried being nice to her, and asked how she and her family were doing. Her lack of response and demeanor indicated her inner struggles were compounded. Once Lucinda returned, the work situation went back to being difficult. Soon afterward, Ollie and Marty were taken off the rail job, and I became the main ground-person, again.

Lucinda was the one to finally present the procedure-change form that explained using train air brakes with our primitive locomotive was no longer mandatory, and requested Arnold and me to sign it. I had some major safety and liability concerns both with not using train air brakes and in how these documents were worded. I tried explaining my concerns to Arnold and Lucinda, but they didn't care.

Instead, they both reminded me that I was permitted to write a statement on the procedure-change form noting my concerns along with my signature, which I also knew was permissible. After I initially signed the form, I had second thoughts and then crossed out my signature. I also understood that even with a statement under my signature, once signed, any hope of addressing my safety and liability concerns would be gone.

Ollie and Marty were never required to sign this procedure-change form, which was another infraction of the safety procedure rule, as they were working the rail job when the procedure change was implemented per Nabal's email.

How documents and agreements are worded is so very important, but even more so with a signature as acknowledgment. This statement comes into play even more significantly now.

The minutes of the hazard risk meeting clearly documented that the operators (rail workers) were the ones who admitted the stopping distance of railcars was compromised without the use of train air brakes. The procedure-change form the rail workers were directed to sign reaffirmed what was documented in these meeting minutes and what Nabal stated in his email, including what was in parenthesis: "Air brakes are not required while using the locomotive. Air brakes may be used if desired by operators (i.e., air brakes are already connected on incoming cars, or the operator feels the quantity of cars is sufficient enough that the stopping distance may be compromised)."

Even though the rail workers admitted to the safety risks when not using train air brakes, this did not deter management from regressing in safety by no longer mandating the use of train air brakes. Management knew that with so many supporting documents, they were well protected from all liability.

If a significant incident happened on the rails that even remotely suggested train air brakes could have prevented, the last sentence in parenthesis threw all the liability for the final decision back on the rail workers, and exempted management totally from all liability for their own regressed safety decision to no longer mandate the use of train air brakes.

Lucinda informed Nabal that I crossed out my signature from the procedure-change form that same day and never gave me a heads-up. I was blindsided when Nabal called me into his office and closed the door for a one-on-one meeting. Instantly, I became leery and on guard, especially knowing that target was on me. I knew it would come down to my word against his. Although I am forever accountable to God for all I say and do, others do not always understand this, and many feel exempt from such Divine accountability themselves.

During this meeting, Nabal went over the procedure-change form asking for an explanation as to why I refused to sign it. I explained in simple terms my major safety concerns with not using train air brakes, the liability being thrown back on the rail workers, and my added concern for purposely creating another contention scenario on the rails. I explained what I knew he did not know: There must be agreement and cooperation between the ground-person and locomotive driver using the train airbrakes for these brakes to function correctly. I reminded him that it was well known by then that Lucinda had problems with following my directions on the rails while I worked as the ground-person.

Nabal encouraged me to contact him whenever there was a problem on the rails. I told him I've done that and it backfired. He claimed he didn't know when that happened. *Right!*

I then reminded him how annoyed he was when I tried addressing my concerns that the integrity of the damaged coupler was compromised, which resulted in the June meeting. He claimed he didn't remember that. *Right!*

When I realized Nabal was adamant I sign this procedure-change form, I compromised by asking only for the last sentence in parenthesis to be deleted: "The operator feels the quantity of cars is sufficient enough that the stopping distance may be compromised."

I knew that I would insist on using train air brakes while working as the ground-person. I have been dealing with Lucinda's attitude all this time on the rails. Somehow, I would cover myself and trust the Lord for His protection. Nabal said he would get back to me on my concerns and a possible revision of the form.

Meanwhile, Chief had contacted me asking if I was willing to attend the higher-wage arbitration scheduled the following week. Newbie had made it clear to me that he didn't want me present at the mediation or the arbitration, but he changed his mind for some reason. I knew it took a lot for Chief to contact me because of that rift between us, and he did so only because Newbie told him to. I told Chief I would get back to him with an answer.

The following day, Nabal called me back into his office for another one-on-one meeting. Once again, I was leery and on guard. He explained that the decision to not require the use of train air brakes was not going to be reversed, and the form was not going to be revised in any way. The last sentence that I requested to be deleted as my compromise would remain.

Nabal told me: "You can sign it with a statement below noting your concerns, or I can go back and tell them you won't sign it."

I asked Nabal: "Who are 'they' who are making the decision that this wording cannot be deleted?"

He was adamant that he was not going to tell me who was behind making these decisions. I was adamant that I was not signing this form as it was worded.

This same afternoon was the goodbye party for Adrianne on the first floor in the same building that Nabal's office was in. She really was a special person and well-loved, and so many people came out to send her off into retirement with well-wishes.

I walked down the stairs after leaving Nabal's office, and while I was still in the stairwell, I saw Jezebel and Chief in the hallway speaking outside where Adrianne's retirement gathering was taking place. The only thing I heard said between them was Jezebel telling Chief: "She won't sign it." I only guessed it was about me.

I called Chief afterward and told him that I would attend the arbitration. Chief never mentioned his conversation with Jezebel. I knew if I asked him anything about it, he would explode in anger without answering me. So, I didn't mention it either.

Chapter 101
The Trap

The following day was Friday. Nabal showed up first thing in the morning at the handler building to speak with me again about the procedure-change form. He directed me into an empty office and closed the door. Even more so today, I was leery and on guard with meeting him one-on-one. He then proceeded to tell me: "They are viewing your refusal to sign the procedure-change form as insubordination. I'm giving you another chance to sign the form."

I asked again: "Who are 'they' that are making these decisions, and the decision that the wording absolutely cannot change? I would like to speak to them myself."

At this, Nabal got mean: "I'm not telling you who is making these decisions. I'm just telling you that it's being viewed as insubordination, and if you're telling me that you are not going to sign the form, I'll let them know. I don't know where this is leading. But I'll let them know."

Nabal just lied to me. Imagine that! He knew exactly where this was leading. At this point, I decided this one-on-one meeting needed to end for my own protection. I said nothing more but opened the door and left.

After Nabal left the building, I logged on to the computer and sent Ferengi a quick email letting him know what Nabal had just told me. I explained to Ferengi what I knew he already understood while being in charge of the plant-wide procedure committee: Procedures were supposed to be written with openness as to the wording and considering the ramifications for those who did the job on a consistent basis. Maybe he would remember the confined space entry procedure I was instrumental in revising for the benefit of everyone involved. I didn't wait around for his response; I left to do my job.

While on my way to where my job responsibilities were that morning, Nabal came driving around in his Kubota looking for me. When he spotted me, he drove up to where I was and told me to get in the Kubota stating that Jezebel wanted to meet with me, but he didn't tell me where or why. I climbed into the Kubota with another leery feeling; I was sure this was not going to end well. All this was happening so fast without any real time to digest anything.

Nabal drove to his office building and parked in the lot. I followed him into the building and up the stairs. When we reached his office, he directed me in where I found Jezebel sitting at a table facing the door, obviously just waiting for me. Instantly, I realized I just walked into a trap.

But it was too late! Nabal was closing the door behind me!

Before the door closed completely, Jezebel started speaking: "Angelika, Nabal told me that you are refusing to sign the procedure-change form. We are viewing this as insubordination. I am going to ask you to clock out and leave the plant."

No sooner did Jezebel finish her last word, without thinking or uttering a single word, I spun around, opened the door, and I was out of there before either of them knew what hit them.

As I was heading down the hallway at a fast pace, my brain heard Jezebel in the background but refused to respond: "Angelika, stop! Where are you going? I asked you to clock out and leave the plant!"

Exactly! Now that was a really stupid question she just asked me! Where could she think I was going, but to clock out and leave the plant? My only thought was getting out of that trap and away from her and Nabal as soon as possible before either of them could claim I said or did anything. It was two against one, and I didn't like the odds.

In order to leave the plant, I had to get my belongings and car keys which were in the handler building, a good distance away from Nabal's office building. Once I was outside of the building, I pulled out my cell phone. My first call was to Newbie. Even though I had been out of the office of union president for over a year, Jezebel was still in the habit of contacting Newbie every time I was involved in anything. And of course, Newbie saw my name on caller ID. *I knew he wouldn't answer!*

As I walked at a fast pace through the Darkly Graveyard towards the handler building, my second call was to Chief. I told Chief what happened and that I needed a union rep right then. He said he was on his way.

Meanwhile, Jezebel got in her car and headed me off reaching the handler building before I did. As I approached the handler building, I saw Jezebel standing by the only door that I could use to get in. There was no way I was approaching her! There was no way I was going into that building, have her follow me inside, and be alone with that woman where no one could see or hear what was happening! God only knew what she would have claimed I said or did once we were alone. *This is turning ugly!*

I turned around and started walking back the way I came. Jezebel hollered at me again: "Angelika, stop! I told you to clock out and leave the plant."

Now I turned to speak to her: "And where's the union rep? You know better than to throw someone out of the plant without a union rep present!"

I turned again and continued to walk away from her going back through the Darkly Graveyard towards the building where Nabal's office was. Jezebel started to follow me. She was refusing to leave me alone, while I was refusing to be alone with her.

Finally, Jezebel gave up her pursuit and headed back to her car. I took this opportunity to make a priority stop in the women's locker room and ran into a few people along the way. I greeted them as though nothing unusual was happening. With my priority stop taken care of, I headed back towards the building that Nabal's office was in and waited outside for Chief to show up.

And far into the distance, I spotted him. *Here comes the Cavalry to the rescue!* Chief was driving a forklift, as his department was a good distance away. Once he reached me, the first thing I asked him pointing to the forklift: "Is this the best you could do?"

We both laughed, but then had a short, tense conversation.

After I confronted Chief on speaking to Jezebel the day before, he admitted that he purposely did not tell me anything. His excuse was his misunderstanding of my last email I sent to him and Pres before leaving the office of union president. He told me that his interpretation of that email was that I did not want any union representation should management ever approach them with their intentions to throw me out of the plant.

I responded, "Read the email again! That was not at all what I stated or meant." It was not the first time he misunderstood something I said, either in an email or in person.

But I wasn't quite grasping everything Chief was referring to, and it was a good thing I did not at that time. I told Chief that Jezebel had no business asking me to leave the plant without a union rep present, that she knew better. Chief never told me that Jezebel had called him that morning, and that he was the one who refused to be present. I would learn all about what really happened much later. I kept calm knowing that this was not the time to argue this out.

I told Chief: "We need to forget about personal issues between us; because right now, I need a union rep."

Chief suggested I just sign the procedure-change form so that I would not get thrown out of the plant. He told me exactly what everyone else had said and which I also understood: I could write a statement under my signature noting my concerns. It was only during this conversation that I learned that Chief had no idea what the procedure change was. My side of the story and safety concerns were never relayed to him, and apparently, he never cared enough to ask.

Because our relationship over the last few weeks had become strained, and my last attempt to address safety backfired on me that resulted in the June meeting, neither did I contact him regarding my concerns with this procedure change.

When Nabal showed up, Chief asked him for a copy of the form. As Chief followed Nabal into the building and up the stairs to his office, I followed behind. While in Nabal's office, he started to hand Chief the form as I reached out to intersect it with resignation and stated, "Let me just sign it now."

With this, Nabal quickly pulled back the form and clutched it close to his chest as though he were a little boy protecting his prize toy from a mean monster. He flexed his muscles, and in his mean tone stated, "NO! You're not signing it now! You can sign it on Monday!"

Chief never once spoke in my defense; he never once insisted to Nabal to let me sign the form right then to avoid being thrown out of the plant. Chief was never good at assertively confronting management, even though the labor laws allowed him to without consequence. Jezebel was present when Nabal pulled back the form and reiterated what he just told me: I would not be allowed to sign the form until Monday.

Chief and I then left Nabal's office and the building. We headed towards the handler building to get my belongings before I could leave the plant. We walked through the Darkly Graveyard of solid concrete and through the area where proud buildings once stood, some dating back to the era of WWII, now ground to smithereens and dispersed all over. I could almost smell the Darkly pancakes that permeated from the concrete as a reminder of what this area once was. I gave a quick thought: *What if Darkly had never shutdown?* But for those who love God and are called according to His purpose, there are no "what-ifs." (Romans 8:28.) I had no doubt that God was still in this—somehow.

Once I got my belongings and before I left the handler building, I decided to log on to the computer to check if Ferengi had responded to my earlier email. Chief started nervously pacing the floor while reminding me that I needed to leave the plant and not check emails. I ignored him and his nervous pacing and continued checking my emails. *He needs to calm down; I am the one being thrown out of the plant—not him!*

And there it was, Ferengi's response: "Angelika, I would recommend that you sign the procedure-change form to show that you understand the information communicated. You can also add a statement with your concerns. Then we won't have to continue to spend time on this issue or pursue any other action. The ball is completely in your court to resolve this situation."

Apparently, Ferengi had a different thought pattern than Jezebel and Nabal. Sometime along the way, the ball jumped out of my court and flew out the window. Maybe it would catch up with all the past good-faith gestures that I had made through the years that also flew out the windows, never to rebound.

I sent a hasty email back and copied everyone he did, and included Gremlin, and Theodore, who was now the vice president of the company. I let everyone know that "they" refused to let me sign the form now, but instead, I was being thrown out the plant. I also let everyone know that I was going to file NLRB charges, and would address this as far as I could.

Chapter 102

Betrayal

Most of these procedures' changes that involved signing these procedure-change forms had to do with major changes or new equipment being installed, that if workers were not properly trained before implementing the change or using the equipment, or the procedure was not properly followed, it would adversely change our products or cause major safety hazards.

In contrast, this train air brakes procedure change was regressing in safety by no longer mandating the use of train air brakes when moving railcars full of dangerous chemicals, yet also allowed the option to continue using the train air brakes. Although I was infuriated with everything that transpired, I had the undeniable peace from God that surpasses all comprehension.

Both Nabal and Jezebel stated that I would be allowed to sign the form on Monday, as Chief witnessed. Jezebel had sent an email to my home email address and denied she told me this. She left me hanging for four days before sending to my home email address a step-three DML (decision making leave) discipline letter, which included three days off without pay. At no time in the past was a discipline letter ever sent to an employee's home email address, or sent through any email. This was a direct violation of our contract.

This same management was adamant during our last contract negotiations that I was involved in, that their corrective action policy would be noted in our contract and precisely adhered to for all steps in the discipline process. This policy clearly stated: "In all corrective action steps, a union official must be present unless expressly refused in writing by the employee."

Not one union rep copied on Jezebel's discipline email, which included Newbie, addressed her contract violation, or reneging on her agreement that I could sign the form on Monday. This was not the first time these union reps knew of this same management violating our contract regarding how they administered discipline; I knew all about this firsthand.

That evening after I received this DML discipline letter, Newbie met with those who would testify at the higher-wage arbitration scheduled the following day. When everyone left this meeting, I stayed behind to discuss with Newbie what happened the previous Friday. During our conversation, Newbie was sure to remind me: "You know the rule: obey now and grieve later."

It is a long-standing rule that every union rep makes clear to rank-and-file union members to avoid insubordination discipline: If told to do something they do not want to do, just do it and file a grievance later. But Newbie conveniently neglected to remember the one significant exception to this rule: disobey when safety is compromised.

As far as I was concerned, the safety of everyone at our plant site was compromised by no longer mandating the use of train air brakes while moving large quantities of railcars that were fully loaded with dangerous chemicals, and especially moving them through congested pedestrian and vehicle traffic areas.

And I knew these union reps were not going to address any of my concerns with a grievance. Just as they did not address my safety concerns with Virgil, or the damaged coupler that resulted in the June meeting and my emotional meltdown, and nothing was addressed since my return to work from my sick leave.

Newbie had not changed at all, especially regarding me, and I knew him well. He was governing behind the scenes again. He was taking the position that I was the one in the wrong again. He was not taking into consideration any of my safety or liability concerns.

Newbie had already judged me before we discussed this—without hearing my side of the story.

No doubt, Newbie conversed with his allies prior to them issuing a DML discipline letter. Had management terminated my employment under insubordination, they all knew that Newbie would have had no choice but to arbitrate such a termination. And management's sliver of hope to win an arbitration to secure my termination was obliterated with Ferengi's email and my response.

Just like Cain, Newbie would not lose face with his favored Joab by blowing a sure-to-win arbitration for terminating an employee for a lame excuse of refusing to sign a regressed in safety procedure change form. However, management also knew that Newbie had no qualms with forcing me to "eat" another discipline letter. All this was confirmed in how the events unfolded.

At the corporate building for the higher-wage arbitration the following day (and not surprisingly, we lost the arbitration), I ran into Jezebel in the restroom as she stood in front of the mirror. I greeted her with a simple hi. She said nothing, but tensed up and gave me a mean stare only through the mirror.

The day after arbitration, Thursday, we had a meeting before I was allowed back into the plant. Sabrina, Audrey and Nabal were at this meeting from management. Pres, Chief and Newbie were present as my union reps.

Audrey started off rehashing the June meeting and her emails with expectations that Lucinda was supposed to direct the handler workers as the trainer/production tech. I voiced my previous well-known objection: Union employees were not to be in roles as salaried supervisors, period. No union rep supported me on this.

Audrey stated if there was a disagreement with Lucinda and what she directed, or if I had any safety concerns, I should reach out to Nabal, and if he wasn't available, I should reach out to her. She made it clear that this could also be done by radio contact.

Apparently, no one present remembered the recent past when I voiced my disagreements and safety concerns before, and how they backfired on me. Or were they purposely ignoring the facts of the past now? Nabal regularly monitored our radio conversations, and as of yet, he made no attempts to address anything. I knew nothing was going to change in the near future.

I expressed to Audrey and all present my safety concerns with the procedure change for no longer mandating the use of the train air brakes, and my concerns with how this procedure was worded. I also stated that there were discrepancies between the General rail operations manual obtained from the company's other plant site and the Liquid Handler rail procedures manual that Lucinda revised, and that these were significant discrepancies that posed major safety hazards. I reminded them that we were supposed to reference both these manuals for our procedures working the rails.

No one seemed to even hear what I had to say, let alone care. Everyone there had only one concern: I sign the procedure-change form. They all reaffirmed, including the union reps present, that I could write a statement under my signature noting my concerns.

I finally signed this form with my statement underneath and gave it to Nabal with a request for a copy. It was no more than a minute from when Nabal left the room to make a copy, that he was back in the room along with Sabrina and Audrey. All of them were now telling me that I had to cross out my added statement: "pending addressing my concerns," and initial the cross out.

I was so angry and countered, "Wait a minute! You ALL told me I could write a statement expressing my concerns under my signature! Now you're telling me to cross it out? I've got concerns I want addressed!"

They were all adamant that I cross out my statement they didn't want kept in there or deal with, and until I did, I would not be allowed to go back to work.

My union reps never spoke in my defense. *I cannot believe this is really happening! What is wrong with these people? Doesn't anyone care at all about what concerns I have?*

Newbie told me to just use one line to cross out my statement so it could still be read in case we needed it for later, trying to give me the impression that he would support me in this; I knew better.

He's eating another canary!

After the salaried personnel left this meeting, I had a heated discussion with these union reps. I pointed out the violations of our contract regarding how this discipline was handled, and how Jezebel made sure no union reps were present when she knew she was going to throw me out of the plant.

Chief finally confessed that Jezebel did call him on Friday morning asking for his presence before she met with me, and that he was the one who refused to be present on my behalf. He stated, "I told her if you wanted me there, you would call me. And when you did, I came as soon as I could."

I was infuriated and extremely upset over everything, but especially the betrayal of my union reps; the very ones I worked with side by side for many years.

Pres finally spoke and criticized my last email I sent to these reps before I left the office of union president. He said I sent them an email offering my help, and then sent another email telling them I didn't want their representation should management approach them that they were going to throw me out of the plant. I told Pres that was not at all what I wrote in the email. He was adamant that his interpretation was correct, and then added in his angry tone: "I bet you still have a copy of that email!"

Apparently, he didn't keep a copy. I responded, "As a matter of fact, I do have a copy." But by this time, I was completely done with these guys and couldn't say too much more. I needed out of there and away from these so-called union reps.

At the arbitration the day before, the union's main defense to justify a higher wage was claiming how dangerous the rail job was. After I walked out of this meeting very visibly upset, Newbie sent Pres and Chief after me to make sure I was okay, but he took his time doing so.

They caught up to me in their Kubota as I was walking through the Darkly Graveyard heading to the handler building, about one-third of a mile from where the meeting was. Chief was the one who spoke: "Newbie wanted us to check on you. We just told everyone yesterday how dangerous it was out on the rails, and he was concerned with you being so upset. Are you okay?"

You guys really don't care! I kept my thoughts to myself and stated the obvious: "NO! I am not okay! Just leave me alone!"

I turned and walked away from these guys who were supposed to represent me. I was so tired of the hypocrisy and contradictions of everyone involved. No one was listening to me at all about my safety concerns, what I was going through working this job, or dealing with a dictator union employee who seemed to get so confused herself, and who refuses to follow my directions while it was my job and life on the line moving these railcars.

Once I got to the handler building, no one spoke to me, and I spoke to no one; it was better that way. I still did my job to the best of my ability. When it came to getting any handler training, it didn't matter what Nabal told Lucinda on how he wanted me trained. Her responses to me afterward once he was gone were always: "Get the procedures and self-train."

So, I did what I could on my own. With Samson still off on sick leave, I continued to do the brunt of the ground-person duties working the rails. The working atmosphere was at its worst, as was the RSD condition, as was the torment witnessing so many near misses while working the rails.

Chapter 103

Near Misses

Ever since the rail job was added to the Liquid Handler Department, I witnessed many near misses on the rails that upset me and could have caused a serious incident or injury.

When Tara was trying to train Lucinda as the ground-person at the beginning, while I was driving the locomotive, a man was crossing the tracks where he should not have been while seemingly oblivious to the locomotive. Tara directed me to move ahead with her back to the locomotive and didn't see the man. Had I not seen him before following Tara's direction to move ahead, he could have been seriously injured or killed.

Another near miss involved a contractor spraying a chemical for killing weeds around the rail tracks. His hose was strung across the tracks with his truck on the road. He too was oblivious to the locomotive, until it drove up to him—this put a scare in him.

Lucinda was responsible for contractors and work permits, but didn't understand the importance of issuing a work permit in this case, or the safety procedure of locking out the tracks for everyone's safety. Tara tried explaining to her what she should have done in this case, but Lucinda just argued with her.

After I came back from being thrown out of the plant, a rash of near misses escalated my torment and safety concerns on the rails. Causes of these were operator error, poor communications, and a few were from Lucinda's bad attitude.

The gatehouse guard was supposed to keep the ground-person informed whenever the railroad company was passing through on their main track in our plant that we also used, to avoid any near misses. Whenever Lucinda drove the locomotive, she insisted on listening to the handler radio channel on the radio she wore, while also listening to the rail channel on the radio in the locomotive cabin. The ground-person only conveyed directions on the rail channel. Listening to both channels at the same time proved to cause her more confusion.

One day, the guard told only Lucinda on the handler channel that the outside railroad company was coming through. I had no clue that this was happening, until I saw them moving railcars on the track I was directing Lucinda to move on. When I questioned the guard why this happened, his excuse was that he told Lucinda they were coming through. *But Lucinda isn't the ground-person, and she didn't relay that message to me!*

Around this same time, when Lucinda was driving and I was in the cabin, I witnessed her looking straight at a private vehicle ready to cross the tracks, but made no attempts to brake or blow a warning whistle. This driver decided he could beat the locomotive and crossed the tracks dangerously close in front of us. Had his vehicle stalled, it would have been smashed along with him inside.

Another near miss involved a rail track switch that was not locked in any position. When I visually checked this track switch per our procedure, the flag indicated it was locked in place on the track I was directing the railcars to move on. It was only after the railcars went over this track switch, and I went to switch it to another track that I realized it had not been locked in place.

Had the railcars been going the opposite direction over this track switch, it would have caused severe damage to the switch and a derailment of the railcars. As the ground-person, I would have been blamed for all damages. I never found out who was responsible for leaving this track switch unlocked. I thought of this incident often afterward, and wondered if it was purposely left unlocked knowing I was always the ground-person responsible?

643

After this last incident, I became even more vigilant while checking everything beyond what our procedures would dictate that normally, I would not have had to check. I wanted to make sure nothing else was out of the normal operating positions, that there would be no possible incident or error on my part knowing that target on me was even bigger now than ever before. This made for an even more stressful work environment.

Tara and Samson weren't always safe on the rails either. Tara didn't always feel the need to apply hand brakes when needed, and Samson had no qualms about texting on his phone while driving the locomotive. They also had many other unsafe practices that concerned me.

But there was one sure thing Tara and Samson understood very well: The ground-person was the eyes of the locomotive driver. The only time the locomotive driver should not follow the direction of the ground-person was if there was a hazard not known to the ground-person. When the ground-person directed the locomotive driver to stop, it meant immediately and without debate. Lucinda never understood this. And there was more than one near miss when Lucinda became confused and moved railcars in the opposite direction I had given her. I understood very well that anyone could make mistakes while working on any job. But there were times when Lucinda refused or debated my directions.

One incident happened when Lucinda was going way too fast when moving railcars to hook-up. I told her to stop the locomotive to get these railcars under control, and then directed her to move slower for the hook-up. She argued with me afterward. Lucinda insisted I only needed to tell her how many cars there were before she needed to stop for the hook-up. When I explained she was going too fast, she continued her argument that was habitual with her: "I'm the driver. That's my job. I know how fast I was going. Don't tell me to just stop anymore."

If Lucinda had smashed into these railcars too fast and went over the track-end stopper, as Tara and Samson once did, it would have been my job forfeited, not hers.

Everyone who monitored radio communications heard this conversation, including Nabal and Audrey. As I walked away after securing these railcars for a much-needed work break, I saw Audrey driving her Kubota. She gave me a pathetic look that told me she heard everything, but nothing was ever addressed.

I saw Pres driving around his Kubota afterward and asked to speak to him over the issue. He told me he didn't have time right then, but would catch up with me later; that later never came.

Someone once told me that they would laugh at the radio conversations that Lucinda and I had on the rails. I didn't find any of this funny at all. Under the best working conditions, working around and moving railcars was a dangerous job. Something bad was going to happen. Someone was going to get hurt. Soon, one of these near misses would hit their mark, and I could be it.

I was being tormented while working in the most perilous, hostile and physically demanding job I have ever worked in my entire life. I was constantly praying for my protection and others out on the rails and at other times.

My dad was killed because of the negligence of a coworker. It would only be with Divine protection that my life would be safeguarded from ending in the same way.

And that target on me only made matters worse. This last discipline letter was my last chance. The next step in the corrective action policy was automatic termination. Maybe questions would be asked afterward, but I doubted it. If management thought they had even a sliver of a chance to get away with terminating my employment, they would have jumped on it—that I had no doubt. With management knowing that my union reps refused to support me, it seemed to be only a matter of time now.

Chapter 104

My Grievance Meeting

*A*fter that last heated conversation with these union reps, I again sent them that email they referenced supporting their actions and beliefs that I did not want their representation until after management actually threw me out of the plant. Pres and Newbie never responded. Chief responded but initially held to his interpretation.

I responded to Chief as patiently as I could while expressing that he really misunderstood what I said in the email, but since it happened the way it did, we needed to deal with it now—together. Finally, Chief's light bulb turned on, but it didn't change how this discipline letter was addressed, as Newbie took the lead.

I wrote out the grievance myself, and worded it simple and short as compared to so many other grievances and remedies of past grievances that I wrote over the years. I just didn't have God's direction to write out in detail everything. God had other plans yet unbeknown to me, and He knew in the grand scheme at the end of all this, none of this was going to matter anyway.

Once the grievance was filed, Jezebel was adamant that the contractual steps of grievance meetings be bypassed, and moved it to the final step before arbitration. She justified her decision stating that all DML discipline letters were automatically moved to this final step. I was opposed to this and sent her via email two past DML discipline letters that were settled in the lower grievance steps, and copied the union reps. She forgot I was the union president for two terms! Her nasty-gram response didn't inspire the union reps to speak in my defense to follow our contractual steps for processing grievances, not even when I asked them to.

Neither did the union reps speak in my defense when I later tried again bringing forth my safety concerns on the rails, and the contradictions between the two rail procedures' manuals we were supposed to follow. This lack of union representation was now habitual and well known. I knew Newbie planned on forcing me to eat this discipline letter, just as he predetermined I would eat the last one on my so-called unethical behavior.

It was shortly after receiving the discipline letter that I met with a lawyer apart from the union, who attentively listened to my whole story without saying too much during my discourse. I started with my lack of training, my safety concerns with the damaged coupler, went through the June meeting and my emotional meltdown, and ended with being thrown out of the plant and disciplined for refusing to sign a procedure-change form until my safety and liability concerns were addressed.

When I finished speaking, this lawyer asked me one question that told me he heard everything I said: "What happened to the conflict resolution meeting that was supposed to take place?"

This lawyer gave me a clear direction and good advice: "File a formal OSHA complaint under their whistleblower protection program against management."

This OSHA whistleblower protection program investigates and addresses all alleged employers' retaliation against any employee who has brought forth safety concerns or other violations of the Occupational Safety and Health Act in the workplace. Although this lawyer's advice was correct as to who could address everything successfully, when I prayed about this path forward, I did not have God's direction to pursue this OSHA complaint at that time.

I knew filing OSHA complaints were drastic actions with ramifications that could have a domino effect throughout the entire plant site. This was not a simple record keeping non-compliance violation, such as untimely supplying me with copies of the OSHA 300 logs I once requested. Without God's direction to move forward with this OSHA whistleblower complaint, I would not do so. I continued to pray for God's direction in this situation while constantly keeping vigilant on my job. I wisely told no one of my contact with this lawyer.

The grievance meeting was scheduled soon after I met with the lawyer. As was normal practice, I met with the union reps just before this meeting for a last-minute discussion on how this was going to be addressed. Newbie, Chief, and Alvin, as vice president in place of Pres, were my union reps.

During this meeting, Chief admitted to Alvin that he misunderstood my email referring to my direction for any future discipline or being thrown out of the plant. It wasn't the first time Chief had different interpretations to what was really meant or said. I initially said nothing to what Chief now admitted.

However, before our long journey down the hallway to the HR conference room where this grievance meeting was going to be held, I started to think of what I could say to convince these reps to at least try to win this grievance. Newbie had already made it clear that he had no intention of supporting me during our first discussion on this discipline letter.

I decided to bring up Chief's prior knowledge and purposely not telling me that I was going to be thrown out of the plant. I didn't remind him that he also chose initially not to be present as my union rep. I regretted bringing this up as soon as I saw Chief's saddened expression. But I didn't have a chance to voice my regret before Newbie blew up in hot anger at me that I would dare bring up what was obvious to everyone—poor union representation.

While still raging at me, Newbie threw it back that I made the decision, and I should take all the blame for my actions—and I knew this. But no one was taking into consideration the principle concerns and safety compromise involved for the real reason I refused to sign that form in the first place. These union reps also conveniently forgot I was willing to sign this form before being thrown out of the plant, but Nabal and Jezebel refused to let me sign it. Chief also witnessed that with no objections in my defense.

Newbie's anger being aroused just before going into this grievance meeting was not a good start. I needed union reps willing to speak in my defense, as the next step in this corrective action policy was automatic termination of employment.

Ferengi and Jezebel were present during this grievance meeting, along with Audrey and Nabal. The start of the meeting did not go well. In front of everyone, Newbie and I started off with a debate as to who should speak first. *This is a no-brainer!*

Many times over, Newbie had made it clear that I should not represent or speak for myself in such issues, not even when I was the union president. Now he wanted me to speak first? This debate only reaffirmed that he had no intention of supporting me or speaking in my defense. I insisted on Newbie speaking first.

Newbie stated, "We are asking for reconsideration given the circumstances and events that went down on how this discipline was administered. Angelika will now speak on the corrective action policy."

I was on my own again, speaking for myself!

I spoke to Jezebel first: "The corrective action policy clearly states that in all steps, a union official must be present unless expressly refused in writing by the employee. This corrective action policy is now part of our contract language. It was a violation of our contract not to have a union rep present. Instead, I got thrown out of the plant, left hanging for four days, and then received a decision-making-leave discipline letter sent to my home email address! How many other employees get discipline letters sent to their home email address? This was not following the company's corrective action policy."

Jezebel tilted her head and gave me her "dumb expression" look without saying a word.

I then spoke to Audrey and Nabal: "I was told that I could write a statement on the procedure-change form noting my concerns along with my signature, only to be told after I did, that I had to cross out my statement, or I would not be allowed to go back to work! I have safety and liability concerns I want addressed with no longer mandating the use of train air brakes. There are also discrepancies between the General rail operations manual from the other plant site and the Liquid Handler rail procedures manual that pose major safety concerns that need addressed. We are supposed to reference and use both manuals for our procedures while performing our rail job. You people have no idea how dangerous it is out there working the rails."

Audrey had her own expression of showing disinterest in a subject matter that was being discussed: She would roll her eyes looking up into the air as if she was watching something else going on. She responded with her rolled eyes.

After each statement I made, Ferengi would ask, "Is there anything else to share?"

All Ferengi wanted was to be done with this meeting, and with me. He obviously already had his mind made up, as did everyone else in management, as did Newbie. Chief never spoke a word. Alvin was the only rep who spoke just a few words in my favor.

I directed my last statement only to Ferengi, who I knew was so ticked off at me for filing another board charge: "A man was smashed while two railcars were being coupled together some years ago at this plant site. How would you feel if someone was killed out on the rails? How could you live with yourself then?"

His response was the same: "Is there anything else to share?"

Ferengi was the man who was always so big on safety in the plant. Yet, it was Ferengi who drove his van through deep standing water under the plant overpass during a torrential downpour, instead of going an alternative route. He and six occupants had to climb out the windows and tread water to safety. And it was Ferengi who drove around the plant site with bald front tires on his SUV.

However, Ferengi was relentless in pursuing someone to discipline after even the smallest safety infraction; unless they were one of his favored employees—and obviously, I was not.

Ferengi was the man who headed the plant-wide procedure committee that I was part of for years by this time, and the man who told me the ball was in my court to resolve this situation. All I had to do was sign the form, I could add my statement under my signature, and nothing else would happen.

It seemed no one was listening to me. No one cared to even acknowledge any of my concerns, let alone address them. Most of these people just wanted me to go away—permanently. I left that meeting believing that had I been hurt or killed on the rails, there were some present who would not have cared one way or another.

Chapter 105
Divine Ambush

I knew the NLRB charge was not going anywhere. I was well versed on what they would deal with. I knew that without being a union official anymore, they wouldn't deal with this discipline letter, or any safety or liability concerns I had. But I also knew without a doubt that the board charge was something God directed me to follow through with.

This board charge took only one phone call. Just two days later, my case was assigned to a board agent, Peter. But it took several phone calls trying to contact Peter before we connected. He explained his delay was due to being on vacation. Now that we connected, he wanted to meet and rush through this charge sooner than I wanted to. Reluctantly, I agreed to a meeting the following week. The dining area at an Ikea store halfway between where I lived and where Peter worked in Pittsburgh served well for a meeting place several times before dealing with board agents. So we agreed on a date and time to meet there.

I arrived at Ikea first and waited on Peter, who I didn't know to recognize. When Peter showed up a few minutes later, he recognized me and remembered that we spoke one time before. Peter was the board agent on duty working the information desk when I went there for my first board charge while still union president. He was never assigned to any board charges of the past. But by Divine appointment, he was assigned to this last one.

I related my story to Peter as I did with the lawyer, starting from the training issues, through the June meeting, and ended with the reason I filed the board charge: I was thrown out of the plant and disciplined for refusing to sign a procedure-change form until my safety and liability concerns were addressed. He listened as attentively as the lawyer did, and then made a nice comment after I finished speaking: "You articulate very well."

I responded with astonishment, and then acknowledgment to the One who was the giver of all gifts in my life: "Thank you! No one has ever told me that before. But really, it's a gift from God's Holy Spirit."

This opened the door that allowed a beautiful sharing time of our faith and belief in the same Lord and Savior, Jesus. Peter was a born-again Christian living his life for the Lord. I don't believe in coincidences; this was Divine appointment. Peter gave me the same advice as the lawyer: I should have filed a formal complaint with OSHA under their whistleblower protection program. I told him I still could. He didn't respond. He knew the time limit was thirty days for filing an OSHA complaint. But what he didn't know was that God had a grand scheme in all of this that He was working on for my career and life. I would pray about this later.

But for right then, I told Peter that if nothing else came out of this current storm I was facing except meeting him, it would have been well worth everything. We parted on good terms rejoicing in the Lord, and with the understanding that I would withdraw the board charge.

That evening during my quiet time with God, I sought His direction on a path forward. Now I had God's direction to file this OSHA whistleblower complaint. I counted down the days, and if the date of when Jezebel sent the discipline letter to my home email address was used, it would be just under the thirty-day limit.

The following day, I phoned OSHA and heard a recording that the contact person to file complaints with would not be available until the next day. But the next day was too late! Tenacious me would not give up until I spoke with a real person.

It took some doing, but I finally reached Douglas, the head of OSHA. After explaining to him the recorded message, I stated, "Today is the last day I can file this complaint."

Douglas responded, "The time limit just stopped with this phone call."

Butch was the OSHA agent who was assigned to my case and contacted me by phone as a follow-up to my conversation with Douglas. When Butch sent the preliminary complaint based on our phone conversation, there were so many mistakes that I contacted him via email. It was through his email that he stated he was going on a three-week leave of absence. I contacted him back asking because of his leave, would I have extra time to prepare my full complaint statement? His answer was "yes." I believed I also had extra time for the initial complaint form I was required to sign and send in after my first phone contact with Douglas.

It was the Lord who reminded me, although I had more time to prepare my full complaint statement, my initial complaint form must be sent within OSHA's ten-day time limit for doing so, or it would be dismissed for being untimely filed. After sending in my initial complaint form, I started working on my whistleblower complaint statement.

Jezebel had quoted an OSHA regulation in the discipline letter that she claimed my refusal to sign this procedure-change form would have violated.

Along with my twenty-four-page complaint statement, I included copies of my discipline letter, the procedure-change form with my signature and one line crossed-out statement, and other company-generated documents. These supported my safety and liability concerns, and supported my allegations of retaliatory discipline for trying to address my concerns. I was very thorough while using these documents to clarify that management were the ones who violated Jezebel's quoted OSHA regulation with how they implemented the train air brakes procedure change, and violated their own plant procedures and policies while doing so.

I also included with my statement copies of other procedure-change forms and documents of recent past procedures' changes that supported how these were also implemented in a way that violated Jezebel's quoted OSHA regulation, and supported how management was habitual in violating their own plant procedures and policies at the same time. I took great care while referencing every document in my statement in such a way as to make sure all my allegations were credible.

I discussed this OSHA complaint with no one, either prior to filing it or afterward. When OSHA sent management the notice of my initial complaint (OSHA whistleblower complaints are not anonymous), it was a Divine ambush to everyone involved. Everything seemed to be timed just right, and I really believed God was directing everything in His way and timing, and that this OSHA complaint would come to fruition.

Before management knew of my OSHA complaint, they had already sent their grievance answer: It was denied. None of my safety or liability concerns were given a second thought.

At the next union membership meeting, without naming me as the grievant, Pres announced that the e-board voted not to take my grievance for this DML discipline letter to arbitration.

When I requested how many e-board officers were present for this vote, he said only three members were present. This was less than half the quorum needed to have an e-board meeting; therefore, the vote was not valid. Newbie later told me that he was the one who made the final decision not to arbitrate my grievance.

I had no doubts that this grievance could have been won in arbitration. To sum it all up, nothing was done contractually correct, or according to plant procedures, or according to OSHA regulations. The injustice continued with everyone ignoring my safety and liability concerns, and with poor union representation.

But the real killer was Ferengi's email stating the ball was in my court. All I had to do was sign the form and no further action would be taken against me, even as he reiterated that I could include a statement along with my signature noting my concerns: a statement that I was coerced to cross out after I signed it.

Yep, I had no doubt Newbie was again governing behind the scenes with this discipline letter, and not only by refusing arbitration. And as usual, management knew they had Newbie— another staff rep—supporting them against me.

I could have gone over Newbie's head as I did Cain's, and paid another visit to my dear old friend, Joab, our district director, and forced arbitration. And if Joab didn't agree to this arbitration, I could have filed NLRB charges against these union reps for misrepresentation. But I didn't have God's direction to pursue any of these avenues.

After all my years in this local union, I still believed no one really understood that the Holy Spirit was my driving force, or that I did my best to follow God's direction while making such important decisions. God takes delight in intricately orchestrating my life according to His purpose. What people mean for my harm, God turns it around and uses it for my good. (Genesis 50:20, Romans 8:28.) I have witnessed this many times during God's nurturing of my life.

The Lord God had another direction for my life that as of that time, He had not revealed to me yet. My only obligation was obeying the Lord one step at a time, and then trusting His grace and power to get me through.

Chapter 106

God's Timing

Soon after my initial call to Douglas, someone from OSHA had sent me the Whistleblower Investigation manual that outlined the procedure for investigating such complaints. This manual had a disclaimer: The intent was only to provide guideline instructions regarding some of the internal operations, and was not enforceable by any person or entity. In other words, any deviation from the procedure instructions in this manual was permissible.

OSHA had very heavy workloads and probably still do. It was not unusual to take several months and at times years for complaints to be resolved under their whistleblower protection program. However, OSHA is well known for being very strict on the time limits for filing any complaints. Safety concern complaints that impose imminent danger in any workplace are addressed immediately, as they should be.

I mailed my OSHA complaint via certified return receipt, but before they received it, the U.S. government shut down. This added a longer delay to Butch's three weeks leave of absence. The complaint stayed in limbo during this time, leaving management hanging without knowing the outcome. This was just a bit longer than the four days I was left hanging by Jezebel. Once the government re-opened, it did not take long for Butch to contact me by leaving a voice message asking that I call him to discuss my case. He called at the end of my three-week vacation, the longest vacation time I ever took at one time.

When I contacted Butch at his request before I returned to work, he informed me that my complaint was being dismissed due to being untimely filed.

We had a long discussion over this dismissal decision. I referenced the Whistleblower Investigation manual in relation to how the thirty days were calculated. Accordingly, the day after the decision was made and communicated to the employee of the adverse action being taken was the start date for the thirty days. The manual also stated that if a hostile work environment was proven to exist and retaliation was ongoing, any date of adverse action could be used.

OSHA was using the date I was thrown out of the plant, which made it three days past the thirty-day time limit. I was using the date Jezebel actually sent the discipline letter to my home email address, making the decision and communication for that adverse action on that same day, still within the thirty-day time limit.

The Whistleblower Investigation manual meant nothing in my defense in supporting that I did file my complaint timely. Butch was not satisfied with my reasoning. I was not satisfied with his dismissal decision for my complaint.

Butch explained that I could withdraw my complaint based upon his dismissal decision, in which case it would be as though I had never filed a complaint. Absent this withdrawal, the dismissal decision would stand, but my complaint file would be held for five years and accessible to OSHA during that time, and I would have the option of filing a formal appeal to the dismissal decision.

With my job jeopardized and none of my concerns addressed, in addition to spending so much time and energy on this OSHA complaint statement while submitting so many documents supporting my allegations, I wasn't about ready to just drop this. Therefore, I let Butch know that withdrawing my whistleblower complaint was not an option.

Butch suggested I write to Douglas, his superior who initially took my phone complaint, regarding this dismissal decision—so I did. I wrote another letter and submitted more emails justifying using the later date, which showed that just the day before this later date, the decision to give me the discipline letter had not been made yet. However, even after submitting these additional documents, the decision to dismiss my complaint was still final.

On the initial phone conversation with Butch discussing this dismissal, he informed me that a letter would be sent reiterating this dismissal decision with instructions for filing a formal appeal. I sent a follow-up email to Butch soon afterward asking when I could expect this letter, and I was glad I did (Document Princess strikes again). Butch assured me this letter would be sent out in the near future.

After the dismissal of my complaint, I really believed God had deceived me in this whole situation. I could have filed this complaint well within the thirty-day time limit, but did not do so because God's direction initially was not to file the complaint. Once God gave me the direction to file it, I believed everything was lining up perfectly. Had I met with Peter just one day later, I would have believed the time limit was past for filing this complaint. Had I continued to believe I had more time for the initial phone complaint to be put in writing than just the ten days, it would have been untimely filed.

"So, what happened, Lord? Why have me go through all this for nothing?"

My strong anger over the dismissal of my OSHA complaint was unjustified when I understood the obvious answers. The Lord would never deceive me! My purpose for filing this OSHA whistleblower complaint would not come to fruition, but God's purpose would. I would not understand what God had planned out with all this until further into the future. But I didn't need to understand God's plan just then. All I needed to do was to continue to follow God's directions one step at a time.

I returned to work from my vacation just after speaking with Butch about my OSHA complaint being dismissed. Chief refused to speak to me for a very long time after I filed this complaint. When Chief finally spoke to me, he expressed strong anger and said he would never forgive me for filing my OSHA complaint. Chief's justification was that I put the entire plant site in jeopardy by doing so. I ignored Chief's strong anger and unforgiving attitude. I knew I didn't do anything that required his forgiveness.

These union reps had their chance to address my discipline letter, and my safety and liability concerns. But even before the e-board voted against arbitration without a quorum, and before I filed my OSHA complaint, I knew these union reps were not going to address anything on my behalf, especially with Newbie taking the lead.

The Lord knew that I would have never wanted to jeopardize the plant site as a legacy of my career. My OSHA whistleblower complaint statement and all the documents supporting my allegations could have very well jeopardized the plant.

And my Lord also knew that I would not have filed this OSHA complaint without His direction to do so. The timing was perfectly orchestrated by the Lord and part of His grand scheme. God still sent His message while the ramifications were avoided.

In the end, the Lord used my actions in filing this OSHA whistleblower complaint in a powerful way for my benefit that not even I knew at that time could happen.

Chapter 107
Agenda Against Me

After my DML discipline letter grievance was denied, I tried one final time through an email to address the discrepancies between the two rail operating manuals with Audrey and Nabal, but to no avail. Audrey's nasty-gram response that copied union reps only supported everyone's lack of interest in such a major safety hazard when having to reference and use both manuals' procedures while performing our rail job.

I tried several more times addressing Lucinda's refusal to follow my directions on the rails only with the union reps, but to no avail. I hated my job at this point, more so than ever before. Each day, I would wake up dreading to go to work, yet determined that I was not going to let these people push me out of my job.

Since my OSHA complaint was dismissed, there was a concerted effort at deliberate contractual violations against me personally. I believed that with my union reps' obvious lack of support for me that was well known by this time, the mindset was that no other grievances I might file that had merit would be addressed. I was also sure that management knew of Chief's strong anger towards me over filing my OSHA complaint. All this would have caused management to believe that I was on my own from here on out without any union representation. But none of this deterred me from my legal and contractual rights to file grievances for contract violations against me personally.

There was strong contract language that governed vacation requests and overtime distribution, two treasured and guarded benefits in any union shop. When Samson finally returned to work after being off for over four months, he had a lot of vacation days left that needed used up by the end of the year. Samson was one of those rank-and-file union members who had no qualms about approaching management on his own asking for special deals.

Samson had requested every Monday and Friday off for the next few months until the end of the year, which would use up his vacation days. Since this was not contractually permitted, Nabal and Audrey approached Jezebel, who then approached Chief. Jezebel wanted Chief's agreement to this special deal for their own protection. They wanted to be able to invoke their long-standing defense: "But your union agreed to this."

This special vacation deal was great for Samson, but denied my contractual rights as more senior to Samson to some of these same days off, and some I had requested while Samson was still off but were denied. I amicably pointed all this out to Nabal via email. Nabal responded via email and adamantly denied my requested vacation days off again that contractually, he should have approved.

I filed a grievance over this issue, as I needed one of these days for a trip to New York. During the grievance meeting, Nabal revealed his strong anger over my OSHA complaint as he defended his denial for my vacation days again: "After what you just put me through these past three months!"

What about what I have been going through all these months that you could have addressed but refused? I did not speak what I wanted to tell him, but hoped my looks said it all.

Then Jezebel had one of her conniptions because I sent my vacation requests to Nabal via email instead of word of mouth, and stated that I was no longer permitted to waste time by sending emails to Nabal, or anyone else for that matter. She warned me that going forward, I was only to speak verbally with Nabal.

Silvia was Adrianne's replacement, and very new with these grievance meetings while being present to take notes. Jezebel apologized to Silvia for her angry outburst, expressing that the habit of sending emails hit her nerves. I so much wanted to tell her what I was thinking: *And this is coming from the company's Document Queen herself!* But I knew better than to say anything to Jezebel, as I also knew that emails were an acceptable form of communication at our company. Jezebel didn't like how I used some of these emails recently in my defense. I was sure Ferengi's ball-in-my-court email was at the forefront of her thoughts.

Chief supported my grievance at this meeting, which I am sure was a surprise to everyone—it was to me. He stated that this special vacation deal for Samson that was not contractually permitted, was never meant to deny an older employee their contractual vacation requests. I remembered other "special deals" Chief had agreed to while I was the union president that I had to intervene to stop because they were not contractually permitted, and denied others their contractual rights.

Although Chief supported the merits of my grievance, Jezebel still refused to grant my vacation days off in her grievance answer. In addition, she stated that the special vacation deal with Samson would end because I filed a grievance over the issue, which she knew would cause strife between us and in our department.

My intentions were never to mess up Samson's special deal. I only wanted three vacation days off as compared to his two each week for a few months. After getting the grievance answer, I told Chief to withdraw my grievance and let Samson have his special deal. I would forego my contractual rights to vacation days off for his benefit. This allowed Samson to keep his special vacation deal.

Just before this last vacation grievance meeting, I was denied an overtime opportunity working the rails that was instead given to Lucinda. This was another contract violation against me personally. I tried addressing this also amicably with Nabal via email while there was still time to stop this violation by giving me the overtime instead. But as usual, he just blew me off.

When I gave Chief my bypassed-overtime grievance I wrote up, he again expressed strong anger towards me over my OSHA complaint. It was at this time that I spoke to him about another near miss on the rails, but he didn't seem to care at all. We parted on this bad note between us.

It was the weekend before Veterans Day when I emailed Ferengi letting him know that I was withdrawing from his plant-wide procedure committee. He canceled out the last few meetings for lame excuses. The last procedure we were reviewing was sent out using email asking for feedback. It seemed pretty obvious to me that he was purposely avoiding my presence at any meetings. He was angry with the board charge I filed, but he was irate over my OSHA whistleblower complaint. And such was life!

I reiterated in this email all that went down when I was thrown out of the plant. I reminded Ferengi that he told me the ball was in my court, yet I was refused the opportunity to sign the form to avoid being thrown out. I expressed again my safety and liability concerns on the rails with this procedure change. Being on this committee with Ferengi for a few years should have meant something. We both knew procedures were supposed to be written with openness as to the wording and considering the ramifications for those who did the job on a consistent basis.

I made it clear to Ferengi that I was accountable to the Lord God in ways no one could understand, and had I followed the advice of the outside lawyer to file the OSHA complaint instead of waiting on the Lord's direction to do so, there would be a full-blown OSHA investigation throughout the plant site that everyone would be dealing with. I told Ferengi that any decision not to file a formal appeal to the OSHA dismissal decision would be at the direction of the Lord, and not for anyone else.

Why was I willing to share all this with a man who had been an adversary for so many years? It was the Lord's leading, as I also shared with Ferengi why: "Because after all these years of knowing you, I know there is another side of you, another side that believes you are doing right, another side that believes in Jesus. I believe we were both caught in a circumstance that took us off guard that neither one of us wanted. I will continue to follow the Lord in His next direction in all this, and will pray that you do also."

Ferengi's response surprised me, as he asked that I reconsider withdrawing from the procedure committee while expressing that I had provided valuable input in the past that he believed would continue. I didn't commit to a final decision right then.

It was the Thursday after Veterans Day, and towards the end of the shift, Nabal and I spoke about the heavy workload on the rails the following day. My RSD condition had been getting considerably worse over the last several months, and I was going to be the only available ground-person while Lucinda was the locomotive driver. Samson was off, and Arnold was never physically capable of doing the rail job. The grievance meeting on the bypassed overtime issue was also going to take place first thing in the morning.

All of this really concerned me, so very much that I wanted to just pick up the phone and report off for that Friday. With our new contract language that allowed report-offs to be converted to personal single vacation days at the employee's request, my report-off would not have been considered unexcused.

However, I didn't have God's permission to do so. I resigned myself to going to work and dealing with everything as it came. I trusted the Lord knowing that He knew what was going to happen, and that He had everything under His control.

Chapter 108

Last Battle

I walked into work that Friday as the cold November morning aggravated my RSD condition. I wondered, but not for the first time: *How am I ever gonna handle working another winter outside on the rails?* And it wasn't even the dead of winter yet. And it wasn't just the rail job work that aggravated the RSD. Unloading the styrene-railcars was proving to take its toll on my arms and hands.

Lucinda and I made some rail moves early before the scheduled bypassed overtime grievance meeting, which caused me to be late for the meeting. Audrey, Nabal and Chief were present. Nabal mentioned that Lucinda had some medical issues that would be preventing her from learning and doing the ground-person work on the rails indefinitely; this information was offered on his own. It was always much easier to just drive the locomotive while the ground-person did the brunt workload.

After the bypassed overtime issue with the grievance was discussed, we ended the meeting with Nabal stating he would get some contractor area log paperwork from the handler building that justified his decision to give Lucinda the overtime instead of me, since part of her job dealt with contractors.

Outside the office building after the grievance meeting, I spoke with Chief again about the rail safety issues and some recent near-misses that I stated would have caused a derailment of the railcars. He was still very angry over my OSHA complaint that he wasn't hearing anything I said. We parted again on this bad note.

Later that afternoon, I walked in on Nabal speaking with Lucinda and Arnold in the handler building as he held the area logs he was supposed to get for the grievance. Nabal had always instigated the friction between Lucinda and me at every possible opportunity; I believed this was always intentional. Whatever Nabal had said to Lucinda set her off into one of her tantrums.

The door hadn't closed from Nabal leaving the building before Lucinda lashed out on me: "Ange, you're walking a fine line. You screwed up Samson's vacation deal, and now you turned me in."

No doubt, Nabal had discussed both my grievances with Lucinda, which past practice was not done until after they were settled. Nabal's selective information he discussed didn't include my withdrawal of my vacation grievance to ensure Samson kept his special deal, even though contractually, I was entitled to my vacation requests.

I kept calm as I told Lucinda: "I did not screw up Samson's vacation deal, and I had every right to file a grievance over a contract violation in how overtime was distributed. This had nothing to do with turning you in."

This didn't settle Lucinda down one bit. I didn't try telling her that I withdrew my vacation grievance so Samson could keep his special deal. I knew her well enough to know, in her current state of mind, Lucinda would only hear what she wanted to hear. These confrontations were becoming habitual!

As I walked away, she followed behind me and continued her ugly accusations and threats: "I'm going to get your union card pulled for turning me in. You went from being a union president to a non-union member."

I told Lucinda to stop. She continued, "I'm never going to speak to you again unless Chief is present. You turned me in, and you were a union president!"

I told Lucinda again to stop, but she continued with her tantrum. Finally, I told her what I always knew to be true but never brought it up until now: "You are the one who has constantly turned me in to Nabal, Audrey and other supervisors for my harm."

Lucinda's response only supported my accusations: "Prove it."

This confrontation was not going to end well unless the Lord intervened. Lucinda continued her tantrum even as I continued to tell her to stop with my attempts to remain patient and calm quickly edging away. In exasperation, I finally told her harshly: "SHUT UP!"

It was not how I wanted to end this, but enough was enough. This harshness only fueled Lucinda's aggression. She literally got in my face now, provoking me: "Make me shut up, baby doll."

Forty-plus years ago on the streets of the South Bronx, I threw a punch into a girl's stomach for provoking me just as Lucinda did.

Arnold had been in the background all this time, hands on his hips, chubby-belly sticking out with a great big smile on his face while observing everything, hoping I would do something stupid that would justify terminating my employment.

Forty-plus years later—a lot has happened in my life!

With the power of God's Holy Spirit now ruling my heart, I said nothing in response, but turned my back to Lucinda and walked away.

As I grabbed my safety gear to get ready to go back out on the rails after such a hostile ordeal, I came against the real enemy, binding and rebuking Satan and his demons in the name of the Lord Jesus Christ, and letting them all know that they were not going to have the victory over this battle.

I then prayed for God's protection for all of us, as I knew Lucinda, in her current state of mind, was not going to follow my directions on the rails even if my life depended on it. Only by the grace of God was I able to continue my job that afternoon.

There were still many railcar moves yet to be made on the rails, including moving twelve fully loaded styrene-railcars to the styrene unloading rack. This involved walking the longest distance along the tracks just a few feet ahead of the moving railcars, through the most congested pedestrian and vehicle traffic areas of the plant, while remaining ever vigilant so that no one would get in harm's way.

But before these railcars could be moved, there were many dangerous tasks that I needed to do while I walked up and down a line of twenty-plus railcars: make sure they were hooked together, go in between them to connect air hoses, check that each cock valve was in the correct position, jump on and off of them to release hand brakes, make sure the pressured air was charged for the train air brakes.

To complete this move successfully and safely, it was absolutely imperative that the communications between the locomotive driver and ground-person were carefully understood and followed. This did not happen well that afternoon!

Out on the rails, I gave Lucinda the same direction three times over the radio to move the railcars to ensure all the brakes were released, but she never responded. I finally asked her if there was something wrong that was causing her not to be able to move the railcars as I directed. Her response told me she was again questioning my directions on her own.

It took some time before Lucinda finally started moving the railcars as I directed her for this move. I began counting off the twelve railcars to separate them from the twenty-plus in this string of connected railcars as they passed me.

Just before I was done with the count, Lucinda stopped the railcars on her own. Following was a round of confusing communications between the gatehouse guard, Lucinda, the railroad company locomotive driver, and me. All this confusion was the result of the outside railroad moving on the main track that our railcars were already moving on.

These confusing communications resulted in putting the twenty-plus string of railcars back where they started from, and starting and stopping the move several more times. With each restart of the move, I had to recount the twelve railcars needed. I was frustrated and worn out even before I had to walk the long journey to the unloading rack.

Finally, we reached the styrene unloading rack with these twelve fully loaded railcars. The train air brakes were applied to each railcar connected in the string when the air hose on the first railcar nearest the locomotive disconnected as the locomotive pulled away.

I left the cock valve in the open position on this first railcar so as not to bottle-in the train air on the whole string of connecting railcars. The last railcar at the end of these twelve railcars had its cock valve closed.

This simple action caused Lucinda and I to have another disagreement: She insisted the cock valve should be left in the closed position. As I was still on the ground, I explained over the radio that the General rail operations manual made it clear that one cock valve needed to be left open on one end on the string of connected railcars once the train air brakes were applied. Otherwise, if the train air was left bottled-in, the air would bleed off causing the train air brakes to be released, which in turn could cause the string of railcars to run-away. This explanation was heard by everyone who monitored radio communications at this plant site, including Nabal.

After I jumped into the locomotive, there was no shouting match, but our disagreement continued. Lucinda was adamant that I follow the Liquid Handler rail procedures manual, which stated the cock valves on the end of the first and last railcar in a string of connecting railcars were to be left in the closed position. I was adamant that I was going to follow the General rail operations manual, which was written by those who had more experience using train air brakes than Lucinda and those working at our plant site had.

Once again, I explained to Lucinda the safety hazard of the train air brakes being released as the air bled off from being left bottled-in. For one last time, I stated that there were significant discrepancies between these two different rail operation manuals that posed major safety hazards, yet it was still mandatory that we referenced both while performing our rail job.

She responded, "Then why didn't you tell anyone?"

I could not believe what she just asked me! Lucinda was privy to every safety and liability concern I tried getting addressed these last several months.

I responded, "I did! But no one ever listens to me!"

And with that said, I decided it was best to get off the locomotive and away from Lucinda, and as I did, I shook the dust off my feet and walked away. (Matthew 10:14.)

I was so done by then, physically and emotionally. While every limb was screaming out in pain, my heart was screaming out a warning: I needed to stop working the rails for that day.

Chapter 109

Divine Rescue

After I left Lucinda in the locomotive, I tried to contact Nabal to ask if the rest of the rail moves that needed done could wait till Monday. I walked to his office but he wasn't there. The secretary thought he was taking care of a priority run. I waited for a while, but Nabal never showed up. I sent an email using my cell phone knowing that in the past he responded on his cell phone, but never received a response. I texted him and then called his cell phone. If he was receiving my contact, he was choosing not to respond. This practice of ignoring my contact was something Lucinda was habitual in doing.

The only method to contact Nabal that I did not try was over the plant radio. My main reason was that I didn't want Lucinda to hear me and think I was contacting Nabal about her. When all my attempts to contact Nabal failed, I had no doubts he was with Lucinda, who already had his ears about my refusal to follow the Liquid Handler rail procedures manual she had originally revised to include the train air brakes procedures.

Abby had always told me, if I had any problems working the rails physically due to the RSD, I was to let her know. Since I could not get a hold of Nabal after several tries with so much time that past, and I did not want to get fired for not completing my work, I went to the plant medical building hoping Abby would be there.

Abby was ready to leave when I showed up. I tried making my situation clear without giving out too much detail. I told Abby: "I am not saying that I cannot do my job long term. I am not saying that I cannot do my job on Monday. What I am saying is for right now, I am done. The pain is so bad that I cannot make any more rail moves today. And I tried, but I cannot contact Nabal to get his permission to leave the rest of the rail moves till Monday."

I wasn't with Abby long before Nabal finally texted me back. But his timing was too late! My text response was to call Abby.

Abby was a born-again Christian who always meant well and really cared for the employees; although she tended to err on the side of caution too much. Because Abby did not want to make the decision herself to allow me to work the rails on Monday, she contacted Dr. Willy. Upon her insistence, I agreed to see him that same afternoon. Dr. Willy and I always had a good rapport, and he understood RSD to some extent.

Chief had texted me earlier letting me know that he already had a copy of the grievance answer from that morning over being bypassed for the overtime. I had planned on stopping over to see him for my copy after my shift had ended. But when Dr. Willy wanted to see me as the last patient before the weekend, I didn't have time for this meeting with Chief. I understood later that this was again Divine intervention. Nothing good was going to come out of meeting with Chief while he was still very angry over my OSHA complaint, and after everything else that happened that day.

I gathered all my belongings, made sure all my lockers were locked, and left the plant in haste, almost imagining how the Israelites left Egypt. My full shift was completed as I carded out the gatehouse and drove straight to Dr. Willy's office. Walking into the medical building with me was an army of angelic warriors, their swords unsheathed and already battling the evil forces. Unbeknown to me at the time, I was walking into a demons' lair.

I explained to Dr. Willy the extreme pain I was dealing with in my limbs, how it had been progressively getting worse over the last few months, and how my toes had been turning blue. After each explanation of my symptoms, Dr. Willy would tap his temple with his index finger, and with a strange expression and authoritative but strange tone declared, "It's all up here."

This meeting with Dr. Willy was bizarre. Something with him had changed, as he was definitely not the same doctor I knew from visits before. He was from the Orthodox faith, and we had shared about God on many occasions. But I could not shake the turmoil during this visit that something was so wrong with him.

Dr. Willy made the decision that I was unfit for my work duties, and would not agree to allow me back into the plant in any work capacity with the RSD symptoms I was experiencing. He never once mentioned his new faith of Qigong as he did the last time we met, and neither did I. But by his actions, I was guessing he knew I never read up on the Qigong book he recommended during my last visit.

Meanwhile, the angelic warriors gained the upper hand in their battle against the resident demons in this place. But as I left this appointment, I could not shake off the spiritual turmoil I had while meeting with this doctor, which stayed with me the entire time I was driving home.

Abby asked me to call her as soon as the appointment was over. While speaking with Abby, I shared with her the extreme turmoil I was experiencing right then, and told her something was so wrong with this meeting that I had never experienced before with this doctor.

After this appointment, I decided to order the Qigong book Dr. Willy had recommended before. The little I read proved to me that this "Qigong Heal Yourself," was definitely demonic dabbling, and something I should not entertain at all. As a matter of fact, the Lord directed me to get rid of this book within less than twenty-four hours after receiving it.

It was much later that I remembered the Qigong convention Dr. Willy told me back in July, that he was excited about attending in October. It was now the second week of November. I've been to different conventions and understood firsthand how exhilarating and influential they can be. I could only imagine the demons that were invited into this man's life from such an experience.

None of this knowledge was going to change the circumstance I found myself in. I was out of the plant for God only knew how long. This became a time of really seeking the Lord for His next direction. I understood it could have been so much worse.

My employment could have been terminated rather than just medically being put out of the plant. I could have lost a limb or even my life. Maybe someone else could have been hurt, or a serious incident could have happened.

Less than two weeks after Dr. Willy put me out of the plant, there was a serious derailment of the railcars. While at the YMCA for my pool therapy for the RSD, I ran into someone who worked at the plant who shared this derailment incident with me. He didn't know the particulars, but any particulars would not have mattered. Had I been working the rails, and most likely I would have been, my employment would have been terminated over this incident without a doubt. Maybe questions would have been asked later—maybe not. Only the Lord would know for sure.

The Lord God pulled me out of the most perilous, hostile and physically demanding job environment I had ever worked in, and just in time before something really bad happened that I could have been involved in. That meeting with Chief was also never supposed to happen—this I was also sure of.

God proved He was still in control of my life. Although I found myself in limbo, I believed God was going to lead and direct me, as sure as He was protecting and nurturing me. I needed more than ever before to be attuned to God's Holy Spirit, and to follow His directions exclusively and precisely.

Chapter 110
Another Nightmare

Abby was adamant that I find a medical specialist who would oversee my care with the RSD while on sick leave. It didn't matter that it was the company's doctor who made the decision to keep me out of work, or that this was all work related. I had already started on my own doing pool therapy before I was put out of work. This helped before with the RSD when I was first diagnosed, and I believed it would help again.

The prospects, though, of trying to find a medical specialist to treat the RSD didn't appeal to me. But since I had to consider securing my employment, I had no choice. I had to find someone who knew enough about RSD to effectively treat this off-the-wall neurological pain disorder that I have been dealing with for almost fourteen years by this time, with the hopes that I would eventually be able to return to work. I believed that was the goal.

I reluctantly made an appointment to see a neurologist who my personal doctor had recommended. Dr. Nero was with the same group of doctors that my last treating neurologist was with, but whose knowledge of RSD was not up-to-date; that doctor had since left the group.

I was given a stack of paperwork to fill out in the waiting room. And lo and behold, there they were again—the naked-genderless-people form. Nothing had changed over the years with this form: "Please circle every part of the diagram below that corresponds to where you are experiencing pain." Yep, I was sure the copyright owner was a millionaire by this time. I filled out this form even knowing it was for naught.

While in the examining room, I watched my toes turn blue as I waited for Dr. Nero, who showed up with a demeanor that told me his mind was already made up. He spoke with authority from years of knowledge in his field to the point that his pride reared up as arrogance. I soon realized that he didn't understand RSD any more than his long-gone counterpart did years earlier.

Dr. Nero was determined that he was going to diagnose something else causing the pain other than RSD. My years of experience living with this painful condition meant nothing to this doctor. But hey, he was the doctor—I was not!

Dr. Nero was not going to treat me in any way until an EMG (Electromyography) was performed. Inquisitive as I am, I asked for an explanation as to how this EMG was done. I did not at all care for his answer: "Little needles will be inserted up and down your legs and feet, and then electrical shocks will be sent through these needles to record how your nerves react."

My thoughts went into high alarm mode knowing my little nerves would never tolerate such an abuse without a vengeful reaction. I expressed my concern to this doctor: "That will aggravate the RSD even further."

His insensitivity to my concern only irritated me: "Well, you've had flare-ups before. Another one would be no different."

Duh! Maybe he doesn't understand what brought me here? I tried again voicing my concern: "I am here now because of an aggravation of the RSD. I don't want to aggravate it further from a test that will not support a diagnosis of RSD."

But he didn't care about anything that I had to say. I asked that he order a bone scan to be done, thinking if this doctor didn't believe I had RSD, maybe that would settle it, as it did before. But he ignored me.

After he was done with me and started leaving the room, I asked again about a bone scan. Although he turned back to face me while holding the door, his demeanor and lack of response before he left told me I was out of line questioning his expertise in his profession. After all, he was the doctor—I was not!

I left this appointment very upset but absolutely determined: There was no way I was going to allow anyone to stick little needles in my legs and feet to send electrical shocks to aggravate the nerves and RSD further. It simply was not going to happen! Once this test was over, I was the one who was going to have to deal with the aggravated pain, not this doctor. And if he didn't believe me now, neither would he believe me when this pain went berserk even further. I needed time to pray and think this through.

I had thought of going back to Dr. Donna for a specialist, the neurologist who first confirmed the diagnosis of RSD. I found her obituary when I looked her up on the Internet for contact information. It had only been a few weeks since she had died suddenly while riding a bike; she was only fifty-two.

I decided to schedule an appointment with the group Dr. Donna had worked with, hoping that with my history in their computer system they would be willing to help me. These doctors were in Pittsburgh, an hour's drive from my home without traffic.

As I waited in the examining room, an intern doctor in training came in while I was still filling out some of the forms I was given. I completely ignored the naked-genderless-people form. Dr. Intern examined my legs and saw my blue toes, but he didn't say much about what he saw. I explained my whole situation to him to the best of my ability as to how I ended up to where I was while still wondering what happened myself.

Dr. Intern wanted to prescribe Neurontin. I told him I had tried it before and couldn't take it. He wanted me to come to his facility two to three times a week for physical therapy. I told him I was doing pool therapy myself, and really, it was too far from my home to come that often, especially when I would be back to work.

It wasn't long before Dr. Real came in, who didn't bother examining me at all, not even with a quick look. When I received her report much later, I read that she stated she did her own exam in addition to Dr. Intern's exam. *Why do some doctors lie?*

I listened as Dr. Intern explained to Dr. Real my case accurately. He explained that I had tried Neurontin before but found I couldn't take it. Dr. Intern also stated I was doing pool therapy myself, and that I expressed the distance was too far for me to come often for physical therapy at their facility.

After hearing Dr. Intern's report, Dr. Real spoke to me: "We're going to prescribe Neurontin, and physical therapy two to three times a week at our facility. I prefer you take this therapy here so that we can know for sure you are getting what is needed."

Is this selective hearing, or prideful arrogance?

I repeated my concerns again, hoping she would understand a second time coming from me: "I couldn't take Neurontin before and prefer not taking it again. I am doing pool therapy myself closer to home. This helped before and I believe it will again. It's too far to come here so often, especially when I return to work."

Dr. Real didn't care what I had to say. She claimed she couldn't confirm the RSD and would not agree to the diagnosis. I then requested her to please, fill out my work paperwork regarding my sick leave agreeing that I could return to work, but she refused. She was not going to take any responsibility for my condition one way or another unless I agreed to her demands for treating this, whatever she wanted to believe I had.

I was making no headway, either in finding a treating doctor, getting the required sick leave paperwork filled out, or getting the RSD under control. Only twenty minutes on my feet was causing unbearable pain by this time, not to mention what the rest of my limbs were doing.

Chapter 111

I Was Done

During this season of my life, while dealing with so much more aggravated pain, dealing with the stress of trying to find a specialist, and being in limbo with my job and life, I would often be overwhelmed by God's presence and peace during my quiet time with Him. It was the Lord's way of assuring me that He was in all this; He was still in perfect control. I was in limbo, but only by my own understanding.

After much prayer, I decided to see Dr. Saul, who did the IME years ago as arranged by the workers' comp insurance company. I did not want to submit to that exam, as I was sure this doctor was going to lie on behalf of those who paid him. However, the Lord had made it clear that He wanted me to submit to that IME.

Dr. Saul was honest with the diagnosis of RSD, but refused to treat me because he did the IME. Now over twelve years later, I reasoned that enough time had gone by that he would be willing to treat me. When I couldn't get an appointment with Dr. Saul, I settled for his partner, Dr. Shultz. I was so sure Dr. Shultz would accept his partner's diagnosis, that I went to the appointment armed with my copy of the IME report for him to read.

As I waited in the examining room smelling the familiar scent of a doctor's office, feet dangling and toes turning blue, I said a little prayer as I examined the floor tile. I found this practice was habitual by then. *Is this real linoleum or vinyl? Is there a distinct pattern or random pattern?* What I didn't want to think about was being in limbo with my condition, my job and my entire future.

When Dr. Shultz walked in, I explained that I had been able to deal with the RSD all these years on my own. I told him now my situation had drastically changed, and I needed a doctor who understood RSD and was willing to take on my treatment, at least until I could get this under control again.

Dr. Shultz agreed to take me on as a patient. He prescribed the drug Lyrica and wanted to see me back in a few weeks. In his report, he noted the blue toes and skin changes in my legs that were indicative of RSD, and had agreed with the diagnosis.

Lyrica made me feel high, and I didn't want to take drugs again that altered my mind. In addition, my employer-controlled health insurance refused to pay for it. I could have appealed the decision but didn't want to. I needed something to help calm the RSD pain without addicting side effects so I could get back to work sooner rather than later. I believed that was the goal at the time.

After my initial appointment with Dr. Shultz, his practitioner, Ms. Sidekick, shared with my treatment. After several different trials with other drugs over the course of a few months, I became increasingly frustrated with the lack of improvement, especially as I witnessed one of my toenails becoming deformed and ready to fall off. I always knew there were possibilities that RSD could cause deformities, but until then, I had never experienced this.

I discussed my concern with the progression of the RSD with Ms. Sidekick, who suggested that maybe another series of nerve blocks would stop the progression. I never wanted to go through getting nerve blocks again, but something needed done. Any deformities caused by RSD may prove irreversible.

When the last medication prescribed had an adverse side effect that caused me to yawn uncontrollably for long periods of time, I called the office to express my concerns. The nurse who answered the phone spoke with Ms. Sidekick, who encouraged me to make an earlier appointment to see Dr. Shultz—so I did. This involved a much longer trip to another location that Dr. Shultz would be available at for this earlier appointment.

While I waited in the examining room for Dr. Shultz, not knowing his reaction to an earlier appointment, I got a little nervous. I did my normal exam of the floor tile while talking to the Lord: "What am I doing here, Lord? How did this RSD get so bad that now my toenail is deformed? What is this doctor going to say? Please don't let me say anything I should not say, but only what I should say and in the way I should say it." I waited for Dr. Shultz with my thoughts racing as I watched my toes turn blue.

Dr. Shultz finally made his entrance, but he seemed annoyed that I was there. I wasted no time explaining the uncontrollable yawning the last medication prescribed was causing, asking that he agree I wean off of it and try something else. I wasn't prepared for his response, "There is no other medication left that I know of that you can try. You just have to stay on it."

This didn't satisfy me. I brought to his attention my toenail: "Look at my toenail. It's getting deformed, ready to fall off."

His response only told me what I already knew: "The RSD is the cause of the toenail becoming deformed."

Duh! I know that! But what are you going to do about it? He answered my thought without me asking: "I do not treat RSD. I only help manage the pain."

You have got to be kidding me! Did I hear him right? I was dumbfounded but kept my thoughts to myself. I specifically asked his staff when I made the first appointment if this doctor treated RSD, and I was told he did. *Now what?*

He responded before I did: "More nerve blocks at this point will not help. The RSD is too widespread. You just need to keep taking the medication. The yawning will eventually slow down."

Obviously, Dr. Shultz had his mind made up before he came into this room. He seemed annoyed that I would dare come to see him before my later scheduled appointment. Did he know that I came at the advice of his staff? He was obviously too busy with other patients giving his nerve blocks that meant more money to him than to be troubled with me for a measly appointment.

Once he left the room, I stayed there for some time trying to process everything he said. *Where do I go from here?* I had a priority stop I needed to make before traveling the long distance home. When I left the restroom, I spotted Dr. Shultz coming out of a treatment room wearing his surgical garb, which told me it was a room he used for nerve blocks. Our eyes locked for a few seconds speaking silently before I turned and walked away.

I decided on a Plan B. I saw another pain doctor for a second opinion after this appointment with Dr. Shultz. I explained to Dr. Colts everything I had been experiencing thus far since I had been off work. I told him that I was seeing Dr. Shultz but felt I needed another opinion. I also stated that I asked Dr. Shultz to wean me off the medication I was on because of the uncontrollable yawning, but he refused to agree to it. Whenever one doctor refers to another by first name, it only proves that they are well known to each other; such was the case here.

Dr. Colts said Markus would have agreed to wean me off the medication I was currently on; all I had to do was ask him. Another doctor who obviously didn't hear what I said!

I didn't elaborate about my last appointment with Dr. Shultz; there was no value in it. Dr. Colts agreed I could wean off the medication, but referred me to another neurologist to confirm the diagnosis of RSD before prescribing a replacement medication.

Dr. Little, this new neurologist, was another doctor who had his mind made up before he saw me. Once in his examining room, the nurse made a point to tell me that there was no need to take my shoes or socks off. After she walked out, I took them off anyway. This doctor needed to see my toes, feet and legs to help diagnose the RSD for a treatment plan.

It wasn't long after Dr. Little came in that I realized I could have saved myself the effort. Dr. Little never once looked at my feet. As a matter of fact, he didn't examine me at all. All he said was that he was ordering an EMG test before he would treat me. *Were these doctors conferring with each other without a chance for an independent, unbiased exam for their own knowledge?*

I left Dr. Little's office extremely upset but once again very determined—I was not getting an EMG test. It was just not going to happen! If no one believed that I was dealing with so much pain by this time, no one would believe the aggravated excruciating pain I would be dealing with after this EMG test.

I went back to Ms. Sidekick and asked for some kind of medication that would help the pain when it got at its worst, hoping this would at least calm it down. I reminded her of my allergy to morphine that affected my breathing. Ms. Sidekick then prescribed a medication that clearly had a warning on the label that it should not be taken by anyone allergic to morphine.

I tried contacting Ms. Sidekick about this allergy warning. She left her answer on my answering machine: "That allergy alert was only put there for purposes of covering themselves. The amount of the ingredient to be concerned about is so little. But, if you start having an allergic reaction, then just stop taking the medication."

Well, that would prevent future allergic reactions! But what about the allergic reaction from what is already in my system? After Ms. Sidekick's message, I refused to take the medication.

I was living the same nightmare I did years ago when I was first diagnosed with this off-the-wall neurological pain disorder. The aggravation and frustration of dealing with all these doctors who either didn't believe I had RSD, didn't know how to help me, or didn't want to help me, finally reached the climax.

Once again, I was done with them all!

Chapter 112

God's Decision

From the very beginning of when I was put out of work, I searched God's heart earnestly in prayer for my job and life that by my own understanding was in limbo. But the Lord God knew everything that He was doing. All I needed to do was to follow His directions exclusively and precisely, one step at a time—and I did.

Just two months into this sick leave, I had contacted Chief and asked that he continue to process my last grievance regarding being purposely bypassed for the overtime that I was entitled to, when it was instead given to Lucinda. He said he would. It had been on hold because I was off work.

After going through the grievance process without a settlement, the union e-board decided that this grievance had merit to pursue to arbitration, and without my input. Allowing the trainer/production techs to get overtime others were entitled to was a direct violation of our contract. It went against past practice and affected every department at the plant site. The arbitration was not for my benefit, but for the union's benefit. However, it was another grievance that had merit going to arbitration with my name as the grievant, even while I was out on sick leave.

But once again, Newbie took the lead, and this arbitration never happened. When Chief contacted me to let me know it was canceled, he said it wasn't because it was my grievance, but that everyone agreed: They would not have given Lucinda the overtime if someone other than myself was involved. So in essence, the arbitration was canceled because it was my grievance.

Chief asked if I would be satisfied with a settlement for the lost overtime, which I refused to accept. I told him truthfully, it was more important to me that our contract was going to be honored going forward. He assured me it would.

The Lord also directed me to file a workers' comp claim just under the expiration of the time limits to do so for this current work-related aggravation of my RSD condition. Even though I knew this claim would be denied, I followed God's direction.

I also contacted Butch again, the OSHA agent who was assigned to my case, asking about that letter he promised would be sent in the near future outlining the steps for a formal appeal to the dismissal decision for my whistleblower complaint. Butch referred my email to Douglas, the head of OSHA. It took two more emails and a week later before I finally received the letter. It was now over five months from when my whistleblower complaint was dismissed. I guessed that OSHA had a different meaning of "near future" than I did!

OSHA gave me just fifteen days to file this formal appeal once I received the letter outlining the steps I needed to take. I saw that OSHA had also sent Ferengi a copy of this letter. Following God's direction, I didn't pursue an appeal to my case. God's purpose for filing this OSHA complaint and requesting the appeal letter while I was off work all came to fruition in His grand scheme for my career and life.

Not too long into this sick leave, Abby had told me that I would not be allowed back to work in any capacity as long as my current RSD symptoms continued. She said this decision was supported by Dr. Willy. I believed management was part of this decision as well.

As long as I needed to secure my employment, I was trapped with the need to treat with a doctor per the requirements of my sick leave benefit. Without my employment, I would be able to go out on my own again dealing with my RSD condition without a treating doctor, and with God's help try to at least get it calmed down to a tolerable pain level for a near-normal lifestyle again.

For years, I had it in my heart to retire at the earliest possible age permitted per our contract agreement. Looking back now, I understand this too was from God. He gives us the desires of our hearts, but I also believe as we earnestly follow Jesus as Lord of our hearts and lives, He also puts His desires in our hearts.

My industrial chemical job career supplied me with a good livelihood and great benefits for many years. But such a major decision needed to be without doubt. I didn't want to remove myself from a war zone that God wanted to keep me in. Staying in the Lord's perfect will had to be the priority of my life, and should be for every follower of Jesus. The Lord knew that being sure of His will at that time was important to me before making such a life-altering decision.

God took His time through these several months I was off from work as He gradually led in another direction for my life, gently yet firmly, knowing that I needed that time of adjustment.

In God's timing, I had no doubt in His direction: I was going to terminate my employment and take early retirement. The freedom in this decision alone gave me tremendous peace.

I had no doubt that management was so elated by my decision to take early retirement, that they did their best to do right by me to make sure everything was going to work out to that end. I didn't discuss my decision with anyone from the union.

Ironically, and to the dismay of many involved from management, I had the legal right to represent myself during my retirement severance, and I chose to do so. I made sure all the documents were worded to my complete satisfaction before I signed off on anything, which was very important to me. And management and their lawyers were very accommodating to my requested revisions.

That adamant belief that I could never represent myself or speak on my own behalf flew out the window. But I was sure it would have plenty of company with all those past good-faith gestures I had made over the years with management that also flew out the windows, never to rebound. And by this time, they had that ball that jumped out of my court and also flew out the window to play with.

The Lord God allowed me to fully understand by now, how certain scenarios orchestrated by His direction that I obediently followed through during the last several years of my career and while I was off work, played a vital role in His grand scheme for securing my retirement severance on His terms and no one else's; although some of these scenarios never came to fruition as I would have wanted them to.

God always proved faithful in working everything together for my best, and according to His purpose and call on my life. There were many battles lost, along with some powerful victories. But the triumphal end of my career was the fulfillment of God's promise to me so long ago: "No weapon formed against you will ever prosper." (Isaiah 54:17.)

During this time, Theodore was the company vice president, and Ferengi was once again under him in their chain of command. Roles in life change often, and God's providence intervened again! I believe things would have turned out much differently had Ferengi still been on top of the chain of command.

After my retirement, I wrote to each person in management a nice thank you letter while expressing the intervention of the Lord Jesus for allowing such a peaceful end of my career. I was sure everyone understood—it was on the path to end much differently.

By this time, Jezebel moved up to corporate and away from the plant site. Sabrina took Jezebel's place as HR leader. Initially, Sabrina refused my earlier request to come into the plant and retrieve a Bible from one of my lockers, even though someone from the company would have accompanied me. After speaking a few words to Albert, another company lawyer, I was permitted back in the plant to gather up all my belongings for myself from the various lockers I had. For one final time, as God commanded my strength, my tenaciousness proved stronger than Sabrina's!

Gertrude, the shift coach, escorted me back into the plant site for this final time. It was a Saturday with only those working shifts being present in their departments. I didn't see anyone else as I went through all my lockers separating what was mine from what needed left as company property. Afterward, I asked Gertrude for a last drive through the plant site that had been my place of employment for over twenty-four years; she was more than happy to oblige.

We drove past the Rail Prince and styrene unloading rack that was instrumental in securing my position in the Liquid Handler Department. I saw the primitive locomotive and remembered conversing in jest to the Lord: "Is this REALLY what You want me to do for the rest of my working career?" I'm sure the Lord just chuckled then, as He knew exactly what He was planning for my career and life.

As we drove past the warehouse docks, I remembered all those semi-trailers I had to learn how to perfectly spot at the loading doors, believing then that the Lord knew at some point in my future I was going to need that experience. I remembered how frustrated I was with the mundane task of loading these semi-trailers for our customers one bag at a time with a forklift, especially after being a lead operator in Darkly.

Then we drove past the Darkly Graveyard where my career began. I had moved up through the ranks from an entry-level material packager, to being the first and only woman Darkly chem tech and lead operator dealing with reactors, extruders and hotcutters. I had spent almost twenty years working in that department, dealing with the critical situations that left only minutes to respond to avert a catastrophe.

I could almost hear the Westminster Chimes blaring out their warning alarm, and smell the faint aroma of the pancakes permeating from the concrete. *What if Darkly had never shutdown?* Then I remembered again: *There are no "what-ifs" for anyone who loves God and are called according to His purpose.* (Romans 8:28.)

I had no regrets for leaving all this behind me, no aching feelings in my heart as I did when I left the Army. I had the Lord God's great peace that surpasses all comprehension in this decision to terminate my career with early retirement.

I have great anticipation for God's plans for my future! The most adventurous years of my life serving my Lord Jesus is yet to come! My accountability to my Lord God will always be above all. I must always obey God's voice, unconditionally submit to His will, and embrace all aspects of His prophetic call.

Anyone can believe and live the ultimate truth! Our lives are God's gift meant to live intimately with Him: to love, worship and serve Him for His praise, honor and glory. The Lord God created us for His pleasure! Apart from God, no life would exist.

Our future begins now! It's our free choice to embrace Jesus as our Lord and Savior for the fulfillment of God's purpose for our lives. There are no words to adequately describe God's precious love for those who embrace Jesus, for those who love Him and are called according to His purpose.

Epilogue

Just two weeks after my retirement, I showed up at the annual union-family picnic, and was received warmly by Chief and many others. Some folks expressed concern for my well-being, while others expressed thankfulness that I made it to retirement and were sincerely happy for me.

Some folks expressed their appreciation for my service as the workers' comp rep and president. A few who knew the inner circle of the union's dealings acknowledged that I dealt with some tough issues as president, and at times without any support from others.

The encouragement that the Lord had given me through these people was special. I left there remembering that it was all about being the servant to the Lord Jesus first and foremost, and then the servant to the membership of our union. I may not have been the best union president, but I can honestly say I did my best, and I always tried to rely on God's Holy Spirit as my driving force.

The RSD has calmed down since retirement. But I will always have to deal with the unpredictable nature of this off-the-wall neurological pain disorder. And the Lord has been unwilling to relax His spanking rod in my life!

It has been several years since I started this book. In the last few months of preparing this manuscript for publication, I find myself again in God's "fire of affliction and judgment." The Lord God has made me profoundly aware why His severest yet justified spanking looms over me. I cannot get into particulars at this time. But to be sure, it's not a matter of if—but when the Lord is ready!

During this season of anticipating God's looming spanking, in extraordinary ways the Lord has manifested His presence to me, assured me of His love and forgiveness, and has been drawing me closer to Himself as never before. The Lord also shared His heart with me, that I have deeply hurt Him, and that it grieves Him when He must spank me. Yet, the Lord has made it undeniably known to me: He will never relent with His spankings!

Knowing how my disobedience and sins of my heart deeply hurt my precious Lord God, and how the consequences from which grieves Him, brings a new depth of sorrow to my heart!

So why does the Lord God deal so severely with me and in such humiliating ways that He then leads me to openly share? Because the Lord God will not allow any pride—not even a trace—to be in my heart. Pride untunes us to God's Holy Spirit!

There can be no doubt in my heart that I am so incredibly unworthy and inadequate for God's prophetic call. It is only by the grace of God I am what I am! I must depend solely on the Holy Spirit as my driving force to reach the goal of fulfilling God's purpose for my life, in the way that pleases Him the most, and only for His praise and honor and glory. The Lord God will never share His glory with anyone! (1 Corinthians 15:10; Acts 1:8.)

God demands perfect obedience from His prophets, and will not tolerate anything less. Yet no one can be perfect in this world! This only reinforces my need and thankfulness to the Lord Jesus for His atoning sacrifice for my sins, and because of which, I am assured of God's mercy and forgiveness.

But this I also know: Nothing has ever happened in my life, nor will ever happen in my life, apart from the Sovereignty of the Lord God of my life.

God's forgiveness in Jesus will always be ours once we confess and repent of our sins, and ask for His forgiveness. But even with God's forgiveness, there may still be consequences for us to deal with once we sin against such a holy, righteous and just God.

The agony that Jesus suffered, and His precious and holy blood shed as the atonement for our sins was never meant to issue anyone a license to sin. The atoning sacrifice of the Lord Jesus

Christ—the Lamb of God—was meant for our reconciliation with His Holy Father to become His children.

God has a purpose for each of His children, and customizes His relationship and nurturing with each accordingly. As our Heavenly Father, all His children will in some way experience His discipline, and only because of His great love that He has for us through Jesus. (Hebrews 12:5-11.) And the closer we grow to such a precious, holy and righteous Lord God, the less tolerant He is of any sin in our lives, and the more accountable we are to Him.

We all have just one life journey through this world; however short or long that journey may be. Just one life to invest for the glory of our Lord Jesus Christ and our eternal future. We do this by living with the purpose of serving our Lord Jesus, and being a witness of His love and Gospel to a dying and lost world.

Our relationship with Jesus, the choices we make and the people our lives touch, the experiences we have and how we deal with them, will all play a role in what awaits us for all eternity.

For no matter what anyone believes during their life, every single person will at some point in time, give an account to the Lord Jesus Christ for their lives. Jesus alone has been appointed as Judge for all mankind. (2 Corinthians 5:10.)

For anyone who may not have accepted Jesus Christ as Lord and Savior, I implore you to wait no longer. Once your life in this world ends, it will be too late! The alternative to accepting Jesus as Lord and Savior is living an eternity separated from God, and in torment in Hell with Satan and his demons.

Please, if you have not done so already, turn to the Lord Jesus. Confess and repent of all your sins, and ask Jesus to forgive you for your sins, and eternal life in His Paradise of Heaven will be yours. Here is a simple prayer for salvation that must be sincere:

"Lord Jesus, I confess that I am a sinner. I believe that You suffered and died for my sins, and that You rose again from the dead. I believe it is only through You that I can be forgiven for my sins and reconciled to God the Father, and by doing so, I will receive eternal life in Your Paradise of Heaven. I repent of all my sins and ask You to please, forgive me for all my sins, and come into my heart to be my Lord and Savior. Thank You, Lord Jesus!"

Once you have embraced Jesus as Lord and Savior, God fills you with His Holy Spirit. But you cannot stop there! You need to get involved in a true Gospel preaching church, and obtain a good translation of the Bible for reading and studying. As a priority, you need to spend quality time in fellowship with God in prayer, and get to know your Heavenly Father and your Lord Jesus while submitting to His authority and perfect will for your life.

God so desires to nurture all His children, to speak to us, and to be intimately involved with every aspect of our lives. But we must be attuned and obedient to God's Holy Spirit, and this will be even more crucial in the days ahead.

We are living in the very last days of our world as we know it, and to ignore the signs of the times is dangerously wrong. No one knows the day nor the hour that the Lord Jesus will return, but we have never been closer to that powerful day than we are right now.

There are so many real and powerful adversaries against the followers of Jesus: Satan and his vast army of demons are the strongest. These evil forces know very well that their time is short, and they are currently in a frenzy of rage in the spiritual realm. They are very adept in using people and circumstances as their spiritual and physical weapons, and are playing havoc with the world system. These evil forces are prowling about like a roaring lion, just waiting for someone to devour, deceiving and destroying all who get in their way.

But we know the end of the story!

Jesus already won the victory against Satan and his demons when He died on the cross at Calvary. His resurrection is the proof of His victory. And when Jesus returns, He will be the Ruler of a new Earth and of all nations.

But until then, the trials and adversaries for the followers of Jesus in the years ahead are going to be too powerful for us without complete dependence on the Lord Jesus Christ, and on the power of God's Holy Spirit as our driving force.

All that awaits the children of God and the world that we live in, and all that will transpire in the future before the Lord Jesus Christ returns . . . That will be for another book!

But know this much: God continues orchestrating everything according to His Master Plan, setting the stage, putting everything in place while the world races towards the final days and hours before the return of the Lord Jesus Christ.

On that day Jesus returns, every eye shall see Him, even those who pierced Him; every knee shall bow, even those who hated Him; every tongue shall confess, even those who did not believe Him, that Jesus Christ is Lord, all to the Glory of God the Father. (Romans 14:11; Philippians 2:10-11; Revelation 1:7; Isaiah 45:23.)

As the world continues in this difficult time in history, remember this one absolute truth will never change:

The only One-Triune Lord God of the Universe is Sovereign, and He rules over all, in all, and will for all eternity. (Psalms 103:19, 115:3, 135:6.)

Nothing has ever happened, nor will ever happen, without the Lord God allowing it to happen, and according to His Master Plan—end of story, period.

Author's Appreciation

I praise and thank my precious Lord God for the completion of this book. It has been a humongous undertaking for years that I could not have accomplished apart from the Holy Spirit's help. I have committed this book and all the consequences that will come with it—good and bad—completely to my Lord God.

In sharing my life story for anyone to read, I have shared God's heart as He nurtures my life for His prophetic call; but I have done so by His leading, with His blessings, and only for His purpose. Yet, above all else that He may call me to be, I will always be my Lord God's little daughter.

I would like to thank everyone who has taken the time to read my autobiography. The Lord God knows my prayers offered to His throne for all those who read this book.

Witness of God's Voice is a prelude to my next book:
God's Voice Crying Out
It will be a prophetic message for those who will be here for God's great "Day of the Lord" event.

In the Service of Our Lord Jesus Christ,

Angelika Mitikas

If you have enjoyed this book, I would appreciate very much if you would leave a book review.

Thank you!

ISC-01/IS-02

www.ingramcontent.com/pod-product-compliance
Lightning Source LLC
Chambersburg PA
CBHW020832120526
44590CB00034BA/363